THE COMPLETELY UPDATED AND REVISED MUST-HAVE COMPANION FOR SCRABBLE® PLAYERS AT EVERY LEVEL

EVERYTHING SCRABBLE®
Fourth Edition

Learn to think like a SCRABBLE® champion,
immediately improve your scoring average,
and elevate your game with indispensable tools like these:

- ❑ Comprehensive word lists, including two-letter words, Q words, top ten most useful six-letter stems
- ❑ Hints for managing your rack: rearrange tiles to your advantage, know when to exchange your letters, and prepare for a bingo
- ❑ Four rules for your two best friends, the blank and the S—find seven-letter bonus plays and maximize your score

PLUS ALL NEW TIPS, STRATEGIES,
AND MUCH, MUCH MORE!

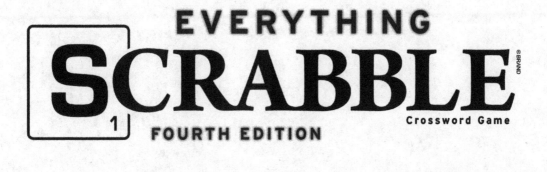

EVERYTHING SCRABBLE®BRAND Crossword Game

FOURTH EDITION

EVERYTHING SCRABBLE® BRAND Crossword Game

FOURTH EDITION

NOW UPDATED AND REVISED!

70TH ANNIVERSARY EDITION

JOE EDLEY and

JOHN D. WILLIAMS, JR.

GALLERY BOOKS

New York London Toronto Sydney New Delhi

Gallery Books
An Imprint of Simon & Schuster, Inc.
1230 Avenue of the Americas
New York, NY 10020

This Gallery Books trade paperback edition October 2018.

Tilez font designed by Randy Ford

Puzzle design by Sally Ricketts and Patty Hocker

Text design by Stanley S. Drate / Folio Graphics Co. Inc.

Manufactured in the United States of America

10 9 8 7 6 5 4 3 2 1

Library of Congress Cataloging-in-Publication Data

Names: Edley, Joe, author. | Williams, John D., Jr., author.
Title: Everything scrabble : crossword game / updated and revised Joe Edley and John D. Williams, Jr.
Description: New York : Gallery Books, 2018.
Identifiers: LCCN 2017058398 | ISBN 9781501175473 (paperback)
Subjects: LCSH: Scrabble (Game) | BISAC: GAMES / Reference. | GAMES / Word & Word Search. | GAMES / Board.
Classification: LCC GV1507.S3 E354 2018 | DDC 793.734—dc23 LC record available at https://lccn.loc.gov/2017058398

ISBN 978-1-5011-7547-3

ISBN 978-1-4391-3862-5 (ebook)

I dedicate this book to my parents, Marian and Morris Edley, my wife, Laura Marlene Klein, alias "Keen Animal Allurer," and my six-year-old daughter, Amber, who is a joy to love. Also to John D. Williams, Jr., for giving me the opportunity, joyfully, to promote the game and for his efforts to make this book a comprehensive and entertaining read. Finally, to all the ardent fans, who share the joy and camaraderie of this wonderful word game.

—Joe Edley

I would like to thank my father, who gave me a love of words; Jane Ratsey Williams, who gave me encouragement and more; Kristen and Alexandra, who grew up in "SCRABBLE Central"; and Joe Edley, who made me a serious player. Also thanks to Alfred Mosher Butts, who started it all.

—John D. Williams, Jr.

The authors would like to acknowledge Jerry Lerman and Rita Norr for their excellent advice; Sally Ricketts for her patience and fine work; our editors Paul McCarthy and Eric Tobias; Regula Noetzli, who kept the faith; and Cathy Meredith, who saw the wisdom in all of this.

CONTENTS

PART ■ 2

PART ■ 3

PART ■ 4

ABOUT THIS BOOK:
What It Is and How to Use It

This is the most comprehensive book ever published about the SCRABBLE® game. Authored by a three-time winner of the National SCRABBLE® Championship and the executive director of the National SCRABBLE® Association, it was written to increase your knowledge of virtually every aspect of the game, from the SCRABBLE game's history and culture to learning how to increase your vocabulary; from learning how to manage your rack to understanding what it takes to become national champion. And to make this educational book fun, we have included puzzles. This book was written for anyone who has ever played a SCRABBLE game, from novice to expert.

We expect that some people will read the book straight through and others will simply want to browse and use it as a reference. With all these readers in mind, we have divided the book into six parts.

Sprinkled throughout the book are puzzles of varying difficulty designed to help you retain what you will learn from reading the text. If you spend time trying to solve them, you will learn more. If you can't solve a puzzle within a reasonable amount of time, you might want to look up the answer. We've suggested a time limit in most cases. At some point in the future you might try the puzzles again to see if you can solve them faster or without looking up the answers. Doing so will help develop your abilities even further.

As you will see throughout the text, there will be talk of "bingos"—that is, scoring a 50-point bonus for using all seven letters on your rack in one play. For expert and championship players, bingos are an essential, constant part of the game. For less experienced players, this fact may seem a little intimidating, as many of them have never seen, let alone scored, a bingo.

The examination of bingos is not intended to intimidate, but to encourage you to reach beyond your current skills. You may surprise yourself!

Part 1 (chapters 1–8) is devoted to teaching you the basic SCRABBLE® Brand Crossword Game skills. For the novice, a thorough understanding of the principles of this section will raise your scores considerably with very little effort. Please remember to use the Glossary at the end of the book, if necessary. We introduce many commonly used SCRABBLE terms that may be unfamiliar.

Part 2 (chapters 9–15) delves deeper into more advanced concepts of play. While we recommend that both novices and experts read these chapters, you will get more out of them after you've practiced the exercises in Part 1.

Part 3 (chapters 16–18) is loaded with puzzles that will tease, test, and develop your skills. Try them! The puzzles are graded—the more stars, the harder the puzzle.

Part 4 (chapters 19–25) will take you beyond your living room for a glimpse of the game's inventor, Alfred Butts, the SCRABBLE culture, and competitive SCRABBLE game club and tournament play. We also include fifty-five examples of outstanding SCRABBLE game play, and a special chapter on how to introduce the game to children. The game can help teach a variety of skills and combines learning with fun! This edition also includes a chapter on how to approach finding the best play.

For those of you who haven't yet seen an *Official SCRABBLE® Players Dictionary (OSPD)* or its sixth edition *(OSPD6)*, we recommend that you read **chapter 1** to familiarize yourself with the ins and outs of using the *OSPD6*.

Chapter 2 is devoted to teaching novices how to form words on the board and how to understand the notations used throughout this book. Make sure you understand this chapter before reading further.

We recommend **chapter 3** for everyone who hasn't yet learned the 107 two-letter words. They are the foundation for virtually all SCRABBLE game skills. In fact, we suggest that you play the SCRABBLE game with the two-letter word list in front of you until you learn them all by heart.

We'll bet that **chapter 4** is more important than most of our readers will immediately think. If you don't frequently rearrange the tiles on your rack, you will miss many easy high-scoring plays. Check out this chapter, whether you're a novice or an expert.

Chapter 5 is, broadly speaking, at the heart of excellence in the SCRABBLE game. If you are able to see and utilize the open bonus squares, also known as "hot spots," you will consistently score more points. We present several puzzles here that will help you develop your skills. Novices and experts alike can learn from this chapter.

Chapter 6 is all about the dreaded Q. Sure it's worth 10 points, but if you don't have a U, you'll probably be in a quandary about what to do. Believe it or not, you don't need a U to play the Q! Play your next game armed with this chapter's information and the Q won't seem so daunting.

Chapter 7 will show you how to earn big scores! Most people we've talked with don't know how to find seven- and eight-letter bonus plays, known as "bingos," which earn an extra 50 points. It's not difficult, but it does require that you learn and remember a few common combinations of letters. If you solve the puzzles in this chapter, we predict that you'll dramatically increase your bingo output.

Chapter 8 will show you that each play has two parts: the score and the "leave." The leave is the set of letters remaining on your rack after you've played, but before you've drawn new tiles. Your skill at the game will develop quickly as you learn how to combine scoring big and saving good combinations of letters.

In **chapter 9,** we explore in more depth how to think like a topnotch player. We recommend reading this chapter carefully. Look at each example rack and think about what you would do before you go on to read the analysis. Then incorporate our suggestions into your thinking.

Chapter 10 goes into depth about when you should exchange tiles. Most novices we've encountered are hesitant to do so, thinking that it's always better to score *some* points in a round rather than *no* points. Wrong!

Chapter 11 explores how you can make the most of both of the super tiles: the blank and the S.

Chapter 12 will give you insights into how the champions learned the words, and how you can, too, painlessly, and even have fun doing so.

Chapter 13 will show you how to take advantage of the J, X, and Z. You can learn all the unusual three- and four-letter J, X, and Z words by solving the puzzles while referring to this brief list.

Chapter 14 will show you how to take advantage of the developing spatial patterns on the board as the game progresses. Knowing how to "open" or "close" the board can give you a decided advantage, even if you're behind.

Chapter 15 is all about phoney words. In SCRABBLE club and tournament play, if a phoney word is played, it remains in play unless challenged off the board. We present several examples of when you might want to play a phoney or challenge your opponent. For tournament players, whether you're a novice or expert, this chapter is a must.

Chapter 16 will show you that it's not enough just to know the words; you'll want to be able to find them on your rack. This chapter has several different kinds of puzzles designed to improve your overall word-finding ability.

Chapter 17 will give you extensive practice finding words and the best places to play them.

Chapter 18 is for the word buff who likes real challenges. This chapter has some stumpers that will keep you busy for many hours.

In **chapter 19,** we'll introduce you to Alfred Butts, the inventor of the SCRABBLE game.

In **chapter 20,** you'll learn all about clubs and tournaments. Those of you who are thinking about entering organized competitive SCRABBLE play will have the most to gain here.

Chapter 21 is for budding experts only. We lay our tiles on the table in this chapter. If you want to be one of the best players, this chapter will tell you how! Most people have the capacity to become SCRABBLE experts. It simply takes time, practice, and learning the proper skills. It's all here.

Chapter 22 will show you exactly the kinds of skills the top players have. Here are fifty-five wonderful plays that we hope will convey why we think the SCRABBLE game is so exciting.

Chapter 23 will show you how to introduce the SCRABBLE game to children. Whether you want to start your five-year-old with SCRABBLE® for Juniors, or your eight-year-old with the regular SCRABBLE® Brand Crossword game, this chapter will give you many of the dos and don'ts. It also talks about the successful and highly acclaimed National School SCRABBLE® Program.

In **chapter 24,** we share with you the funny, unusual, poetic, and always fascinating situations that occur in the world of SCRABBLE crossword games.

In **chapter 25,** you will be faced with twenty positions to find the best play, giving you a lot of practice learning how to decide which of several plays are best.

Chapter 26 gives you an inside look at the tournament experiences of three player directors and the 2017 National SCRABBLE® Championship runner-up.

Chapter 27 (Part 5) can turn a rank beginner into an expert at anagramming—that vital skill all good players develop. There are thousands of practice puzzles designed to gently increase your skills.

Appendix 1 clarifies many often-asked questions about the rules of the game. **Appendix 2** presents a variety of facts and figures that will delight trivia buffs. **Appendix 3** is all about the North American SCRABBLE® Players Association (NASPA). What does it do? How can you join? If you have any questions about the SCRABBLE game, we're your definitive resource. **Appendix 4** contains some extremely useful word lists drawn directly from *The Official SCRABBLE® Players Dictionary*. You will probably want to refer to these lists frequently. **Appendix 5** shows you SCRABBLE champ Joe Edley's tried and true method for learning how to find words during game play—practicing with flashcards twenty minutes a day can turn you into a pro quickly! **Appendix 6** gives you a handy guide to the odds of your opponent's having any given letter in his or her rack.

The **Glossary** contains all the definitions for the SCRABBLE game lingo we've used throughout the book.

Enjoy!

INTRODUCTION

"Spellbound."

It was the middle of the night, and I was certain my wife was asleep. So I was startled when she abruptly sat up in bed and squinted at me through the dim haze of my night-light. As she stared at me, her look became a blend of bewilderment and disdain. "Has it come to this?" she finally said.

She did not even wait for a reply as she rolled back over to sleep. With luck, she'd spend a few more hours in a dreamworld where husbands don't wake up in the middle of the night to study secret word lists.

There was no denying it: After years of being on the fringes of the national SCRABBLE scene, I had become a bona fide "word nerd." And, like people all across the U.S. and Canada, I was preparing for my first official SCRABBLE tournament. This meant committing to memory words that most people never heard of, would never use, and lived very happily without knowing. But to the SCRABBLE enthusiast, they are critical. Among the basics were the Q words without a U and the two-letter words. And these were only the beginning.

Actually, my wife was getting off easy. She could have married the retired military officer who spent his days calculating the probability of seven-letter plays on the first draw. Almost every day he'd spend a couple of hours drawing seven SCRABBLE tiles out of a bag and writing down the letters. Then he'd see if there was indeed a seven-letter play in the combination. Next, he'd put the tiles back in, shake the bag, and start the process all over again. By his own calculation, he had done this several thousand times, recording each "play."

With reams of crumpled paper from yellow legal pads as proof, he determined there is a 10 percent probability that SCRABBLE experts should expect a seven-letter play—a bingo—to start their game. It should come as no surprise that this man once described his apartment in the following way: SCRABBLE draperies, a SCRABBLE wastebasket, a SCRABBLE bedspread. He slept in SCRABBLE pajamas.

While this gentleman's love of the game tended toward the obsessive, his dedication was by no means rare. We are a country of special-interest groups, and the SCRABBLE world is like any other, whether it be Elvis fans, sky divers, baseball card collectors, Trekkies, or golfers. We have our own superstars, prodigies, groupies, and leaders. We have a body of knowledge—word lists, strategies, training techniques—that dazzles everyone from the humble inventor of the game himself to the casual living room player.

Like most subcultures, our membership cuts across a wide cross-section of the continent. It includes celebrities, prison inmates, doctors, teachers, truck drivers, teenagers, the old and the young, the expert and the amateur, and just about everyone else. Some of us got here because we love words, others because we love games. Still others play because they love people. Some play occasionally; some play every single day of their lives. When a human being is not available to compete, a computer opponent will more than test one's skill.

Before you get too overwhelmed by all of this, here is the most important thing of all to know about the SCRABBLE game: The game is a classic, which means two things. The first is that it's completely different every single time you play it. The second is that you can enjoy it at every level, whether you play once a year on a rainy summer day, once a month on a visit to your aunt, or every day of your life. This book is meant to celebrate all of those levels and the people at them.

I turned back to my wife, who was still sleeping peacefully. Looking at things objectively, I guess I could understand her amusement at my growing fascination with competitive SCRABBLE. It was getting late and I really needed sleep. Turning off the light, I decided I'd had enough of word lists for the night. Maybe just a few anagrams before drifting off . . .

JOHN D. WILLIAMS, JR.

I have always been a game player. In fact, the first memory I have of playing a game was at five years old. Our extended family of ten people—including aunts, uncles, and cousins—all played a game of Monopoly®. Working as a team, my father and I won by being the first to build on the purples—Mediterranean and Baltic.

From there, I graduated to chess, pocket pool, table tennis, and a variety of other board games such as backgammon, Othello®, and Mastermind®. One of my diversions, as a rather unusual teenager, was solving puzzles, including finding the smaller words that could be formed from the letters in larger words. Though I eventually studied mathematics in college, my heart wasn't in it.

During my twenties, while studying psychology and philosophy and trying to "find myself," I learned the correct approach to a winning competitive attitude. When I heard about the first National SCRABBLE Championship in 1978, I believed in my heart that I could become a SCRABBLE game expert and that this might ultimately lead to a profession. My head told me that was ridiculous, for although I had played many different games, I'd never focused on one game long enough to consider making it my profession.

To realize my goal, late in 1978 I took a job as a night watchman and studied SCRABBLE on the job. In 1980, I won the National SCRABBLE Championship. That's a long story in itself. I hope to put it into print someday. I was the runner-up in 1985 and finished third in 1983. In 1988, John Williams needed an expert to be part of the administration at the National SCRABBLE® Association. Now, for more than twenty years, John and I have devoted our time to promoting and improving the organized SCRABBLE scene.

After directing a number of national tournaments, I came back to play in 1992 and won my second National SCRABBLE Championship. In Providence, RI, in 2000, at our record-breaking National SCRABBLE Championship with over 600 players, I was fortunate enough to win a third time. It's been my goal for years to be able to expand the SCRABBLE game population. This book represents a significant part of my continuing efforts toward that goal. Whether you want to be a champion or just want to beat your uncle Jim, we're sure you'll find some useful information and improve your abilities by reading this book.

JOE EDLEY

The History of SCRABBLE®

Ironically, the entire world has heard of the SCRABBLE® Brand Crossword game, but hardly anyone knows how it got here. Many people assume it has existed for centuries—most certainly invented by the Romans or, at the very least, the English. Actually, the story is an American classic.

The year was 1931, during the depths of the Great Depression. Alfred Mosher Butts was a young out-of-work architect living in his hometown of Poughkeepsie, New York. In an attempt to earn some extra money, he set out to invent a game. Butts had always liked doing anagrams and crosswords, so he used that talent as his inspiration.

Analyzing existing games, Butts determined that they fell into three basic categories. There were "numbers" games, such as bingo and dice. There were "move" games, such as chess and checkers. And then there were "word" games, such as anagrams and crossword puzzles. Between his interest in words and his architect's love of structure and order, Butts decided to work on a word game that utilized a grid concept. In addition, he wanted to create a game that combined both luck and skill, with stronger emphasis on skill. He also liked the idea of 100 tiles. As he began his first set of sketches, Butts called his boardless anagram game idea Lexiko, which later evolved into the board game Criss Cross Words.

Alfred M. Butts next began an exhaustive analysis of the English language, particularly examining word structure. The most obvious dynamic, he knew, was that while there were twenty-six letters in the language, some appeared far more frequently than others. For example, he quickly determined that vowels were used far more frequently than consonants, with the vowel E being the most common. To verify his theories, Butts painstakingly studied the front page of the *New York Times*, doing letter-by-letter counts. He kept detailed charts of how many times each letter appeared—or didn't appear!

It was this research that enabled Butts to assign values to each letter in a SCRABBLE game, while also determining how many of each should be available as game pieces. Hence, there are twelve Es, worth only 1 point each, and only one Z, worth 10 points. Butts's basic cryptographic analysis of our language and his original scheme for the distribution have stood the test of time for three generations of SCRABBLE game players and billions of games played.

The game boards for the prototype of Criss Cross Words were hand-drawn with architectural equipment, reproduced by blueprinting, and pasted on folding cardboard checkerboards. The tiles were blueprinted and then glued to quarter-inch plywood and cut into squares to match the size of the board.

Throughout the years, the physical aspect of the game went through some subtle changes. For example, one version of the game had 109 letters and one blank. Another prototype began play in the upper left-hand corner of the board—similar to the way one traditionally starts a crossword player. However, the basics have remained the same.

From about 1932 through 1938, Alfred Butts continued to make the Lexiko sets by hand and to give them to friends, many of whom became instant devotees of the new game. To his disappointment, however, almost every single established game manufacturer in the United States turned down the new idea. Most found it interesting but felt it did not have the elements for mass appeal. In 1938, Butts stopped producing Lexiko, and then sold to individuals its offspring, Criss Cross Words, until 1942. That was when he met a bookseller named Charles Ives, who began manufacturing Criss Cross Words until the war forced him to stop in 1943. It was at that time that Butts was introduced to an entrepreneur named James Brunot, an owner of one of the few original Criss Cross Words game sets. In time, Brunot was to add his marketing genius to the project.

Sidelined by World War II and an infusion of new work, both Butts and Brunot were forced to keep the project as a low priority until 1947. Then the pair made progress. First, some refinements were made in the basic play of the new game. For example, the partners agreed to rearrange the premium squares—Triple Letter, Double Word, etc.—for more exciting and varied scoring opportunities. They also simplified the rules, which had been lengthy and complicated. The rules were fine for someone as brilliant as Alfred Butts and his friends, but not for a mass market.

Next Brunot and Butts agreed on a new name—SCRABBLE Brand Crossword Game. It was then that Brunot and his family became convinced that the game was ready for the mass market. Alfred Butts, who had very little time to develop the game, quickly authorized Brunot and his wife to produce and sell it. With this in mind, the ambitious young couple formed the Production and Marketing Company and set up shop in their Newtown, Connecticut, home.

Before long, game production became too complicated for the Brunots' home. They rented a small abandoned schoolhouse in Dodgingtown, Connecticut, where they and a friend turned out about twelve games per hour, stamping letters on the wooden tiles one at a time. Later, boards, boxes, and tiles were made elsewhere and sent to the fledgling factory for assembly and shipping.

The first four years were a struggle, so Brunot kept his other job to support the family. In 1949, for example, the Brunots made 2,400 sets but lost $450. But year by year, the number of orders increased as news of this wondrous new game began to spread, chiefly by word of mouth.

By 1952, the Brunots acknowledged they could no longer keep pace with the growing demand. They reached an agreement with Selchow & Righter, a Bay Shore, New York, game manufacturer, to market and distribute the game in the United States and Canada. Founded in 1867, Selchow & Righter was a family business, best known for manufacturing the game classic "Parcheesi®, A Royal Game of India." The Brunots would retain the rights to the SCRABBLE name.

Selchow & Righter had another classic on its hands. By the mid-1950s, in fact, SCRABBLE had become a bona fide national craze, as stories praising it appeared in newspapers and magazines and on television. The demand was so great that for three years game orders were very carefully allocated in order that all areas of the continent could receive their fair share. By 1954, more than four million sets had been sold.

Over the next two decades, it seemed as if everyone in the United States owned a SCRABBLE game. Sales remained steady, and the game eventually expanded into versions in Spanish, Italian, Russian, Hebrew, French, Braille, and large type. In 1972, Selchow & Righter purchased the trademark "SCRABBLE" from James Brunot's Production and Marketing Company, giving it exclusive rights to all SCRABBLE brand products and entertainment services in the United States and Canada. Two other companies were to divide the rights for the rest of the world.

In 1986, Selchow & Righter was sold to Coleco Industries, manufacturers of Cabbage Patch dolls. Three years later, Coleco declared bankruptcy, and its primary assets—most notably SCRABBLE and Parcheesi®—were purchased by the nation's leading game manufacturer, Hasbro, Inc.

Hasbro, Inc., also realized the value of competitive SCRABBLE game play for keeping alive the "SCRABBLE game culture" in the United States and Canada. The company helps underwrite the National SCRABBLE Association, based in Greenport, New York, and hosts the biennial National SCRABBLE

Championship. The company also created the respected National School SCRABBLE® Program, a classroom-tested curriculum that utilizes the word game as a learning tool in the nation's schools. As of this writing, Hasbro, Inc., sponsored the sixteenth National School SCRABBLE® Championship in May 2017. While Hasbro, Inc., prefers not to discuss sales figures, it's safe to say SCRABBLE is not only very much alive, but still growing.

In 2009 Hasbro chose to stop funding the National SCRABBLE Association. After a meeting of representatives of the NSA and several of its tournament directors and advisory board members, Hasbro gave its blessing to Chris Cree, then the NSA's player ombudsman, and John Chew, NSA webmaster, to lead the newly formed North American SCRABBLE Players Association (NASPA). Previous committees and activities would remain to help govern and administer clubs and tournaments. Hasbro would continue to help fund the National SCRABBLE Championship, now an annual event, with a first prize of $10,000.

PART • 1

GETTING BETTER QUICKLY: One Good Turn Follows Another

These first eight chapters are especially written both for novice players and for those more experienced players who've never used *The Official SCRABBLE® Players Dictionary, Sixth Edition* (*OSPD6*).

We've simplified and included in these chapters all the basic skills you'll need in order to enjoy playing an exciting and skillful SCRABBLE game.

- ❑ Learn how the *OSPD6* differs from other dictionaries.
- ❑ Learn the 107 two-letter words.
- ❑ Learn how to rearrange your tiles on your rack so that words will appear effortlessly.
- ❑ Learn how to use the bonus squares to maximize your score.
- ❑ Learn the Q words that don't use a U, as well as all the three-, four-, and five-letter Q words.
- ❑ Learn how to find seven- and eight-letter words with your rack.
- ❑ Learn how to save good combinations of letters to increase your odds of drawing better tiles.

1 LOOK IT UP: *The Official SCRABBLE® Players Dictionary, Sixth Edition*

If you want to get serious about the SCRABBLE game, sooner or later you are going to need *The Official SCRABBLE® Players Dictionary (OSPD)*. It's the "bible" of SCRABBLE word game enthusiasts and, like any important book, has a story.

Back in the dark ages, if two people were playing the SCRABBLE game, chances were they occasionally had an argument about which words were acceptable. To help decide these arguments, there has always been a variety of excellent dictionaries on the market. But while Aunt Ethel from Wyoming always used one dictionary, Uncle Dave from Nebraska used another. Invariably you could watch them battle the merits of their favorite words or nonwords late into the evening.

To clear this potential word-game roadblock, Selchow & Righter, the game's manufacturer, decided in 1975 to publish an official SCRABBLE dictionary. One of the challenges facing the company was how to get the word experts to agree upon the entries. Should it be an unabridged dictionary? Or should it simply contain the words used in everyday English?

The end result—*The Official SCRABBLE Players Dictionary*—fell somewhere in between the two extremes. Based on listings from five popular dictionaries, it lists only two- to eight-letter words. Longer words are included as inflections of shorter words (UNLIKELIEST is the superlative of UNLIKELY). To be included in the *OSPD*, a word had to be found in two of the five most popular American dictionaries. At the time, that collection of five was composed of *Webster's Seventh Collegiate Dictionary, Webster's New World Dictionary, Random House Collegiate Dictionary, American Heritage Dictionary,* and *Funk & Wagnalls College Dictionary*.

When it was finally published in 1978, the *OSPD* included more than 100,000 words. This was a SCRABBLE game player's dream!

As one might imagine, there are arguments over why certain words are included or excluded. With the number of unusual words, some people are unconvinced that the words come solely from popular dictionaries. Yet, for all its faults, the *OSPD* is the breakthrough that SCRABBLE needed to surge in popularity. Now any two North Americans could play using the same word source.

There are still the occasional gripes over the brief or unusual definitions (KANE is defined as KAIN, which you then have to look up to discover is "a tax paid in produce or livestock"), and few people are certain how to pronounce many of the words, since there are no pronunciation marks in the *OSPD*. However, the original *OSPD* edition in 1978 was generally praised as an excellent reference source for settling any SCRABBLE game word disagreement.

In 1991, Hasbro, Inc., the game's new manufacturer, and Merriam Webster published *The Official SCRABBLE Players Dictionary, Second Edition*, which was followed by the third edition in 1995, the fourth edition in 2005, and the fifth edition in 2014, and now the sixth edition in 2018.

Here are some hints on using *The Official SCRABBLE Players Dictionary, Sixth Edition:*

A) Only one definition is given for each word. Often the common meaning will be bypassed to illustrate an unusual usage. For example, IMP is listed as a verb, and is defined: "to graft feathers onto a bird's wing." The verb usage is necessary to show that IMPED and IMPING are acceptable. For the purposes of the game there was no need to mention other definitions.

B) There are special RE- and UN- lists, which include hundreds of words not defined in the text. Make sure you look at both the text and the list when verifying RE- or UN- words. The lists are printed right after the text entries for RE and UN.

C) Unless an -ING word is defined as a noun, it doesn't take an S. For example, PLAY is defined as a verb. As such, PLAYING is the present participle and is acceptable. Instead of listing PLAYING separately, it is simply shown as: "PLAY -S, -ED, -ING, to engage in amusement or sport." Since there is no separate listing for PLAYING as a noun, PLAYINGS is not acceptable. However, FLYING is acceptable, as it is listed as a noun—"*n*: pl. -S the operation of an aircraft"—and so its plural FLYINGS is acceptable.

D) If a word is listed in boldface, or as an inflection of a boldfaced word, then it is acceptable. *Example:* FOCUS is listed and so it is acceptable. Also listed and acceptable are: FOCUSED, FOCUSING, FOCUSES, FOCUSSED, FOCUSSING, and FOCUSSES.

E) There are many verbs that take an ER at the end to form a noun. After all, if you can PLAY, then there can be a PLAYER. One can BAKE, and s/he is a BAKER. However, not all verbs can be so altered. One may HELM a ship, but there is no HELMER listed in the *OSPD6*. All cases in which verbs may be made into nouns by adding ER are listed in the *OSPD6*.

F) Although foreign words are not generally considered acceptable, there are many words in the *OSPD6* that seem foreign. That's because if a word has no adequate equivalent in English, then the original foreign word is considered acceptable. For example, almost all names of foreign coins are acceptable; you will find words like PESETA (a monetary unit of Spain) and XU (a Vietnamese coin) acceptable. Also, foreign titles are acceptable, such as QAID (a Muslim leader) and SAHIB (sir; master—used as a term of respect in colonial India).

G) Some words are listed in boldface more than once. For instance, BRITTLE is listed as an adjective and shows the inflections BRITTLER and BRITTLEST. If someone challenges BRITTLED, an inexperienced word judge might assume, after seeing this entry, that BRITTLED is unacceptable. Wrong! BRITTLE is *also* listed separately as a verb and can be inflected as BRITTLED, BRITTLING, and BRITTLES. So when you can't find an entry, be sure you check before and after the expected alphabetic positioning of a word for an alternate listing.

While there may always be discussions about which words should or should not be acceptable, we must always defer to the *OSPD6*, so that we are all playing by the same rules. We should not forget that the *OSPD6* allows equal chances to all players.

Now that you've been introduced to the *OSPD6*, let's look at a few basic SCRABBLE game rules that you'll need to know.

One last comment for those who once used the *OSPD2:* DA, DEI, DES, KEV, VIN(S) and VON were all removed from the *OSPD3*. These words were reviewed and ultimately rejected as unacceptable by both the Merriam-Webster Company and the NSA's Dictionary Committee. For the *OSPD4* EMF was deemed a mistake as well, and so removed. For the *OSPD5*, DA(S) and VIN(S) were added back.

2 THE ABCs: How to Make Plays and Score Bonus Points—A Word About Notations, Diagrams, and Puzzles

Below is a representation of a SCRABBLE® Brand Crossword game board. Following it are explanations for some of the symbols used in this book.

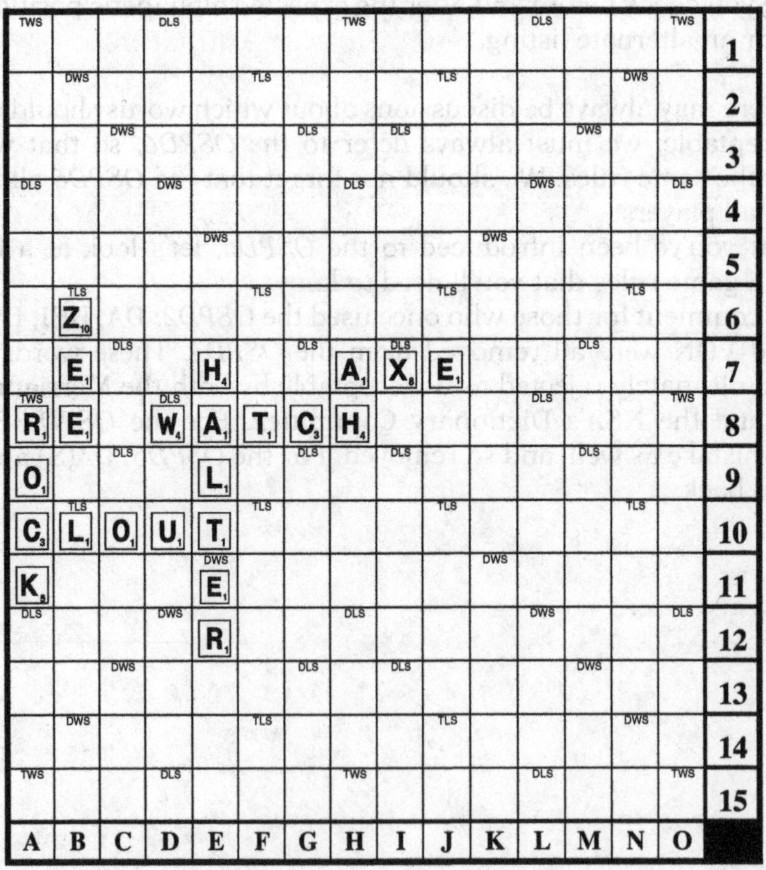

A B C D E F G H I J K L M N O
1 2 3 4 5 6 7 8 9 10 11 12 13 14 15
TWS
DWS
TLS
DLS

DIAGRAM 2-1

TWS = TRIPLE WORD SCORE

When a TWS square is covered, the player covering it scores triple the value of the sum of the individual letters of the word covering the TWS. *Example:* Adding the letters R, O, and K in Diagram 2-1, forming ROCK, scored 1 (R) + 1 (O) + 3 (C) + 5 (K) = 10 x 3 = 30 points. Notice that ROCK was played after CLOUT but before ZEE.

DWS = DOUBLE WORD SCORE

When a DWS square is covered, the player covering it scores double the value of the sum of the individual letters of the word covering the DWS. *Example:* The play of HALTER in Diagram 2-1 scored 4 (H) + 1 (A) + 1 (L) + 1 (T) + 1 (E) + 1 (R) = 9 x 2 = 18 points.

TLS = TRIPLE LETTER SCORE

When a TLS square is covered, the value of the letter covering the TLS is tripled. *Example:* For the play of ZEE in Diagram 2-1, the Z alone was worth 3 x 10 = 30 points.

DLS = DOUBLE LETTER SCORE

When a DLS square is covered, the value of the letter covering the DLS is doubled. *Example:* For playing AXE in Diagram 2-1, the X alone was worth 8 x 2 = 16 points.

It's also wise to keep in mind another way to score points quickly. As mentioned earlier, there is an additional 50-point bonus if you use all seven tiles on your rack in one play, commonly known as a bingo.

? = BLANK

The blank tile is worth zero points and is represented in the text as a question mark: "?". In diagrams, a blank has a black background.

Recording Plays

Notice the numbers 1–15 printed down the right side of the board on Diagram 2-1, as well as the letters printed across the bottom. With their help we can describe any square of the board with only a letter and number. Thus, the center square is represented as either 8H or H8.

When the *number* is listed first, the play is *horizontal.* That shows that the word is played across a row. When the *letter* is listed first, the play is *vertical.* That shows that the word is played down a column.

Example

In Diagram 2-1 the opening play of WATCH is recorded as: WATCH 8D. The 8D represents the square that is in the eighth row and intersects the D column, and is the location of the *first letter* of the word. The second play, HALTER, is recorded as HALTER E7. The E7 represents the square that is in the E column and intersects the seventh row, and is the square on which the word begins.

Who Plays First?

Here's how you determine who plays first at the start of the game: Each of the players randomly chooses one tile from the pool. The player who draws the letter closest to the beginning of the alphabet plays first. Drawing a blank tile automatically earns first play. If the drawn tiles are identical, the players draw again. After it is determined who goes first, all drawn tiles are returned to the pool and the first player draws seven new tiles to start the game.

Whoever is first to play begins the game by forming a word with two or more letters, playing it horizontally or vertically so that one of the letters covers the pink center Double Word Score square.

Note that in most diagrams in this book we make the first play horizontally. We've found that most people play the first word that way, though there is absolutely nothing wrong with starting vertically. Also note that we often print the score of a play next to the beginning square. *Example:* PARTY 8D 26 points. This signifies that the word "party" was played beginning on the 8D square, moving across the board horizontally, and earned 26 points.

Basic Play-Making 101

After the first play, there are *four ways* to add words to the board. The official rules included with the game mention only three. We haven't changed the rules; we're just redefining those three ways to make it even easier to understand.

1. Play *through* an existing word.

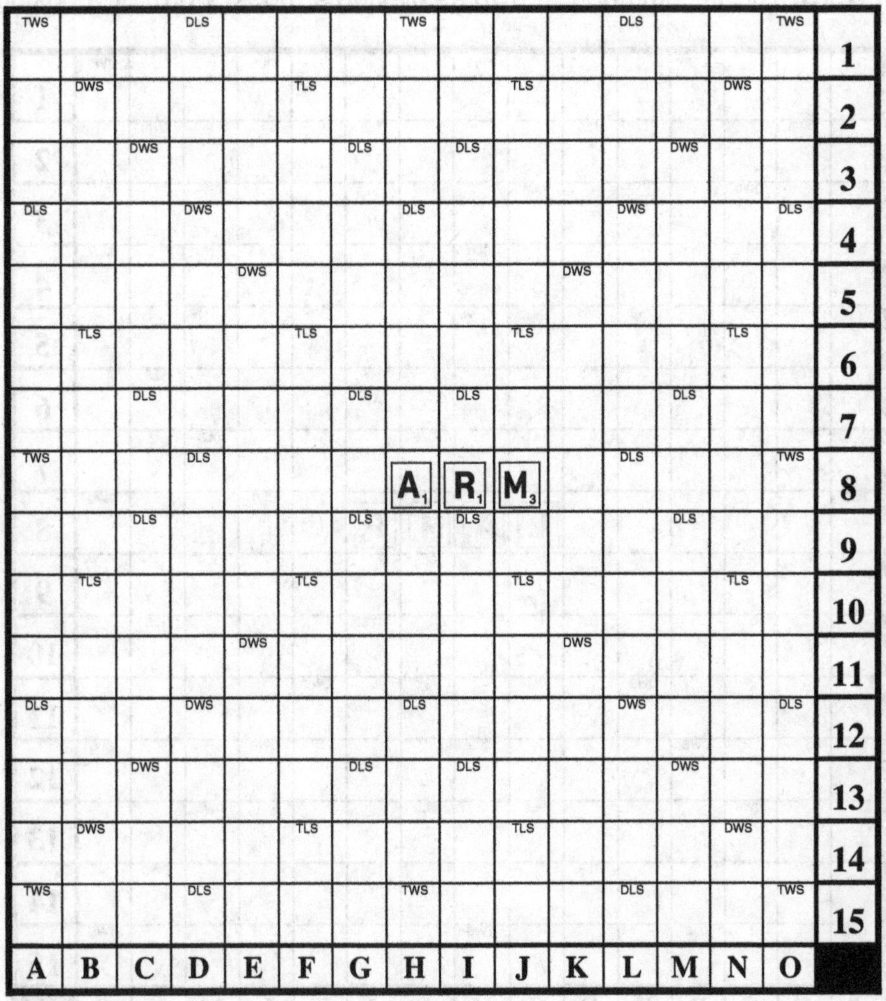
A B C D E F G H I J K L M N O
1 2 3 4 5 6 7 8 9 10 11 12 13 14 15
TWS
DWS
TLS
DLS
A 1
R 1
M 3

DIAGRAM 2-2

Example

Imagine that Diagram 2-2 is your game position. Your rack: **C G H I L N Y**

What would you play?

You may play *through* one of the letters of the word ARM to form your play. Some choices are: CLANG H6 8 points, HIM J6 16, RICH I8 10, CHAIN H6 10, and LAYING H7 12.

2. *Add* a letter to the front or back of an existing word and play perpendicular to that word. This is commonly known as playing a "hook" word, or "hooking."

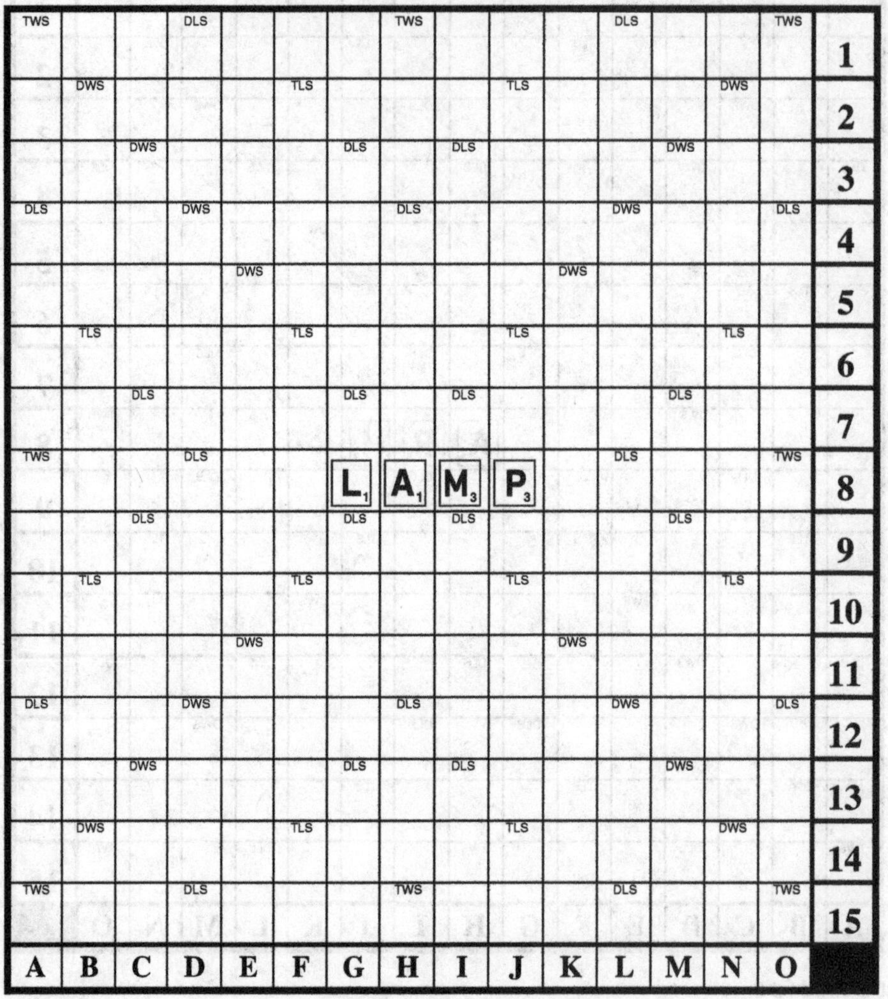
TWS DLS TWS DLS TWS 1
DWS TLS TLS DWS 2
DWS DLS DLS DWS 3
DLS DWS DLS DWS DLS 4
DWS DWS 5
TLS TLS TLS TLS 6
DLS DLS DLS DLS 7
TWS DLS L1 A1 M3 P3 DLS TWS 8
DLS DLS DLS DLS 9
TLS TLS TLS TLS 10
DWS DWS 11
DLS DWS DLS DWS DLS 12
DWS DLS DLS DWS 13
DWS TLS TLS DWS 14
TWS DLS TWS DLS TWS 15
A B C D E F G H I J K L M N O

DIAGRAM 2-3

Example

Imagine Diagram 2-3 is your game position. Your rack: **A B C L N O Y**

What would you play?

You may add a C to LAMP to form CLAMP and form another word played vertically on the board. Some choices are: CLAY F8 22 points, BACON F6 28, COB F8 24, COY F8 27, and LACY F6 22.

3. *Extend* a word by adding letters either to the front or back, or to both the front and back.

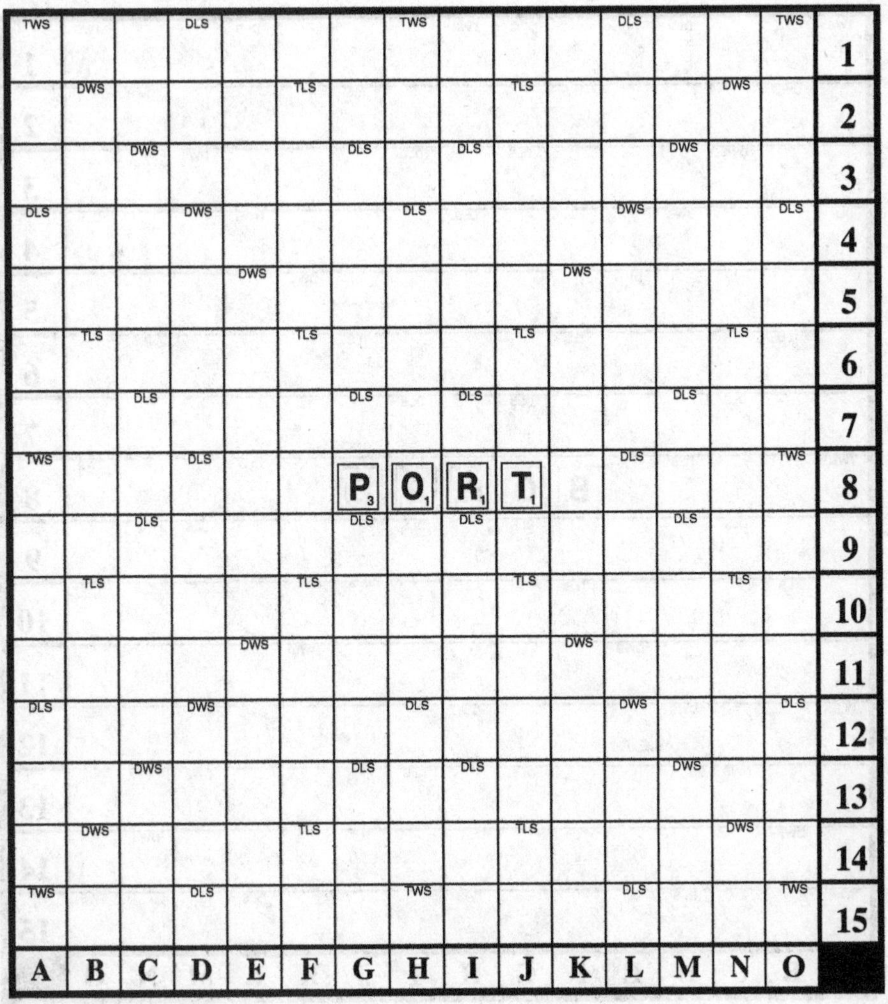
PORT
A B C D E F G H I J K L M N O
1 2 3 4 5 6 7 8 9 10 11 12 13 14 15

DIAGRAM 2-4

Example

Imagine Diagram 2-4 is your game position. Your rack: **ADEEIMR**

What would you play?

You may extend PORT in a variety of ways: REPORT 8E 8 points, DEPORT 8E 9, PORTER 8G 9, REPORTED 8E 13, IMPORT 8E 10, IMPORTED 8E 15, and REIMPORTED 8C 18.

4. Play *parallel* to an existing word, forming two or more words on the same play.

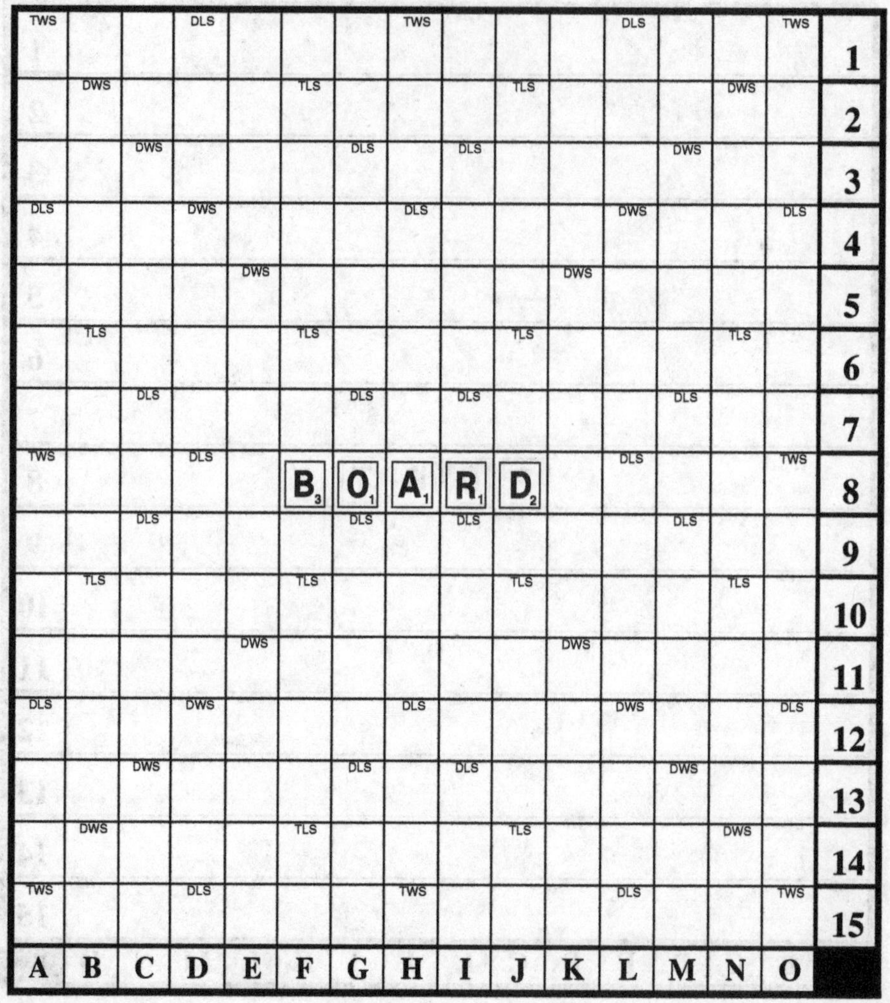
TWS DLS TWS DLS TWS 1
DWS TLS TLS DWS 2
DWS DLS DLS DWS 3
DLS DWS DLS DWS DLS 4
DWS DWS 5
TLS TLS TLS TLS 6
DLS DLS DLS DLS 7
TWS DLS B O A R D DLS TWS 8
DLS DLS DLS DLS 9
TLS TLS TLS TLS 10
DWS DWS 11
DLS DWS DLS DWS DLS 12
DWS DLS DLS DWS 13
DWS TLS TLS DWS 14
TWS DLS TWS DLS TWS 15
A B C D E F G H I J K L M N O

DIAGRAM 2-5

Example

Imagine Diagram 2-5 is your game position. Your rack: **A C E R T T X**

What would you play?

You may play parallel to BOARD, with several choices: CRATE 9B 12 points, which also forms BE; CATER 9C 18, which also forms BE and OR; and TEXT 9E 42, which also forms BE, OX, and AT.

Once you learn that BA is acceptable (it means "the eternal soul in Egyptian mythology"), then TAX 9E 39 points is possible, which forms OX as well.

With both plays, TEXT 9E and TAX 9E, the X is played on a Double Letter Score and helps form two words simultaneously. This means that the X is scored as a double letter (16 points) for *each* word it helps form. This is important to remember, since once you learn this principle, you'll be able to score 32 points for just the X when it forms two words at once. And on a Triple Letter Score, the X can score you 48 points when it spells two words at once!

But remember, once a letter is played, later words that use that letter don't earn the bonus square it covers. That bonus is good only the first time it's used.

Knowing the rules in this chapter is your starting point for SCRABBLE excellence. Your first step forward is learning the 107 two-letter words in chapter 3.

3 IT TAKES "TWOS" TO TANGLE

The two-letter words are without question the most critical building blocks to improving your game. In fact, NASPA routinely advises new members that learning "the twos" will almost automatically increase their scoring average by 30 to 40 points a game.

These two-letter gems are priceless, for a couple of reasons. First, they will increase your scoring opportunities by allowing more parallel plays. Second, knowing the twos opens up many more spots for scoring, often allowing you to play a bingo where there would otherwise be no place on the board. Few things in the game are more frustrating than holding a bingo with nowhere to play it!

It's also encouraging to realize that you already know many of the two-letter words, and that the rest are relatively easy to learn. For example, there are several common sources of two-letter words.

One is the diatonic musical scale: DO, RE, MI, FA, SO, LA, TI. Another is the Greek alphabet, a terrific source for both twos and unusual threes, such as XI, MU, NU, RHO, CHI, and more. Then there is the English alphabet itself, where most letters have their own spellings. For example, all of the following are real words: EF (F), EM (M), EN (N), AR (R), ES (S), and EX (X). Some threes include CEE, DEE, GEE, VEE, and ZEE. Here is an example of how a two-letter word can make a +50-point play all by itself:

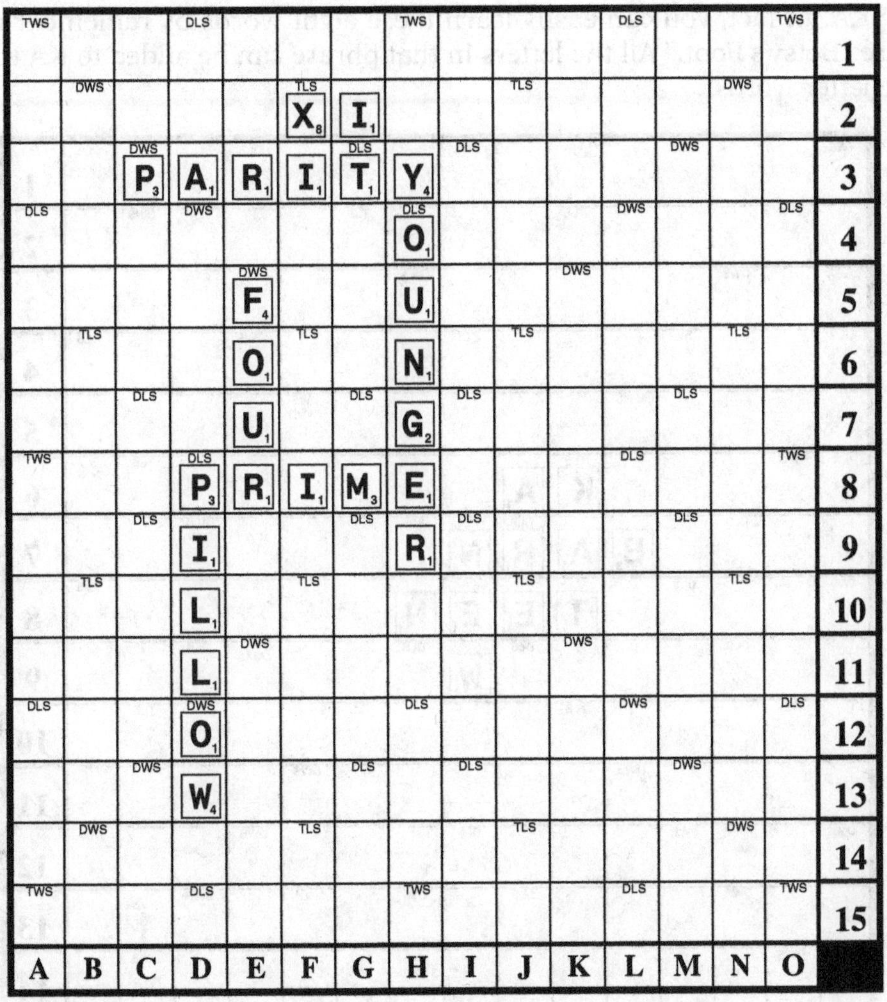
XI
PARITY
YOUNGER
FOUR
PRIME
PILLOW

DIAGRAM 3-1

As you can see in Diagram 3-1, playing the word XI above and parallel to the word PARITY allows you to score with the X in both directions, making for a 52-point play. You could have also played XU in the same spot, assuming you had also learned the two-letter word UT. This would have not only scored big, but also enabled you to get rid of the X and U, both tough letters to carry on your rack if you are trying to build a seven-letter word and earn the 50-point bonus for using all your tiles. (See chapter 7.)

Diagram 3-2 shows an example using the word KA, a favorite of many SCRABBLE players. That's because it can take a third letter to form several three-letter words. They include: KAB, KAE, KAF, KAS, KAT, KAY, OKA, and SKA. In fact, you can easily learn these eight words by remembering the phrase "Betsy's Foot." All the letters in that phrase can be added to KA to form three-letter words!

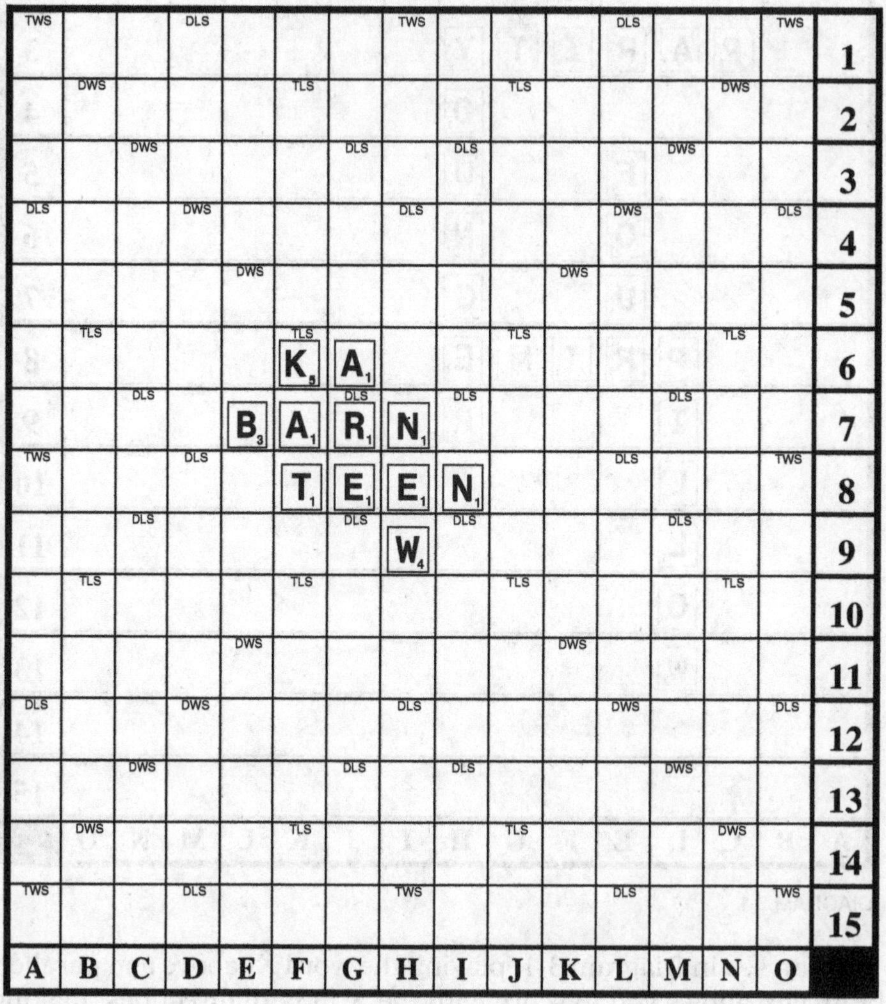

K A
B A R N
T E E N
W
A B C D E F G H I J K L M N O
1 2 3 4 5 6 7 8 9 10 11 12 13 14 15

DIAGRAM 3-2

Just played: KA 6F 36 points

In Diagram 3-2, knowledge of the two-letter words pays off with the 36-point play of KA. It also points out another good function of the twos: allowing you to score well without opening up much scoring opportunity for an opponent. And while you don't want to play your entire game in such a "closed" fashion, there are definitely situations when it makes good sense strategically. (See chapter 14 on open and closed boards.)

As we said earlier, the two-letter words are also valuable because they open up opportunities. Diagram 3-3 shows an example of how knowledge of the twos results in a high-scoring play on a somewhat closed board.

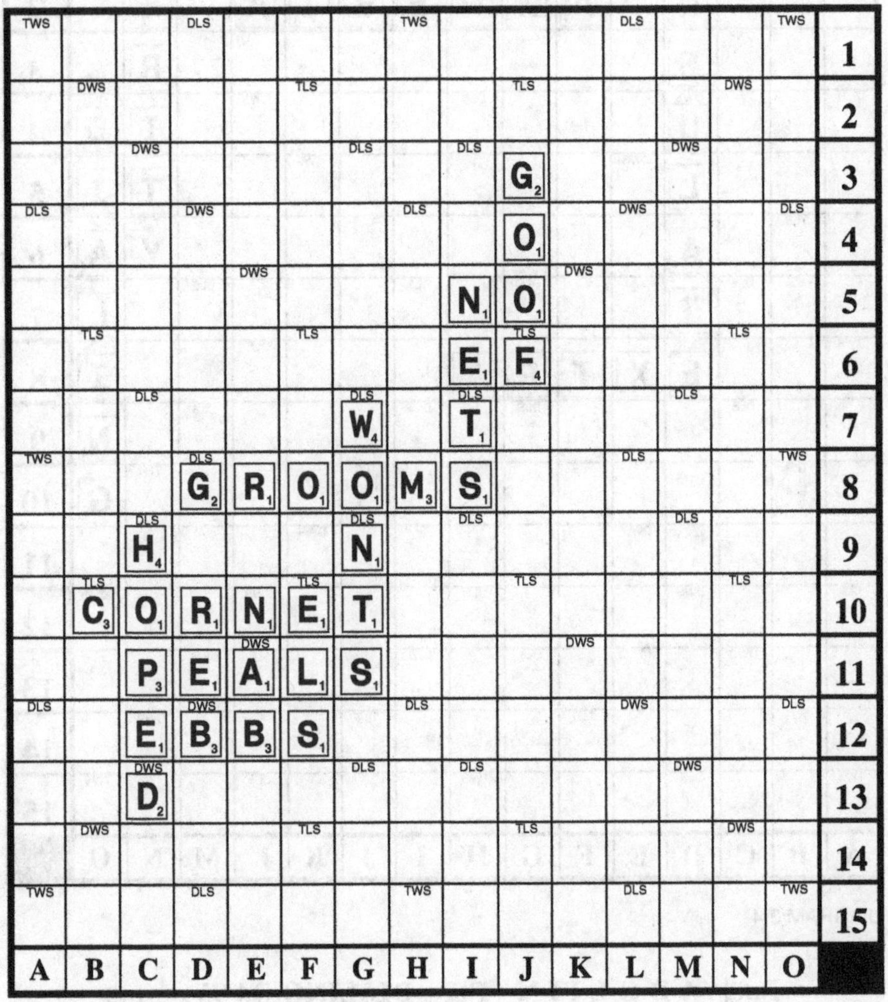

GOOF
NETS
WONTS
GROOMS
HOPED
CORNET
PEALS
EBBS
A B C D E F G H I J K L M N O
1 2 3 4 5 6 7 8 9 10 11 12 13 14 15

DIAGRAM 3-3

Rack: **A F G L O O V** Play: **GOOF** J3 31 points

In Diagram 3-4 is an example of how knowledge of the twos allowed a player not only to score a bingo for an extra 50 points, but to earn a Triple Word

Score as well. Note that DIALING could also be played at 9H, but for far fewer points.

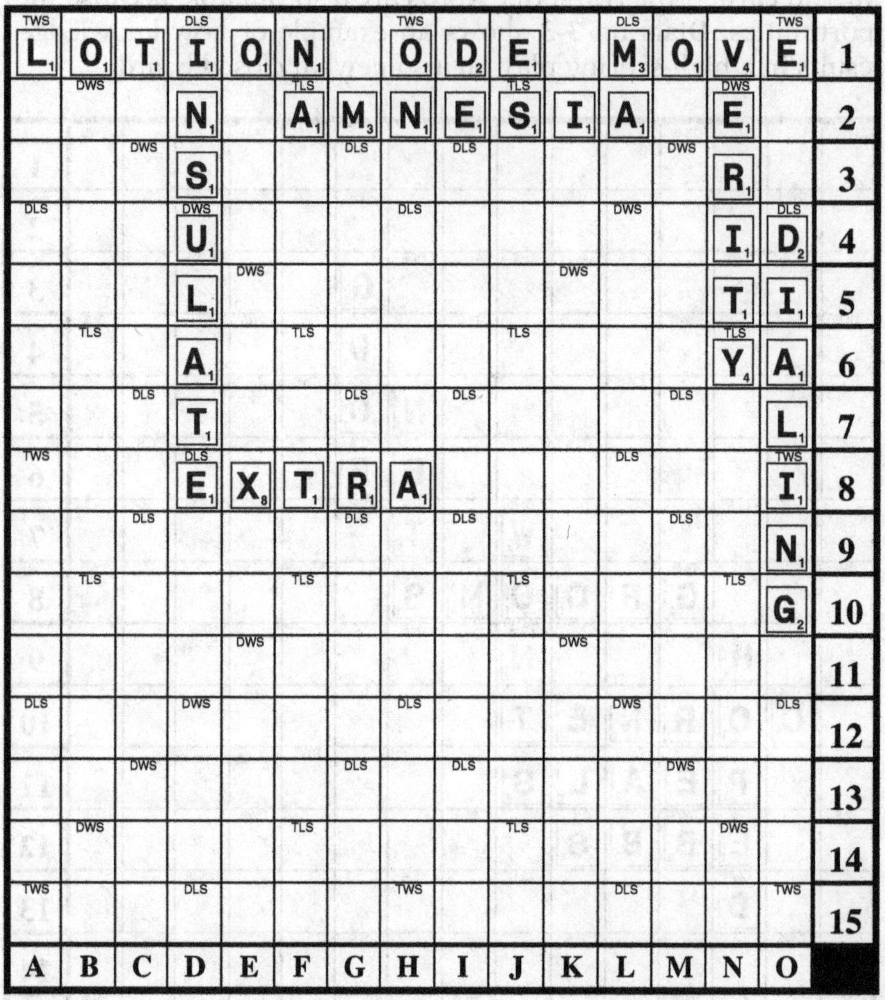

DIAGRAM 3-4

Rack: **A D G L I I N** Play: **DIALING** O4 95 points

You can see why when someone asks us how s/he can become an expert, the first thing we say is: Learn the twos.

Following is a list of all 107 two-letter words in *The Official SCRABBLE® Players Dictionary*. Next, you will want to be able to find those high-scoring plays that will take advantage of your knowledge of the twos. To do that means learning how to rearrange the tiles on your rack. Next stop: chapter 4.

The 107 Acceptable Two-Letter Words

AA: *n* pl. -S rough, cindery lava
AB: *n* pl. -S an abdominal muscle
AD: *n* pl. -S an advertisement
AE: *adj* one
AG: *adj* pertaining to agriculture
AH: *interj*—used to express delight, relief, or contempt
AI: *n* pl. -S a three-toed sloth
AL: *n* pl. -S an East Indian tree
AM: present 1st person sing. of BE
AN: *indefinite article*—used before words beginning with a vowel
AR: *n* pl. -S the letter R
AS: *adv* to the same degree
AT: *prep* in the position of
AW: *interj*—used to express protest, disgust, or disbelief
AX: *v* -ED, -ING, -ES to work on with an ax (a type of cutting tool)
AY: *n* pl. -S aye
BA: *n* pl. -S the eternal soul in Egyptian mythology
BE: *v* AM, ARE, ART, WAS, WERE, WAST, WERT, BEEN, BEING to have actuality
BI: *n* pl. -S a bisexual
BO: *n* pl. -S a pal
BY: *n* pl. -S a pass in certain card games
DA: *n* pl. -S dad
DE: *prep* of; from—used in names
DO: *n* pl. -S the first tone of the diatonic scale
ED: *n* pl. -S education
EF: *n* pl. -S the letter F
EH: *interj*—used to express doubt
EL: *n* pl. -S an elevated railroad or train
EM: *n* pl. -S the letter M
EN: *n* pl. -S the letter N
ER: *interj*—used to express hesitation
ES: *n* pl. ESES the letter S (also spelled ESS)
ET: a past tense of EAT
EW: *interj*—used to express disgust
EX: *n* pl. EXES the letter X
FA: *n* pl. -S the fourth tone of the diatonic musical scale
FE: *n* pl. -S a Hebrew letter
GI: *n* pl. -S a white garment worn in martial arts
GO: *v* WENT, GONE, GOING, GOES to move along
HA: *n* pl. -S a sound of surprise
HE: *n* pl. -S a male person
HI: *interj*—used as a greeting
HM: *interj*—used to express thoughtful consideration
HO: *interj*—used to express surprise
ID: *n* pl. -S a part of the psyche
IF: *n* pl. -S a possibility
IN: *v* INNED, INNING, INS to harvest
IS: present 3rd person sing. of BE
IT: *pron* the 3rd person sing. neuter, all three cases
JO: *n* pl. -ES a sweetheart
KA: *n* pl. -S the spiritual self of a human being in Egyptian religion
KI: *n* pl. -S the vital force in Chinese thought

LA: *n* pl. -S the sixth tone of the diatonic musical scale
LI: *n* pl. -S a Chinese unit of distance
LO: *interj*—used to attract attention or to express surprise
MA: *n* pl. -S mother
ME: *pron* the objective case of the pronoun I
MI: *n* pl. -S the third tone of the diatonic musical scale
MM: *interj*—used to express assent or satisfaction
MO: *n* pl. -S a moment
MU: *n* pl. -S a Greek letter
MY: *pron* the possessive form of the pronoun I
NA: *adv* no; not
NE: *adj* born with the name of (also NEE)
NO: *n* pl. NOS or NOES a negative reply
NU: *n* pl. -S a Greek letter
OD: *n* pl. -S a hypothetical force of natural power
OE: *n* pl. -S a whirlwind off the Faeroe Islands
OF: *prep* coming from
OH: *v* -ED, -ING, -S to exclaim in surprise, pain, or desire
OI: *interj*—OY
OK: *n* approval
OM: *n* pl. -S a mantra used in contemplation of ultimate reality
ON: *n* pl. -S the side of the wicket where a batsman stands in cricket
OP: *n* pl. -S a style of abstract art
OR: *n* pl. -S the heraldic color gold
OS: *n* pl. -S ORA, OSSA, or OSAR either an orifice, a bone, or an esker
OW: *interj*—used to express sudden pain
OX: *n* pl. OXEN or OXES a hoofed mammal or clumsy person
OY: *interj*—used to express dismay or pain
PA: *n* pl. -S a father
PE: *n* pl. -S a Hebrew letter
PI: *v* PIED, PIEING, PIING, or PIES to jumble or disorder
PO: *n* pl. -S a chamber pot
QI: *n* pl. -S the vital force that in Chinese thought is inherent in all things
RE: *n* pl. -S the second tone of the diatonic musical scale
SH: *interj*—used to urge silence
SI: *n* pl. -S ti
SO: *n* pl. -S the fifth tone of the diatonic musical scale
TA: *n* pl. -S an expression of gratitude
TE: *s* pl. -S ti
TI: *n* pl. -S the seventh tone of the diatonic musical scale
TO: *prep* in the direction of
UH: *interj*—used to express hesitation
UM: *interj*—used to indicate hesitation
UN: *pron* pl. -S one
UP: *v* UPPED, UPPING, UPS to raise
US: *pron* the objective case of the pronoun we
UT: *n* pl. -S the musical tone C in the French solmization system, now replaced by do
WE: *pron* the 1st person pl. pronoun in the nominative case
WO: *n* pl. -S woe
XI: *n* pl. -S a Greek letter
XU: *n* pl. XU a monetary unit of Vietnam
YA: *pron* you
YE: *pron* you
YO: *interj*—used to call attention or express affirmation
ZA: *n* pl. -S pizza

4 REARRANGING YOUR TILES MAKES WORDS APPEAR!

We have observed many new SCRABBLE game players struggling unnecessarily to find words with their seven tiles. Why do they struggle? That's easy! They think that a word will simply occur to them if they sit and *stare* at their rack of seven letters. That's definitely *not* the best way to go about finding good plays.

We advise that you get into the habit of moving the tiles around on your rack frequently, often randomly. Words will appear before your eyes, often like magic! As you become more experienced, you will learn which combinations of letters will produce more words than others.

Let's show you what we mean. This might be a good time to pull out your own SCRABBLE set and use an actual rack and letters. Try to spell a common seven-letter word with these letters:

A E G N O S T*

Below are some sample arrangements. Examine each one only briefly before going on to the next one. After you become experienced moving tiles on your rack, finding such words may become commonplace. The answer is at the end of this chapter.

AEGNOST	TONAGES	TEAGONS	ETAGONS
NOGATES	STONAGE	GANTOES	SENTAGO
GETANOS	OGENTAS	ANTOGES	ENGOATS
NOSTAGE			

* TANGOES is now acceptable because it was added to the *OSPD5*. Let's assume that you cannot play TANGOES.

Following is a surefire system for moving tiles on your rack in order to be thorough in your search for words.

Imagine you have just four tiles on your rack: A, B, D, and E. These can be arranged into twenty-four different possible arrangements. How fast can you form all twenty-four arrangements? Experts can do it in their heads in just a few seconds. If you can manipulate the tiles quickly enough, checking for words as you go, you can probably learn to do it in less than a minute. Start by putting them in alphabetical order. Note any letters that form a word. Here's the list: ABDE, ABED, ADBE, ADEB, AEBD, AEDB, BADE, BAED, BDAE, BDEA, BEAD, BEDA, DABE, DAEB, DBAE, DBEA, DEAB, DEBA, EABD, EADB, EBAD, EBDA, EDAB, EDBA.

Of course, in one turn you'll never be able to form all the arrangements of a typical rack of seven different letters (there are 5,040 of them). But as you learn how to combine letters, you usually won't need to use this systematic approach for more than four letters at a time.

To really burn this system into your memory, try the following exercise just once: Take the lettered tiles A, E, P, R, and S and form all 120 arrangements. Start with AEPRS, AEPSR, APERS, etc. This exercise will give you the experience and practice you need to know how to move your tiles on your rack. While you're doing it, try to recognize the twelve acceptable five-letter words spellable with these exact letters. Only eight of them are common words. You'd need an unusually good vocabulary to recognize the rest. You'll find all twelve words at the end of this chapter.

To help develop your word-finding ability, we suggest practicing with the following chart. Find several words that use each pair or triplet of consonants. By knowing how consonants go together, you'll become more efficient at rearranging combinations of letters to form words. For example: Using the B, you might find BLACK, BLIMP, BLUE, CLIMB, LAMB, SYMBOL, BROWN, BRICK, HERB, CURB, and MARBLE.

Once you're able to find the words on your rack, you will want to be able to use the bonus squares on the board to boost the scores of your words. Chapter 5 will show you exactly how to do that.

Common Combinations of Consonants

2-LETTER COMBOS

B: BL, MB, BR, RB
C: CH, CK, CL, CR, NC, RC, SC, CT
D: DL, DG, DR, LD, ND, RD
F: FL, LF, FR, RF
G: GH, DG, GL, LG, GN, NG, GR, RG
H: CH, GH, PH, SH, TH, WH
K: CK, LK, KL, NK, KN, RK, SK
L: BL, CL, DL, LD, FL, LF, GL, LG, KL, LK, LM, PL, LP, RL, LS, SL, LT, TL, LV, WL
M: MB, MP, LM, RM, SM
N: NC, ND, NG, GN, NK, KN, RN, NS, SN, NT, WN
P: PH, PL, LP, MP, RP, PR, SP, PT
R: BR, RB, CR, RC, DR, RD, FR, RF, GR, RG, RK, RL, RM, RN, PR, RP, RS, RT, TR, RV, WR
S: SC, SH, SK, SL, LS, NS, SM, SN, SP, PS, RS, ST, SW
T: CT, FT, TH, LT, TL, NT, PT, TR, RT, ST, TW
V: LV, RV
W: WH, WL, WN, WR, SW, TW

3-LETTER COMBOS

CHR, CKL, GHT, LCH, LTH, NCH, NDL, NGL, NKL, NTH, RCH, RDL, RGL, RST, RTH, SCH, SCR, SHR, SPL, SPR, STR, TCH, THR

ANSWERS: CHAPTER 4

AGENOST = ONSTAGE

AEPRS = APERS, APRES, ASPER, PARES, PARSE, PEARS, PRASE, PRESA, RAPES, REAPS, SPARE, SPEAR

5 MAXIMIZE YOUR SCORING: Head for the "Hot Spots"

In theory, there are often several hundred different possible plays you can make on any one turn. How should you choose which ones are the best? Naturally, your first priority is the score. The higher the score, the better the play—usually. This chapter is devoted to helping you find those high-scoring plays. In chapters 8 and 9 we'll explore how to determine which of those choices is best strategically. We suggest you use a board and have a set of tiles in front of you when you try some of the puzzles in this chapter. You're more likely to have an easier time solving them, as well as better success simulating actual game situations.

Very simply: **Use the bonus squares!** We also call them "hot spots," because they can lead you to earn an explosive number of points. They are where the action is! And while one bonus square is good, we advise, if you can: **Cover Two Bonus Squares at Once!**

1. Bonus Squares and Parallel Play

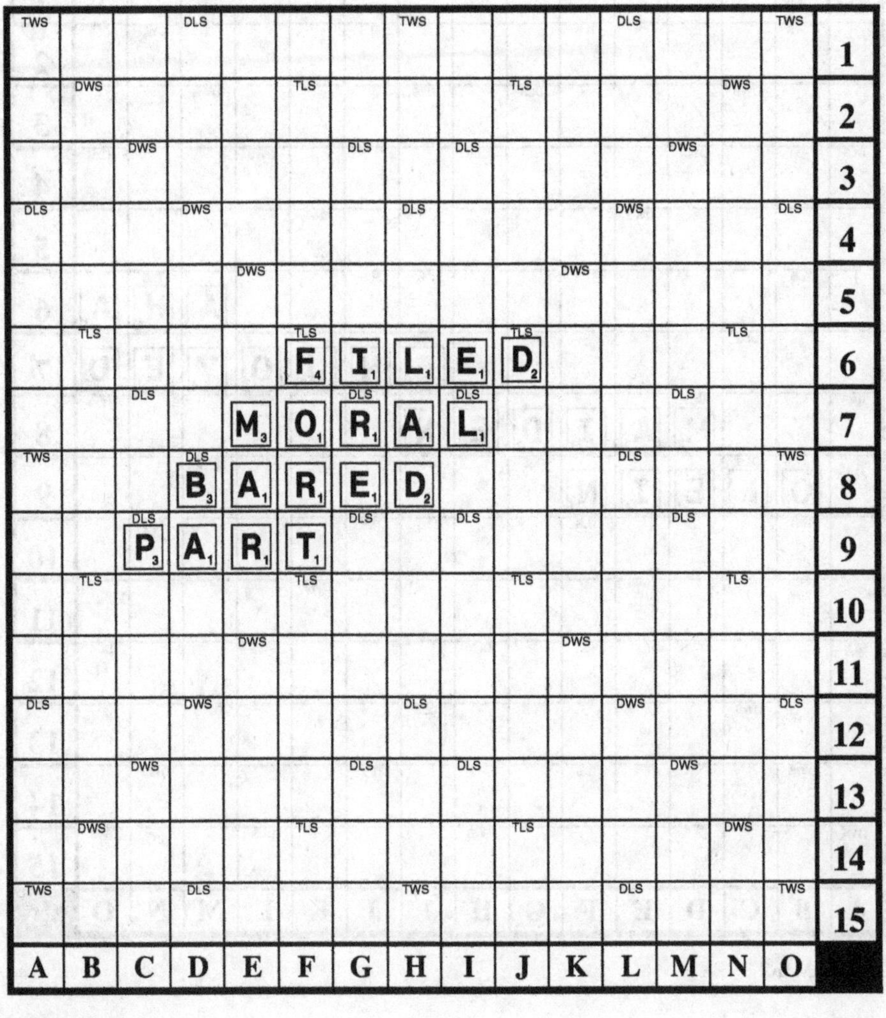
FILED
MORAL
BARED
PART
A B C D E F G H I J K L M N O
1 2 3 4 5 6 7 8 9 10 11 12 13 14 15

DIAGRAM 5-1

Always look for plays parallel and adjacent to words already on the board. Often such plays will score many more points than most others. *Example:* In Diagram 5-1, the play of PART also formed BA, MAR, and FORT, scoring a total of 25 points, whereas PART itself scored only 9. That's a bonus of 16 extra points for playing parallel to another word.

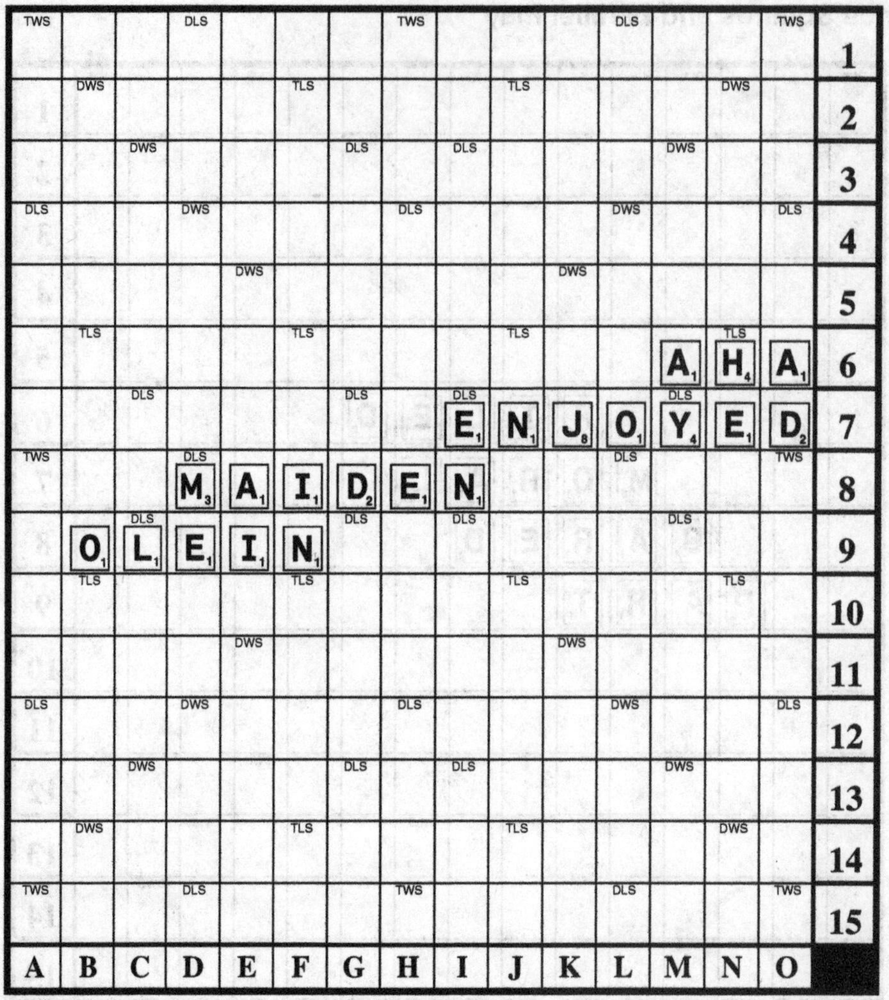
AHA
ENJOYED
MAIDEN
OLEIN

DIAGRAM 5-2

Find an outstanding way to play each of the following words onto Diagram 5-2. As you find a place for each word, remove the word from the position and go on to the next word. The answers are on page 55.

Time limit: 20 minutes

1. REND
2. DOUBTS
3. NONSKID
4. QUITE

2. Triple Letter–Triple Letter

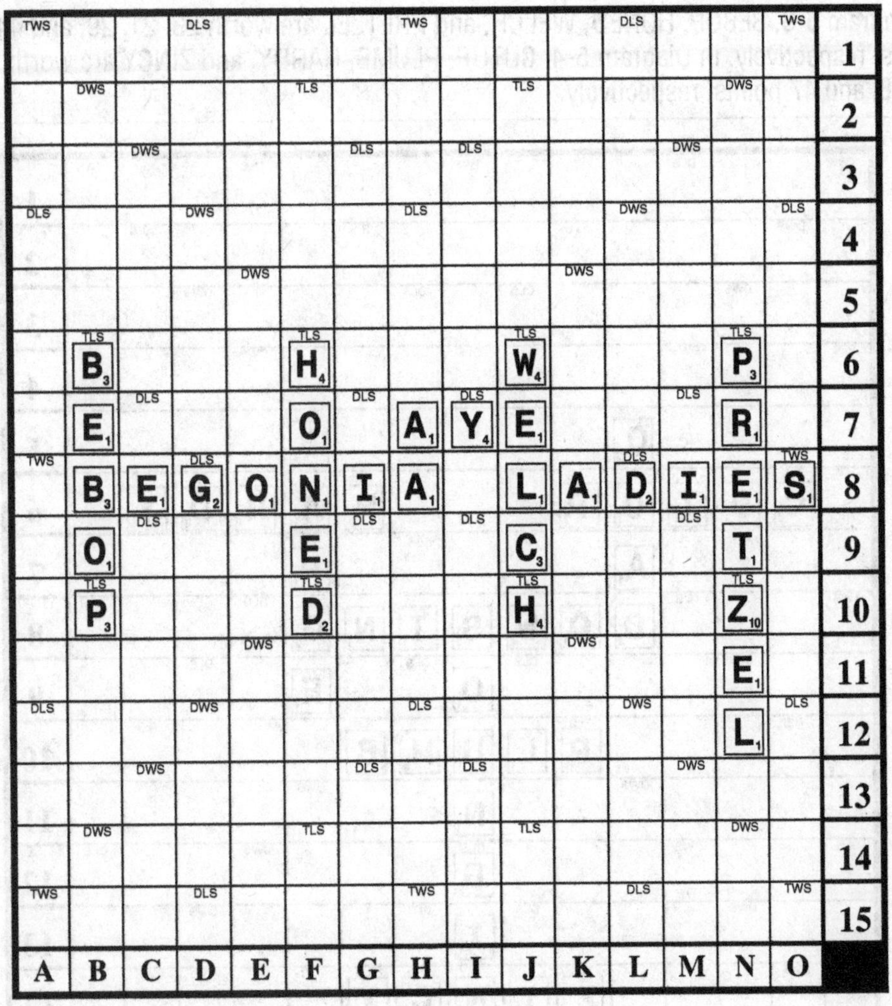

BEBOP
HONED
AYE
WELCH
PRETZEL
BEGONIA
LADIES
A B C D E F G H I J K L M N O

DIAGRAM 5-3

Because the twelve Triple Letter Score squares are aligned in the same four rows and columns, look for opportunities to use two of them when you have several high-point tiles. These combinations can be formed on the B, F, J, and N columns, as well as on rows 2, 6, 10, and 14.

Examples

In Diagram 5-3, BEBOP, HONED, WELCH, and PRETZEL are worth 23, 21, 29, and 44 points, respectively. In Diagram 5-4, CUTUP, PLUMB, HARDY, and ZINCY are worth 21, 23, 28, and 47 points, respectively.

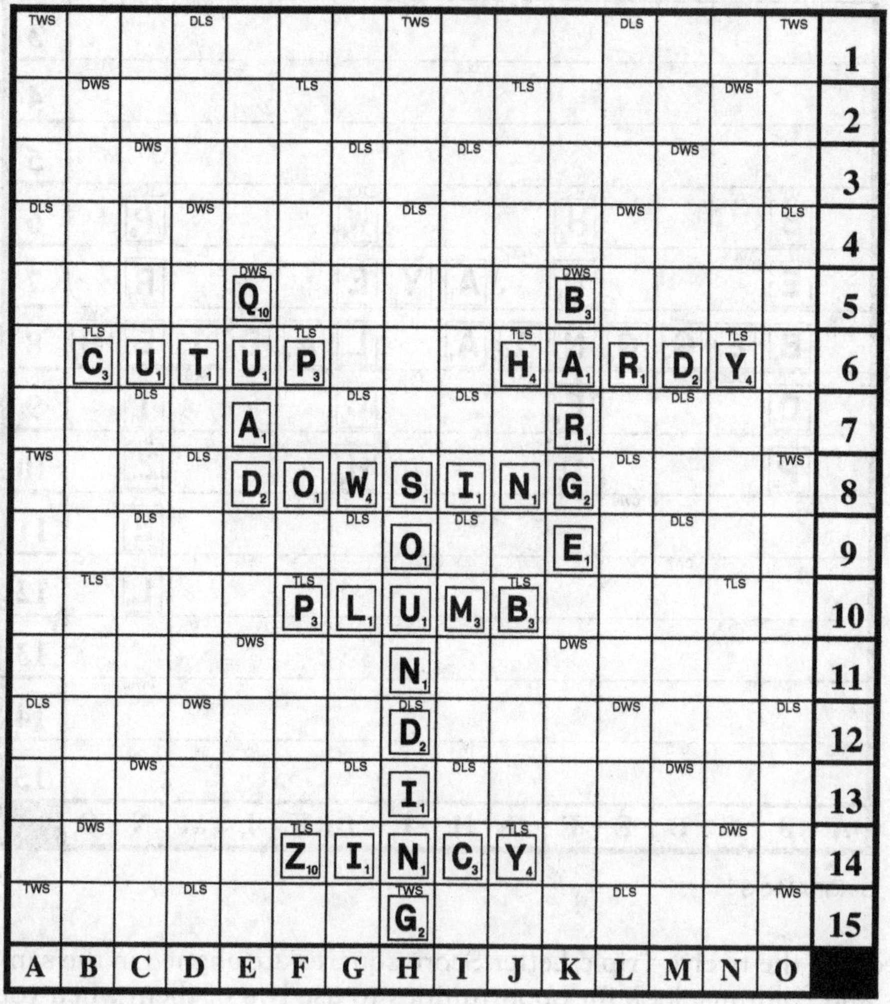

CUTUP
HARDY
QUAD
BARGE
DOWSING
SOUNDING
PLUMB
ZINCY
TWS
DWS
TLS
DLS
A B C D E F G H I J K L M N O
1 2 3 4 5 6 7 8 9 10 11 12 13 14 15

DIAGRAM 5-4

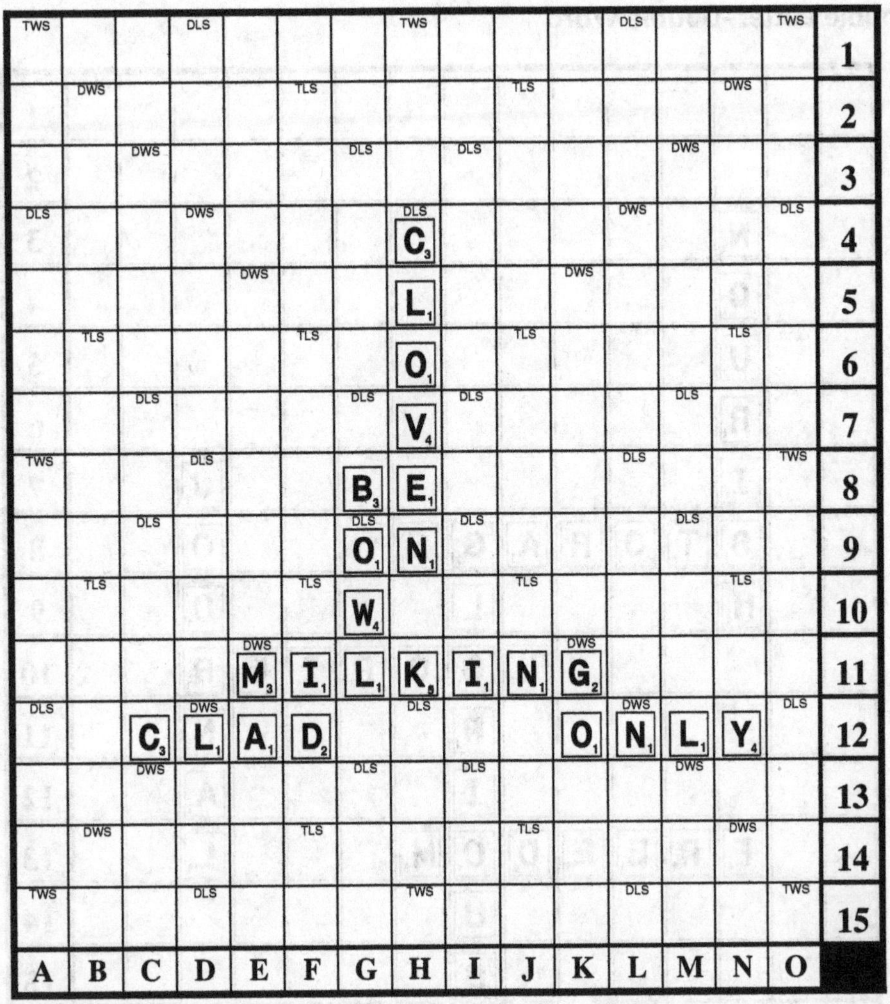

DIAGRAM 5-5

Your rack: **I M N P P R T**

Use Diagram 5-5 and the letters IMNPPRT to find a play covering two TLSs. The highest-scoring, common-word answer is on page 55.

Time limit: 10 minutes

3. Double Letter–Double Word

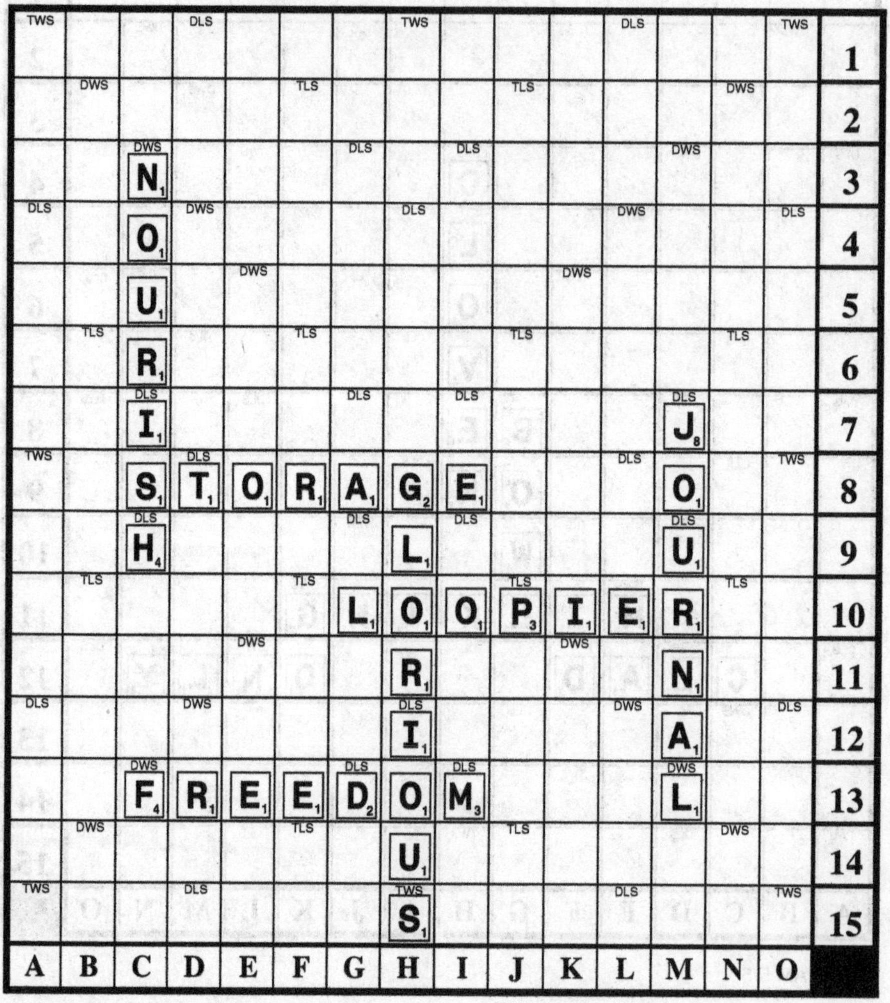
NOURISH
STORAGE
GLORIOUS
LOOPIER
JOURNAL
FREEDOM

DIAGRAM 5-6

When you have opportunities to use a Double Word Score square, don't overlook using the Double Letter Score squares as well. You may even have an opportunity to use *two* DLSs with one DWS. These can be commonly formed on rows 3 and 13 or columns C and M. Less frequently, you may be able to use two DLSs in one play on rows 4 and 12 or on columns D and L.

Examples

In Diagram 5-6, NOURISH, FREEDOM, and JOURNAL are worth 30, 36, and 46 points, respectively. In Diagram 5-7, FEELING, CRYPTIC, and ZANIEST are worth 28, 40, and 54 points, respectively.

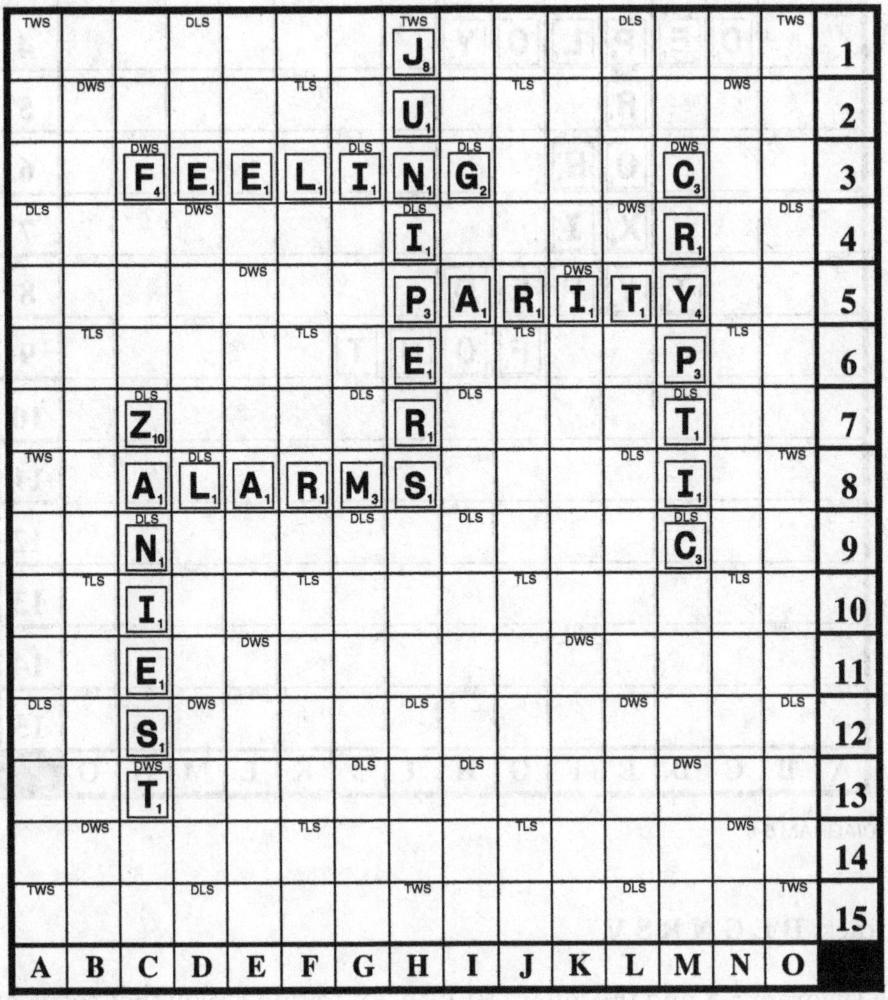

DIAGRAM 5-7

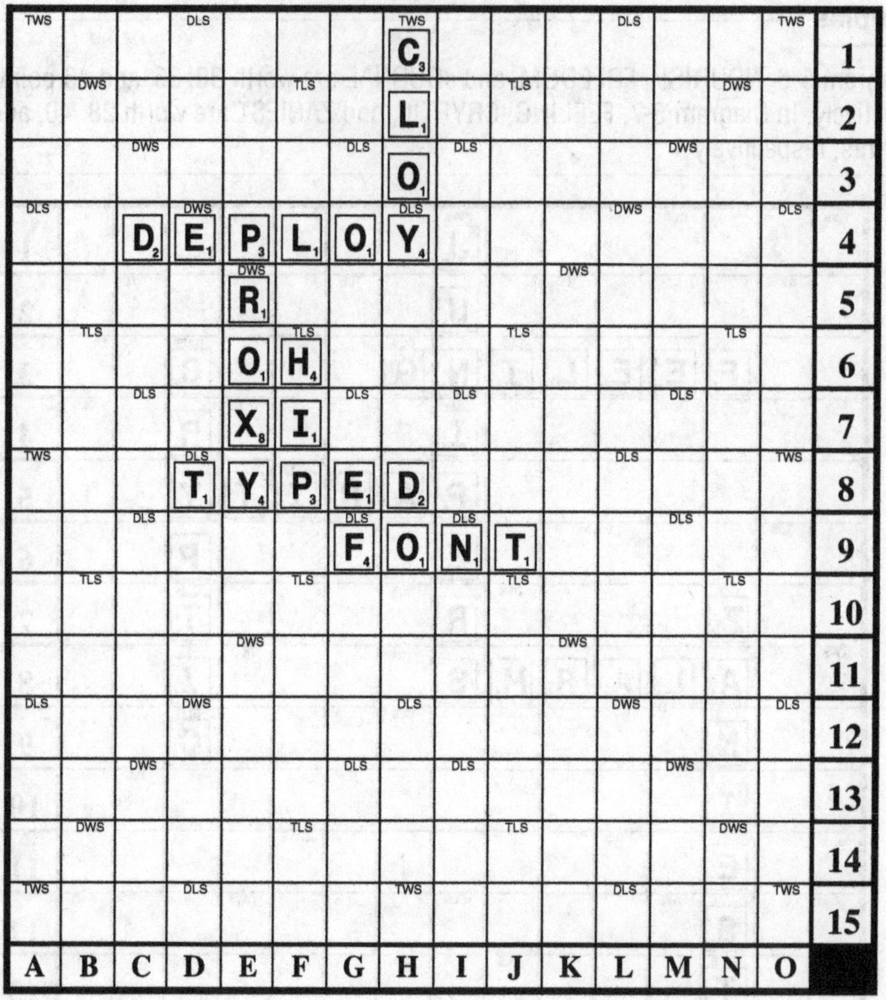
C
L
O
DEPLOY
R
OH
XI
TYPED
FONT
A B C D E F G H I J K L M N O
1 2 3 4 5 6 7 8 9 10 11 12 13 14 15

DIAGRAM 5-8

Your rack: **B E G N R S V**

Use Diagram 5-8 and the letters BEGNRSV to find a play that earns at least one DLS and one DWS. The answer is on page 55.

Time limit: 10 minutes

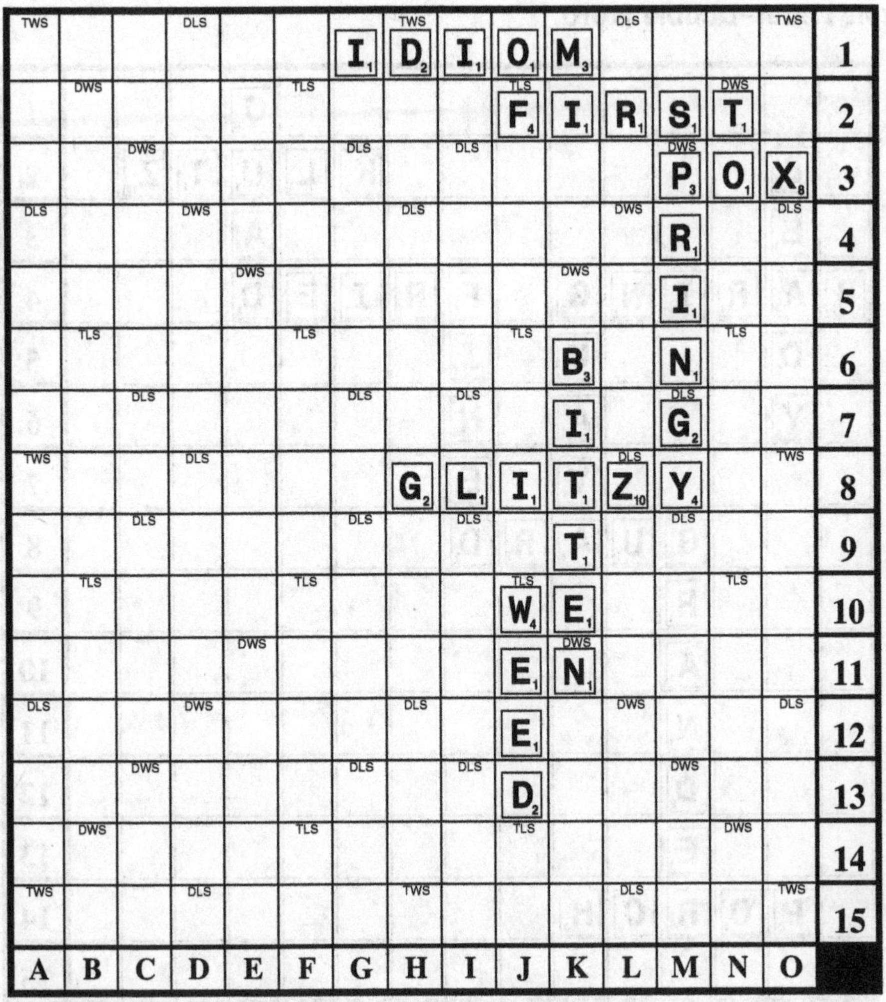
IDIOM
FIRST
POX
SPRINGY
BITTEN
GLITZY
WEED

DIAGRAM 5-9

Your rack: **A E F I O P R**

Use Diagram 5-9 and the letters AEFIOPR to find a play that earns at least one DLS and one DWS. The highest-scoring common-word answer is on page 55.

Time limit: 10 minutes

4. Triple Letter–Double Word

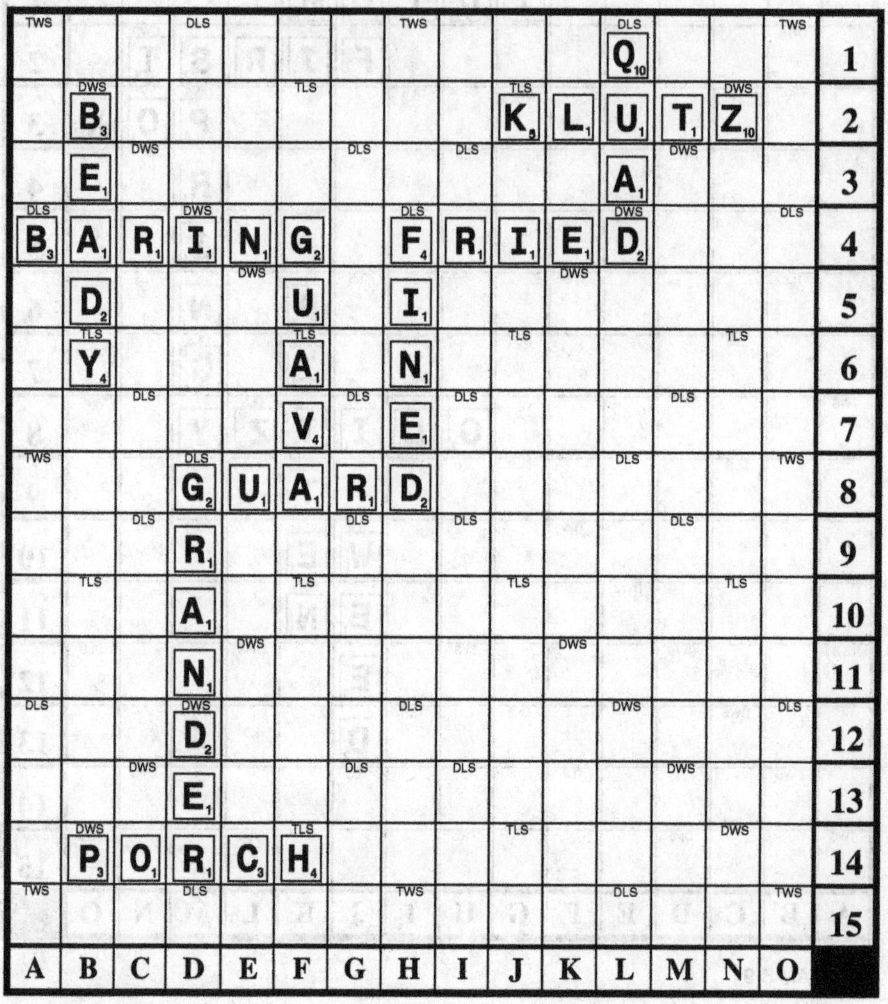

Q
KLUTZ
BEADY
BARING
FRIED
QUAD
GUAV
FINED
GUARD
GRANDE
PORCH
TWS
DWS
DLS
TLS
A B C D E F G H I J K L M N O
1 2 3 4 5 6 7 8 9 10 11 12 13 14 15

DIAGRAM 5-10

Four of the DWSs have Triple Letter Score squares four spaces away. By combining these two squares, you can score as much as 70 points or more with a Q or Z. With the 4-point tiles (F, H, V, W, and Y) you can often score more than 30 points. These combinations can be formed on rows 2 and 14 and on columns B and N.

Examples

In Diagram 5-10, BEADY, PORCH, and KLUTZ are worth 38, 40, and 56 points, respectively. In Diagram 5-11, BELOW, QUIET, and IODIZED are worth 32, 68, and 76 points, respectively.

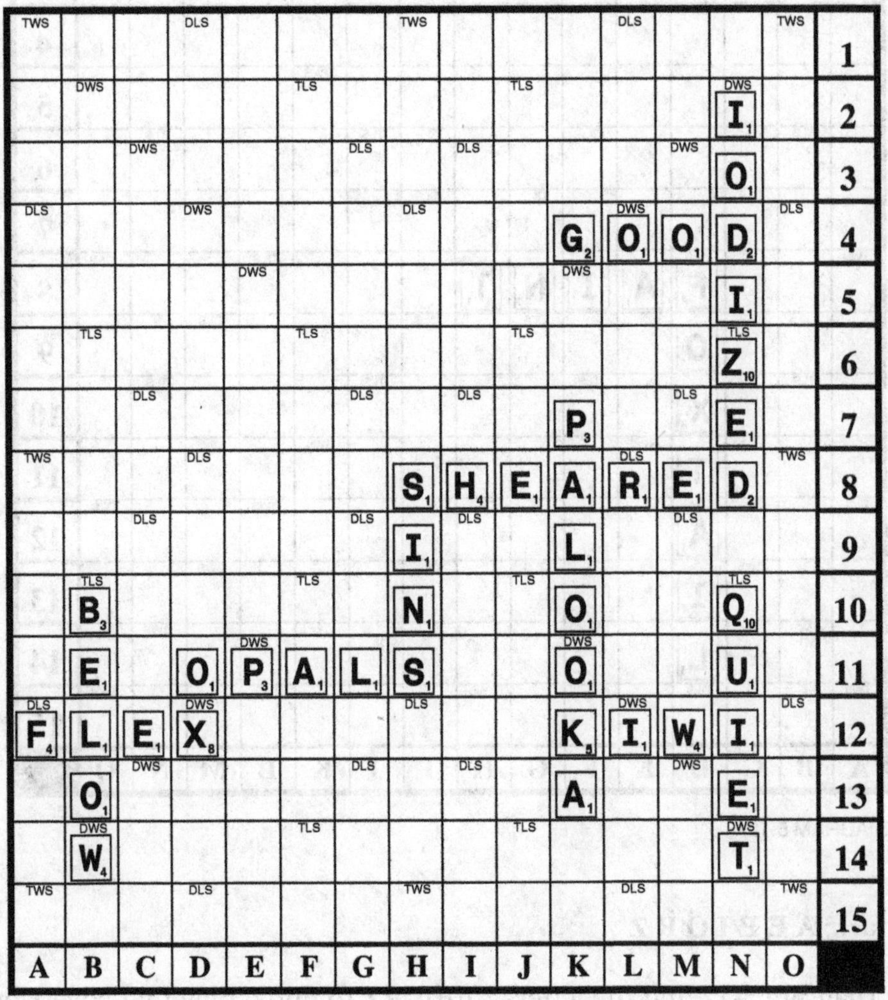

TWS DLS TWS DLS TWS
DWS TLS TLS DWS
DWS DLS DLS DWS
DLS DWS DLS DWS DLS
DWS DWS
TLS TLS TLS TLS
DLS DLS DLS DLS
TWS DLS DLS TWS
DLS DLS DLS DLS
TLS TLS TLS TLS
DWS DWS
DLS DWS DLS DWS DLS
DWS DLS DLS DWS
DWS TLS TLS DWS
TWS DLS TWS DLS TWS
I O
G O O D
I Z
P E
S H E A R E D
I L
B N O Q
E O P A L S O U
F L E X K I W I
O A E
W T
1 2 3 4 5 6 7 8 9 10 11 12 13 14 15
A B C D E F G H I J K L M N O

DIAGRAM 5-11

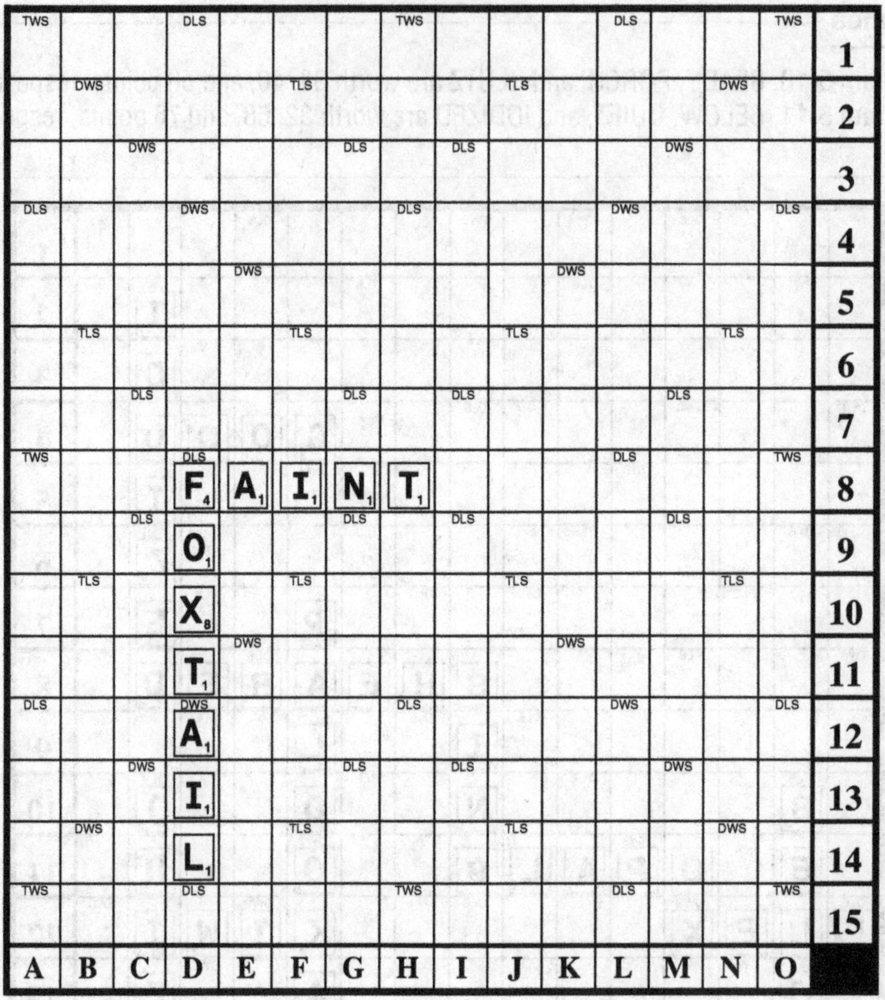
F A I N T
O X T A I L

DIAGRAM 5-12

Your rack: **A E E I O R Z**

Use Diagram 5-12 and the letters AEEIORZ to find a play that covers both a DWS and a TLS. The highest-scoring answer is on page 55.

Time limit: 10 minutes

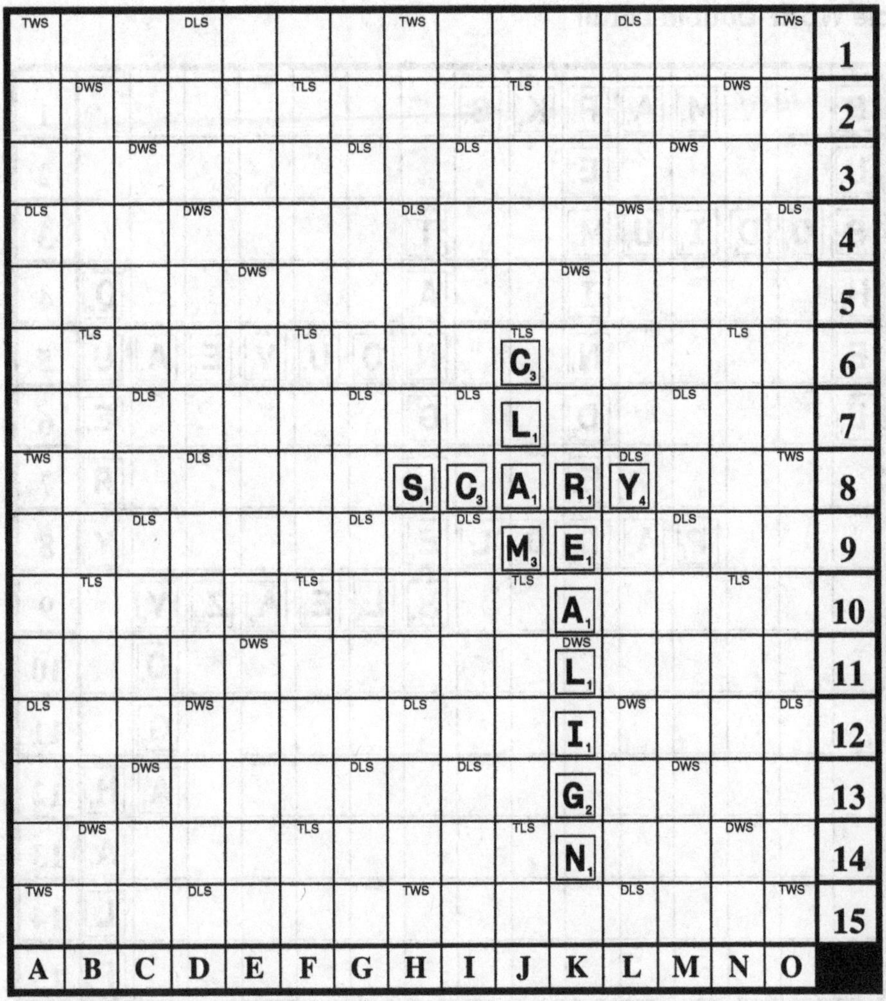
S C A R Y
C L A M
R E A L I G N
A B C D E F G H I J K L M N O
1 2 3 4 5 6 7 8 9 10 11 12 13 14 15

DIAGRAM 5-13

Your rack: **A E K N O P W**

Use Diagram 5-13 and the letters AEKNOPW to find a play that covers both a TLS and a DWS. The highest-scoring answer is on page 55.
Time limit: 10 minutes

5. Triple Word–Double Letter

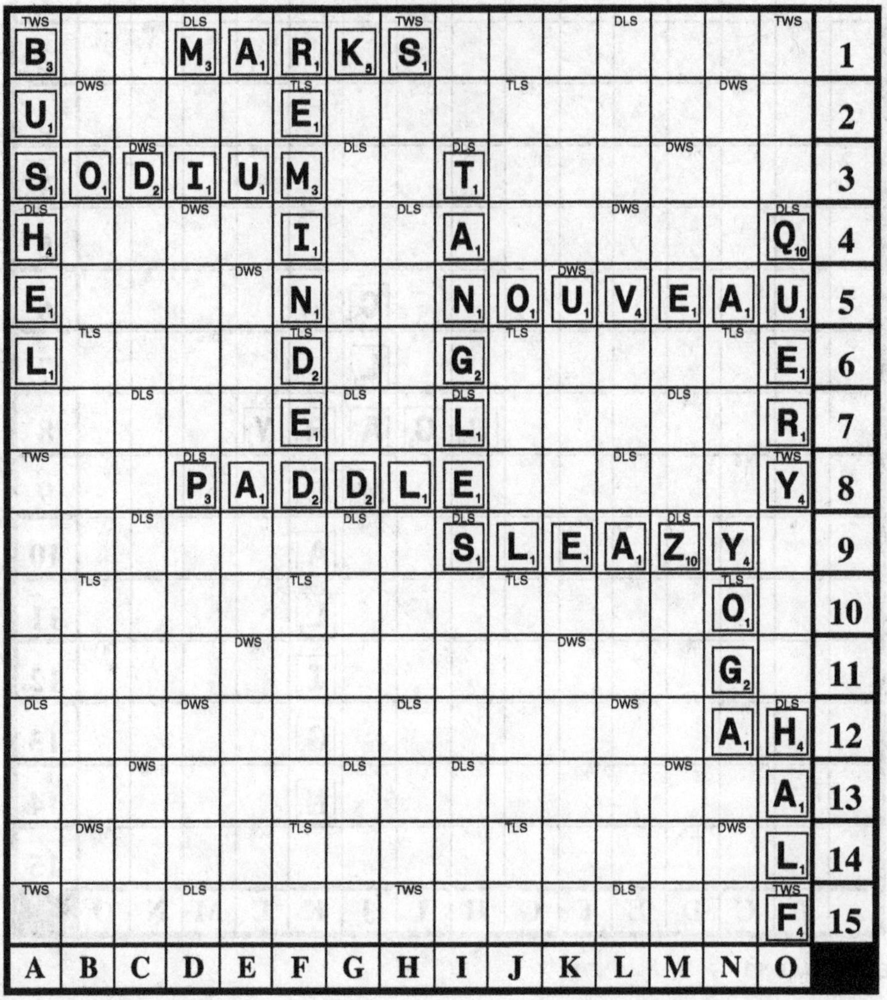

MARKS
SODIUM
NOUVEAU
PADDLE
SLEAZY
BUSHEL
REMINDED
TANGLES
QUERY
YOGA
HALF
TWS
DWS
TLS
DLS
1 2 3 4 5 6 7 8 9 10 11 12 13 14 15
A B C D E F G H I J K L M N O

DIAGRAM 5-14

The TWS can be a potent weapon for earning high scores. Try to use it with the Double Letter Score square a few spaces away. You can form such combinations in two different ways. One way is along the edges of the board on rows 1 and 15 and columns A and O. The other way is to cover one of the middle TWS squares at either 1H, A8, H15, or O8 while playing toward or away from the center of the board.

Examples

In Diagram 5-14, MARKS, BUSHEL, HALF/AH, and QUERY score 42, 45, 51, and 81 points, respectively. In Diagram 5-15, BIND, HECKLE, and ZONE score 30, 60, and 69 points, respectively, while GOLFS/WORMERS is worth 51 points.

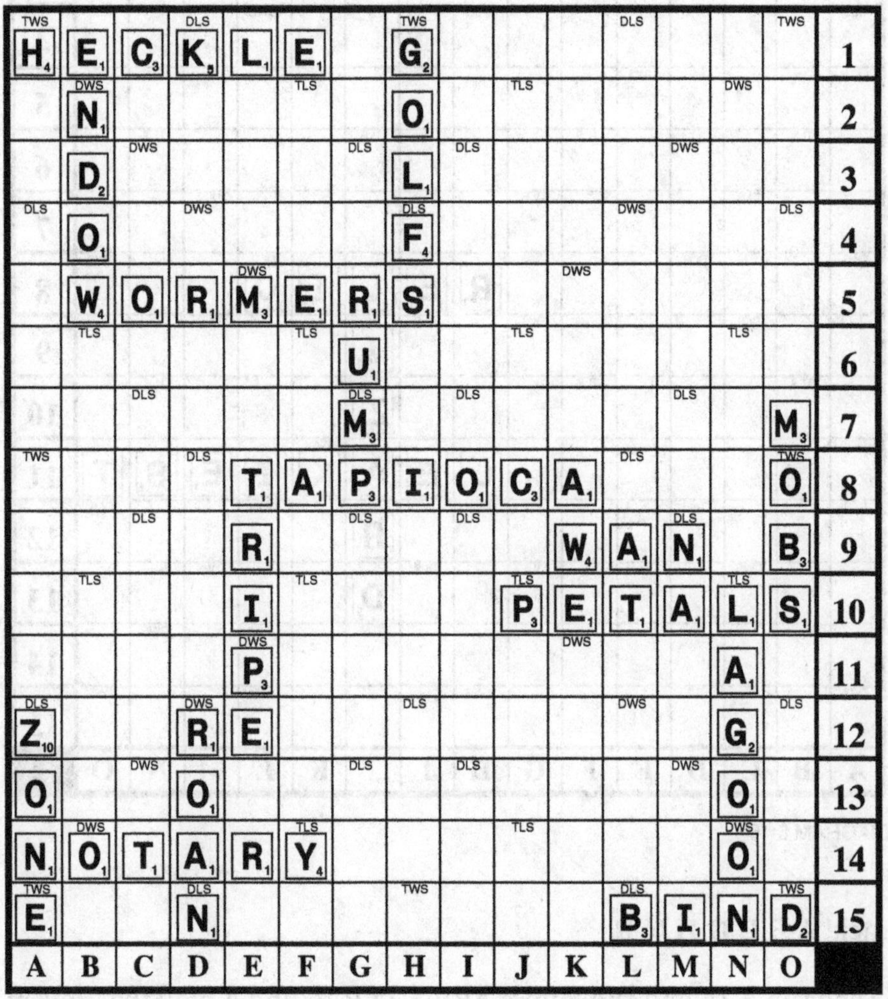
HECKLE
GOLFS
ENDOW
WORMERS
RUM
MOBS
TAPIOCA
TRIP
WAN
PETALS
LAGOON
RE
ZONE
ROD
NOTARY
BIND

DIAGRAM 5-15

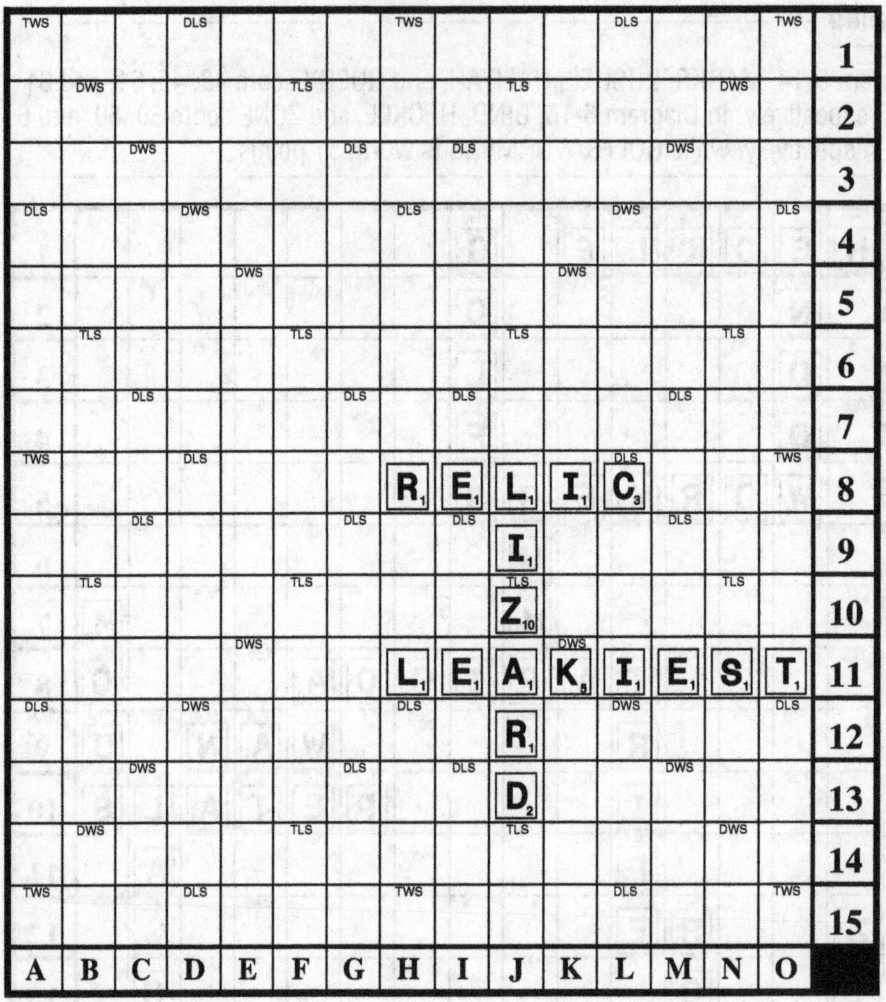

R E L I C
I
Z
L E A K I E S T
R
D
A B C D E F G H I J K L M N O

DIAGRAM 5-16

Your rack: **A B E G H N R**

Use Diagram 5-16 and the letters ABEGHNR to find a play that covers both a TWS and a DLS. The highest-scoring answer is on page 55.

Time limit: 10 minutes

6. Double-Doubles (DWS-DWS)

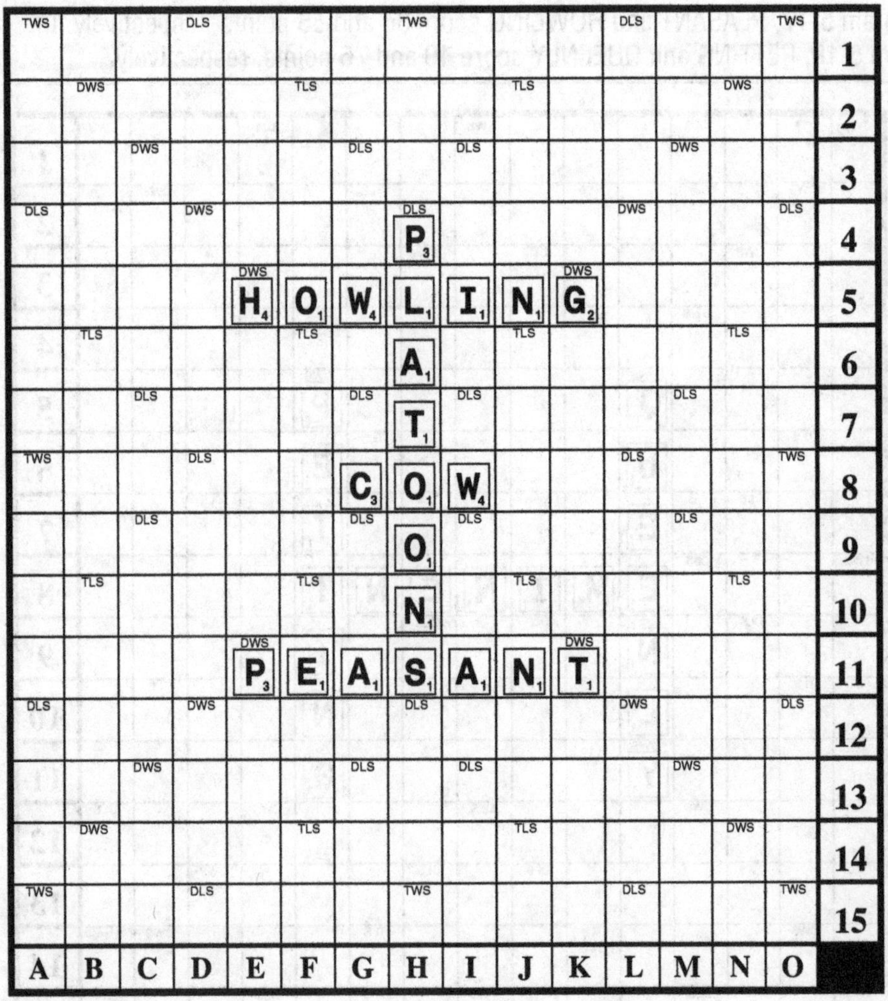

HOWLING
PLATOON
COW
PEASANT
1 2 3 4 5 6 7 8 9 10 11 12 13 14 15
A B C D E F G H I J K L M N O

DIAGRAM 5-17

Covering two Double Word Score squares at the same time is called playing a "Double-Double," and written as DWS-DWS, or 2x2.

There are four places that account for almost all Double-Doubles (see Diagrams 5-17 and 5-18).

The DWS-DWS is worth **four** times the value of the sum of the tiles. If all seven tiles are 1-pointers, that's 28 points. However, play a DWS-DWS with a Q or Z and you can score 64 points without even using all your tiles!

Examples

In Diagram 5-17, PEASANT and HOWLING score 36 and 56 points, respectively. In Diagram 5-18, PETTING and QUEENLY score 40 and 76 points, respectively.

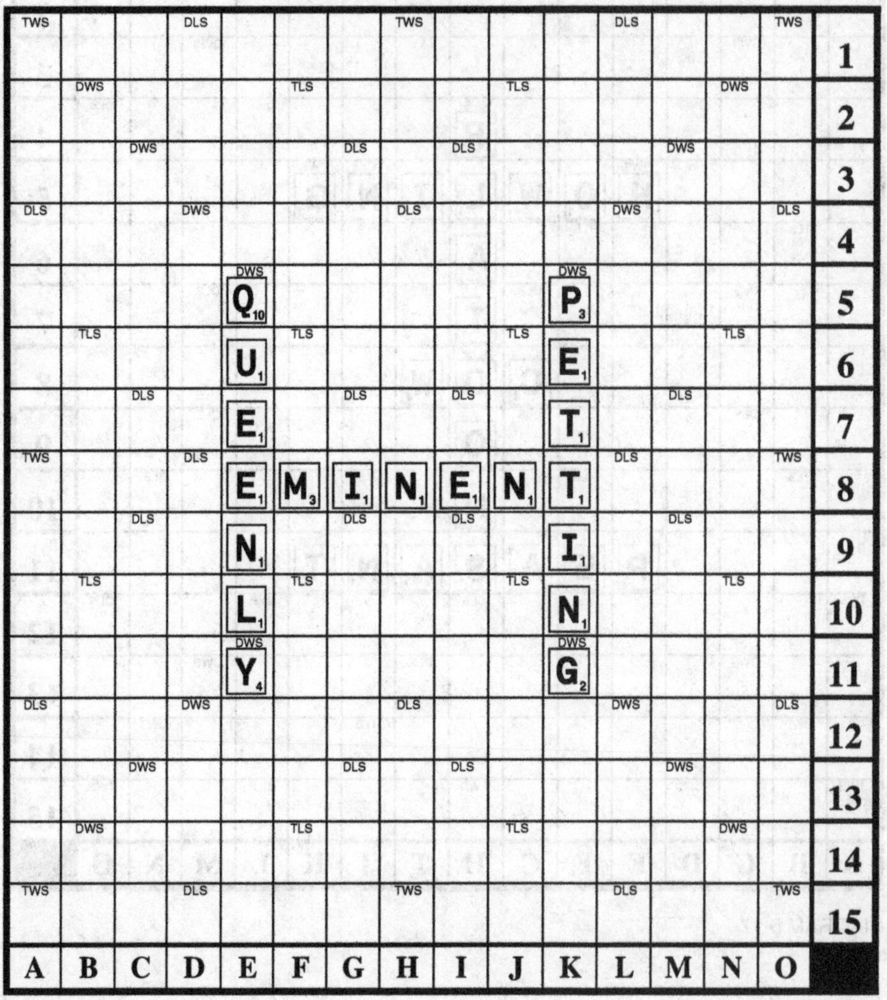

QUEENLY
EMINENT
PETTING
A B C D E F G H I J K L M N O
1 2 3 4 5 6 7 8 9 10 11 12 13 14 15

DIAGRAM 5-18

Double-Doubles can happen as early as the second play of a game. If the first player covers any Double Letter Score square along the eighth row (8D or 8L) or the H column (H4 or H12), the second player will have a chance for a DWS-DWS.

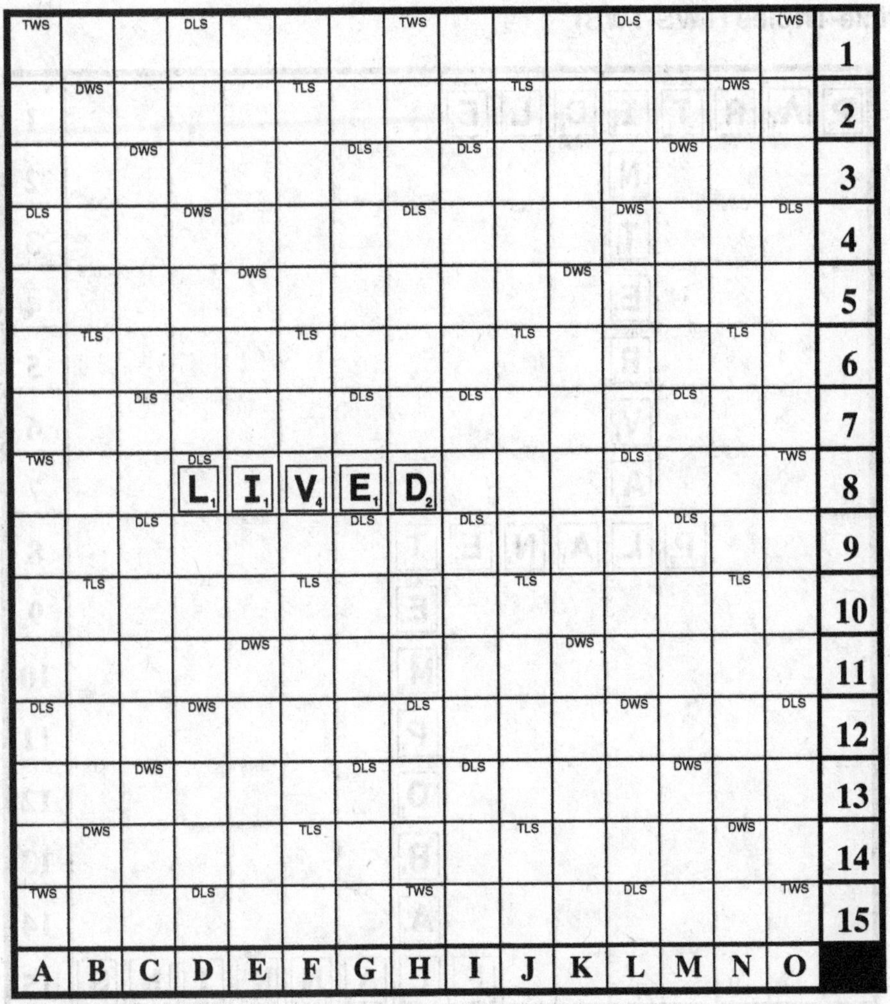
L I V E D
A B C D E F G H I J K L M N O
1 2 3 4 5 6 7 8 9 10 11 12 13 14 15
TWS
DWS
TLS
DLS

DIAGRAM 5-19

Your rack: **A D E E H T V**

Use Diagram 5-19 and the letters ADEEHTV to find a play that covers both DWSs along the E column. The answer is on page 55.

Time limit: 10 minutes

7. Triple-Triples (TWS-TWS)

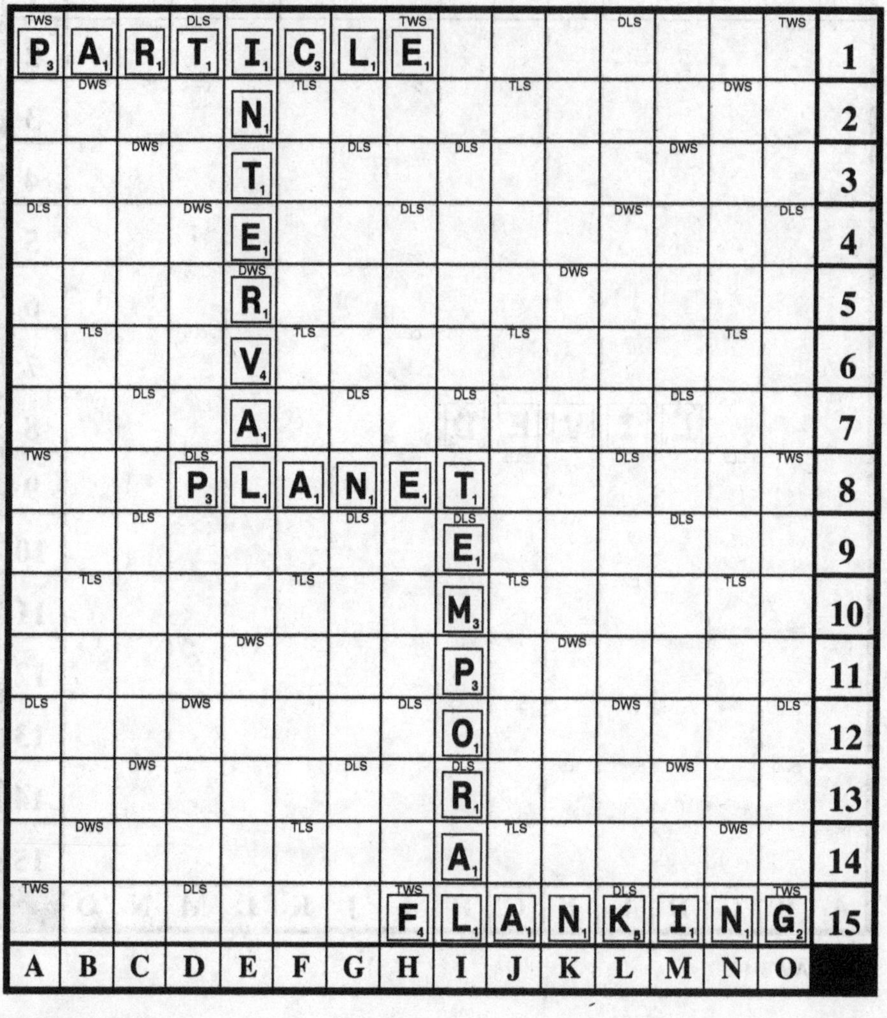

TWS
DLS
TWS
DLS
TWS
P A R T I C L E
1
DWS
TLS
TLS
DWS
N
2
DWS
DLS
DLS
DWS
T
3
DLS
DWS
DLS
DWS
DLS
E
4
DWS
DWS
R
5
TLS
TLS
TLS
TLS
V
6
DLS
DLS
DLS
DLS
A
7
TWS
DLS
DLS
TWS
P L A N E T
8
DLS
DLS
DLS
DLS
E
9
TLS
TLS
TLS
TLS
M
10
DWS
DWS
P
11
DLS
DWS
DLS
DWS
DLS
O
12
DWS
DLS
DLS
DWS
R
13
DWS
TLS
TLS
DWS
A
14
TWS
DLS
TWS
DLS
TWS
F L A N K I N G
15
A B C D E F G H I J K L M N O

DIAGRAM 5-20

A Triple-Triple is the pinnacle of the SCRABBLE scoring experience. That's when you play across two red Triple Word Score squares on the same play, giving you **nine** times the value of the sum of your letters. At a minimum, when you don't use all your letters and two blanks are employed, your score will be 54 points. Commonly, a TWS-TWS, or 3x3, will earn about 122 to 140 points (this includes the 50-point bonus for using all your tiles). Because it's worth so much, you should always take some time to look for one if it seems you have a chance.

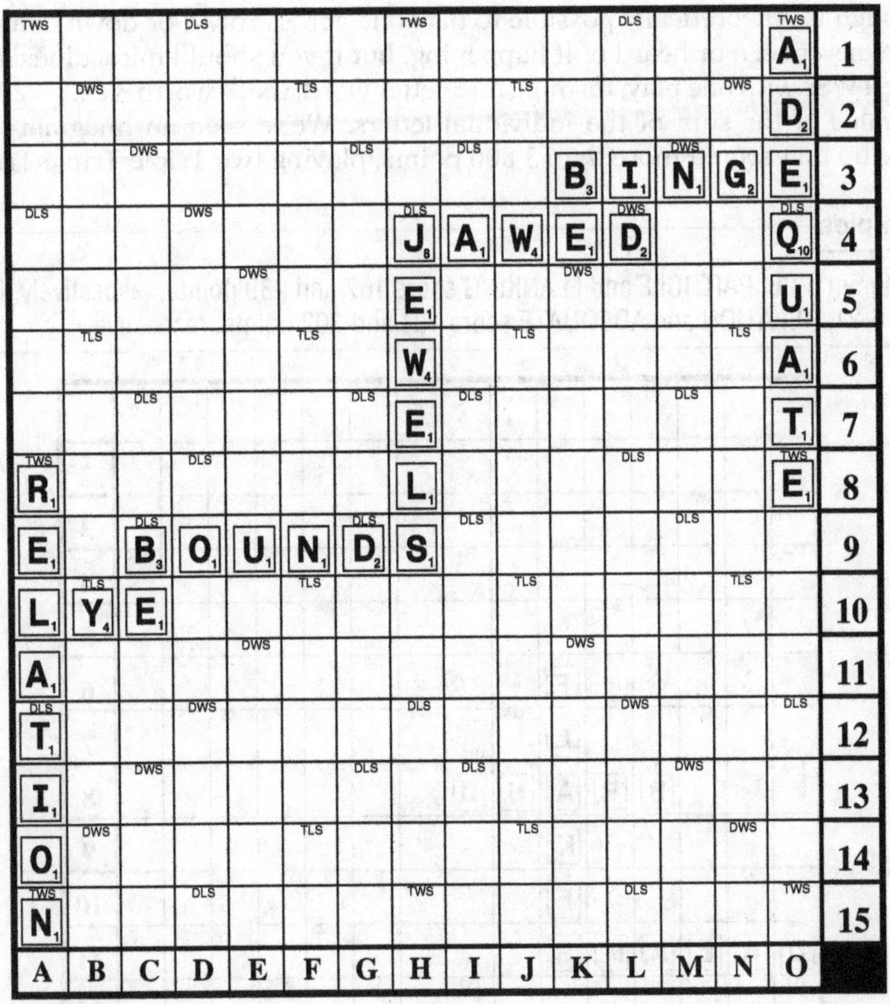

DIAGRAM 5-21

It may take hundreds of games before you ever have the luck to play one, because most players avoid giving their opponents such opportunities. And when they do, you're not likely to have just the right tiles you'll need. But when it does happen, watch the points pile up!

Lest you think that you won't ever play a Triple-Triple, we're happy to tell you that at virtually every SCRABBLE game tournament there are a few Triple-Triples played. At most tournaments, the highest single play is often worth more than 130 points.

You'll play Triple-Triples almost always on rows 1 and 15 or columns A and O, although it's theoretically possible to play one across row 8 or down column H. We've never seen or heard of it happening, but if you should miraculously cover three TWSs with one play, forming a 15-letter word, that's worth 3x3x3 = 27 times the value of the sum of the individual letters. We've seen an imaginary game made up that scored more than 3,800 points, playing two Triple-Triple-Triples!

Examples

In Diagram 5-20, PARTICLE and FLANKING score 167 and 239 points, respectively. In Diagram 5-21, RELATION and ADEQUATE score 131 and 302 points, respectively.

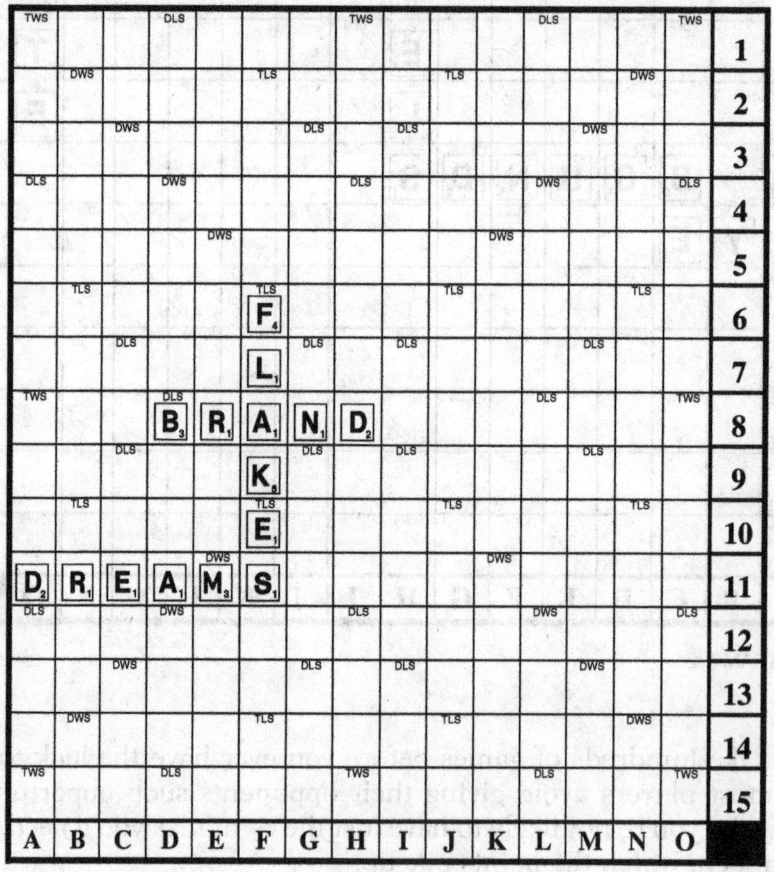

FLAKES
BRAND
DREAMS

DIAGRAM 5-22

Your rack: **G I I M N O S**

Use Diagram 5-22 and the letters GIIMNOS to find a TWS-TWS play. The answer is on page 55.

Time limit: 10 minutes

Bonus Square Bonanza

In each of the following diagrams, use the given rack to find a play that covers the two bonus squares listed. The answers are on page 55.

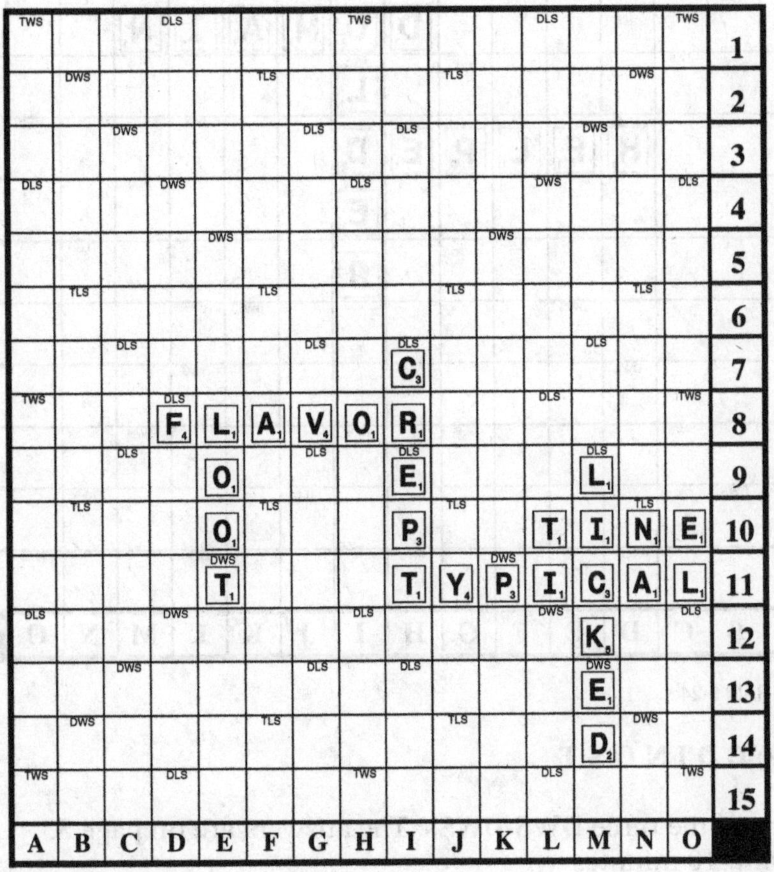
FLAVOR
COREPT
FOOT
TINE
TYPICAL
LICKED
A B C D E F G H I J K L M N O
1 2 3 4 5 6 7 8 9 10 11 12 13 14 15

DIAGRAM 5-23

Your rack: **E H N R S S T**

Find the TWS-TWS. The answer is on page 55.

Time limit: 10 minutes

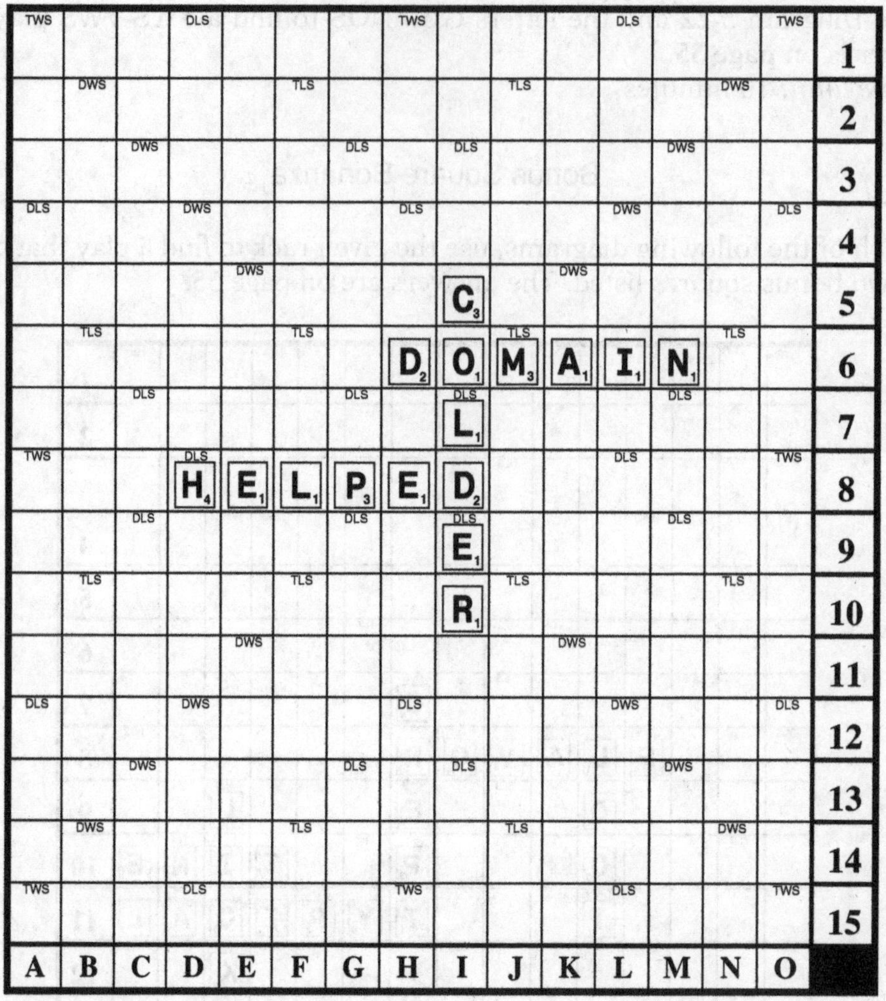
DOMAIN
COLDER
HELPED
A B C D E F G H I J K L M N O
1 2 3 4 5 6 7 8 9 10 11 12 13 14 15

DIAGRAM 5-24

Your rack: **B D I N O S T**

Find one of the three DWS-DWSs. The answers are on page 55.
Time limit: 10 minutes

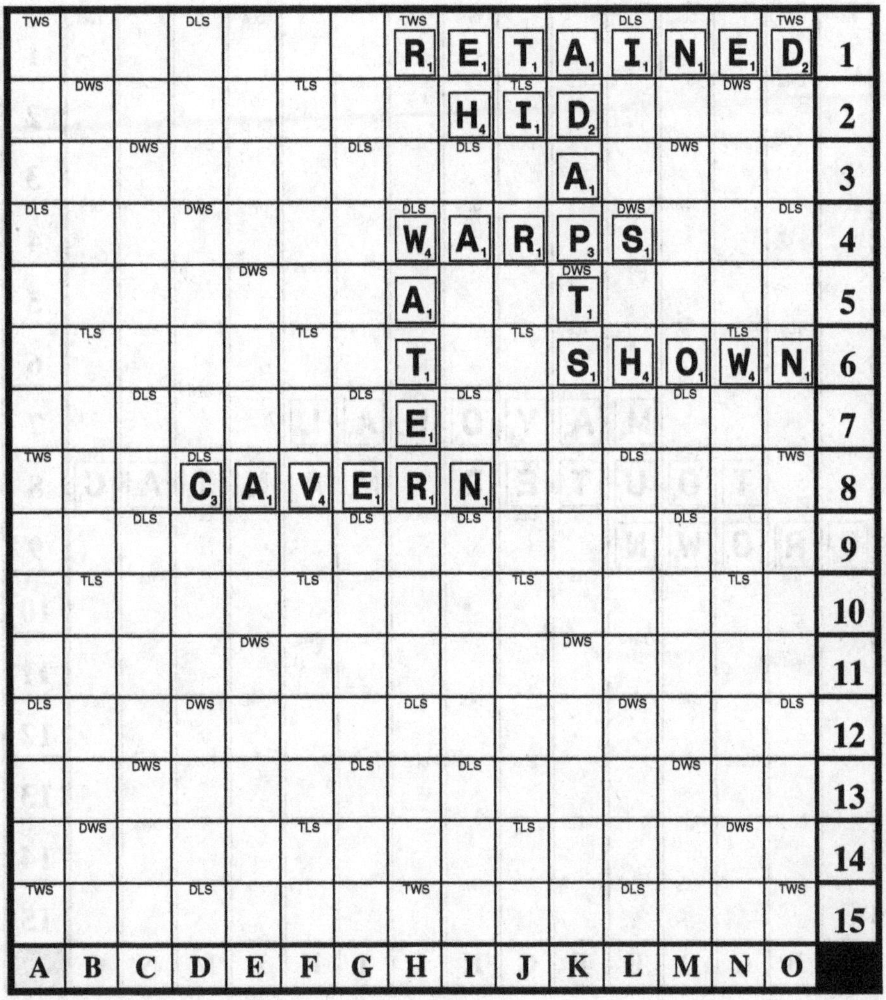
RETAINED
HID
WARPS
SHOWN
CAVERN
1 2 3 4 5 6 7 8 9 10 11 12 13 14 15
A B C D E F G H I J K L M N O

DIAGRAM 5-25

Your rack: **A G H M T U Y**

Find the highest-scoring TWS-DLS. The answer is on page 55.
Time limit: 10 minutes

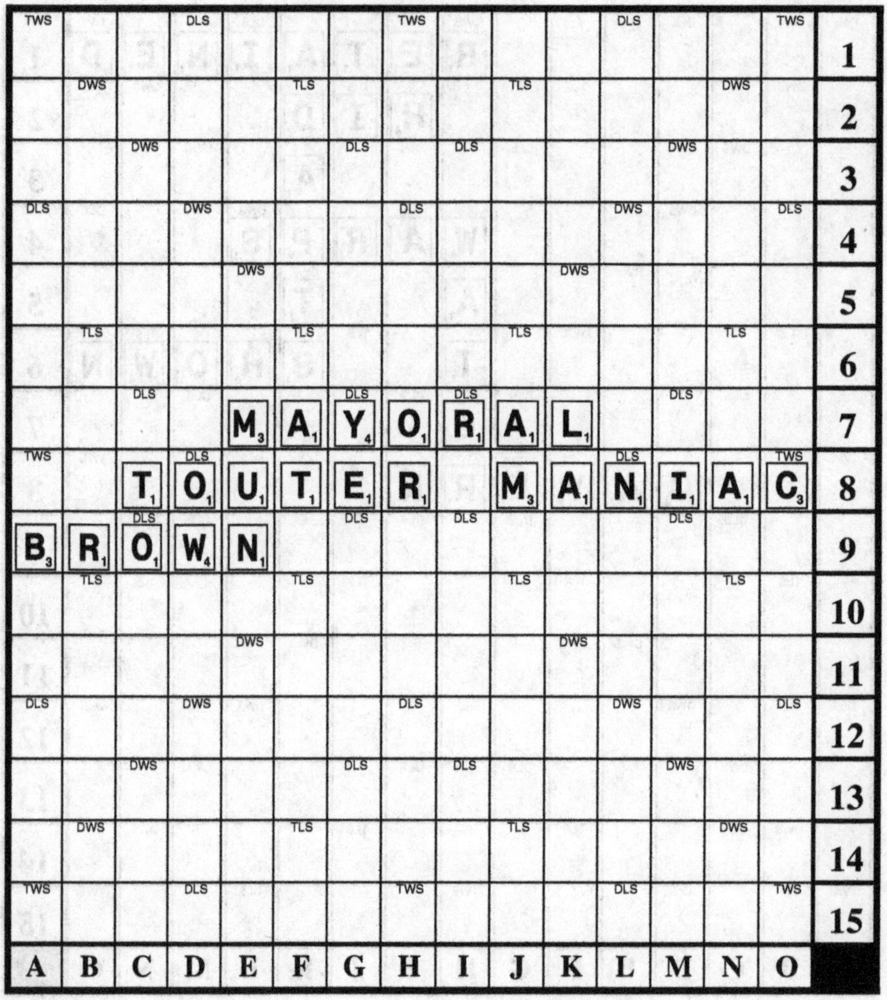
MAYORAL
TOUTER
MANIAC
BROWN
A B C D E F G H I J K L M N O
1 2 3 4 5 6 7 8 9 10 11 12 13 14 15

DIAGRAM 5-26

Your rack: **C I O Q S T U**

Find the highest-scoring DWS-TLS. The answer is on page 55.
Time limit: 10 minutes

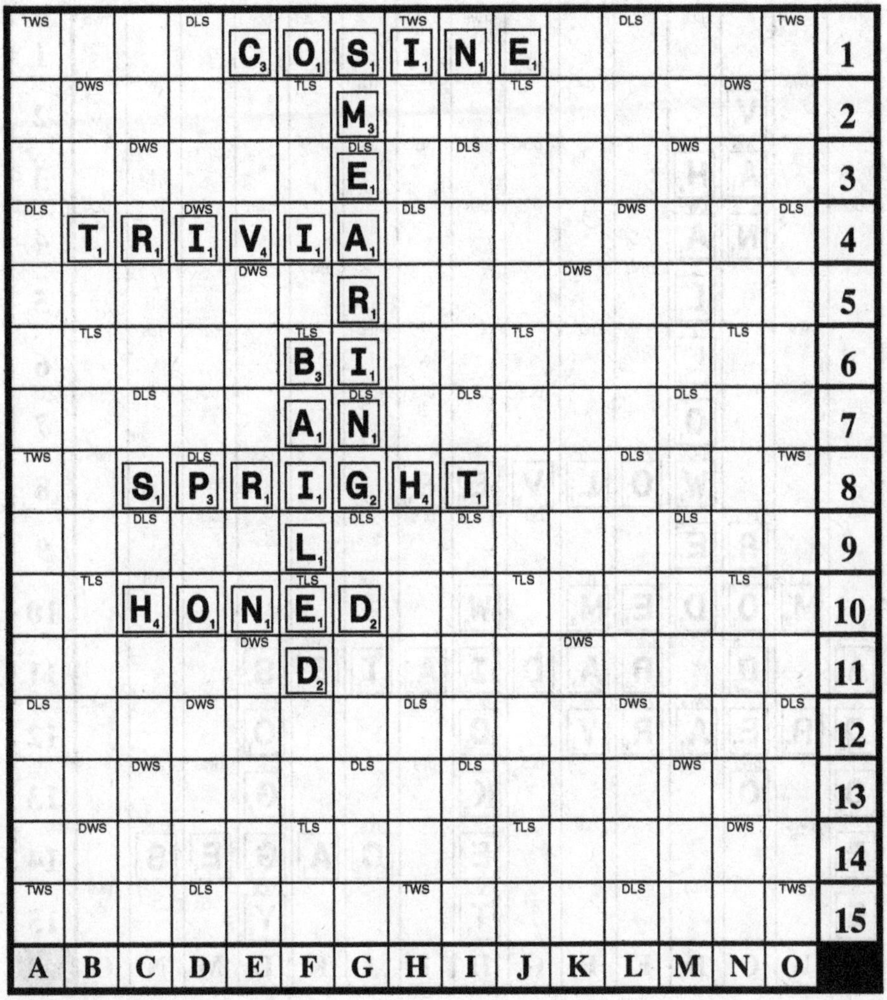
COSINE
SMEARING
TRIVIA
BAILED
SPRIGHT
HONED
A B C D E F G H I J K L M N O
1 2 3 4 5 6 7 8 9 10 11 12 13 14 15

DIAGRAM 5-27

Your rack: **B C E G I K U**

Find the highest-scoring DWS-DLS. The answer is on page 55.
Time limit: 10 minutes

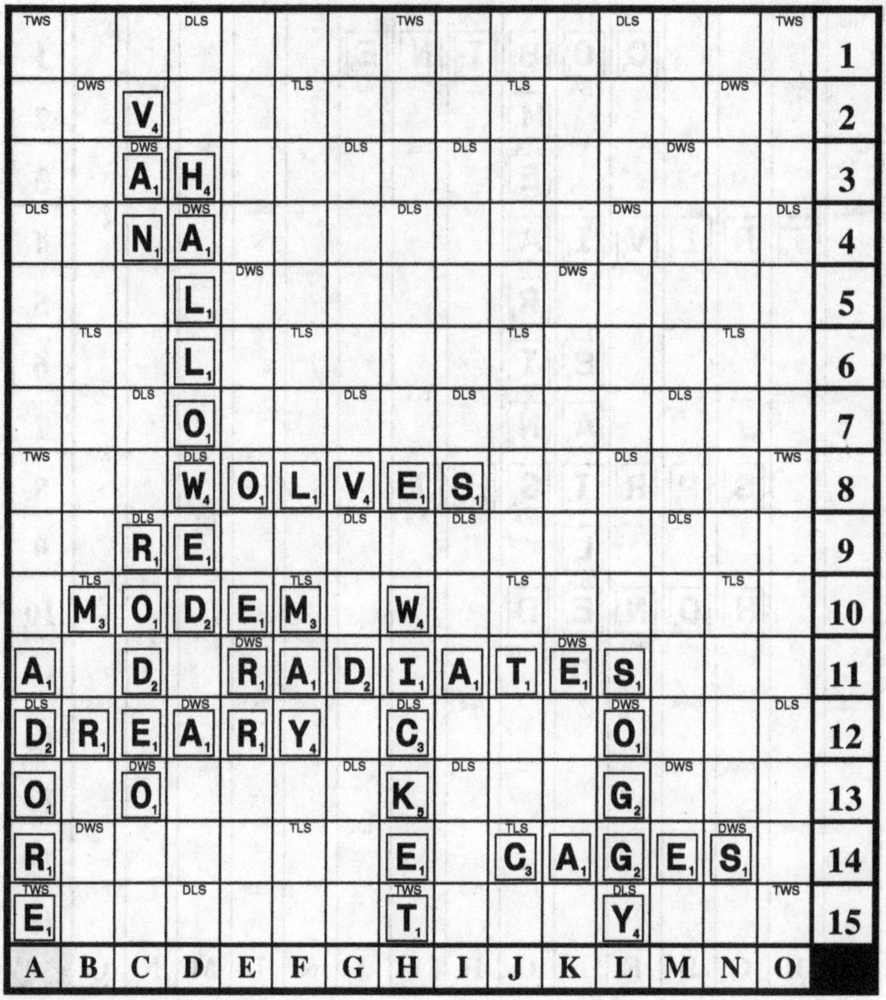

DIAGRAM 5-28

Your rack: **A E F I L O P**

Find the highest-scoring TLS-TLS. The answer is on page 55.
Time limit: 10 minutes

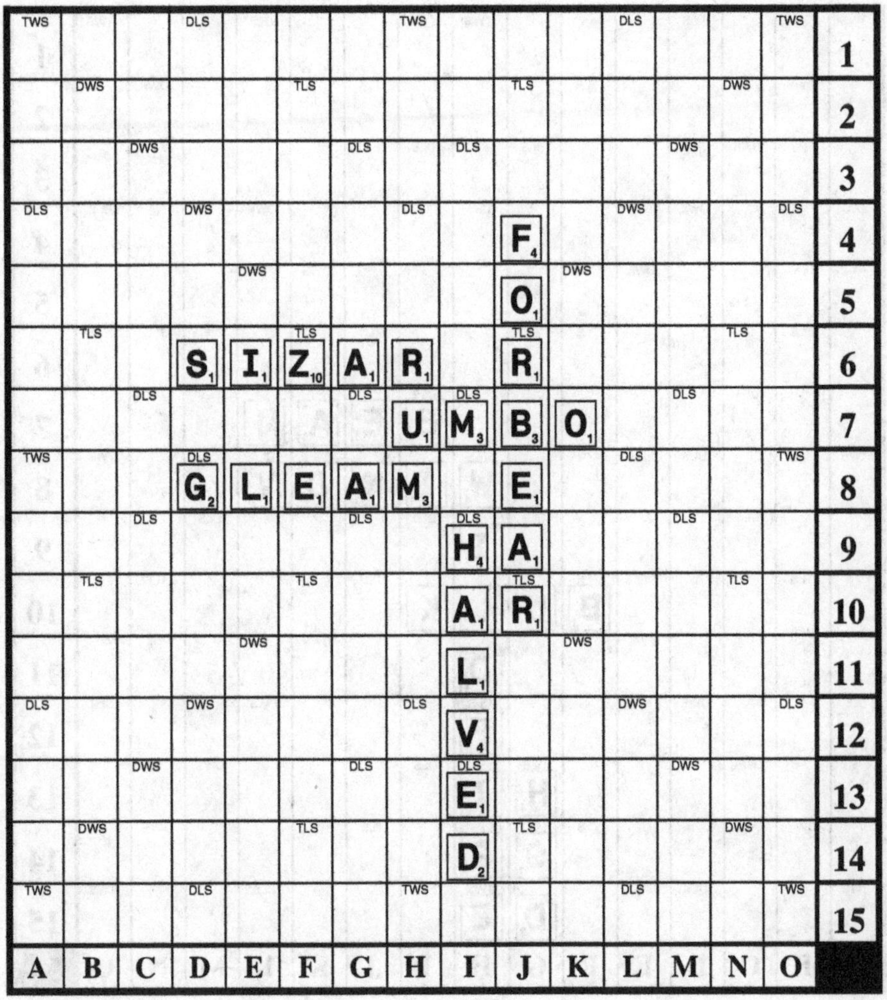
F
O
SIZAR R
UMBO
GLEAM E
HA
AR
L
V
E
D
1 2 3 4 5 6 7 8 9 10 11 12 13 14 15
A B C D E F G H I J K L M N O

DIAGRAM 5-29

Your rack: **A D E E R R R**

Find the outstanding parallel play. This is a toughie! The answer is on page 55.
Time limit: 15 minutes

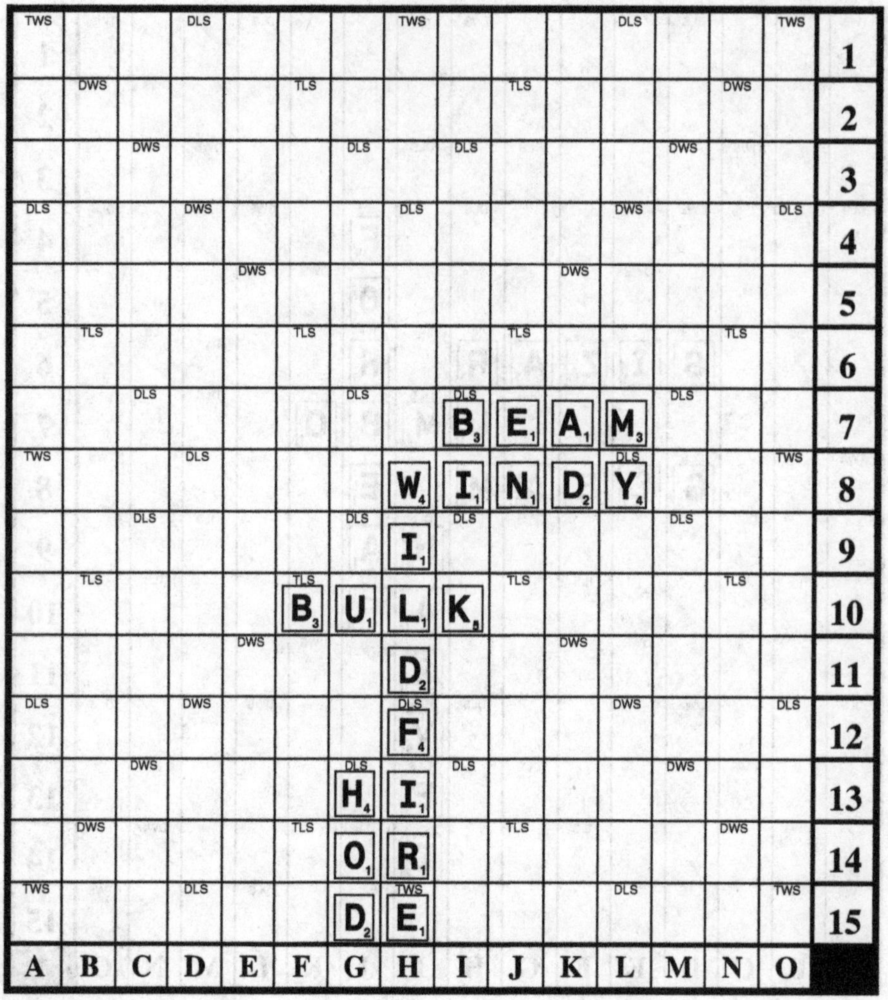
BEAM
WINDY
BULK
WILDFIRE
HOD
A B C D E F G H I J K L M N O
1 2 3 4 5 6 7 8 9 10 11 12 13 14 15

DIAGRAM 5-30

Your rack: **A A D L M P R**

Find the outstanding parallel play. The answer is on page 55.
Time limit: 10 minutes

One of the major stumbling blocks to scoring well is drawing the Q without a U. Chapter 6 shows you some important words that will quickly help clear your rack of the Q.

ANSWERS: CHAPTER 5

DIAGRAM 5-2: 1. REND 8L 48 points; 2. DOUBTS 5J 36; 3. NONSKID 10B 105; 4. QUITE 6F 43.
DIAGRAM 5-5: PROMPT 6F 24.
DIAGRAM 5-8: GOVERNS 3G 39.
DIAGRAM 5-9: FAIRER 4H 26.
DIAGRAM 5-12: REALIZE 14A 72.
DIAGRAM 5-13: KNOWN 14J 44.
DIAGRAM 5-16: BREATH O7 45.
DIAGRAM 5-19: DEVIATE E5 44.
DIAGRAM 5-22: MISDOING A8 167.
DIAGRAM 5-23: SHELTERS O8 108.
DIAGRAM 5-24: BANDITS K5 40; BASTION K5 36; BANDITOS K5 94.
DIAGRAM 5-25: NAUGHTY O6 54.
DIAGRAM 5-26: ACQUITS N8 76.
DIAGRAM 5-27: BRICKS C3 36.
DIAGRAM 5-28: PILAF 6B 24.
DIAGRAM 5-29: REORDER K5 50.
DIAGRAM 5-30: MILD 9G 33.

6 YOUR FOURTH-GRADE TEACHER, MRS. KLEINFELDER, LIED TO YOU: You *Can* Have Words with a Q and No U

In years gone by, the Q was both loved and hated by most players. If you had a U and another vowel or two, the Q could usually be played for 25 to 40 points. If so, you loved it. Even without a U, if you had an AT or an AID, you could play QAT, an evergreen shrub, or QAID, a Muslim leader. But you never knew when you'd draw it, and sometimes, after it had been exchanged a couple of times during a game, it came back to haunt you at the end and you'd get 20 points subtracted from your score. Okay, now you really hated it!

Not anymore. Or, shall we say, 99 percent of the time, you'll *never* have to get stuck with the Q again! Don't believe us? Well, armed with the most commonly played word in SCRABBLE game land, QI, you can prove it to yourself!

QI, a variation of CHI, or life force, in just a couple of short years has transformed the game enormously. Now if you draw the Q, you either have an I ready to play QI or there's one on the board that you can use to dump the Q for at least 11 points.

Nowadays, experts have learned to get rid of the U as soon as they draw one, because the U is a really poor bingo tile. And if they have to keep the Q on their rack for a turn or two while they wait for an I or a U, it's not so bad anymore, because there are thirteen combined Is and Us to draw.

In addition, once the Q is on the board, you should be thinking about how you can get an I down right in front of it, playing parallel to it and scoring many more points. And if that isn't enough, look out for Triple Letter Score squares that sit in front of an I, because if you or your opponent draws the Q, you'll then be able to play QI for 64 points! Wow! That's almost as good as most bingos! At the same time, you should be careful of playing an I next to that TLS, because you don't want to give those 64 points to your opponent.

What QI does do is give everyone a powerful new weapon with which to score points. Sometimes you'll use it, and sometimes your opponents will. But overall, just knowing it's there can give you a feeling of being in greater control of your own fate over the board and that you won't be at the whim of the tile gods when you draw the Q and no U. Because of this, the game just got more fascinating and engrossing!

And for the same reason, the other *big* new two-letter word ZA (slang for pizza, which originally came out of the Southern California campuses in the 1970s) made the Z just that much easier to play.

Below are all of the Q words that don't require a U. This is an invaluable list, so you might want to memorize it.

CINQ: *n* pl. -S the number five
KAMOTIQ: *n* pl. -S an Inuit sled
MBAQANGA: *n* pl. -S a South African dance music
NIQAAB, NIQAB: *n* pl. -S a veil worn by some Muslim women
QABALA, QABALAH: *n* pl. -S cabala (an occult or secret doctrine)
QADI: *n* pl. -S a Muslim judge
QAID: *n* pl. -S variation of CAID, a Muslim leader
QAJAQ: *n* pl. -S a kayak
QANAT: *n* pl. -S a system of underground tunnels and wells in the Middle East
QAPIK: *n* pl. -S GOPIK, a unit of currency
QAT: *n* pl. -S variation of KAT, an evergreen shrub
QAWWALI: *n* pl. -S a style of Muslim music
QI: *n* pl. -S the vital force that in Chinese thought is inherent in all things
QIBLA: *n* pl. -S the direction in which Muslims face to pray

QIGONG:	*n* pl. -S a Chinese system of physical exercise
QINDAR:	*n* pl. -DARs or -DARKA variation of QINTAR, a monetary unit of Albania
QINTAR:	*n* pl. -S see above
SHEQEL:	*n* pl. SHEQALIM, SHEQELS, an ancient unit of weight
TRANQ:	*n* pl. -S variation of TRANK (i.e., tranquilizer)
QOPH:	*n* pl. -S variation of KOPH, a letter of the Hebrew alphabet
QWERTY:	*n* pl. -S a standard keyboard
FAQIR:	*n* pl. -S variation of FAKIR, a Hindu ascetic

Also of note: BUQSHA(s), BURQA(s), QIVIUT(s), SUQ(s), UMIAQ(s), and QAMUTIK(s)

Here's one more hint to keep in mind: Be mindful of the words AID and AT. These two words can be used by either you or your opponent to dump the Q. So whenever you are about to play either of them, ask yourself if it will help or hinder your efforts to win.

In general, whenever you get the Q, try to get it off your rack by whatever means possible, and as soon as possible. That's how to use the Q to your advantage.

Playing the Q

With each of the following four-letter combinations, a Q may be added to form a word after rearranging the five letters. Review the list of Q words on page 57 and above before trying this exercise. You may want to redo these puzzles occasionally in the future until you can determine all the words without reviewing the list. The answers are on page 59.

1. EIRU	6. EOTU (2 words)	11. HOTU	16. ANRT
2. AIMU (2 words)	7. ESUU	12. HRSU	17. EORU
3. ANTU	8. IPUU	13. INOU	18. AKUY
4. EEUU	9. AANT	14. AISU (2 words)	19. AENU
5. ASTU	10. ETUU	15. EFIU	20. EIPU (2 words)

3-, 4-, and 5-Letter Q Words

QAT	AQUAE	QUAFF	QUERN	QUOIT
QIS	AQUAS	QUAGS	QUERY	QUOLL
QUA	BURQA	QUAIL	QUEST	QUOTA
SUQ	CINQS	QUAIS	QUEUE	QUOTE
AQUA	COQUI	QUAKE	QUEYS	QUOTH
CINQ	EQUAL	QUAKY	QUICK	QURSH
QADI	EQUES	QUALE	QUIDS	ROQUE
QAID	EQUID	QUALM	QUIET	SQUAB
QATS	EQUIP	QUANT	QUIFF	SQUAD
QOPH	FAQIR	QUARE	QUILL	SQUAT
QUAD	FIQUE	QUARK	QUILT	SQUAW
QUAG	MAQUI	QUART	QUINS	SQUEG
QUAI	NIQAB	QUASH	QUINT	SQUIB
QUAY	PIQUE	QUASI	QUIPS	SQUID
QUEY	QADIS	QUASS	QUIPU	TOQUE
QUID	QAIDS	QUATE	QUIRE	TRANQ
QUIN	QAJAQ	QUAYS	QUIRK	TUQUE
QUIP	QANAT	QUBIT	QUIRT	UMIAQ
QUIT	QIBLA	QUEAN	QUITE	USQUE
QUIZ	QOPHS	QUEEN	QUITS	
QUOD	QUACK	QUEER	QUODS	
SUQS	QUADS	QUELL	QUOIN	

While you may now be able to make good 25- to 35-point plays, your next jump will take you further than you imagine. Anybody can learn how to find seven- and eight-letter words! You need only to practice looking for them with the right tools. Up ahead—chapter 7!

ANSWERS: CHAPTER 6

1. QUIRE
2. MAQUI, UMIAQ
3. QUANT
4. QUEUE
5. SQUAT
6. QUOTE, TOQUE
7. USQUE
8. QUIPU
9. QANAT
10. TUQUE
11. QUOTH
12. QURSH
13. QUOIN
14. QUAIS, QUASI
15. FIQUE
16. TRANQ
17. ROQUE
18. QUAKY
19. QUEAN
20. EQUIP, PIQUE

7 BINGOS: How to Make 7- and 8-Letter Plays

A bingo is a play that uses all seven letters of a player's rack in one turn. This scores 50 extra bonus points and is at the heart of consistent winning. Experts usually play two or three bingos in an average game, and they are constantly thinking about how to develop a bingo rack.

We've known many casual players who've never laid down a bingo. What's the secret to finding these plays? It's actually not all that mysterious. First, know which letters commonly combine together to form easy-to-see word beginnings and endings. Then look for them on your rack.

Example

The three letters G, I, and N can be combined as ING to form the ending of many words. ENDING, HAVING, FLOWING, and COMING are just four of the thousands of words ending in ING. Once you see ING on your rack, all you need to do is rearrange the other four letters (remember from chapter 4 that there are only twenty-four possible arrangements), which shouldn't take more than a minute to explore once you're experienced at it.

Some of the other most common endings are: ED, ER, IER, IEST, and IES. Of word beginnings, UN and RE are two of the most frequently played. An extensive list of such word beginnings and endings appears on page 71. The more familiar you are with them, the quicker you'll achieve those 50-point bonuses. By moving the tiles around on your rack, you will learn to see the useful letter combinations without much effort.

BINGO PRACTICE #1

Find the common word that can be spelled with each set of letters below. In each case the word will either begin or end with one of the following sets of letters:

Beginnings: **EM, EN, EX, FORE, HAND, HEAD, IM, IN, ISO, MID**
Endings: **ED, EE, ENCE, ENT, ER, EST, FORM, FUL, GHT, ISH**

We recommend that you play with actual tiles on a rack as you would while playing a game, instead of trying to find the words in your head. The answers are on page 72.

Example

In Set A, #1 is ABELMMS. If you compare these seven letters with the possible beginnings and endings above, you may notice that the answer word can begin only with EM, since there is no other matching beginning or ending.

Time limit per set: 30 minutes
Average score: 5 correct *Good score:* 7 correct *Expert score:* 8 correct

SET A	SET B	SET C	SET D
1. ABELMMS	1. BEIILMMO	1. AEFOPRW	1. AEILOSST
2. EIOOPST	2. ADEEHST	2. AEELMNS	2. ADDEHOR
3. ADEINPRS	3. ACDEEINU	3. EGLNPRU	3. EEINNPTT
4. FIMNORU	4. AEGSTUV	4. EEIORRTX	4. EEELMOPY
5. CEEEILNN	5. BEIKLNR	5. IIMNOPRS	5. AGHIRSY
6. EFHLLPU	6. AGHIRSTT	6. DEFLLOU	6. ACEFORST
7. GHIILRS	7. ACEHNNT	7. ACEEINRS	7. AABDHLLN
8. AGHILRT	8. BDEMSTU	8. ACDEHKLO	8. DGHIIMNT

BINGO PRACTICE #2

Beginnings: **MIS, NON, OUT, OVER, POST, PRE, RE, SEA, SUB, UN**
Endings: **ATE, GRAM, IA(L), IBLE, IC, ICAL, IER, IES, IEST, IFY**

The answers are on page 72.

SET A	SET B	SET C	SET D
1. BEEIORTV	1. ABEGINO	1. ADINNORY	1. EIIPRSTU
2. AEHIOPRU	2. EINNSSTU	2. EEEIMPRR	2. ABDEILU
3. ACIILNOR	3. DEENNOPU	3. DFIILOSY	3. ACELNNU
4. ABEELSSU	4. EGHIOSTU	4. ADEEMORT	4. EEGIPRST
5. DEEEINRR	5. ABDEILMN	5. AEEGLMRT	5. CDEEIIMP
6. EENNNOSS	6. ADELNORV	6. AEEHORSS	6. AEFNORST
7. EEIILLRV	7. ACDOPRST	7. ACCILMO	7. BEEGMRSU
8. AAEGILTT	8. AMORSTTU	8. CDEIMOST	8. ACEILMPS

FINDING BINGOS OVER THE BOARD

Use the following diagrams as your board positions. Try to find the playable eight-letter bingos with each of the three given racks. This will teach you to use an existing letter on the board plus your seven-letter rack. We list the choice of beginnings or endings to use in the answers. The answers are on page 72.

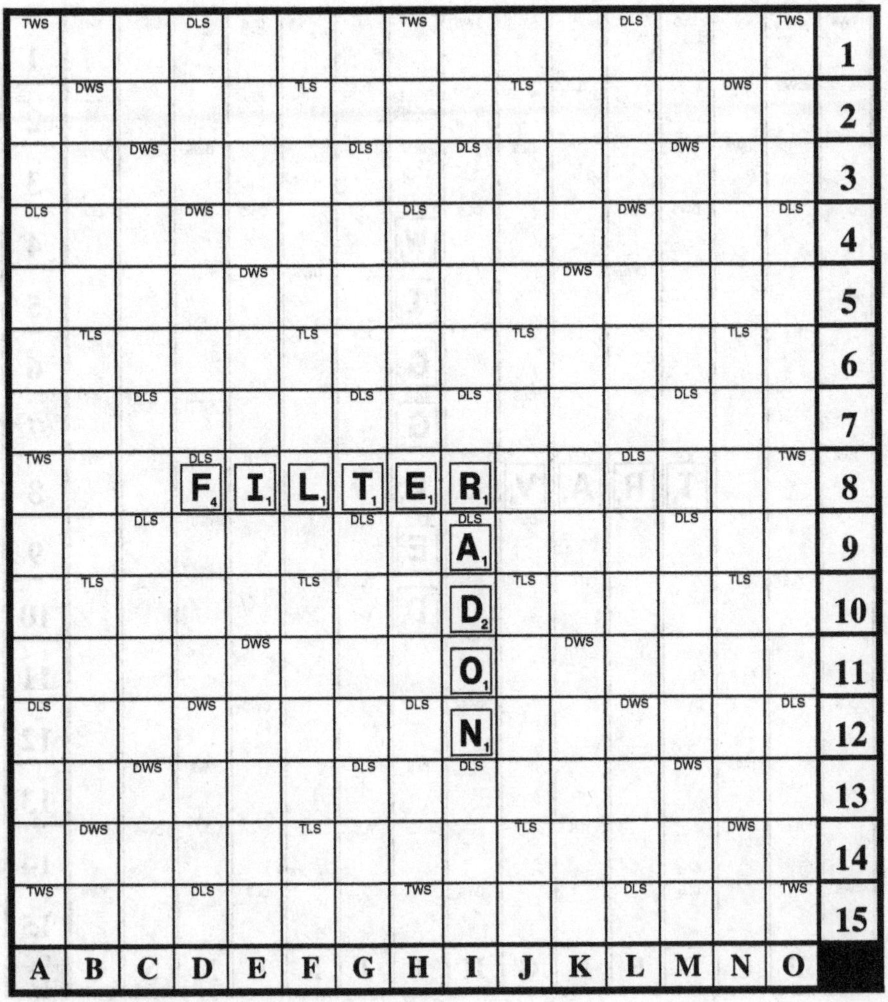

DIAGRAM 7-1

Beginnings: **CON, IN, OUT, RE, UN**
Endings: **ABLE, ED, ENT, IES, TION**
Rack #1: **D D E E F I R**
Rack #2: **A E I N R T V**
Rack #3: **A A C N O T V**

Time limit: 20 minutes
Average score: 1 correct *Good score:* 2 correct *Expert score:* 3 correct

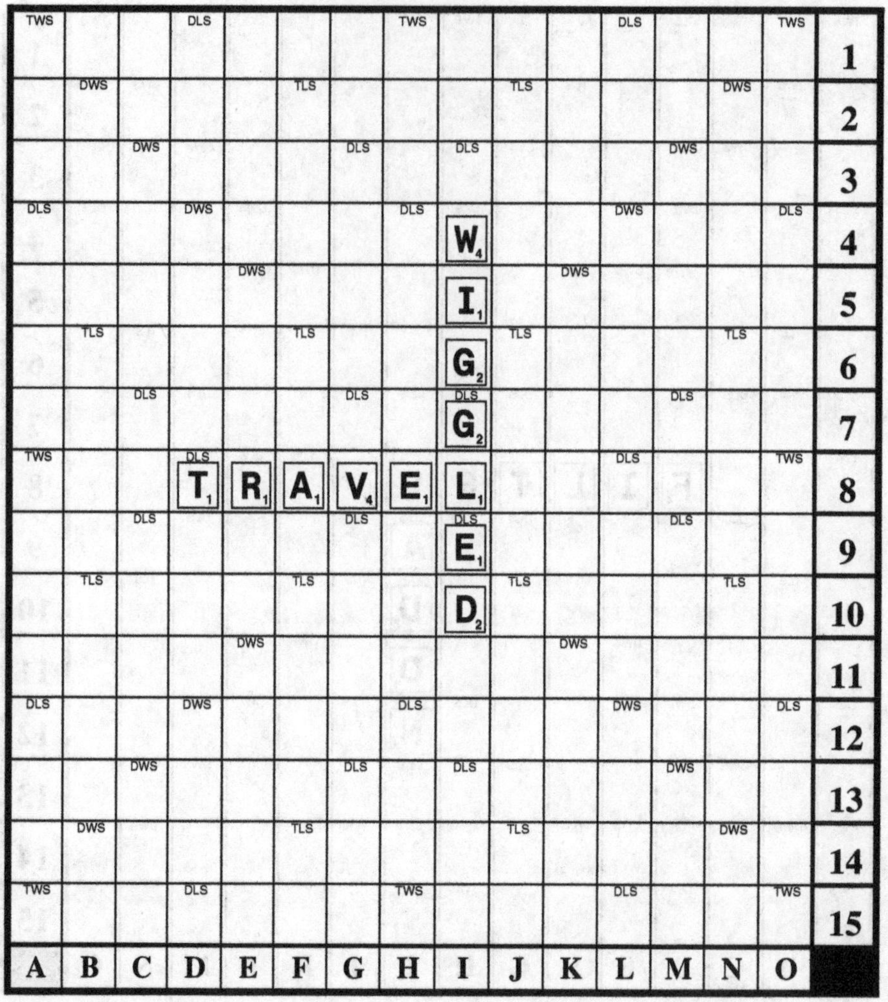
W I G G L E D
T R A V E L

DIAGRAM 7-2

Beginnings:	**CON, IN, OUT, RE, UN**
Endings:	**ABLE, ED, ENT, IES, TION**
Rack #1:	**D E N R U W Y**
Rack #2:	**I L N O O S U**
Rack #3:	**B D E E L L O**

Time limit: 20 minutes

Average score: 1 correct *Good score:* 2 correct *Expert score:* 3 correct

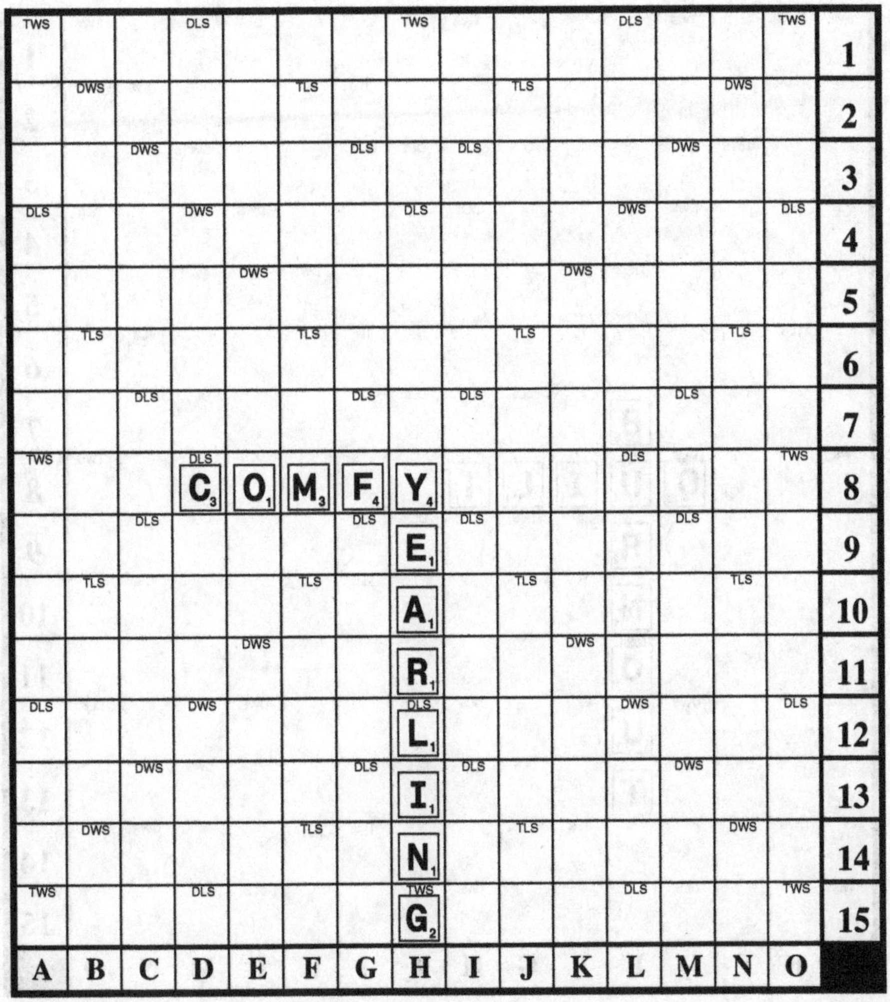
C O M F Y
E
A
R
L
I
N
G
A B C D E F G H I J K L M N O

DIAGRAM 7-3

Beginnings: **CON, IN, OUT, RE, UN**
Endings: **ABLE, ED, ENT, IES, TION**
Rack #1: **C E N O O R T**
Rack #2: **E E I N P T T**
Rack #3: **D E N O S U V**

Time limit: 20 minutes
Average score: 1 correct *Good score:* 2 correct *Expert score:* 3 correct

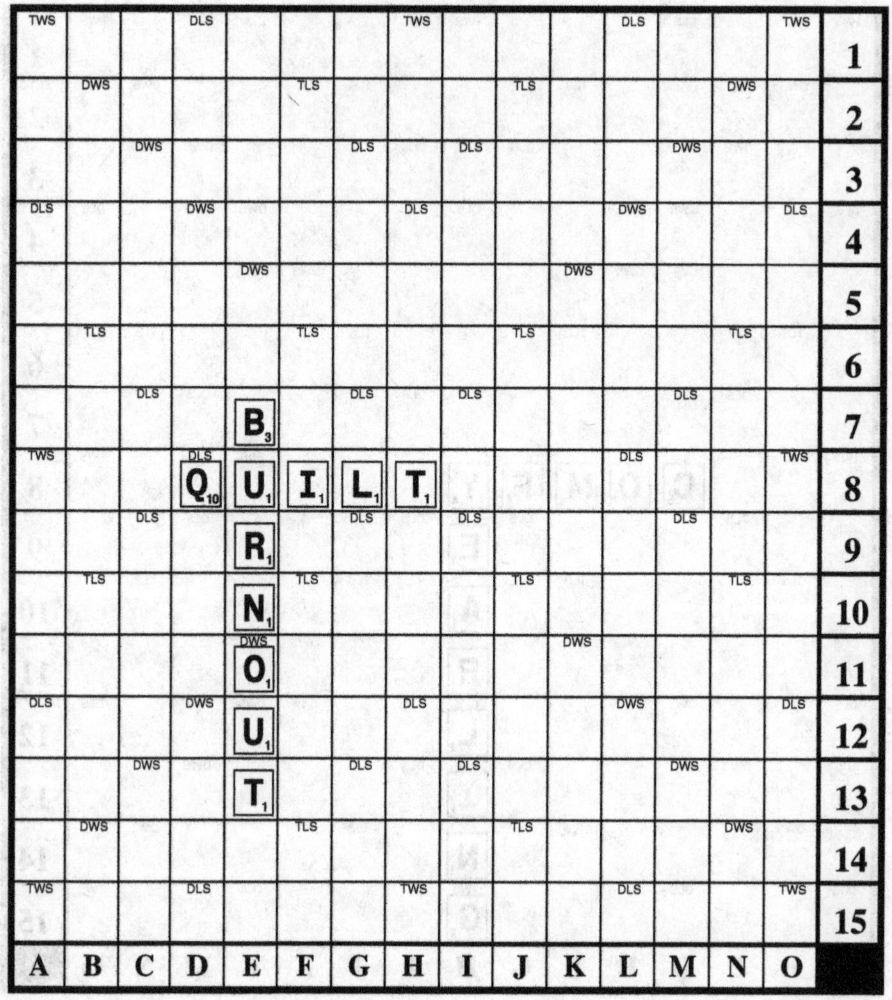
TWS
DLS
DWS
TLS
Q
U
I
L
T
B
R
N
O
U
T
A B C D E F G H I J K L M N O
1
2
3
4
5
6
7
8
9
10
11
12
13
14
15

DIAGRAM 7-4

Beginnings: **CON, IN, OUT, RE, UN**
Endings: **ABLE, ED, ENT, IES, TION**
Rack #1: **G I L N O T Y**
Rack #2: **A B D E F I N**
Rack #3: **A B C E I N T**

Time limit: 20 minutes
Average score: 1 correct *Good score:* 2 correct *Expert score:* 3 correct

HOPEFUL
BUCKING

DIAGRAM 7-5

Beginnings: **CON, IN, OUT, RE, UN**
Endings: **ABLE, ED, ENT, IES, TION**

Rack #1: **A A E E N R W**
Rack #2: **A A D I L M S**
Rack #3: **A C F I I P S**

Time limit: 20 minutes
Average score: 1 correct *Good score:* 2 correct *Expert score:* 3 correct

It's one thing to find a seven-letter word on your rack; it's another to find a place for that bingo on a board crowded with letters. The secret is to look for hook words and parallel plays. Look at the following diagrams and follow the directions. In each case you will be asked about finding a place for your bingo. The answers are on page 72.

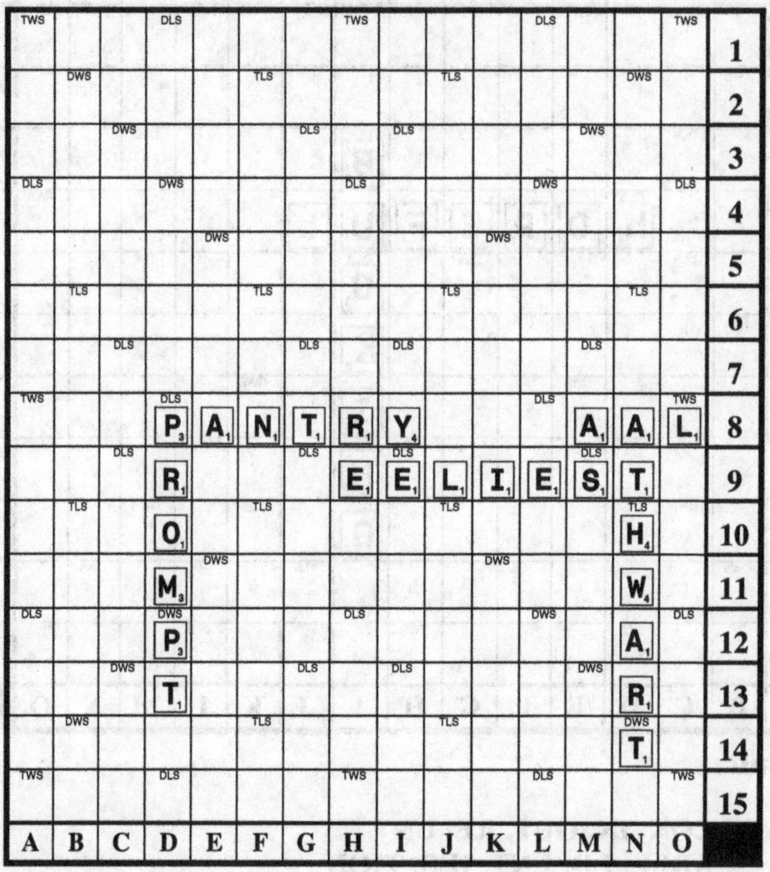
PANTRY
AAL
EELIEST
PROMPT
ATHWART
A B C D E F G H I J K L M N O
1 2 3 4 5 6 7 8 9 10 11 12 13 14 15

DIAGRAM 7-6

Your rack: **E A R D R U M**

Find an allowable place to play the bingo EARDRUM in Diagram 7-6.
Time limit: 10 minutes

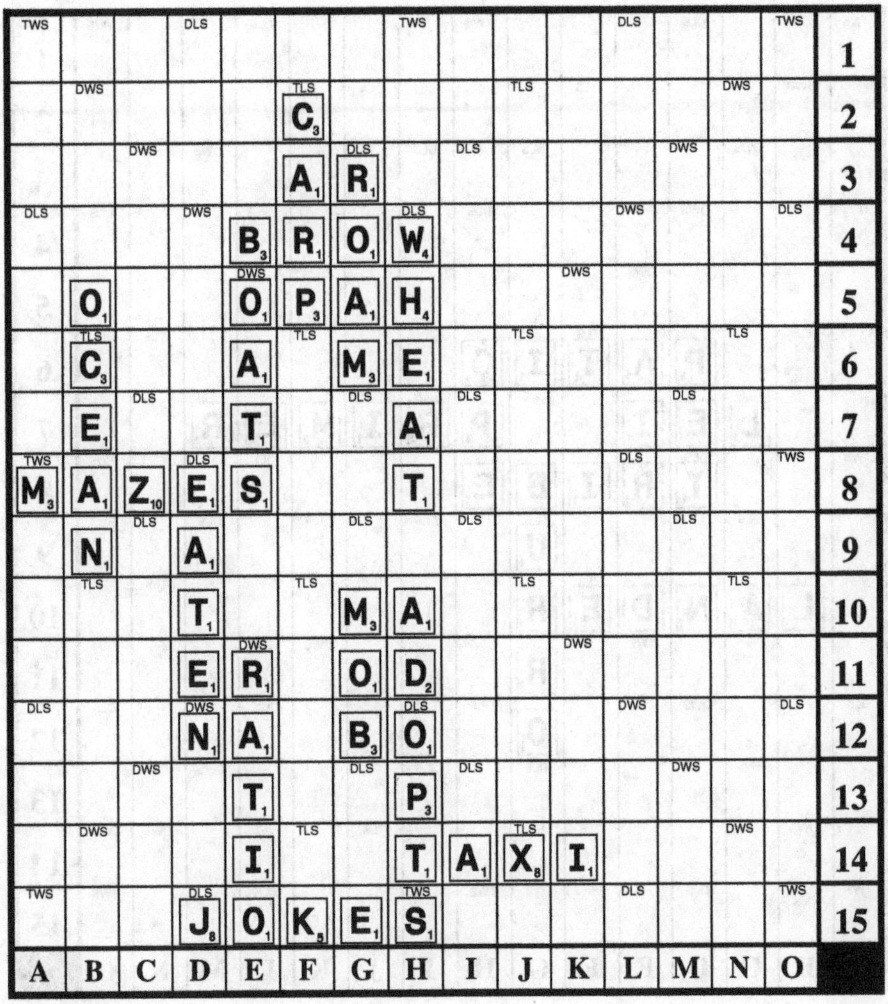

DIAGRAM 7-7

Your rack: **T R A I N E D**

At what place in Diagram 7-7 can you play TRAINED, using all seven tiles in the rack and forming only acceptable words?

Time limit: 10 minutes

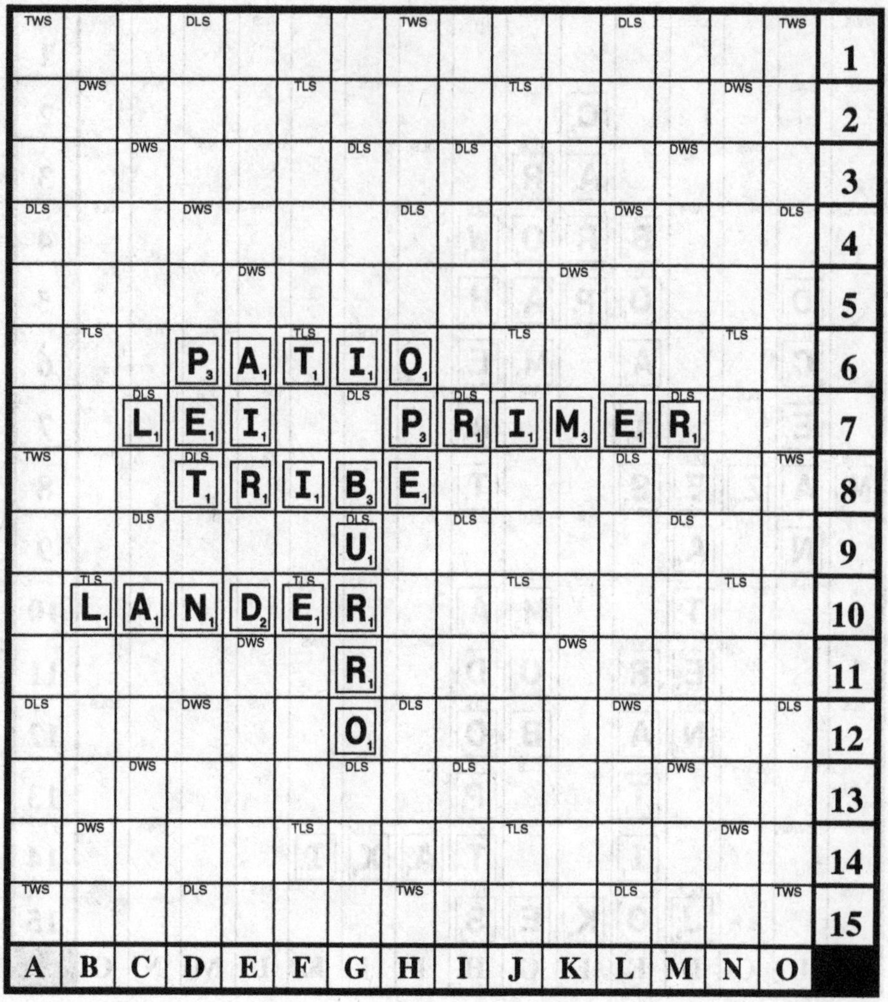

DIAGRAM 7-8

Your rack: **F E L L O W S**

There are five common ways to position your bingo in Diagram 7-8. Where are they, and which one gives you the most points?

Time limit: 15 minutes

BINGO PRACTICE #3

Now that you've had some practice finding seven- and eight-letter words, go back to diagrams 2-2, 2-3, 2-4, and 2-5 in chapter 2. Try to find the playable bingo with each of the given racks. In diagrams 2-2 and 2-4, there are two common playable bingos each.

The answers are on page 72, listed under their respective diagrams.

Time limit: 30 minutes
Average score: 2 correct *Good score:* 3 correct *Expert score:* 4 correct

Diagram 2-2: Rack: **C G H I L N Y**
Diagram 2-3: Rack: **A B C L N O Y**
Diagram 2-4: Rack: **A D E E I M R**
Diagram 2-5: Rack: **A C E R T T X**

Common Word Beginnings and Endings

Beginnings: AB, AD, AIR, ANTI, BE, BI, COM, CON, DE, DIS, EM, EN, EX, FORE, HAND, HEAD, IM, IN, ISO, MID, MIS, NON, OUT, OVER, POST, PRE, RE, SEA, SEMI, SUB, TRI, UN, UP

Endings: ABLE, AGE, AL, ANCE, ANE, ANT, ARY, ATE, DOM, EAU, ED, EE, ENCE, ENT, ER, EST, FISH, FORM, FUL, GHT, GRAM, HOOD, IA(L), IBLE, IC, ICAL, IER, IES, IEST, IFY, ILE, ILY, INE, ING, ION, ISE, ISH, ISM, IST, ITE, ITY, IUM, IVE, IZE, LAND, LESS, LET, LIKE, LOGY, LY, MAN, MEN, MENT, NESS, OID, OSE, OUGH, OUS, OUT, SHIP, SIS(SES), SOME, TURE, WARD, WEED, WISE, WOOD, WORM

There is only one more step to learn in Part 1. You won't often find bingos to play unless you save on your rack the common letters that frequently form them. Chapter 8 tells you how to do it.

BINGO PRACTICE #1:

A.	B.	C.	D.
1. EMBALMS	1. IMMOBILE	1. FOREPAW	1. ISOLATES
2. ISOTOPE	2. HEADSET	2. ENAMELS	2. HOARDED
3. SPRAINED	3. AUDIENCE	3. PLUNGER	3. PENITENT
4. UNIFORM	4. VAGUEST	4. EXTERIOR	4. EMPLOYEE
5. LENIENCE	5. BLINKER	5. IMPRISON	5. GRAYISH
6. HELPFUL	6. STRAIGHT	6. DOLEFUL	6. FORECAST
7. GIRLISH	7. ENCHANT	7. INCREASE	7. HANDBALL
8. ALRIGHT	8. DUMBEST	8. HEADLOCK	8. MIDNIGHT

BINGO PRACTICE #2:

A.	B.	C.	D.
1. OVERBITE	1. BEGONIA	1. NONDAIRY	1. PURITIES
2. EUPHORIA	2. SUNNIEST	2. PREMIERE	2. AUDIBLE
3. IRONICAL	3. UNOPENED	3. SOLIDIFY	3. UNCLEAN
4. SUBLEASE	4. TOUGHIES	4. MODERATE	4. PRESTIGE
5. REINDEER	5. MANDIBLE	5. TELEGRAM	5. EPIDEMIC
6. NONSENSE	6. OVERLAND	6. SEASHORE	6. SEAFRONT
7. LIVELIER	7. POSTCARD	7. COMICAL	7. SUBMERGE
8. TAILGATE	8. OUTSMART	8. DOMESTIC	8. MISPLACE

DIAGRAM 7-1: 1. DIFFERED D5 or D6 82 points. Give yourself extra credit for also finding REDEFIED H2 68 and/or FRIENDED 12E 78; 2. INTERVAL F1 71; 3. VACATION E3 76.

DIAGRAM 7-2: 1. UNDERWAY F2 69; 2. SOLUTION D4 66; 3. BELLOWED 4D 80, or BOWELLED 4G 80.

DIAGRAM 7-3: 1. CONCERTO D8 76 or D5 74 points; 2. PENITENT, 14B 74; 3. UNSOLVED 12D 74.

DIAGRAM 7-4: 1. OUTLYING 12D 82; 2. FINDABLE G2 69; 3. INCUBATE 12B 76.

DIAGRAM 7-5: 1. REAWAKEN 10D 69. Notice that AWAKENER 10G 69 points is also possible. 2. MALADIES G2 64; 3. PACIFIES G2 68.

DIAGRAM 7-6: EARDRUM 7G 86.

DIAGRAM 7-7: TRAINED I6 85.

DIAGRAM 7-8: The five starting squares are: A4, 13A, 13B, N1, and 5E. FELLOWS 5E scores the most, 126. Give yourself extra credit for finding FELLOWS N3. PRIMERO is a type of card game.

DIAGRAM 2-2: CHARMINGLY 8F 116. ACHINGLY H8 104.

DIAGRAM 2-3: BALCONY 9C 88.

DIAGRAM 2-4: DIAMETER J3 69, or DREAMIER I1 63 or I7 65.

DIAGRAM 2-5: EXTRACT E4 91.

8 MINDING YOUR Ps, Qs, AND EVERYTHING ELSE: Introduction to Rack Management

No matter how skilled you are at word games, as a SCRABBLE® Brand Crossword Game player you will be at the mercy of the tiles you draw. You might be an expert, but if you draw TUUVVWW (a well-known expert once drew this opening rack) and your novice opponent draws AEINRST, you probably won't be leading after the first play. Of course, during a series of games the luck factor is less important, since generally each player will get his or her fair share of blanks and Ss. The expert, however, knows how to manage his or her rack consistently well. We often hear about experts at tournaments from their opponents: "S/he drew all the good tiles! I couldn't do a thing!" While this can and does happen, there are ways to enhance your chances of drawing a balanced, high-scoring rack.

To balance your rack means to save the better combinations of letters. The ideas in this chapter are so important for improving your SCRABBLE game skills that we've created a handy anagram to help you remember:

UNBALANCED RACK = CAN EARN BAD LUCK

We'll use a question-and-answer approach to express some of the ideas in this chapter.

Novice: I have trouble with Cs on my rack. Someone once said that a C is a good letter and better than a P, but I like Ps much better. What's really true?

Expert: Each person's vocabulary will, to a certain extent, determine how valuable each letter is to him or her. Hence, the best play for one person may not be the best play for someone else. Computer tests based upon the results of thousands of SCRABBLE games show this order of most- to least-valuable letters: Blank, S, E, X, Z, R, A, H, N, C, D, M, T, I, K, L, P, O, Y, J,* F, B, G, W,

* Originally the list was mistyped by the computer analyst, who set the J several places to the left on the list. We have finally corrected it for this edition

U, V, Q. However, you should be warned that this list was generated by a computer knowing *all* the words in the *OSPD*.

Novice: Why should that matter?

Expert: Suppose you want to become a good SCRABBLE game player and so you start, for some odd reason, by learning all the words spelled with a V. After you have learned them all, you may find that the V is a very valuable letter, much more valuable than the C. That's because whenever you draw the V, you can almost always use it to get a good score, since you know so many words using it. When you draw a C, on the other hand, you don't know many words using it, so you have more difficulty with the C than with the V.

Novice: How do I determine which letters are best for me?

Expert: Though you may usually rely on the list on page 73, instead of focusing too much energy on individual letters, we advise you to spend some time during each turn determining which *combination of letters* you'd like to have left on your rack *after* your play.

For example, you have AABIILN. You see the play BANAL for 25 points. That's not a bad score. However, you notice that ALIBI will score 20. Which do you choose? Look at the difference between the "leaves" for both plays. (A leave is the group of letters left on your rack *after* you have made a play and *before* you have replenished your rack.) After BANAL, you will be left with II. After ALIBI you have AN. Which do you think will reap better results on your next turn?

If you don't know, try this experiment: Choose five random tiles from the tile bag and add the II combination to form a new seven-letter rack. Find your best play using a position from any SCRABBLE game in progress. Now take away the II and add the AN to form a slightly different rack. Find your best play again on the same game in progress. Repeat this experiment twenty times with twenty random racks and keep track of how many points you scored with both the II rack and the AN rack. It should be apparent that the AN is much more likely to help you score well than the II. Is the AN leave worth the 5 points you will lose by playing ALIBI? Most times it will be worth it! Think of a good play as having two parts—what you score, and what tiles are left on your rack. This example demonstrates, in part, a worthwhile principle to remember: ***You don't want to duplicate any letter on your rack unless it's an E.*** Duplicate letters take away your flexibility to form more words. So, if you have two of any letter but the E, make sure you look for plays that use at least one of these letters.

Novice: What if I have two Ss? I know that Ss are valuable tiles. Should I save two of them at the cost of a few points?

Expert: It's true that Ss are very valuable. However, two Ss don't necessarily make for a better rack. If you can get an extra 3 or 4 points for the second S, we suggest you use it. See chapter 11 for a more detailed discussion on how to use Ss.

Another principle we can learn from the preceding example is to ***keep approximately the same number of vowels and consonants in your leave.*** This means that if you play five tiles, keep one vowel and one consonant. If you play three tiles, keep two vowels and two consonants. If you play only one tile, you should probably be close to a bingo, and your chances will be enhanced if you save three vowels and three consonants.

When you must leave an odd number of tiles on your rack, it's usually a good idea to leave one extra consonant. That's true largely because there are more three-, five-, and seven-letter words with one extra consonant than an extra vowel. Another reason is that if you draw too many vowels, which are worth only 1 point each, you won't often have a high-scoring play; whereas, if you have too many consonants, you're more likely to make a good play, since you may have one or more high-point consonants to use on a bonus square.

One last principle to remember is: If possible, ***hold as few high-point tiles as possible in your leave.*** The high-point tiles and their values are: B (3), C (3), D (2), F (4), G (2), H (4), J (8), K (5), M (3), P (3), Q (10), V (4), W (4), X (8), Y (4), and Z (10). The high-point tiles are worth more because they are generally less frequently used to spell words. So, the more high-point tiles you have in your rack, the fewer choices you'll have for plays.

Those of you who hesitate to believe this principle may point to all the times you've had several letters like the X, Z, M, and P and one or two vowels that enable you to make a play of 30 or more points. It's true: Having three or four high-point tiles *in addition to* a few vowels may give you points galore. However, if you don't draw vowels with those consonants, you may be wishing you had used those high-pointers earlier. Plus, you will find that bingos are *much* harder to draw with three or more high-point tiles. Therefore, we advise you to try to keep a good balance of 1-point tiles.

One last reason to use those high-point tiles is that you'll rarely be able to play five or six tiles with three or more high-pointers in your rack. Keep in mind that your best bet to draw the Ss, blanks, a steady flow of Es, and the X and Z is by playing more, rather than fewer, tiles each turn.

Novice: Okay, I understand that I should save the good combinations. But which are they?

Expert: That's a good question. Before we tackle it, here is one important point to remember: Any accurate assessment of how you should manage your rack in any *specific* position must include the configuration of the words on the game board. That's because you may want to make certain plays for reasons other than rack balance. Having said that, we'll assume for this discussion that none of the board positions has distinguishing features that will influence the rack leave, unless we say otherwise.

LEAVE: 1 LETTER

If you're using six tiles and leaving one, you can look at the list on page 73 to see which letters are more valuable. The blank, S, E, and X are the four best tiles to keep. Imagine your rack is AEGLNPT and you're trying to decide between playing TANGLE or PLANET, and each is about the same number of points. The list shows that the P is generally more useful than the G, so play TANGLE.

The blank and S are the two most valuable tiles. If you are able to make a good play with six tiles and still keep the blank or S, you are accomplishing the typical rack-balancing goal. Nonetheless, check the board carefully to see if you may have overlooked a really outstanding play using the S or blank.

It's a good idea to think "two words" whenever you have an S, because adding an S to a word on the board and playing perpendicular to it is one of the best ways to score more points.

With the blank on your rack, if you don't see a bingo, you should ask yourself if you can score at least 20 to 30 more points using the blank. If so, play it. If not, save it for a later play.

Chapter 11 discusses how to use Ss and blanks to find bingos.

LEAVE: 2 LETTERS

We've already said that it's better to save one vowel and one consonant. Which ones are best? Use the valuable-letter list on page 73 to determine which vowels and consonants are best to keep. If you're trying to decide between leaving AL and ER, you can see that the E is better than the A, and the R is better than the L, so ER is a better leave than AL. Similarly, HI is a better leave than GO.

For someone just beginning to learn how to play, this method of evaluation is an excellent guide. But keep in mind that it's not perfect. For instance, though the list shows otherwise, most experts would keep DE instead of CE, and AL instead of AK. In both cases, the expert is thinking about playing bingos. We'll discuss more about rack balance and bingos in chapter 9.

LEAVE: 3 OR 4 LETTERS

In general, the best leaves have combinations of one or two vowels (preferably the E and A, or two Es) and two of the following consonants, in decreasing order of preference: S, R, N, T, and L. Why is this a good formula for a three- or four-tile leave? Mostly because you'll draw bingo racks more often if you save these letters. Furthermore, if you draw one or two high-point tiles and no bingo, then these three or four 1-pointers will usually combine well with them to form good-scoring five- or six-letter words.

There is one exception to this three-tile-leave rule. The E is such a useful letter that keeping it with another vowel and a consonant for a three-tile leave is not often discouraged, although other factors may affect your decision.

LEAVE: 5 LETTERS

Not counting the variety of special-scoring and board considerations that can occur, there are a limited number of reasons for playing only two tiles and leaving five:

1. You keep five dynamic tiles, such as AERST, with the hope that you will draw a bingo on your next turn. This is called "fishing." In that case you need only learn: Which five-tile combinations are worthy of fishing with?

There aren't many we would waste a turn to fish with, but here are most of them: AERST, AENST, AELST, ADEST, ADERS, AELRS, EIRST, EINST, EORST, ENOST, EENST, EERST, AENRT, and EINRT. Keep in mind that the first six are the best, and the last two are the least desirable. There are exceptional situations in which certain letters already on the board may inspire you to fish with less spectacular leaves. However, as a general rule, we don't suggest developing this habit.

2. You earn a good score with a two-letter word. Example: You play AH for 28 points, EX for 36, WE for 24, or JO for 52. When you play any of these or similar choices, chances are you're not keeping AERST. In the majority of cases you simply want to keep a balance of two or three vowels and three or two consonants. *Example:* AABEHIR. You play AH for 28 points, keeping ABEIR. However, if you have AAEHIOR, playing AH leaves you with AEIOR, which is very unbalanced and may lead to a horrible next rack. You might instead want to sacrifice as many as 5 or 10 points to keep a much better leave. For instance, playing ARIA for 20 points, and thus keeping EHO, gives you much better chances for a higher score next turn.

LEAVE: 6 LETTERS

As with the five-tile leave, you should avoid using only one tile unless you score really well or you are fishing for a bingo. Here are ten six-letter leaves that you can comfortably fish with: AEINST, AEIRST, AEINRT, AEINRS, EINORS, EINOST, AENRST, EINRST, ENORST, and AEERST. Appendix 4 lists all the bingos that can be formed with these leaves. Such a six-letter leave is often called a "six-letter stem," since each is the foundation for many bingos.

To those of you who've never played a bingo: We suggest that if you follow all of these rack-balancing guidelines and review, even occasionally, Appendix 4, you will soon surprise yourself with your increased scores.

This completes Part 1—your first course.

PART • 2

ADVANCED PLAY: Graduating to the Next Level

What distinguishes a good home SCRABBLE game player from an experienced club player? Chapters 9–15 will answer that question and show you how to improve your play even further. Expect, however, greater complexity in our discussions. These chapters are not intended for beginners. Our intention in Part 2 is to take an experienced player one step or more ahead toward becoming an expert. However, we do encourage novices to read these chapters, since there are many insights here that can be grasped by anyone.

Chapter 9 discusses rack balancing in more depth. Chapter 10 presents ideas that may change your thinking about exchanging tiles. Chapter 11 is a must for anyone who wants to score more points with the S and blank tiles. In chapter 12, we'll show you which words you should learn to help you the most, while four top players give you their secrets for word power. Chapter 13 adds yet more words to your arsenal—the three- and four-letter J, X, and Z words. Chapter 14 will explain "open" and "closed" boards and teach you how you can take advantage of them to win more games. Chapter 15 will give you the information you need about those phoneys that every topnotch player knows and will use against you.

9 ADVANCED RACK MANAGEMENT: Points vs. Leave

In this chapter we want to explore further the concept of rack balancing by giving you several racks and several choices for plays. Then we'll tell you how the expert thinks about each rack. Advanced players strive to build bingo racks as quickly as possible. In general, the major concern is twofold: How many points is each play worth, and how good is the leave? Whether it's better to score more points or to keep a better leave is not always easy to answer, even by the best players.

Here are a few other things to keep in mind as you read this chapter:

Our analysis assumes that the reader is at least familiar with the ideas in chapters 7 and 8. If you haven't read those pages, you definitely won't benefit as much from this chapter.

For the purposes of learning these specific ideas, the reader should consider only the choices provided and disregard other plays s/he might find. Unless we specify otherwise, assume that when a play is suggested, all the letters come from the given rack.

For any specific board position and rack, there will be a variety of other considerations besides rack balance that can affect your decisions. In these pages, we delve into these ideas enough to get you started thinking along winning ways. Ultimately, you will have to learn by experience how to choose the best plays. And since SCRABBLE game strategy is by no means complete, we leave it to the aspiring player to discover new ideas that expand the boundaries of current theory.

Finally, we advise you to read our analysis while simultaneously assessing your ability to follow our advice. For example, if you haven't yet tried any of the bingo exercises in chapter 7, and if you haven't yet become familiar with how to find bingos, some of the analysis found in this chapter may not exactly apply to you. Once you are able to find bingos with the more common letters, the 1- and 2-point tiles (ADEGILNORSTU), you may find this chapter more useful. To help your bingo skills grow, we've designed an exercise at the end of chapter 11 that can show you just how powerful having three vowels, three consonants, and a blank can be. It will be well worth trying. Note that in this chapter the leave after each play is given in parentheses.

Rack #1: A B C E I N V

Novice: I see VICE (ABN), VIBE (ACN), CAB (EINV), CAVE (BIN), and CABIN (EV), all for 16 to 20 points. Which should I play?

Expert: You might choose any of the words but CAVE or CABIN. After CABIN, the EV leave makes your rack particularly vulnerable to bad luck, since you'll have five chances to draw high-point tiles. The V does not usually combine well with other high-point tiles, unless you draw the OR for the prefix OVER-. After CAVE, the BIN leave is far inferior to the other leaves.

Otherwise, consider: You have three high-point tiles (B, C, and V) that don't combine well together. Your goal should be to use at least two of them for your next play. That's because, in general, you should never leave two high-point tiles on your rack. It reduces your bingo chances enormously. (The CH combination is a notable exception.)

Each of the first three words gives you a reasonable leave. Let's compare VICE and VIBE: Which is the better leave, ABN or ACN? In general, we would choose to play VIBE, since the C is much superior to the B. That's particularly true when you're looking for bingos; many more seven- and eight-letter words have a C than a B.

Now compare VIBE with CAB: Some experts might instead play CAB in order to keep the balanced EINV leave, which is bingo-prone if you don't draw another high-point tile. But your best decision will depend on an honest evaluation of your own vocabulary. So if you know many seven- and eight-letter words spelled with the V, the EINV will lead you to a bingo often enough to make this leave worthwhile.

As you might guess from our lack of a definitive answer, not all experts will agree on how to play this rack. We wanted to show you from the start that there is often a wide range of opinions on what to play. We believe that what's most important is for us to show you the thought process behind the decision, rather than that there is always only one right answer.

Rack #2: A A M O O T T

Novice: I see ATOM (AOT) 20 points, MOTTO (AA) 18, and TOMATO (A) 16. I'm not sure which is best.

Expert: Though only 16 points, TOMATO is the best choice. The most important reasons are that it allows you to draw six new tiles and it minimizes the duplication of letters. In general, it's better to play six tiles instead of four in order to have a better chance to draw the blanks and Ss and the valuable J, X, and Z. The only common exceptions are when you play four tiles and save three terrific letters, such as ERS, ENS, EST, ERT, ENR, or ENT, to name a few. When you save these tiles you give yourself a good chance either to draw a bingo or to make a five- or six-letter follow-up play.

Rack #3: E H I I O U V

Novice: I see HIVE (IOU) 20 points, HOVE (IIU) 20, and VIE (HIOU) 12. What should I do?

Expert: Sometimes you have to trust that your letters will improve. In this case that means playing HIVE (not HOVE because of the II leave) for 20 points, even though you keep the horrible IOU leave. You can expect that you may have to exchange letters next turn if you don't draw well, but taking 20 points now and hoping to draw well next turn is better than taking zero now and risking who-knows-what-you-will-draw next time.

Even as we say this, there are probably a few experts who would exchange five tiles, keeping the EH. That's a decision often made based on other considerations, such as who's ahead, by how much, and what tiles have already been played.

Rack #4: A E L O S T T

Novice: Should I play TO (AELST) 6 points or TOTAL (ES) 15?

Expert: Even if you can't find an eight-letter bingo using a tile on the board, you should realize that you are very close to a seven-letter bingo. Assuming there are at least two places on the board to play bingos, you should rid yourself of just two tiles, saving AELST, and hope for a bingo next turn. As we discussed in chapter 8, this is called fishing, and all the best players do it occasionally. AELST is a powerful five-letter leave. There are 245 different seven-letter words that include these letters. See page 77 for other strong five-letter leaves.

Rack #5: A B E L R R V

Novice: I have three different ways to play the word VERBAL. One way uses only the BLRV, saving AER and scoring 25 points. Another way is to play VERBAL using all six tiles from my rack, saving an R, and scoring 25. The last way is to play through an E on the board, keeping ER and scoring 24. Both blanks and one A have already been played, but no Ss or Rs are on the board yet, and this is only my fourth play of the game. I can also play BRAVER and keep the L, scoring 28. All my choices seem nearly equal, since they all keep the board open for seven-letter words. Is one of my plays better than the others?

Expert: You can eliminate BRAVER, since the L leave is much inferior to any of the others. The extra point or two does not make it worth keeping the L. Using six tiles and keeping the R isn't bad, but it doesn't compare to either other leave, ER or AER. The ER combination is so dynamic that you should try to keep these letters even at the cost of a few points. The only question now is whether you should keep the A or not. The AER combination is quite good, as long as you don't draw too many vowels. Since there are plenty of As left in the bag, I advise you to play yours, keeping only ER. If you were to perform a thousand trials that compared drawing to ER or AER at this stage of the game, you'd find that you would generally have more balanced racks after keeping ER than AER.

Rack #6: L N O R V W ?

Novice: I see VOWER or VOWEL, both through an existing E on the board. Both plays score 22 points. I also see VOW for 26 points and WON for 28 points, both using three of my tiles. With all these choices, it's not at all clear to me what to do.

Expert: What's most important here? With a blank on your rack, your priority is to build a bingo in the next few turns! To that end you must make the play that gives you the best leave without sacrificing too many points. Of the choices listed, VOWEL gives you the best leave (NR?). Why? Because after VOW and WON, the three consonants left (LNR or LRV) make it harder to draw a bingo rack next turn. While after VOWER, the LN? leave is somewhat less powerful than the NR? leave after VOWEL. You can assume that because the R is much closer to the beginning of the most- to least-valuable letter list.

Rack #7: A I L O S S Y

Novice: My choices are SOYA (ILS) 22 points, SILO (ASY) 20 points, NOISY (ALS) 20 points (N on the board), SLAYS (IO) 35 points, and LOYAL (ISS) 23 points, with an L on the board. I'd like to play an S, but I don't think I should use both of them. Is that true?

Expert: This is a typical choice for many double-S racks: There is a variety of plays using one S for about the same number of points; there is one play not using either S, and a play using both Ss for many more points. The decision you reach will depend on factors other than simply rack balance. However, if rack balance is your only concern, then our opinion is to choose the SAL leave over all others and play NOISY. That's because you have a better chance to bingo after this leave than with any other.

Keep in mind that if you think you won't need a bingo to win or that you won't be able to play one later in this game, you will probably want to take the points with SLAYS. That's because you don't need to save the Ss for a bingo. Some novices get caught up with the idea of saving Ss and forget that the *S is for Scoring!*

Rack #8: A A A D E R W

Novice: This is my first rack of a game, and I am first to play. I see AWARD (AE) 8H 22 points, and WARED or WADER (AA) 8D 26. I like getting rid of two As with AWARD. It's probably worth it to lose 4 points and have a better leave.

Expert: You're right! AWARD is better than either WARED or WADER. However, there's an even better play! If you have looked at the two-to-make-three letter list, you may have noticed the word AWA. It's an adverb meaning "away." As an opening play, it scores only 12 points. Most players discount AWA immediately, since it scores so many fewer points than the other plays. But oddly, this play has been shown by computer analysis to be best. However, before we explain why, we will repeat what we said earlier: The computer analysis is based upon the player's knowing all the bingos. If you haven't developed your bingo skills, you may not actually benefit as much as some other players from AWA.

Here's the reason AWA is so good: After playing AWA 8F for 12 points, you have the very powerful ADER leave. If you played this exact position a thousand different times, each time drawing three tiles to ADER, you would find that your rack created a second-turn bingo a significant fraction of times. Your overall two-turn total after turns one and two would, in general, be more than after any other first play.

The other significant difference between AWA and the five-tile plays is that AWA gives away fewer scoring opportunities to your opponent. That means your opponent will generally score fewer points after you play AWA than s/he will after WARED, WADER, or AWARD.

Rack #9: E I N O R S Y

Novice: I see OY (EINRS) 10 points, IRONY (ES) 30, and NOISY (ERS) 20, which uses an S already on the board. Which do you prefer?

Expert: All three plays leave dynamic tiles. The ERS leave is the best three-letter leave you can have without a blank. However, with most positions and scores, you should simply play IRONY for 30 points. That's because the ES leave after playing IRONY is also excellent. And in most cases, the extra 10 points are worth taking. But if IRONY were only 22 to 25 points, you might seriously consider playing NOISY and keeping the ERS instead.

If you're behind in the score so much that you must play a bingo to win, play OY. The EINRS leave is better than just ERS. But in most other cases, when the score is closer, you sacrifice too many points by playing OY for only 10 points.

Rack #10: E F I L N O P

Novice: I see several plays: FLOP (EIN) 28 points, FELON (IP) 34, FILE (NOP) 24, FOP (EILN) 28, and FLOE (INP) 30. There are sixty-five tiles on the board already, and neither blank has been played. I'm ahead by 30 points before my play.

Expert: Since you're going to be nearly a bingo ahead after your turn, your main concern is how to stay ahead. By playing five tiles (FELON 34) and keeping IP, you maximize your chances of drawing a blank, which is vital if you want to keep your opponent from playing a bingo. The IP leave, though not as bingo-prone as EIN or EILN, will generally allow you a decent play next turn. Plus, FELON is your biggest-scoring play. That's important!

Rack #11: B D I O P T X

Novice: The board is fairly open, with several bonus squares available. The only choices I see are BIPOD (TX) 30 points and two different places for POX (BDIT), worth either 36 points or 35 points. I think I should take the extra 6 points, but the leave, BDIT, isn't that great. The score is about even. Neither blank and only one S has been played.

Expert: You should sacrifice the points to play BIPOD. That's because on the open board you're likely to play the X next turn for at least 36 points. And the TX leave is much superior to BDIT, while you have two extra chances to draw an S or blank.

Rack #12: C E I L O W Y

Novice: The game is three-quarters over, with the blanks and Ss on the board. I don't see any places to put a bingo even if I had one, though there are two TLSs open next to As. I'm ahead by 5 points. I have several choices: COWY (EIL) 30 points; YOWIE (CL) 28; YOWL (CEI) 32; WILCO (EY) 28; YOW (CEIL) 28.

Expert: Without the prospect of a bingo, you want to make as good a play next turn as you will this turn. With that in mind, play WILCO. The EY leave will allow you to play parallel to a TLS for at least 28 points, since YA and YE are both acceptable twos.

Rack #13: A D E I R V Y

Novice: We've each taken only five turns, playing two bingos apiece. The score is very close, but the board is wide open. There is an open D, S, and T in separate parts of the board that can be used to spell eight-letter bingos. I see IVY (ADER) for 20 points, DAVY (EIR) for 30, and VARIED (Y) for 35.

Expert: The ADER leave after IVY is the best of your three leaves. However, because the score is close, you need every point you can get, while still giving yourself bingo chances. That's why you should choose DAVY. With three useful consonants open, the EIR leave acts effectively like a leave of DEIR, EIRS, or EIRT, any one of which could earn you a bingo next turn.

Finally, even though VARIED is 5 points more, the Y leave has much less potential for scoring a bingo, even if it does earn 28 points next turn.

Rack #14: A A E N O T Z

Novice: I'm behind by 80 points with only twenty-five tiles left to play, though the board is fairly open for playing bingos. Both blanks and three Ss are on the board already. My choices are AZOTE (AN) 40 points, ZOA (AENT) 32, or ZONATE (A) 36.

Expert: You're far enough behind so that you need a bingo to win. In order to build a bingo, you must sacrifice the extra points by playing ZOA. The AENT leave is too good to pass up. By comparison, playing ZONATE effectively gives up the game. That's because you're using all your good tiles and are unlikely to draw a bingo with just the A leave. And while AZOTE is 10 extra points with a decent leave, you're still far less likely to bingo than after playing ZOA.

Others may argue that by playing more tiles you give yourself a better chance to draw the last S. That's true. But drawing the S doesn't guarantee a bingo, and we simply wouldn't pass up the powerful AENT leave.

Rack #15: A H I J M O W

Novice: I'm behind by about 50 points with a very open board. There are lots of good bonus squares to play on. I have three plays that score from 30–35 points: HAJ (IMOW) 32, HAJI (MOW) 33, and MHO (AIJW) 34. Plus, three words—MOW (AHIJ) 34 points, HOW (AJIM) 35, or JOW (AHIM) 39—can be played vertically down the board starting on the same square, K9, which places the O alone on row 10 just to the right of a Triple Letter square. Playing HAJ sets up the I hook for HAJI, but my opponent might have an I and take it.

Expert: You won't be any closer to a bingo after any of your choices, so that shouldn't be your major concern. Instead, ask yourself how each of your plays will set up a play for your other high-point tiles next turn. You're right to be afraid of the HAJ/I setup. In another position, with different scores, you might consider it. Instead, by playing HOW and leaving AJIM, you may be able to play JO across, while coming down with JAM parallel to HOW and score more than 55 points. There is no reason to assume your opponent will block your setup with so many other bonus squares to choose from. And even if your opponent takes your setup, you'll likely score at least 30 points on this open board, which is all you'd expect after making any other play now.

No matter how well you balance your rack, you're bound to draw poor tiles occasionally—everyone does. Is it advisable to exchange tiles, or is it more important to play a word, any word? Chapter 10 will show you how to determine when to exchange tiles.

10 BAG IT! When to Exchange Your Tiles

Chances are that at one time or another during most SCRABBLE games you will say to yourself: "I can't find a decent play. Maybe I should exchange tiles." (Actually, we've known some players whose language in these situations is a lot more colorful.) We're going to show why it's to your advantage to exchange tiles more often than you'd probably expect. Then we'll explain when to do it.

We will explain the main factors to consider on the following pages.

SCRABBLE

1. What are your options for plays, and how many points are they worth?

Whenever your rack of letters looks really hopeless (say you have 3 Is and 2 Os), you should still take time to find whatever plays are possible. One of the characteristics that distinguishes the better players from the novices is the ability to take seemingly terrible combinations of letters and find plays that score well. You won't be able to make a good, sound decision about whether to exchange or not until you know all your choices.

Let's look at an example:

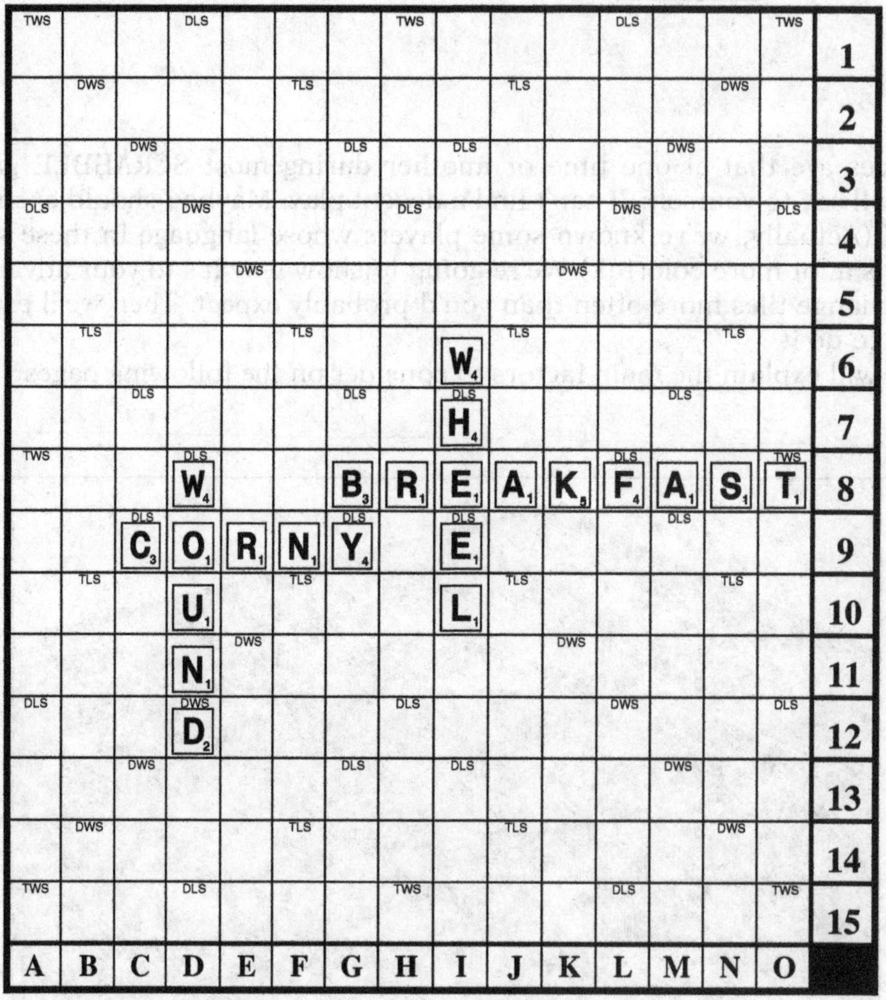

W H E E L
B R E A K F A S T
C O R N Y
W O U N D
A B C D E F G H I J K L M N O
1 2 3 4 5 6 7 8 9 10 11 12 13 14 15

DIAGRAM 10-1

Your score: 40 *Opponent's score:* 113
Rack #1: **AFIIIOO** Rack #2: **ADIIIOO**

What would you do with each rack, faced with the position shown in Diagram 10-1?

Rack #1: First look at your choices. Three choices are FA, OF, or IF. These can be played parallel to BREAKFAST, with the F falling on the 7M square. Considering the score of these plays—between 20 and 23 points—one might think they're not so bad. However, as we've seen from chapter 9, the five-vowel leave is so bad that on the next turn you're not likely to improve your rack. Being as far behind as you are, you can't expect to win this game unless you play a bingo. Keeping five vowels is not the way to do that!

What are the other common word choices? OAF at C11, WOO 6I, SOFA N8, ALOOF 10H, WAIF 6I, and INFO 11C. You would be left with: IIIO, AFIII, IIIO, III, IIOO, or AIIO. Each of these is so weak that, given the few points you'd be scoring, you are much better off trying to draw Ss and blanks by exchanging tiles. A good rule of thumb is: Unless you score 20 points or more, don't ever leave yourself with three vowels and no consonants, especially if you need a bingo to win. Also, avoid leaving one consonant and three vowels, unless the score is relatively close and you see no better choice. See page 102 for the answer.

Now imagine that you have Rack #2: **A D I I I O O.**

If you know the word OIDIA (*n* pl.; a type of fungus), that is an excellent play and much better than exchanging tiles. OIDIA plays best at either J10 or H2. Though we don't recommend keeping two vowels, you have good bingo chances if you draw three consonants. However, there is an even better play available—a four-voweled, six-letter word with which many of our readers are familiar. Can you find it? The answer is on page 102.

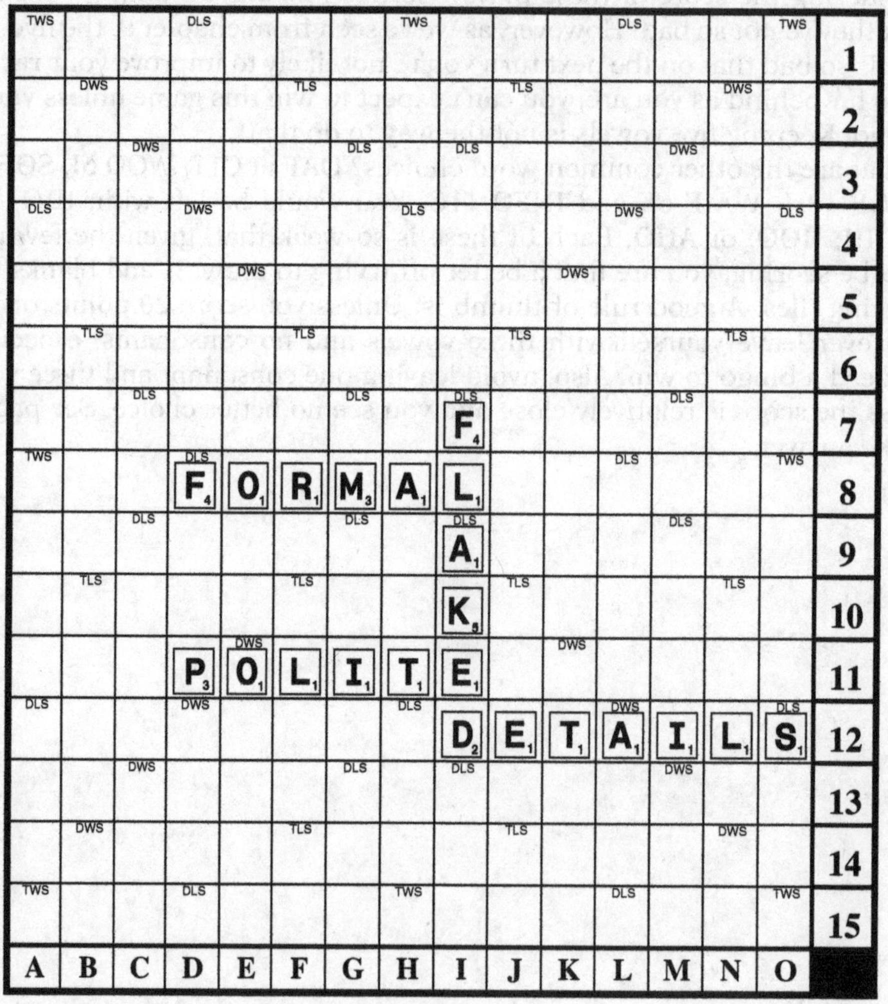
F O R M A L
F L A K E
P O L I T E
D E T A I L S
A B C D E F G H I J K L M N O
1 2 3 4 5 6 7 8 9 10 11 12 13 14 15

DIAGRAM 10-2

Rack: **A L N U U U U**

Using Diagram 10-2, what would you do?

It's worth noting another example of a mistake that novices often make. Big-Ego Bob has just drawn all four Us! His rack reads ALNUUUU. He's silently bemoaning his fate and waiting for his opponent to play so that he can exchange tiles. When his opponent finally does play, it is a bingo—DETAILS, for 66 points, which opens up the S in the middle of a Triple-Triple column. Of course, he congratulates his opponent and says, sarcastically, "That was tough to find!" Then Bob exchanges seven tiles rather quickly. But what did he miss? Had he taken some time to look, he probably would have seen a good common-word play, for a reasonable 21 points, that would have dumped six of his tiles! Can you find it? The answer is on page 102.

The point of this example is to make you aware that your opponent's play may turn your poor rack into a diamond-in-the-rough! Always look to see how your opponent's last play has changed the board for you.

2. If you exchange now, what will your chances be on your next turn to make a significantly better play?

On each turn, try to estimate the chances of your playing a bingo in the next several turns, both after exchanging and after playing a word on the board. Ask yourself one or both of the following questions:

A) "Suppose I make a play now. If I draw average tiles, will I be able to play a bingo next turn? How about the following turn?" If the answer is yes, then you may want to play a word.

B) "After making this play, will my leave be so awkward that even after a reasonably good draw I will still take more than two turns to bingo?" If so, then you may want to exchange now.

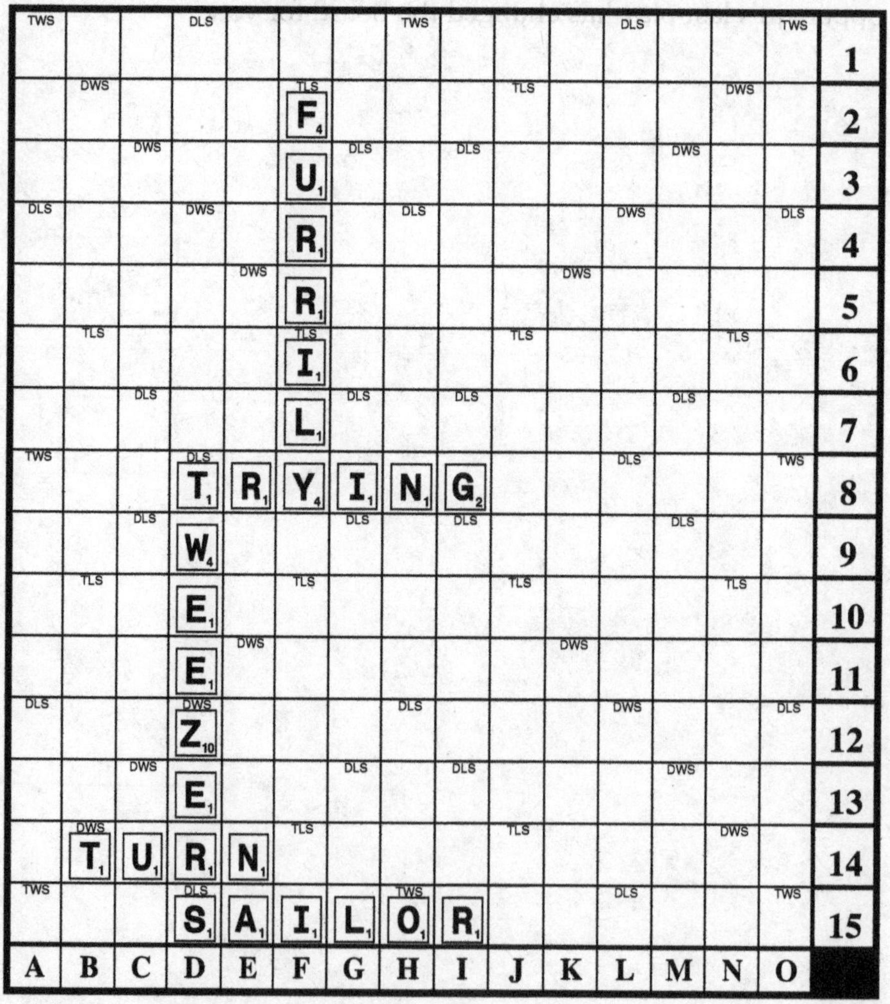

FURRIL
TRYING
TWEEZERS
TURN
SAILOR
1 2 3 4 5 6 7 8 9 10 11 12 13 14 15
A B C D E F G H I J K L M N O

DIAGRAM 10-3

Your score: 37 *Opponent's score:* 149
Rack: **A B F K M V W**

What would you do?

Using Diagram 10-3, if you make the nice-looking play of FAME 13A 28 points, your rack leave will be BKVW. These are extremely awkward tiles. Even with the best of draws you won't bingo for at least two turns, and more probably three or four. Since you won't win without a bingo, being so far behind, you can't afford to play FAME. You must either exchange all seven tiles or keep the AM combination for use on row 13 next turn. However, our preference is to exchange all seven tiles, especially with the blanks missing. Who knows? Maybe you'll draw the X and use row 13 anyway for 40-plus points! *Note:* If you were only 40 to 60 points behind, then FAME would be a terrific play. It's only because you need a bingo so desperately that you must exchange.

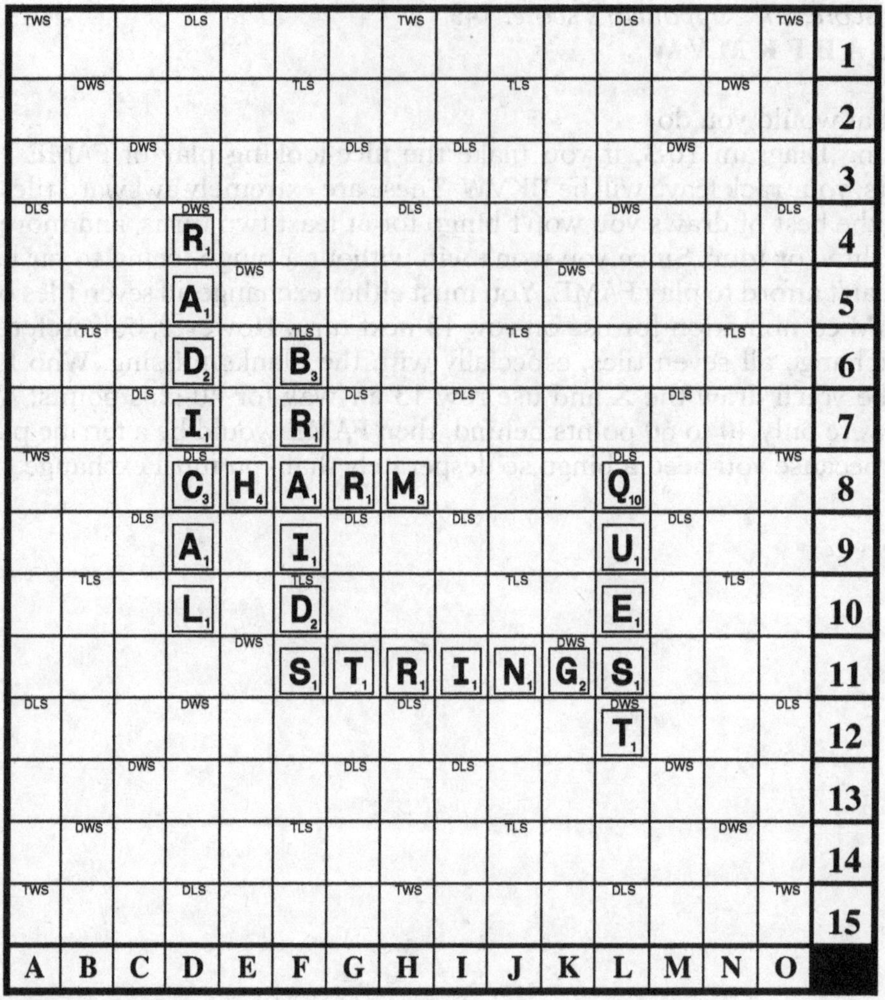
A B C D E F G H I J K L M N O
1 2 3 4 5 6 7 8 9 10 11 12 13 14 15
TWS
DWS
TLS
DLS
R A D I C A L
B R A I D
C H A R M
Q U E S T
S T R I N G S

DIAGRAM 10-4

Rack: **L M R R T T U**

The score is even. What would you do?

Bonus question: What high-scoring word can you play with an O added to your rack?

Refer to Diagram 10-4. Should you exchange? If so, what? The most apparent play seems to be TRAM 5B 12 points. Other plays just don't score as well or use enough tiles to balance the rack adequately. MURAL 5A 14 points is not as tempting, because you open the TWSs for a paltry 14 points. While you shouldn't avoid playing to the board edge when scoring well, there is no reason to give your opponent such a juicy opening without compensation. Two extra points are not enough!

But what will happen the next turn after TRAM? By scoring 12 points, now you keep LRTU. Let's look at the hot spots. You will have only three chances to draw an I to make QUIT 8L 39 points, and only three chances to draw an A or an E plus a high-point consonant to make a five-letter word starting at C9 and playing down to the DWS at C13.

There's one other nice hot spot for which you need only one tile. Add an O to your rack and you can score 45 points. Can you guess what the play is? Even if you don't know the word, which is somewhat obscure, creative players will often look for the chance to add prefixes or suffixes to words already played, even if they're not certain of their validity. The answer is on page 102.

Now let's imagine that you do exchange five tiles and then play one of these high-scoring possibilities next turn. We suggest that your score for your next turn alone will probably total more than both turns together if you play TRAM now. The odds of drawing an I or O after an exchange of five tiles at this point in the game is roughly 62 percent to 64 percent.*

Because of that, we don't suggest playing. Instead we suggest you exchange five tiles, saving the TU. That's because LRTU is not a good leave—you won't often draw a bingo to these tiles, and even if you do, unless you draw an S, there are few places to play a bingo on this board. Second, having five chances to draw either an O or I or other good combinations outweighs the 12 points gained now. Keep in mind that if the O-play or QUIT or the C-column hot spots weren't available, then TRAM might very well have been a better play.

**Alert:* The above was written in 1993, before the regular use of computer simulations. Now, extensive analysis of this position shows clear results. TRAM is far superior to exchanging. The reason? You get 12 points *and* chances to draw the I and O. The extra two tiles that you'd get by exchanging five doesn't overcome the 12 points, the score you'll get after saving LRTU. Plus, many times the LRTU leave will result in either QUIT 8L 39 or OUTCHARM 8A 45, or even a bingo. Furthermore, keeping RT instead of TU is superior! That's because without the I or O draw, you'll likely get an A or E, significantly increasing your bingo chances.

For more information or practice with simulated positions, see *The Official SCRABBLE® Puzzle Book*, published by Pocket Books, chapters 13 and 14.

3. How many points will you score for both this turn and next turn, in total, if you don't exchange now?

Say that you don't exchange but instead play for 10 points. Next turn your rack doesn't improve that much, and you are forced to play for 10 points again, for a total of 20 points in two turns. Now, suppose that you exchange this turn, scoring zero points. Your rack improves significantly, so that you score 30 points next turn. That's a total of 30 points for the two turns. We can say that exchanging was worth 10 extra points to you.

Of course, you may be wondering: "If I think about exchanging now, how am I going to determine how many points I'll score next turn, when I don't know what my letters will be?"

The luck of the draw keeps you from knowing exactly what you'll have. But with time and experience, you will probably develop a good idea about your scoring chances in most positions if you do the following:

Imagine that you play this exact position and rack a thousand times. Imagine the varieties of racks you'd draw. If you exchange five hundred times, you will naturally draw a blank and/or an S a certain number of times. You'll also draw a well-balanced rack a certain number of times. And you'll draw the good 3- and 4-point tiles a certain number of times in order to make good four-, five-, or six-letter plays that justify your exchange. Of course, you'll also draw poor combinations of letters some number of times, but fewer times than most people imagine! Likewise, imagine making a play five hundred times drawing to the weak leave. What kinds of plays will you usually have next turn?

It would also help you to understand this principle of "imagining" by actually taking one position and rack and replaying it fifty to a hundred times just to gain experience about what can happen. This process will give you invaluable insight that you'll be able to use in your real games! After you have enough SCRABBLE game experience, it's likely you'll develop a strong sense of the probabilities for drawing tiles. It's very much like the experienced gin rummy or poker player who knows his chances of getting a good card. Of course, it also helps to have an awareness of what tiles have already been played. You can read more about that in chapter 21.

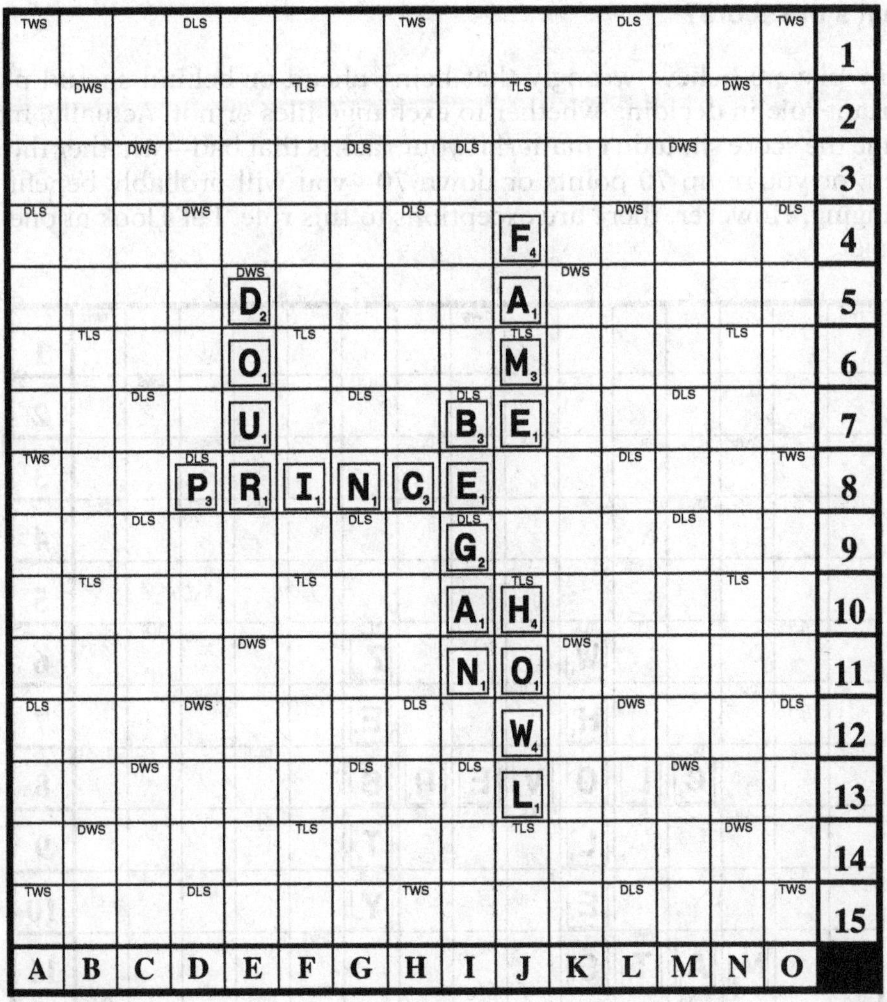

DIAGRAM 10-5

Rack: **A A A A L O O**

The score is even.

What would you do?

Some potential plays are: ALOOF 4F 9 points, FOAL 4J 14, MOOLA 6J 9, WOOL 12J 14, or AAL K5 19. Most experts would tell you that regardless of the score, they would rather exchange five tiles (keeping AL) than take points now and keep three or four vowels. There are blanks and Ss and Es to be drawn. If you play a word now, you have little chance of playing a bingo soon.

4. What's the score?

Many players believe wrongly that being ahead or behind should play an important role in deciding whether to exchange tiles or not. Actually, most of the time the score shouldn't matter! If your rack is that bad—whether the score is even, or you're up 70 points or down 70—you will probably benefit from exchanging. However, there are exceptions to this rule. Let's look at one more example.

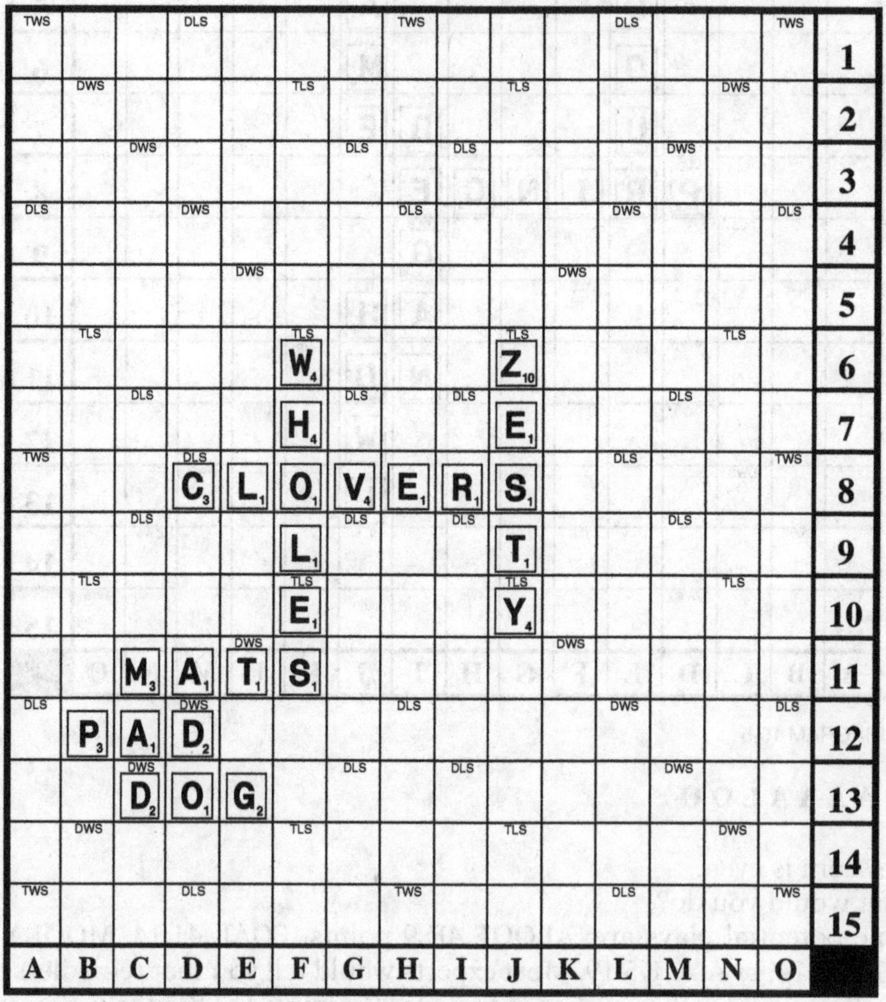
CLOVERS
WHOLES
ZESTY
MATS
PAD
DOG
A B C D E F G H I J K L M N O
1 2 3 4 5 6 7 8 9 10 11 12 13 14 15

DIAGRAM 10-6

Rack: **C D M O R T V**

Consider Diagram 10-6 when:

A) You're 70 points ahead. What would you do?

B) You're 70 points behind. What would you do?

Analysis: A) The board is not conducive for playing bingos. Because of that, and because you're ahead, you want to close the board down as much as possible, even if you don't score many points. Your opponent can play a bingo down the H column. If you can block this, it's going to be very difficult for him or her to place a bingo on the board, and your chances of winning increase dramatically. Which play blocks the best and results in the best leave? Some choices are: DROVE (CMT), COVER (DMT), CORVET (DM), VECTOR (DM), MOVER (CDT), and COVERT (DM). Of these choices, we like COVERT because it uses five tiles and keeps two consonants instead of three. It also leaves no new openings. The weaker VECTOR allows for an S-hook, since VECTORS is also a word, while CORVET opens up the letter C for bingos.

B) If you are 70 points down, the last thing you want to do is close up the board. You'll need an open board to play your bingo—if and when you develop one. We suggest exchanging five or six tiles (keep R or RT, since by counting letters we know that the vowel–consonant ratio of the tiles in the bag is about 1–1).

SUMMARY FOR WHEN TO EXCHANGE

1. **What are your options?** It's important to be systematic and examine all the rows and columns for scoring potential.

2. **How quickly will you bingo?** Consider playing a word. If you estimate that it will take at least three or four turns to develop a bingo rack, and you can't find a play that satisfies you, then seriously consider exchanging now.

If you are like most casual players, who don't average at least one bingo a game, please be patient. As you practice the exercises in chapters 7 and 26, your bingo skills will grow.

3. **Compare your total score for this and your next turn:**

A) after you've exchanged.

B) when you form words both turns.

Compare (A) and (B). If you think there is a very good chance that you'll score enough points in the future by exchanging now, then seriously consider doing so.

Since you can't know for certain what possibilities your opponent will open up for you, assume that what's available now is all there will be next turn. You might even consider that one of the hot spots available now won't be there next turn. In the end, it all boils down to experience and paying attention to the probabilities.

There will be times when instead of wanting to exchange, you'll have the opposite challenge: too many choices for good plays. That may be particularly true when you draw a blank or an S. It's not always easy to find a bingo with a blank. And with an S on your rack, you may be torn between playing it and saving it. Chapter 11 will show you what to do.

ANSWERS: CHAPTER 10

DIAGRAM 10-1: AIKIDO K6 22

DIAGRAM 10-2: UNNUSUAL O9 21

DIAGRAM 10-4: OUTCHARM 8A 45

11 YOUR TWO BEST FRIENDS—THE BLANK AND THE S

When you draw the blank, it will be the most valuable tile on your rack. Why? Because you will be able to form more bingos with a blank on your rack than with any other tile!

Now that you have practiced finding bingos in chapter 7, let's see how the blank can help even more (note that "?" will represent the blank):

Suppose you have the rack BDNORW?. You have only one vowel, so the chances are that if there is a bingo, the blank will have to be used as a vowel. Notice the D on the rack. From the list of common endings, you know that ED is a great combination. Try it; you just have to rearrange BNORW. The answer is on page 116.

Of course, this was a relatively easy example; there weren't too many choices for what to make the blank. Unfortunately, however, it won't always be this easy.

The key to finding bingos with the blank is to be systematic and thorough. Follow these guidelines and you will improve your blank–bingo skills over time.

Guidelines for Finding Bingos with Blanks

1. Check your vowel–consonant ratio.

Here are some general rules to follow:

If you have **six vowels,** you most probably won't have a bingo; there are only a handful of eight-letter words with six vowels. (See Appendix 4.) With **five vowels** you may have one of the few five-vowel seven-letter words, such as SEQUOIA or MIAOUED. Or perhaps you may have one of the 300 or more five-vowel eight-letter words, like AQUANAUT or PEEKABOO. Otherwise, you aren't likely to have a bingo. If you have **four vowels,** the blank will probably need to be a consonant. If you have **three vowels,** the blank may be either a vowel or consonant. If you have only **two vowels,** the blank will probably be a vowel. However, there are many seven-letter words with only two vowels. Here you should see how your consonants fit together. Do you have the TCH or GHT combination? These can lead you to words such as WATCHES or SIGHTED. If you have only **one vowel,** the blank will almost always have to be a vowel. Of course, there are exceptions. There are some six-letter words with only one vowel that take an S to form a bingo. *Examples:* FRIGHT, SPRAWL, STRING, and SCRIMP.

2. Which of the bingo-prone tiles do you already have?

The letters that work best to form seven- and eight-letter words, beginning with the best in each category, are the vowels E, A, and I; and the consonants S, R, N, T, and L. The D also works really well, but mostly if you have an E for the ED ending. Finally, the G is excellent, although usually only when you have ING or the less useful ending AGE.

What we mean is that if you are looking for the "right" vowel, imagine the blank is first an E, then an A, and then an I. If you need a consonant, imagine the blank is first an S, then an R, N, T, and finally L.

If you already have some of these letters, then go on to the next letter. That's because *you're much more likely to find a bingo with seven different letters than with one letter that's repeated.* The only exception to this is with the letter E. If you have one, you can easily have a bingo with a second E. That's because the E is extremely versatile. For example, hundreds of words either begin with RE or end in ER or ED—or, for that matter, with the E alone.

Example 1

You have **A E I N S V ?.** What should you imagine the blank to be—a vowel or a consonant? First notice that you have three vowels and three consonants, so the blank might easily be either. In this case, we advise looking at the consonants first. Why? Remember guideline #1: You already have the three common vowels. Plus, it is very common for bingos to have at least two of the four letters **L N R T.** As we look at the most bingo-prone letters—E, A, I, S, R, N, T, and L—notice that you are missing the R, T, and L. Since the R is the first consonant listed that we don't already have, let's try it first. Can you find a seven-letter word with the letters A E I N S V by adding an R?

Again, we advise that you take the actual tiles and move them around on your rack. The answer is on page 116. Now try the blank as a T. There are three common words using the letters A E I N S V and a T.

Can you find them? The answers are on page 116.

Example 2

Your rack is **B E M N O R ?**. Can you find a seven-letter word with these tiles?

Since you have only two vowels, your last letter will probably be a vowel. But which? First try B E M N O R + E, then B E M N O R + A, and finally B E M N O R + I. Give yourself at least a minute with each combination before going on to the next, moving the tiles around at least every few seconds. The answers are on page 116.

3. Use your high-point tiles to help lead you to a bingo.

One of the reasons that some tiles are worth more points than others is that they aren't as frequently found in the English language and are harder to use. However, each of the sixteen high-point tiles (B, C, D, F, G, H, J, K, M, P, Q, V, W, X, Y, and Z) has its own particular style of showing up in seven- and eight-letter words. Each is commonly found in certain arrangements with other letters. For example, the B will often be paired with the R or L to form BR or BL combinations such as BROWN, BRICK, BLUE, or NIMBLE. The F will often be combined with a T or a Y, or even the UL duo, to form FT, FY, or FUL combinations such as LOFT, RIFT, NOTIFY, EDIFY, CAREFUL, or HARMFUL. See pages 23 and 71 for a list of useful combinations.

Example 3

You have the rack **H I N R S U ?**. As soon as we notice that we don't absolutely need to have an extra vowel, we should automatically look to use our one high-point tile, the H, in one of its familiar "settings." On page 71 we see that the H can often be placed after IS at the end of a word. Let's see how that affects our search. We have NRU? left. Try playing with these tiles! If you look at NISH first, you may find more than one bingo. See page 116 for the complete list.

Other bingos with a blank will likewise be easier to find if you use your high-point tile to guide you.

4. Remember the common beginnings and endings, and then use them to find your blank bingos.

To summarize what we've said:

How to Find Bingos Using a Blank

1. Consider the vowel–consonant ratio.
2. Look for the best bingo tiles: vowels E, A, and I; and consonants S, R, N, T, and L. Avoid duplicating a letter already on your rack unless it's an E.
3. Use your high-point tiles to guide your search.
4. Remember the common beginnings and endings and use the blank to form them. *Example:* IE? can be imagined as IED, IER, or IES.

Quiz: Test yourself again and find the bingos by using the following sets of six letters and a blank tile. In each case there is only one common word to be found. We suggest using actual tiles to help simulate playing the game. We also suggest that after three to five minutes of searching, you look at the hint on page 116. We list the letter the blank must be to spell each word.

This quick search-and-look-up method can both train your mind to find the common letter arrangements and help you to avoid becoming too frustrated with *not* finding the words. It's better to look it up and move on!

BLANK BINGO QUIZ

1. CIRRTU?	6. ADEHMT?	11. EEFLMS?	16. EGPSTU?
2. CFILNY?	7. AGMSTU?	12. EEFFIT?	17. EGNOTV?
3. ANOOTV?	8. ALLRTY?	13. EEISTZ?	18. ENNOTV?
4. AEGSVY?	9. DEELNV?	14. EEKOTY?	19. IIOTTU?
5. ADFHLN?	10. DLLNOW?	15. EENNTU?	20. IMNORT?

The answers are on page 116.

A Blank Without a Bingo

What happens when you have a blank, but you can't find or play a bingo? The answer depends on two conditions:

1. Do you have a play using the blank that scores at least 20 to 30 points more than if you don't use your blank? Look at Diagram 11-1.

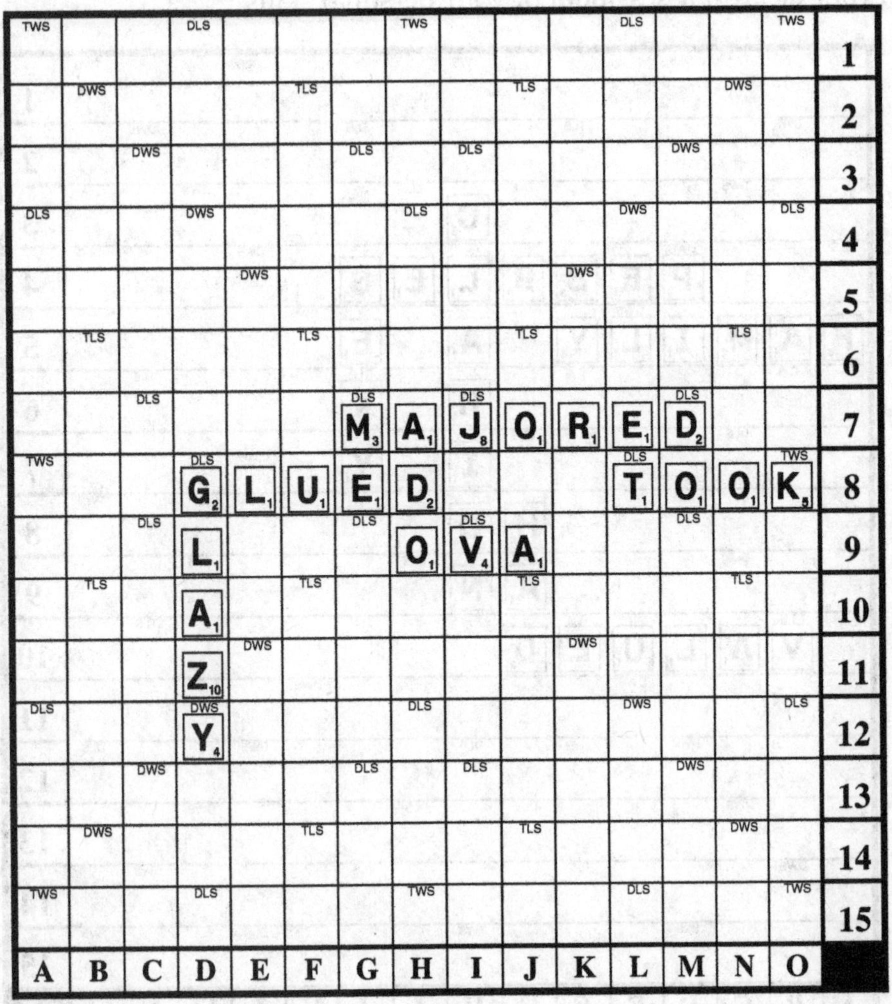

MAJORED
GLUED
TOOK
OVA
LAZY

DIAGRAM 11-1

Your rack: **L N O O R X ?**

What should you do? You can play XU 10J and score a huge 49 points. Or you can simply play LOX K9 and score only 27, but hope to bingo next turn. The best answer to this question may differ for each player. If you are able to find bingos with ease, and think you will have no trouble finding one next turn, then you should probably sacrifice the points this turn. However, if you haven't yet mastered the skills involved in finding bingos, you might want to take the extra points now. In each case, you will be making the best decision based upon your clearest assessment of your personal skills.

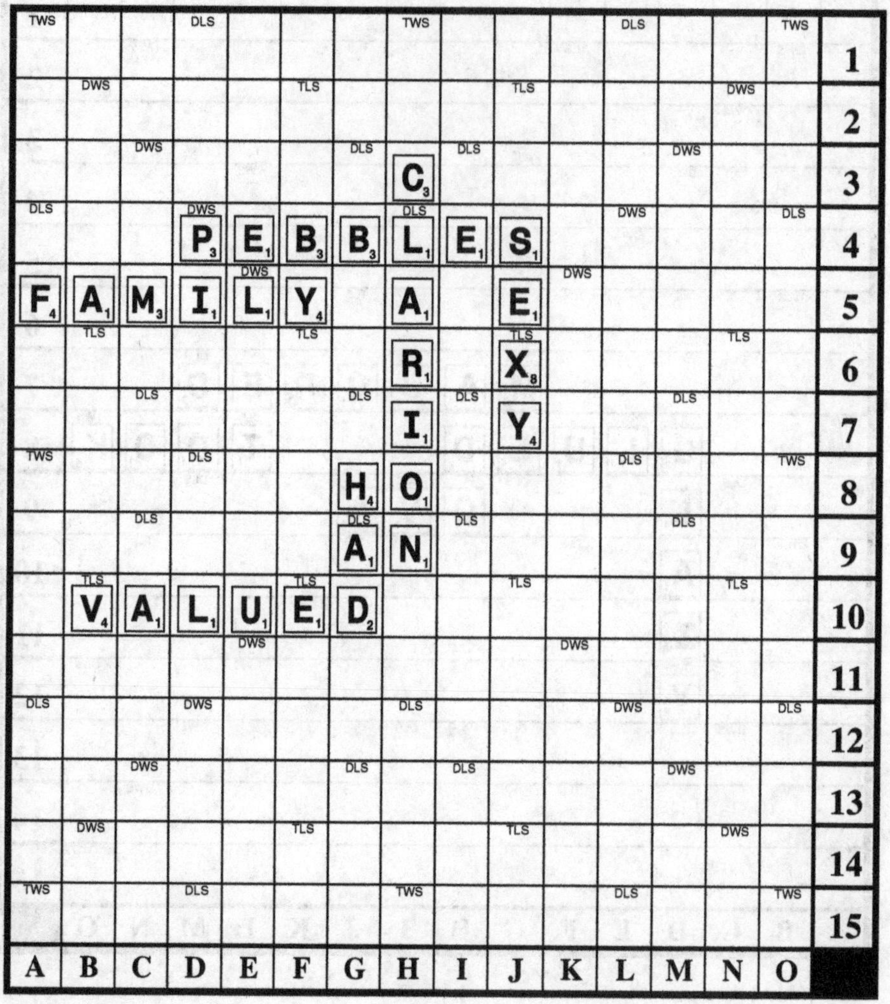

PEBBLES
FAMILY
CLARION
SEXY
HO
AN
VALUED
A B C D E F G H I J K L M N O
1 2 3 4 5 6 7 8 9 10 11 12 13 14 15

DIAGRAM 11-2

Your rack: **L M O O P Z ?**

Using Diagram 11-2, you can play TOPAZ B2 70 points. That's like playing a bingo! There is no other play available that scores 40 points without using the blank. You should jump at the chance to make this play!

2. What are your winning chances with or without a bingo?

If you can assess that you don't need a bingo to win, you might simply want to make your highest-scoring play. However, if you realize that you need a 70- to 90-point play to win the game, then you must sacrifice the points now in order to have a good chance later on to get that bingo.

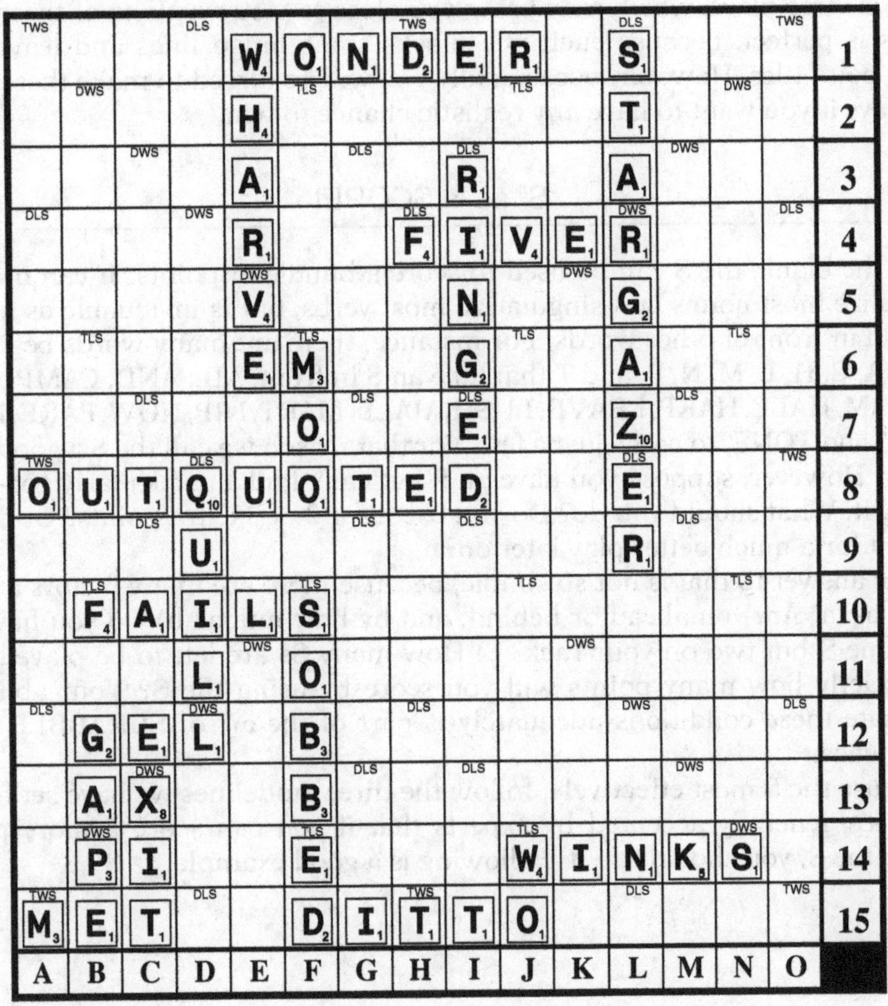

A B C D E F G H I J K L M N O
1 2 3 4 5 6 7 8 9 10 11 12 13 14 15
TWS
DWS
TLS
DLS

DIAGRAM 11-3

Your rack: **C E I J P R ?**

You're behind 80 points and playing on Diagram 11-3. You see three excellent plays: PROJECT C2 40 points, JAPER 4A 42, and JEEPS 8K 39. But you need to use your blank for each of them. If you play any of these, you'll be 60 to 70 points down after your opponent's next play and have little chance to play a bingo without the blank. And you will definitely need the bingo to win. So these options don't leave much hope of your winning. What are your other choices? You can play JIN L12 20 points, JEU B6 26, or JERK M11 30. By not using your blank, you now have a reasonable chance to build a bingo within two or three plays, which may bring you close to victory. None of these three plays is perfect, because each one blocks some bingo lines and leaves two high-point tiles. However, occasionally you will be forced to make these kinds of plays if you want to have *any* realistic chance to win.

"S" as in SCORE!

Like the blank, the S can be used to score a bundle of points. It can not only pluralize most nouns and singularize most verbs, but is invaluable as a letter to add in front of other words. For instance, there are many words beginning with A, C, H, L, M, N, P, and T that take an S in front: AIL, AND, CAMP, COW, CREAM, HALE, HARP, LEAVE, LUSH, MALL, MART, NIP, NOW, PARE, PELT, TILT, and TONE, to name just a few. For that reason we call the S a good hook letter. However, suppose you have an S but can't find a particularly good play using it. What should you do? Do you use it for 2 or 3 extra points? Or do you save it for a much better play later on?

The answer to that is not so simple, because there are many factors at play, such as: a) Are you ahead or behind, and by how much? b) Do you have not just one S but two on your rack? c) How many Ss are left to be played? and d) Exactly how many points will you score by using the S? Your ability to evaluate these conditions adequately is part of the art of SCRABBLE game excellence.

To use the S most effectively, follow the three guidelines we have set forth:

1. It's generally accepted by experts that if you can score 8 more points using the S, you should use it. Following is a good example:

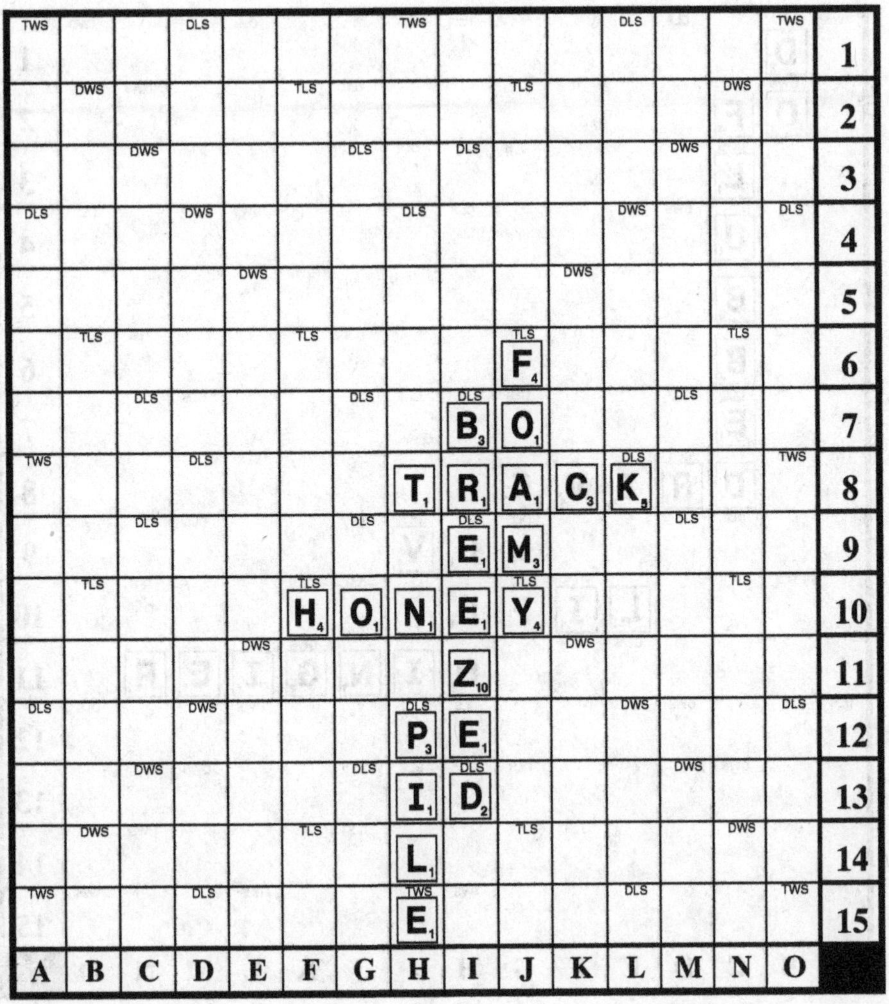

F
B O
T R A C K
E M
H O N E Y
Z
P E
I D
L
E
A B C D E F G H I J K L M N O
1 2 3 4 5 6 7 8 9 10 11 12 13 14 15

DIAGRAM 11-4

Your rack: **A I L O S U V**

Playing on Diagram 11-4, if the choices you find are VIOLA K2 or 11B for 21 points or VIOLAS M3 32, you can be comfortable playing away the S for 11 extra points. Of course, if you see the word SOUVLAKI L2, you'll earn a whopping 80 points.

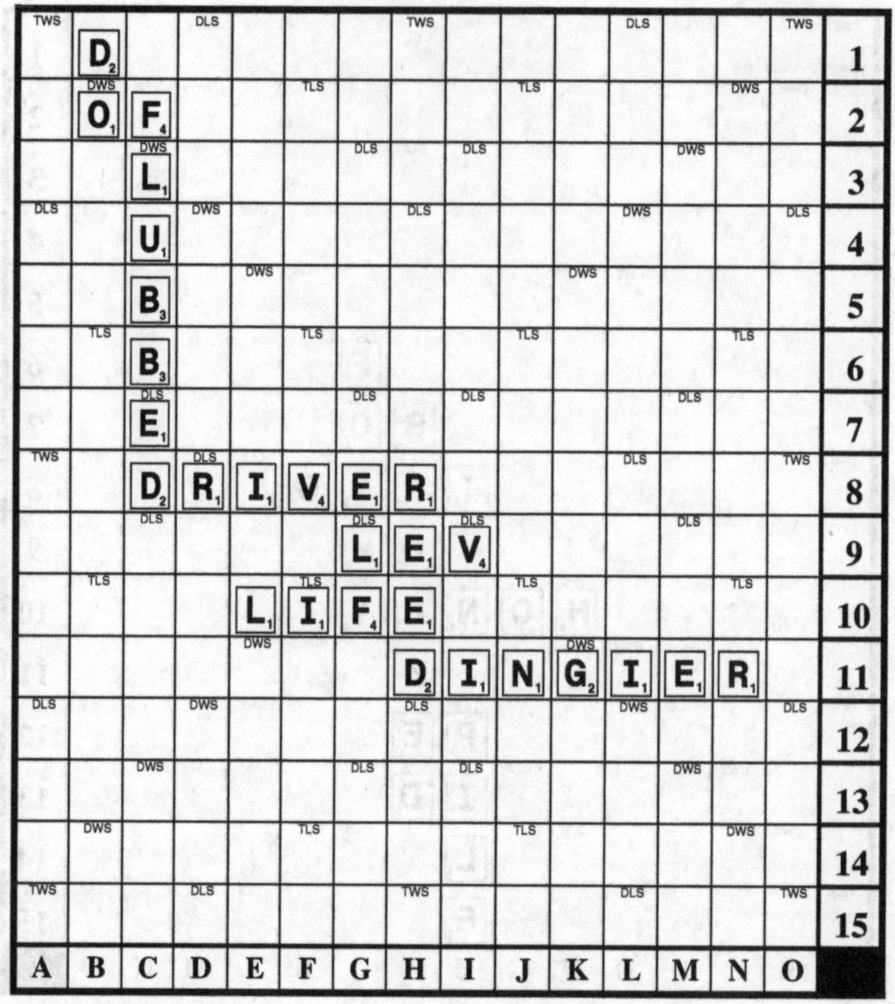

DIAGRAM 11-5

Your rack: **A E I N N O S***

In Diagram 11-5, the score is nearly even. You see either ANIONS 12C 21 points or ION 11D 12. Though the S gives you 9 extra points, the letters AENS remaining on your rack after playing ION are so bingo-prone that many experts would choose the lower-scoring move.

*NONARIES, NONARY are now acceptable, per the *OSPD5*. Let's assume you don't know that for this example.

2. If you have two Ss, you may part with one of them for less than 8 extra points. Because the second S usually doesn't help you much to build a bingo, you're better off getting rid of it for a few extra points. The exception to this rule is if you have one of the endings LESS or NESS. In that case you should examine your rack thoroughly for a bingo. Let's look at an example:

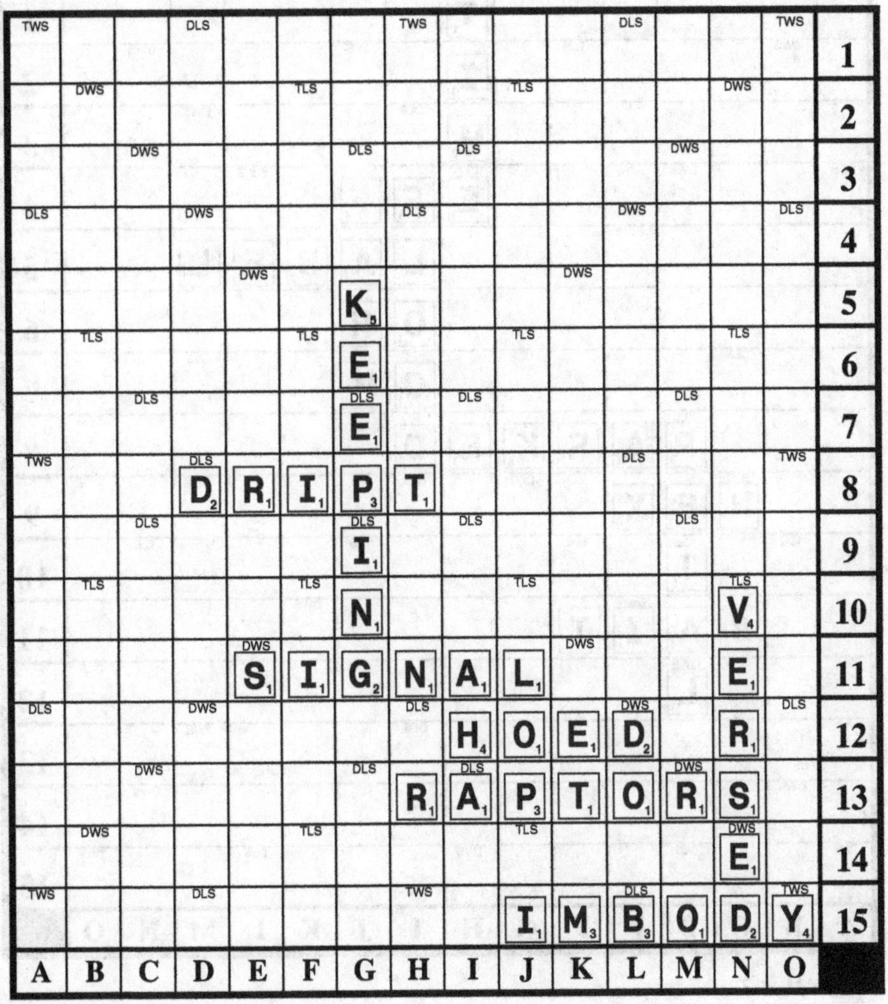
KEEPING
DRIPT
SIGNAL
HOED
RAPTORS
VERSE
IMBODY
A B C D E F G H I J K L M N O
1 2 3 4 5 6 7 8 9 10 11 12 13 14 15

DIAGRAM 11-6

Your rack: **A D G M O S S**

Playing on Diagram 11-6, you find DOGMA H1 42 points. But you can score 5 more points with DOGMAS in the same place. Should you? Yes! Saving the extra S here isn't worth sacrificing 5 points.

3. If you don't have a bingo, but you do have *nearly* a bingo, then you may want to play off one tile or two tiles, saving the S and other bingo-prone letters in order to try to bingo next turn. This is called "fishing" and was discussed in chapter 8.

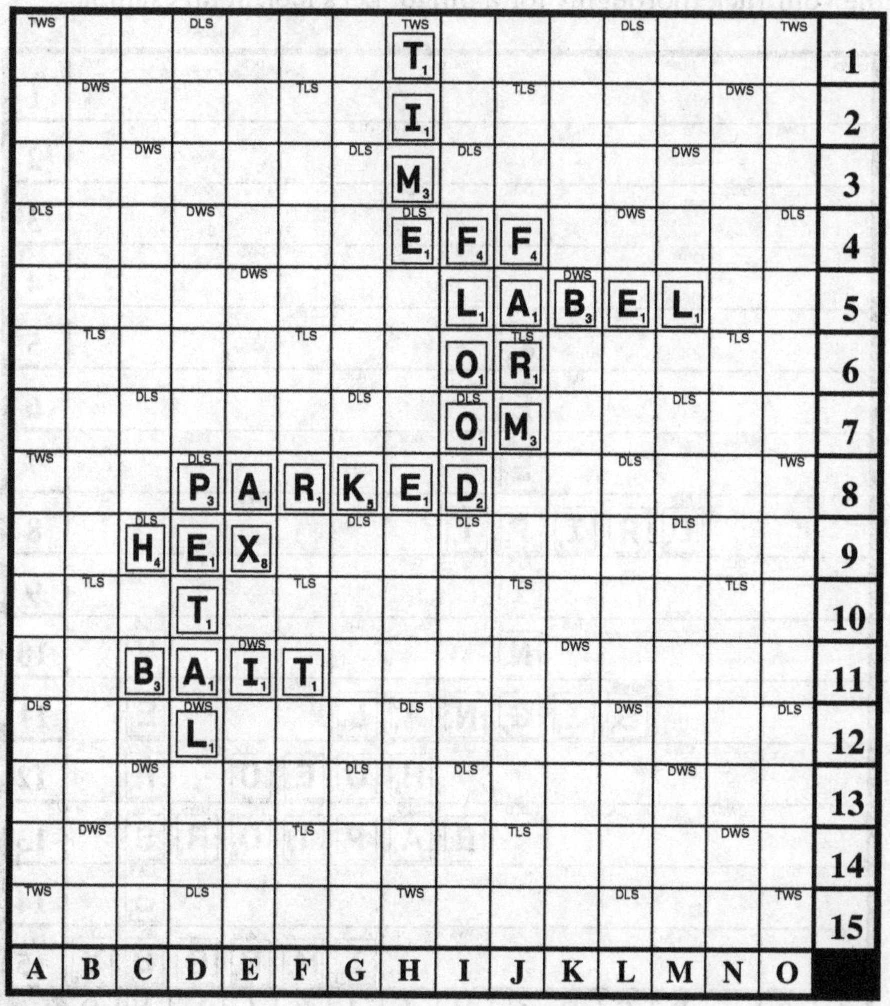
TIME
EFF
LABEL
OR
OM
PARKED
HEX
T
BAIT
L
A B C D E F G H I J K L M N O
1 2 3 4 5 6 7 8 9 10 11 12 13 14 15

DIAGRAM 11-7

Your rack: **E E I N Q R S**

You are playing on Diagram 11-7. Because you can't play the Q, and because the EEINRS leave is so strong, you would be wise to sacrifice a turn to exchange the Q. The odds are very high that you will have a bingo next turn. Note that some experts prefer exchanging EQ, saving EINRS.

Now that QI is available, play QI 2G 11 points, because EEINRS will draw a bingo a significant number of times *and* you'll have those extra points. QIS 13B 32 is also a good play.

One-Point-Tile Bingo Practice

Imagine that you have an E and a blank on your rack. Now combine any one of the two-letter vowel combinations below on the left with any one of the three-letter 1-point-consonant combinations on the right. With *every* such seven-letter rack, there will *always* be a bingo. And in almost every case, there will always be a *common-word bingo* available. The exceptions are: E? + EULST = ELUATES, TELEDUS, EUSTELE, UNSTEEL, or ELUENTS; + IULNR = URNLIKE or PURLINE; + EOLNT = TOLUENE; + EULNT = TEENFUL, TOLUENE, ELUENTS, or UNSTEEL. In some cases there are more than fifty bingos available! (See Appendix 4.) See page 116 for one example of each of the 100 combinations. How many can you find? We suggest you spend about ten to fifteen minutes with each combination, trying to find at least one bingo.

E ? +

A	E		L	N	R
A	I		L	N	S
A	O		L	N	T
A	U		L	R	S
E	I		L	R	T
E	O		L	S	T
E	U		N	R	S
I	O		N	R	T
I	U		N	S	T
O	U		R	S	T

As we've seen in this chapter, you don't have to memorize the dictionary to hone your SCRABBLE game skills. However, there are a few types of unusual words that you will enjoy knowing. Learning new words will give you more choices for each turn, which will increase your opportunity for developing your decision-making abilities. Chapter 12 will show you what words to focus on.

ANSWERS: CHAPTER 11

BDNORW?: BROWNED or RUBDOWN

AEINSV?: EVANISH, NAVVIES, VAHINES, INVADES, ALEVINS, EVASION, NAIVEST, NATIVES, RAVINES, SAVINES, VAINEST, VALINES, and VINASSE

BEMNOR?: EMBROWN, EMBRYON, and BROMINE

HINRSU?: UNHAIRS, BURNISH, URCHINS, FURNISH, RUNTISH, RUSHING, NOURISH

BLANK BINGO QUIZ: HINTS (blank given): 1. E; 2. A; 3. I; 4. O; 5. U; 6. C; 7. N; 8. E; 9. I; 10. A; 11. A; 12. N; 13. R; 14. N; 15. A; 16. A; 17. I; 18. C; 19. N; 20. O

BLANK BINGO QUIZ: ANSWERS
1. RECRUIT; 2. FANCILY; 3. OVATION; 4. VOYAGES; 5. HANDFUL; 6. MATCHED; 7. MUSTANG; 8. ALERTLY; 9. LIVENED; 10. LOWLAND; 11. FEMALES; 12. FIFTEEN; 13. ZESTIER; 14. KEYNOTE; 15. UNEATEN; 16. UPSTAGE; 17. VETOING; 18. CONVENT; 19. TUITION; 20. MONITOR

ANSWERS TO ONE-POINT-TILE BINGO PRACTICE
E? **AELNR** = RELEARN; + **AELNS** = ENABLES; + **AELNT** = LEANEST; + **AELRS** = LEADERS; + **AELRT** = LEATHER; + **AELST** = RELATES; + **AENRS** = ENDEARS; + **AENRT** = GREATEN; + **AENST** = NEGATES; + **AERST** = CREATES; + **AILNR** = LANKIER; + **AILNS** = SALIENT; + **AILNT** = INFLATE; + **AILRS** = DERAILS; + **AILRT** = RETAILS; + **AILST** = DETAILS; + **AINRS** = ARSENIC; + **AINRT** = FAINTER; + **AINST** = SEATING; + **AIRST** = WARIEST; + **AOLNR** = LOANERS; + **AOLNS** = RELOANS; + **AOLNT** = TOENAIL; + **AOLRS** = ORACLES; + **AOLRT** = GLOATER; + **AOLST** = LOCATES; + **AONRS** = REASONS; + **AONRT** = SENATOR; + **AONST** = DONATES; + **AORST** = COASTER; + **AULNR** = UNCLEAR; + **AULNS** = UNSEALS; + **AULNT** + ANNULET; + **AULRS** = SURREAL; + **AULRT** = TEARFUL; + **AULST** = SULFATE; + **AUNRS** = SAUNTER; + **AUNRT** = URINATE; + **AUNST** = PEANUTS; + **AURST** = STATURE; + **EILNR** = RELINED; + **EILNS** = LICENSE; + **EILNT** = TENSILE; + **EILRS** = REPLIES; + **EILRT** = REPTILE; + **EILST** = LEFTIES; + **EINRS** = EROSION; + **EINRT** = TRAINEE; + **EINST** = INTENSE; + **EIRST** = RECITES; + **EOLNR** = ERELONG; + **EOLNS** = ENCLOSE; + **EOLNT** = TOLUENE; + **EOLRS** = RESOLVE; + **EOLRT** = ELECTOR; + **EOLST** = OMELETS; + **EONRS** = ENDORSE; + **EONRT** = OFTENER; + **EONST** = DENOTES; + **EORST** = STEREOS; + **EULNR** = UNREELS; + **EULNS** = UNREELS; + **EULNT** = TOLUENE; + **EULRS** = REPULSE; + **EURLT** = LECTURE; + **EULST** = UNSTEEL; + **EUNRS** = ENSURED; + **EUNRT** = TENURES; + **EUNST** = ENTHUSE; + **EURST** = REQUEST; + **IOLNR** = LOONIER; + **IOLNS** = LESIONS; + **IOLNT** = ELATION; + **IOLRS** = BOILERS; + **IOLRT** = POLITER; + **IOLST** = VIOLETS; + **IONRS** = SENIORS; + **IONRT** = ORIENTS; + **IONST** = NOTICES; + **IORST** = LOITERS; + **IULNR** = URNLIKE; + **IULNS** = LINEUPS; + **IULNT** = UTENSIL; + **IULRS** = LEISURE; + **IULRT** = REBUILT; + **IULST** = LUSTIER; + **IUNRS** = INJURES; + **IUNRT** = TRIBUNE; + **IUNST** = MINUTES; + **IURST** = GUTSIER; + **OULNR** = LOUNGER; + **OULNS** = COUNSEL; + **OULNT** = OUTLINE; + **OULRS** = OURSELF; + **OULRT** = TROUBLE; + **OULST** = LOUDEST; + **OUNRS** = SURGEON; + **OUNRT** = FORTUNE; + **OUNST** = TONGUES; + **OURST** = DETOURS

12 IT'S YOUR WORD AGAINST MINE: Building a Better Vocabulary

You are playing your next-door neighbor in your weekly best-two-out-of-three SCRABBLE games match. You are both reasonably competitive and intelligent, and have equal understanding of the fundamental game strategies. Who's usually going to win?

Given these conditions, the two most important factors that will determine the victor in these games are tile selection and vocabulary. Short of using X-ray vision, there is very little you can do about assuring yourself great tiles every time you play. So the single best thing you can do is learn as many words as possible.

This means quality as well as quantity. For example, it is far better that you know the fifty Q words without a U (see chapter 6) than a few hundred nine-letter words. And you'll be far better served knowing words with a high proportion of vowels (see Appendix 4) than you will knowing a handful of impressive, but obscure, medical terms.

The first place to start in building a SCRABBLE vocabulary is the two-letter words, which we discussed in chapter 3. The next step is to learn the 900-plus three-letter words in *The Official SCRABBLE® Players Dictionary*. These are the centerpiece of NASPA's beginner's word sheet, and they are listed in Appendix 4.

Also in NASPA's New Member Kit is a sampling of what the experts call "vowel dumps." Anyone who has played even a few games knows the frustration of having a rack that is reminiscent of "Old MacDonald Had a Farm"—EIEIO—or for that matter, the letters AUAUA. This vowel-heavy situation is inevitable for SCRABBLE players at all levels, and the best way to be prepared is to know these invaluable words.

NASPA's list of important words to memorize also includes the most common and/or short usages of the heavy artillery—the J, Q, X, and Z. These are about 375 words that you will use again and again as you try to match the high-scoring tiles on your rack with open "hot spots" on the board. Many of these are discussed in chapters 6 and 13.

Before you get too intimidated by all these lists and how long they seem, it's important to put everything in perspective. For example, all the specialized words we've just talked about come to a total of 1,200 or so. Even better, there is a very good chance you already know at least half of them. Don't believe it? As you use Appendix 4, go ahead and cross out in pencil all the words you already know. You'll be surprised.

Now you are faced with learning only 500–750 new words, a very achievable task. Given the natural interest in words that helped draw you to the SCRABBLE game in the first place, this should not be too difficult. And consider the rewards. We estimate that you'll increase your SCRABBLE scoring average a full 100 points a game if you learn these starter lists and use the words effectively.

Learning new words can be approached in any number of ways. Following are some ideas that have worked over the years for champions and casual players alike.

GENERAL CURIOSITY

People remember unusual words for a variety of reasons. Many know them from years of doing crossword puzzles. Some have areas of expertise—medicine, gardening, zoology—which expose them to hundreds of uncommon words and terms. Still others seem to know indiscriminately or discover strings of related words.

For example, John Williams has always been fascinated by the "genie family," as he calls it. Everyone knows that word, of course, as the creature who rose from Aladdin's lamp, in addition to other appearances throughout folklore and mythology. However, the term provides word magic as well; using both singular and plural forms, it has all the following alternative spellings:

GENIE: genies, djin, djins, djinn, djinns, djinni, djinny, jin, jins, jinn, jinns, jinnee, and jinni.

That's fourteen different forms of the same word! More important, it gives you many different options when you have the J, a high-scoring tile.

A favorite example of Joe Edley's is a G word—ganef. It means a "thief," and its variations include:

GANEF: ganefs, ganev, ganevs, ganof, ganofs, gonef, gonefs, gonif, gonifs, goniff, goniffs, gonof, gonofs, gonoph, and gonophs.

There are countless other examples of these types of words throughout *The Official SCRABBLE® Players Dictionary*. They are particularly easy to learn, because they are inherently interesting, and one form of the word is usually an extension or twist on another. While this is an admittedly arbitrary and random form of learning new words, it is certainly effortless. You should be propelled by your curiosity alone!

Another random method of learning new words is simply to read the dictionary. Many players buy an extra copy of *The Official SCRABBLE® Players Dictionary* and black out all the words they already know. Then, over time, in fifteen-minute or half-hour doses, they browse through the book. It offers brief definitions—as opposed to pure word lists—and many people find that helpful as well.

Remember, of the 100,000 or more words in the *OSPD,* chances are you know as many as one-third of them already. In fact, everybody knows more words than they think; they just don't use many of them on a regular basis—until they start playing the SCRABBLE game. To prove this, sit down with a friend and open up *The Official SCRABBLE® Players Dictionary*. Choose six pages at random and test how many of the words you know between the two of you. You'll be very surprised.

It's also important to know that when you are learning new words for the purpose of playing the SCRABBLE game, you don't necessarily have to take time to learn meanings. You have to know only if a word takes an S, ING, or other inflection. Understandably, word purists take offense at this idea.

HINTS FROM THE EXPERTS

If you have your sights set on becoming a legitimate, top-ranked SCRABBLE expert, you are going to have to employ some of the more systematic methods of learning new words. It is like training for an athletic competition. Some people can swim laps for hours, while others would rather run ten miles than swim a hundred feet. So find a regimen to learn words that is best suited to your personality.

We have interviewed four of the most renowned word experts in the history of competitive SCRABBLE play and asked each to give us his secret for adding to one's vocabulary. Following are some of their recommendations.

Peter Morris, an English teacher and writer from Michigan, has been a SCRABBLE expert since he was a teenager. He is one of only six people to have won both the American National SCRABBLE Championship (1989) and the

World SCRABBLE® Championship (1991). An avid sports fan and a player of many games, Peter is the first to admit he does not like to study or learn new words as much as most other experts seem to. As a result, he has developed ways he feels are time-efficient for learning new words.

The first thing Peter recommends is simply to go to the nearest SCRABBLE game club in your area. (A North American club roster listing every club is available with NSA membership.) "After each game, wander around and look at all the boards," he advises. "You will see the same words appear over and over again, simply because these words have letters that players save, and so, inevitably, they are played repeatedly."

He especially emphasizes that you should always keep an eye out for words that get rid of bad tiles. A perfect example would be the words JUBA or VUG. The latter is especially good because its reverse—GUV—is good as well. In fact, reversible words or words that use the same letters as each other are some of the easiest to learn and remember. Other examples are:

KOA, OAK, OKA
AVER, RAVE, VERA
CHI, HIC, ICH
ELMY, YLEM

It's Peter's feeling that some people spend too much time learning obscure seven- and eight-letter words that will hardly ever be used. It's better that you learn the ones that will most likely appear again and again. For instance, AEEINRT will occur on your rack repeatedly as you learn to save these excellent letters. So you would do well to learn the following three words: RETINAE, TRAINEE, and ARENITE. His advice to beginners: Play a lot, learn from those better than you, and study board positions.

We have one word of caution for you, however, when learning new words from other players' boards: *Make sure you look up the unfamiliar words, since some players get away with phoneys!*

Joel Wapnick, a retired music professor at McGill University in Montreal, is renowned in the SCRABBLE world for his enormous vocabulary. He was the 1983 National SCRABBLE Champion and the 1999 World SCRABBLE Champion. He is said to have learned up to 15,000 new words in the six months prior to winning the national championship.

Joel says one of the first things he did was to go through the entire *Official SCRABBLE® Players Dictionary* and identify all the two- to five-letter words that he did not know. He then took these words and put them into a list to study. As he recorded a word, he would also note any good anagrams of the word beside it. It's Joel's theory that you might as well learn both the word and its anagrams at the same time. A couple of examples would be:

ALIEN:	ALINE, ANILE, ELAIN, LIANE
COSINE:	CONIES, ICONES, OSCINE

Joel says time management is the key to learning new words. He often carries word lists with him and uses stolen moments to hone his vocabulary. A long wait in a doctor's office, a traffic jam, or a late-starting meeting are all small opportunities to learn a couple of new words. "Find your own area of weakness and create your own list and exercise," Wapnick suggests. He also mentions learning niche categories, like the Q-without-U list and words that don't take an S. These are especially helpful for defensive play.

Mike Baron, a clinical psychologist in Albuquerque, New Mexico, is one of America's best-known SCRABBLE players and foremost word experts. His popular *Word List Book* has been a bible to tournament players for years. Mike has also run one of the oldest and most successful SCRABBLE game clubs in America, introducing scores of "living room" players to the world of competitive SCRABBLE.

A veteran of more than twenty National SCRABBLE Championship tournaments, Mike has written more about words and word lists than anyone else. Like Peter Morris, Mike believes the goal is "to get the best payoff with the least amount of studying." As a result, his specialty is breaking down words into logical groupings and analyzing their letter patterns for easy learning.

Consistent with NASPA's dictum, Baron says to learn the two- and three-letter words first. He feels the best way to do this is to write out the two- and three-letter word lists twice from memory, studying the omissions after each effort. Along with the threes and the J, Q, X, and Z lists, Baron feels four-letter words are more important than many players realize. Why? He maintains that in any given SCRABBLE game, 75 percent of the words will consist of two, three, or four letters. After you master these, Baron advises that you should learn the top 100 "bingo stems," which will be discussed in the advanced-strategy chapters.

Joe Edley, the coauthor of this book, is the 1980, 1992, and 2000 National SCRABBLE Champion. Trained as a mathematician, Joe takes a very systematic but fun approach to learning new words.

"Basically, I just play a variation of the word game many of us played as children. It's played by choosing a large word and then seeing how many smaller words you can make from it." Joe says it's fast and easy and captures the essence of SCRABBLE—making new words from a jumble of letters. "Do this fifteen to twenty minutes a day several times a week," Joe says, "and within a year you'll not only know hundreds of new words, but you'll be able to find them on your rack!" At first, it will help you learn all the two- and three-letter words; then with practice the fours and fives.

When Joe practices this exercise, he invariably uses a nine- or ten-letter word. However, here is an example of a very common word—HANDLE—and all the words that can be made from it. In all, there are sixty-two words contained in its letters!

ad	ane	deal	el	hade	he	laden	lend
ae	da	dean	elan	hae	head	lah	na
ah	dah	del	eland	haed	heal	land	nae
ahed	dahl	den	eld	haen	held	lane	nah
al	dal	dhal	en	hale	hen	lea	naled
ale	dale	ed	end	haled	la	lead	ne
an	dan	edh	ha	hand	lad	lean	
and	de	eh	had	handle	lade	led	

Of course, you are going to need a method to check and see how many of the possible words you have found. There are several options for this. One is to use the *Webster's Word Game Word Finder,* by Bruce Wetterau; another is a good anagramming computer program. Membership in NASPA also offers an excellent word list–building program that creates pretty much any word list you can imagine. We use it all the time. It's called Zyzzyva. Each will help you gauge your progress. Whatever your method for learning new words, do it! Because if you want to get better, and beat your opponents, it all comes down to your word against theirs.

WACKY DEFINITIONS

Creating wacky definitions is an excellent way to remember if a word is acceptable or not. The National SCRABBLE Association's *SCRABBLE® News* has had several contests that asked for the most creative definitions for unusual words.

For example, we can't possibly forget the word ZENAIDA after Luise Shafritz (PA) defined it as meditating to certain types of music.* Or when Rick Wong (CA) defined ACHOLIA as something men say to their first dates at the end of the evening.

If you can develop the ability to imagine silly definitions for obscure words, you'll be much more likely to remember the word in the heat of a competitive game. And you'll have fun remembering, too!

Examples:

ADZUKI: an advertisement for a popular Japanese motorcycle (Bill Hunter, TX)

AEQUORIN: the favorite of squirrels everywhere (Doug Pike, AZ)

ALLEES: a rack of tiles only slightly better than all Is (Siri Tillekeratne, AL)

APROTIC: a well-paid athletic insect (John Feneck, NJ)

BEDU: the residue on a honeycomb (Richard Bowers, NJ)

BLASTIE: a golf club that hits harder than a mashie (Joe Singer, NY)

BOPEEP: a nervous condition exhibited by the misplacing of woolen objects (Bob Aleksiewicz, CT)

BOREEN: a common youth retort to an adult suggestion (Jim Kramer, MN)

BUDWORM: one who obsessively reads beer labels (Paul Terry, NV)

CANOODLE: the act of sketching various landscapes while simultaneously paddling a canoe (Dan Townsend, NC)

COINVENT: the opening in a piggy bank (Jim Pate, AL)

COLEAD: a commercial for cabbage (Alice Goodwin, WA)

COOKTOP: chef's tall hat (Lois Molitors, OH)

*ZEN is a religion/philosophy that includes meditation among its practices, while *AIDA* is one of the most famous operas performed on stages worldwide.

CRAMOISY: a whole class of students who study at the last minute (Matt Laufer, NY)

DIALYZE: an optometrist's telephone number (John Robertson, ONT)

DYNEIN: boycott restaurants (Dick Lazaro, FL)

ECHELLE: back covering of turtle (Patricia Holmes, MO)

ERGATIVE: not to argue, to urge you (F. I. Fragee, IL)

EXEDRA: and so forth (Alice Goodwin, WA)

FALAFEL: how you feel when you're really sick (Richard Ross, FL)

FIBRANNE: newest high-fiber cereal (Louis Schecter, NY)

GALYAK: girl talk (Jonathan Jensen, MD)

GLASNOST: having a fragile schnozz (Grace Stinton, KY)

HAHNIUM: an element comprising the half-life of a laugh (Matt Laufer, NY)

MERLOT: parking area for certain aquatic creatures (Stu Goldman, CA)

MOBLED: when the other two stooges got a little too rough (Margie Gordon, CA)

NEARSIDE: a popular comic strip about humans (Joseph Schwarz, NY)

NOISETTE: a small racket (Diana Grosman, MD)

OPIOID: a fan of the young Ron Howard (Jim Kramer, MN)

OXO: symbols used in the game of tic-tac-toe (Mary Ellen Lester, HI)

PORCINI: an Italian sports car in the shape of a pig (Luise Shafritz, PA)

PREQUEL: the nighttime sniffly, sneezy, so-you-can-rest medicine that you take before you come down with the symptoms (Diane Firstman, NY)

PRUNUSES: recipes that promote digestive health and well-being (Luise Shafritz, PA)

PYCNOSIS: an inflammation of the nasal passages caused by frequent introduction of the fingertip (Jonathan Jensen, MD)

RAUNCH: a very high-class dude ranch for English nobility (Beth Fleischer, CA)

TANGRAM: grandma after a week in Hawaii (Stu Goldman, CA)

TILLITE: how long teenagers stay out on prom night (Tom Titus, CA)

TRISHAW: an evening performance of three short plays (Joe Edley, NY)

TUCKSHOP: plastic surgeon's operating room (Richard Bowers, NJ)

UPLINK: What "U" do before you start taking piano lessons (Vail Palmer, Jr., OR)

UROPYGIA: the practice of insulting a date (Dick Lazaro, FL)

Mnemonics

Mnemonics is a technique that uses words or phrases to serve as memory aids. Creating and using mnemonics can be very useful. Consider KNIGHT SWAM. This was the first mnemonic Joe Edley ever created, back in 1978, when he first starting studying the *Official SCRABBLE® Players Dictionary (OSPD)*. The group of consonants in that phrase are the only letters that can be added to the front of the word AE to form a list of acceptable three-letter words. KAE, NAE, GAE, etc., are all acceptable. Furthermore, two of the 1-point consonants in that group (S & T) form three-letter words that can't be pluralized, while all of the others take an S (KAES, GAES, HAES, WAES, MAES, NAES).

Some players have gone so far as to create mnemonics to learn which letters can be added to certain six-letter combinations to form a seven-letter word. Mike Baron (NM), Bob Lipton (FL), and Zev Kaufman (ONT) are three who pioneered this method. For instance, the six letters AEINRV, rearranged to spell VAINER, can be paired with the phrase I LOVE A SMUDGE. Each of the consonants in this phrase, and only these consonants, can be added to VAINER to form at least one seven-letter word: RAVELIN, VERVAIN, RAVINES, VERMIAN, INVADER, VINEGAR.*

This can be helpful if your opponent lays down INCARVE and you're wondering if it's good. By remembering the mnemonic, you'll be certain that it's a phoney. Likewise, if you have AEINRV with an M, you'll know that you should look carefully at your letters, rearranging them on your rack until you find the seven-letter word—because you know it's there. Note that when no vowels are among the bingo letters to be learned, then, conventionally, the mnemonic will use all five vowels. It usually is easy to distinguish such mnemonics from those where all five vowels are actually used as bingo tiles.

A word of warning about mnemonics: They can be an exciting tool for learning, but with the huge number of potential popular six- and seven-letter combos to learn, you may find that it takes constant review just to remember the mnemonics. And you'll still need to find the word once you know it's there.

*RAVINED and REAVING are two others.

Instead of learning hundreds of these memory aids, we recommend learning only a few of the most common and productive ones.

Here are some of the most useful "anamonics," as they are often called. Thanks go to Nick Ballard (CA), Jim Kramer (MN), Charlie Carroll (MN), and others who created these and hundreds of others, as they popularized this method of study.

To learn what the words actually are, look at Appendix 4.

Example:

For the six letters RETINA, every one of the letters found in the phrase THE RED PUPIL PREFERS MUCH WINKING can be used with RETINA to form a seven-letter word: NITRATE, HAIRNET (INEARTH, THERIAN), TRAINEE . . . etc.

6-to-make-7's

DIALER: CALL YOUR BIG BRAVE DOG SPOT
NAILER: VEXES SPOCK MIGHTILY
ORATES: ADAMANT PREACHER CLANS BRAG
RAINED: DIDN'T POUR MUCH, BUT HAD A VIGOROUS SOUND
REGINA: PERFECT ANGEL BEHEADS MEN THAT GAZE AND WAVE
RETAIL: CHUMPY LENDER TURNS BUCKS
RETINA: THE RED PUPIL PREFERS MUCH WINKING
SATIRE: BAD SPEECH REVIEW: FLAMING WIT
SENIOR: VIGOROUS OLD CHAP'S JOWLS MATCH
TISANE: MAKES EXCELLENT HERB TEA, GIVING FOOD A POWERFUL JET BUZZ

7-to-make-8's

EASTERN: BROUGHT JOVIAL FACES
ENTRIES: GUV MARKEDLY FIXED CONTEST
NASTIER: WICKED HORRIBLE FANG STUMP
REALIGN: JILL ENJOYS EXAMS VILIFYING ALPHABETICAL ORDER
RENAILS: BOXES, CHESTS MIGHTY IMPROVED
SAINTED: BEGETS IMPROVED TOUCH
SARDINE: PROVEN SALTED GRUB
SERIATE: HELPED MY NEW TERMS
STONIER: ROCKY JUNGLES HAVE BENT STEPS
TRAINEE: CHIMP'S KID GIRL

We present a couple of other mnemonics just to show you how easy they are to do:

Imagine a WEE EEL on a RUG drinking TEA. This shows you that TWEE, TEEL, and TRUG are acceptable. (Helga Williams, BC, CAN)

Joe Connelly (CA) found the mnemonic A SHINY DUCHESS, which shows the ten letters that can be added to SILVER to form seven-letter words. All the vowels are used as well.

Following are all of the "SILVER" bingos:

SILVER +

A: REVISAL
C: CLIVERS
D: DRIVELS
E: LEVIERS, RELIVES, REVILES, SERVILE, VEILERS
H: SHRIVEL
I: LIVIERS
N: SILVERN
S: SLIVERS, SILVERS
U: SURVEIL
Y: SILVERY, LIVYERS

Letter Patterns

Generating lists of words that include specific vowel or consonant patterns can be a helpful way to remember some words. For instance, when Joe Edley thinks of the consonants DNPS, he always remembers several very unusual words: DIAPASON, ISOPODAN, and IODOPSIN. He had never heard of these words before playing the game, and he doesn't know what they mean without looking them up. However, he'll never forget them because none of them has an E; they all have four vowels and some combination of the four consonants D, N, P, and S; as well as two or three of the vowels A, I, and O. He can also remember that simply changing the As in DIAPASON, one at a time, first to an O and then to an I, will give you ISOPODAN and then IODOPSIN. Similarly, CAVORTER, OVERCOAT, and CAVEATOR all have combinations of CRTV and AEO. As he thinks of one, it's easy to recall the others.

How can you generate such lists? One way is to go to www.hasbro.com. There you can type in up to eight letters, and you will get back all the words that you can form with those eight letters. You can also use Zyzzyva, which NASPA members can download free. The free phone app Word List Pro is also a good source.

This is a list of seven-letter words that can be made using any of the letters AEIOULNRT exactly once. These words occur frequently as playable bingos in actual games. How quickly can you find those that are anagrams of one another?

AILERON	NEUTRAL	RELIANT	TOENAIL
ALEURON	OUTEARN	RETINAL	TORULAE
ALIENOR	OUTLAIN	RETINOL	TRENAIL
ALUNITE	OUTLIER	ROUTINE	URALITE
ELATION	OUTLINE	RUINATE	URANITE
ELUTION	RAINOUT	TAURINE	URINATE
LATRINE	RATLINE		

Short Word Lists

1. There are twenty-four acceptable words that end in F and do not take an -S back hook, but they do take a -VES after dropping the F. For instance, ELVES is acceptable and ELFS is not. Thanks to Lewis Martinez (CA) for this list. (Reprinted from *SCRABBLE News,* 149.)

AARDWOLF	FLYLEAF	NONSELF	WEREWOLF
BEHALF	HALF	OURSELF	WERWOLF
BOOKSHELF	LIVERLEAF	QUARTERSTAFF	YOURSELF
BROADLEAF	LONGLEAF	SHELF	
CORF	MANTELSHELF	SUGARLOAF	
DEAF	MEATLOAF	THEIRSELF	
ELF	MOONCALF	THIEF	

2. There are sixteen words that take OVER at either the beginning or the end. For example, ALLOVER and OVERALL are both acceptable. Thanks to Kathy Gray (GA) for this list. (Reprinted from *SCRABBLE News,* 148.)

ALL	HAND	LAY	SLIP
BOIL	HANG	PASS	SPILL
CUT	HOLD	RUN	TAKE
FLY	HUNG	SLEEP	TURN

Of the new words we advise you to learn, the short J, X, and Z words will be among the most useful. With the help of some puzzles, chapter 13 will teach these words to you.

13 THE HEAVY ARTILLERY— J, X, AND Z

While the 10-point Q is often a difficult tile to play, the other high-point tiles—the J, X, and Z—are generally much easier to place for large scores. Using those tiles on bonus squares can earn 40 to 80 points in one play! Learn the unusual, but acceptable, three- and four-letter J, X, and Z words listed on page 135. Opportunities to play these words will occur repeatedly.

New players frequently ask which one of these high-point tiles is the best. The X is by far the best, due to its versatility. Because AX, EX, OX, XI, and XU are all acceptable, you will often be able to form plays worth 36 to 52 points by using the X on one of the bonus squares and making parallel plays with letters already on the board. The Z is second to the X, followed by the J.

To help you learn the unusual four-letter words containing J, X, and Z, first review the four-letter word list on page 135. Keep referring back to the list when you have trouble remembering the words.

Each of the following three-letter combinations takes either the J, X, or Z to form a four-letter word. Most of the time you'll have to mix up the letters to spell the word properly. We've marked either a 2 or 3 next to a letter combination if two or three of the letters J, X, or Z can be added to form a word. A star (*) next to a number means that one of the answer words has an anagram. *Example:* In number 45, EST will form words with any of the letters J, X, or Z, and one of the words has an anagram.

Most of the answer words are obscure, so please review the word list on page 135 before trying this exercise.

J X Z QUIZ

1. CEH	*11. AOT	21. ELO	31. ADH	41. OOR
2. EMY	12. DOY -2	22. ACR	32. IOR	*42. EIN -2
3. BEU -2	13. GIN	23. AIR	33. AOS	43. AIO
4. IIT	14. OOU	24. EFU	34. AAL	44. EPR -2
5. EEF	15. ALR	25. STY	35. INY	*45. EST -3
6. ETU	16. IPY	*26. AEL -2	36. ORY	46. EOY -2
7. ACL	17. ART	*27. ANO -2	37. DIN	47. BEI -3
8. AAT	18. EOP	28. ISY	38. AEE	*48. AEN
9. DIO	19. OKU	29. ABU	*39. APU	*49. ENO -3
10. IRT	20. AII	30. EHU	40. ILL -2	*50. ADE -3

As you repeat the exercise in the future, your word knowledge will improve, until such time that you'll probably find you won't need the list at all!

The answers to this quiz are on page 136.

Following are three more puzzle diagrams to practice using the J, X, and Z. In each case, the answers will list a variety of plays not asked for specifically, in order to give you an idea of the numerous choices available in each position.

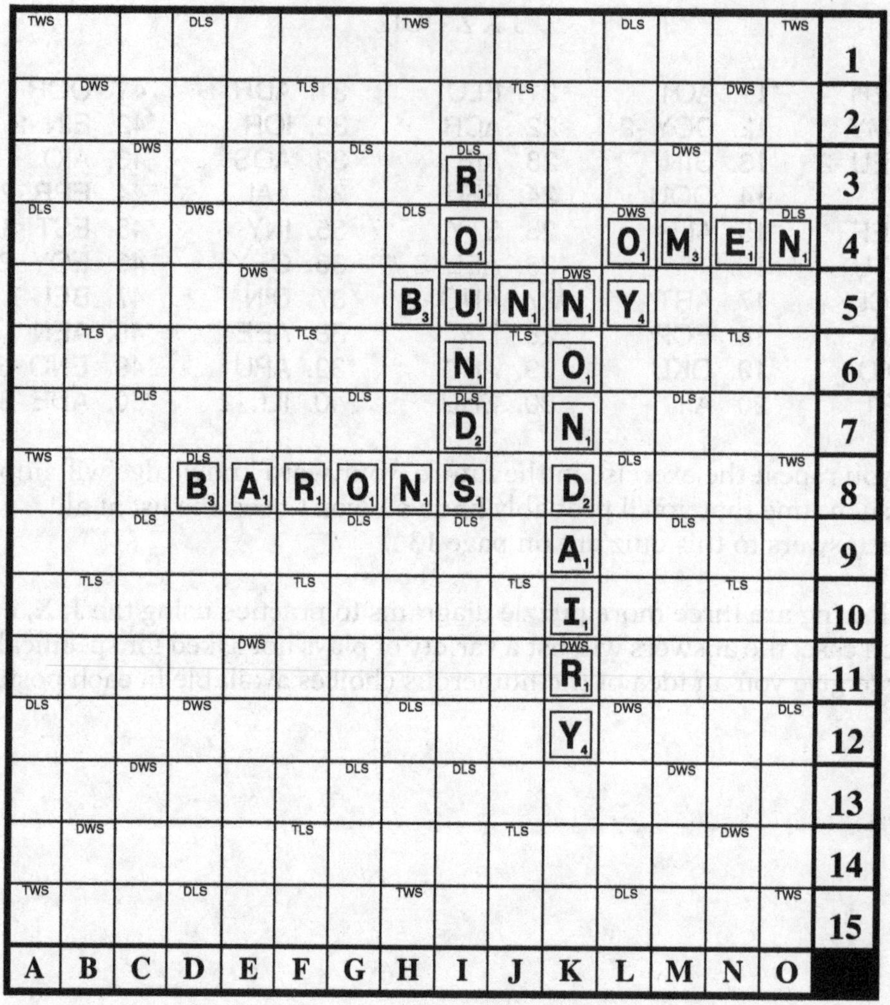
ROUNDS
OMEN
BUNNY
NONDAIRY
BARONS
1 2 3 4 5 6 7 8 9 10 11 12 13 14 15
A B C D E F G H I J K L M N O

DIAGRAM 13-1

Your rack: **A D E G G I J**

There are many excellent plays available on Diagram 13-1 using the given rack. In fact, there are at least three different places on the board where you can make plays worth 36 points or more. Can you find them? The answers are on page 136.

Time limit: 20 minutes

Average score: 1 correct *Good score:* 2 correct *Expert score:* 3 correct

HOPED M
E E
N T
T R
PILLOW
TRIBES A
T N
S T
E
D
A B C D E F G H I J K L M N O
1 2 3 4 5 6 7 8 9 10 11 12 13 14 15

DIAGRAM 13-2

Your rack: **A G I M O U X**

Diagram 13-2 is open for many high-scoring X plays. As you explore, try to find several 50-plus-point plays. The answers are on page 136.

Time limit: 20 minutes

Average score: 1 correct *Good score:* 2 correct *Expert score:* 3 correct

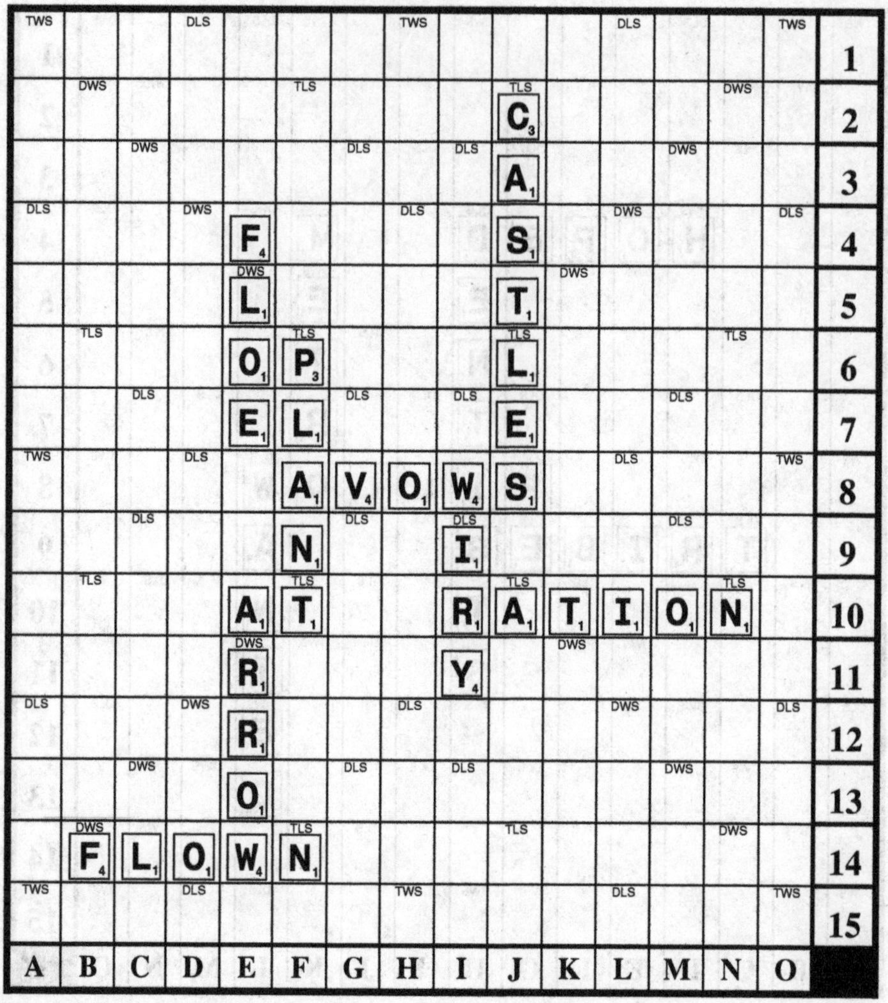

DIAGRAM 13-3

Your rack: **E N O O T Y Z**

Use Diagram 13-3 to find the four different hot spots for which each will allow you to make at least one play of 50-plus points. The answers are on page 136.

Time limit: 20 minutes

Average score: 1 correct *Good score:* 2 correct

Expert score: 3 or 4 correct

It takes more than word knowledge to win SCRABBLE games. After the first thirty or so tiles are on the board, it's often an advantage for either player to know how and where to play to prepare the board's open spaces for the latter stages of the game. In chapter 14 we show you how to "open" or "close" the board and when to do it.

The 3- and 4-Letter J X Z Words

J					X				Z			
AJI	AJIS	JEAN	JINX	JUDY	AXE	SEX	DOUX	MOXA	ADZ	AZON	MAZE	ZEDA
HAJ	DJIN	JEED	JIRD	JUGA	BOX	SIX	DOXY	NEXT	AZO	BAZZ	MAZY	ZEDS
JAB	DOJO	JEEP	JIVE	JUGS	COX	SOX	EAUX	NIXE	BIZ	BIZE	MEZE	ZEES
JAG	FUJI	JEER	JIVY	JUJU	DEX	TAX	EXAM	NIXY	COZ	BOZO	MOZO	ZEIN
JAM	GOJI	JEES	JOBS	JUKE	FAX	TIX	EXEC	ONYX	CUZ	BUZZ	NAZI	ZEKS
JAR	HADJ	JEEZ	JOCK	JUKU	FIX	TUX	EXED	ORYX	FEZ	CAZH	OOZE	ZEPS
JAW	HAJI	JEFE	JOES	JUMP	FOX	VEX	EXES	OXEN	REZ	CHEZ	OOZY	ZERK
JAY	HAJJ	JEHU	JOEY	JUNK	GOX	VOX	EXIT	OXER	SEZ	COZY	ORZO	ZERO
JEE	JABS	JELL	JOGS	JUPE	HEX	WAX	EXON	OXES	FIZ	CZAR	OUZO	ZEST
JET	JACK	JEON	JOHN	JURA	KEX	XED	EXPO	OXIC	TIZ	DAZE	OYEZ	ZETA
JEU	JADE	JERK	JOIN	JURY	LAX	XIS	FALX	OXID	WIZ	DITZ	PHIZ	ZIGS
JIB	JAGG	JESS	JOKE	JUST	LEX	ZAX	FAUX	OXIM	WUZ	DOZE	PREZ	ZILL
JIG	JAGS	JEST	JOKY	JUTE	LOX	APEX	FIXT	PIXY	YEZ	DOZY	PUTZ	ZINC
JIN	JAIL	JETE	JOLE	JUTS	LUX	AXAL	FLAX	PLEX	ZAG	FAZE	QUIZ	ZINE
JOB	JAKE	JETS	JOLT	KOJI	MAX	AXED	FLEX	POXY	ZAP	FIZZ	RAZE	ZING
JOE	JAMB	JEUX	JOOK	MOJO	MIX	AXEL	FLUX	PREX	ZAS	FOZY	RAZZ	ZINS
JOG	JAMS	JIAO	JOSH	PUJA	MUX	AXES	FOXY	ROUX	ZAX	FRIZ	RITZ	ZIPS
JOT	JANE	JIBB	JOSS	RAJA	NIX	AXIL	HOAX	SEXT	ZED	FUTZ	SIZE	ZITI
JOW	JAPE	JIBE	JOTA	SOJA	TIX	AXIS	IBEX	SEXY	ZEE	FUZE	SIZY	ZITS
JOY	JARL	JIBS	JOTS	SOJU	OXO	AXLE	ILEX	TAXA	ZEK	FUZZ	SPAZ	ZIZZ
JUG	JARS	JIFF	JOUK		OXY	AXON	IXIA	TAXI	ZEP	GAZE	TIZZ	ZOEA
JUN	JATO	JIGS	JOWL		PAX	BOXY	JEUX	TEXT	ZIG	GEEZ	TZAR	ZOIC
JUS	JAUK	JILL	JOWS		PIX	BRUX	JINX	VEXT	ZIN	GRIZ	WHIZ	ZONA
JUT	JAUP	JILT	JOYS		POX	CALX	LUXE	WAXY	ZIP	HAZE	YUTZ	ZONE
RAJ	JAVA	JIMP	JUBA		PYX	COAX	LYNX	XYST	ZIT	HAZY	YUZU	ZONK
TAJ	JAWS	JINK	JUBE		RAX	COXA	MAXI		ZOA	IZAR	ZAGS	ZOOM
AJAR	JAYS	JINN	JUCO		REX	CRUX	MINX		ZOO	JAZZ	ZANY	ZOON
AJEE	JAZZ	JINS	JUDO		SAX	DEXY	MIXT		ZUZ	JEEZ	ZAPS	ZOOS
									ZZZ	LAZE	ZARF	ZORI
									ADZE	LAZY	ZEAL	ZOUK
									AZAN	LUTZ	ZEBU	ZYME

ANSWERS TO J X Z FOUR-LETTER WORD QUIZ: 1. CHEZ; 2. ZYME; 3. JUBE, ZEBU; 4. ZITI; 5. JEFE; 6. JUTE; 7. CALX; 8. TAXA; 9. OXID; 10. RITZ; 11. JOTA, JATO; 12. DOXY, DOZY; 13. ZING; 14. OUZO; 15. JARL; 16. PIXY; 17. TZAR; 18. EXPO; 19. JOUK; 20. IXIA; 21. JOLE; 22. CZAR; 23. IZAR; 24. FUZE; 25. XYST; 26. AXEL, AXLE, LAZE, ZEAL; 27. AXON, AZON, ZONA; 28. SIZY; 29. JUBA; 30. JEHU; 31. HADJ; 32. ZORI; 33. SOJA; 34. AXAL; 35. NIXY; 36. ORYX; 37. DJIN; 38. AJEE; 39. JAUP, PUJA; 40. JILL, ZILL; 41. ORZO; 42. NIXE, ZEIN, ZINE; 43. JIAO; 44. PREX, PREZ; 45. JEST, JETS, SEXT, ZEST; 46. JOEY, OYEZ; 47. JIBE, IBEX, BIZE; 48. JANE, JEAN; 49. JEON, EXON, OXEN, ZONE; 50. JADE, AXED, ADZE, DAZE

ANSWERS TO J X Z, DIAGRAM 13-1: Four plays worth 36 points or more are: DJIN O1 36; JADING 7G 42; JAGGED (or JIGGED) 2F 43; and JADE 3L 50. Other high-scoring plays are: JAGGED E7 32; JAGGIER 3C 34, or F2 34; JIG 10J 27; JEAN 01 33; JAGG 2F 38; JAG 9C 26.

DIAGRAM 13-2: Three 50-plus X-plays are MOXA or MAXI at 5C 53 points and AXIOM 8A 54. Other high-scoring plays are: MOXA L1 40, or L3 45, or M12 36; XU M9 36; AXIOM 5A 41, or L1 42; and GOX (or MIX) 5C 45 (47) or L3 39 (41). Advanced players may discover OXIME 5D 59.

DIAGRAM 13-3: The four highest-scoring hot spots are: across row 15 beginning at 15F; down from D1–4; down from H11–15; across row 4H–L. The plays are: OOZY or OYEZ 15F 50 points; ZONE D1 56; ZESTY 4H 54; and OZONE H11 77. Other high-scoring plays include: COZEY 2J 38; OOZE 15F 41; OOZY H10 38; TROOZ 12D 48; SNOOZY 4J 44; ZONER 12A 48; ZONATE 10B 35; ZOO D2 34; OZONE 15F 44; ZOOEY or ZOOTY M9 54.

14 SPACE EXPLORATION: When the Board Is Open or Closed

Look at the following two board positions:

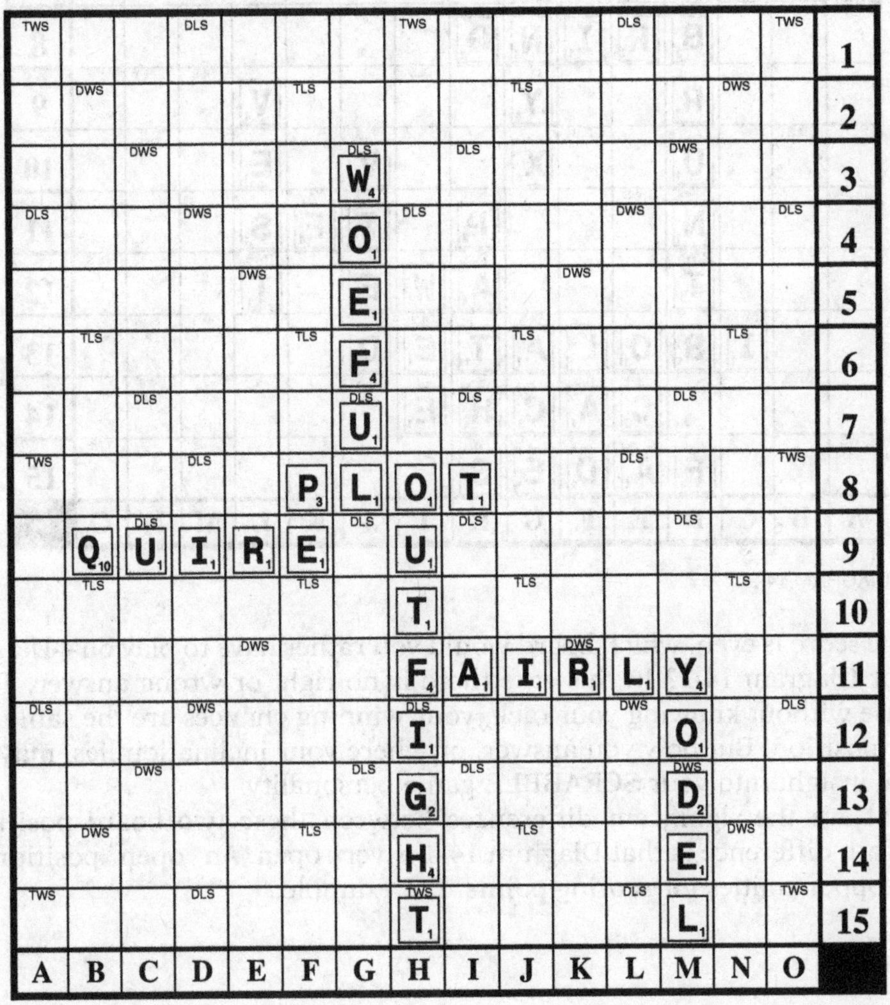
WOEFUL
PLOT
QUIRE
OUTFIGHT
FAIRLY
YODEL
A B C D E F G H I J K L M N O
1 2 3 4 5 6 7 8 9 10 11 12 13 14 15

DIAGRAM 14-1

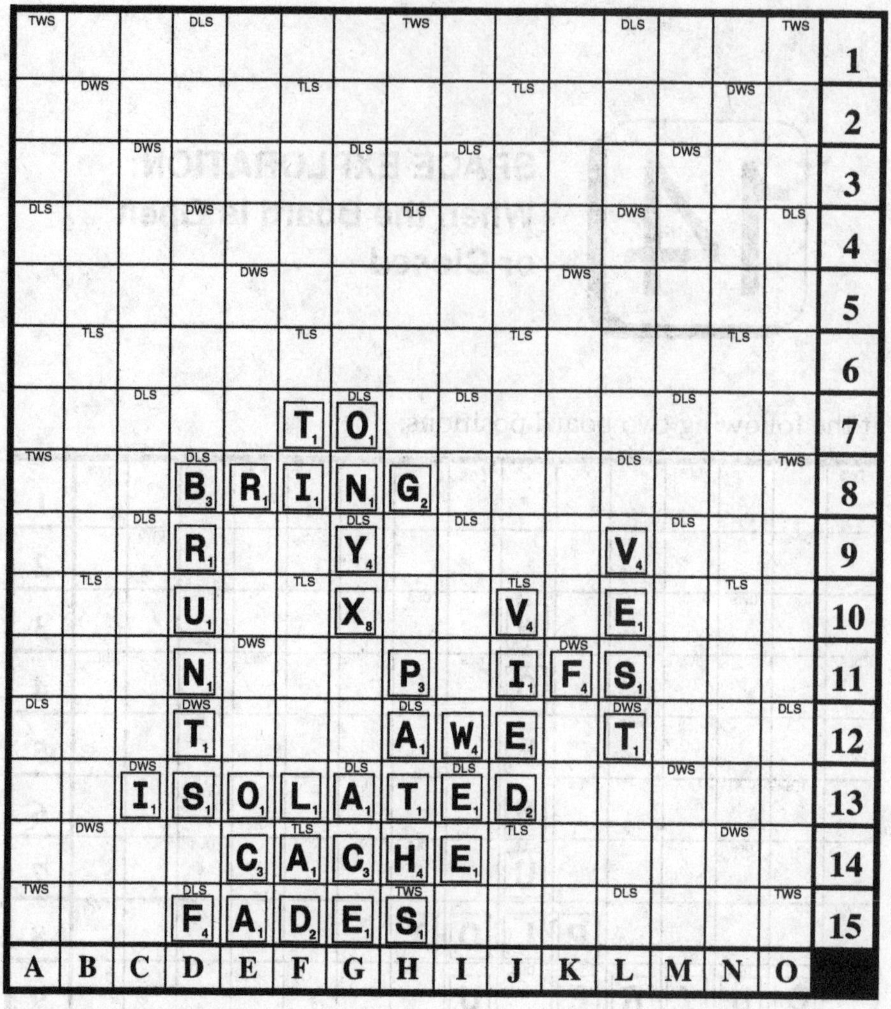

DIAGRAM 14-2

If the score is even, which board would you rather have to play on—Diagram 14-1 or Diagram 14-2? In this case there is no right or wrong answer. That's because without knowing your rack, your winning chances are the same with either position. But how you answer, or where your inclination lies, may give you an insight into your SCRABBLE game personality.

What are the significant differences between these two board positions? The main difference is that Diagram 14-1 is very open. An "open" position has many opportunities for scoring points. For example:

1) With an S you can play SQUIRE and spell another word vertically on column A, earning a Triple Word Score—for example, DOGS A6 33 points.
2) You can play at H1–4—for example, PLOW H1 53.
3) If you have an IN combination, the G on 13H might help you form an ING bingo at 13A–H.
4) A high-point tile can play on 14J–N—for example, JIBED 14J 62.
5) You might find a Double-Double playing through the E at 5G.
6) You can play at 15L–O; for example, FLEX 15L 54.

With all these possibilities, both players may score many points as the game progresses.

Now consider Diagram 14-2. It is a very closed board on which there are very few scoring possibilities. Can you find any rows or columns open for earning large scores? If either player has an S, then column I allows for bingos ending in S, by forming BRINGS. There is one other possible bingo line: H1–8. An ING bingo would fit very nicely from H1–8 and open up rows 1–5. Otherwise, a word like TIME or TIMED starting at F7 might give someone as much as 26 or 28 points.

As we have said, your chances on either of these boards are about equal. Regardless of how "lucky" your tiles are, opening up the board or closing down existing hot spots will often determine the outcome of your games. While it's not in the scope of this book to explain fully every conceivable nuance of strategy, there are a few basic ideas that you should know.

One general principle is this: **When you are ahead, you want to limit your opponent's chances to catch up,** so you want to **keep the board closed.** This usually forces your opponent to open the board. When s/he does, you hope to take advantage of those openings to increase your lead.

When you are behind, you need to keep the board open to allow you to score enough to overtake your opponent. That means you will sometimes want or need to risk opening the board for your opponent.

When the score is close, with neither player ahead by more than 30 points, it's not always clear what to do. Many times you will simply disregard the concept of "openness" or "closedness" and just make your best play, taking into consideration only how much you score and how good your leave is.

How can you create the kind of board position that's advantageous for you? Let's look at two examples.

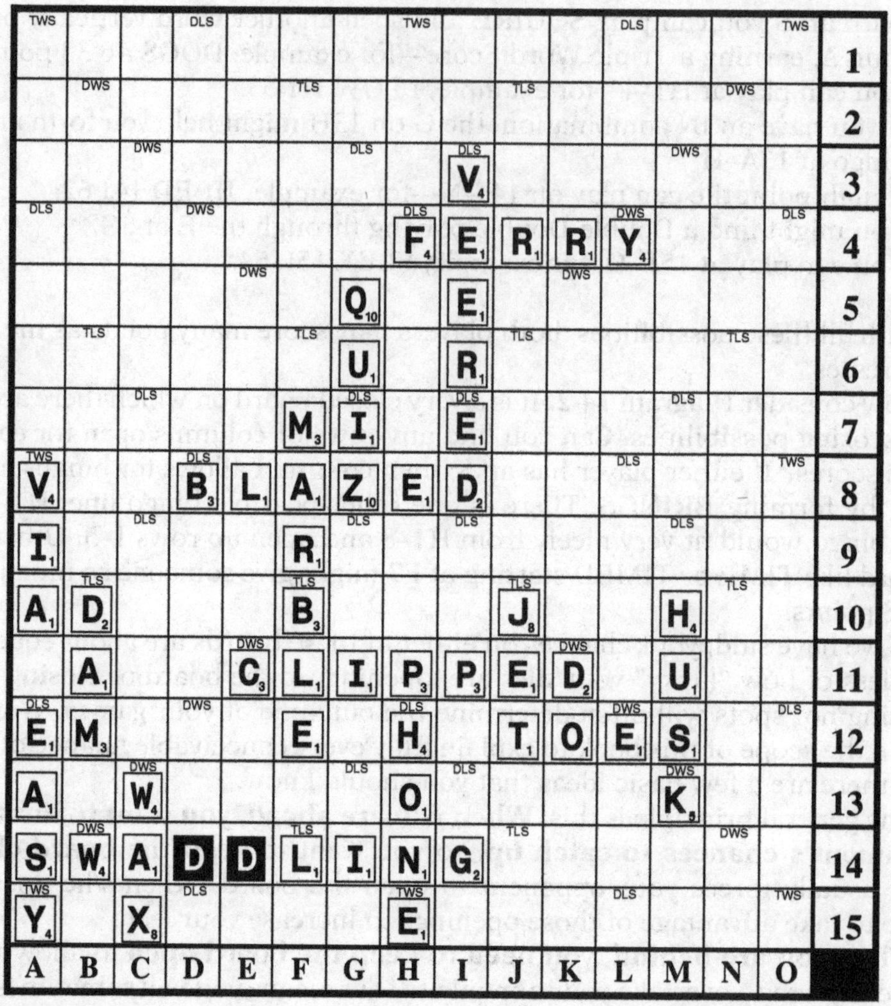

DIAGRAM 14-3

Your rack: **A E F I N S T**
Your score: 220 *Opponent's score:* 300

Using Diagram 14-3, what would you play with the above rack?

ANALYSIS: You're too far behind to win without playing a bingo. You have very good tiles. In fact, you have the bingo FAINEST, meaning "gladdest," but it doesn't play. Here are the bingo hot spots: 1) through the R or Y on the K or L columns; 2) down to or through B on the D column; 3) across row 3 ending in

Note: In a diagram the blank tile is blackened.

IVE through the V at 3I (forming IF and ER as well); and 4) down column N to the H and/or U in HUSK. Despite having four bingo spots, if your opponent plays through the R at 4K, two of those spots will be gone. And you're unlikely to be able to use the B at D8 unless you draw an L for an -ABLE or -IBLE word.

So, realistically, your best chance to bingo is on column N. Now, suppose your opponent decides to play down the L column, ending his or her word in an E on L10 and forming EH, which doesn't take an S. You'll have only the V or B to bingo through. That's not promising either!

Therefore, what you must do is create a new opening for yourself, while keeping most of your bingo-prone tiles. First off, which tiles should you consider playing? Ideally, you would play off just the F. By keeping SATINE you give yourself the best chance to bingo next turn. See Appendix 4 for all the possible bingos using the six SATINE letters.

However, the problem is that you won't open any new bingo lines for yourself if you play off just the F (look at EF 7I or H8). The next-best thing to do is play off the FI. There are several ways to do this. Do you see how one of them opens a dynamic bingo line? Look for the answer labeled Diagram 14-3 on page 146.

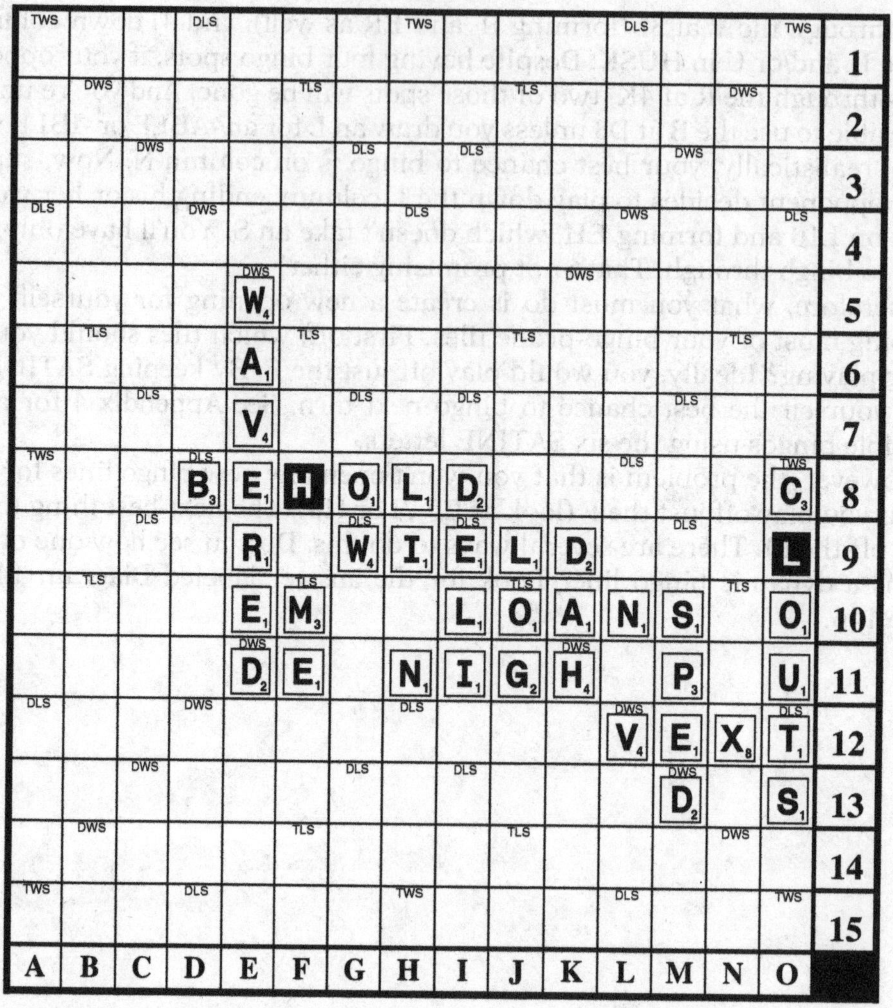

DIAGRAM 14-4

Your rack: **A B E G H I L**

You are 70 points ahead playing on Diagram 14-4. What would you do?

ANALYSIS: This board is nearly closed down. There are two places for opening up the game. You can take a 100-point lead by playing NEIGH H11 30 points, and keeping ABL. Or you can take the TLS at 6F, using BAGEL F2 25 or EH F5 31, or play on the DWS at D4 with BLAH D3 28, BAH D4 26, or even BELGA D1 27. Other plays don't score nearly enough to justify themselves.

Which of the choices do you like?

ANSWERS: Because you are ahead by so much, you don't want to give your opponent a chance to catch up by giving him or her a potentially large comeback play or bingo, which could happen if you open up several letters to play through. So, plays like NEIGH, BAGEL, and BELGA are eliminated; they are much too dangerous. Note that if the board were wide open, any of these might be the best play. But because there is so little chance for scoring, and you're so far ahead, you want to keep it that way by limiting your opponent's options.

Of the other choices, BLAH leaves an unbalanced rack with too many vowels and no scoring prospects for the next turn. So, we are left with either EH or BAH. The leave after BAH (EGIL) is better than the leave after EH (ABGIL), mainly because the E is such a useful letter. However, we would choose EH over BAH only because the F2–F6 line, the best hot spot for your opponent after your BAH, will give away too many points. Try drawing several random racks and see how many points you can score along the F column after BAH! After EH, though the D column is open, it will tend to score fewer points for your opponent. Note that FEH, PEH, and YEH are all good words, but they are not so dangerous because your opponent is unlikely to win this game by playing a bingo beginning with either an F, P, or Y.

Whether you agree or disagree with BAH or EH, either one is an excellent choice. Of course, if you knew and found GALABIEH 6B 74 points, you would quickly play it.

Now imagine that you're *behind* by 70 points in Diagram 14-4 with the same rack. Disregarding the obscure bingo for the moment, you would definitely want to open up the board by playing NEIGH H11 30 points. That's because any play on the D or F column will either not be worth as much as NEIGH or will block the board unnecessarily. Unless you open it up, you'll surely lose.

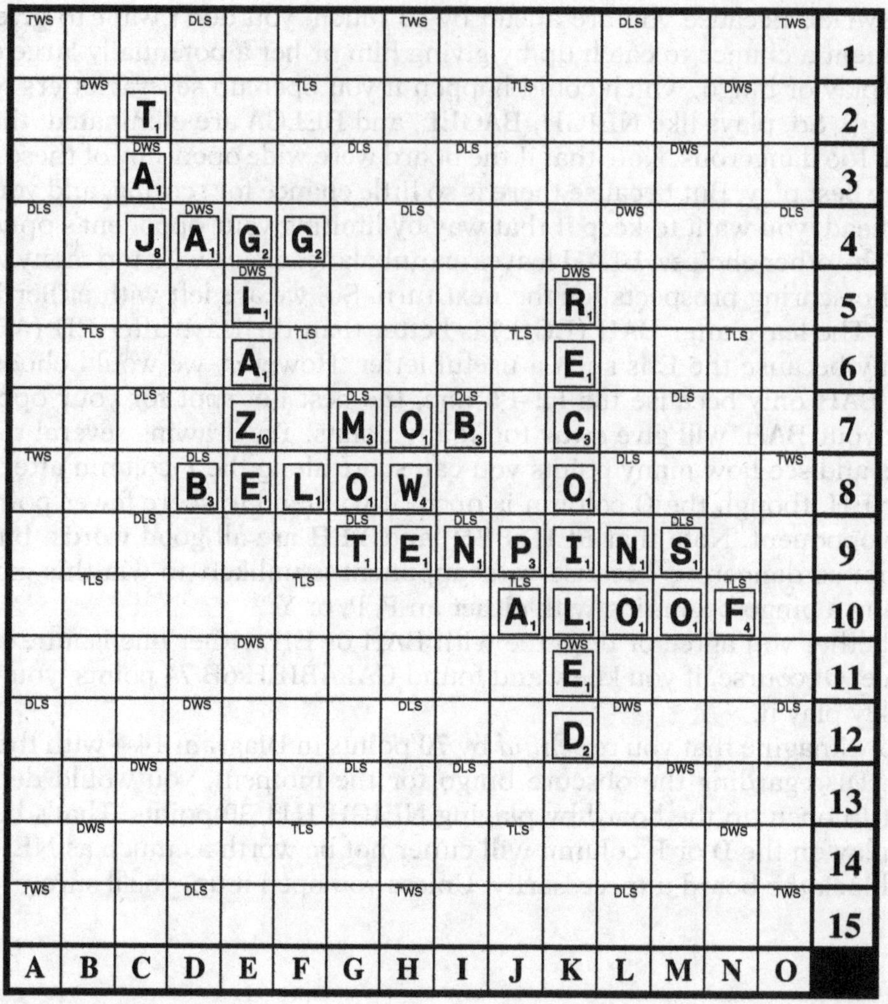

DIAGRAM 14-5

Your rack: **A A C G K L N**

You and your opponent are within 30 points of each other playing on Diagram 14-5. What do you do?

Suppose you are trying to decide between two plays: BLACK D8 26 points and FLACK N10 28. Which one do you prefer?

ANALYSIS: Either of these plays allows you a reasonably good leave: AGN. Since FLACK is worth 2 more points, one might argue that it is the better play.

But look closely at what FLACK does to the board. If your opponent has an S, s/he could then play along the bottom of the board, earning a TWS that might make the difference in who wins the game.

While BLACK allows the opponent an S-hook, row 13 is not nearly so dangerous. That's because the DWS and DLS at 13C and 13G are relatively hard to use to make large scores, whereas after FLACK, all your opponent has to do to score more than 34 points is play a four-letter word with S as the third letter, and the first letter being any tile worth more than 1 point. Also, it is much easier to end bingos with an S than it is to have the S in the first, second, third, or fourth position. Your opponent will bingo much more often after FLACK than after BLACK. You could wind up losing the game on this one play.

One more point: If you have an S on your rack instead of the N (AACGKLS), you might want to consider playing FLACK, because you have an immediate opportunity to score on row 15. However, how will you feel if your opponent takes the spot with his or her own S? What this means is that while some of the time you'll benefit from setting up your S, other times you'll get burned. Only your own experience—and knowing how many Ss and blanks are still out—can help you to learn what to do in situations like this.

SUMMARY FOR SPACE EXPLORATION

Deciding whether to leave the board more or less open after your play is one of the most difficult decisions a player will encounter. Even the top experts think there is still a great deal to learn in this area. However, if you use the following guidelines, you won't go far wrong:

1. When you are far ahead (70 or more points), you should generally close down the board as best you can, even at the expense of a few points. Wouldn't you be happy costing yourself 5 or 10 points if you could keep your opponent from playing a bingo?

2. When you are 70 or more points behind, keep the board fairly open to bingos or high-scoring J, Q, X, or Z plays.

3. When you and your opponent are about even or are within 30 points of each other, always weigh these two factors: the openings you leave your opponent vs. your rack leave. When you have bingo-prone tiles, you may often decide to keep the board more open so you can play your bingos; when you have poor letters, you may want to keep the board more closed.

4. Always remember to use the preceding guidelines in the context of how your opponent plays. Against some opponents you might fare better by not making the theoretically "best" play. Again, only your own experience will help you make that determination.

Even when you've played your very best and taken a huge lead, your opponent may try to trick you with phoney words. Or, even if you are so far behind that you want to give up and start another game, you may be able to catch up and win with a phoney word. Does that seem unethical to you? Who plays phoneys and why? We'll give you the inside scoop about playing phoneys in chapter 15.

ANSWERS: CHAPTER 14

DIAGRAM 14-3: Play FIB D6 8 points. This opens up the excellent C column (C1–C7) for any bingos ending in ES (forming EF and SI). Now there are *two* excellent bingo columns available for you. Your opponent won't be able to block them both, so you will have a decent chance to catch up next turn.

15 IS IT A SOUTH AMERICAN SHRUB OR A PHONEY WORD?

In North American SCRABBLE® Players Association game clubs and tournaments, it is within the official rules to play phoney words. However, if your opponent challenges, the phoney creation comes off the board and you lose a turn. On the other hand, if your play is found acceptable, the challenger loses his or her turn. So there is a definite risk for the challenger.

In this chapter we'd like to discuss three major issues concerning phoneys.

1. Is it ethical to play phoneys?

Many players who have yet to play at NASPA game clubs and/or tournaments think it is unethical to play a nonword purposely. Many of these same people play the game in part to learn new words, and often enjoy conversing with their opponents about words during a game. If a word is played and they are unfamiliar with it, they might ask the player what the word means, fully expecting an accurate answer.

If this sounds like you or your friends, please know that you aren't alone! There are thousands of people who enjoy playing this way. We applaud this style and urge you to continue enjoying yourselves.

In fact, when children or young adults play the game, we recommend the dictionary as a tool. This way they are regularly encouraged to look up words they don't know. (However, we want to make it clear that we're not recommending that they browse through the dictionary looking for words to make a better play.) Later on, when their vocabulary is extensive enough, they might prefer to play with more "challenging" dictionary rules.

Organized competitive SCRABBLE game play in the United States and Canada is very different from the typical "living room" play. Players must not only learn which words are acceptable, but also be able to recognize phoney words. Here word meanings are less important, since no one has to define the words they play. Players consider it a valued skill to be able to challenge a nonword off the board. Because of this, the attitude of most club and tournament players is that any kind of play is acceptable as long as your opponent doesn't challenge.

Admittedly, this can lead to some higher scores, especially when an expert plays against a novice. Because the novice quickly becomes wary of challenging the expert after the first incorrect challenge, the expert can make virtually any play s/he wants, knowing the opponent won't dare question it. Because of the enormous advantage the expert has, most don't consider it ethical to play phoneys against novices. In order to even the match, many experts handicap themselves by allowing the novice free challenges. Regardless of your attitude toward playing phoneys, club and tournament players are happy being "challenged" in this way!

2. There are several situations during a game when you may benefit from playing a phoney word.

When You Have Little to Lose

Sometimes your game will seem hopelessly lost. For instance, suppose you're 150 points behind. At that point you notice that you can play an "almost" real word for a bingo or high score that might give you an outside chance to win. Since you have little to lose, you might as well try it! What's an "almost" real word? It's a phoney that looks and sounds as if it might or should be an acceptable word, but isn't, or you are *almost* sure isn't. For example, one expert tried the phoney PARODIZE against another expert in a crucial tournament game. Although it was eventually challenged and removed from the board, it cost the opponent eight minutes of precious time on his game clock just to ponder the acceptability of a "word" that could easily have meant "to make a parody of."

In general, plausible phoneys are frequently "words" that have common prefixes or suffixes, so they seem familiar. RE, ER, or UN words are particular favorites. Would you be willing to challenge PARTERS, RETILES, or UNCARED*? None of these were acceptable in 1995. RETILES was one of the more notorious phoneys, since most everyone could think of a sensible meaning and may even have used the "word" occasionally. We have seen many games won with this tactic that wouldn't have had a chance otherwise. Incidentally, PRATERS, LEISTER, STERILE, and DURANCE are the acceptable anagrams of those phoneys that won't be challenged off the board.

*RETILES was finally made acceptable in 1995 upon the publication of the *OSPD3*. PARTERS and UNCARED became acceptable with the *OSPD5*.

We suggest that you be aware that the reverse tactic has also been used. Suppose your opponent lays down ZIGWURST. Would you know that it was a phoney? To us it seems so outrageously phoney that even an experienced player might reason: "That's so weird that my opponent must surely know it's good and is simply laying a trap for me!" While the opponent *is* laying a trap, s/he *knows* that it is a phoney.

We recall a tournament game between two experts in Reno, Nevada, in which the bingo FOGHATS was played. In fact, it was an important play that helped win that game for the victor. The losing player knew he had seen the word before but forgot that he had seen it on a special list of outrageous phoneys, instead of in the dictionary.

Several years later, another top expert was the victim of FOGHATS at the very same hotel and tournament in Reno. And he, too, recalled seeing the word in print. Of course, the original story had been talked about and published in *SCRABBLE News,* the official newsletter of the National SCRABBLE Association. Over time, the details of the true events had been forgotten, but the word was remembered as being acceptable.

When You Want to Test Your Opponent

Suppose you are playing someone you've never played before. Does this person typically challenge words s/he doesn't know? You may have no idea. If you have the first turn, you might open the game with a phoney just to see what s/he does. If s/he doesn't challenge, this gives you valuable information about him or her. If s/he does challenge, what have you lost? Often, losing the first move is inconsequential.

Incidentally, you might want to open a game with a phoney because you know that your opponent *will* challenge. Here's why. We know a player who, in the 1993 World SCRABBLE Championship, opened a game with the word GARROT. His rack included another T. He knew that GARROTTE is a good word. He was hoping that his opponent would challenge, remove his word, and then play an E in his first word, allowing him to play his eight-letter bingo next. Since there are 12 Es, that possibility was not so far-fetched.

Unfortunately for this expert, in the World Championship the British-based *Chambers English Dictionary* was also used as a word source at that time, and GARROT was listed in it. When the challenge came back *acceptable,* he was, ironically, somewhat disappointed. We should also add that because most of the contestants were playing with thousands of words they weren't necessarily familiar with, the rules were adjusted so that there was no penalty for an incorrect challenge.

When Your Opponent Has Just Lost a Challenge

You've just played MACRONS. Your opponent challenges and it is found acceptable! Now you've drawn letters that don't quite work together well, but you see a phoney that looks like a plausible word. Should you try it?

One of the best times to play a phoney is right after your opponent has just lost a challenge. After feeling the sting of one lost turn, s/he may not want to test the waters again just yet. We've seen this ploy used successfully hundreds of times!

When You Have a Variety of Good Plays

You have a blank and have found several playable bingos. Yet you see a phoney bingo that scores 15 more points than any of the other real words. Do you play it? Answer: only if you think that your opponent will see your legitimate bingos. In that case s/he might assume that you wouldn't try a phoney when you have all those perfectly good words to play.

We don't advise using this strategy unless you are familiar with how your opponent usually thinks.

When You Score Few Points

You have an average rack and see no spectacular plays. However, you do see a phoney that looks plausibly like a real word. It scores 10 to 20 points and leaves you with a much better leave than any other play.

Often an opponent won't challenge a low-scoring play because s/he will assume that the player probably has several acceptable low-scoring plays and wouldn't take a chance on losing a turn unless the phoney was worth something substantial. Once again, it pays to know your opponent's thinking habits and level of word knowledge before you try this.

When You Want the Game Decided on One Play

Let's say you have a moderate lead of 50 points. If you play a phoney bingo and raise that lead to 130 points at the halfway mark of the game, this can demoralize a less-than-expert opponent and make it extremely difficult for him or her to win. You may be able to coast to a victory. If you lose the challenge, what have you lost? You'll probably still have a lead after your opponent plays, though it may be a narrower one. But if your phoney uses a blank, you may be confident you'll play a bingo later and win anyway. Playing the phoney simply puts enormous pressure on your opponent *right at that moment.*

One well-known expert is known for occasionally playing phoneys against other experts in championship play. In one national championship he knowingly used a blank to play the phoney SALTANTS to take a 100-point lead in the crucial final game. He was fairly certain that his opponent would know the word SALTANT (which means "dancing and singing"), but not know that it is an adjective and does not take an S. In that situation, even if he had lost the turn, he would retain the blank and the lead, and so maintain good winning chances.

When You Want a Higher Point Spread

Tournaments are often won on "point spread." Point spread is the amount of points by which a game is won or lost. If you win 400–300, then your point spread for that game is +100 and your opponent's is -100. After each game your "total point spread" goes up or down, depending on whether you win or lose. Someone who has eight wins and a point spread of 609 points places higher than someone who finishes with eight wins and a point spread of 467. Therefore, when some players are fairly certain they will win a game and can afford to lose a turn, they may take a chance in playing a phoney in order to win by a larger margin!

When the Game Is Nearly Over

At the end of the game, one player may be stuck with a tile and not be able to play out. This infrequently happens with the Q. At this point the opponent may continue taking turns until s/he plays all of his or her tiles on the board. If you see a phoney or a word you're not sure of that scores well, why not try it? Losing a turn in this situation won't hurt at all. But be careful! If six consecutive turns score zero points, the game is over. That means if your opponent passes three times in a row, and you play three consecutive challenged phoneys, the game is over.

3. When should you challenge a word you think is a phoney?

If you are certain a play is unacceptable, then it's usually right to challenge it. The only exception is when the phoney allows *you* to make a great play that you wouldn't have otherwise. Even then you should calculate exactly what advantage you gain from allowing the phoney. An example of this is in Diagram 15-1.

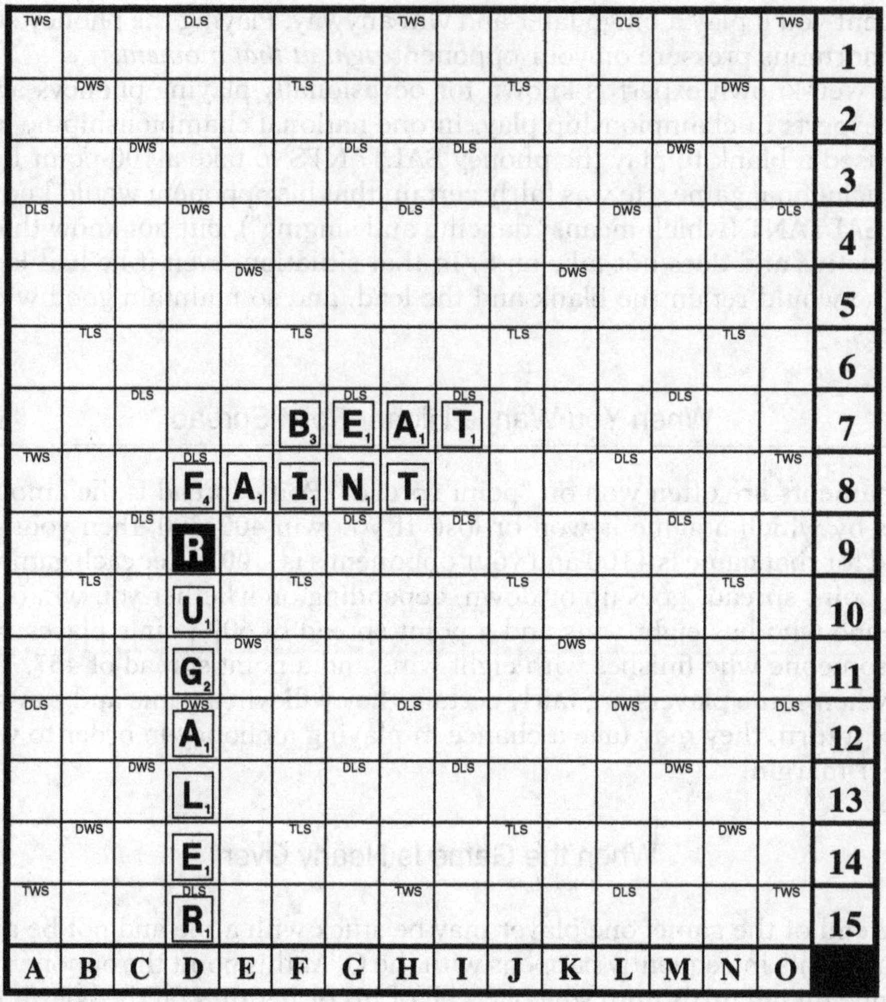

DIAGRAM 15-1

Your rack: **A A E E G S V**
Your score: 17 *Opponent's score:* 24 (or 98)

What do you do on Diagram 15-1?

Your opponent has just played FRUGALER. You immediately think, "No way!" But then you might ask, "If someone can be frugal, why can't they be frugaler?" Having looked at your -ER list recently, you're fairly certain that it just didn't make it into the *OSPD6*. However, you notice that your opponent has other bingos, such as GRATEFUL or REGULAR, which would have been safer plays. Still undecided? Look at your rack and see what's possible for you after

FRUGALER. Suddenly, you see a Triple-Triple through the R for 158 points! Clearly, you don't want to challenge your opponent's play, since it allows you to take a considerable lead. What is your big move? The answer is below.

When deciding whether to challenge or not, keep in mind the following:

If you aren't sure that a word is a phoney, first consider who your opponent is and what his or her habits are concerning phoneys. Does s/he frequently or rarely play them? How sophisticated is his or her thinking? How strong is his or her word knowledge? Is s/he using any of the ploys mentioned in this chapter? If you don't challenge, do you have a reasonable chance to win? If not, then challenge. How often are your decisions correct when you have a strong desire to challenge? If your intuition is sometimes wrong, be wary! Finally, *always* challenge the last play unless you are 100 percent sure it's good. You've nothing to lose.

The extent to which you can answer these questions accurately will determine whether you should challenge your opponent.

One final thought about phoneys: Although we've shown you many different scenarios about using phoneys purposely to your advantage, the most common reason people play a phoney, *by far,* is because they think the play is or may be acceptable. So when you aren't sure about a word, consider how frequently your intuition has been accurate in previous situations. Take a few seconds to ask yourself if, deep in your heart, you believe the word is acceptable, or if you're indulging in wishful thinking. If you have a good track record, you might want to take the chance and make the play. If you're usually making up the words, then take extra time to consider alternate plays.

This ends Part 2. We invite you to test yourself with the puzzles found in Part 3. They're designed to be fun while increasing your skills. Enjoy!

ANSWER: CHAPTER 15

DIAGRAM 15-1: AVERAGES 15A 158 points

PART • 3

PUZZLES: Learning Can Be Fun!

In Part 3 we have assembled a wide variety of puzzles. Solving these puzzles will serve four functions:

1. It will be fun.
2. It will build vocabulary skills.
3. It will assess your word-finding abilities.
4. It will be more fun.

We've also suggested a time limit and an average, good, and expert score for most sets of puzzles so that you can gauge how well you're developing. We suggest you repeat any sets you find difficult. In this way you'll be able to measure your progress over time.

In chapter 16 we have created four kinds of puzzles and assigned to each a level of difficulty based on a three-star scoring system. The more stars, the greater the difficulty. In chapter 17 you will be challenged to find words over-the-board. These puzzles will better prepare you for your toughest opponent! Chapter 18 has some very tough puzzles. Check your schedule before beginning any of these. If you spend time trying to solve them, we believe your anagramming skills will greatly improve.

16 HOOK WORDS, ANAGRAMS, FILL-INS, AND FRONT EXTENSIONS

In this chapter we're going to test your word-finding abilities in four different ways. We suggest that if you can't solve any given puzzle in a reasonable length of time, look up the answer. Then, at a much later time, try to solve it again. For most people it's surprisingly easy to forget the answers, so you'll be able to test how well you've improved over time. Our experience has shown that by practicing in this fashion you will be training yourself to find these same types of answers during actual game play. Time and again we've seen novices, who typically take five minutes or more to find a seven-letter word with their rack of letters, speed up their skills by a factor of ten in the course of a year or two.

HOOK WORDS

Find the one letter that can be added to the front of each of the following words to form a very common word. For each individual puzzle, a different letter may be needed. For instance, __ A G O N and __ A G M A take different first letters, a W and an M, respectively, and so on. We've deliberately presented many obscure, less common words so that, by association, you'll find it easier to remember both words. Our puzzle sections are designated with stars; the more stars, the harder the puzzles. The answers are on page 167.

5-Letter Words*

Time limit per set: 20 minutes
Average score: 6 correct *Good score:* 8 correct *Expert score:* 10 correct

SET A

1. __ HONG
2. __ AGON
3. __ IMID
4. __ ANTA
5. __ VIES
6. __ BACK
7. __ VARY
8. __ FOUL
9. __ PRIG
10. __ EGER

SET B

1. __ PERM
2. __ HIDE
3. __ PALS
4. __ AGMA
5. __ HOST
6. __ AGUE
7. __ IWIS
8. __ KING
9. __ PLAT
10. __ LAKY

SET C

1. __ NOME
2. __ OMIT
3. __ HILI
4. __ HEIR
5. __ PICE
6. __ LAID
7. __ DEAL
8. __ RIAL
9. __ RIMY
10. __ ROOD

SET D

1. __ EYED
2. __ FIRE
3. __ FOOT
4. __ CONS
5. __ GAPE
6. __ LOBE
7. __ GREE
8. __ MAGE
9. __ HEAP
10. __ HEFT

SET E

1. __ LEFT
2. __ LIEN
3. __ GLOW
4. __ LOFT
5. __ LORY
6. __ LUNT
7. __ HANT
8. __ MELL
9. __ RUTH
10. __ NAVE

SET F

1. __ RUSK
2. __ MIRK
3. __ TROP
4. __ VAIL
5. __ BONY
6. __ VERY
7. __ APSE
8. __ VOWS
9. __ WEAK
10. __ WELT

6-Letter Words**

Time limit per set: 20 minutes
Average score: 5 correct *Good score:* 7 correct *Expert score:* 9 correct

SET G	SET H	SET I
1. __ ACTOR	1. __ ANTIS	1. __ BLEST
2. __ ADIOS	2. __ APTLY	2. __ BORTS
3. __ AGLET	3. __ ARBOR	3. __ CRAWL
4. __ AIVER	4. __ ARGLE	4. __ CURVY
5. __ ALARY	5. __ ARGON	5. __ DRIFT
6. __ ALDER	6. __ ARSON	6. __ EAGER
7. __ ALIGN	7. __ ASCOT	7. __ EAGLE
8. __ ALOES	8. __ ATMAN	8. __ EBBED
9. __ AMBIT	9. __ AWFUL	9. __ EDUCT
10. __ AMENT	10. __ BATED	10. __ EGRET

SET J	SET K	SET L
1. __ ELECT	1. __ HOSEN	1. __ LORAL
2. __ EMBER	2. __ HUBBY	2. __ OSMIC
3. __ ENURE	3. __ HYING	3. __ OVINE
4. __ ERROR	4. __ INDOW	4. __ QUATE
5. __ EVERT	5. __ IRADE	5. __ RALLY
6. __ EXIST	6. __ KETCH	6. __ RAYON
7. __ GREED	7. __ LAPSE	7. __ RIFLE
8. __ HADED	8. __ LINGY	8. __ RIGID
9. __ HOOEY	9. __ LIVES	9. __ SABLE
10. __ HORAL	10. __ LOGAN	10. __ UNSET

7-Letter Words**

Time limit per set: 20 minutes
Average score: 5 correct *Good score:* 7 correct *Expert score:* 9 correct

SET M

1. __ AGNATE
2. __ ANTRUM
3. __ ARMFUL
4. __ ARRANT
5. __ AUDING
6. __ ENFOLD
7. __ ETHANE
8. __ GAINST
9. __ LATTEN
10. __ STOUND

SET N

1. __ LEANLY
2. __ LIABLE
3. __ LISTEN
4. __ LOWERY
5. __ LUMPEN
6. __ MARTEN
7. __ MONGST
8. __ NEATEN
9. __ OFTEST
10. __ VENUES

SET O

1. __ OXTAIL
2. __ PENDED
3. __ RECKED
4. __ REPAID
5. __ RACKET
6. __ RATIFY
7. __ PRAISE
8. __ REASON
9. __ REFACE
10. __ PREACH

SET P

1. __ RIDENT
2. __ ROUBLE
3. __ RUDELY
4. __ RUMPLE
5. __ SCENDS
6. __ SPOUSE
7. __ LAYOFF
8. __ THEISM
9. __ OOLOGY
10. __ VERBID

Anagrams

Each of the following less common words has exactly one very common word as an anagram. For example, the anagram of CHAY is ACHY. Your task is to find the common words. After one or more trial runs through each set of puzzles, you may learn to go through this list fairly quickly. You then might want to test your recall of these obscure words by looking at the common words on the Answers page and trying to find their anagrams on this page. The answers start on page 168.

4-Letter Anagrams*

Time limit per set: 20 minutes
Average score: 6 correct *Good score:* 8 correct *Expert score:* 10 correct

SET A	SET B	SET C
1. CHAY	1. ORAD	1. LATH
2. POLY	2. EGAL	2. HILA
3. SIMP	3. KOTO	3. PIAL
4. BLAW	4. EPHA	4. IMAM
5. BAHT	5. WONK	5. VINA
6. ALEC	6. LAZE	6. MOLA
7. CAPH	7. FIAR	7. PALY
8. CAKY	8. AGIN	8. MYNA
9. MARC	9. GAOL	9. PRAM
10. YALD	10. HANT	10. NONA

SET D	SET E
1. AWRY	1. OYER
2. DOBY	2. NEIF
3. BENE	3. FROE
4. BREE	4. KEPI
5. BONK	5. HYTE
6. CEIL	6. METH
7. POCO	7. PLIE
8. EDDY	8. LWEI
9. DELF	9. NEUK
10. OHED	10. FILO

5-Letter Anagrams**

Time limit per set: 20 minutes
Average score: 5 correct *Good score:* 7 correct *Expert score:* 9 correct

SET F

1. AAHED
2. DAMAR
3. MALAR
4. BALDY
5. RABID
6. TUBAE
7. BIALI
8. CAGER
9. CHELA
10. CHARE

SET G

1. MACLE
2. ECLAT
3. COMAE
4. GAMIC
5. MOCHA
6. NATCH
7. ORACH
8. MALIC
9. TAROC
10. MUSCA

SET H

1. LAMED
2. DRAVE
3. HYDRA
4. VIAND
5. AROID
6. PAVID
7. MONAD
8. EGRET
9. ENATE
10. FLEAM

SET I

1. NAEVI
2. ANOLE
3. UVEAL
4. YAMEN
5. TRAVE
6. TAWER
7. IMAGO
8. TONGA
9. GOWAN
10. THRAW

SET J

1. LARUM
2. BEDEL
3. BERME
4. BOSUN
5. LUDIC
6. SODIC
7. PUDIC
8. TEUCH
9. CIVET
10. VOCES

SET K

1. LICHI
2. ONTIC
3. RUNIC
4. CUTIN
5. MONDE
6. FONDU
7. IMIDO
8. REIFY
9. GOFER
10. FLYTE

SET L

1. GREGO
2. GENOM
3. MOHUR
4. EPHOR
5. THROE
6. VOILE
7. OWLET
8. SLYPE
9. SULFO
10. LOUGH

7-Letter Anagrams***

In sets M–O, the common-word anagrams all have either common beginnings or common endings (see page 71 for the list). We strongly recommend using letter tiles on a rack to solve these puzzles. Doing this will better simulate game play. An alternate method is to use pencil and paper and record different letter arrangements while trying to find the anagrams.

Time limit per set: 20 minutes
Average score: 3 correct *Good score:* 5 correct *Expert score:* 8 correct

SET M	SET N	SET O	SET P
1. BISNAGA	1. AVODIRE	1. NILGHAI	1. USURPER
2. CATALOS	2. OVERSAD	2. NILGHAU	2. ANTISAG
3. VEDALIA	3. TEREFAH	3. SAINTLY	3. SPATHAL
4. DRAYAGE	4. HALTERE	4. SAVIOUR	4. CARIBES
5. ANAPEST	5. FINAGLE	5. BIOGENY	5. ABRIDGE
6. DOGBANE	6. REFUTAL	6. TUBULIN	6. BRAILLE
7. AMBONES	7. RIVAGES	7. RESTYLE	7. REBOANT
8. ECHIDNA	8. MUTAGEN	8. MITOGEN	8. HARICOT
9. CUMARIN	9. NEGATON	9. WETTISH	9. FAIENCE
10. OCTANOL	10. PREWRAP	10. NIVEOUS	10. GYRATED

SET Q	SET R	SET S	SET T
1. PAROLED	1. STYLATE	1. NOCTUID	1. DINKEYS
2. PANDITS	2. SURNAME	2. THICKEN	2. DUMMIES
3. DALTONS	3. FUNFAIR	3. POLEMIC	3. DENSITY
4. MADRONO	4. OOMPAHS	4. EXOTICS	4. VIROIDS
5. REAVING	5. OPUNTIA	5. COLONES	5. PERLITE
6. ALLONGE	6. ISSUANT	6. MONOECY	6. VESPINE
7. IMPASTE	7. BUNDIST	7. EMERSED	7. QUERIER
8. LATHERY	8. TURBINE	8. PREDIVE	8. PROETTE
9. SENHORA	9. RAILBUS	9. PUNGLED	9. FLEMISH
10. APLENTY	10. NUCLIDE	10. WOODHEN	10. THEGNLY

Fill-Ins

Simply seeing the consonants in their correct position in a word can lead to finding the word. Using only vowels (and no Ys), fill in the blanks to form common words. The answers are on page 169.

Time limit per set: 30 minutes
Average score: 5 correct *Good score:* 7 correct *Expert score:* 9 correct

SET A**	SET B**
1. B__ SC__ __ T	1. CR__ N__ __ M
2. __ LM __ N__ C	2. M __ __ LB__ X
3. R__ __ DW__ Y	3. S __ __ S__ CK
4. H__ __ RS__ Y	4. PL __ G__ __ D
5. V__ N__ LL__	5. R __ T__ ND__
6. __ N__ T__ MY	6. __ ST __ __ ND
7. T__ BL__ __ D	7. __ NF__ D__ L
8. C__ R__ F__ L	8. P__ __ NF__ L
9. C__ H__ __ TS	9. N__ M__ R__ L
10. M__ S__ C__ L	10. F__ RT__ L__

Time limit per set: 30 minutes
Average score: 3 correct *Good score:* 5 correct *Expert score:* 7 correct

SET C***	SET D***
1. __ MN__ S__ __	1. R__ R__ __ T__
2. C__ __ R__ G__	2. F__ __ NC__ __
3. S__ __ W__ __ D	3. L__ M__ __ D__
4. __ RD__ __ S	4. T__ __ N__ __ L
5. T__ __ T__ M__	5. __ N__ W__ R__
6. P__ R__ L__ __	6. __ SC__ P__ __
7. B__ S__ __ G__	7. M__ T__ N__ __
8. T__ P__ __ C__	8. N__ __ V__ T__
9. __ __ TM__ __ L	9. F__ T__ G__ __
10. G__ N__ __ N__	10. B__ C__ __ S__

Front Extensions

Sometimes you'll have an opportunity to extend from the front of a word already on the game board. This is particularly true when the opening play is a five-letter word starting on Double Letter Score square 8D or H4. You can then extend that opening play to a Triple Word Score square, either at 8A or H1. Below we show you what your rack is and what has already been played. Add three letters of the given rack to the front of the five-letter word to form a common eight-letter word. The answers are on page 169.

Time limit per set: 30 minutes
Average score: 4 correct *Good score:* 6 correct *Expert score:* 8 correct

SET A**

	RACK	WORD
1.	ACEGMNR	___ ___ ___ ACING
2.	EGILOPR	___ ___ ___ AMBLE
3.	ACMORUV	___ ___ ___ AMENT
4.	EILNTUV	___ ___ ___ AMINS
5.	EGHMNOR	___ ___ ___ ANTIC
6.	CDEILNW	___ ___ ___ ANGER
7.	AEGIORT	___ ___ ___ BORNE
8.	CEFILNP	___ ___ ___ CITED
9.	ABELMRU	___ ___ ___ DOWNS
10.	ACGINPT	___ ___ ___ EATER

SET B**

	RACK	WORD
1.	ADGLMOU	___ ___ ___ FIGHT
2.	ACDILRT	___ ___ ___ FULLY
3.	DEGILMR	___ ___ ___ HEADS
4.	GIMOPST	___ ___ ___ HOLES
5.	ABCDLMP	___ ___ ___ HOUSE
6.	AHILOTW	___ ___ ___ LIGHT
7.	ACDELMT	___ ___ ___ ORATE
8.	CEHNPRV	___ ___ ___ OVATE
9.	ABLNORW	___ ___ ___ RAGES
10.	CEFIOPR	___ ___ ___ RIDGE

SET C**

	RACK	WORD
1.	ABEGINU	___ ___ ___ ROWTH
2.	EHLMPRY	___ ___ ___ SERVE
3.	AEFGLMS	___ ___ ___ TIFFS
4.	BENPRTU	___ ___ ___ TONED
5.	AELPRUV	___ ___ ___ TICAL
6.	CDIMPSU	___ ___ ___ TINCT
7.	ABFLMOP	___ ___ ___ TONIC
8.	EKLMOPR	___ ___ ___ TALLY
9.	AEHLMNR	___ ___ ___ TORIC
10.	CEIKLNT	___ ___ ___ WELLS

For the following five sets, there is only one set of three letters that will extend the given word from the front to form a common word.

Time limit per set: 30 minutes
Average score: 4 correct *Good score:* 6 correct *Expert score:* 8 correct

SET D***

1. __ __ __ ALATE
2. __ __ __ ALFAS
3. __ __ __ AMIDS
4. __ __ __ AMITY
5. __ __ __ ARGOT
6. __ __ __ AWFUL
7. __ __ __ BARBS
8. __ __ __ BATHE
9. __ __ __ BRUSH
10. __ __ __ CHASE

SET E***

1. __ __ __ CHILD
2. __ __ __ COAST
3. __ __ __ COUGH
4. __ __ __ CUTER
5. __ __ __ DRAIL
6. __ __ __ DUSTS
7. __ __ __ EMBER
8. __ __ __ EVERY
9. __ __ __ GLARY
10. __ __ __ GRATE

SET F***

1. __ __ __ GULAR
2. __ __ __ HANDS
3. __ __ __ HILLS
4. __ __ __ HOMED
5. __ __ __ HOVER
6. __ __ __ IODIC
7. __ __ __ KLONG
8. __ __ __ KNIFE
9. __ __ __ LIFTS
10. __ __ __ LOUGH

SET G***

1. __ __ __ LUTED
2. __ __ __ MOILS
3. __ __ __ NEVER
4. __ __ __ NIVAL
5. __ __ __ OLEUM
6. __ __ __ OVALS
7. __ __ __ PARDY
8. __ __ __ PLASH
9. __ __ __ RATOS
10. __ __ __ REDLY

SET H***

1. __ __ __ AMOUR
2. __ __ __ ROILS
3. __ __ __ ROUGH
4. __ __ __ PLUGS
5. __ __ __ SHALL
6. __ __ __ SOLED
7. __ __ __ TEMPT
8. __ __ __ VERBS
9. __ __ __ WHERE
10. __ __ __ TROYS

HOOK WORDS: 5-LETTER WORDS

SET A	SET B	SET C	SET D	SET E	SET F
1. THONG	1. SPERM	1. GNOME	1. KEYED	1. CLEFT	1. BRUSK
2. WAGON	2. CHIDE	2. VOMIT	2. AFIRE	2. ALIEN	2. SMIRK
3. TIMID	3. OPALS	3. CHILI	3. AFOOT	3. AGLOW	3. STROP
4. MANTA	4. MAGMA	4. THEIR	4. ICONS	4. ALOFT	4. AVAIL
5. IVIES	5. GHOST	5. SPICE	5. AGAPE	5. GLORY	5. EBONY
6. ABACK	6. VAGUE	6. PLAID	6. GLOBE	6. BLUNT	6. EVERY
7. OVARY	7. KIWIS	7. IDEAL	7. AGREE	7. CHANT	7. LAPSE
8. AFOUL	8. EKING	8. TRIAL	8. IMAGE	8. SMELL	8. AVOWS
9. SPRIG	9. SPLAT	9. GRIMY	9. CHEAP	9. TRUTH	9. TWEAK
10. LEGER	10. FLAKY	10. BROOD	10. THEFT	10. KNAVE	10. DWELT

HOOK WORDS: 6-LETTER WORDS

SET G	SET H	SET I	SET J	SET K	SET L
1. FACTOR	1. MANTIS	1. ABLEST	1. SELECT	1. CHOSEN	1. FLORAL
2. RADIOS	2. RAPTLY	2. ABORTS	2. MEMBER	2. CHUBBY	2. COSMIC
3. EAGLET	3. HARBOR	3. SCRAWL	3. TENURE	3. SHYING	3. BOVINE
4. WAIVER	4. GARGLE	4. SCURVY	4. TERROR	4. WINDOW	4. EQUATE
5. SALARY	5. JARGON	5. ADRIFT	5. REVERT	5. TIRADE	5. ORALLY
6. BALDER	6. PARSON	6. MEAGER	6. SEXIST	6. SKETCH	6. CRAYON
7. MALIGN	7. MASCOT	7. BEAGLE	7. AGREED	7. ELAPSE	7. TRIFLE
8. HALOES	8. BATMAN	8. WEBBED	8. SHADED	8. CLINGY	8. FRIGID
9. GAMBIT	9. LAWFUL	9. DEDUCT	9. PHOOEY	9. OLIVES	9. USABLE
10. LAMENT	10. ABATED	10. REGRET	10. CHORAL	10. SLOGAN	10. SUNSET

HOOK WORDS: 7-LETTER WORDS

SET M	SET N	SET O	SET P
1. MAGNATE	1. CLEANLY	1. FOXTAIL	1. TRIDENT
2. TANTRUM	2. PLIABLE	2. UPENDED	2. TROUBLE
3. HARMFUL	3. GLISTEN	3. WRECKED	3. CRUDELY
4. WARRANT	4. FLOWERY	4. PREPAID	4. CRUMPLE
5. LAUDING	5. PLUMPEN	5. BRACKET	5. ASCENDS
6. TENFOLD	6. SMARTEN	6. GRATIFY	6. ESPOUSE
7. METHANE	7. AMONGST	7. UPRAISE	7. PLAYOFF
8. AGAINST	8. UNEATEN	8. TREASON	8. ATHEISM
9. FLATTEN	9. SOFTEST	9. PREFACE	9. ZOOLOGY
10. ASTOUND	10. AVENUES	10. UPREACH	10. OVERBID

ANAGRAMS: 4-LETTER WORDS

SET A	SET B	SET C	SET D	SET E
1. ACHY	1. ROAD	1. HALT	1. WARY	1. YORE
2. PLOY	2. GALE	2. HAIL	2. BODY	2. FINE
3. IMPS	3. TOOK	3. PAIL	3. BEEN	3. FORE
4. BAWL	4. HEAP	4. MAIM	4. BEER	4. PIKE
5. BATH	5. KNOW	5. VAIN	5. KNOB	5. THEY
6. LACE	6. ZEAL	6. LOAM	6. LICE	6. THEM
7. CHAP	7. FAIR	7. PLAY	7. COOP	7. PILE
8. YACK	8. GAIN	8. MANY	8. DYED	8. WILE
9. CRAM	9. GOAL	9. RAMP	9. FLED	9. NUKE
10. LADY	10. THAN	10. ANON	10. HOED	10. FOIL

ANAGRAMS: 5-LETTER WORDS

SET F	SET G	SET H	SET I
1. AHEAD	1. CAMEL	1. MEDAL	1. NAIVE
2. DRAMA	2. CLEAT	2. RAVED	2. ALONE
3. ALARM	3. CAMEO	3. HARDY	3. VALUE
4. BADLY	4. MAGIC	4. DIVAN	4. MEANY
5. BRAID	5. MACHO	5. RADIO	5. AVERT
6. BEAUT	6. CHANT	6. VAPID	6. WATER
7. ALIBI	7. ROACH	7. NOMAD	7. AMIGO
8. GRACE	8. CLAIM	8. GREET	8. TANGO
9. LEACH	9. ACTOR	9. EATEN	9. WAGON
10. REACH	10. SUMAC	10. FLAME	10. WRATH

SET J	SET K	SET L
1. MURAL	1. CHILI	1. GORGE
2. BLEED	2. TONIC	2. GNOME
3. EMBER	3. INCUR	3. HUMOR
4. BONUS	4. TUNIC	4. HOPER
5. LUCID	5. DEMON	5. OTHER
6. DISCO	6. FOUND	6. OLIVE
7. CUPID	7. IDIOM	7. TOWEL
8. CHUTE	8. FIERY	8. YELPS
9. EVICT	9. FORGE	9. FOULS
10. COVES	10. LEFTY	10. GHOUL

ANAGRAMS: 7-LETTER WORDS

SET M	SET N	SET O	SET P
1. ABASING	1. AVOIDER	1. HAILING	1. PURSUER
2. COASTAL	2. SAVORED	2. HAULING	2. AGAINST
3. AVAILED	3. FEATHER	3. NASTILY	3. ASPHALT
4. YARDAGE	4. LEATHER	4. VARIOUS	4. ASCRIBE
5. PEASANT	5. LEAFING	5. OBEYING	5. BRIGADE
6. BONDAGE	6. TEARFUL	6. UNBUILT	6. LIBERAL
7. BEMOANS	7. GRAVIES	7. TERSELY	7. BARONET
8. CHAINED	8. AUGMENT	8. EMOTING	8. CHARIOT
9. CRANIUM	9. TONNAGE	9. WHITEST	9. FIANCEE
10. COOLANT	10. WRAPPER	10. ENVIOUS	10. TRAGEDY

SET Q	SET R	SET S	SET T
1. LEOPARD	1. STATELY	1. CONDUIT	1. KIDNEYS
2. SANDPIT	2. MANURES	2. KITCHEN	2. MEDIUMS
3. SANDLOT	3. RUFFIAN	3. COMPILE	3. DESTINY
4. DOORMAN	4. SHAMPOO	4. COEXIST	4. DIVISOR
5. VINEGAR	5. UTOPIAN	5. CONSOLE	5. REPTILE
6. GALLEON	6. SUSTAIN	6. ECONOMY	6. PENSIVE
7. PASTIME	7. DUSTBIN	7. REDEEMS	7. REQUIRE
8. EARTHLY	8. TRIBUNE	8. DEPRIVE	8. TREETOP
9. HOARSEN	9. BURIALS	9. PLUNGED	9. HIMSELF
10. PENALTY	10. INCLUDE	10. HOEDOWN	10. LENGTHY

FILL-INS

SET A	SET B	SET C	SET D
1. BISCUIT	1. CRANIUM	1. AMNESIA	1. REROUTE
2. ALMANAC	2. MAILBOX	2. COURAGE	2. FIANCEE
3. ROADWAY	3. SEASICK	3. SEAWEED	3. LIMEADE
4. HEARSAY	4. PLAGUED	4. ARDUOUS	4. TOENAIL
5. VANILLA	5. ROTUNDA	5. TEATIME	5. UNAWARE
6. ANATOMY	6. ASTOUND	6. PAROLEE	6. ESCAPEE
7. TABLOID	7. INFIDEL	7. BESIEGE	7. MATINEE
8. CAREFUL	8. PAINFUL	8. TAPIOCA	8. NAIVETE
9. CAHOOTS	9. NUMERAL	9. OATMEAL	9. FATIGUE
10. MUSICAL	10. FERTILE	10. GENUINE	10. BECAUSE

FRONT EXTENSIONS

SET A	SET B	SET C	SET D
1. MENACING	1. DOGFIGHT	1. INGROWTH	1. ESCALATE
2. PREAMBLE	2. ARTFULLY	2. PRESERVE	2. ALFALFAS
3. ARMAMENT	3. REDHEADS	3. MASTIFFS	3. PYRAMIDS
4. VITAMINS	4. POTHOLES	4. BUTTONED	4. CALAMITY
5. ROMANTIC	5. MADHOUSE	5. VERTICAL	5. ESCARGOT
6. ENDANGER	6. TWILIGHT	6. DISTINCT	6. UNLAWFUL
7. AIRBORNE	7. DECORATE	7. PLATONIC	7. RHUBARBS
8. ELICITED	8. RENOVATE	8. MORTALLY	8. SUNBATHE
9. RUBDOWNS	9. BARRAGES	9. RHETORIC	9. AIRBRUSH
10. ANTEATER	10. PORRIDGE	10. INKWELLS	10. PURCHASE

SET E	SET F	SET G	SET H
1. GODCHILD	1. SINGULAR	1. POLLUTED	1. PARAMOUR
2. SEACOAST	2. COWHANDS	2. TURMOILS	2. EMBROILS
3. HICCOUGH	3. ANTHILLS	3. WHENEVER	3. THOROUGH
4. EXECUTER	4. FATHOMED	4. CARNIVAL	4. EARPLUGS
5. HANDRAIL	5. PUSHOVER	5. LINOLEUM	5. MARSHALL
6. SAWDUSTS	6. PERIODIC	6. REMOVALS	6. CONSOLED
7. REMEMBER	7. WEEKLONG	7. JEOPARDY	7. CONTEMPT
8. THIEVERY	8. PENKNIFE	8. WHIPLASH	8. PROVERBS
9. BURGLARY	9. AIRLIFTS	9. VIBRATOS	9. ANYWHERE
10. EMIGRATE	10. FURLOUGH	10. SACREDLY	10. DESTROYS

17 DIAGRAMS: Finding Plays Over-the-Board

PLACE THE WORD

Using the following four diagrams, locate where on the board the given word will score the most points. You may sometimes use tiles already on the board to spell the given word. For example, in Diagram 17-1, WAPITI will require all six letters beginning at 14B but only five at E2 to the I at 7E; however, WAPITI will earn more points at a third spot. As a hint, we show you how many points the word can score. You should refer to the list of two-letter words on pages 19–20 to verify any potential parallel plays.

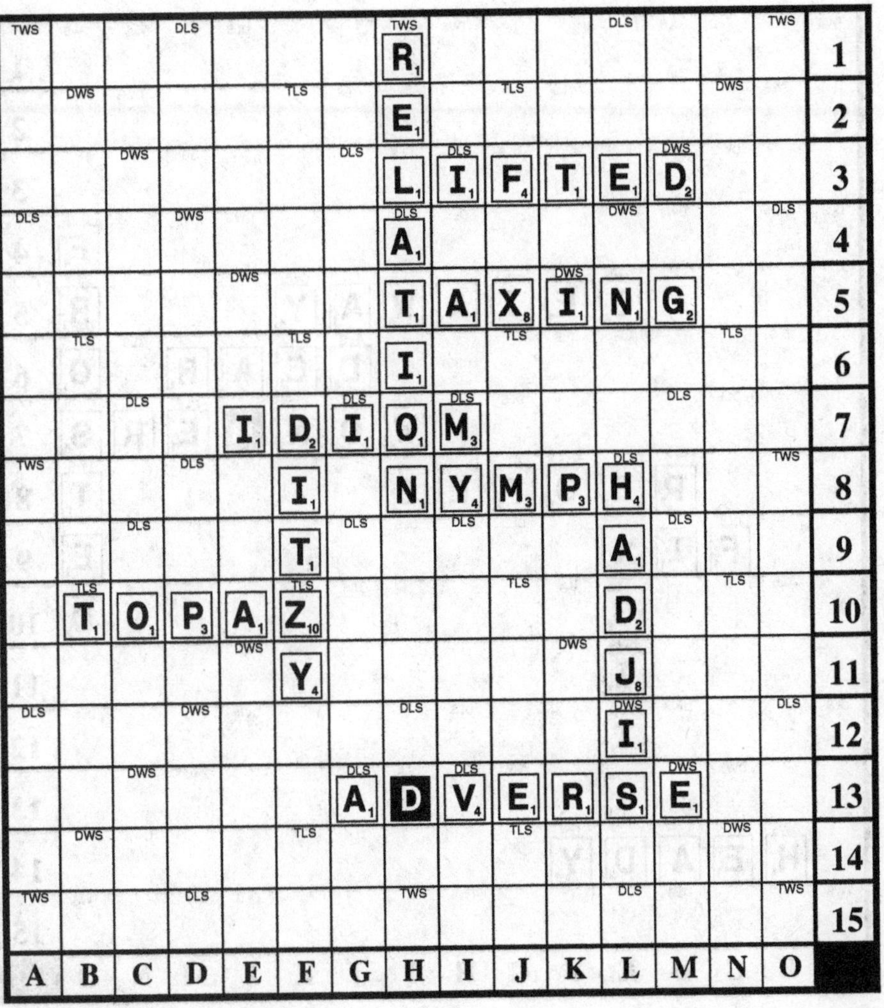

DIAGRAM 17-1

Where on Diagram 17-1 can the following words be played for the most points? The answers are on page 191.

Time limit: 25 minutes
Average score: 2 correct *Good score:* 3 correct *Expert score:* 4 correct

1. L E O N E 23 ___________
2. W A P I T I 38 ___________
3. O I D I A 31 ___________
4. V O D K A 36 ___________

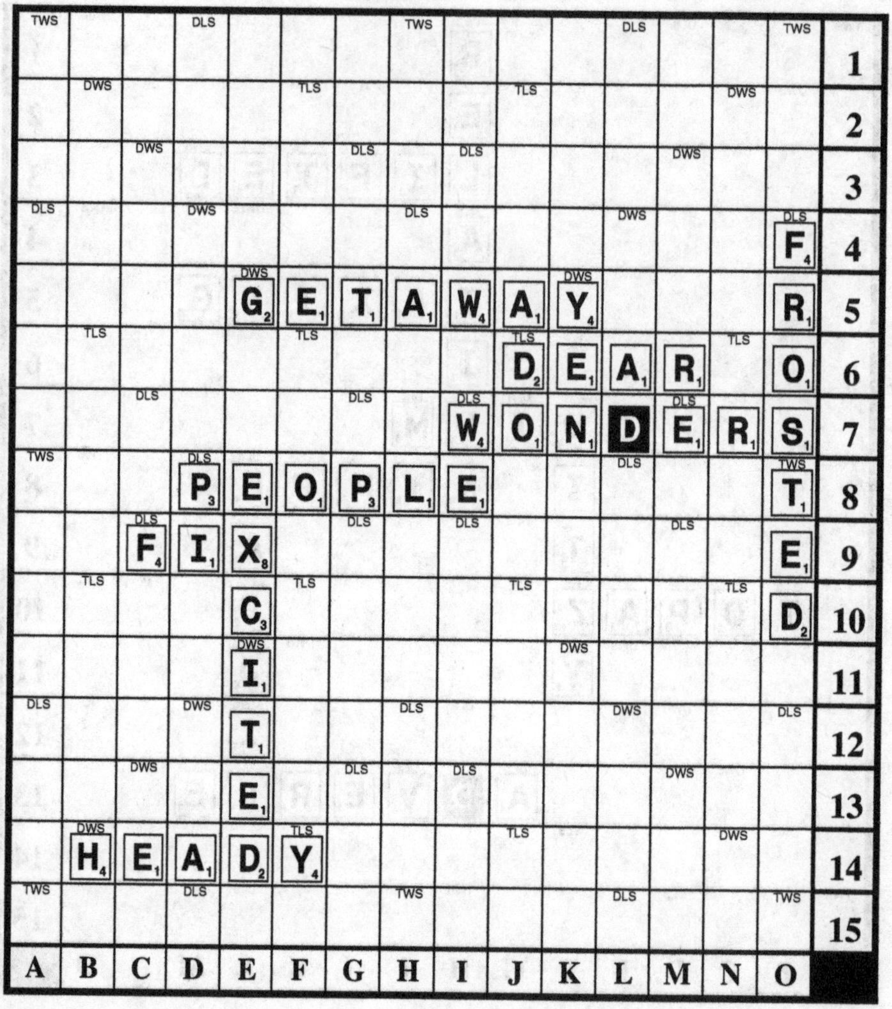
GETAWAY
DEAR
WONDERS
PEOPLE
FIX
CITE
HEADY
FROSTED

DIAGRAM 17-2

Where on Diagram 17-2 can the following words be played for the most points? The answers are on page 191.

Time limit: 25 minutes
Average score: 2 correct *Good score:* 3 correct *Expert score:* 4 correct

1. GAMUT 30 ______
2. ASIDE 23 ______
3. HERD 42 ______
4. BLOOM 34 ______

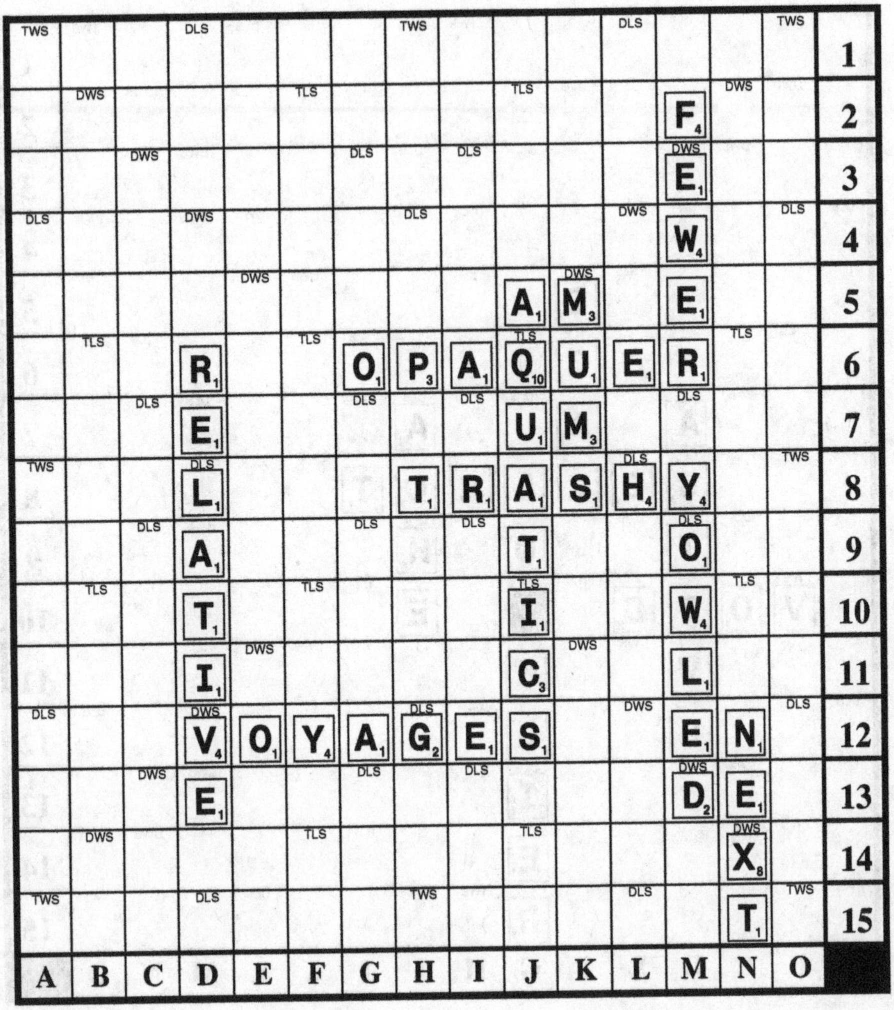

DIAGRAM 17-3

Where on Diagram 17-3 can the following words be played for the most points? The answers are on page 191.

Time limit: 30 minutes
Average score: 2 correct *Good score:* 3 correct *Expert score:* 4 correct

1. B I O 36 ________
2. D O D O 34 ________
3. F O L D 36 ________
4. C A R O M 39 ________

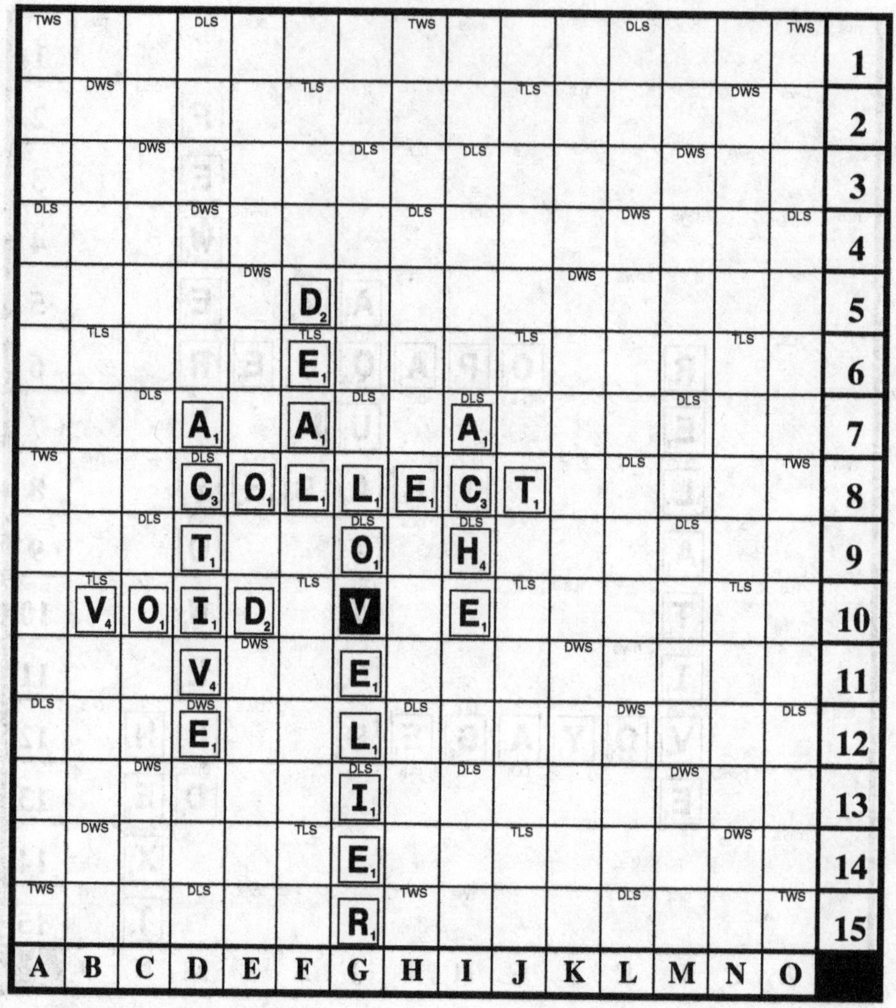

DIAGRAM 17-4

Where on Diagram 17-4 can the following words be played for the most points? The answers are on page 191.

Time limit: 30 minutes
Average score: 2 correct *Good score:* 3 correct *Expert score:* 4 correct

1. LITRE 33 __________
2. FRAME 42 __________
3. HELP 34 __________
4. UNTIL 20 __________

BONUS SQUARES

In each of the following four diagrams, you have different racks and are asked to find the highest-scoring common-word play that covers two specified types of bonus squares. As a hint, we show you the score you're looking for.

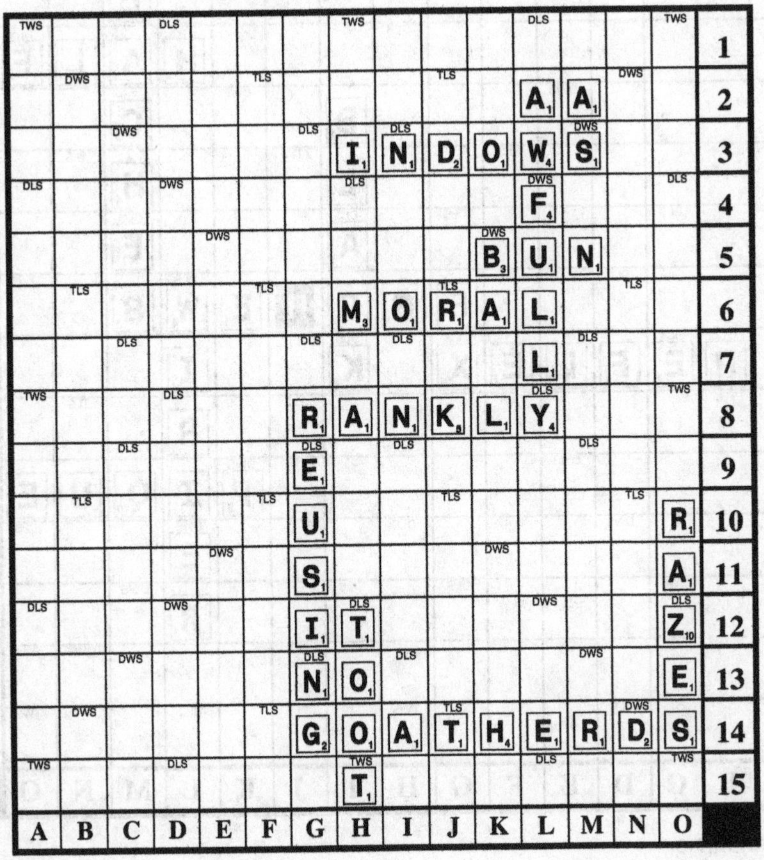

A A
I N D O W S
F
B U N
M O R A L
L
R A N K L Y
E
U
S
I T
N O
G O A T H E R D S
T
R
A
Z
E
1 2 3 4 5 6 7 8 9 10 11 12 13 14 15
A B C D E F G H I J K L M N O

DIAGRAM 17-5

Time limit: 30 minutes
Average score: 2 correct *Good score:* 3 correct *Expert score:* 4 correct

1.	A D E E F M U	53	Find the high-scoring TLS-TLS.	______
2.	B F L N P R T	36	Find the high-scoring TWS-DLS.	______
3.	B E F H L O S	39	Find the high-scoring DWS-DLS.	______
4.	A B C C G I O	23	Find the high-scoring TLS-TLS.	______

The answers are on page 191.

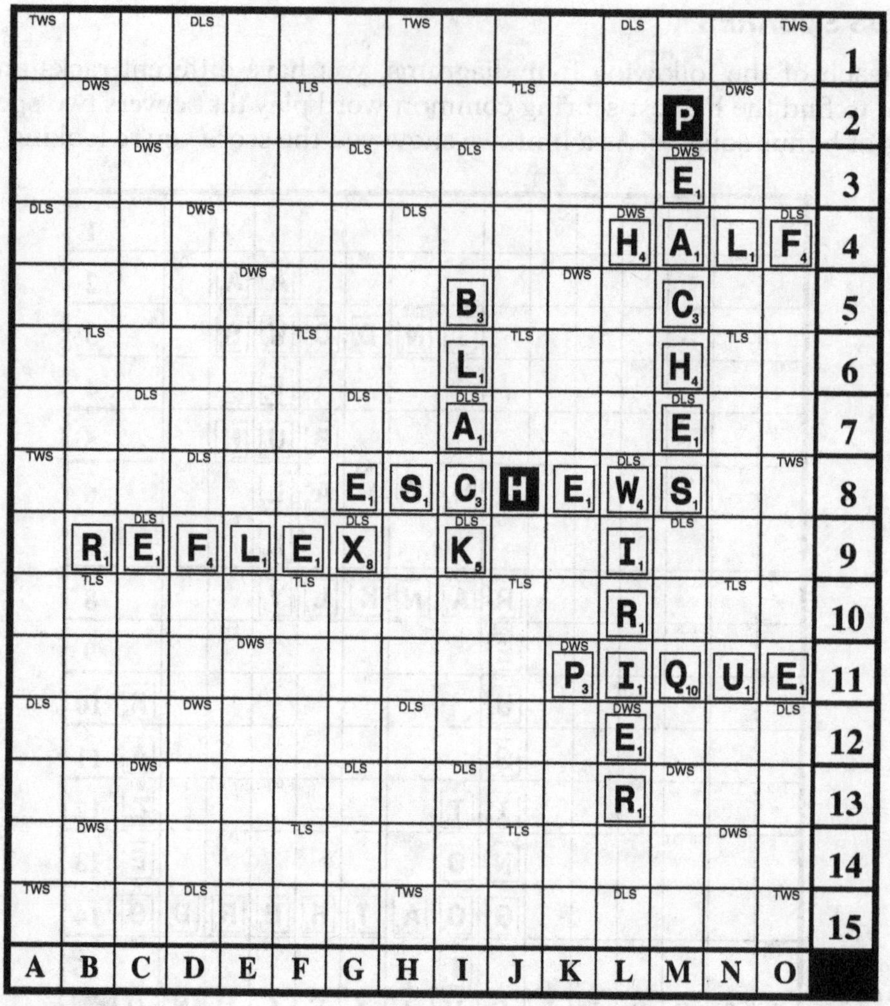

DIAGRAM 17-6

Time limit: 30 minutes
Average score: 2 correct *Good score:* 3 correct *Expert score:* 4 correct

1. AJLNOPU	32	Find the high-scoring TLS-TLS.	________
2. ELNOPUZ	52	Find the high-scoring TWS-DLS.	________
3. AGLMPRV	51	Find the high-scoring TWS-DLS.	________
4. EGLMRTU	48	Find the high-scoring DWS-DWS.	________

The answers are on page 191.

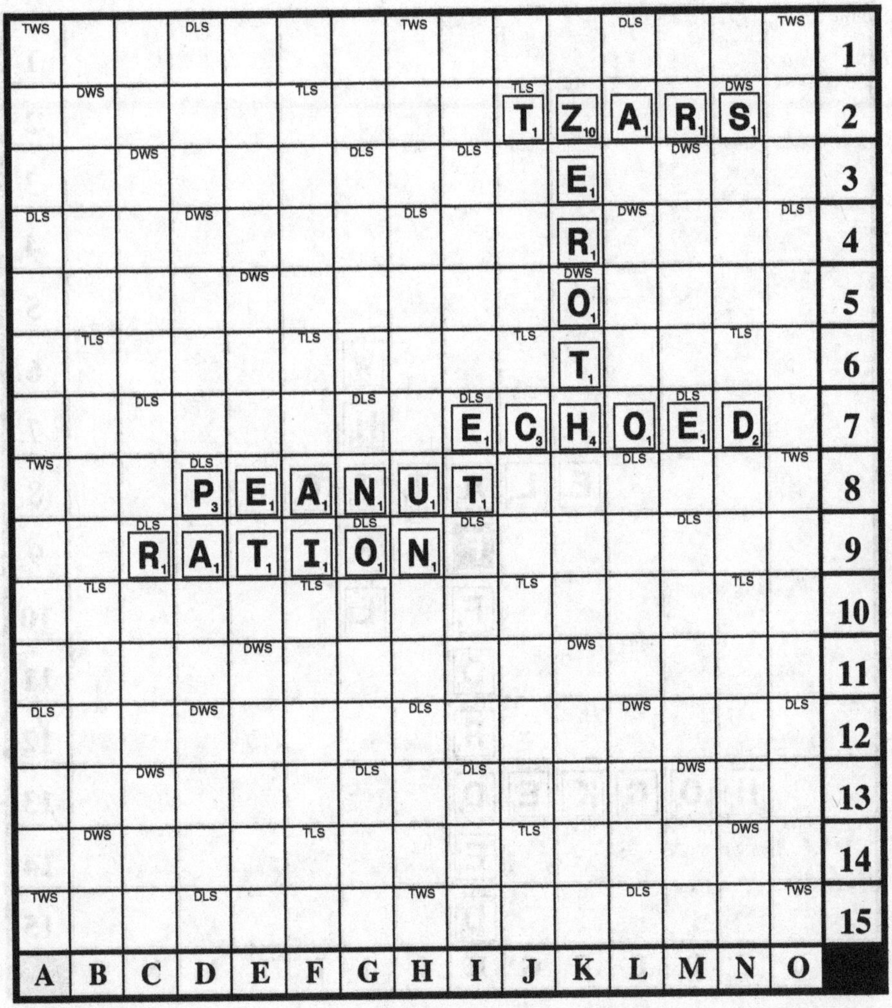
TZARS
E
R
O
T
ECHOED
PEANUT
RATION
A B C D E F G H I J K L M N O
1 2 3 4 5 6 7 8 9 10 11 12 13 14 15

DIAGRAM 17-7

Time limit: 30 minutes
Average score: 2 correct *Good score:* 3 correct *Expert score:* 4 correct

1.	A C H L O T V	34	Find the high-scoring TLS-TLS.	________
2.	B C E F G I M	34	Find the high-scoring DLS-DWS.	________
3.	D K L O P W Y	48	Find the high-scoring DLS-TWS.	________
4.	B E F G I L N	48	Find the high-scoring DWS-DWS.	________

The answers are on page 191.

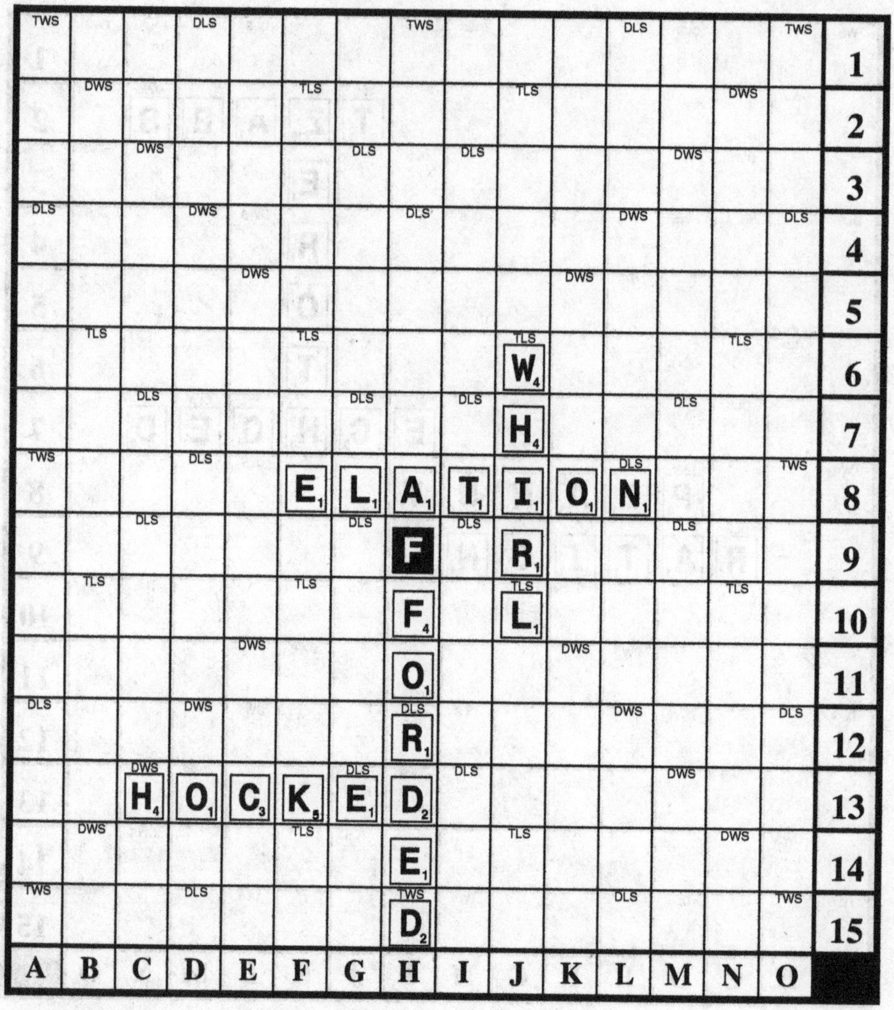
ELATION
WHIRL
FFORDED
HOCKED

DIAGRAM 17-8

Time limit: 30 minutes
Average score: 2 correct *Good score:* 3 correct *Expert score:* 4 correct

1. A A D F H I U 28 Find the high-scoring TLS-TLS. ________
2. E G H M O R W 45 Find the high-scoring DWS-DLS. ________
3. A C E G H S V 49 Find the high-scoring TLS-DWS. ________
4. E E F M R R S 48 Find the high-scoring DWS-DWS. ________

The answers are on page 191.

Your Move!

In an actual game situation, you probably won't be given any clues as to what your best play is. With that in mind, the remaining diagrams present typical game situations and ask you to find the best common-word play.

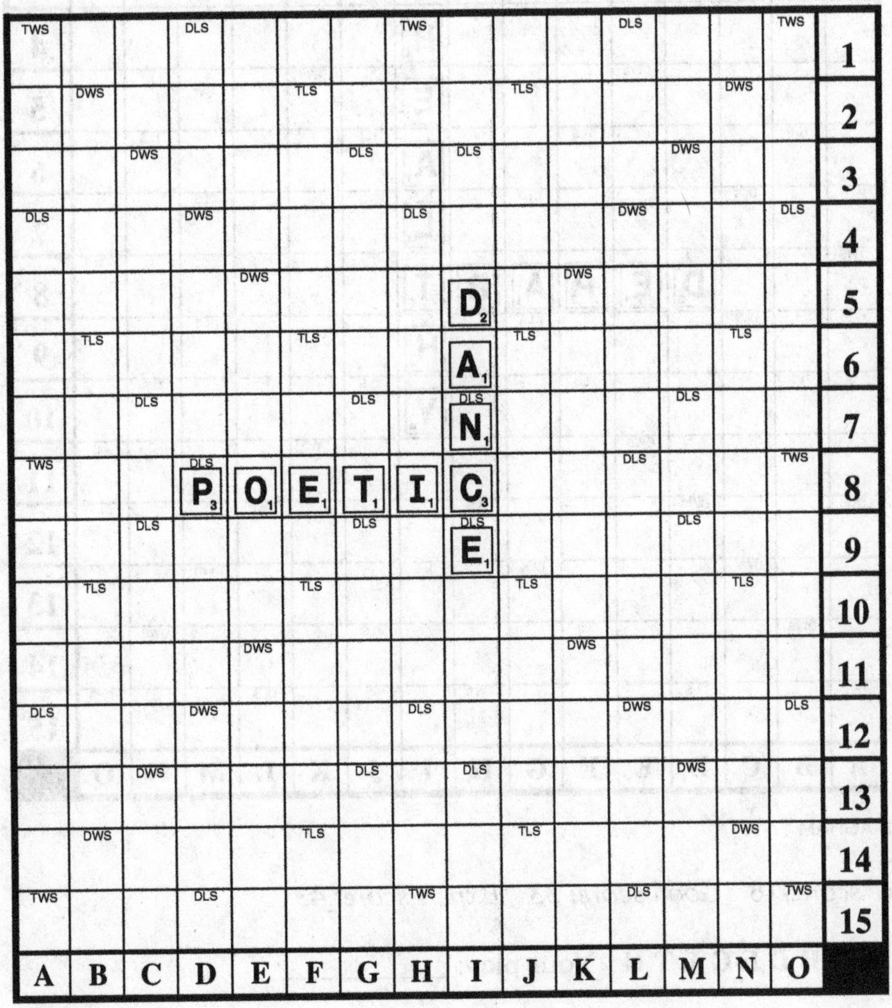
D
A
N
P O E T I C
E
A B C D E F G H I J K L M N O
1 2 3 4 5 6 7 8 9 10 11 12 13 14 15

DIAGRAM 17-9

Average score: 22 *Good score:* 29 *Expert score:* 40

Your rack: **A D M N O R U** Your play: ___________

The answer is on page 191.

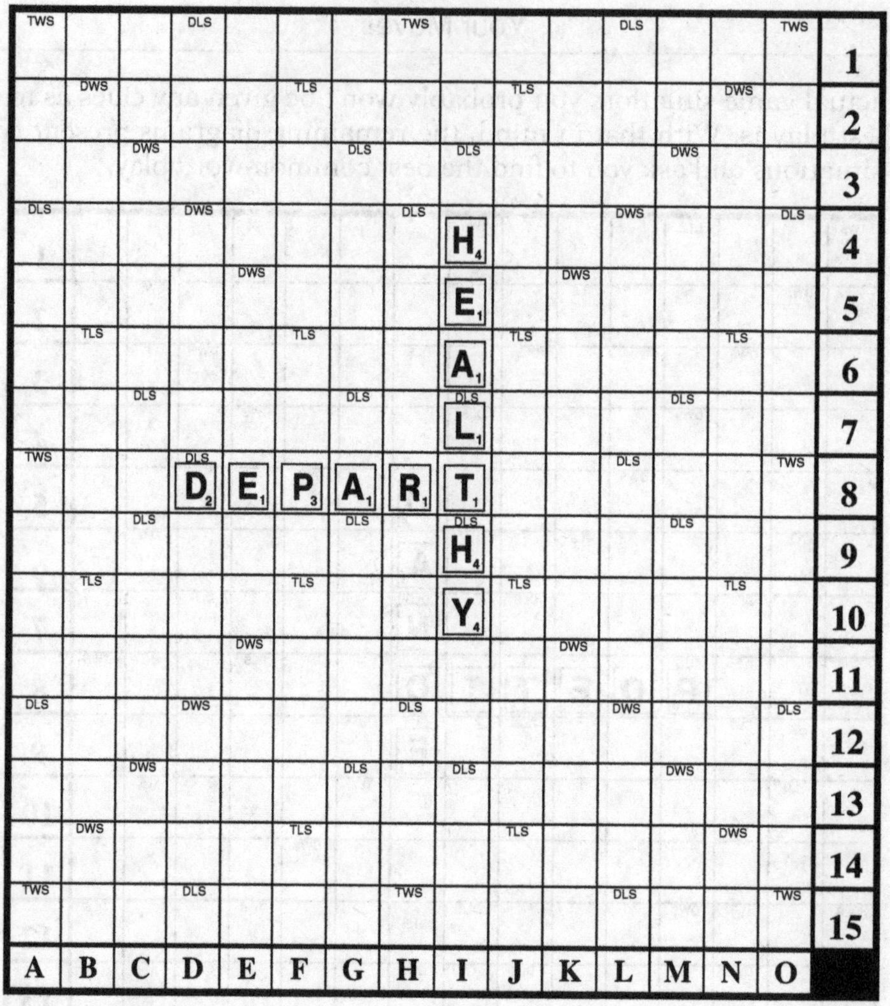

DEPART
HEALTHY
TWS
DWS
TLS
DLS
1
2
3
4
5
6
7
8
9
10
11
12
13
14
15
A B C D E F G H I J K L M N O

DIAGRAM 17-10

Average score: 16 *Good score:* 33 *Expert score:* 43

Your rack: **B D E G L T U** Your play: ________

The answer is on page 191.

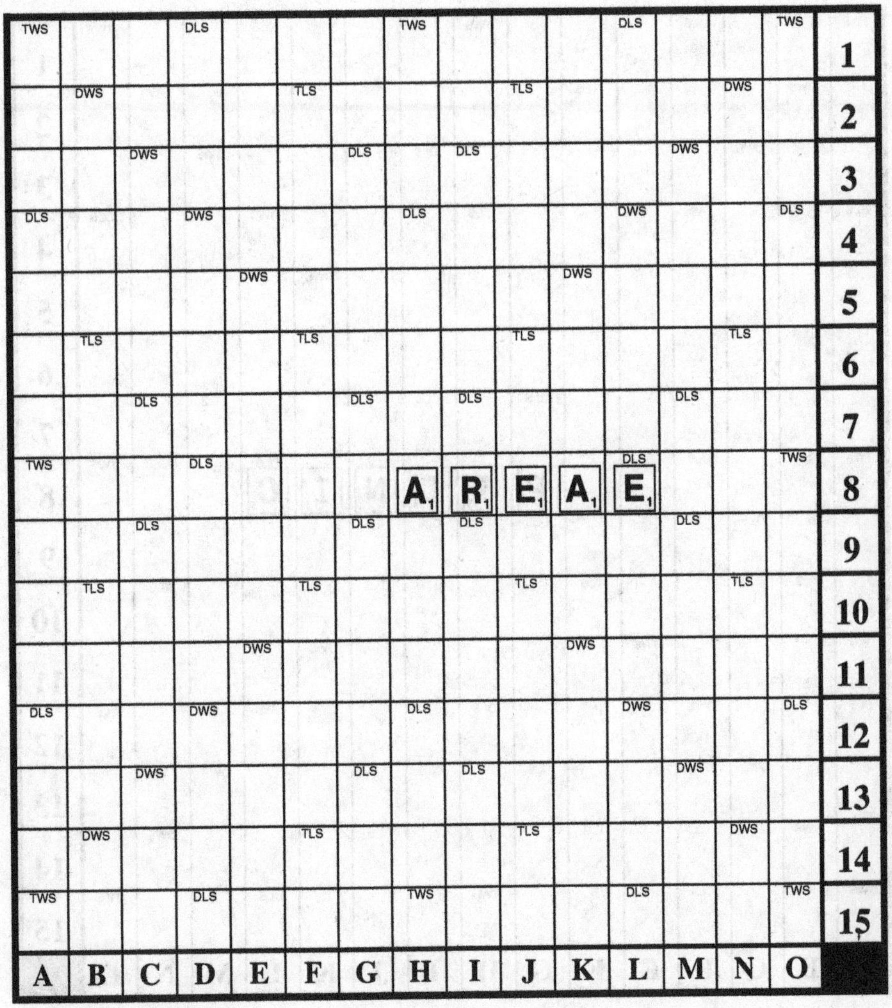
A R E A E
1 2 3 4 5 6 7 8 9 10 11 12 13 14 15
A B C D E F G H I J K L M N O

DIAGRAM 17-11

Average score: 20 *Good score:* 24 *Expert score:* 29

Your rack: **A F H L O R T** Your play: ____________

The answer is on page 191.

PICNIC

DIAGRAM 17-12

Average score: 32 *Good score:* 34 *Expert score:* 60

Your rack: **D E I K L Q U** Your play: ________

The answer is on page 191.

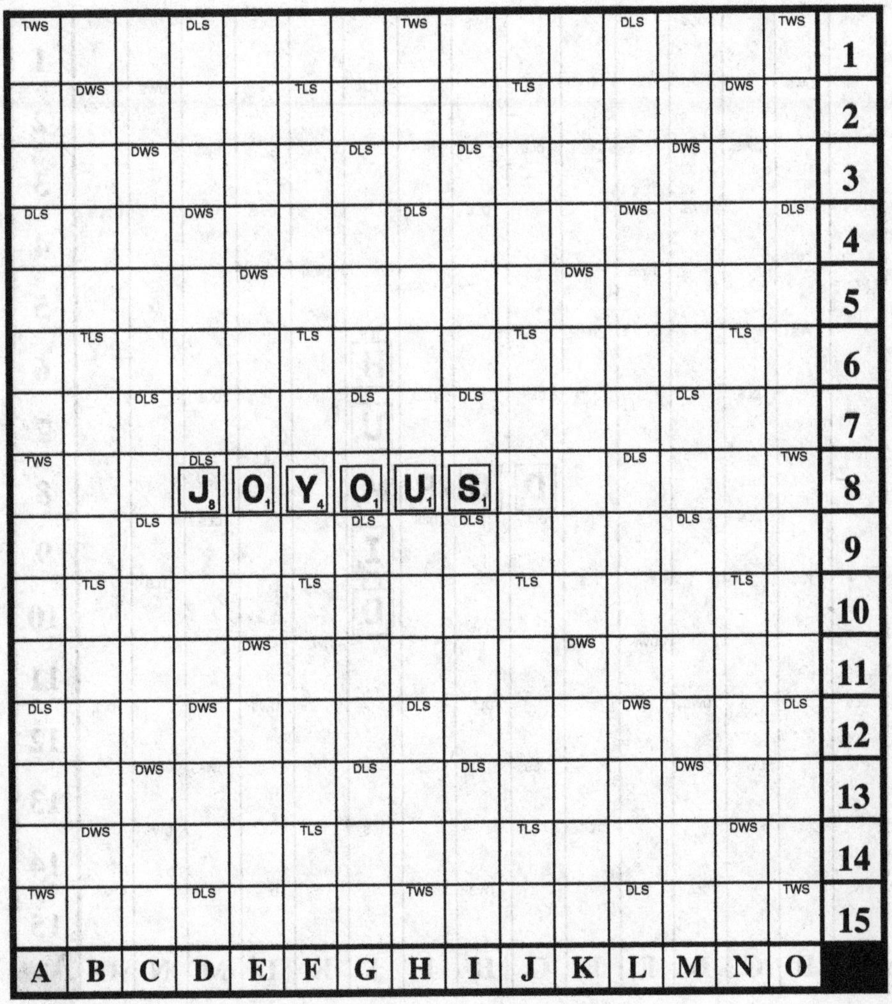
J O Y O U S

DIAGRAM 17-13

Average score: 30 *Good score:* 34 *Expert score:* 48

Your rack: **B D E L M O W** Your play: ___________

The answer is on page 192.

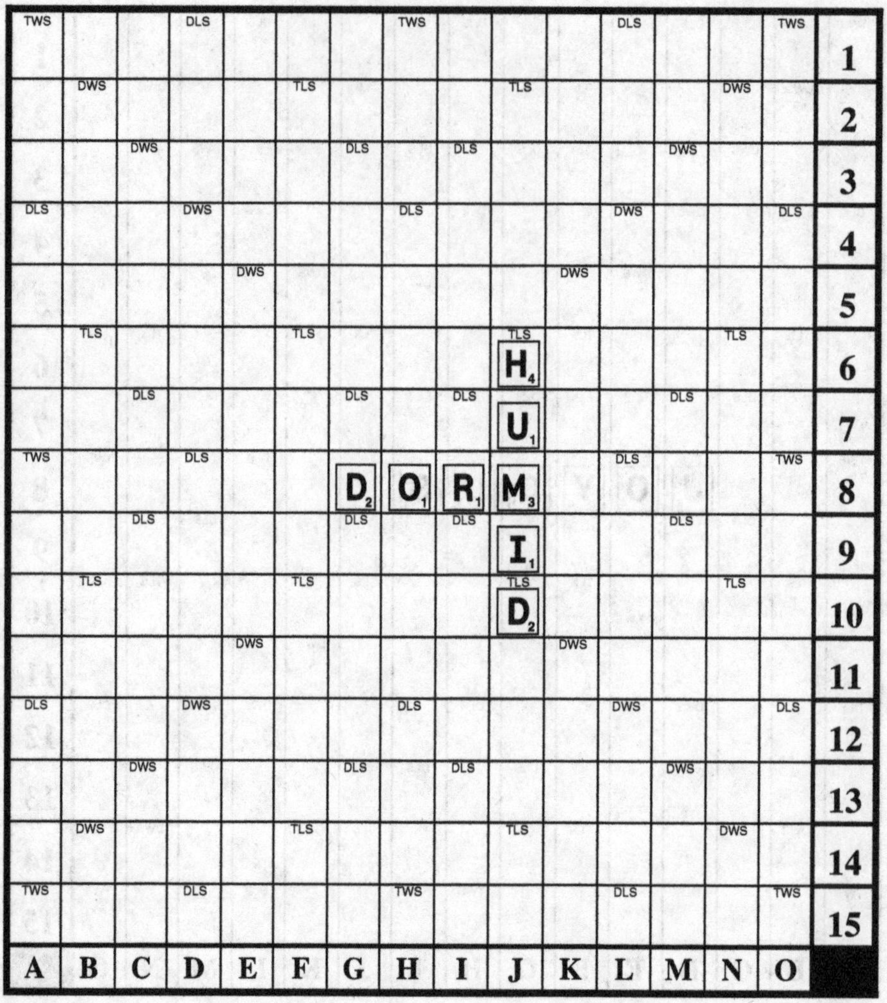
TWS
DLS
DWS
TLS
D
O
R
H
U
M
I
D
1 2 3 4 5 6 7 8 9 10 11 12 13 14 15
A B C D E F G H I J K L M N O

DIAGRAM 17-14

Average score: 14 *Good score:* 19 *Expert score:* 48

Your rack: **C E I O R T Y** Your play: __________

The answer is on page 192.

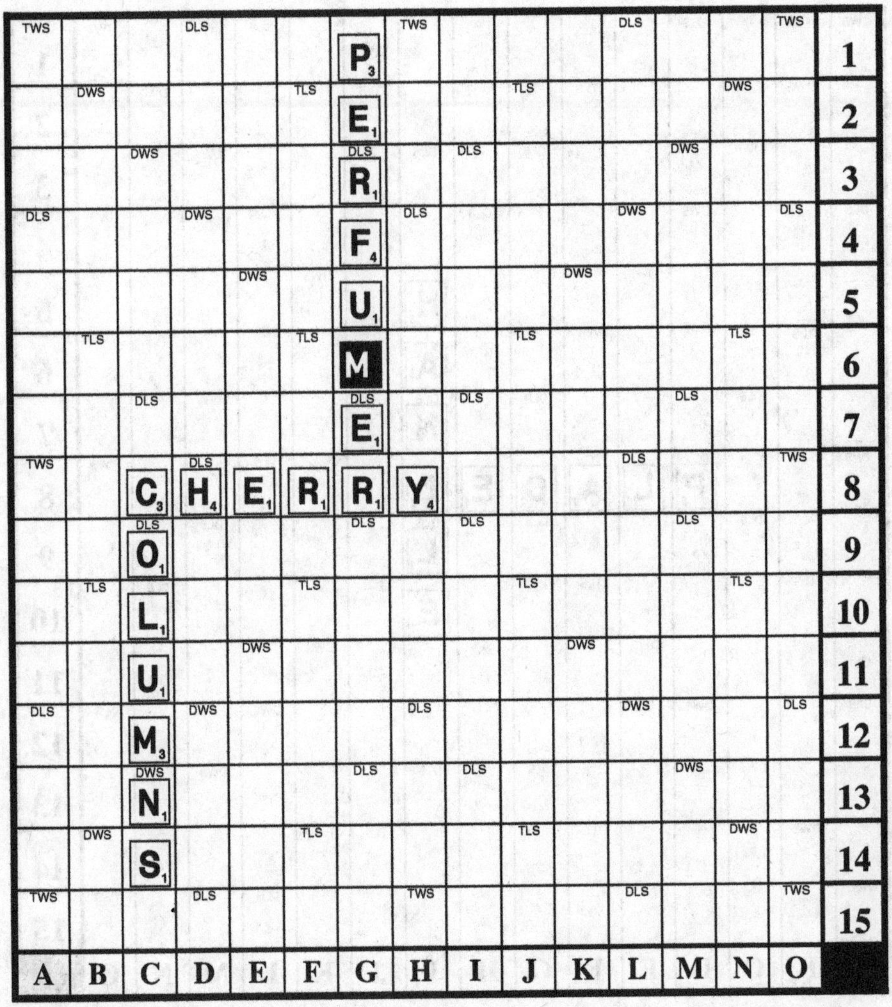
TWS
DLS
DWS
TLS
P3
E1
R1
F4
U1
M
E1
C3
H4
E1
R1
R1
Y4
O1
L1
U1
M3
N1
S1
A B C D E F G H I J K L M N O
1 2 3 4 5 6 7 8 9 10 11 12 13 14 15

DIAGRAM 17-15

Average score: 30 *Good score:* 54 *Expert score:* 60

Your rack: **E I K M N P U** Your play: ___________

The answer is on page 192.

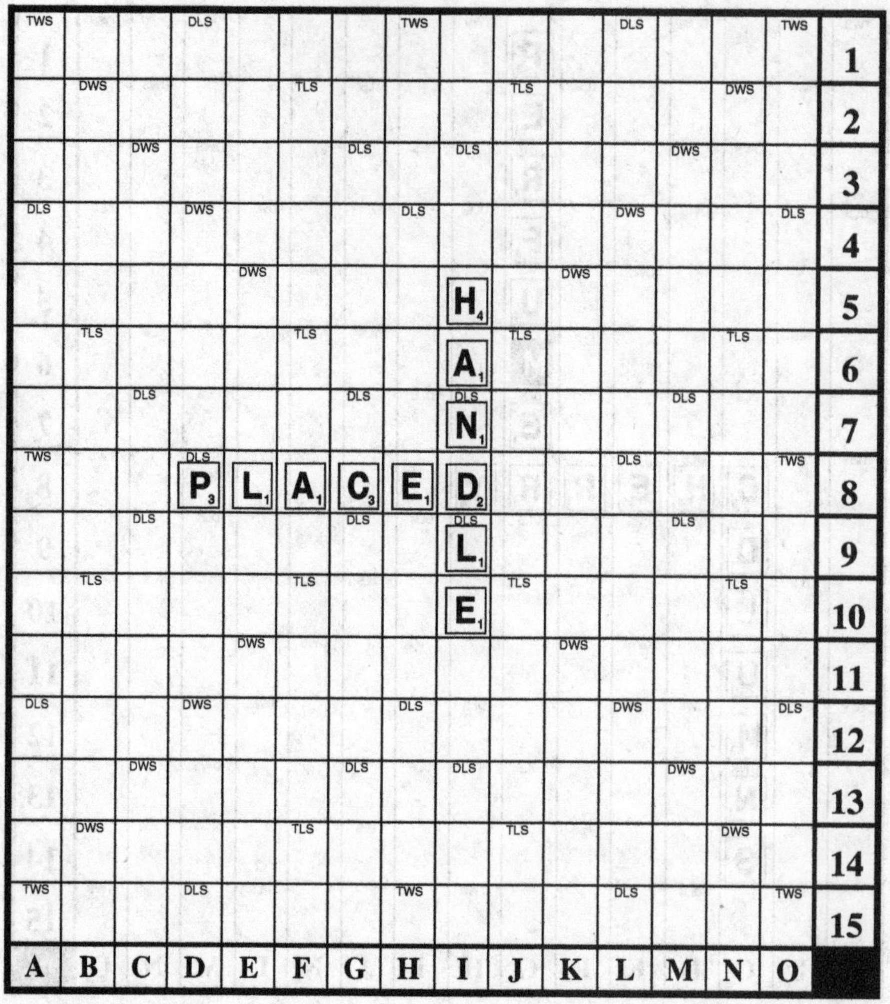

TWS
DLS
DWS
TLS
P
L
A
C
E
D
H
N
1
2
3
4
5
6
7
8
9
10
11
12
13
14
15
A B C D E F G H I J K L M N O

DIAGRAM 17-16

Average score: 29 *Good score:* 40 *Expert score:* 38

Your rack: **A E I M O T V** Your play: __________

The answer is on page 192.

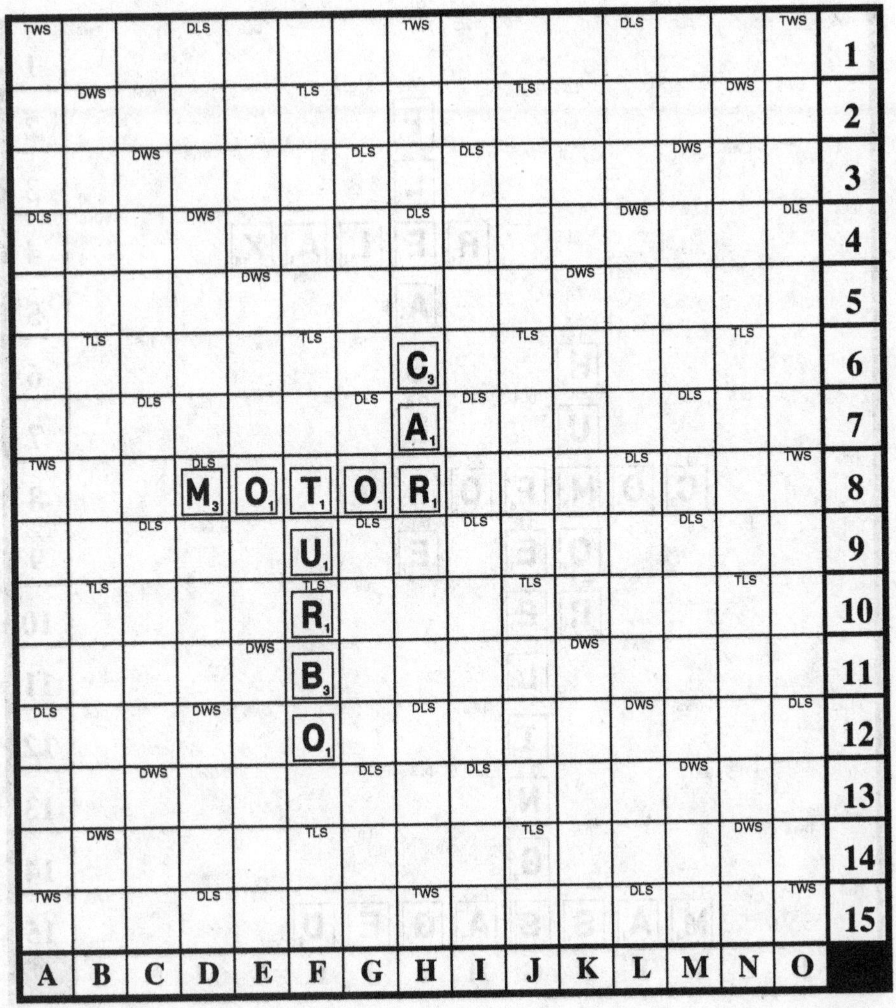
M O T O R
C A R
T U R B O
A B C D E F G H I J K L M N O
1 2 3 4 5 6 7 8 9 10 11 12 13 14 15

DIAGRAM 17-17

Average score: 24 *Good score:* 32 *Expert score:* 72

Your rack: **C E J L O S T** Your play: ________

The answer is on page 192.

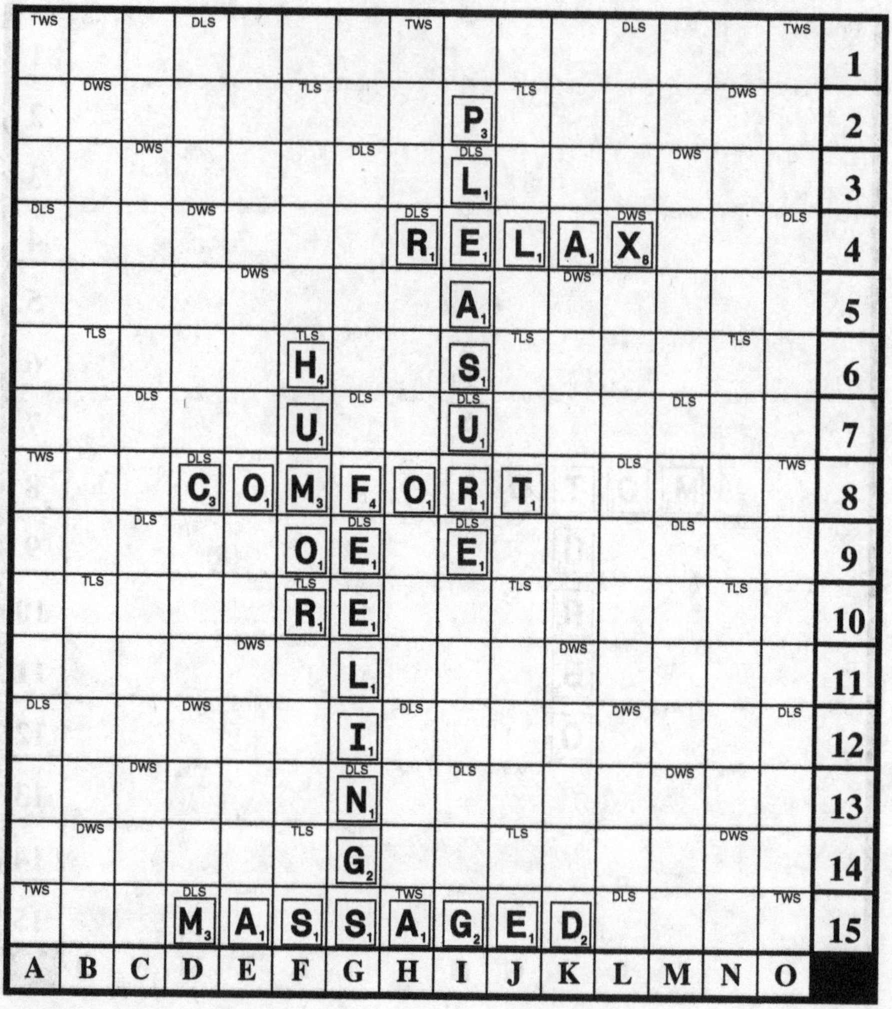
RELAX
PLEASURE
HUMOR
COMFORT
FEELING
MASSAGED
A B C D E F G H I J K L M N O
1 2 3 4 5 6 7 8 9 10 11 12 13 14 15

DIAGRAM 17-18

Average score: 28 *Good score:* 40 *Expert score:* 57

Your rack: **D E H L N O R** Your play: ____________

The answer is on page 192.

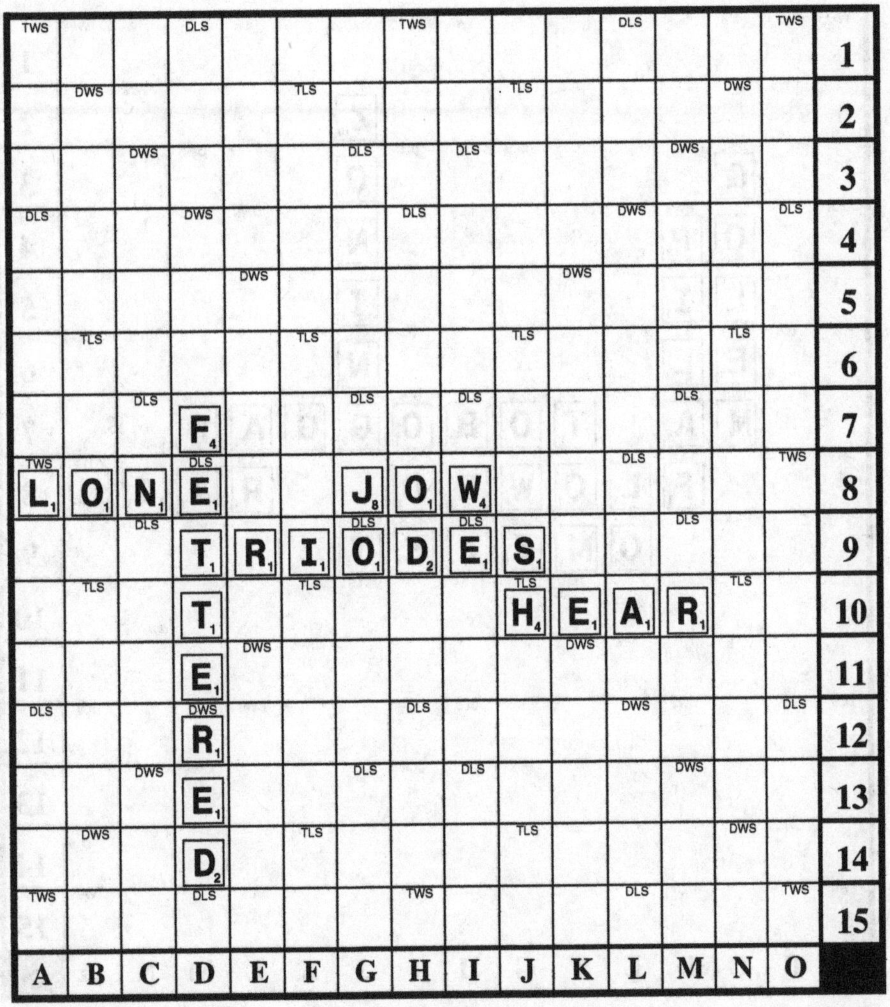
LONE
JOW
TRIODES
HEAR
FETTERED
A B C D E F G H I J K L M N O
1 2 3 4 5 6 7 8 9 10 11 12 13 14 15

DIAGRAM 17-19

Average score: 25 *Good score:* 33 *Expert score:* 39

Your rack: **A B D I L L S** Your play: ________

The answer is on page 192.

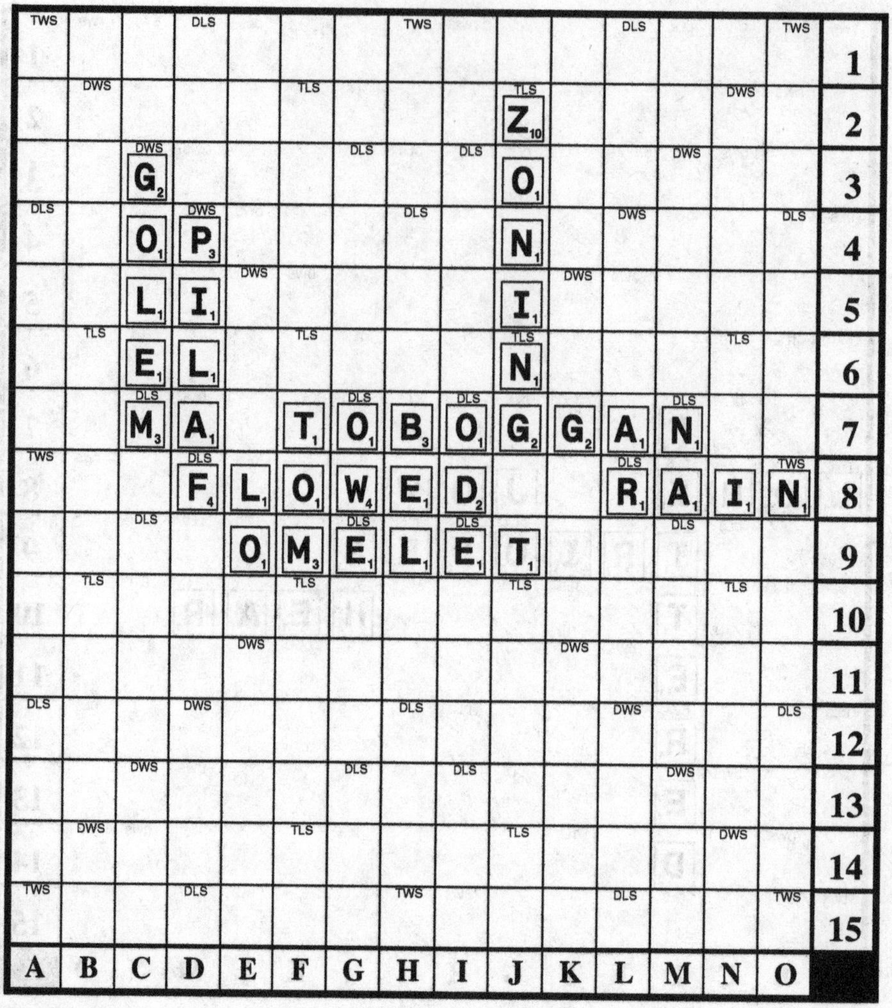

DIAGRAM 17-20

Average score: 20 *Good score:* 30 *Expert score:* 40

Your rack: **G I M N N S U** Your play: ________

The answer is on page 192.

We invite you to try the more demanding puzzles in chapter 18. Those of you who spend time with them will have the opportunity both to learn new words and to develop a better understanding of what is possible in the world of SCRABBLE game puzzles. Besides providing the familiar fill-ins, eight- and nine-letter anagrams, and high-scoring plays, we include a contest from *SCRABBLE News* that may keep you busy for hours, as well as several innovative puzzles designed to improve your anagramming skills.

ANSWERS: CHAPTER 17

DIAGRAM 17-1: 1. M9; 2. 8A; 3. 2J; 4. H11

DIAGRAM 17-2: 1. 4D; 2. 15F; 3. 15A; 4. 6B

DIAGRAM 17-3: 1. O13; 2. L1; 3. L12; 4. N1

DIAGRAM 17-4: 1. H11; 2. A8; 3. F11; 4. J6

DIAGRAM 17-5: 1. DEFAME F6; 2. FLIP H1; 3. SHELF 4D; 4. CUBIC 10F

DIAGRAM 17-6: 1. JOURNAL B6; 2. ZONE 8A; 3. REVAMP O10; 4. GRUMBLE 5E

DIAGRAM 17-7: 1. HAVOC B6; 2. FAME L1; 3. PLOY 8L; 4. FLEETING E5

DIAGRAM 17-8: 1. AHEAD 14F; 2. WHOM 12A; 3. CHASE B10; 4. REMORSE 11E

DIAGRAM 17-9: RANDOM H1 40

DIAGRAM 17-10: BUGLED H10 43 or BUDGET H10 43

DIAGRAM 17-11: FORTH 7H 29

DIAGRAM 17-12: PICNICKED 8G 60

DIAGRAM 17-13: BLOOMED E5 48

DIAGRAM 17-14: DORMITORY 8G 48

DIAGRAM 17-15: PUMPKIN 1D 60

DIAGRAM 17-16: There is a choice of several excellent plays: VIOLATE E5 40, MOTIVE H10 40, or MOVIE H1 38. We prefer MOVIE because its AT leave is better than the M leave after VIOLATE. Plus, it blocks the TWS square at H1, preventing your opponent from using it. If MOVIE were 3 points less, we would play VIOLATE. Furthermore, MOTIVE keeps the board wide open, allowing many more scoring chances. We prefer MOVIE to reduce the opponent's opportunities.

DIAGRAM 17-17: OBJECTS 11E 72

DIAGRAM 17-18: HONORED E5 57

DIAGRAM 17-19: ODDBALLS H8 39

DIAGRAM 17-20: LINGUINIS 5C 40

18 TOUGHIES! Puzzles That Are Seriously Fun!

Far-Sight***

In each case use only the letters of the given rack to fill in the blanks below to form thirty common words. The answers are on page 229.

Time limit per set: 30 minutes
Average score: 3 correct *Good score:* 5 correct *Expert score:* 8 correct

Rack: **A C L N O R W**

SET A

1. P __ __ T __ __ I __
2. V __ __ C __ __ I __
3. B __ __ __ A __ __ E
4. __ A __ E __ D __ __
5. __ __ __ __ I __ ET
6. __ U __ I __ __ __ Y
7. __ __ U __ __ HE __
8. __ O __ __ TI __ __
9. F __ __ ME __ __ __
10. P __ __ __ A __ __ E

SET B

1. B __ __ __ H __ __ D
2. __ __ __ K __ O __ D
3. __ B __ __ __ MA __
4. H __ __ MO __ __ __
5. L __ __ D __ __ __ D
6. M __ T __ __ __ __ Y
7. M __ __ O __ __ I __
8. N __ __ G __ __ __ E
9. __ __ __ D __ M __ Y
10. T __ __ E __ __ __ T

SET C

1. __ __ __ __ __ E __ Y
2. __ __ __ __ __ D __ Y
3. I __ __ __ __ __ __ D
4. F __ __ __ __ __ E __
5. __ __ __ P __ __ __ D
6. __ __ __ __ B __ L __
7. __ __ __ __ __ DE __
8. __ __ __ __ ME __ __
9. __ I __ __ __ T __ __
10. __ __ __ E __ __ __ K

Anagrams

Each of the seventy words below has exactly one very common word as an anagram. How many of them can you find? The answers are on page 229.

Time limit per set: 30 minutes
Average score: 3 correct *Good score:* 5 correct *Expert score:* 8 correct

SET A***	SET B****	SET C****	SET D****
1. ADVANCES	1. ARMONICA	1. URANYLIC	1. IMAGINER
2. TRAPPEAN	2. DRAINAGE	2. DEMERSAL	2. HAPPIEST
3. BIOCIDAL	3. HOGMANAY	3. SULFATED	3. OXHEARTS
4. DECIMATE	4. AMANITIN	4. DISHWARE	4. SARKIEST
5. DECIGRAM	5. FIREBOAT	5. HANDOUTS	5. TALEYSIM
6. DEACONRY	6. AMBIVERT	6. GENERATE	6. ALUNITES
7. CHIVAREE	7. CRATONIC	7. OVERLATE	7. VENATION
8. MINACITY	8. EXCLAIMS	8. EARSTONE	8. SENORITA
9. ADHEREND	9. SAUCIEST	9. MEDALING	9. WORKMATE
10. TARRAGON	10. RUSTICAL	10. UNMARRED	10. PSORALEN

SET E****	SET F****	SET G****
1. TOLUIDES	1. HUNTSMAN	1. CRISPENS
2. INSUREDS	2. ROYALIST	2. ORCHITIS
3. EINSTEIN	3. DEBRIDES	3. REFUNDED
4. GUNFIRES	4. BLOTTIER	4. DISPLODE
5. HEISTING	5. DEMOTICS	5. OVERIDLE
6. KINGLIER	6. CENTROID	6. DESPITES
7. EMPTINGS	7. CLEVEITE	7. FINISHED
8. ORNITHES	8. TECHIEST	8. PIEDFORT
9. POLEMIST	9. ISOCLINE	9. EPHEDRAS
10. ROARINGS	10. COTERIES	10. DUODENAL

Rearrange the letters in each two-word phrase below to spell a common eight- or nine-letter word. The answers are on page 229.

Time limit per set: 30 minutes
Average score: 3 correct *Good score:* 5 correct *Expert score:* 8 correct

SET H***	SET I***	SET J****
1. LAVA GNAT	1. SLID HOME	1. COSY DRIVE
2. TEA MYTHS	2. OPEN LATE	2. CLAY FAULT
3. TAUT DIET	3. USED CARS	3. EARTH WIND
4. BEST NAME	4. HOLD PINS	4. OLIO STAIN
5. FIND BEER	5. LEG ZONES	5. DAY REPORT
6. ENEMY ORC	6. COME RIDE	6. HEAR SCORE
7. SOUL MICE	7. LARGE HUT	7. DEEP RIDGE
8. LION CAMP	8. LIVE FAST	8. LIMP AURAS
9. BEAN SOUP	9. ACE PILOT	9. TIRE CATCH
10. RING LADY	10. CHIC NAME	10. ART POSTER

Blanagrams

Sometimes, by pairing one word with another that has *almost* the same letters, you can also remember more easily the words. "Blanagram" gets its name from the use of a blank to transform one word into another and was coined by 1997 World SCRABBLE Championship winner Joel Sherman (NY).

Imagine two words for which there is only one different letter. For example: Change the U of BUOYAGE to a P and you spell PAGEBOY. So, BUOYAGE and PAGEBOY are blanagrams of each other. In the following sets, we give you the first word and tell you which letter to drop and which to add in order to find one of its blanagrams. All of the answers (see pages 229–30) are common words. How many can you find?

7-Letter Words

SET A

WORD	MINUS/PLUS
1. UNITAGE	- N + F = ?
2. HAGRODE	- G + R = ?
3. CODEINA	- C + D = ?
4. ISOTACH	- I + M = ?
5. THERIAC	- T + V = ?
6. DATURIC	- I + S = ?
7. MACHREE	- R + T = ?
8. ABIOSES	- O + D = ?
9. SANDBUR	- R + H = ?
10. DIABOLO	- O + T = ?

SET B

WORD	MINUS/PLUS
1. TANAGER	- R + P = ?
2. MANSARD	- S + B = ?
3. CALATHI	- H + P = ?
4. AIRBOAT	- I + C = ?
5. AMBARIS	- S + D = ?
6. CITHARA	- I + E = ?
7. DIORAMA	- I + T = ?
8. AMREETA	- E + U = ?
9. LAMINAR	- N + A = ?
10. OBLASTI	- T + H = ?

SET C

WORD	MINUS/PLUS
1. AMIDONE	- E + D = ?
2. LINEAGE	- I + T = ?
3. PHASEAL	- A + Y = ?
4. VULGATE	- L + S = ?
5. ESTUARY	- Y + E = ?
6. ECBOLIC	- O + Y = ?
7. BIOTECH	- O + W = ?
8. DEBRIDE	- D + N = ?
9. ZEBROID	- Z + L = ?
10. BURSEED	- E + O = ?

SET D

WORD	MINUS/PLUS
1. DEHISCE	- H + T = ?
2. CLONKED	- N + W = ?
3. PERCOID	- I + U = ?
4. CONIDIA	- A + T = ?
5. LECTERN	- R + G = ?
6. FRESHED	- F + U = ?
7. ELOINED	- O + V = ?
8. EMEROID	- I + F = ?
9. ERODENT	- T + S = ?
10. SOUGHED	- G + I = ?

SET E

WORD	MINUS/PLUS
1. TERGITE	- G + P = ?
2. SVELTER	- T + O = ?
3. UMPTEEN	- N + A = ?
4. TYPESET	- Y + M = ?
5. PIEFORT	- P + F = ?
6. SWITHLY	- W + S = ?
7. THIONYL	- I + M = ?
8. SPUTNIK	- U + E = ?
9. SURTOUT	- U + I = ?
10. SANTOUR	- A + I = ?

8-Letter Words

SET A

	WORD	MINUS/PLUS					
1.	SEABOARD	-	S	+	L	=	?
2.	ARBALEST	-	T	+	E	=	?
3.	PLACENTA	-	T	+	Y	=	?
4.	ACAULINE	-	E	+	T	=	?
5.	DIAPAUSE	-	U	+	R	=	?
6.	ECDYSIAL	-	Y	+	P	=	?
7.	CHRESARD	-	R	+	E	=	?
8.	MUSCADET	-	M	+	E	=	?
9.	BRACONID	-	B	+	S	=	?
10.	ESCHEWAL	-	W	+	O	=	?

SET B

	WORD	MINUS/PLUS					
1.	HARDEDGE	-	D	+	T	=	?
2.	DEMENTIA	-	N	+	R	=	?
3.	TAUTENED	-	U	+	V	=	?
4.	AMIDOGEN	-	M	+	Z	=	?
5.	REIMAGES	-	M	+	D	=	?
6.	VERNACLE	-	C	+	D	=	?
7.	OPERETTA	-	P	+	L	=	?
8.	ESCARGOT	-	C	+	H	=	?
9.	ROSULATE	-	T	+	C	=	?
10.	PARVENUS	-	P	+	O	=	?

SET C

	WORD	MINUS/PLUS					
1.	LOTHARIO	-	H	+	V	=	?
2.	ANEURISM	-	E	+	U	=	?
3.	STASIMON	-	S	+	C	=	?
4.	ANVILTOP	-	V	+	Y	=	?
5.	RUMINANT	-	R	+	O	=	?
6.	BRUCINES	-	U	+	I	=	?
7.	BUTTOCKS	-	T	+	H	=	?
8.	BESOOTHE	-	H	+	L	=	?
9.	BLOUSIER	-	R	+	L	=	?
10.	SNOWBIRD	-	D	+	A	=	?

SET D

	WORD	MINUS/PLUS					
1.	CRENELED	-	L	+	A	=	?
2.	PERCOIDS	-	I	+	A	=	?
3.	CHEVERON	-	V	+	T	=	?
4.	UNHEROIC	-	U	+	L	=	?
5.	ISOMERIC	-	I	+	P	=	?
6.	TINCTURE	-	E	+	S	=	?
7.	INEDIBLE	-	B	+	S	=	?
8.	ANDESITE	-	A	+	M	=	?
9.	INDORSEE	-	I	+	A	=	?
10.	TRUSTEED	-	T	+	G	=	?

SET E

	WORD	MINUS/PLUS					
1.	UREDINIA	-	A	+	Q	=	?
2.	DORMIENT	-	R	+	A	=	?
3.	PHARISEE	-	A	+	D	=	?
4.	OHMMETER	-	M	+	S	=	?
5.	TWEETING	-	W	+	V	=	?
6.	NESCIENT	-	C	+	L	=	?
7.	PILLIONS	-	P	+	U	=	?
8.	MISPOINT	-	N	+	T	=	?
9.	UNSPOILT	-	P	+	O	=	?
10.	POSTRIOT	-	T	+	M	=	?

Words-in-Words

By taking a longer word and looking for all the shorter words in it, you engage in the one essential act that, to a large degree, will determine your skill at the SCRABBLE game. *SCRABBLE News* had lots of this type of practice in each issue. For instance, the word STARED contains many smaller words that can be formed with these letters: STAR, RATE, TREAD, RED, DEAR, etc.

Here's how to use the words-in-words idea to pair words and remember them: When you find an unusual word, see if you can subtract a letter, then rearrange the remaining letters to find a word. If you can, you've now discovered a useful word pair to aid your memory.

Following are some useful uncommon words for which if you **subtract** the given letter, you'll be able to rearrange the letters to spell a very common word.

There may be one or more anagrams for each answer. The answers are on page 230.

SET A

	WORD	MINUS	
1.	ENAMINE	- N	= ?
2.	RADIALE	- D	= ?
3.	COTERIE	- E	= ?
4.	MIAOWED	- I	= ?
5.	TOLUATE	- L	= ?
6.	ANDIRON	- N	= ?
7.	OUTLIER	- U	= ?
8.	AGNATIC	- A	= ?
9.	MOONLIT	- L	= ?
10.	THERETO	- O	= ?

SET B

	WORD	MINUS	
1.	GRIESEN	- R	= ?
2.	BEVOMIT	- B	= ?
3.	FUSTIAN	- U	= ?
4.	EUCLASE	- E	= ?
5.	COMATIC	- C	= ?
6.	WOMANED	- W	= ?
7.	DAPSONE	- N	= ?

8. ANVILED - L = ?
9. WINDAGE - E = ?
10. RESIDUA - E = ?

8. OLIVINE - E = ?
9. TETANAL - A = ?
10. VENTAIL - L = ?

SET C

WORD	MINUS	
1. READMIT	- M	= ?
2. CAIRNED	- A	= ?
3. THEROID	- O	= ?
4. IGNEOUS	- O	= ?
5. ANVILED	- L	= ?
6. GRANULE	- A	= ?
7. TENSIVE	- I	= ?
8. UNLOBED	- N	= ?
9. INFLECT	- F	= ?
10. GORMAND	- G	= ?

SET D

WORD	MINUS	
1. CORDAGE	- O	= ?
2. SUNDIAL	- L	= ?
3. SUEDING	- N	= ?
4. TRAGEDY	- D	= ?
5. PLATEAU	- U	= ?
6. PANDOUR	- P	= ?
7. SUBEDIT	- T	= ?
8. VACUITY	- U	= ?
9. BARCHAN	- A	= ?
10. DEODARA	- A	= ?

SET E

WORD	MINUS	
1. REUNIFY	- U	= ?
2. PINNACE	- P	= ?
3. LEWDEST	- L	= ?
4. BREWAGE	- G	= ?
5. PLACATE	- T	= ?
6. IMPOUND	- N	= ?
7. MUDHOLE	- H	= ?

Trivia

It's fun to create questions that test your friends' word knowledge and also improve your memory. It is not our intention for most people to know the answers to these questions without much prior *Official SCRABBLE® Players Dictionary* experience. They are intended to allow players to *review,* or, in other words, test themselves, after the answers are known. In this way the words will be at your fingertips when you need them in a game.

We've credited each question to authors not on the staff of the NASPA. The answers are on pages 230–31.

1. What do the following words have in common, besides baseball: COACH, CURVE, DRIVE, FIELD, FLY, HIT, HOMER, LINE, PITCH, PLAY, RUN, SCORE, START, THROW, TRADE, WALK?
2. Fifty-nine less common two-letter words as well as a few very common words are spelled correctly within the following list of words. If you review these periodically, you'll implant them more firmly in your memory. Refer to the answers first if you don't already have our list of all the twos memorized. *Example:* AMMO contains three acceptable words: AM, MM, and MO.

1. AGHA:	2	13. WEFT:	2	25. AALII:	3
2. AMMO:	3	14. ENOW:	3	26. REHEM:	4
3. AHOY:	3	15. YETI:	3	27. ELIDE:	4
4. LOOM:	2	16. DEER:	2	28. BASIC:	3
5. BOUT:	2	17. JOES:	3	29. NEXUS:	4
6. MUMS:	2	18. ALAE:	3	30. ABATE:	4
7. WOOD:	2	19. PIKA:	2	31. YOWED:	4
8. OPAL:	3	20. UNAI:	3	32. FEODS:	2
9. OHMS:	2	21. AWAY:	2	33. ZAIKAI:	4
10. BUHR:	1	22. NAOS:	2	34. BOILS:	2
11. PEAR:	2	23. NUBIA:	2	35. QINTAR:	4
12. TAXI:	3	24. YAMUN:	4	36. KITED:	4

3. There are exactly twenty-one five-letter words that contain only one consonant. How fast can you find them, given only the consonant: C (two words), D (three words), L (four words), M (one word), Q (two words), R (eight words), and Z (one word). Most of these words are obscure, so if you don't have NASPA's one-page "Important Words to Know" list, provided free with your NASPA membership and that has these "vowel dumps" listed, we recommend that you look at the answers and then come back to this question at a later date to test yourself.

4. ABEORS is a very interesting six-letter stem. You may add any of the common letters E, I, N, R, and T to ABEORS to form several seven-letter words, but it also takes each of eight high-point tiles: C, G, J, P, V, X, Y, and Z. Virtually all of the words are uncommon. (Jan Dixon, DE)
5. Rearrange the following brand names to form acceptable words. We've starred the obscure words.

1. LEXUS*	10. FRITOS*
2. PONTIAC	11. NABISCO*
3. ARMANI	12. PEPSI
4. LACOSTE	13. EVIAN
5. NORELCO*	14. AMSTEL
6. SANKA*	15. SEAGRAM'S
7. LIPTON*	16. ENDUST*
8. NESCAFE*	17. PINE-SOL*
9. FOLGERS	

6. The V doesn't combine well with the F, H, or K, especially in four-letter words. There are only four words that use both the V and F, only four V-with-K words, and only five V-with-H words. Many of these are obscure.
7. There are eleven four-letter verbs ending with an E that you might expect would have to drop the E when adding ING to form the present participle, but they don't necessarily do so. They are BLUE, CLUE, DEKE, DELE, GLUE, LUGE, SABE, SHOE, SPAE, TRUE, and VISE. *Examples:* BLUEING, CLUEING . . . VISEING are all acceptable. Which five of them also drop the E?
8. When a five-letter word has an H and a G, usually the G comes first in the word. There are only six such words that don't begin with H and don't end in S or NG in which the H comes first. Only two are common. Can you find all six?
9. There are only twelve six-letter words that don't end in S and use exactly two three-point tiles (BCMP), two four-point tiles (FHVWY), and two vowels (AEIOU). Only four are common words. Can you find them?
10. What are the two unhookable three-letter words that begin with Y?
11. We wonder how many of our readers get confused with EI or IE spellings. There are seven five-letter words that are spelled ?EI?E, in which the ? can be any letter. Only two of these words are very common.
12. There are eight five-letter words that are spelled ?IE?E. Two of them start with common three-letter words: PIECE and DIENE. The other six are "Saturday Night Live" repeats, meaning that they begin with the letters SNLSNL. Can you find them? Only three are common words.

13. Which of the following words take an S? ONEFOLD, TWOFOLD, THREEFOLD, FOURFOLD, FIVEFOLD, SIXFOLD, SEVENFOLD, EIGHTFOLD, NINEFOLD, or TENFOLD.
14. The six-letter words ENATIC/ACETIN will make a bingo with, among others, any of the letters U, V, X, Y, and Z added to them. Can you find them? Only one is a common word.
15. Which of the following are acceptable words: NORTHINGS, EASTINGS, SOUTHINGS, or WESTINGS?
16. All but one of the following words take an S. Do you know which? BENZAL, BENZOL, BENZOLE, BENZOYL, or BENZYL.
17. Of the following five words, which are nouns that take an S? BICORN, BICRON, BICORNE, TRICORN, TRICORNE.
18. The sequence of letters ILLIONS takes five different one-letter front hooks. Do you know which?
19. Which seven-letter word may be spelled out in SCRABBLE game tiles so that each tile has a different point value? Careful, this is tricky! The answer is not a common word. (Al Weissman, RI)
20. Do you know the one and only three- to eight-letter acceptable word (not counting plurals) that begins with each of the following two letters? Virtually all are obscure words.

1. BD	7. LW	13. PN	19. UI
2. GJ	8. MH	14. QO	20. YL
3. IH	9. MM	15. QW	21. YP
4. IW	10. MN	16. TM	22. YW
5. JN	11. NT	17. UF	23. ZW
6. KB	12. OQ	18. UH	24. ZZ

Common 8-Letter Words

Here are thirty words—whose rearranged letters are laid out in alphabetical order—that any average eight-year-old child knows. Can you unscramble these common, everyday words? Here's a hint: They are *all* compound words. We suggest you take tiles and use them to switch the letters around. Though the words themselves are simple, they aren't easy to find!

1. ACDHINSW
2. AABEHLPT
3. AENOOPST
4. AADDEMRY
5. ACEEHLOS
6. IIMSSTUW
7. ABDEKORY
8. DHIKNOOW
9. EEFNORTU
10. BEHINOSW
11. EHKMOORW
12. ABDHIRTY
13. AEEHNRWY
14. AADILORR
15. EHLLNSTU
16. AEFORSTW
17. ABELOPTT
18. ABDEGOPR
19. EFLORSUY
20. AEEFLLRW
21. CEHNSTTU
22. ABEMMNOO
23. EFOOPSTT
24. AADDEHMN
25. AABBELLS
26. HMMOORSU
27. ADEINRVY
28. AILNOPTY
29. ACEHOSSW
30. EEGHISST

Two-Rack Play***

Following are two racks. Start with an empty board and form a play with Rack #1. Then use Rack #2 to form a second play on the board. What's your two-turn total score? The answer is on page 232.

Average score: 52 *Good score:* 58 *Expert score:* 72

Rack #1: **A B C D E F G**
Rack #2: **P Q R S T U V**

Six-Rack Play****

Following are six racks. Start with an empty board and form a play with Rack #1. Leaving the first play on the board, follow it with a second play, using only Rack #2. Continue in this fashion until you've made your sixth play with Rack #6. Our best solution uses two smaller words (each less than five letters long) that are obscure. The answers are on page 232.

Average score: 369 *Good score:* 458 *Expert score:* 602 *Our Best score:* 809

Rack #1: **D E I I N R W**
Rack #2: **A I N O P T ?**
Rack #3: **E F L S T U Z**
Rack #4: **A E G I N R T**
Rack #5: **A I I I L N T**
Rack #6: **C N N O O S U**

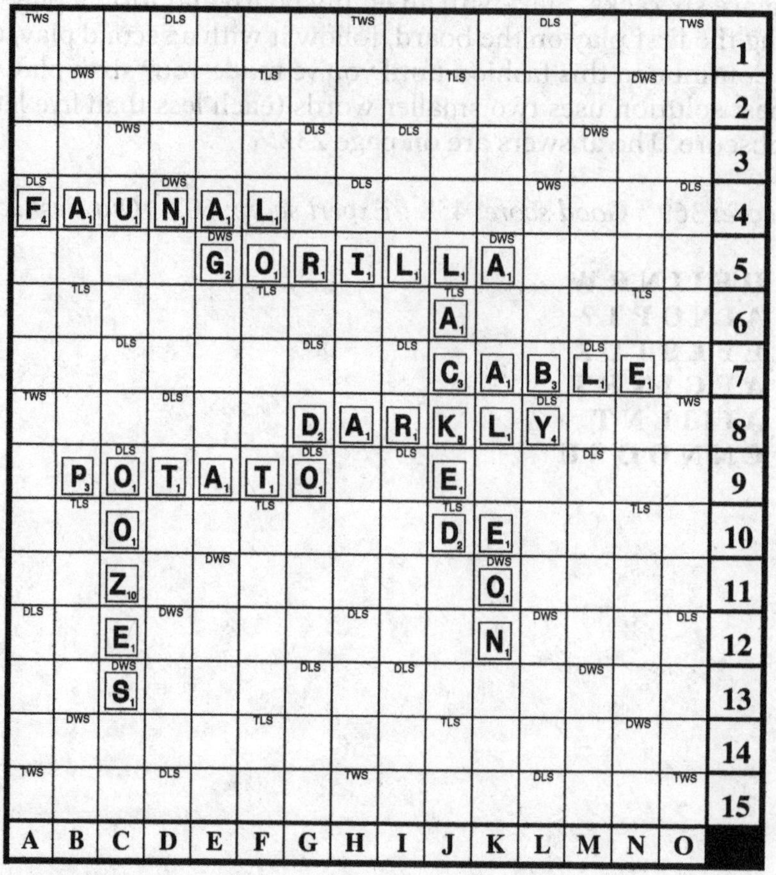

DIAGRAM 18-1

Using any or all of the given letters, find the highest-scoring play on Diagram 18-1 with each rack below. The answers are on page 232.

Note: Once you've found a play for Rack #1, don't add it to the board. Always use Diagram 18-1 for each rack.

Average score: 165 *Good score:* 195 *Expert score:* 210 *Our Best score:* 235

Rack #1: **G I L O T T U**
Rack #2: **B G H M N R Y**
Rack #3: **I I L N O P U**
Rack #4: **D E E H L M S**
Rack #5: **D E F L O R V**

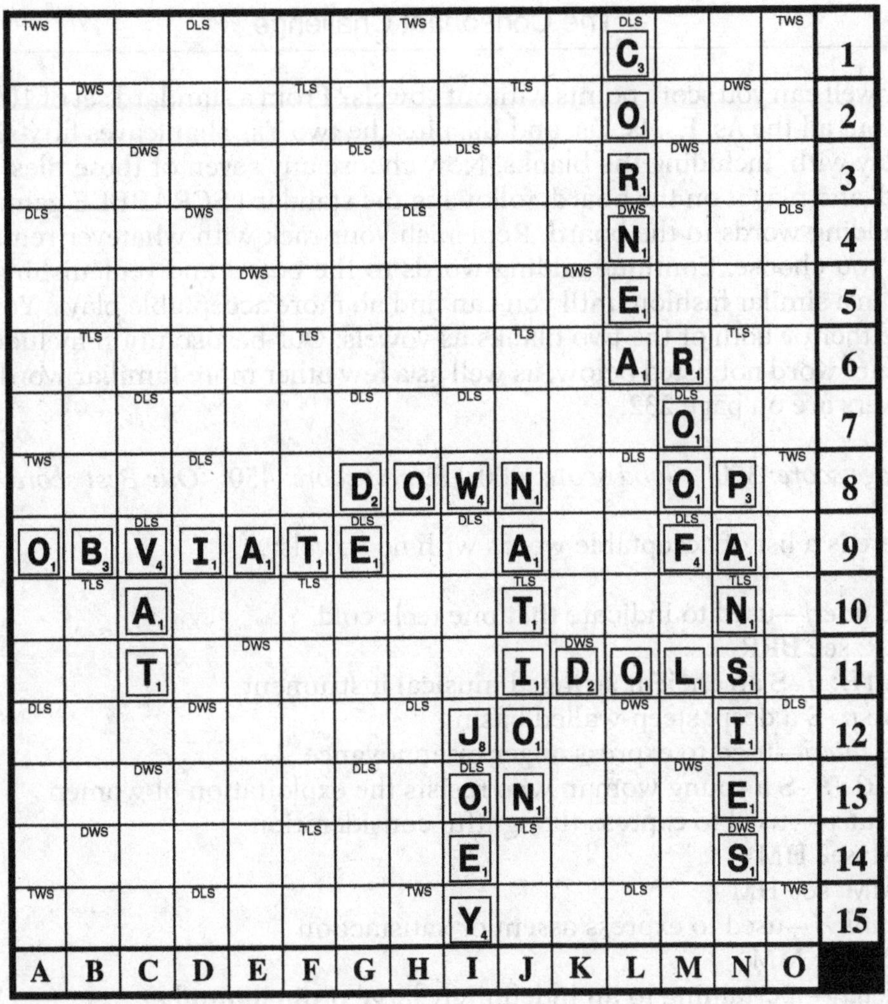
CORNEA
ROOF
PANSIES
DOWN
OBVIATE
VAT
NATION
IDOLS
JOEY
JO
ON
A B C D E F G H I J K L M N O
1 2 3 4 5 6 7 8 9 10 11 12 13 14 15

DIAGRAM 18-2

Find the highest-scoring play on Diagram 18-2 with each rack below. The answers are on page 232.

Average score: 220 *Good score:* 300 *Expert score:* 350 *Our Best score:* 409

Rack #1: **A C E L M O W**
Rack #2: **C D E M N O S**
Rack #3: **E I I N N O V**
Rack #4: **D D E M O R Y**
Rack #5: **E E H L N P T**

The Consonant Challenge

How well can you score points without vowels? From a standard set of 100 tiles, take out all the As, Es, Is, Os, and Us, plus the two Ys. That leaves fifty-six tiles to play with, including the blanks. Now choose any seven of these tiles, find a word, and play it on the board, following the standard SCRABBLE game rules for adding words to the board. Replenish your rack with whatever remaining tiles you choose. Continue adding words to the board and replenishing your rack in a similar fashion until you can find no more acceptable plays. You may use either or both of the two blanks as vowels. Our best solution includes one obscure word not listed below, as well as a few other more familiar words. The answers are on page 232.

Average score: 350 *Good score:* 400 *Expert score:* 450 *Our Best score:* 522

Here is a list of acceptable words with no vowels:

BRR: *interj*—used to indicate that one feels cold
BRRR: see BRR
CRWTH: *n* -S an ancient stringed musical instrument
CWM: *n* -S a deep, steep-walled basin
GRR: *interj*—used to express anger or annoyance
GRRRL: *n* -S a young woman who resists the exploitation of women
HM: *interj*—used to express thoughtful consideration
HMM: see HM
HMMM: see HM
MM: *interj*—used to express assent or satisfaction
MMM: see MM
NTH: *adv*—pertaining to an indefinitely large ordinal number
PFFT: *interj*—used to express a sudden ending
PHPHT: see PHT
PHT: *interj*—used as an expression of mild anger or annoyance
PSST: *interj*—used to attract someone's attention
PST: see PSST
SH: *interj*—used to urge silence
SHH: see SH
TSK: *v* -ED, -ING, -S to utter an expression of annoyance
TSKTSK: *v* -ED, -ING, -S to tsk
ZZZ: *interj*—used to suggest the sound of snoring

The Alphabet Caper

SCRABBLE News used to have a contest in each issue. We present here Contest #6. Using each letter of the alphabet and one blank tile (twenty-seven tiles total), score as many points as you can playing a typical SCRABBLE game. Two readers, Stephen Root (MA) and Gene Gruhn (AZ), tied for first place, having identical solutions of 714 points. Can you find their solution or do better? They play only two unusual words, one four- and one eight-letter word. The eight-letter word uses two of the J, Q, X, and Z. The answer is on page 232.

Average score: 410 *Good score:* 550 *Expert score:* 714

Below is a sample solution: (See sample Diagram 18-3, page 237.)

1. JUMPY 8D	54
2. QURSH E7	34
3. CHALKING 11D	86
4. FIX I10	13
5. FIXT I10	15
6. ADZ F11	13
7. ADZE F11	16
8. WOVE 14C	10
9. BY H7	7
10. ADZE*S* F11	14
Total:	262

Clabbers Word Search**

Clabbers is a form of wordplay that doesn't require the words to be spelled correctly. The letters may be in any order as long as they can all be arranged in some sequence that spells a word. Example: EENUQ is a valid word, as is UNEQE, both representing QUEEN, in Clabbers play.

To play, find and circle the words below, displayed Clabbers-style in the grid. The letters for each word are all adjacent in a line, horizontally, vertically, or diagonally. When you have circled all but *two* of the words, the remaining letters, not in a line, may be rearranged to spell the remaining two words. Which of those two words' letters are found in a smaller rectangle? The answers are on page 232.

Novice: 40 minutes *Intermediate:* 20 minutes *Expert:* 15 minutes

Words to find:

DANGEROUS	MONETIZE	BEACON	WOFUL	TRAIT
SOMERSAULT	POCKET	YEOMAN	HELP	BRIO
CREAMERY	POSITION	WISELY	DIDO	SAG
TREADMILL	ALMOND	HOSEY	NUMB	VID
DELICATE	PLANET	EAU	ULU	LUV
MELANOID	GLOBAL	ENVY	LYCH	ENUF
HEBDOMAD	WUD	THOU	KNOW	RITZ
RELATIONS	NYMPH	HOWF	MOGUL	TOME
WORKMAN				

T	S	I	I	T	N	O	O	P	W	W	E	F	B	C	1
L	C	M	E	O	A	N	Y	N	F	O	U	R	Y	R	2
N	O	Y	V	N	Y	E	R	U	A	N	O	L	O	K	3
A	F	D	A	M	L	M	L	N	E	I	H	S	W	A	4
P	W	B	A	E	O	O	M	U	L	U	E	O	G	I	5
E	H	D	D	A	R	L	I	O	L	S	N	S	V	B	6
O	N	M	K	D	I	M	U	O	U	M	N	D	C	I	7
A	L	L	T	D	E	T	R	T	D	Y	G	E	D	E	8
R	L	I	O	P	H	H	M	E	H	D	A	O	T	O	9
I	A	T	C	H	S	L	M	M	A	O	O	M	U	E	10
T	G	E	P	L	A	R	P	A	N	U	O	U	B	N	11
T	O	A	E	E	T	V	U	L	O	E	E	R	U	T	12
D	B	L	K	I	E	E	D	C	A	I	L	T	M	M	13
A	W	R	Z	A	I	S	N	O	R	T	E	L	N	Z	14
E	G	U	Y	E	O	S	H	E	Y	S	I	W	L	N	15
A	B	C	D	E	F	G	H	I	J	K	L	M	N	O	

Recognizing Long-Word Anagrams*

Record in the spaces next to the numbered words all the lettered words on the list at the right that are anagrams (exact same letters rearranged). Example: CHARM and MARCH are anagrams. The answers are on page 232.

Novice: 5 minutes *Intermediate:* 3 minutes *Expert:* 1 minute

1. URANYLIC	A. TOENAILS
2. MIDRANGE	B. PRETRIAL
3. MOORWORT	C. RUFFIANS
4. PALTRIER	D. RESAILED
5. DRAWBORE	E. LITANIES
6. INSOLATE	F. CULINARY
7. FUNFAIRS	G. TOMORROW
8. SIDEREAL	H. DREAMING
9. ENTAILED	I. WARDROBE
10. ALIENIST	J. DATELINE

Recognizing Blanagrams*

Which words on the right-hand list match up as blanagrams of the words on the left? A "blanagram" is a word that has all of the same letters but one of another word and has the same number of letters. KNEELS and KENNEL are blanagrams because only the S and second N are different—all but one of the letters are the same: KNEEL. The answers are on page 232.

Novice: 10 minutes *Intermediate:* 5 minutes *Expert:* 2 minutes

1. PARTICLE	A. FINAGLES
2. SANDWICH	B. PEDALOES
3. LIFESPAN	C. PRESPLIT
4. COMPLAIN	D. ANTIHERO
5. PIANISTS	E. CLARINET
6. DEVELOPS	F. COWHANDS
7. HOPELESS	G. ANIMATES
8. SLIPPERY	H. ISATINES
9. MANIFEST	I. PESTHOLE
10. OVERTHIN	J. PALOMINO

Clabbers Word Search (Level 2)**

The words below can all be found in the grid under the following conditions: Each word will be found Clabbers-style (disordered), completely filling a rectangle of some size. Rectangles may also be in a line; for instance, the rectangle defined by the boundary squares 1D and 1G completely encloses the word WASH. Or the rectangle defined by the opposite corners D4 and F5 completely includes the word MANORS (or RANSOM). As you find the words below, you may cross them off the grid, for the letters won't be used in more than one word. How quickly can you find all of the words below? The answers are on page 232.

Novice: 40 minutes *Intermediate:* 30 minutes *Expert:* 15 minutes

Words to find:

DELINEATE	STRAIGHT	PEOPLED	ALMUCE	MOGHUL
RELIEF	DUVET	PORCELAIN	VIOLATED	MONETIZE
EXAMINE	VACUUM	APPLET	DELIRIOUS	TENORITE
WITHHELD	PLEDGEE	MOLTEN	RUMPUS	WHAMO
FRUITFUL	RESEARCH	INEQUITY	SLEIGHT	ARISEN
RUMBA	PLASTICS	IRONCLAD	FORGIVEN	AMOEBIC
SANDWORM	FURY			

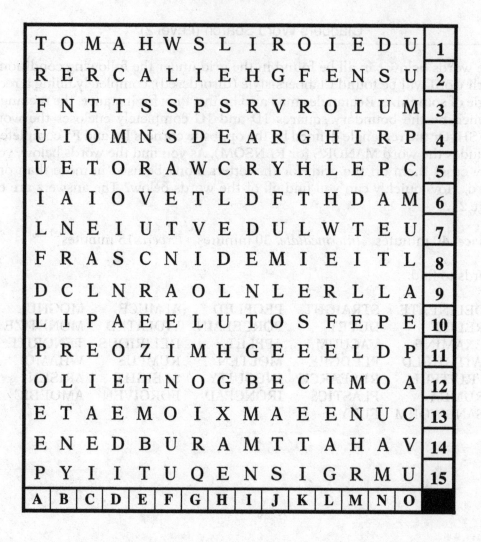

T	O	M	A	H	W	S	L	I	R	O	I	E	D	U	1
R	E	R	C	A	L	I	E	H	G	F	E	N	S	U	2
F	N	T	T	S	S	P	S	R	V	R	O	I	U	M	3
U	I	O	M	N	S	D	E	A	R	G	H	I	R	P	4
U	E	T	O	R	A	W	C	R	Y	H	L	E	P	C	5
I	A	I	O	V	E	T	L	D	F	T	H	D	A	M	6
L	N	E	I	U	T	V	E	D	U	L	W	T	E	U	7
F	R	A	S	C	N	I	D	E	M	I	E	I	T	L	8
D	C	L	N	R	A	O	L	N	L	E	R	L	L	A	9
L	I	P	A	E	E	L	U	T	O	S	F	E	P	E	10
P	R	E	O	Z	I	M	H	G	E	E	E	L	D	P	11
O	L	I	E	T	N	O	G	B	E	C	I	M	O	A	12
E	T	A	E	M	O	I	X	M	A	E	E	N	U	C	13
E	N	E	D	B	U	R	A	M	T	T	A	H	A	V	14
P	Y	I	I	T	U	Q	E	N	S	I	G	R	M	U	15
A	B	C	D	E	F	G	H	I	J	K	L	M	N	O	

Name Blanagram****

Each first name and surname of ten famous people have been modified by changing just one letter and rearranging the letters. Can you determine whose names we've doctored? By the way, in *no way* are the modifications necessarily any true representation of how we think about these famous people. The answers are on page 232.

Novice: 60 minutes *Intermediate:* 40 minutes *Expert:* 15 minutes

1. NOISY LOCALE (A good ear for talent.)
2. FATHOM VIDEOS (He lit up our lives!)
3. LEAKY CALDRONS (But not the songs! See number 1.)
4. ROMAN GUIDE (There's no place like homer!)
5. QUAIL RESORTS (We'd go to any resort with her!)
6. REPORT BINDER (We'd want him on our side in any bind.)
7. RHYME SPRITE (There's no doubt her skills are extraordinary.)
8. DIVAS GIRDLE (Has a light weapon.)
9. MAROONED INVALID (Centuries ahead of his time.)
10. BARELY SENTIENT (Quite the opposite!)

Which State?**

Each of the following words can be formed from the letters of only one U.S. state name. Which states are they? Consider "North," "South," "West," and "New" to be parts of the state names. The answers are on page 232.

Novice: 40 minutes *Intermediate:* 30 minutes *Expert:* 15 minutes

1. ZOARIA
2. COWMEN
3. FALCON
4. GOON
5. NIGHT
6. YOGI
7. CASTS
8. MANNA
9. TENSION
10. SONICS
11. ACHING
12. NAIAD
13. CHOLA
14. BARK
15. LIAISON
16. AWARD
17. DROOL
18. VOTE
19. SURIMI
20. LAMB
21. PIP
22. AGGIE
23. SAX
24. RADIO
25. AMOK
26. SENTE
27. CUTEY
28. THANK
29. KUDOS
30. WISH
31. STRANGE
32. DRAMA
33. WEENY
34. LEVY
35. WONKY
36. DELIS
37. INTENT

Which Nation?***

Which nation names' letters can generate the following words, some of which are admittedly quite obscure? Use repeat letters only if the nation name has those repeats as well. None of the nations use more than thirteen letters or include more than two words. The answers are on page 233.

Novice: 60 minutes *Intermediate:* 40 minutes *Expert:* 20 minutes

1. EVASION
2. ZOMBIE
3. ACRIMONIES
4. NUTRIMENTS
5. UNSTEADIEST
6. TACTICIAN
7. MINUTIA
8. NAUTILI
9. NINETIETHS
10. FRACTIOUS
11. FANTASIA
12. ROMANCE
13. DIMINUENDO
14. DRAWLIEST
15. GALATEA
16. COMEDIAN
17. UNIALGAL
18. AERATING
19. SALARIAT
20. HANDBAGS
21. ELEVEN
22. GRAPY
23. HIPLINES
24. GENUINE
25. CARIOCAS
26. ENSNARLED
27. ORGANISE
28. GAVIALS
29. ONRUSH
30. BATONS

City Blanagrams***

Each of the words below is a blanagram of a well-known American city. How many can you find? Example: SANDAL is a blanagram of DALLAS because all but one of the letters is the same. Two include more than just one word. The answers are on page 233.

Novice: 60 minutes *Intermediate:* 30 minutes *Expert:* 10 minutes

1. TABOOS
2. GNOCCHI
3. EDITORS
4. UPSHOOT
5. BLATANT
6. LOCUSTS
7. HIPBONE
8. DIAMOND
9. ATHLETE
10. PRONATED
11. CANCELLED
12. HALFLIVES
13. GALLSTONES
14. SUPERTIGHT
15. DECATHLONS

Mystery Phrases****

Every clue below describes from a skewed point of view a commonly used two-word phrase. The number of letters in each word is given, as are all the letters, though, in at least one case, appropriate punctuation between the words may be missing. Find these "mystery phrases." The answers are on page 233.

Novice: 60 minutes *Intermediate:* 40 minutes *Expert:* 20 minutes

1. Whose candidate was Tony the Tiger? (5, 6)*
   AAAILMNPRTY: _____ ______

2. Child absorber (8, 4)*
   BCGIKLNOOOOR ________ ____

3. Ubiquitous news (5, 4)**
   AEHILMNOP _____ ____

4. Folded newspaper falling from a plane onto a crowded street (9, 5)**
   ADEEGIMNORSSTU _________ _____

5. Getting ready to work, for many, since the early 1990s (4, 7)**
   DEINNOOPSWW ____ _______

6. Philanthropist (8, 11)***
   BCEEFINNOOQRRRTTTUU
   ________ ___________

7. Ali Baba (6, 10)****
   ADDDEGGIIILNRUUV ______ __________

8. Happily ever after (9, 6)****
   BDEGIKNNOOORSTY _________ ______

9. Sidewalk (6, 6)***
   CDGMMNNOOORU ______ ______

10. What champions do (7, 6)***
    EEEFFMOPRRSTU _______ ______

Switch Words***

Move one letter from the word on the left to the word on the right, and also move one letter from the word on the right to the word on the left. This switches one letter of each word. Now rearrange the letters within each group to spell a word. In each case there is only one pair of switchable letters that turn the two groups into words. The answer is on page 233.

Novice: 25 minutes *Intermediate:* 15 minutes *Expert:* 5 minutes

1. BEACH	FLUID
2. POLIO	NORTH
3. PUTRID	ENERGY
4. COMFIT	FAITHS
5. ECBOLIC	SYMBOLS

Dominords****

A "dominord" is two sets of three letters. By combining all six letters of each dominord and rearranging them, you can spell a common six-letter word. The puzzle is to determine which sets of three letters go with which other adjacent three-letter sets. Sets are paired only horizontally or vertically. For example, in the puzzle below, FOT, in the upper left, can be paired with REG to spell FORGET, or it might instead be paired with SNE to spell SOFTEN. There is only one correct way to divide these three-letter sets into their proper pairs. Circle the pairs when you think you know where they are. The answer is on page 233.

Novice: 60 minutes *Intermediate:* 40 minutes *Expert:* 20 minutes

FOT	REG	HOP	AST	DNO	URA
SNE	BDL	EIO	CVN	SSA	EUB
OYV	ELR	BNO	HPU	EMS	APT
AEG	BRY	ALE	ABC	EHL	AIN
LTU	AAC	NRT	CNU	GMP	LMY
BER	DEW	ATY	AHP	AIR	HPS

EXTENSIONS****

Many smaller words can be extended to the right or left, or to both the right and the left to form longer words. Such extension words are sometimes difficult to find and not always available, but when they are, and if they reach to Triple Word Score or Double Word Score squares, you'll find yourself one happy camper!

Below are ten racks. Each may be used to extend at least one of the words shown on the right to form a longer word. We've printed the blank spaces surrounding each word to show you exactly how many letters need to be placed and where. When you've successfully finished, each rack will have been used exactly once, and each word will have been extended once as well. The answers are on page 233.

Novice: 60 minutes *Intermediate:* 40 minutes *Expert:* 20 minutes

1. DEIIINV	A. _ _ _ _ _ POWER
2. EHLMORS	B. _ _ _ _ _ WEIGHT
3. CDEGIST	C. _ _ _ _ _ SHIRT
4. AECNNOT	D. _ _ _ SULTAN _
5. AGHILMT	E. _ _ _ _ _ _ DUALITY
6. BEILMNT	F. _ _ _ _ _ COLOR
7. IKMOPRT	G. _ _ _ _ _ EWE _ _
8. AENRSTW	H. _ _ _ TURBAN _ _
9. BDELMTU	I. _ _ _ AIRMEN _
10. AENRTUW	J. _ _ OPERA _ _ _

Making Music****

Change one letter of each of the words below to the correct letter and rearrange to form the name of a musical instrument. In other words, find the musical instrument blanagram of each word below. They are arranged in increasing order of difficulty. Can you find them all? Example: Given RANGE, change the E to an O and form ORGAN. The answers are on page 233.

Novice: 60 minutes *Intermediate:* 40 minutes *Expert:* 20 minutes

1. IRON	11. TRAIN
2. BEANO	12. SALOONS
3. AMINO	13. HERMIT
4. ALIVE	14. RELATION
5. LETUP	15. GENIPAP
6. LOCAL	16. SPUTTER
7. RATING	17. NONVALID
8. LIVING	18. MOULDIER
9. ORGANIC	19. ANTEPAST
10. MACARONIS	20. ALOPECIA

Halphagrams

A "halphagram" divides a longer word into two parts, front and back, by drawing a line between two interior letters and rearranging both the front set of letters (those to the left of the line) and the back set of letters (those to the right) into their respective alphagrams. They might be described as half-alphagrams—thus, halphagrams. For instance, take a nine-letter word and divide it into two groups, the first consisting of four or five letters, and the second of five or four letters. Using the word RHAPSODIC, if we divide it between the P and S (like this: RHAP | SODIC), we form AHPR (from RHAP) and CDIOS (from SODIC) and print it as AHPR | CDIOS. We have divided two hundred common nine-letter words into the halphagrams below. The object in each of the puzzles is to determine the original word.

Even though nine-letter words are much harder to unravel than smaller words, you already have a good deal of experience in unraveling eights, so use your knowledge of edges to help solve many of these puzzles. And be on the lookout for a few compound words with no edges, and even a few words that have neither common edges nor are compounded. The answers are on pages 233–35.

SET A	SET B	SET C	SET D
1. ACHR | AALNT	1. ACENT | EINR	1. ACHR | AEGLN	1. AGLS | AERSW
2. AADNV | AEGT	2. ABILR | AINR	2. AIPRT | ACHR	2. AELNP | ARTY
3. ACHM | EELNO	3. ACEHT | ADLR	3. ASTW | ADELN	3. ANOR | AGNTU
4. ABLMU | ACEN	4. ACEF | AEIRT	4. ADERV | ARSY	4. ACELT | EMOR

SET E	SET F	SET G	SET H
1. AMRS | AILPU	1. AEMPR | ERTU	1. ACDHR | EORV	1. ACEPR | ENRT
2. BSSTU | ACEN	2. BIOST | AENT	2. DENU | ACENR	2. CEENS | ARSY
3. ACESS | ELOR	3. MOOT | ABORT	3. CENOS | ADRY	3. COPR | AEILN
4. AILN | BEIRT	4. ACRS | CEORW	4. ACERT | EGLN	4. AEHR | BNRTU

SET I	SET J	SET K	SET L
1. ALNOS | GHTU	1. AEGMN | IMST	1. ACERT | TINY	1. COSTU | AMRY
2. CHRSU | AEGR	2. GHINT | AEMR	2. ACPS | EISTU	2. DEIS | AEGNT
3. APRT | ELMNO	3. AGPS | EHITT	3. CIOPT | AIRL	3. EMOPR | ADEN
4. AESTW | HOPS	4. SFRU | AERTT	4. AEHR | CIKST	4. ENTU | ACHIL

SET M

1. ESTY | ADERY
2. AGNR | DEIHS
3. APRT | DEIGR
4. DIMS | AEMRT

SET N

1. DEIM | AORTT
2. AEFT | EFILR
3. EEGLT | AHPR
4. CEHOR | ARST

SET O

1. AEFT | GLORW
2. AELST | EILT
3. EIMST | AERV
4. BDEIS | EFIL

SET P

1. ALMPS | ADEH
2. ADRT | AEKMR
3. ALPP | ADERU
4. EIPRT | AILN

SET Q

1. AADMR | ILLO
2. DEPR | AORTY
3. BEIR | ACEFS
4. ARST | ANOTU

SET R

1. AELT | AENRT
2. EOPS | AGHSU
3. AEMST | FLRU
4. AIRST | AEMR

SET S

1. AINV | AGORT
2. AAMRP | NOTU
3. EEPRS | ANOS
4. EOPR | AEITV

SET T

1. AEIPR | EMNR
2. EENSS | AILT
3. EENPR | AILN
4. EIRV | ADEHR

SET U

1. ADHS | BOOWX
2. ARTT | BEITU
3. EINT | ACEFR
4. ERSU | ACEFR

SET V

1. CEPST | ACEL
2. ACEGR | EIRV
3. EPRT | ELMOU
4. EISTX | EHNT

SET W

1. DLMOU | HOTU
2. CILOS | IORT
3. CEIRT | INOR
4. EINT | CERST

SET X

1. EIMNR | CEIS
2. EHNOP | AEMN
3. HOLW | AEELS
4. EHMOS | AEKR

SET Y

1. AEPSS | EGNR
2. ENOTU | AEGR
3. EILN | AEGNT
4. EFILS | AERV

SET Z

1. ADIMS | INOS
2. DHRY | AINOT
3. EEGLN | ADRY
4. CFFOS | EENR

SET AA

1. CKORS | DEIL
2. EIPST | CDEI
3. CEOR | CEILN
4. DIPS | BEERW

SET AB

1. AORST | MNOY
2. HIOST | AINR
3. AHMS | GNRTU
4. AIMST | GHTU

SET AC

1. EPSU | ARRST
2. AGLO | HIMRT
3. MOSU | AEPRT
4. EINP | ALNSU

SET AD

1. ADLNO | ENRW
2. ADELM | ILNO
3. DHISW | AERT
4. AILR | DEFIT

SET AE

1. FLOO | ADEGT
2. ADEPR | ERTU
3. DILPS | AEES
4. EMOPR | ADEN

SET AF

1. EILPR | ADER
2. DEEPS | ADOR
3. CINOT | ALNU
4. AGMNY | CIST

SET AG

1. CEIST | ALNO
2. AIMR | CEIST
3. AEMRV | LOSU
4. EMMNO | ARTY

SET AH

1. EPSU | ANORV
2. ANORR | ESTW
3. AFGIR | ILTY
4. AORY | EILST

SET AI

1. EINUV | ALRS
2. IMST | AELTU
3. ENOPT | AILT
4. AMNOR | EILZ

SET AJ

1. EIMOT | ALNO
2. AILRT | ELRY
3. IINS | AENTU
4. AIIMN | ERTU

SET AK

1. OSTU I AEHST
2. EHORS I ALPY
3. AERT I HMORW
4. EHRT I AIPST

SET AL

1. EQSU I AHIMS
2. HIMSS I AENP
3. HIPSS I AEHP
4. HIMU I AEILT

SET AM

1. ORRSU I AEGT
2. AGINS I ERTU
3. AEGMN I IMSU
4. EENT I AINRT

SET AN

1. AERW I EIMOS
2. EELPT I AHTY
3. EEGN I AORRT
4. EEMNU I AERT

SET AO

1. GIMR I AELOR
2. AELL I GIRST
3. GIIMM I AERT
4. AGLSU I EHRT

SET AP

1. AELS I GILRS
2. HIRS I AEGKN
3. GHIL I AETVW
4. AGNSY I EGOU

SET AQ

1. EGGOR I AHPY
2. AEFT I NNOOR
3. FMOR I AELTU
4. AEKLP I FOOR

SET AR

1. AFMR I EKORW
2. EFORS I ALLT
3. EFIMS I AILN
4. EIMNS I AFHT

SET AS

1. AEGRS I FHIT
2. ENPSW I AEPR
3. AERT I EMNTT
4. AFIMN I AEMR

SET AT

1. AEMSU I EMNT
2. EPPR I AELTU
3. AEOSW I ELMY
4. EELS I AKLPW

SET AU

1. AJMO I EERTT
2. EESTY I AINR
3. AIOPP I EENT
4. AERSV I EILT

SET AV

1. AEHRW I EOSU
2. AEMNW I EHIL
3. EGLNT I AEMN
4. ANRRU I DNOU

SET AW

1. BEMOO I AGNR
2. ABEGS I HRSU
3. AGILL I AORT
4. ARSTT I AEGM

SET AX

1. AINRW I AERT
2. ABETU I FILU
3. ABHMU I EGRR
4. AAMPR I EERT

One-Offs

Insert the letter in parenthesis into the word immediately next to it, and remove a different letter of that word. After doing so with both words, rearrange the letters of each new combination as necessary to form a familiar phrase. The "theme" is a clue to the answer. Unlike halphagrams, these puzzles get progressively harder.

For example: (I) MEAT SLICE (F) (theme: a saying). Replace the A of MEAT with an I, giving you MEIT, and the C of SLICE with an F, giving you SLIFE, and rearrange each new set of letters to spell TIME FLIES. The answers are on pages 235–36.

SET A	THEME
1. (F) LOUD SOFT (H)	SPORTS
2. (K) CROP DEAN (B)	MUSIC
3. (G) YARD WEAR (C)	TRAVEL
4. (S) TREE PEST (O)	TRAVEL

SET B	
1. (L) COIN ANTE (M)	NATURE
2. (L) FOUL ROOM (N)	LIGHT
3. (K) ALTO OWLS (H)	MEDIA
4. (R) SODA GAME (R)	DRIVING

SET C	
1. (F) THIS AUNT (K)	PET, HOME
2. (F) EAST ROOF (D)	SUSTENANCE
3. (T) WEAK FIRE (V)	BREAK
4. (T) OPEN DATE (F)	DISABILITY?

SET D	
1. (M) LIFE FORCE (S)	MUSIC
2. (M) BURRO MAIL (L)	COMMUNICATION
3. (N) BUILD PLOT (S)	DRIVING
4. (G) THIRD NURD (T)	DRIVING

SET E

THEME

1. (N) PLEA HEARD (A) WISDOM
2. (S) FRUIT BATS (E) SPORTS
3. (V) HYENA DUST (Y) INTENSITY
4. (D) LUSTY HULA (L) SCHOOL

SET F

1. (L) PIRATE PALS (Y) SPORTS
2. (F) AUTHOR POND (W) SPORTS
3. (E) BUTLER LEFT (C) MUSIC
4. (M) UNCLES NOSE (T) ANATOMY

SET G

1. (H) SOLVED WOES (N) ACTIVITY
2. (E) DOLLAR TACO (S) FOOD
3. (E) ETCHES FACE (K) FOOD
4. (T) POORER ROAD (C) SCHOOL

SET H

1. (A) PINE FILLER (E) HEALTH
2. (D) ORGAN PANIC (O) MUSIC
3. (G) STEAL CARGO (T) PERSON
4. (P) SPARE ELBOW (T) CLEANING

SET I

1. (T) MACHO TONIC (P) SPORTS
2. (O) CORAL DECOR (D) DESIGN
3. (F) SERVE CHIPS (T) INTENSITY
4. (L) THOSE TIMES (U) SHELTER

SET J

1. (N) RABBI SUAVE (W) NATURE
2. (O) PLAIN PRUNE (T) PERSON
3. (S) BITE FINGERS (D) PEOPLE
4. (W) IDOL MADONNA (B) INTENSITY

SET K	THEME
1. (N) ALIEN CLONES (T)	HOME
2. (N) INGEST HORSE (S)	ATTIRE
3. (I) ALERT PLAYER (W)	PERSON
4. (L) SPACE LODGER (H)	SUBSTITUTE

SET L	
1. (B) LATENT RAYON (L)	WAR
2. (W) OLDER SEXIER (S)	SPORTS
3. (P) HERON MANURE (B)	COMMUNICATION
4. (D) ARGON CRAYON (N)	NATURE

SET M	
1. (V) RETAIL GUILD (E)	PERSON
2. (K) POETIC NIECE (F)	AMERICAN DREAM?
3. (T) INSANE BLOKE (W)	CONDITION
4. (S) POSTED ALIAS (D)	FOOD

SET N	
1. (U) HORSE TREATS (R)	AT HOME, PERMANENTLY
2. (H) SWAN HOLSTER (C)	CHORE
3. (L) INSECT GIANT (H)	SONG
4. (S) THICK FINGER (U)	SUBSTITUTE

SET O	
1. (K) CAPOTE FIEND (K)	THING
2. (S) RECENT SHAVE (R)	COMPUTERS
3. (H) TIRED FEEDER (G)	COMMUNICATION
4. (I) VARMINT FLIP (L)	HEALTH

SET P	
1. (H) UNCLEAN RUST (F)	ACTIVITY
2. (C) LORD SENATOR (G)	PLACE
3. (G) SNIPER BEARD (K)	VACATION
4. (E) NEUTRAL VOTE (L)	GOAL

SET Q	THEME
1. (N) BEAM ROUTINE (C)	PERSON
2. (E) THEIR THESIS (W)	MYTHIC GIFT
3. (V) SINCERE CLAW (L)	HELP
4. (R) PATSY ALUMNI (A)	PERSON

SET R	
1. (C) WORLD COOLANT (R)	COMMUNICATION
2. (F) FRANTIC GUILT (H)	DRIVING
3. (O) KLEPTO AGENCY (H)	SMALL VALUE
4. (R) ELVISH TUMBLE (L)	ARMS

SET S	
1. (A) FILM EVILDOER (Y)	COMMUNICATION
2. (T) BLOATED STRAW (E)	SUSTENANCE
3. (H) REMOTE TUNDRA (E)	MYTHIC FIGURE
4. (D) ORANGE BARLEY (S)	MYTHIC PERSON

SET T	
1. (I) LAYMAN SETTLER (H)	PLACE
2. (F) PREHEAT DESERT (U)	CLEANER
3. (I) LONGHAIR SNOB (G)	MUSIC
4. (H) ANTELOPE STUD (K)	ANATOMY

SET U	
1. (L) CHOOSY HERETIC (A)	PERSON
2. (C) DIVERT DISPUTE (O)	BANKING
3. (K) EROTIC INCENSE (C)	SUBJECT
4. (U) CENTRAL GEYSER (N)	FUEL

SET V	
1. (N) FIREDOG MYOPIC (L)	POLITICS
2. (R) FLEABAG PLUMBER (O)	SCHOOL
3. (P) MEASURE ACTOR (U)	LAW
4. (T) CELESTIAL KIDS (H)	MEDIA

SET W	THEME
1. (T) PECULIAR PSYCHIC (S)	SUBJECT
2. (I) SOUPSPOON STEAK (N)	NATURE
3. (E) SURPRISE ROCKET (O)	KITCHEN
4. (P) MAGICIAN GRANDMA (E)	PERSON

SET X	
1. (P) REPUTABLE KIMONO (T)	UNATTAINABLE GOAL
2. (I) NIGHTLONG SHRIEKS (T)	NATURE
3. (O) FACECLOTH LICKER (A)	TREAT
4. (N) VARLET MENAGERIE (T)	FOR MUTUAL BENEFIT

SET Y	
1. (R) PLEASANT JAUNDICE (G)	HELP
2. (R) STIFFENED SKATERS (O)	TENDENCIES
3. (E) DISCLOSES ENTRAILS (G)	MATH
4. (W) NOSIEST COMPETITOR (N)	A SAFE PLACE

This concludes Part 3. In Part 4, we show what our SCRABBLE culture is all about. From Alfred Butts, the SCRABBLE game inventor, to SCRABBLE game clubs and tournaments to the experts and their skills, it's all there.

FAR-SIGHT

SET A: 1. PLATONIC; 2. VOLCANIC; 3. BARNACLE; 4. CALENDAR; 5. CLARINET; 6. CULINARY; 7. LAUNCHER; 8. LOCATION; 9. FLAMENCO; 10. PARLANCE

SET B: 1. BLOWHARD; 2. WORKLOAD; 3. ABNORMAL; 4. HORMONAL; 5. LANDLORD; 6. MATRONLY; 7. MONORAIL; 8. NONGLARE; 9. RANDOMLY; 10. TOLERANT

SET C: 1. CLOWNERY; 2. COWARDLY; 3. IRONCLAD; 4. FALCONER; 5. CROPLAND; 6. CORNBALL; 7. COLANDER; 8. CORNMEAL; 9. CILANTRO; 10. LACEWORK

ANAGRAMS

SET A: 1. CANVASED; 2. APPARENT; 3. DIABOLIC; 4. MEDICATE; 5. GRIMACED; 6. CRAYONED; 7. ACHIEVER; 8. INTIMACY; 9. HARDENED; 10. ARROGANT

SET B: 1. MACARONI; 2. GARDENIA; 3. MAHOGANY; 4. MAINTAIN; 5. BIFORATE; 6. VERBATIM; 7. NARCOTIC; 8. CLIMAXES; 9. SUITCASE; 10. CURTAILS

SET C: 1. CULINARY; 2. EMERALDS; 3. DEFAULTS; 4. RAWHIDES; 5. THOUSAND; 6. TEENAGER; 7. ELEVATOR; 8. RESONATE; 9. MALIGNED; 10. UNDERARM

SET D: 1. MIGRAINE; 2. EPITAPHS; 3. THORAXES; 4. ASTERISK; 5. STEAMILY; 6. INSULATE; 7. INNOVATE; 8. NOTARIES; 9. TEAMWORK; 10. PERSONAL

SET E: 1. SOLITUDE; 2. SUNDRIES; 3. NINETIES; 4. REFUSING; 5. NIGHTIES; 6. RINGLIKE; 7. PIGMENTS; 8. HORNIEST; 9. MILEPOST; 10. GARRISON

SET F: 1. MANHUNTS; 2. SOLITARY; 3. BIRDSEED; 4. LIBRETTO; 5. DOMESTIC; 6. DOCTRINE; 7. ELECTIVE; 8. ESTHETIC; 9. SILICONE; 10. ESOTERIC

SET G: 1. PRINCESS; 2. HISTORIC; 3. UNDERFED; 4. LOPSIDED; 5. EVILDOER; 6. SIDESTEP; 7. FIENDISH; 8. PROFITED; 9. RESHAPED; 10. UNLOADED

SET H: 1. GALAVANT; 2. AMETHYST; 3. ATTITUDE; 4. BASEMENT; 5. BEFRIEND; 6. CEREMONY; 7. COLISEUM; 8. COMPLAIN; 9. SUBPOENA; 10. DARINGLY

SET I: 1. DEMOLISH; 2. ANTELOPE; 3. CRUSADES; 4. DOLPHINS; 5. LOZENGES; 6. MEDIOCRE; 7. LAUGHTER; 8. FESTIVAL; 9. POETICAL; 10. MECHANIC

SET J: 1. DISCOVERY; 2. FACTUALLY; 3. HANDWRITE; 4. ISOLATION; 5. PREDATORY or PORTRAYED; 6. RACEHORSE; 7. PEDIGREED; 8. MARSUPIAL; 9. ARCHITECT; 10. PROSTRATE

BLANAGRAMS

7-Letter Words

SET A: 1. FATIGUE; 2. HOARDER; 3. ADENOID; 4. STOMACH; 5. ARCHIVE; 6. CUSTARD; 7. MACHETE; 8. BIASSED; 9. HUSBAND; 10. TABLOID

SET B: 1. PAGEANT; 2. ARMBAND; 3. CAPITAL; 4. ACROBAT; 5. BARMAID; 6. TRACHEA; 7. MATADOR; 8. AMATEUR; 9. MALARIA; 10. ABOLISH

SET C: 1. DIAMOND; 2. ELEGANT; 3. SHAPELY; 4. VAGUEST; 5. AUSTERE; 6. BICYCLE; 7. BEWITCH; 8. INBREED; 9. BROILED; 10. ROSEBUD

SET D: 1. DECEITS; 2. WEDLOCK; 3. PRODUCE; 4. DICTION; 5. NEGLECT; 6. USHERED; 7. LIVENED; 8. FREEDOM; 9. ENDORSE; 10. HIDEOUS

SET E: 1. PETTIER; 2. RESOLVE; 3. AMPUTEE; 4. TEMPEST; 5. FORFEIT; 6. STYLISH; 7. MONTHLY; 8. PINKEST; 9. TOURIST; 10. NITROUS

8-Letter Words

SET A: 1. ADORABLE; 2. ERASABLE; 3. ANYPLACE; 4. NAUTICAL; 5. PARADISE; 6. DISPLACE; 7. SEARCHED; 8. EDUCATES; 9. SARDONIC; 10. SHOELACE

SET B: 1. GATHERED; 2. DIAMETER; 3. VENDETTA; 4. AGONIZED; 5. DISAGREE; 6. LAVENDER; 7. TOLERATE; 8. SHORTAGE; 9. CAROUSEL; 10. RAVENOUS

SET C: 1. VIOLATOR; 2. URANIUMS; 3. MONASTIC; 4. PONYTAIL; 5. MOUNTAIN; 6. INSCRIBE; 7. BUCKSHOT; 8. OBSOLETE; 9. LIBELOUS; 10. RAINBOWS

SET D: 1. CAREENED; 2. SCOREPAD; 3. COHERENT; 4. CHLORINE; 5. COMPRISE; 6. INSTRUCT; 7. SIDELINE; 8. SEDIMENT; 9. REASONED; 10. GESTURED

SET E: 1. INQUIRED; 2. DOMINATE; 3. PERISHED; 4. THEOREMS; 5. VIGNETTE; 6. SENTINEL; 7. ILLUSION; 8. OPTIMIST; 9. SOLUTION; 10. IMPOSTOR

Words-in-Words

SET A: 1. MEANIE; 2. AERIAL; 3. EROTIC; 4. MEADOW; 5. OUTEAT/OUTATE; 6. ORDAIN/INROAD; 7. LOITER; 8. ACTING; 9. MOTION; 10. TETHER

SET B: 1. SEEING; 2. MOTIVE; 3. FAINTS; 4. CLAUSE; 5. ATOMIC; 6. MOANED; 7. SOAPED; 8. INVADE; 9. WADING; 10. RADIUS

SET C: 1. TIRADE; 2. CINDER; 3. DITHER; 4. GENIUS; 5. INVADE; 6. LUNGER; 7. EVENTS; 8. VIOLIN; 9. LATENT/TALENT; 10. NATIVE

SET D: 1. GRACED; 2. UNSAID; 3. GUIDES; 4. GYRATE; 5. PALATE; 6. AROUND; 7. BUSIED; 8. DOUBLE; 9. CLIENT; 10. RANDOM

SET E: 1. FINERY; 2. CANINE; 3. STEWED; 4. BEWARE; 5. PALACE; 6. PODIUM; 7. MODULE; 8. CAVITY; 9. BRANCH; 10. ADORED

Trivia Answers

1. They all take the prefix OUT- to make acceptable words.

2. 1. AG, HA; 2. AM, MM, MO; 3. AH, HO, OY; 4. LO, OM; 5. BO, UT; 6. MU, UM; 7. WO, OD; 8. OP, PA, AL; 9. OH, HM; 10. UH; 11. PE, AR; 12. TA, AX, XI; 13. WE, EF; 14. EN, NO, OW; 15. YE, ET, TI; 16. DE, ER; 17. JO, OE, ES; 18. AL, LA, AE; 19. PI, KA; 20. UN, NA, AI; 21. AW, AY; 22. NA, OS; 23. NU, BI; 24. YA, AM, MU, UN; 25. AA, AL, LI; 26. RE, EH, HE, EM; 27. EL, LI, ID, DE; 28. BA, AS, SI; 29. NE, EX, XU, US; 30. AB, BA, AT, TE; 31. YO, OW, WE, ED; 32. FE, OD; 33. ZA, AI, KA, AL; 34. BO, OI; 35. QI, IN, TA, AR; 36. KI, IT, TE, ED

3. **C:** AECIA, COOEE; **D:** ADIEU, AUDIO, OIDIA; **L:** AALII, AIOLI, LOOIE, LOUIE; **M:** MIAOU; **Q:** AQUAE, QUEUE; **R:** AERIE, AREAE, AURAE, AUREI, EERIE, OORIE, OURIE, URAEI; **Z:** ZOEAE

4. **C:** BORACES; **E:** AEROBES; **G:** BORAGES; **I:** ISOBARE; **J:** JERBOAS; **N:** BORANES; **P:** SAPROBE; **R:** ARBORES; **T:** BOATERS, SORBATE, BORATES, BOASTER, REBATOS; **V:** BRAVOES; **X:** BORAXES; **Y:** ROSEBAY; **Z:** BEZOARS

5. 1. LUXES; 2. CAPTION, PACTION; 3. AIRMAN, MARINA; 4. LOCATES, LACTOSE; 5. CORONEL; 6. KANAS; 7. PONTIL; 8. ENFACES; 9. GOLFERS; 10. FORTIS; 11. BONACIS; 12. PIPES; 13. NAIVE, NAEVI; 14. METALS, LAMEST; 15. MASSAGER; 16. NUDEST; 17. EPSILON, PINOLES

6. FIVE, FAVA, FAVE; VIFF; KAVA, KIVA, KVAS; VOLK, HAVE, HIVE, HOVE, SHIV, VUGH

7. BLUING; CLUING; DEKING; GLUING; TRUING; VISING

8. COHOG; PHAGE; SHOGI; SHRUG; THEGN; THIGH

9. BAYWOP, BEACHY, BEECHY, COWBOY, HYMNIC, MAYHAP, MUNCHY, PEACHY, PACIFY, POACHY; POUCHY, WICOPY, WHOOMP

10. YUM and YEH

11. Three of these words start with an S: SEIZE, SEISE, and SEINE. One other one is also fairly easy: DE-ICE (pronounced de-ICE). The other three are: REIVE, BEIGE, and PEISE. Just remember the consonants in SUPERBAD for the beginning letters.

12. SIEVE, NIEVE, LIEVE, SIEGE, NIECE, LIEGE

13. Only TWOFOLD and TENFOLD are considered nouns. The rest are adjectives.

14. TUNICAE, VENATIC, INEXACT, CYANITE, ZINCATE

15. All of them.

16. BENZAL is the only adjective.

17. All of them are nouns and take an S.

18. B, J, M, P, Z

19. JACKDAW: J (8) A (1) C (3) K (5) D (2) A (using the blank: 0) W (4)

20. 1. BDELLIUM; 2. GJETOST; 3. IHRAM; 4. IWIS; 5. JNANA; 6. KBAR; 7. LWEI; 8. MHO; 9. MMM; 10. MNEMONIC; 11. NTH; 12. OQUASSA; 13. PNEUMA; 14. QOPH; 15. QWERTY; 16. TMESIS; 17. UFOLOGY; 18. UHLAN; 19. UINTAITE; 20. YLEM; 21. YPERITE; 22. YWIS; 23. ZWEIBACK; 24. ZZZ

ANSWERS TO COMMON 8-LETTER WORDS

1. SANDWICH; 2. ALPHABET; 3. TEASPOON; 4. DAYDREAM; 5. SHOELACE; 6. SWIMSUIT; 7. KEYBOARD; 8. HOODWINK; 9. FOURTEEN; 10. WISHBONE; 11. HOMEWORK; 12. BIRTHDAY; 13. ANYWHERE; 14. RAILROAD; 15. NUTSHELL; 16. SOFTWARE; 17. TABLETOP; 18. PEGBOARD; 19. YOURSELF; 20. FAREWELL; 21. CHESTNUT; 22. MOONBEAM; 23. FOOTSTEP; 24. HANDMADE; 25. BASEBALL; 26. MUSHROOM; 27. VINEYARD; 28. PONYTAIL; 29. SHOWCASE; 30. SIGHTSEE

<u>TWO-RACK PLAY:</u> 1. FACED 8D 30; 2. SURFACED 8A 42—TOTAL: 72 points

<u>SIX-RACK PLAY:</u> 1. WINDIER 8F 74; 2. APPOINT 7I 71; 3. ZESTFUL 9I 116; 4. GRAT O4 7; 5. LATI O9 5; 6. CONGRATULATIONS O1 536—TOTAL: 809 points

<u>DIAGRAM 18-1:</u> 1. OUTFIT A1 27; 2. NYMPH B6 38; 3. UNZIP 11A 32; 4. MESHED 4H 58; 5. FLAVORED E7 80—TOTAL: 235 points

<u>DIAGRAM 18-2:</u> 1. CWM H13 61; 2. CONDEMNATIONS J2 82; 3. INNOVATIVE C5 84; 4. DROMEDARY 6F 80; 5. ELEPHANT E4 102—TOTAL: 409 points

<u>THE CONSONANT CHALLENGE:</u> 1. SPRIGHT H3 80; 2. SPRIGHTS H3 13; 3. PFFT 9E 16; 4. IN 6H 1; 5. JIN 6G 9; 6. DJIN 6F 15; 7. DJINN 6E 14; 8. DJINNS 6E 13; 9. CWMS K3 22; 10. CRWTH 3K 26; 11. SCHMALTZ O1 284; 12. TSK 3G 13; 13. BRA 5N 4; 14. BRR M5 6; 15. BRRR M5 6—TOTAL: 522 points. See Diagram 18-4.

<u>THE ALPHABET CAPER:</u> 1. LOCKJAW H8 112; 2. OX I8 34; 3. BY J8 24; 4. VOX I7 16; 5. FOXY 9G 21; 6. AN 13H 3; 7. AND 13H 4; 8. RAND 13G 6; 9. GHI F13 22; 10. MEZQUITS 15A 464; 11. PE B14 8—TOTAL: 714 points. See Diagram 18-5.

<u>CLABBERS WORD SEARCH:</u> ANSWERS DESIGNATE THE BEGINNING AND ENDING SQUARES. SOMERSAULT F11-O2; CREAMERY B2-I9; TREADMILL C6-C14; DELICATE F13-M13; MELANOID E8-L1; HEBDOMAD J12-C5; RELATIONS E14-M14; WORKMAN D7-J1; MONETIZE O7-O14; POCKET D8-D13; POSITION 1B-1I; PLANET A1-A6; GLOBAL B8-B13; WUD A13-15C; NYMPH H11-L7; BEACON J11-O6; YEOMAN C2-H2; WISELY I15-N15; HOSEY D15-H15; EAU J10-L12; ENVY D3-G3; THOU F9-I6; HOWF B3-B6; WOFUL G5-K1; HELP E9-E12; DIDO H6-K9; NUMB N11-N14; ULU I5-K5; LYCH L4-O1; KNOW L6-O3; MOGUL J6-N10; TRAIT A8-A12; BRIO K4-N1; SAG M6-O4; VID M7-O5; LUV G12-I12; ENUF J4-M1; RITZ D14-G11; TOME K12-N9; ALMOND, DEFINED BY THE SIX LETTERS AT 7A, 7B, 4C, 5D, 4E, AND 4F, IS IN A 4 × 6 RECTANGLE (LENGTH IN TERMS OF NUMBER OF LETTERS ON EACH SIDE, NOT BY THE NUMBER OF SPACES BETWEEN THE LETTERS), AND AS SUCH IS MUCH SMALLER THAN THE 8 × 15 RECTANGLE THAT DANGEROUS DEFINES, WHOSE LETTERS ARE AT A14, A15, B15, F10, N8, L10, M11, M12, 15O

<u>RECOGNIZING LONG-WORD ANAGRAMS:</u> 1. F; 2. H; 3. G; 4. B; 5. I; 6. A; 7. C; 8. D; 9. J; 10. E

<u>RECOGNIZING BLANAGRAMS:</u> 1. E; 2. F; 3. A; 4. J; 5. H; 6. B; 7. I; 8. C; 9. G; 10. D

<u>CLABBERS WORD SEARCH (LEVEL 2):</u> ANSWERS DESIGNATE OPPOSITE CORNER SQUARES OF EACH RECTANGLE. DELINEATE B12-D14; RELIEF L8-M10; EXAMINE G13-M13; WITHHELD L4-M7; FRUITFUL A1-A8; RUMBA E14-I14; SANDWORM D4-G5; STRAIGHT J14-M15; DUVET E7-I7; VACUUM N13-O15; PLEDGEE I11-O11; RESEARCH H2-I5; PLASTICS D2-G3; FURY J4-J7; PEOPLED A9-A15; PORCELAIN B9-D11; APPLET N5-N10; MOLTEN I8-J10; INEQUITY B15-I15; IRONCLAD E8-H9; ALMUCE O5-O10; VIOLATED B6-I6; DELIRIOUS G1-O1; RUMPUS N2-O4; SLEIGHT K4-K10; FORGIVEN J2-M3; MOGHUL G10-H12; MONETIZE E10-F13; TENORITE B2-C5; WHAMO B1-F1; ARISEN B7-D8; AMOEBIC I12-O12

<u>NAME BLANAGRAM:</u> 1. SIMON COWELL; 2. THOMAS EDISON; 3. KELLY CLARKSON; 4. AARON JUDGE; 5. JULIA ROBERTS; 6. ROBERT DE NIRO; 7. MERYL STREEP; 8. DAISY RIDLEY; 9. LEONARDO DA VINCI; 10. ALBERT EINSTEIN

<u>WHICH STATE?:</u> 1. ARIZONA; 2. NEW MEXICO; 3. CALIFORNIA; 4. OREGON; 5. WASHINGTON; 6. WYOMING; 7. MASSACHUSETTS; 8. MONTANA; 9. MINNESOTA; 10. WISCONSIN; 11. MICHIGAN; 12. INDIANA; 13. SOUTH CAROLINA; 14. NEBRASKA; 15. LOUISIANA; 16. DELAWARE; 17. COLORADO; 18. VERMONT; 19. MISSOURI; 20. ALABAMA; 21. MISSISSIPPI; 22. GEORGIA; 23. TEXAS; 24. FLORIDA; 25. OKLAHOMA; 26. TENNESSEE; 27. KENTUCKY; 28. NORTH DAKOTA; 29. SOUTH DAKOTA; 30. NEW HAMPSHIRE; 31. WEST VIRGINIA; 32. MARYLAND; 33. NEW JERSEY; 34. PENNSYLVANIA; 35. NEW YORK; 36. RHODE ISLAND; 37. CONNECTICUT

WHICH NATION?: 1. SLOVENIA (L); 2. MOZAMBIQUE (MAQU); 3. MICRONESIA (NONE MISSING); 4. TURKMENISTAN (KA); 5. UNITED STATES (T); 6. VATICAN CITY (VY); 7. MAURITANIA (AAR); 8. LITHUANIA (AH); 9. LIECHTENSTEIN (LEC); 10. SOUTH AFRICA (HA); 11. AFGHANISTAN (GHN); 12. CAMEROON (O); 13. UNITED KINGDOM (TKG); 14. SWITZERLAND (TZ); 15. GUATEMALA (AM); 16. MACEDONIA (A); 17. ANGUILLA (NONE MISSING); 18. ARGENTINA (N); 19. AUSTRALIA (U); 20. BANGLADESH (LE); 21. VENEZUELA (ZUA); 22. PARAGUAY (AAU); 23. PHILIPPINES (PPI); 24. NEW GUINEA (AW); 25. COSTA RICA (T); 26. NETHERLANDS (TH); 27. SINGAPORE (P); 28. YUGOSLAVIA (YOU); 29. HONDURAS (DA); 30. BOTSWANA (WA)

CITY BLANAGRAMS: 1. BOSTON; 2. CHICAGO; 3. DETROIT; 4. HOUSTON; 5. ATLANTA; 6. ST. LOUIS; 7. PHOENIX; 8. MADISON; 9. SEATTLE; 10. PORTLAND; 11. CLEVELAND; 12. NASHVILLE; 13. LOS ANGELES; 14. PITTSBURGH; 15. CHARLESTON

MYSTERY PHRASES: 1. PARTY ANIMAL; 2. COLORING BOOK; 3. PHONE MAIL; 4. DANGEROUS TIMES; 5. OPEN WINDOWS; 6. FREQUENT CONTRIBUTOR; 7. RUGGED INDIVIDUAL; 8. STORYBOOK ENDING; 9. COMMON GROUND; 10. SUPREME EFFORT

SWITCH WORDS: 1. CHAFE, BUILD; 2. PILOT, HONOR; 3. TURNIP, GREEDY; 4. ATOMIC, FIFTHS; 5. BICYCLE, BLOSSOM

DOMINORDS: FORGET, PATHOS, AROUND, BLENDS, NOVICE, SESAME, UPBEAT, VOYAGE, NOBLER, HUBCAP, BARLEY OR BARELY, PHLEGM, MAINLY, ACTUAL, TYRANT, PAUNCH, BREWED, PARISH

E X T E N S I O N S : 1E INDIVIDUALITY; 2A HORSEPOWER; 3H DISTURBANCE; 4D CONSULTANT; 5B LIGHTWEIGHT; 6J INOPERABLE; 7I IMPAIRMENT; 8C SWEATSHIRT; 9G TUMBLEWEED; 20F WATERCOLOR

MAKING MUSIC: 1. HORN; 2. BANJO; 3. PIANO; 4. VIOLA; 5. FLUTE; 6. CELLO; 7. GUITAR; 8. VIOLIN; 9. OCARINA; 10. HARMONICA; 11. SITAR; 12. BASSOON; 13. ZITHER; 14. CLARINET; 15. BAGPIPE; 16. TRUMPET; 17. MANDOLIN; 18. DULCIMER; 19. CASTANET; 20. CALLIOPE

HALPHAGRAMS

SET A: CHARLATAN, ADVANTAGE, CHAMELEON, AMBULANCE

SET B: NECTARINE, LIBRARIAN, CATHEDRAL, CAFETERIA

SET C: ARCHANGEL, PATRIARCH, WASTELAND, ADVERSARY

SET D: GLASSWARE, PLANETARY, ORANGUTAN, LATECOMER

SET E: MARSUPIAL, SUBSTANCE, CASSEROLE, NAILBITER

SET F: PREMATURE, OBSTINATE, MOTORBOAT, SCARECROW

SET G: HARDCOVER, ENDURANCE, SECONDARY, RECTANGLE

SET H: CARPENTER, NECESSARY, PORCELAIN, HEARTBURN

SET I: ONSLAUGHT, SURCHARGE, PATROLMEN, SWEATSHOP

SET J: MAGNETISM, NIGHTMARE, SPAGHETTI, FRUSTRATE

SET K: CERTAINTY, SPACESUIT, PICTORIAL, HEARTSICK

SET L: CUSTOMARY, DESIGNATE, PROMENADE, UNETHICAL

SET M: YESTERDAY, GARNISHED, PARTRIDGE, MIDSTREAM

SET N: MEDITATOR, AFTERLIFE, TELEGRAPH, ORCHESTRA

SET O: AFTERGLOW, SATELLITE, TIMESAVER, DISBELIEF

SET P: LAMPSHADE, TRADEMARK, APPLAUDER, REPTILIAN

SET Q: ARMADILLO, PREDATORY, BRIEFCASE, ASTRONAUT

SET R: ALTERNATE, ESOPHAGUS, MASTERFUL, AIRSTREAM

SET S: NAVIGATOR, PARAMOUNT, PRESEASON, OPERATIVE

SET T: REPAIRMEN, ESSENTIAL, PERENNIAL, RIVERHEAD

SET U: SHADOWBOX, ATTRIBUTE, INTERFACE, RESURFACE

SET V: SPECTACLE, CAREGIVER, PETROLEUM, SIXTEENTH

SET W: LOUDMOUTH, SOLICITOR, CRITERION, INTERSECT

SET X: REMINISCE, PHENOMENA, WHOLESALE, SHOEMAKER

SET Y: PASSENGER, ENTOURAGE, INELEGANT, LIFESAVER

SET Z: ADMISSION, HYDRATION, LEGENDARY, OFFSCREEN

SET AA: ROCKSLIDE, PESTICIDE, RECONCILE, SPIDERWEB

SET AB: ASTRONOMY, HISTORIAN, HAMSTRUNG, MISTAUGHT

SET AC: SUPERSTAR, ALGORITHM, MOUSETRAP, PENINSULA

SET AD: LANDOWNER, MEDALLION, DISHWATER, AIRLIFTED

SET AE: FLOODGATE, DEPARTURE, DISPLEASE, PROMENADE

SET AF: LIPREADER, DESPERADO, CONTINUAL, GYMNASTIC

SET AG: SECTIONAL, ARMISTICE, MARVELOUS, MOMENTARY

SET AH: SUPERNOVA, NARROWEST, FRAGILITY, ROYALTIES

SET AI: UNIVERSAL, STIMULATE, POTENTIAL, NORMALIZE

SET AJ: EMOTIONAL, ARTILLERY, INSINUATE, MINIATURE

SET AK: SOUTHEAST, HORSEPLAY, EARTHWORM, THERAPIST

SET AL: SQUEAMISH, MISSHAPEN, SHIPSHAPE, HUMILIATE

SET AM: SURROGATE, SIGNATURE, MAGNESIUM, ENTERTAIN

SET AN: WEARISOME, TELEPATHY, GENERATOR, ENUMERATE

SET AO: RIGMAROLE, ALLERGIST, IMMIGRATE, SLAUGHTER

SET AP: SALESGIRL, SHRINKAGE, LIGHTWAVE, SYNAGOGUE

SET AQ: GEOGRAPHY, AFTERNOON, FORMULATE, LEAKPROOF

SET AR: FRAMEWORK, FORESTALL, SEMIFINAL, MINESHAFT

SET AS: GEARSHIFT, NEWSPAPER, TREATMENT, MAINFRAME

SET AT: AMUSEMENT, PERPETUAL, AWESOMELY, SLEEPWALK

SET AU: MAJORETTE, EYESTRAIN, APPOINTEE, VERSATILE

SET AV: WAREHOUSE, MEANWHILE, GENTLEMAN, RUNAROUND

SET AW: BOOMERANG, SAGEBRUSH, ALLIGATOR, STRATAGEM

SET AX: RAINWATER, BEAUTIFUL, HAMBURGER, PARAMETER

ONE-OFFS

SET A: 1. FOUL SHOT; 2. ROCK BAND; 3. DRAG RACE; 4. REST STOP

SET B: 1. LION MANE; 2. FULL MOON; 3. TALK SHOW; 4. ROAD RAGE

SET C: 1. FISH TANK; 2. FAST FOOD; 3. TAKE FIVE; 4. TONE DEAF

SET D: 1. FILM SCORE; 2. RUMOR MILL; 3. BLIND SPOT; 4. RIGHT TURN

SET E: 1. PLAN AHEAD; 2. FIRST BASE; 3. HEAVY DUTY; 4. STUDY HALL

SET F: 1. TRIPLE PLAY; 2. FOURTH DOWN; 3. TREBLE CLEF; 4. MUSCLE TONE

SET G: 1. SHOVEL SNOW; 2. ROLLED OATS; 3. CHEESE CAKE; 4. REPORT CARD

SET H: 1. PAIN RELIEF; 2. GRAND PIANO; 3. STAGE ACTOR; 4. PAPER TOWEL

SET I: 1. MATCH POINT; 2. COLOR CODED; 3. FEVER PITCH; 4. HOTEL SUITE

SET J: 1. BRAIN WAVES; 2. PIANO TUNER; 3. BEST FRIENDS; 4. WILD ABANDON

SET K: 1. LINEN CLOSET; 2. TENNIS SHOES; 3. TRIAL LAWYER; 4. PLACE HOLDER

SET L: 1. BATTLE ROYAL; 2. WORLD SERIES; 3. PHONE NUMBER; 4. GRAND CANYON

SET M: 1. TRAVEL GUIDE; 2. PICKET FENCE; 3. TENNIS ELBOW; 4. TOSSED SALAD

SET N: 1. HOUSE ARREST; 2. WASH CLOTHES; 3. SILENT NIGHT; 4. STICK FIGURE

SET O: 1. POCKET KNIFE; 2. SCREEN SAVER; 3. THIRD DEGREE; 4. VITAMIN PILL

SET P: 1. CHANNEL SURF; 2. COLD STORAGE; 3. SPRING BREAK; 4. ETERNAL LOVE

SET Q: 1. BEAN COUNTER; 2. THREE WISHES; 3. SERVICE CALL; 4. PARTY ANIMAL

SET R: 1. CROWD CONTROL; 2. TRAFFIC LIGHT; 3. POCKET CHANGE; 4. SILVER BULLET

SET S: 1. MAIL DELIVERY; 2. BOTTLED WATER; 3. MOTHER NATURE; 4. DRAGON SLAYER

SET T: 1. ANIMAL SHELTER; 2. FEATHER DUSTER; 3. ORIGINAL SONG; 4. ELEPHANT TUSK

SET U: 1. SCHOOL TEACHER; 2. DIRECT DEPOSIT; 3. ROCKET SCIENCE; 4. NUCLEAR ENERGY

SET V: 1. FOREIGN POLICY; 2. ALGEBRA PROBLEM; 3. SUPREME COURT; 4. SATELLITE DISK

SET W: 1. PARTICLE PHYSICS; 2. POISONOUS SNAKE; 3. PRESSURE COOKER; 4. CAMPAIGN MANAGER

SET X: 1. PERPETUAL MOTION; 2. LIGHTNING STRIKES; 3. CHOCOLATE ECLAIR; 4. RENTAL AGREEMENT

SET Y: 1. PARENTAL GUIDANCE; 2. DIFFERENT STROKES; 3. ISOSCELES TRIANGLE; 4. WITNESS PROTECTION

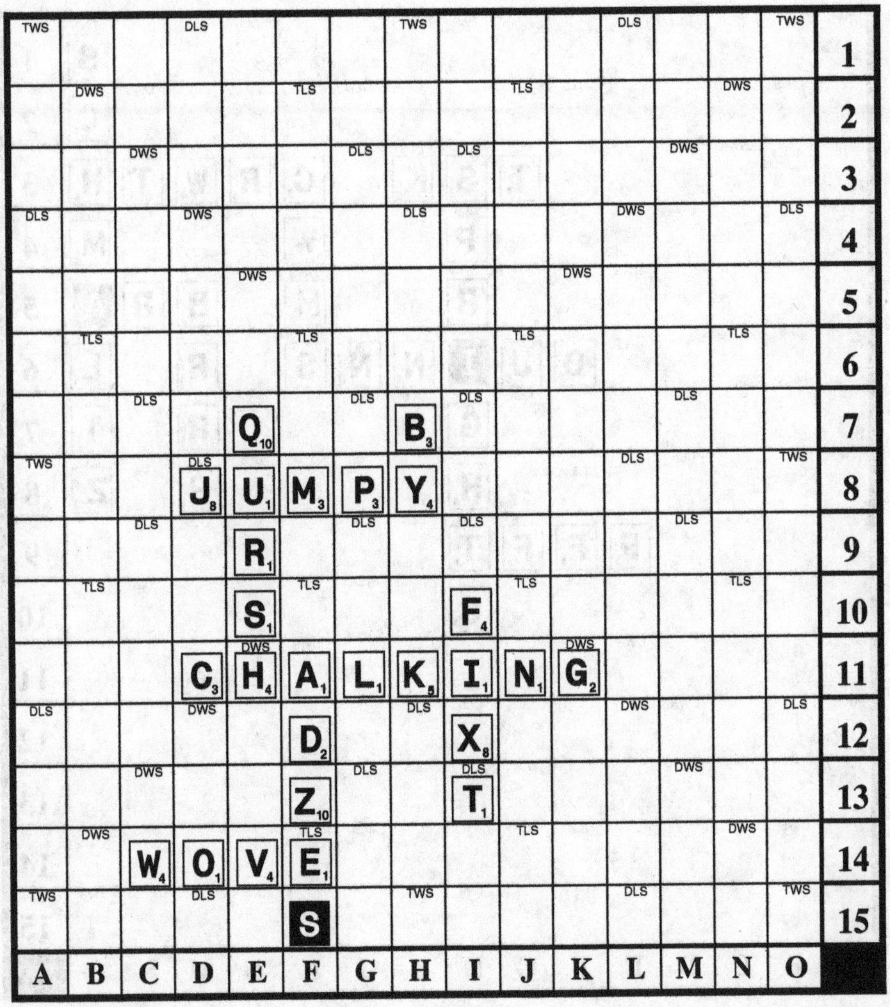

DIAGRAM 18-3

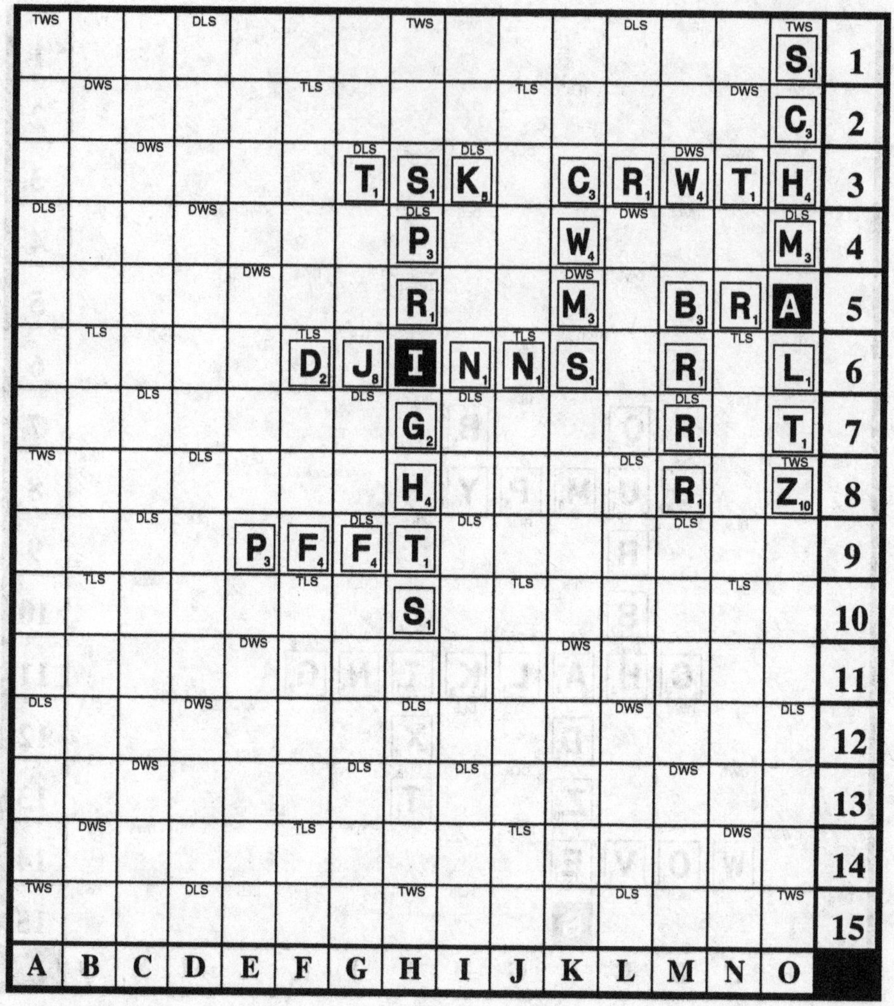

DIAGRAM 18-4

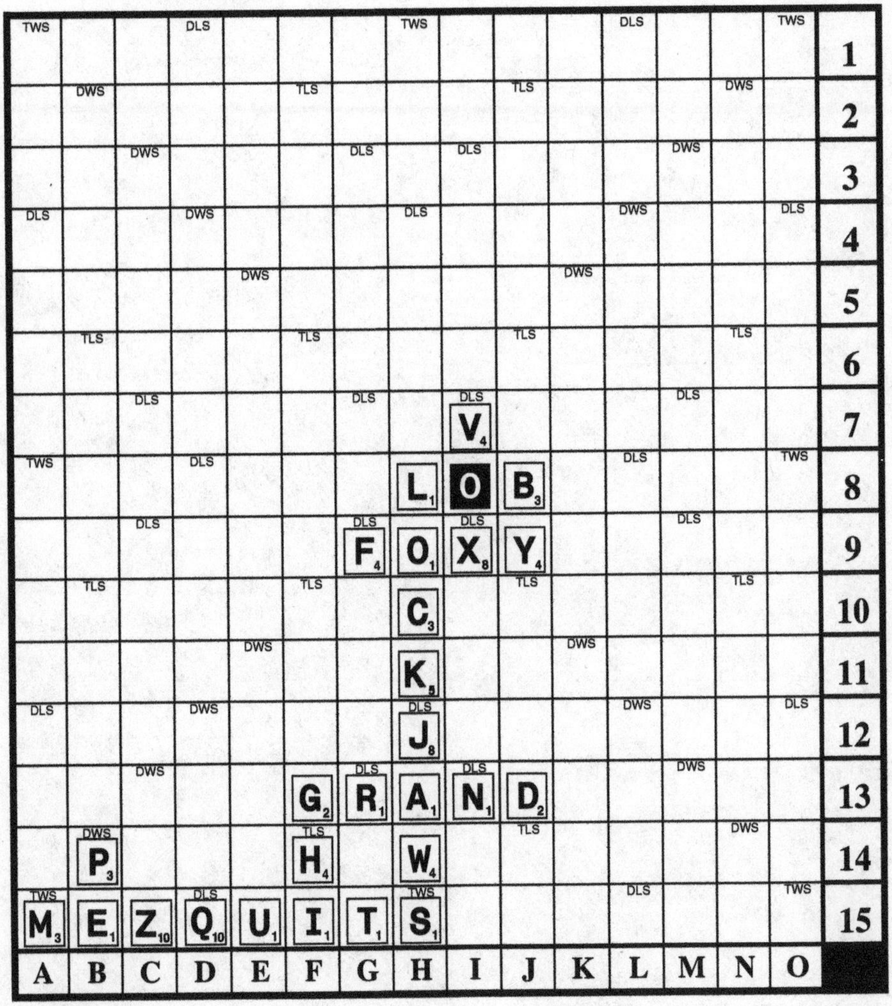

DIAGRAM 18-5

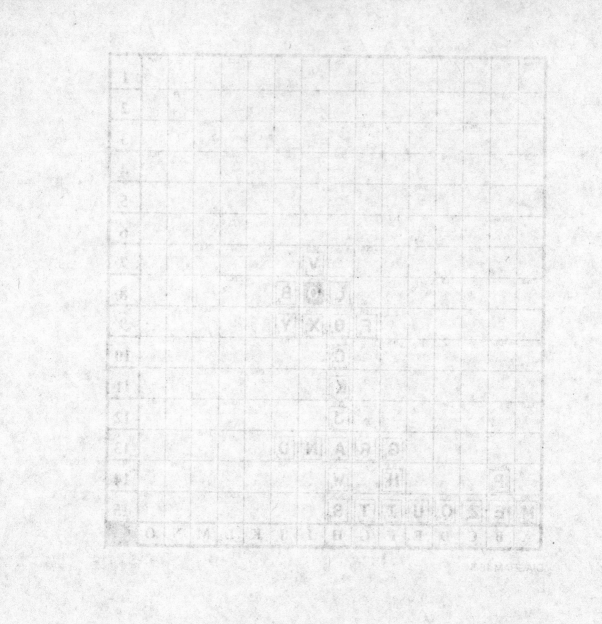

PART • 4

EXPLORING THE WORLD OF SCRABBLE® CLUBS AND TOURNAMENTS

Now that you understand the dynamics of the play of the game, we'd like to show you the larger world of the SCRABBLE game culture.

Chapter 19 introduces you to Alfred Butts, the game's inventor. Chapter 20 will show you what you'll encounter at SCRABBLE game clubs and tournaments. Chapter 21 shows you very explicitly what it takes to become an expert player. Chapter 22 demonstrates just how exciting and beautiful SCRABBLE game play can be, with fifty-five examples of outstanding plays by some of the best players. Chapter 23 shows you how best to introduce the variety of SCRABBLE games to your children.

In chapter 24 we will entertain you with many of the most fascinating true stories that have happened over the board, along with some wonderful poems written by some of our most creative aficionados. In chapter 25 we put you into the middle of a game. There are no obvious best plays. Instead, there are situations where there are several potential best plays. We invite you to think through each position with your best analysis, and then tell you how Joe Edley reasons and decides on his favorite play. In chapter 26 you'll hear from four players about their SCRABBLE game experience. Two are School SCRABBLE kids who are in their late teens and early twenties. The other two are old-timers, both directors, organizers, and long-time players who have had a major impact on our game culture. Enjoy!

19 JOHN WILLIAMS REMEMBERS ALFRED MOSHER BUTTS

It was the summer of 1983, and I had just become involved as a public relations consultant to what was then called SCRABBLE® Crossword Game Players, Inc. The organization was a subsidiary of the game's manufacturer, Selchow & Righter Company. I had just arrived at Chicago's Drake Hotel for the 1983 North American SCRABBLE Championship, where thirty-two finalists from all over the continent were going to compete for a $5,000 first prize and a considerable amount of glory in the game and word subcultures.

On the plane from New York I had tried to memorize all the material I had received about both SCRABBLE and the fledgling tournament scene. Among the sheaves of information was a press release describing the upcoming event. One of its highlights was that the championship would be visited by Alfred Mosher Butts, the inventor of SCRABBLE. Interestingly, this would be the first time Butts would see firsthand the kind of worldwide enthusiasm his idea had spawned.

After checking into my room, I headed down to the tournament room, where officials, press, executives, and players had already convened. After making the rounds, I noticed a frail man, clearly in his eighties, sitting unassumingly in a corner. He was surrounded by several people, but he seemed to be doing more listening than talking. Seconds later, one of my associates informed me that the gentleman was Alfred Butts and asked if I could keep him company for a while.

When the group around Butts dispersed, I walked over to introduce myself. I had not noticed before, but there was a SCRABBLE game in progress on a small table beside him. We had been talking for a few minutes when Alfred asked if I wanted to finish the game with him.

I was stunned. For openers, I had just started to reacquaint myself with the game as part of my new assignment. Second, the prospect of playing SCRAB-

BLE with the game's inventor was more than just a little intimidating. I felt as if I were about to shoot baskets with Dr. James Naismith or change a diaper with Dr. Benjamin Spock.

"I'm really a terrible speller," Alfred told me as we began. I looked at the crush of reporters around the room. "Maybe you shouldn't advertise that fact." The father of SCRABBLE shrugged. "People find out soon enough."

Adding to my sense of intimidation was a prop that Alfred had casually left on the floor beside him. It appeared to be an everyday plastic shopping bag. It contained, however, the first hand-rendered prototype of the SCRABBLE board from decades earlier.

"Shouldn't this be in the Smithsonian or something?" I asked him.

"You really think so?" he replied.

People still ask me how well Alfred Butts played that first day. Frankly, I can't even remember. I'm not sure it really mattered. The next opportunity I had to spend any significant time with Alfred was at the 1985 National SCRABBLE Championship in Boston. It was the largest event in organized SCRABBLE game history, with 302 word experts from dozens of states and several foreign countries competing.

Alfred was even more overwhelmed than he had been at the Chicago tournament a few years earlier, but he loved the attention and VIP treatment he was afforded. He was also introducing a new product, Alfred's Other Game®. It was basically a solitaire version of SCRABBLE, roughly conceived by Alfred and fine-tuned by the people at Selchow & Righter. Each contestant and staff member received a copy of the new game, and Alfred must have signed each one personally during the course of the event.

Happily, there was extensive press coverage of the championship, and Alfred was a focal point of much of it. Although he was an extraordinarily unassuming man, he sat through dozens of interviews and photo sessions, answering the same questions over and over again. It's important to remember that Alfred Butts had no prospect of financial gain from any of this. He had long since stopped receiving royalties on SCRABBLE®; and Alfred's Other Game®, while certainly playable, never threatened to become a classic. Mostly, he was a man in his mid-eighties who was enjoying an unexpected opportunity for some fun and recognition.

It was during the Boston trip that I really spent a lot of time with this American genius. My chief memory was of our visit to a Sunday-morning radio program. We were appearing on a show hosted by a Boston radio legend who called himself "the Culture Vulture." Each Sunday morning he interviewed a featured guest, then opened up the phone lines to his listeners.

It should be noted that WBCN was one of the most famous rock and roll stations in the United States. It's safe to say that many of the listeners were not what you'd characterize as typical SCRABBLE game enthusiasts and that a good portion of them had been awake since the night before.

But Alfred sat there and answered their questions, no matter how outrageous. One caller wanted to know the weirdest word he'd ever played. He couldn't think of any for himself, but he repeated a story about his wife's playing QUIXOTIC against him years earlier. Later, the family had presented her with a custom-made T-shirt with the word emblazoned across the front. Another asked what, if he had to change the SCRABBLE game, he would do. Nothing came immediately to mind, Alfred said. He was sure, however, that his late friend James Brunot would probably have a slew of ideas. An M.I.T. student wanted to know the most points that could conceivably be scored in a SCRABBLE game. Alfred said he had no idea, that it might be too subjective even to figure out. Alfred added that he was happy whenever he scored 300 points.

After the show we received a tour of the radio station, including a peek at what was said to be the largest collection of rock and roll music in the United States. It was a great juxtaposition: eighty-five-year-old Alfred Butts wandering around the bowels of a radio station being introduced to legions of people who looked as if they'd just staggered home from a Grateful Dead concert. People were thrilled to meet the father of SCRABBLE—as in every other setting I'd ever seen him in.

On the way back from WBCN, Alfred asked the driver to pull over when he spotted a huge and impressive example of trompe l'oeil (a photo-realistic mural) on the side of an old brick building. Though a trained architect and accomplished artist, he apparently had not seen that many examples of the form in person; indeed, they are still rare in North America. After we stopped, Alfred got out of the car and walked over to take a closer look. He stood there for a few minutes and admired it, then walked back to the car. "That was really something," he told me.

I agreed.

"How long do you think it took to do that?" he wondered.

I told him I had no idea.

"Do you suppose they had real artists, or just regular sign painters?"

Again, I told him I didn't have a clue. However, there was one thing I *did* realize: A mind like Alfred's was as curious at eighty-five as it ever was!

My last memory of Alfred Mosher Butts is from June 1991. I was in a nursing-home parking lot a few miles outside of Poughkeepsie, NY. Just before we left the car, my host, Alfred's great-nephew Robert Butts, opened the glove compartment of his car and pulled out a giant bag of M&Ms.

"Alfred is ninety-one years old," he said, "and I think these things keep him going."

"Whatever it takes," I told him, hoping *I'm* eating M&Ms at ninety-one.

How ironic, I thought, that the man who invented the SCRABBLE game, Alfred Mosher Butts, was "surviving" on a candy named after a letter of the alphabet.

I had not seen Alfred for three years. He had been involved in an automobile accident while driving at the age of eighty-eight and he did not get around as he once had. Still, it would be a mistake to say he was just sitting around a nursing home and eating candy. As Robert Butts explained, "Alfred now listens more than he talks. But there is still a lot going on in that magnificent brain."

I had hoped to actually play Alfred a SCRABBLE game that day. Robert had told me that his uncle still played an occasional lightning-fast game with nurses and other residents. But Alfred was a little tired that day. As a result, our visit was limited to a half an hour or so, and the conversation, though warm, was mostly me talking and Alfred listening.

While an attendant was checking on Alfred, I experienced a clear and acute sense of privilege just being in the room with him. As he and Robert spoke, I reviewed to myself the remarkable legacy Alfred Butts had created.

A SCRABBLE set was in 30 million American homes; 100 million sets had been sold worldwide. In the United States and Canada alone, there were more than seventy-five official SCRABBLE game tournaments every year and hundreds of official SCRABBLE game clubs. There was a biennial national championship. A typical American championship has 600-plus word experts from forty states and several countries, all of them battling it out for twenty-one rounds in just four and a half days. That's about seven hours of play a day. A recent national tournament in Thailand featured 2,000 players, 95 percent of them schoolchildren.

But this day in 1991 I was delivering a particularly sweet message, a new statistic, to the inventor of the game. I had come to tell Alfred in person that the first-ever World SCRABBLE Championship was going to be held a few months later in London. After the dramatic events around the rest of the world at that time—the Berlin Wall and Lenin's statue had both been toppled—all factions in the SCRABBLE universe had at last agreed on a way to get together and play.

Propped up in his nursing-home bed, Alfred Butts listened as I set the stage. Teams from twenty countries would compete. They would include experts from Sri Lanka, Kenya, Israel, Japan, and Nigeria, as well as the more predictable United States, Canada, England, and Australia. Everyone would, of course, play in English.

However, we would be using both the North American and British dictionaries, which meant all players would try to learn an additional 30,000 words from the "foreign" lexicon. On the final day of the event, two players would battle it out on national television for a $10,000 first prize.

As I expected, Alfred was stunned at the scope and pageantry of this upcoming international event. That he had started it all six decades earlier—in his living room, in the middle of the Great Depression—was almost impossible for him to absorb. Finally, after processing this information for another minute, he looked at me.

"I wish I could be there," he said.

I waited a beat, too.

"Believe me, Alfred," I told him, "you will be."

When Alfred Butts died in 1993, he had already seen SCRABBLE expand worldwide from local clubs and tournaments to national championships to a world championship that included twenty-two nations. Ten years later the World SCRABBLE Championship had grown to have forty-five countries with a $25,000 first prize. The next chapter will give you a good introduction to the world of organized SCRABBLE game play.

20 LEAVING YOUR LIVING ROOM: What You Can Expect

Now that you've read much of this book and are eager to meet new SCRABBLE partners, the world of SCRABBLE game clubs and tournaments is awaiting you! There are more than 300 official SCRABBLE game clubs throughout North America.

The first thing you should know is that every type of person imaginable plays at our clubs! It doesn't matter who you are or whether you're an expert or a novice—if you enjoy the game, you'll be welcome at any of our clubs. We try hard to make sure no one is intimidated, either socially or skill-wise.

PLAYING ONE-ON-ONE

Another thing you should know is that club games are always played one-on-one. One reason is because in two-person games each player has the opportunity to make more plays and has less waiting time between turns. The other chief reason is that in the two-person game it is mostly the players' skills that determine who wins or loses. In three- or four-person games, the luck factor is increased enormously. We estimate that in a two-person game, the outcome is based upon luck 15 percent of the time. In the three- or four-rack game, luck may be an important factor as much as 40 percent of the time.

However, we're not suggesting that you stop playing your four-sided SCRABBLE games if you enjoy them. We just want our readers to know that our clubs provide a venue for players who like the challenge of playing one-on-one.

The only exception to this rule of one-on-one is when two or more players decide to play as a team, pooling their knowledge and competing against another team of players. Often these partnership games are more lively than the regular one-on-one contests. That's because players talk and often joke around with one another about their plays. At the same time, they're trying to avoid telegraphing information to their opponents, which can often produce some clever wordplay, both on and off the game board. This is frequently the way players relax during off-hours at tournaments.

TIMED GAMES

Another important thing you should know about clubs is that most use some sort of device to time the plays. While this isn't universally done, you can expect it at the more established clubs.

There are two types of timers the North American SCRABBLE Players Association recommends. The older method is to use three-minute sand timers. Each player has three minutes to form his or her play on the board and announce the score. The opponent has to warn the player when the sand has almost all run down; otherwise, the player gets a few extra seconds. Games timed this way are ended after an hour, regardless of how many tiles haven't been played.

By ending games after an hour, several can be played during an evening. This allows players a chance to compete against several different opponents. While many of our readers may regularly take two or three hours to complete one game, the timed club play will challenge them to think faster. At first, many new club players have a hard time dealing with the faster pace. But within weeks they are grateful, because they notice a marked increase in their playing speed, which translates into *more playing time*! If you don't believe us, try it at home first.

The newer method for timing SCRABBLE games is to use a chess clock—or, as we like to say, a tournament clock. Clocks are much more popular among tournament players than sand timers are, because they typically give each player a total of twenty-five minutes to complete all of his or her turns. (There is a 10-point penalty for each minute or fraction of a minute used over the allotted twenty-five.) A tournament clock comes in a plastic or wooden frame that houses two individual clocks—one for your time, the other for your opponent's. At the top of each clockface is a button that, when pressed, stops one clock and starts the other. There are also several variations of electronic digital timers now in use in both the SCRABBLE and chess worlds.

The advantage of the clock is that a fast player can make the easy plays in just a few seconds, thus saving up extra time to work on the difficult racks. An added feature is that an inexperienced player can be given more than twenty-five minutes, while an expert may handicap himself or herself by starting with only fifteen or twenty. In addition, using a clock ensures that the game will *always* be played to completion. That doesn't always happen when using sand timers.

Some people initially find the clock intimidating. They're constantly looking to see how much time they have left. And often their opponent has to remind them to press their clock. But after they've played several games and become used to the quicker pace, they settle down and are able to concentrate solely on the game. At first, don't be afraid to ask your club director for more than twenty-five minutes if you're having a difficult time. But don't be surprised when your director urges you, after several weeks of practice, to speed up your pace.

PROTILES

Another thing you should know about club and tournament play is the existence of "Protiles." Robert Schoenman, a businessman who finished eighth in the 1993 World SCRABBLE Championship, created a plastic set of tiles whose lettering cannot be determined from touch alone. Currently, the regular or deluxe set of SCRABBLE tiles that is included with each SCRABBLE game set is engraved. Although most people might not be able to determine which letter they are touching, most people *can* determine whether they have a blank or not. The Protiles are smooth and provide club and tournament players with the security of knowing that their opponents can't feel for blanks as they draw tiles from the bag. Understanding the needs of tournament players, Hasbro, Inc., allows Mr. Schoenman to create these tiles for the several thousand tournament players. Protiles are made in a variety of colors. NASPA has been giving away one set of Protiles to every National SCRABBLE Championship contestant.

SCRABBLE GAME CLUB ATMOSPHERE

Although NASPA has guidelines for sanctioned directors, there remains a wide spectrum of experiences for new club players. Some clubs have a very informal atmosphere. Players at these clubs may play whomever they want, whenever they're available. There may be laughing and talking during play that often helps to develop long-lasting friendships as well as improved word skills.

At the other end of the spectrum, there are other clubs that are more competitive. The players there are very quiet during play—though not between games! New players may be given word lists to help them develop their skills and are often offered instruction. New club players may find themselves losing frequently before they learn enough new words to score between 300 and 400 points a game. Players with patience who can endure losing these early games will reap exhilarating benefits. After some experience, most novices learn the techniques for rack balancing and looking for bingos, and eventually they learn how to win their fair share of games.

Somewhere in between are clubs with both competitive tournament players and informal social players. Often these clubs have enough members to allow the social players to play among themselves and the tournament players to play a more "serious" SCRABBLE game.

Regardless of the type of club you attend, the feedback reaching the North American SCRABBLE Players Association is that the players at successful clubs grow into close-knit families. In order to accomplish this, the savvy director will be guided by his or her players' input. That means that as a new member of a SCRABBLE game club, you should let your director hear your suggestions for improving its operation.

Those readers who live in an area where there are no clubs may develop their own by ordering our SCRABBLE® Game Club Director's Kit (see Appendix 3). It has all you'd want to know about organizing and directing a SCRABBLE game club or tournament.

HOW DO YOU RATE?

We frequently get asked different forms of the same question: "I regularly outscore most of my friends in SCRABBLE. I average 350 to 420 points per game. How good am I? Would I be considered an expert?"

Here's our answer, in two parts: If you've become familiar with most of the two- and three-letter words and your average score is at least 300 points, you'll probably win your share of games at most SCRABBLE clubs. Most clubs have players who average anywhere from 250 to 400 points per game.

Those of you who average 350 to 400 against your friends will probably find that initially your average will go down at a SCRABBLE club and will stay down until you become familiar with your new competitors. Regardless of your average score with your friends, a better judge of skill is your average score per turn. Not counting your exchanges, if you average 25 to 30 points per turn, you may be an expert already! The best players average 30 to 35 points per turn against their toughest competitors.

TOURNAMENT PLAY

For competitive players who thrive on testing their skills, the tournament scene can give you everything you'd expect in excitement, drama, camaraderie, and, of course, SCRABBLE games—and plenty of them! While there may be only a few players who win the top prizes, everyone who plays is a winner in so many other ways. Your character, stamina, and skills will be tested and will likely improve. You'll also meet a variety of interesting people, including some who might become regular playing partners.

Those of you who take the plunge will find that most tournaments have several divisions of expertise. This ensures that you'll be playing against others relatively close to your skill level. After your first tournament, you'll receive a rating that represents your skills in relation to other rated players. After thirty to forty tournament games, your rating will be fairly accurate to within 200 rating points.

Briefly, your initial rating will be based in part upon the average rating of all your opponents. If you finish with five wins and five losses in your first tournament, and the average rating of all your opponents is 1,200, then your first rating will be about 1,200. If instead you finish with six wins and only four losses against the same opponents, your first rating may be closer to 1,300. The ten highest-rated players are rated between 2,030 and 2,200; the lowest ten are below 500.

There are a variety of tournament experiences you may encounter. Some events last only one day and involve playing five to seven games (also called "rounds"). Most last ten to fifteen rounds and are played over a Friday night, Saturday, and Sunday morning. For instance, two of the most popular annual twelve-round tournaments in the country are held near Boston, MA, in early April, and in Atlantic City, NJ, near the end of January. These events have four divisions of players and usually draw more than 150 players each. The top divisions of these events regularly draw many of the top twenty players in the nation.

For specific information on the 300 SCRABBLE game clubs and 200 tournaments run annually in North America, go to www.scrabbleplayers.org or www.cross-tables.com. Cross-tables has all the basic tourney information as well as tourney results and much more. You will find it fascinating as you explore it!

For a more demanding (some say exhilarating) experience, you might like to try the longer events. The annual Western Championship, held in Reno, NV, in July, lasts from eighteen to thirty-nine rounds, depending on the year, has four divisions, draws more than 200 players, and is usually held over a three-day weekend. For a slightly different experience, the twenty-round Dallas Open is held in March each year and has only one division, so anyone might be paired with anyone.

Of course, there are many more excellent tournaments held all across North America. Most of the major cities have annual events. For instance, Phoenix, Los Angeles, Portland, Houston, Chicago, Philadelphia, Fort Lauderdale, Detroit, New York City, Atlanta, Minneapolis, Indianapolis, Cleveland, Pittsburgh, and many others hold tournaments of note. If you haven't already become a member of the North American SCRABBLE Players Association, you may check our website, www.scrabbleplayers.org, for upcoming tournament listings, as well as tournament results. All you need to do to enter a tournament is send the entry fee to the contact person before any announced final registration date, and, of course, show up at the tournament ready to play!

For the ultimate in tournament play, there is the National SCRABBLE® Championship (NSC), held every summer. Provided you are a current member and have earned a rating—any rating—in at least one previous NASPA-rated tournament, you may participate in this incredible event. The NSC is held in a different American city each time, and it extends for thirty-one rounds over five days, usually from Saturday through Wednesday.

Each participant plays seven rounds each of the first four days, then the final three on Wednesday morning. The National SCRABBLE Championship has four divisions, though the winner of the top division is crowned the new National Champion. The divisions are divided strictly by rating, though players may play up one division if they choose. Rating cutoffs for each division of the 2016 NSC were 1,800, 1,400, and 1,100. However, if you were lower-rated you could play up into any of the upper divisions. Including the players who played up from Division 2, there were 100 strong expert players vying for the title in Division 1. These numbers, by the way, represent ratings. It's typical that a player rated 200 points more than another will win approximately 65 percent to 75 percent of their games together.

Our NSC, which regularly draws between 500 and 600 players, is an unforgettable week of eating, breathing, sleeping, playing, laughing, complaining, and talking SCRABBLE. It's a time to reestablish friendships and make new ones, while enjoying one of the best games on the planet. A total of nearly $60,000 in cash and 200 individual prizes were awarded in 2016. The SCRABBLE game is unique in its ability to provide many different inspiring prize categories. Here is a partial list of the prizes awarded in one year in the 1990s.

Division	1st Prize	2nd Prize	3rd Prize
1	$25,000	$10,000	$5,000
2	$5,000	$2,000	$1,200
3	$2,500	$1,500	$1,000
4	$1,500	$1,000	$750
5	$1,200	$800	$600
6	$1,000	$700	$500

Highest-Scoring Game for each round, in each division: $25

Highest-Losing Score for each round, in each division: $20

Highest-Scoring Acceptable Play each day, in each division: $25

Greatest Comeback Award to the player who was furthest behind during a game, then went on to win that game, in each division: $50

Tuff Luck Award to the player in each division who lost six games by the smallest total point spread: $50

Best Win–Loss Record on Day 3 for those in the bottom half of the standings at the beginning of Day 3, in each division: $250

Best Win–Loss Record on Day 4 for those in the bottom half of the standings at the beginning of Day 4, in each division: $150

Lowest-Scoring Win, in each division: $25

Flashiest Bingo, in each division: $50

Best Strategic Play: $250. This must be the best play in the position; must be one of several reasonable playing options; must not be an obvious play, but must be based on clever, thorough, creative, and/or inspired reasoning. The winner is determined by a panel of experts well after the event.

One note on the rules: While tournament play is essentially the same as home play, the rules are designed to encompass many more unusual situations that may arise in a competitive atmosphere. Club and living room play can be informal, but tournament players are sticklers for following the rules. There are several ways that ignorance of the rules can cost you victories, but you can avoid most of the hazards by simply reading the rules a few times. As a new member of NASPA, you can automatically receive a free copy of the *Official Tournament Rules* by downloading a copy from our website, www.scrabbleplayers.org.

Now that you've read about SCRABBLE game experts, you may be curious about what it takes to join their ranks. Chapter 21 will show you exactly what the experts know and how they win.

21 SO YOU THINK YOU WANT TO BE A TOURNAMENT EXPERT? A Word to the Wise

Based on what you've learned so far, you may now want to join the growing number of club and tournament players throughout the world. Some of you may even want to enhance your skills and become a SCRABBLE expert. If so, we'd like to tell you what to expect. Our reason for telling you these secrets is twofold. First, we want to demystify what many articles in the media have tended to show the public—that SCRABBLE game experts are a strange bunch of people who love to memorize obscure words, and that they have amazing word skills that normal people can't possibly develop without studying for hundreds of hours.

Not true! First of all, we know very few players who like to memorize words. Instead, most players simply play the SCRABBLE game and slowly try to remember all the words played against them. They also look at other players' boards to learn new words. If you drop by a club and watch a few games, you'll quickly pick up many new words. However, we'll repeat what we said earlier: Look up all unfamiliar words. You're sure to see some phoneys on many boards.

Do you know anybody who can type sixty to eighty words per minute? Of course. With sophisticated computer keyboards, in fact, many experienced typists do better than that. But you don't develop that skill overnight! The same applies to your SCRABBLE skills. First you have to learn the proper techniques. In typing, it's learning the touch-typing method and practicing it that leads to speed-typing. In the SCRABBLE game, it's learning the fundamentals, then simply practicing by *playing*! While you're at it, toss a few anagrams to your friends and have them likewise test you. It's fun!

We admit that our second reason for presenting this chapter is very selfish. We'd simply like to have more good players to play with! We love to meet new people and have fun playing the SCRABBLE game with them. Since we believe that most anyone can become skilled at the SCRABBLE game—and that with the proper approach it's painless—we want to show as many people as possible how to improve their playing abilities.

A SIMPLE STEP-BY-STEP METHOD

To raise your abilities to the highest level, there are basically four separate skills you'll need to develop. First are the vocabulary and word-finding skills. Second are the over-the-board playing skills, particularly during the endgame. Third are the skills to evaluate your opponent's game strengths and weaknesses and to use that knowledge to your advantage. Fourth, but certainly not least, are the emotional skills, or attitude.

As you read this chapter, please keep in mind that it's our experience that most people, regardless of their initial skills, have the potential to earn an expert rating. In the NASPA, this currently means a rating of 1,600 or higher.

STEP ONE: IMPROVE YOUR VOCABULARY SKILLS

In order to make the jump to become an expert, you can't avoid learning new words. While we've mentioned this earlier—suggesting in chapter 12 which words to learn first—you'll want to know several categories of words. Here are those you should concentrate on, in the approximate order they should be learned.

All 107 two-letter words. You won't find all the great parallel plays unless you know all these words. See chapter 3 for maximizing the usage of the two-letter words.

All the two-to-make-three-letter words. While you won't necessarily need all the three-letter words, you will earn more parallel-play points by learning these gems. *Example:* On our starter sheet, be prepared to begin with each two-letter word and record all its hooks: BA—ABA, BAA, BAD, BAG, BAH, BAL, BAM, BAN, BAR, BAS, BAT, and BAY. When you can create this list accurately and quickly for all the two-letter words, you'll be on a par with the experts.

Most of the three-to-make-four-letter words. The same reasoning as above can be used for these words. Since there are fewer hooks per word, these are actually much easier to learn than the two-to-make-threes.

Most of the four- and five-letter JQXZ non-bingo words. After becoming familiar with this list, you'll be able to take advantage of the many obscure JQXZ words that often form high-scoring plays. Any expert you meet will be able to do this.

The SATIRE, SATINE, and RETINA six-to-make-seven-letter words.

Imagine that after several turns you've been able to save your good letters and finally have the rack AEEIRST. What do you play? Any expert will be able to rattle off instantly the two bingos on this rack: AERIEST and SERIATE. Once you learn these words, look at some of the other high-frequency six-letter stem lists (see Appendix 4, page 515). You'll eventually want to become familiar with most of the words on the top 100 stems—if only to be able to recognize your opponents' phoneys or good words! "High-frequency" stems or bingos are those that show up on racks more often than most others.

Learning these words is actually not as hard as it might appear at first glance. Most of the words have familiar letter arrangements. Once you learn how the various letters combine, remembering or finding these words becomes easier and easier.

RE and UN word lists. By far the most phoneys played are those that begin with RE or UN. You will need to be familiar with the acceptable words in order to know whether you're about to play a phoney, or whether your opponent just has.

Five-letter words with one or more 3- or 4-point tiles (BCMPFHVWY), such as HAKIM or FAKIR. These words are the workhorses that give you 25- to 35-point plays. The more you know, the better you'll be able to score and to rid your rack of awkward tiles.

The words with multiple vowels. Occasionally, all players draw too many vowels. While the novice is apt to exchange them, the expert will be able to find a play that uses several vowels. Become familiar with the words in Appendix 4, pages 520–22; they will show up repeatedly on your rack. As you learn the high-frequency bingos, review the seven- and eight-letter words that have five vowels. You'll be surprised how often they can turn a horrible rack into a 70-point play. The top players typically know most of them.

STEP TWO: IMPROVE YOUR PLAYING SKILLS AND ENDGAME PLAY

There is no substitute for being able to find the high-scoring plays and correctly choosing which one balances your rack the best. But what other strategies are there? We discussed learning how to open and close the board at appropriate times. Is that enough? Can one learn to be an expert without further playing skills? Unless you have the wherewithal to memorize the whole dictionary, the answer is *no*! A further skill the expert develops is how to maximize winning chances when there are very few tiles left to draw.

To illustrate, let's look at the current computer programs and see how their playing abilities compare with those of the best players. From several years of play, we've determined that the computer programs that always make the highest-scoring plays are about as good as the 200th top-rated player. These programs have little concern for rack balance, the endgame, or the openness of a board. That means that if you simply learn all the words in the *OSPD4* and are able to find them over the board, you won't need much strategy to beat most anyone.

Moving up a notch, there are at least two outstanding computer programs that consider rack balancing in their decision-making. These programs play about as well as the 10th top-rated player. There is one program that includes rack balance and plays a nearly perfect endgame. At its highest level, the program plays as well as any human being in the world. It is clear that endgame skills are of vital importance to the very best players.

Given the above, we thought we would provide our readers with some tips on how to improve endgame play.

Incidentally, the endgame is the most difficult, yet often the most aesthetically beautiful, part of SCRABBLE. Many games between experts are won or lost in the last two or three plays. And you don't have to know all the words to enjoy playing a good endgame position.

Tracking Tiles

The first thing to know is that you can't play an endgame well unless you know which tiles are left to play. The expert tracks the tiles played during the game so that s/he always knows what's left to draw. In fact, many players include a list of the 100 tiles (9 As, 2 Bs, etc.) printed on their score sheets. This is called either a "frequency list" or a (preprinted) "tracking sheet." As the letters are played on the board, they are crossed off the list. Many players create their own special tracking sheets, though some directors provide them free at tournaments.

How does tracking help you win games? As most experts can tell you, SCRABBLE is a game of probabilities. You can make more effective decisions regarding your rack leave and your opponent's next play if you know what tiles are left to play. For instance:

A. It might help you to know the precise number of vowels or consonants left to play. *Example:* Your rack is AAEKNPT with three tiles in the bag, and your tracking shows that all the vowels but your three have been played on the board. You should be able to take advantage of the fact that your opponent has no vowels! Look to form setup plays that your opponent can't block because s/he has no vowels. (See chapter 22, Diagram 22-11, page 328, for a good example of a setup play.)

B. Knowing whether you can get stuck with the Q should affect your thinking about the last few plays. *Example:* There is one tile in the bag. Three of the four Us are on the board. There are no Is open for QI, and you don't know where the Q is. You're 60 points ahead. The eight unseen tiles are ADELNQUW. You realize there is no way you can lose the game unless you get stuck with the Q. *Solution:* Pass your turn! Let your opponent either play his or her Q or draw it. While you may win by fewer points (since most of the time your opponent will get a free turn and 25 to 30 free points), you guarantee the win! If your opponent doesn't have the Q, realizes your strategy and passes, just remember that after six passes the game will be over, and you'll win!

Instead, if you make a play on the board, you're likely to win only 87 percent to 95 percent of the time, losing when you get stuck with the Q. That's not nearly as good as 100 percent of the time, as many unlucky players will testify. They'll tell you about the games in which they were 100 points ahead with one tile in the bag, then lost because they drew the Q and couldn't play it. In many of these cases, they simply didn't take the proper precautions.

Questions we often hear from those attempting to learn tracking are:

Q: **What's the use of tracking? I've tried it, and all that happens is I get confused.**

A: That's not uncommon. We find that everyone gets a little rattled when s/he first learns how to track. Although we're not brain scientists, from our own experience it seems that the acts of tracking, scoring, and looking for words utilize different parts of the brain. Doing all three tasks at the same time involves an extra effort—"switching gears," so to speak.

In order to avoid this confusion, track only the ten "power tiles" and the four Us. The power tiles are the two blanks, the four Ss, and the J, Q, X, and Z.

Or if you really want to start slowly, just keep track of the Ss and blanks. Just knowing which of these letters are still available can give you that extra edge in deciding how many tiles to play late in the game. You can learn to track more of the tiles as you gain experience. Many experts will admit it took a year or more before they could track all 100 tiles accurately without negatively affecting their playing skills.

Q: **How can I take advantage of tracking?**

A: Stop to look at your tracking sheet before you make your final decision to play a word. When at least sixty tiles have been played, use your tracking sheet to answer some of the following questions (or others) that may arise as you look for your best play:

1. "Do I need or want to draw the X or E or any other special tile in order to win?" The answer to this question may tell you whether you should play more or fewer tiles per turn.

2. "Do I need to avoid drawing certain tiles [e.g., Q or Z]?" If yes, you may want to play fewer tiles.
3. "Am I far behind, with no bingo in sight?" In that case look for ways to set up the remaining high-point letters, even if you haven't drawn them yet. Remember that even if your opponent draws them, you'd have lost anyway!
4. "Am I way ahead?" If so, do you need to block your opponent from using certain bonus squares? In that case, be aware of hot spots where the unplayed X, Z, or J can earn game-winning scores. Then block those hot spots to keep your opponent from catching up.
5. "What's the vowel–consonant situation?" If one player has either no vowels or no consonants, that could give his or her opponent an enormous advantage in the endgame. You'll also want to be alert to whether your next leave should have more consonants or vowels.
6. "Of the vowels left, which am I likely to duplicate on my rack?" Near the end of the game, if there are five Is, two As, and one E left to play, you probably want to rid your rack of Is.
7. "How many Ns, Rs, and Ts are still available? Which am I more likely to draw?" Since you want to avoid duplication of letters, you can use this knowledge to decide which consonant to play when a choice is available.
8. "Can I afford to pass, hoping my opponent will draw the Q, thereby increasing my chances of winning?" See example **B** on pages 258–59. You may not be able to answer these questions confidently at first. If not, then guess. Later, ask an expert what s/he would have done. The more you ask questions and get good answers, the quicker you'll gain the experience to rely on your own answers. See chapter 22, Diagrams 22-3, 22-10 through 22-15, 22-17, and 22-25 for nine examples of excellent endgame play.

STEP THREE: LEARN YOUR OPPONENT'S STRENGTHS AND WEAKNESSES

As you have seen throughout this book, there are several different skills by which you may measure your opponents. As you recognize each of these skills, or lack thereof, you can play accordingly to maximize your chances of winning.

Bingo vision. Does your opponent have an extensive bingo vocabulary? If so, watch for the telltale one- and two-tile fishing plays. While everyone occasionally fishes for bingos, the true bingo master will more often draw for and then actually play the bingo on the next turn. Much of the time you won't be able to do anything about it. But when you have a choice of plays, consider making a blocking play if your opponent has telegraphed his or her intentions.

On the other hand, the would-be bingo master may have a weakness: overfishing. There are many who rely too heavily on bingos to win their games.

This results in their fishing with a 10-to-15-point play instead of taking a strategically sounder 25-to-35-point play. If you encounter these players, and see that they don't draw their bingos very frequently on their following plays, you can probably rest a little easier about opening the board with a play of 25 to 30 points. In other words: Don't be afraid of opening the board when you have a decent play against those who fish too much!

Defense. There are players who delight in blocking the board. They will often take 10 points instead of 30 just to block the board. If you face one of these people, play as open as you can! They won't take advantage of the opportunities. They'll be too preoccupied trying to block the board. And even if they see their better plays, they'll often be afraid to play them, since they may open the board more!

Turnover. If your opponent plays only two or three tiles per turn, go out of your way to play more tiles whenever you have the choice, even if you score fewer points. That's to ensure that you have a better chance to draw the blanks and Ss ahead of your opponent. The more tiles you play, the better chance you have of drawing the better tiles. However, we caution you to be prudent with this principle, since it's not always optimal. It works best with opponents who generally play too few tiles.

Knowing your opponent. What is your opponent thinking? As in poker, there are telltale signs of body language that can help you read your opponent's thoughts. Every player exhibits different signals unconsciously, so you should approach learning about your opponents individually. Furthermore, some may want to mislead you with a variety of silent mannerisms. The more you play with a variety of opponents, the more experience and skill in this area you'll develop.

How do you take advantage of reading your opponent? Here's one way: If you truly believe your opponent has a bad rack, you should consider making the play that opens the board but gives you the best leave. This puts pressure on your opponent. S/he may think: "Do I exchange tiles and leave the opening for my opponent, or should I make a 12-point blocking play and keep a horrible leave?" By presenting your opponents with such difficult decisions, not only do you take advantage of their poor rack, but you give them a chance to make a mistake.

In conjunction with the above, ask yourself: Do you telegraph your thinking to your opponent? If you do, then you will probably find yourself losing to players with lesser vocabularies and weaker anagramming skills. Try to keep your body movements and facial expressions as neutral as possible. For example, suppose you feel a strong emotional response every time you draw a playable bingo. Many times this won't matter. However, if you show any sign of this emotion when there is only one bingo opening on the board, don't be surprised if the opening is blocked!

Hooks. Some players are known for setting up hook plays. For instance, early in a game at a national championship, one expert played the unusual word OORALIS horizontally. He began this word at 8B, one square to the right of the middle Triple Word Score on 8A. What he was hoping was that his opponent wouldn't know the word WOORALIS, which is a variant spelling of OORALIS. Later, with a W and just a few other letters, he scored 60-plus points with that hook word. This is good strategy if you think your opponent doesn't know a particular word. And even if s/he does, you may be the first one to draw the hook letter.

Knowing when it's advantageous to leave such dangerous hooks means knowing your opponent's temperament and vocabulary. (Is s/he defensive? Does s/he know the word?) As we said above, any play that pressures the opponent may lead to a strategic blunder that gives you better odds of winning.

STEP FOUR: DEVELOP THE RIGHT ATTITUDES

You now have the necessary vocabulary and playing skills, but you still don't win as often as you think you should. You are ready for the last piece from the SCRABBLE game expert's bag of tricks—the right mental approach.

The first thing you need to know—and always remember—is that everybody loses! You may play as well as the best player in the world and still not win. It's just as important to recognize that as it is to realize that most losses are accompanied by playing errors. To help you keep a perspective, you might want to do what some veteran tournament players do. They count how many of the ten power tiles they drew during a loss. If they drew three or fewer, it's likely that luck was definitely against them.

Luck aside, you need to know how you can guard against making mistakes. As a good player, your goals should be as follows:

1. **Always strive to find the best play available to you.**
2. **Once you've found a good play, look for a better one.**
3. **Ask yourself: "How do I know I've found the best play?"**

Let's discuss these elements individually in order to understand them better.

1. Always strive to find the best play available to you.

That may seem like a really silly thing to suggest. We can almost hear the response: "Of course I'm always looking for the best play! You don't need to waste time writing that!"

Our answer is that in the reality of competing against another human being, this simple motto is often forgotten. Here is a collection of thoughts that can interfere with your good thinking:

"Is this a collection of garbage tiles, or what?"

"I'll never win this game! It looks hopeless!"

"If I draw one more U, I'm quitting!"

If you've had these thoughts, or something like them, you're not alone. To compound your task, they're often accompanied by a substantial negative emotional response.

Your ability to find your best play will be affected by how much energy you give to feeling badly about your rack. The more victimized you feel, the more likely your next play will be a poor one.

Watch for these negative thoughts. When they intrude, just notice them dispassionately. Then refocus your attention on your rack and the board. **Stay alert about finding your best play among all the poor options.** Our experience is that you're likely to gather tremendous positive energy from a pure, childlike state of curiosity about what plays are possible in a given situation. Remember, you may lose anyway, but if you find a spectacular play you can more easily accept the loss emotionally.

Here are a few more attitude traps:

"I've never beaten this guy! He knows far more words than I do. Why even bother?"

"Look who my opponent is. This should be a piece of cake!"

There's probably not a player alive who hasn't had one of these thoughts when facing a particular opponent. When you have such thoughts, *beware*! That's because there is an element of luck in SCRABBLE, and almost anybody can beat anyone else on any particular occasion. We've seen players in tournaments repeatedly lose to opponents whom they beat consistently when there is nothing at stake. Thoughts that either overestimate or underestimate your playing skills definitely keep you from the task at hand. So, when you have such thoughts, just smile to yourself and appreciate the fact that you were alert enough to notice them. Then return to looking for the best play.

Here is another attitude trap:

"Look what I missed! What an idiotic play that was!"

Everyone makes mistakes over the SCRABBLE game board. If you should catch one of yours before the game ends, especially one that cost you the game, you'll undoubtedly feel a bit frustrated. We've seen many players lose their cool after an ill-timed challenge or missed bingo. When this happens they're practically guaranteed to make a poor next play. In fact, these negative emotional states can sometimes last for several games. We've seen top players go from six wins and zero losses to six wins and four losses, often due to an accumulation of negative energy. A well-known champion has twice ended important tournaments losing the last three games. In one he still managed to finish in first place. In the other, he finished second by a total of only 30 points. On each occasion, he admitted it wasn't just bad luck; there was an element of negativity in his thinking.

Somehow, you need to recognize that mistakes are a part of the game. All the top players make them occasionally. Sometimes, when they're made in a championship tournament, these errors can cost thousands of dollars. It's our experience that you'll feel better, and your opponents will respect you more, if you just hang tough. This is particularly important when you are playing a series of games, either at home or in a tournament. Most experts simply forget their mistakes and losses and move on to the next game, fully energetic and eager to play!

2. Once you've found a good play, look for a better one.

The expert will continue to look for better plays. Keep in mind that only when you know all the options will you be able to make the best choice. Since you don't have an unlimited amount of time to make each play, our suggestion is that you always look for a play that you consider "adequate." Then continue looking for a better one until you've used up whatever time you've allotted for that play.

We know a top player who, early in his SCRABBLE game career, held the tiles OVERDOS against a strong expert. There was an E on the board between two Double Word Score squares. He was preparing to play OVERDOES for 98 points if his opponent didn't block him. His opponent kindly played the bingo CLEARING on another part of the board, placing the C in the third position between two Triple-Triples. This expert was so eager to play OVERDOES that it wasn't until after he had started his opponent's timer and looked at the C that he suddenly realized what he had done. He asked his opponent sheepishly: "Could I take my play back?" What he had missed was VOCODERS for 185 points! Of course, his opponent wouldn't let him change his play.

3. Ask yourself: "How do I know I've found the best play?"

You will probably never really know for sure if you've found the best play, given the fallibility of the human mind. But we suggest you'll be confident that you did your best if, before you play, you make a systematic search of the board. Experts routinely spend extra time doing exhaustive board searches to find their best plays, especially if they have a blank tile.

Even after a game is over, experts will often review all the significant or questionable plays of the game. By spending five or ten minutes discussing the merits of alternate plays, you'll learn new strategies and develop friendships with your opponents.

Now that we've given you all the tools, we'd like to show you how the best players put it all together. Chapter 22 shows you some outstanding plays from actual tournament play. Enjoy!

22 EXAMPLES OF OUTSTANDING SCRABBLE® GAME PLAY

Though most players don't record the words from their games, many like to recall their favorite plays. The following is a collection of fifty-five examples of excellent expert play. All but a few are taken either from club or tournament play. We offer these positions in order to share with you our appreciation of the possibilities, nuances, and beauty of SCRABBLE play. We also thank our NASPA experts for sharing their talents with you. Enjoy! Unless otherwise specified, the answers are common words.

Example 1

1990 National SCRABBLE Championship, New York: Charlie Carroll, MN (1991 Cincinnati, OH, Masters Champion)

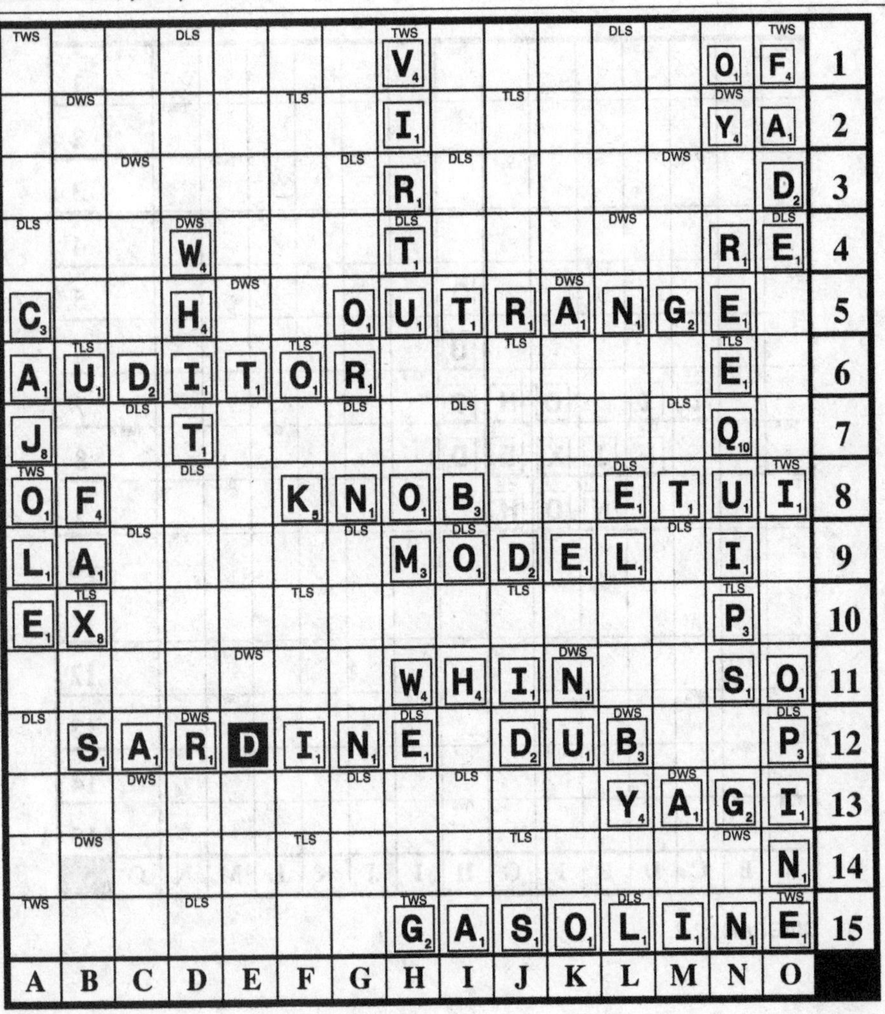

V O F 1
I Y A 2
R D 3
W T R E 4
C H O U T R A N G E 5
A U D I T O R E 6
J T Q 7
O F K N O B E T U I 8
L A M O D E L I 9
E X P 10
W H I N S O 11
S A R D I N E D U B P 12
Y A G I 13
N 14
G A S O L I N E 15
A B C D E F G H I J K L M N O

DIAGRAM 22-1

Carroll's score: 371 *Opponent's score:* 380
Carroll's rack: **A E I L M R T**

Carroll can't bingo, but he does find the second-best play. His play would probably be unanimously voted the "flashiest" of most tournaments. You should have a good working knowledge of the two-letter words in order to find the play. The answer is on page 327.

Example 2

Joe Edley, NY vs. Rita Norr, CT (1987 National Champion)

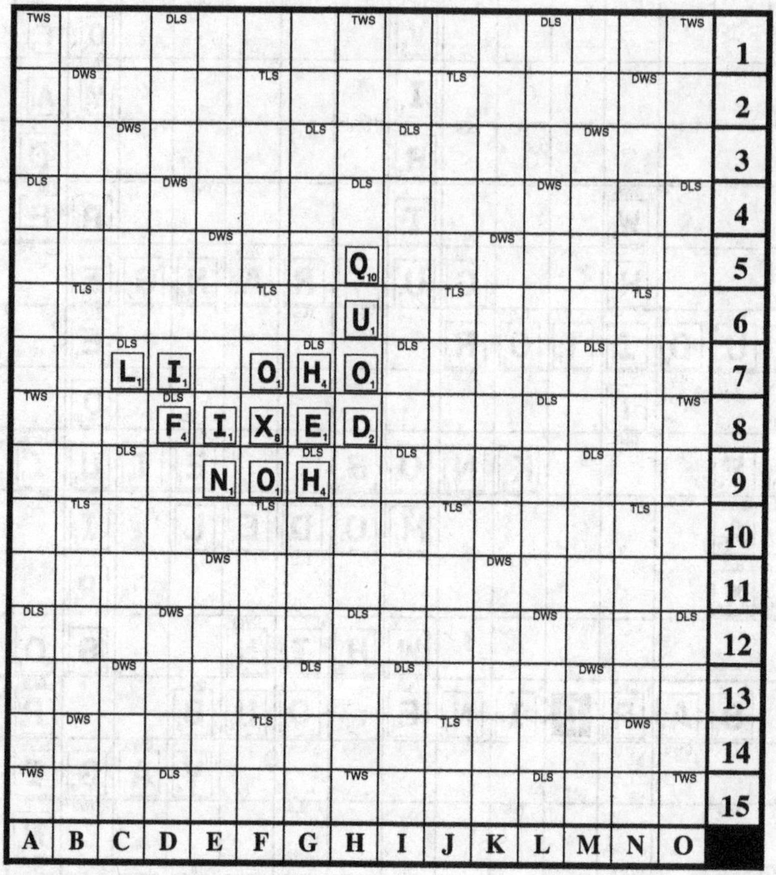
Q
U
L I O H O
F I X E D
N O H
A B C D E F G H I J K L M N O
1 2 3 4 5 6 7 8 9 10 11 12 13 14 15

DIAGRAM 22-2

Edley's score: 79 *Norr's score:* 53
Edley's rack: **D E E L P R S**

Though PEDLERS is an acceptable bingo, it doesn't play. The answer is on page 327.

This game was played during a friendly match prior to an upcoming tournament. Not all of our readers will be familiar with one of the three- or four-letter words considered as a play. We include this example because it shows how a knowledge of hook words can help you score more.

Example 3

Waltham, MA, 2000 championship, Brian Cappelletto, IL vs. Jim Kramer, MN

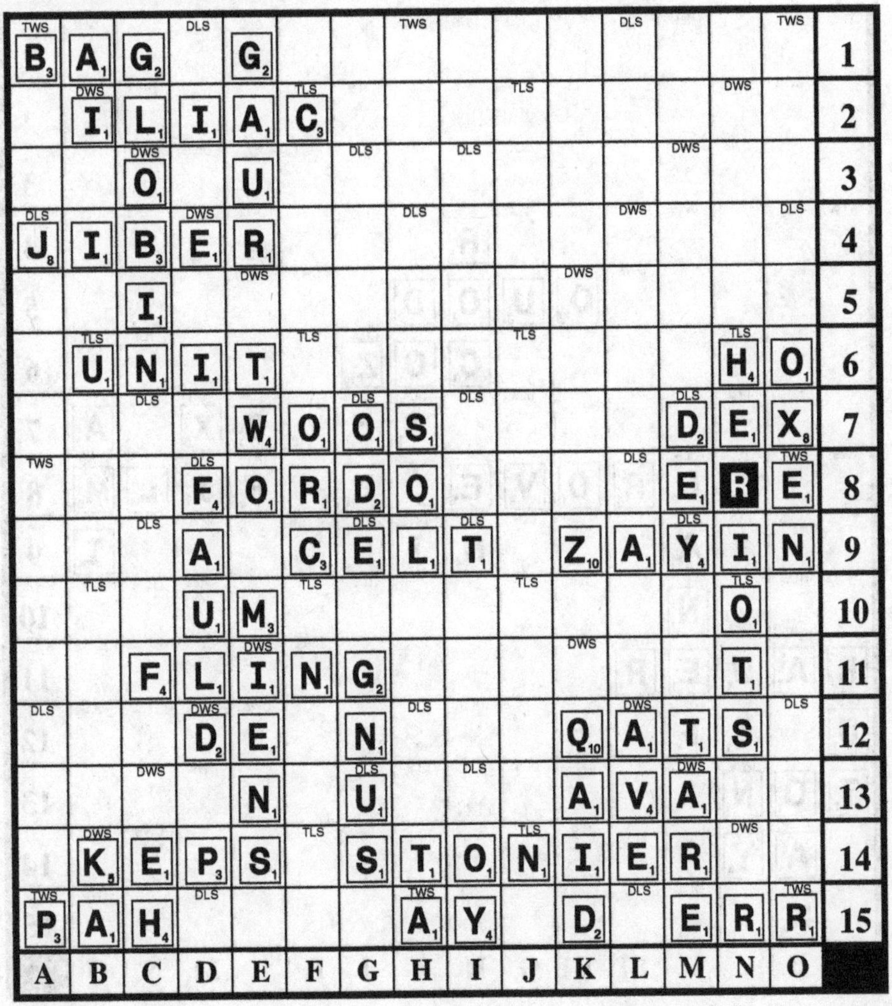
1 B A G G
2 I L I A C
3 O U
4 J I B E R
5 I
6 U N I T H O
7 W O O S D E X
8 F O R D O E R E
9 A C E L T Z A Y I N
10 U M O
11 F L I N G T
12 D E N Q A T S
13 N U A V A
14 K E P S S T O N I E R
15 P A H A Y D E R R
A B C D E F G H I J K L M N O

DIAGRAM 22-3

Cappelletto's score: 335 *Kramer's score:* 357
Cappelletto's rack: **E M N R T ?** Kramer's rack: **E E I L W**

After a first and second glance, this looks impossible for Cappelletto to win. But if you know an unusual five-letter word, it's a sparkling example of how to create "something" from "nothing." The answer is on page 327.

Example 4

1989 National SCRABBLE Championship, New York City: Elaine Glowniak, MI

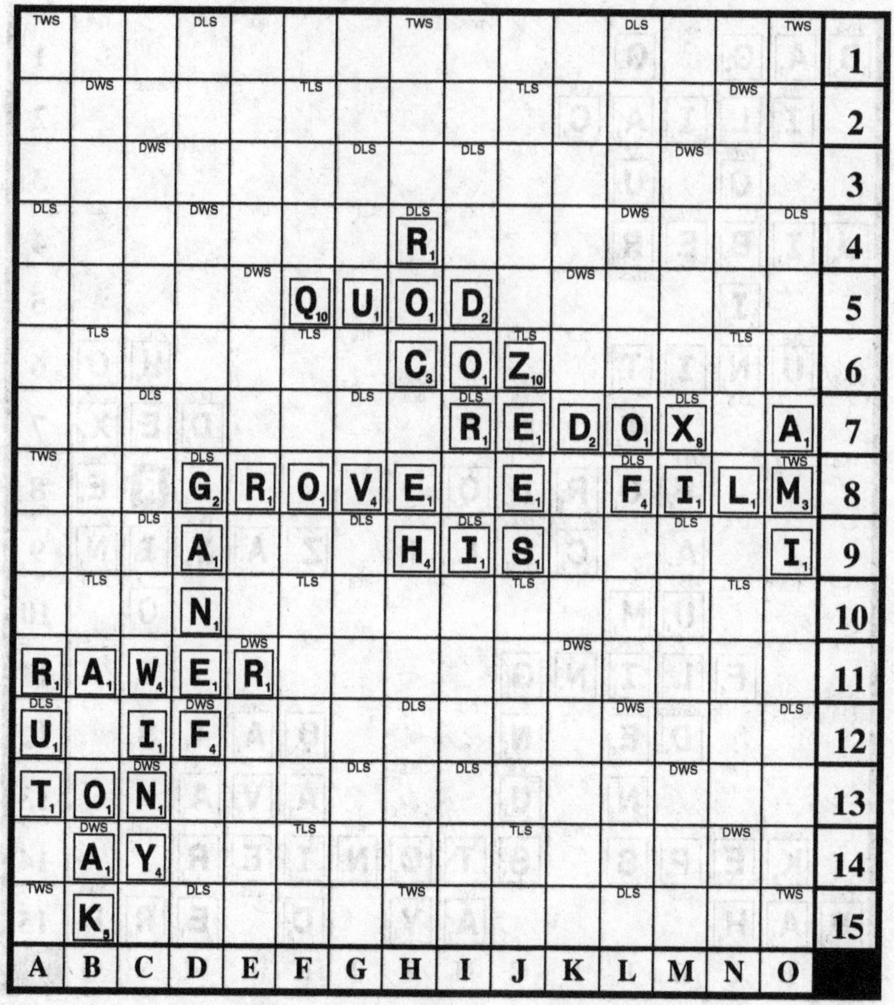

DIAGRAM 22-4

Glowniak's score: 177 *Opponent's score:* 124
Glowniak's rack: **D E H N T U V**

Though there is no bingo, Glowniak finds a very nice way to both balance her rack and score well. The answer is on page 327.

Example 5

1992 Atlantic City Championship, NJ: Robert Felt, CA (1990 National SCRABBLE Champion)

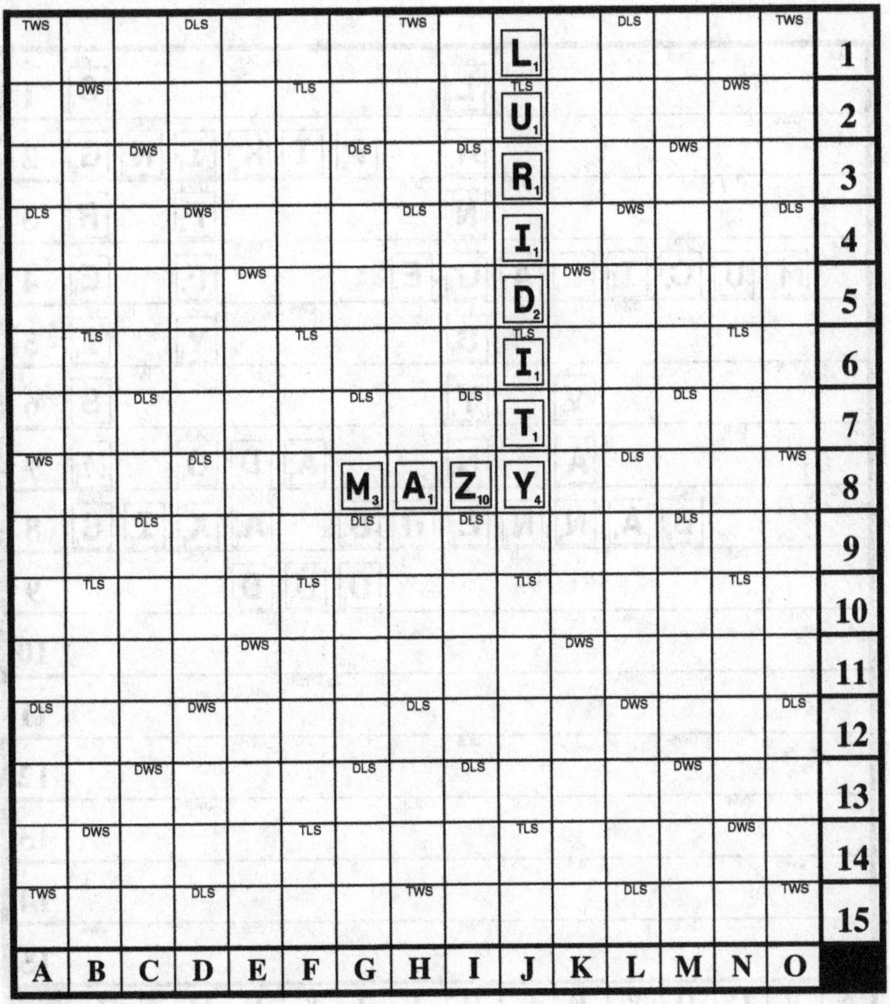
L U R I D I T Y
M A Z Y
A B C D E F G H I J K L M N O
1 2 3 4 5 6 7 8 9 10 11 12 13 14 15

DIAGRAM 22-5

Felt's score: 36 *Opponent's score:* 0 or 66
Felt's rack: **E P P R S T U**

Opponent has just played LURIDITY. Felt called "Hold!" and is certain it is unacceptable. Should he challenge it off the board? He could instead play PURPLEST through the L for 89 points. What did he do? The answer is on page 327.

Example 6

Michigan SCRABBLE Game Club, January 1993: Chuck Armstrong, MI (winner of more than 100 tournaments)

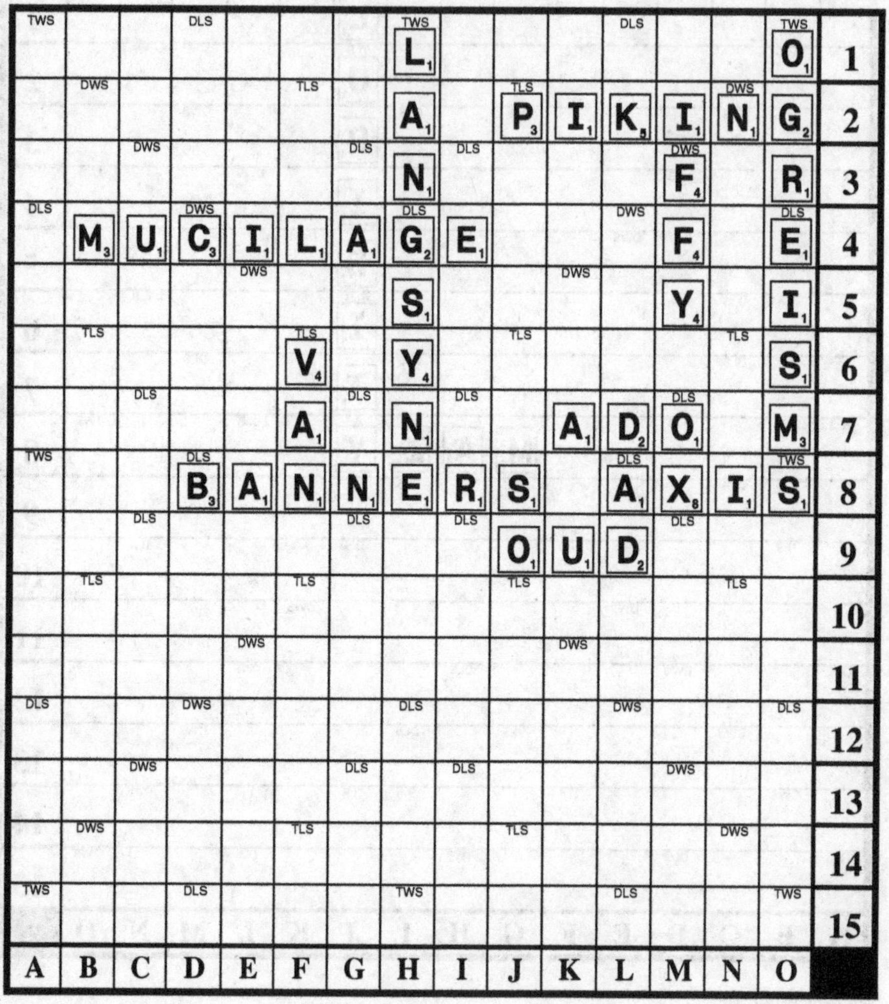

DIAGRAM 22-6

Armstrong's rack: **A E H O P R T**

Armstrong found a very nice common-word bingo. He eventually wound up playing seven bingos in this game. Besides the four already on the board and this one, he later played AWAITER and REOBJECT, to finish with 710 points, a new non-phoney high-scoring record at the time. The answer is on page 327.

Example 7

1987 National SCRABBLE Championship, Las Vegas, NV: Howard Cohen, FL

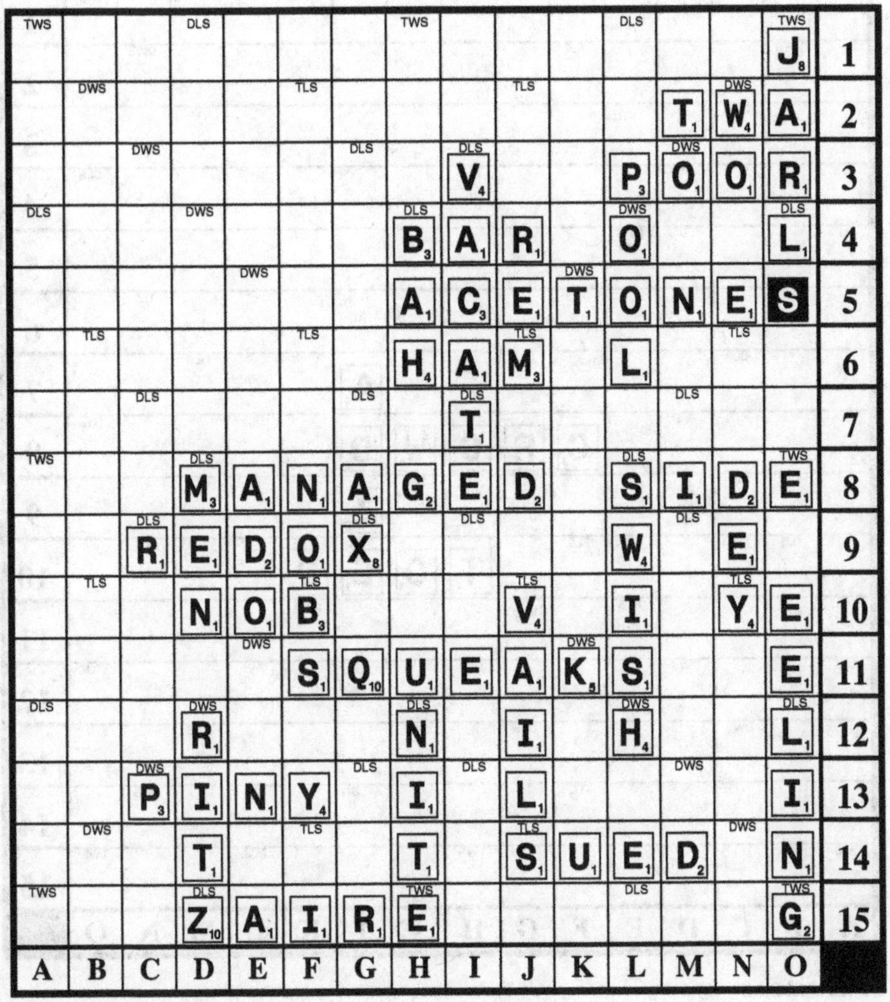

DIAGRAM 22-7

Cohen's rack: **C E O R T U ?**

Cohen is behind by 150 points and knows he can't win; nevertheless, he's able to find a beautiful play that we're sure he'll never forget. The answer is on page 327. (Note that EELING is a phoney.)

Example 8

1989 Grand Canyon Tournament, AZ: Alice Van Leunen, OR

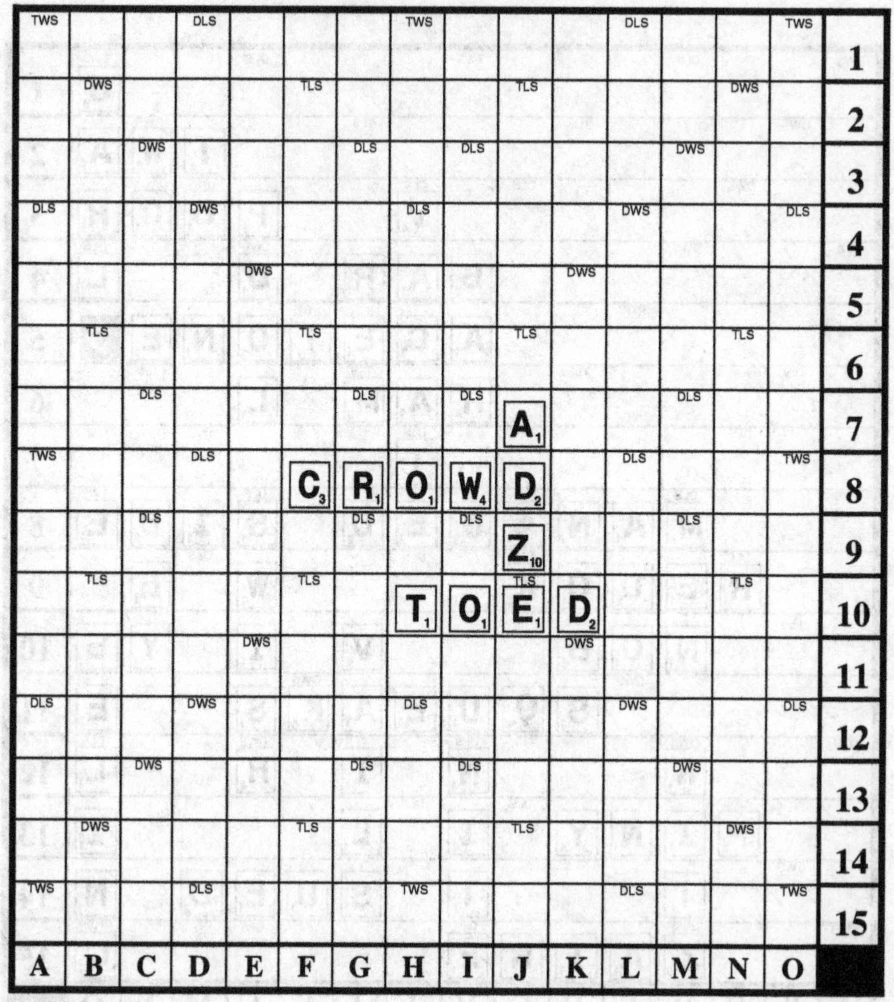
A
C R O W D
Z
T O E D
1 2 3 4 5 6 7 8 9 10 11 12 13 14 15
A B C D E F G H I J K L M N O

DIAGRAM 22-8

Van Leunen's rack: **A C L N R T ?**

There is an excellent bingo that can be played from H1 down to the O on H8. But Van Leunen finds an even better play! The answer is on page 327.

Example 9

1988 Pigeon Forge Tournament, IN: Dee Jackson, NY

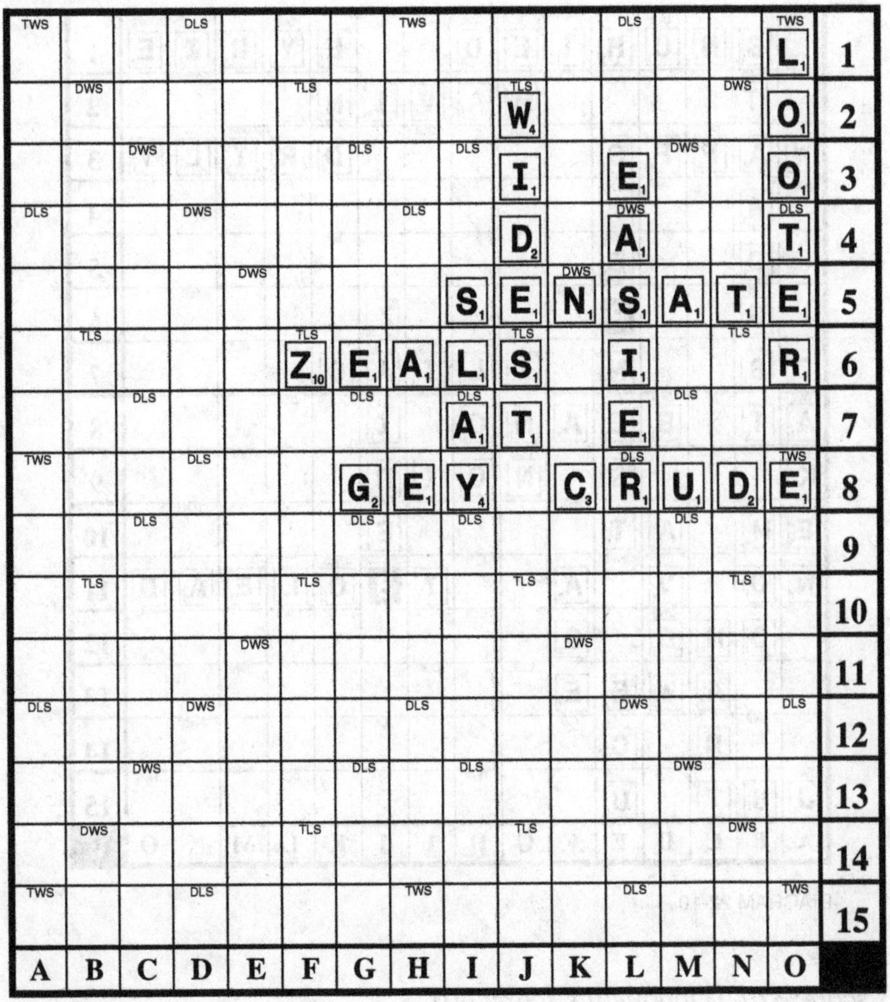

DIAGRAM 22-9

Jackson's rack: **E L N O R V ?**

We believe she found the only bingo! The answer is on page 328.

Diagrams 22-10 through 22-15 show endgame situations. As you're looking at them, keep in mind that the players had no more than five to ten minutes each to find the best play.

Example 10

1991 Atlantic City Tournament: Joe Edley, NY

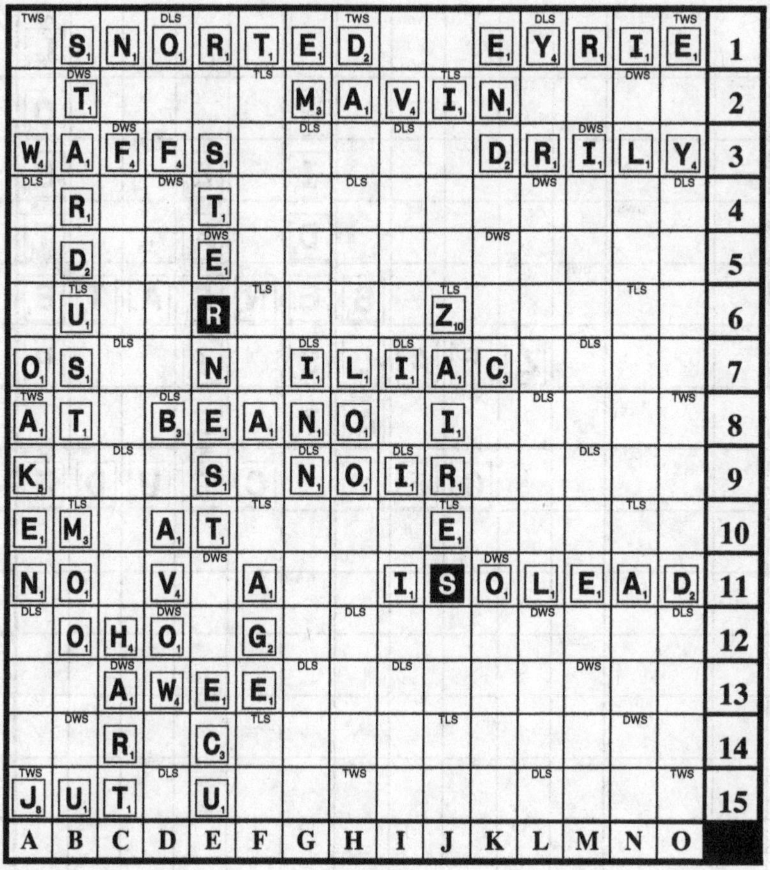

SNORTED EYRIE 1
T MAVIN 2
WAFFS DRILY 3
R T 4
D E 5
U R Z 6
OS N ILIAC 7
AT BEANO I 8
K S NOIR 9
EM AT E 10
NO V A I S OLEAD 11
OHO G 12
AWEE 13
R C 14
JUT U 15
A B C D E F G H I J K L M N O

DIAGRAM 22-10

Edley's score: 329 *Opponent's score:* 401
Edley's rack: **E E H L P U X** Opponent's rack: **G I P Q**

The actual score of the game was different from what is shown above. In actuality, Edley was ahead and had no fear of losing. We adjusted the score for dramatic effect to show you how many points Edley will earn. Given the above score, Edley would still have won. You might encounter an unfamiliar three-letter word while you analyze the position. The answer is on page 328. (Note that QI was not acceptable at that time.)

Example 11

Rita Norr, CT, against another expert at the New York City SCRABBLE Game Club in 1991

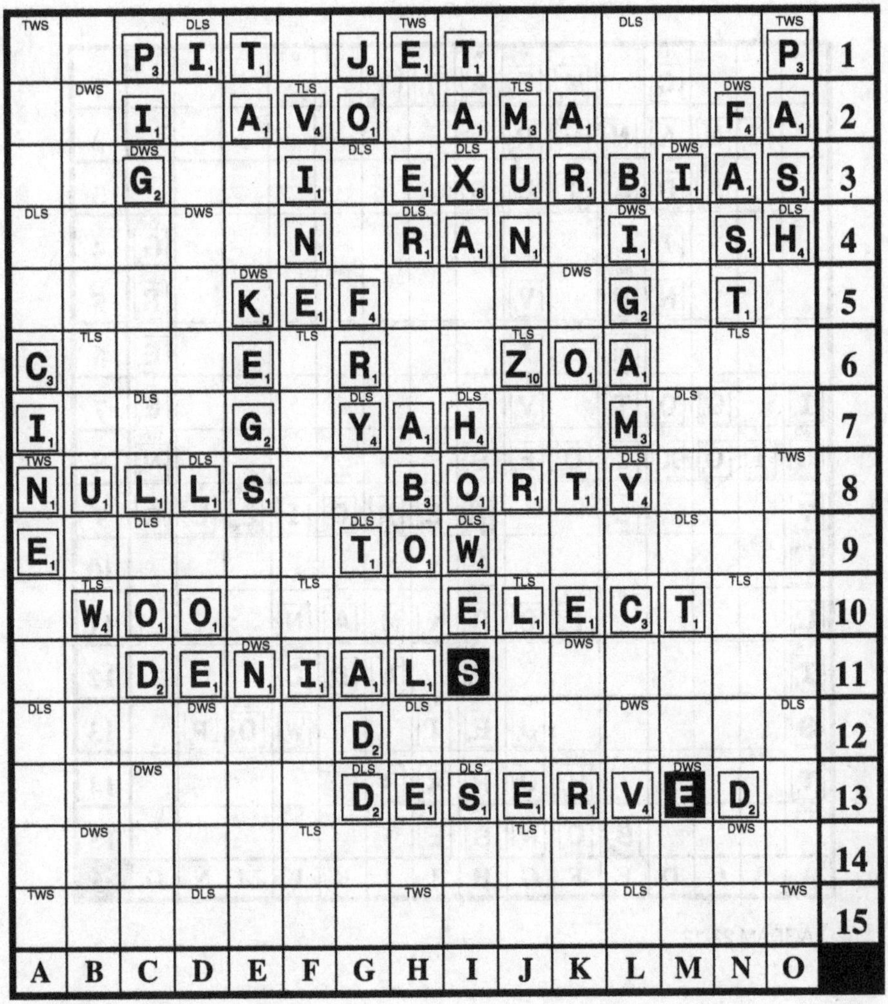

DIAGRAM 22-11

Norr's score: 360 *Opponent's score:* 420
Norr's rack: **E E N O Q R U** Opponent's rack: **I I N O U***

Though technically she has a lost game, Norr gives herself a chance to win by setting a clever trap for her opponent. The answer is on page 328.

*OI and UNI were not acceptable at the time this game was played.

Example 12

1985 National SCRABBLE Championship, Boston: Joe Edley, NY, vs. Ron Tiekert, NY, who won the event with 20 wins and only 2 losses

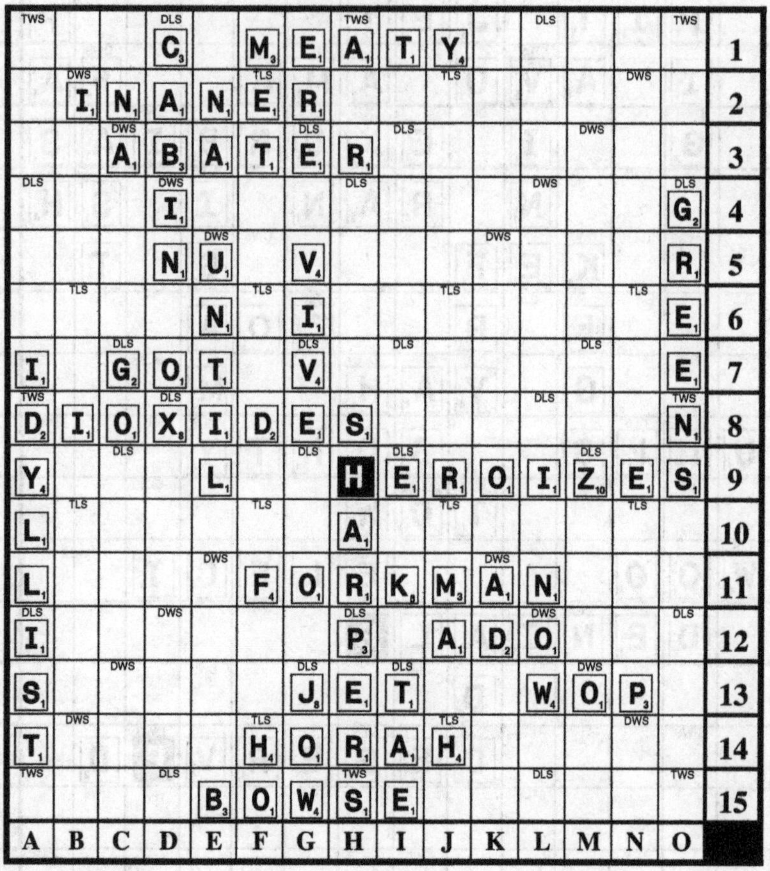
C MEATY
INANER
ABATER
I G
NU V R
N I E
I GOT V E
DIOXIDES N
Y L HEROIZES S
L A
L FORKMAN
I P ADO
S JET WOP
T HORAH
BOWSE
A B C D E F G H I J K L M N O

DIAGRAM 22-12

Edley's score: 326 *Tiekert's score:* 350
Edley's rack: **A D E E L U ?**

There is one tile in the bag, and the unseen tiles are C, F, G, I, Q, T, U, and U. With two minutes left to play, Edley wants to find a sure way to win. Simply playing SAD at 15A for 45 points won't necessarily win if his opponent has a good Q play. The answer is on page 328. (Note that FORKMAN is a phoney and QI was not yet acceptable.)

Example 13

1993 Western Championship, Reno, NV: Brian Cappelletto, AZ

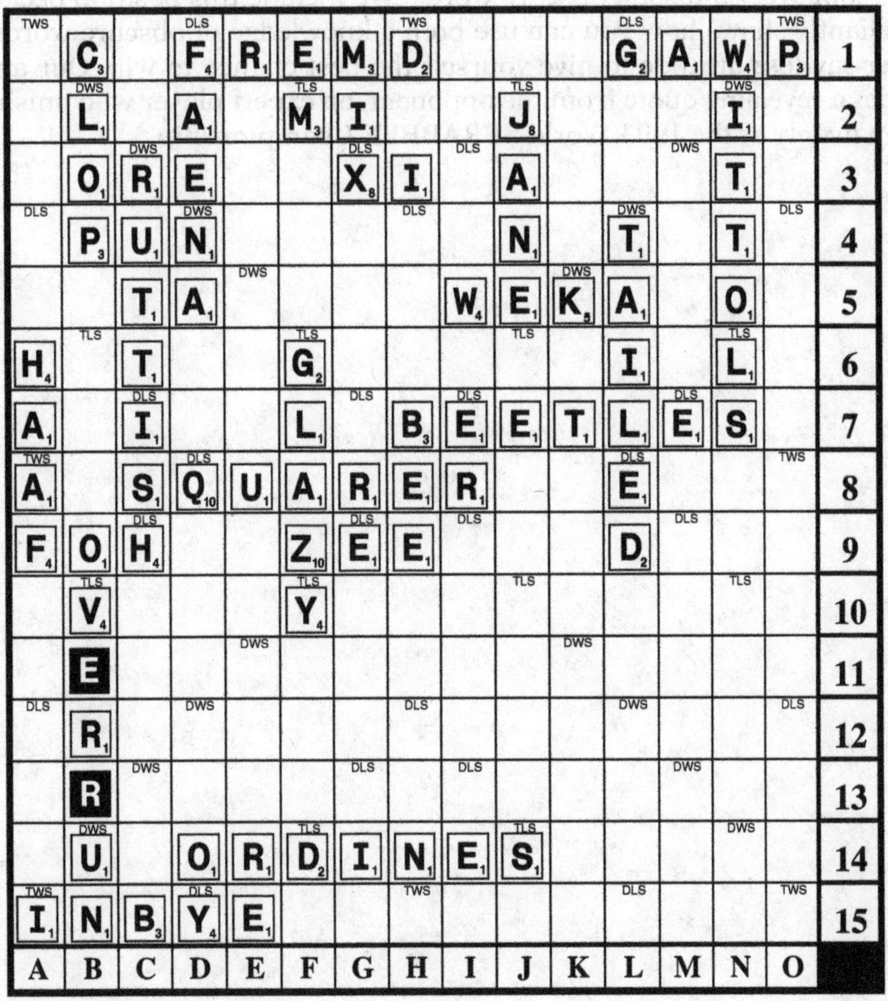

C F R E M D G A W P 1
L A M I J I 2
O R E X I A T 3
P U N N T T 4
T A W E K A O 5
H T G I L 6
A I L B E E T L E S 7
A S Q U A R E R E 8
F O H Z E E D 9
V Y 10
E 11
R 12
R 13
U O R D I N E S 14
I N B Y E 15
A B C D E F G H I J K L M N O

DIAGRAM 22-13

Cappelletto's score: 305 *Opponent's score:* 345
Cappelletto's rack: **A I N O O O S**

There is one tile in the bag. The eight unseen tiles are C, D, G, I, N, O, U, and V. How can Cappelletto play to give himself the best chance of winning? Given the score and his rack, it may seem impossible for him to win, but it's not! Of course, he does need a little help from the "tile gods" and his opponent! The answer is on page 328.

Warning: Our average reader won't find the answer to this one unless s/he knows some very unusual, obscure words. We include this position because it so brilliantly shows how you can use both a knowledge of obscure words and a never-say-lose attitude to give yourself the best chance to win. Our answer includes a revealing quote from the opponent, an expert player who finished in the top twenty at the 1993 World SCRABBLE Championship.

Example 14

1990 National SCRABBLE Championship, Washington, DC: Joel Wapnick, Montreal (1983 National SCRABBLE Champion)

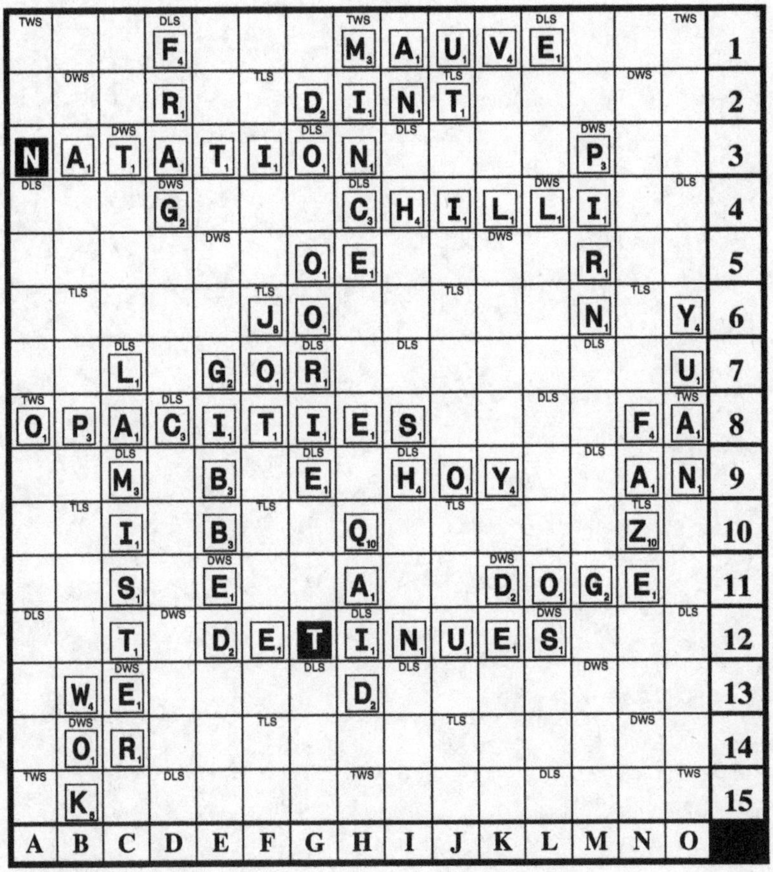

F MAUVE 1
R DINT 2
NATATION P 3
G CHILLI 4
OE R 5
JO N Y 6
L GOR U 7
OPACITIES FA 8
M B E HOY AN 9
I B Q Z 10
S E A DOGE 11
T DETINUES 12
WE D 13
OR 14
K 15
A B C D E F G H I J K L M N O

DIAGRAM 22-14

Wapnick's score: 327 *Opponent's score:* 316
Wapnick's rack: **E E E L S T W**

There are two tiles in the bag. The nine unseen tiles are: A, A, I, N, R, R, U, V, and X. Analysis will involve some uncommon, obscure words. The answer is on page 329.

Wapnick's play won the prize for the Most Strategic Play of the tournament. Watch out! Though it's a common word, it's not an obvious play. None of the expert judges initially thought that Wapnick's play was the best, but after a careful analysis they concluded it was.

Example 15

Played during a friendly match: Mike Baron, NM vs. Jeff Reeves, LA, 1989 (both players are experts and both have won many tournaments)

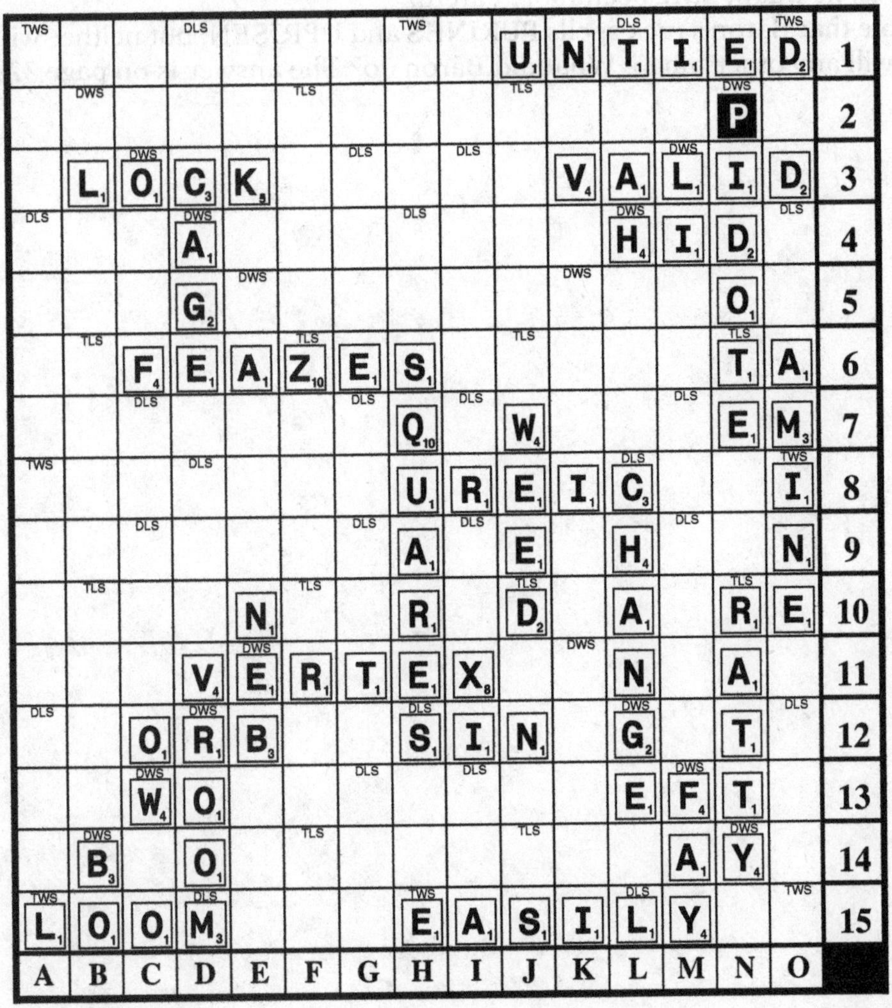

DIAGRAM 22-15

Baron's score: 267 *Reeves's score:* 321
Baron's rack: **E I N P R S U**

There is one tile in the bag. The eight unseen tiles are: A, G, I, J, O, P, T, and the blank. Reeves's last play was LOCK 3B 20 points. Baron finds a very clever way to give himself a chance to win! If Reeves is less than fully alert to Baron's plan, he will lose. Since the game was not played in a tournament, there was no exceptional motivation for winning or losing. We believe *that* played an important part in what transpired—had the game been more important to Reeves, he might have been more careful.

Note that Baron's rack spells PURINES and UPRISEN, but neither will play, nor will any other bingo. What did Baron do? The answer is on page 329.

Example 16

1999 Western Championship, Reno, NV: Stu Goldman, CA

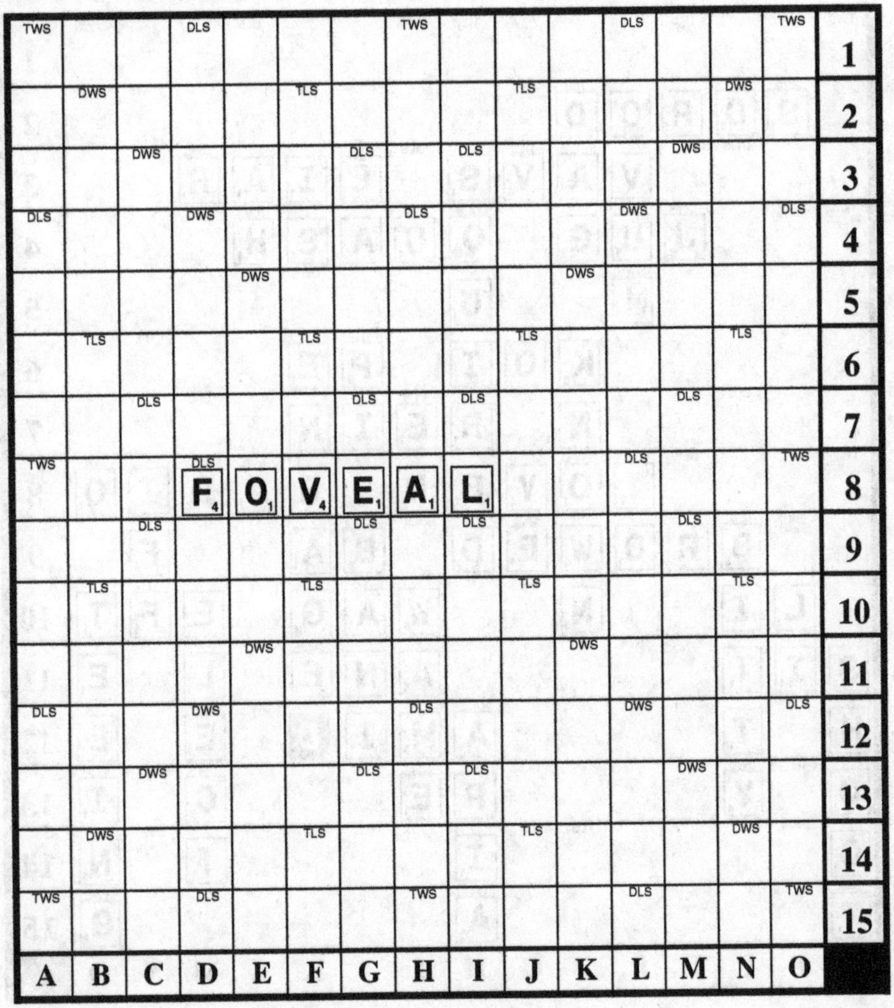
F O V E A L
A B C D E F G H I J K L M N O
1 2 3 4 5 6 7 8 9 10 11 12 13 14 15

DIAGRAM 22-16

Goldman's score: 0 *Opponent's score:* 32
Goldman's rack: **A I J N Q T U**

Should he go for points, get rid of the Q, or what? The answer is on page 329.

Example 17

January 1999, friendly game: James Cherry, ONT, CAN

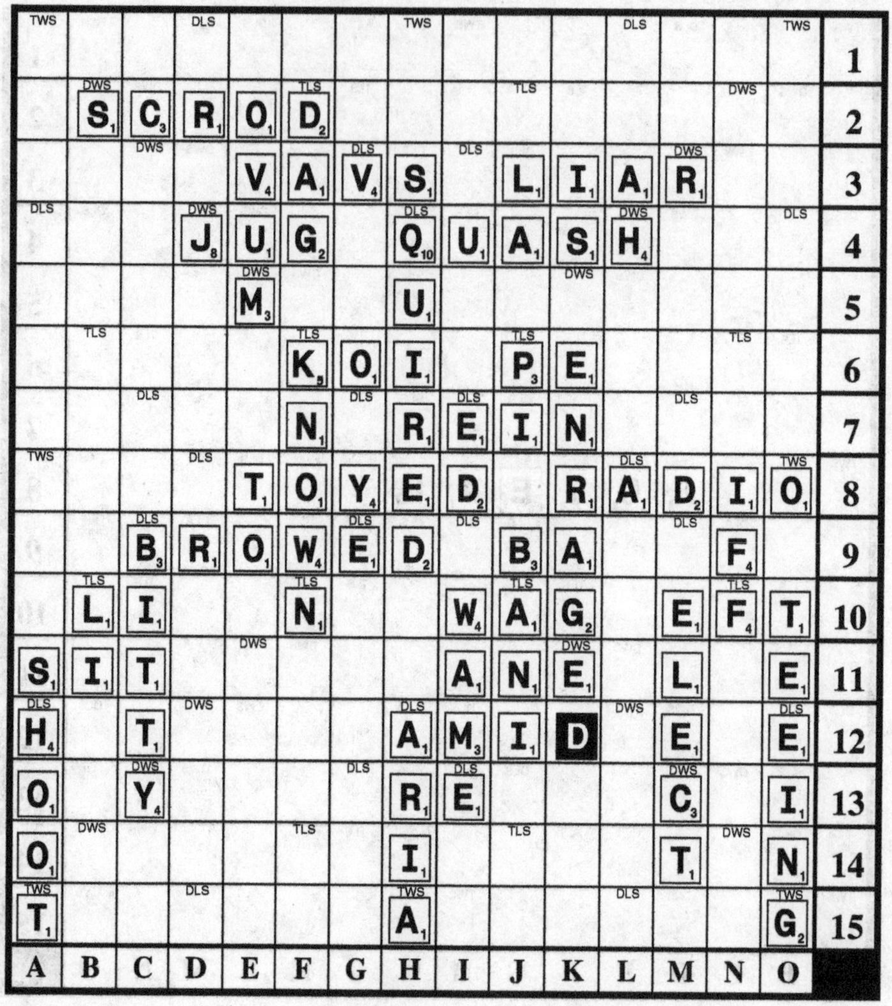
SCROD
VAVS LIAR
JUG QUASH
M U
KOI PE
N REIN
TOYED RADIO
BROWED BA F
LI N WAG EFT
SIT ANE L E
H T AMID E E
O Y RE C I
O I T N
T A G
A B C D E F G H I J K L M N O
1 2 3 4 5 6 7 8 9 10 11 12 13 14 15

DIAGRAM 22-17

Cherry's score: 276 *Opponent's score:* 338
Cherry's rack: **E E L O P Z ?** Opponent's rack: **N U X**

There is a way to win. It entails knowing unusual three- or four-letter words. These types of positions are very rare in actual play, but they are sweet when you do see them. The answer is on page 329.

Example 18

August 1998, friendly game: Christopher Sykes, ONT, CAN

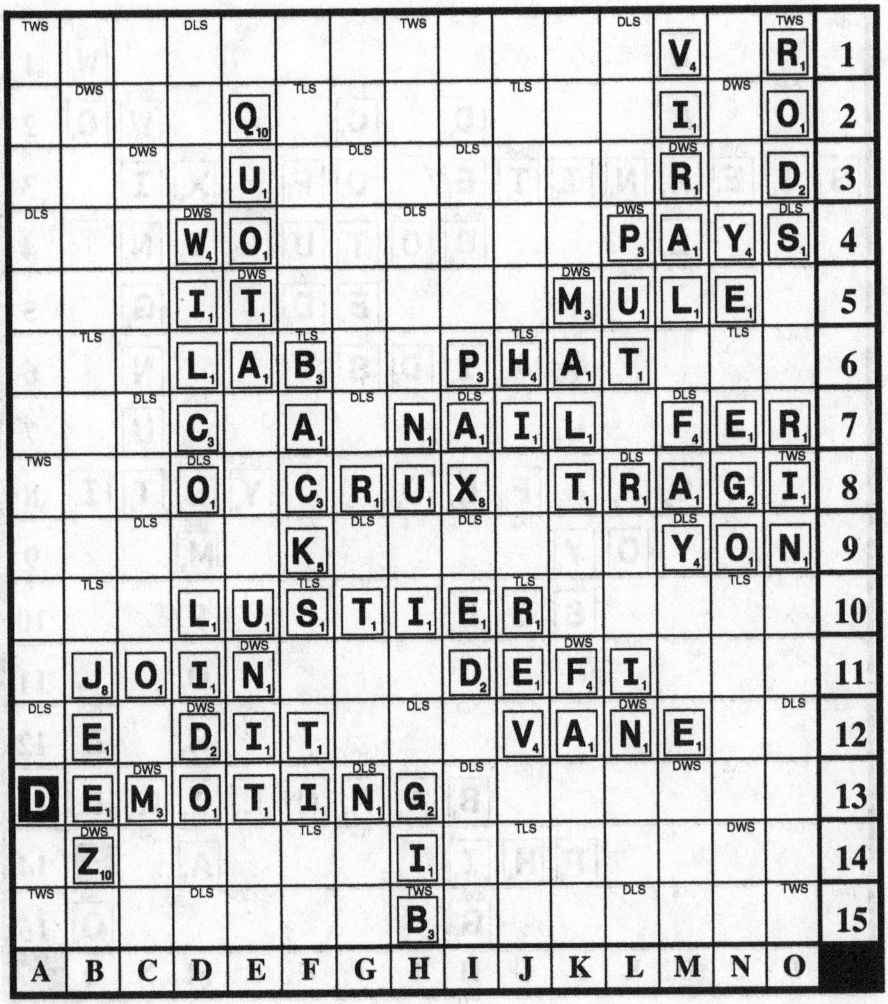

DIAGRAM 22-18

Sykes's score: 317 *Opponent's score:* 345
Sykes's rack: **A D E E N O W**

This position is a good example of how common-word plays are sometimes hard to see, but well worth making that extra effort to find. The answer is on page 330.

Example 19

May 1998, friendly game: Mark Pistolese, HI

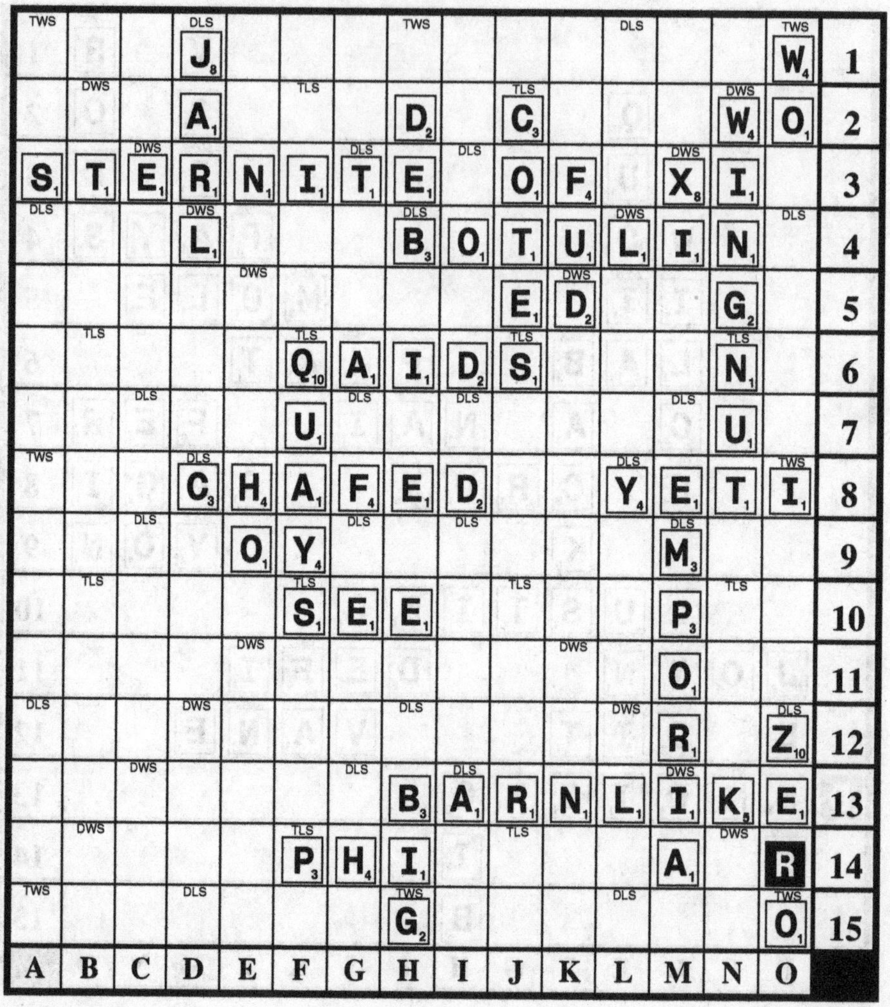

DIAGRAM 22-19

Pistolese's score: 310 *Opponent's score:* 393
Pistolese's rack: **E M N O R T T**

He has TORMENT, but no place to play it. Given how far behind he is, what should his strategy be in order to give himself a reasonable chance to win? The answer is on page 330.

Example 20

Portland, OR, 1997 SCRABBLE club tournament: Karen Merrill

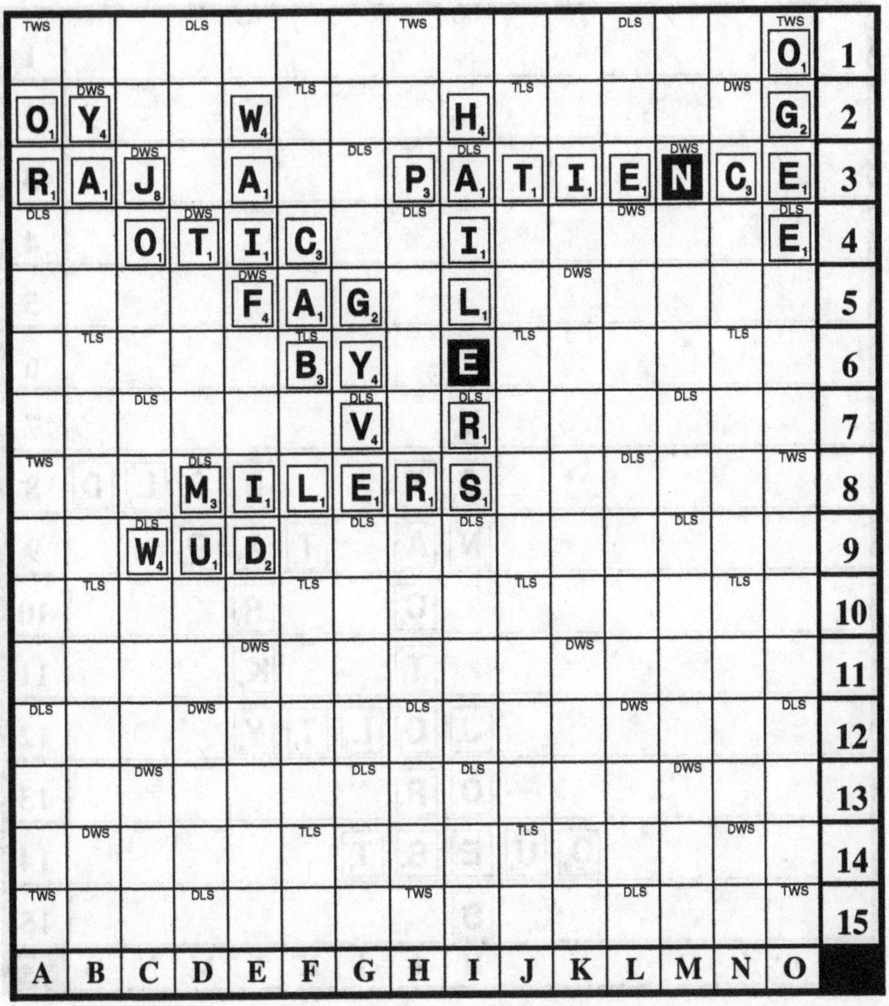
O
O Y W H G
R A J A P A T I E N C E
O T I C I E
F A G L
B Y E
V R
M I L E R S
W U D
1 2 3 4 5 6 7 8 9 10 11 12 13 14 15
A B C D E F G H I J K L M N O

DIAGRAM 22-20

Merrill's score: 187 *Opponent's score:* 159
Merrill's rack: **A D L Q R S U**

Lurking in this quiet-looking position is a whale of a play. It's somewhat of an obscure word, but a record-breaker. The answer is on page 330.

Example 21

1997, New York, friendly game: Randy Greenspan

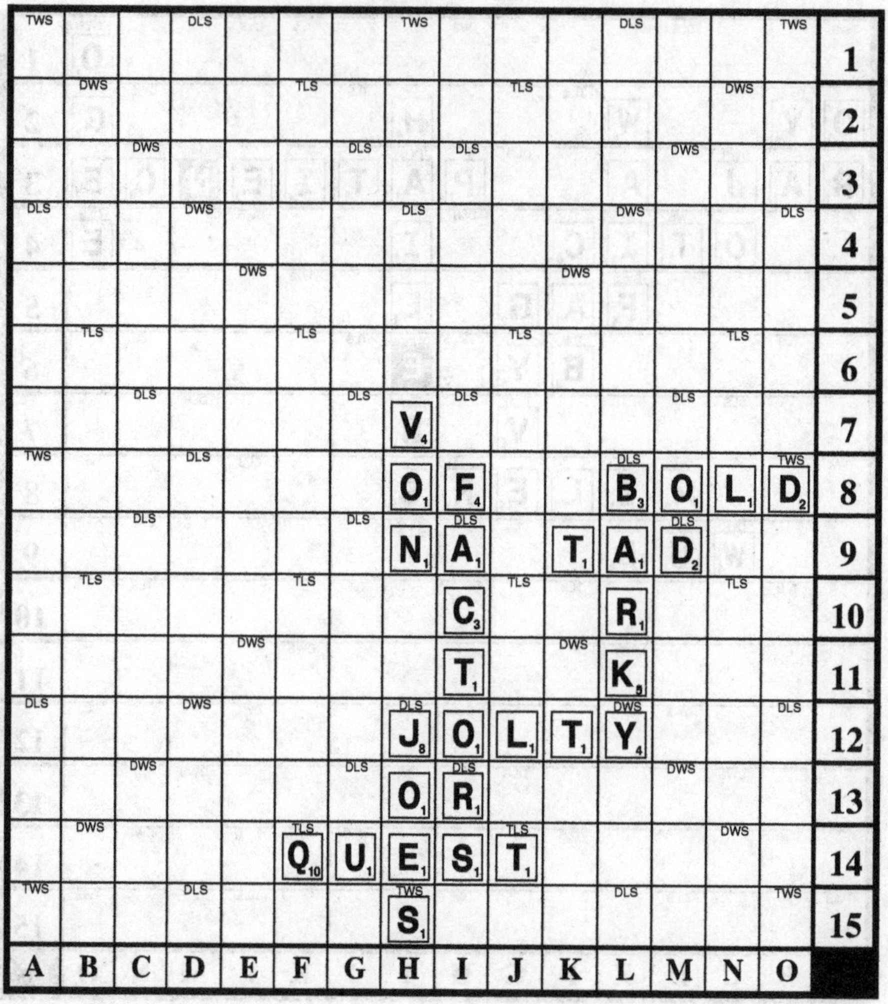

DIAGRAM 22-21

Greenspan's score: 144 *Opponent's score:* 131
Greenspan's rack: **A E I N R S W**

While he's close to a bingo, it's not quite there. Many players would just get rid of one or two tiles. However, there's more to do in this position than fish for bingos. (Note that VON is now a phoney.) The answer is on page 330.

Example 22

1998 Mid-Cities, TX, SCRABBLE Club #248: Carl Hickerson

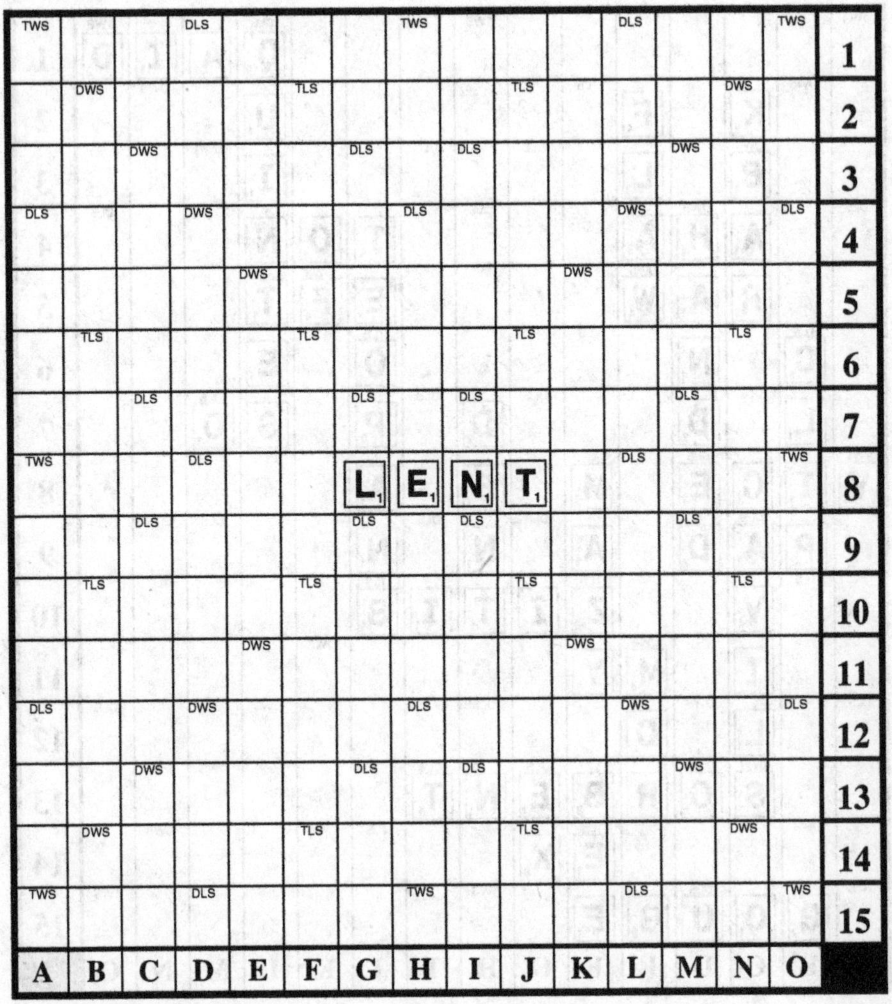
L1 E1 N1 T1
A B C D E F G H I J K L M N O
1 2 3 4 5 6 7 8 9 10 11 12 13 14 15

DIAGRAM 22-22

Hickerson's score: 0 *Opponent's score:* 8
Hickerson's rack: **A E L M O T V**

While there is no bingo, careful examination can lead to a play almost as devastating. The answer is on page 330.

Example 23

August 1996, friendly game: John Luebkemann, OH

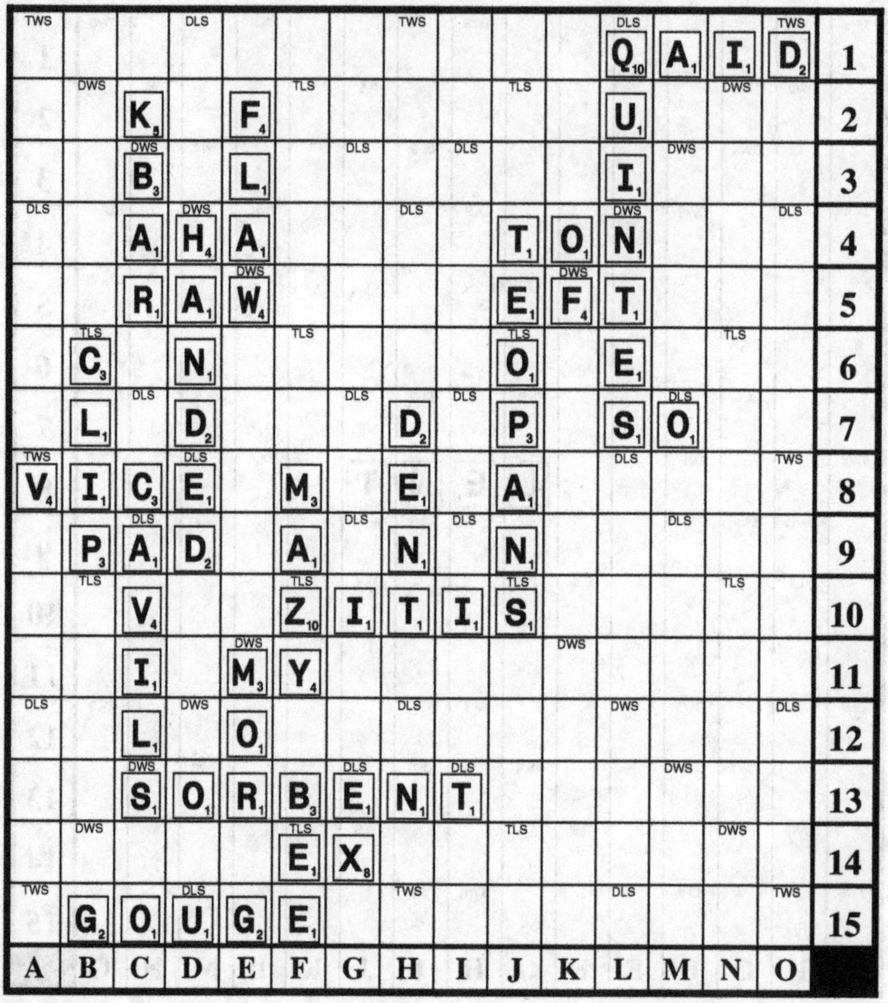

DIAGRAM 22-23

Luebkemann's score: 258 *Opponent's score:* 288
Luebkemann's rack: **A E I L N S ?**

There are clearly a large number of bingos with this fantastic rack. However, can you find his best? The best way to find it is to look for special opportunities that arise from the words already on the board. The answer is on page 330.

Example 24

April 1995, Gatlinburg, TN: Paul Epstein, MI

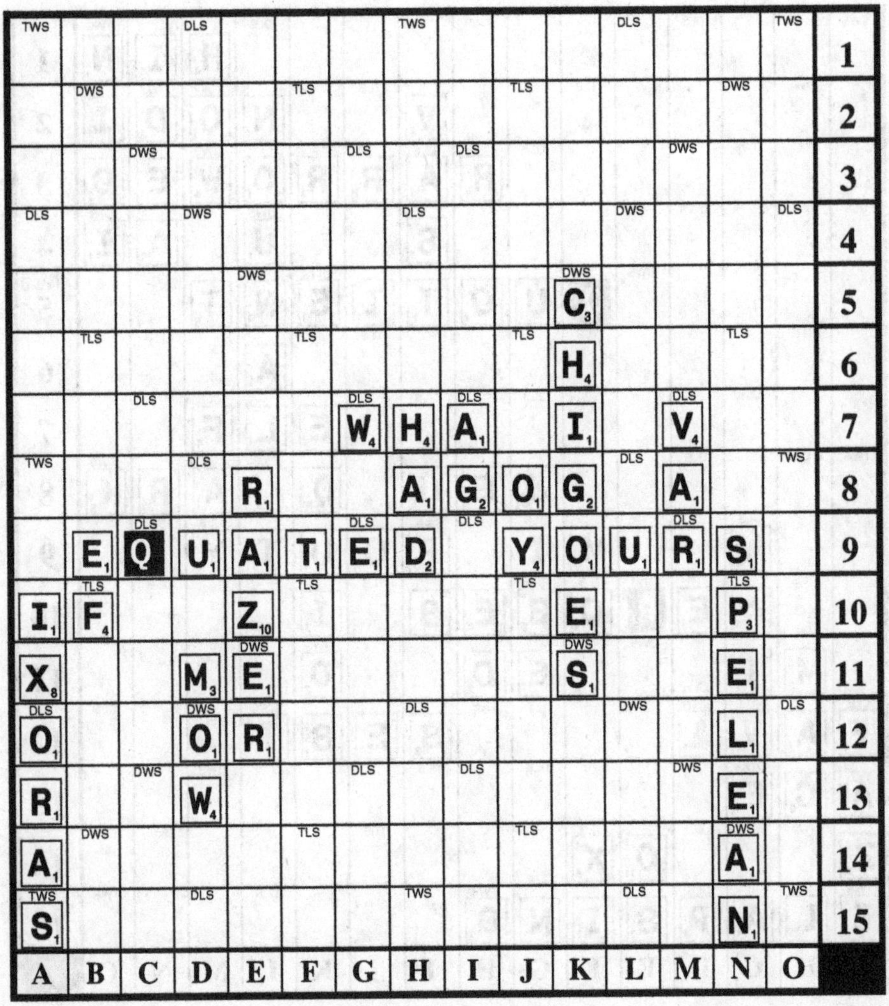
C
H
W H A I V
R A G O G A
E Q U A T E D Y O U R S
I F Z E P
X M E S E
O O R L
R W E
A A
S N
1 2 3 4 5 6 7 8 9 10 11 12 13 14 15
A B C D E F G H I J K L M N O

DIAGRAM 22-24

Epstein's score: 124 *Opponent's score:* 269
Epstein's rack: **D E E E G I T**

He has no bingo and he's being routed. But, as a true expert, he knows how to give himself a slim chance. How should he proceed? The answer is on page 330.

Example 25

March 2000, Portland, OR: Steve Alexander

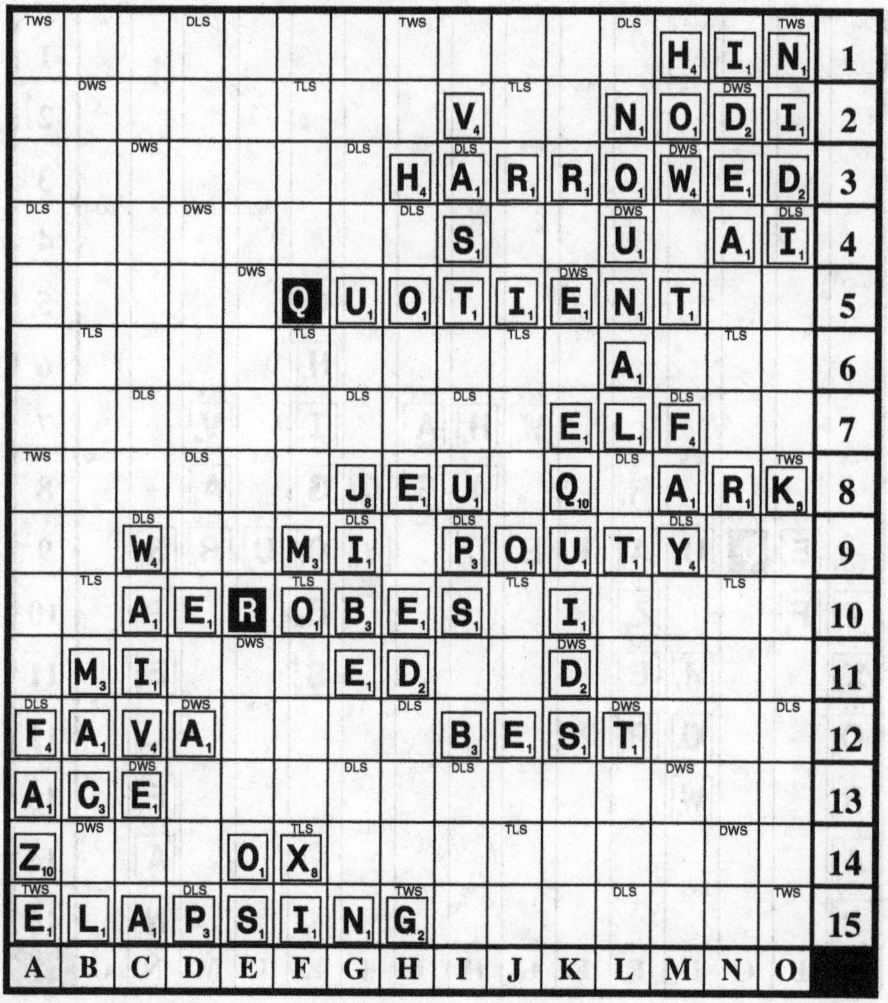

DIAGRAM 22-25

Alexander's score: 346 *Opponent's score:* 406
Alexander's rack: **E E G I O T Y** Unseen tiles: **C G L L N N O R R T** (three in the bag)

With virtually no hope for a bingo, and his opponent not stuck with the Q, this game looks hopeless. Even if his opponent has all consonants, he can score a few points and get rid of some tiles in each remaining turn. So how can Alexander win? The answer is on page 330.

Example 26

June 2000, Calgary, AB: Sam Kantimathi, CA

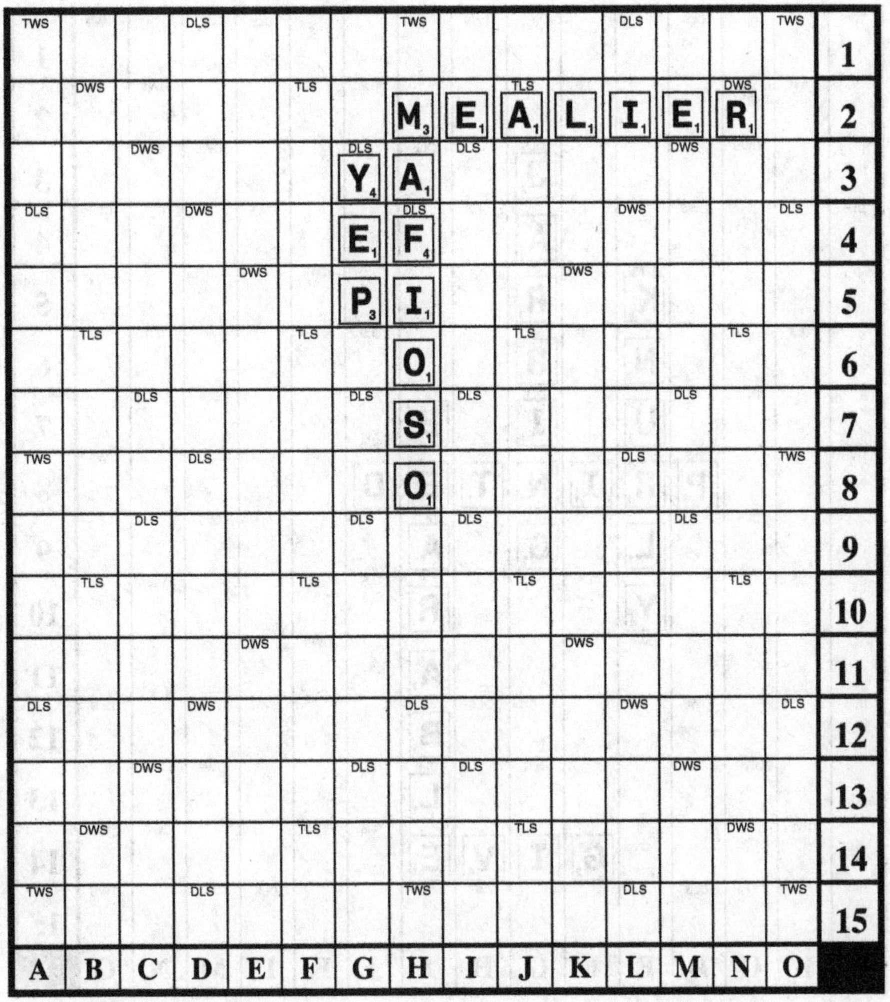

MEALIER
YEP
AFIOSO
A B C D E F G H I J K L M N O
1 2 3 4 5 6 7 8 9 10 11 12 13 14 15

DIAGRAM 22-26

Kantimathi's score: 30 *Opponent's score:* 104
Kantimathi's rack: **A C E E I R ?**

There are many bingos available. However, he found the highest-scoring play, a common word that's very hard to find. The answer is on page 330.

Example 27

June 2000, Lauderhill, FL, SCRABBLE Club #276: Ian Weinstein, FL

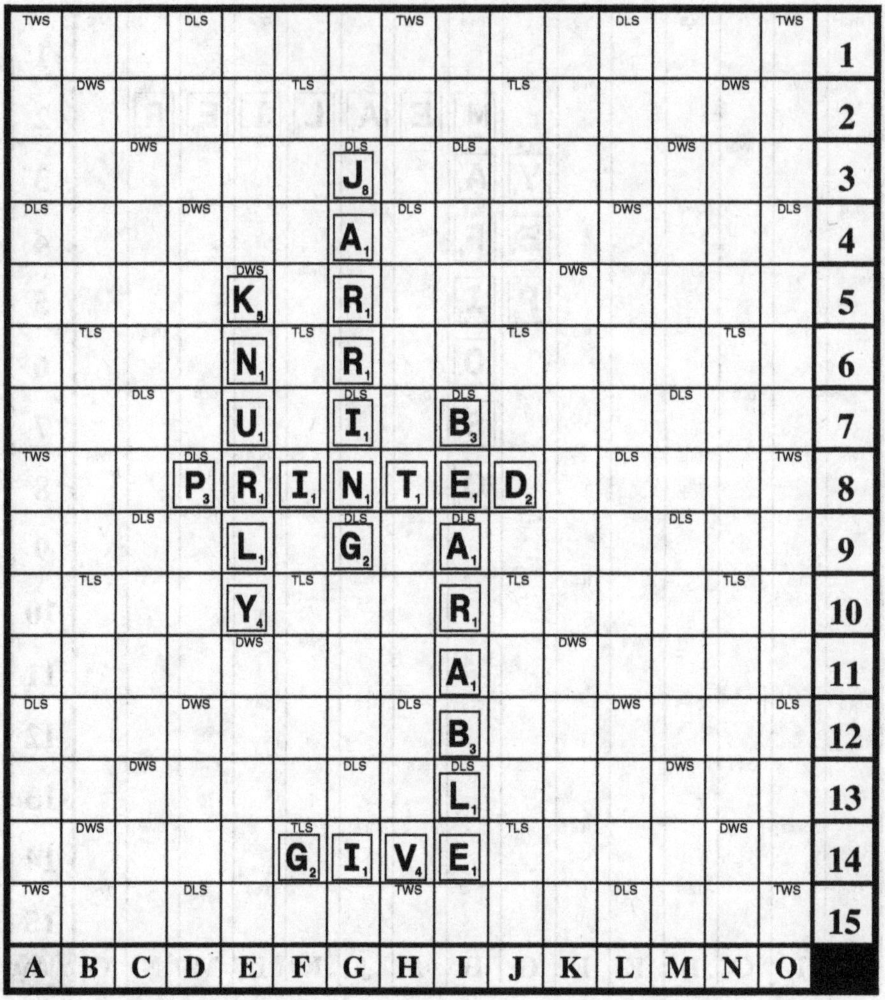

DIAGRAM 22-27

Weinstein's score: 185 *Opponent's score:* 146
Weinstein's rack: **A E H I N O S**

The best play is a relatively common word, but it is definitely not easy to find. We include it here because, in a unique way, it is the first of its kind in club or tournament play. The answer is on page 330.

Example 28

National SCRABBLE Championship 2000, Providence, RI: Joe Edley, NY

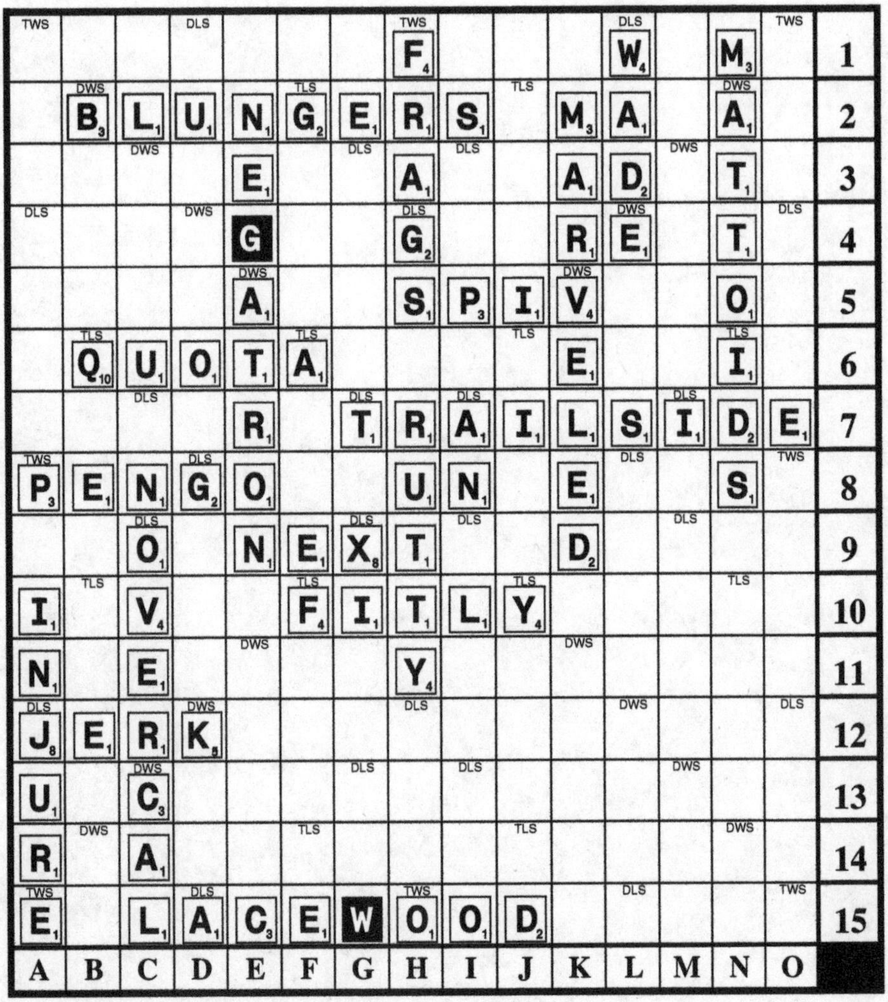

FWM 1
BLUNGERS MA A 2
E A AD T 3
G G RE T 4
A SPIV O 5
QUOTA E I 6
R TRAILSIDE 7
PENGO UN E S 8
O NEXT D 9
I V FITLY 10
N E Y 11
JERK 12
U C 13
R A 14
E LACEWOOD 15
A B C D E F G H I J K L M N O

DIAGRAM 22-28

Edley's score: 407 *Opponent's score:* 425
Edley's rack: **B H I N O W Z** Opponent's rack: **H I I O**

Edley noticed WHIZ 14H 36 immediately, and he thought it would win, especially after verifying to himself that his opponent couldn't go out in one turn. However, in this exhausting thirty-one-game tournament every point counts, since the more you win by, the more tie-break points you earn. At the last minute he took time to look for a better play and found "gold." The answer is on page 331.

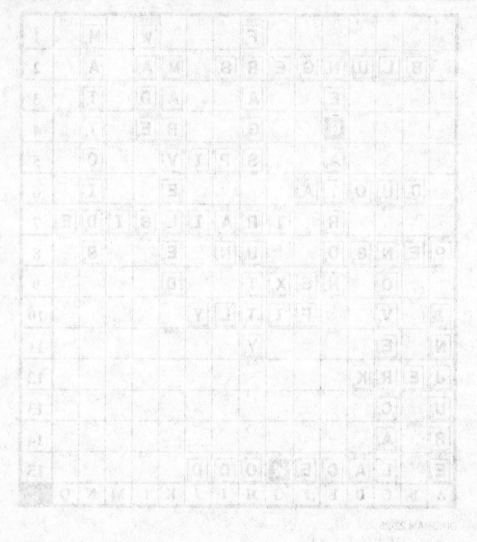

Example 29

July 2002, friendly game: Scott Pianowski

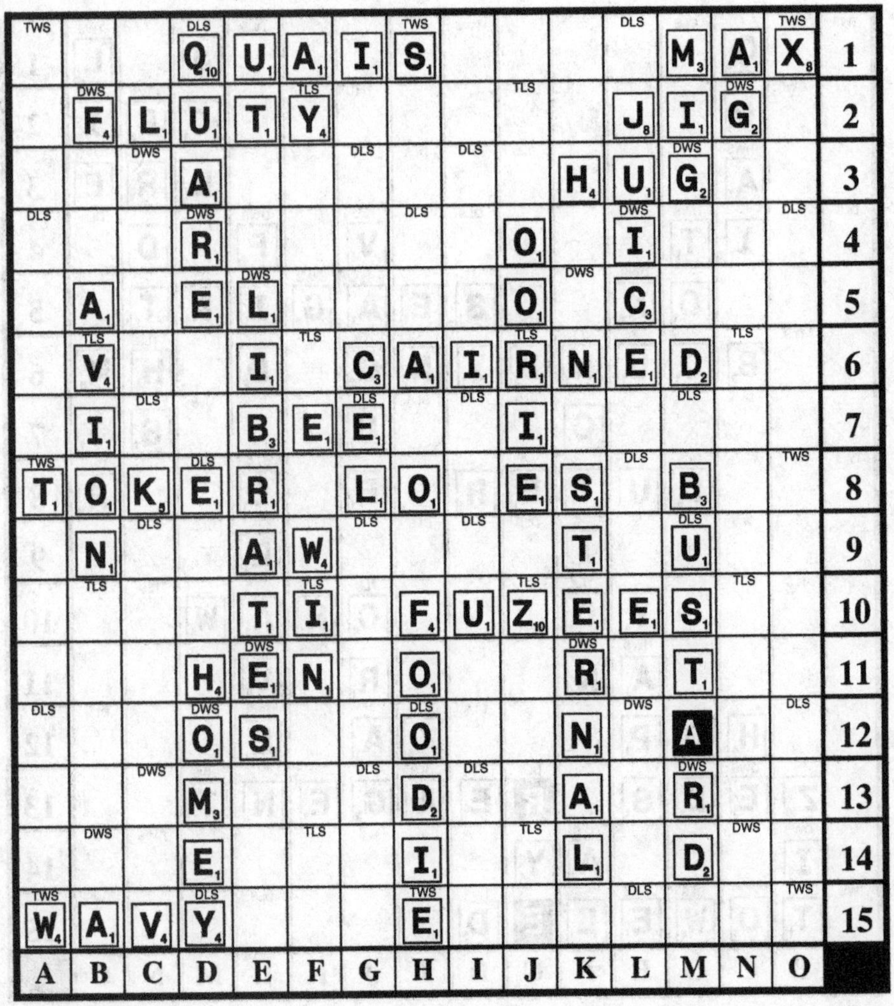

DIAGRAM 22-29

Pianowski's score: 373 *Opponent's score:* 448
Pianowski's rack: **D E N O R T ?**

It looks like there could be a bingo, but where can you play it? Don't forget to check for parallel plays! The answer is on page 331.

Example 30

May 2003, friendly game: Jeff Plake

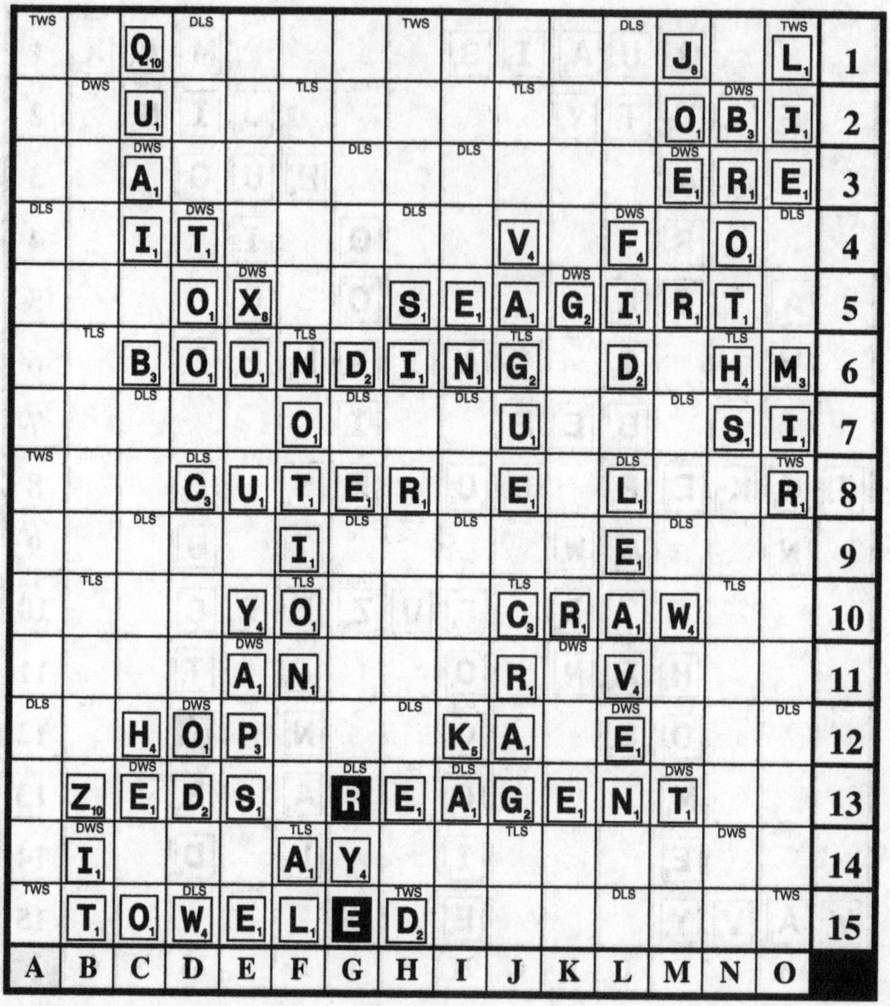

DIAGRAM 22-30

Plake's score: 341 *Opponent's score:* 352
Plake's rack: **A A I L M N P**

If there is no bingo or Q play, he'd at least like to make a very nice parallel play, if possible. The answer is on page 331.

Example 31

October 2002, friendly game: Paul Sidorsky

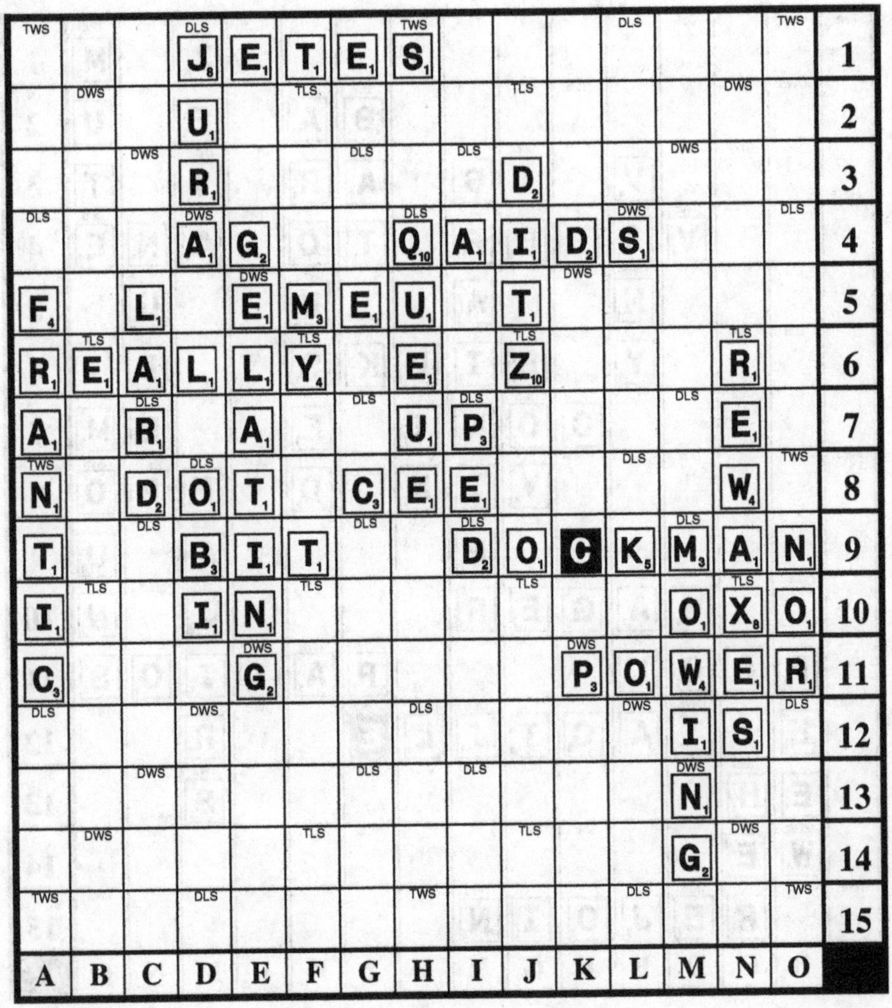

DIAGRAM 22-31

Sidorsky's score: 339   *Opponent's score:* 244
Sidorsky's rack: **E E H O S U ?**

Can he play a bingo? There may be chances for scoring well without one! The answer is on page 331.

Example 32

October 2002, friendly game: Scott Pianowski

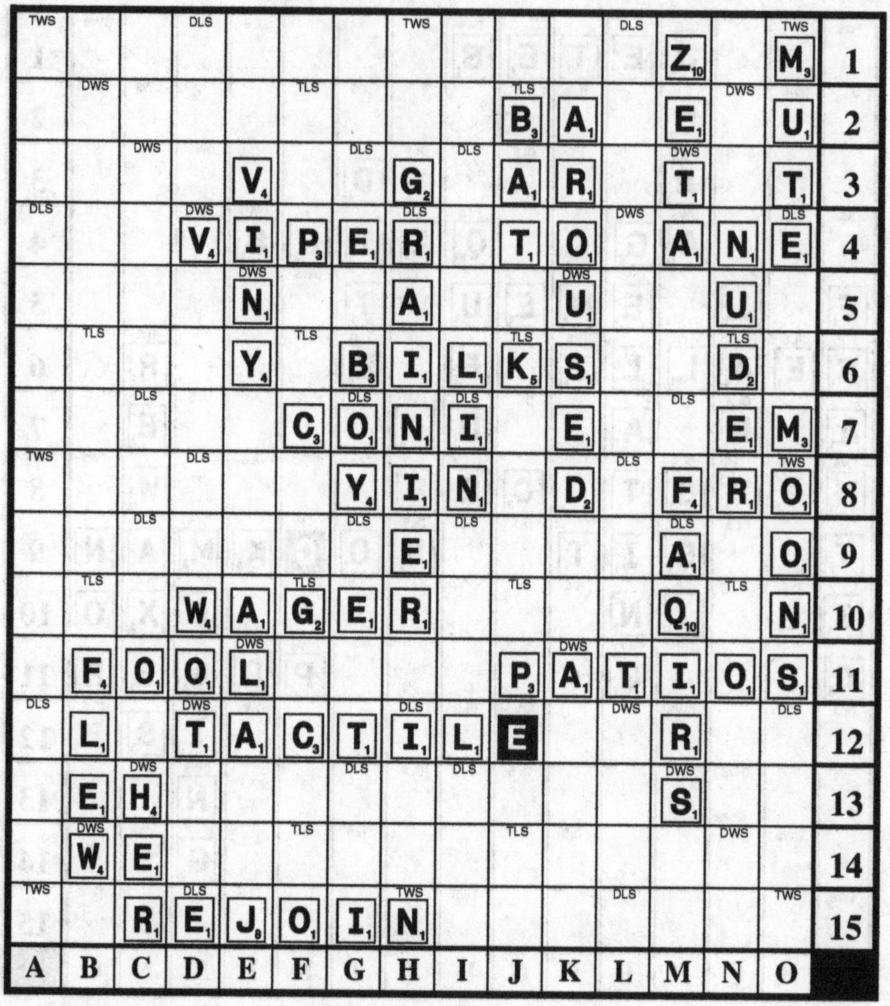

DIAGRAM 22-32

Pianowski's score: 291 *Opponent's score:* 335
Pianowski's rack: **D E E H I I N**

With no bingo, one might think there was little to do but HEN A13 33. One would be mistaken. Let the words already on the board guide you, as they did Scott. The answer is on page 331.

Example 33

September 2002, friendly game: Sharon Hawkes

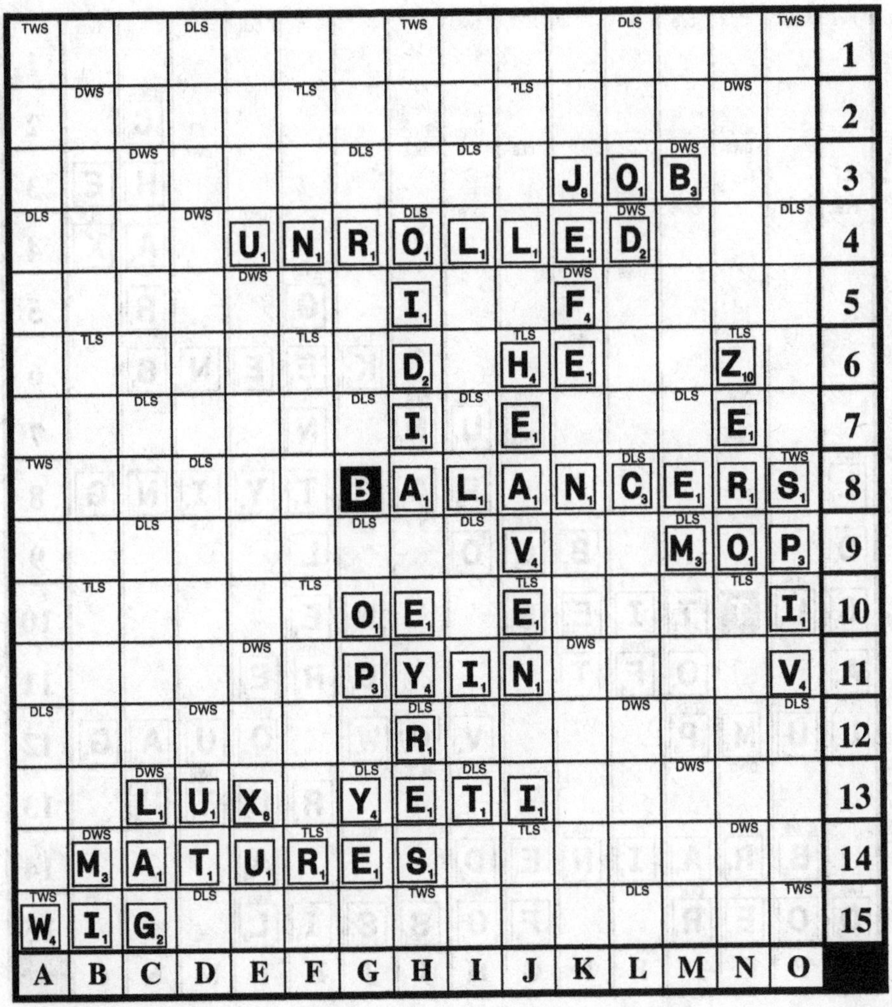

J O B
U N R O L L E D
I F
D H E Z
I E E
B A L A N C E R S
V M O P
O E E I
P Y I N V
R
L U X Y E T I
M A T U R E S
W I G
1 2 3 4 5 6 7 8 9 10 11 12 13 14 15
A B C D E F G H I J K L M N O

DIAGRAM 22-33

Hawkes's score: 309 *Opponent's score:* 219
Hawkes's rack: **A C E G I O T**

Within this quiet position lurks a high-scoring choice. The answer is on page 331.

Example 34

June 2005, Toronto SCRABBLE Club #3: John Robertson

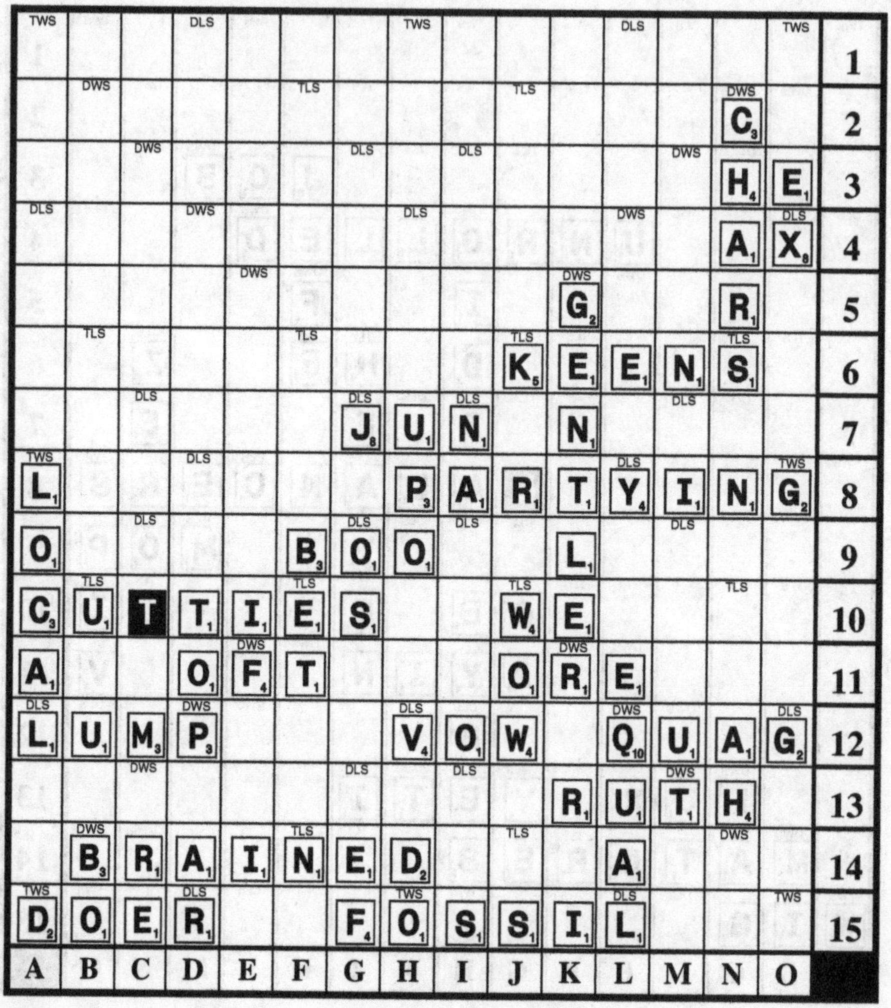
C
H E
A X
G R
K E E N S
J U N N
L P A R T Y I N G
O B O O L
C U T T I E S W E
A O F T O R E
L U M P V O W Q U A G
R U T H
B R A I N E D A
D O E R F O S S I L
A B C D E F G H I J K L M N O
1 2 3 4 5 6 7 8 9 10 11 12 13 14 15

DIAGRAM 22-34

Robertson's rack: **A E I I O V Z**

Hint: One doesn't have to get old to find this play! The answer is on page 331.

Example 35

June 1999, Exeter, PA: Jay Strieb

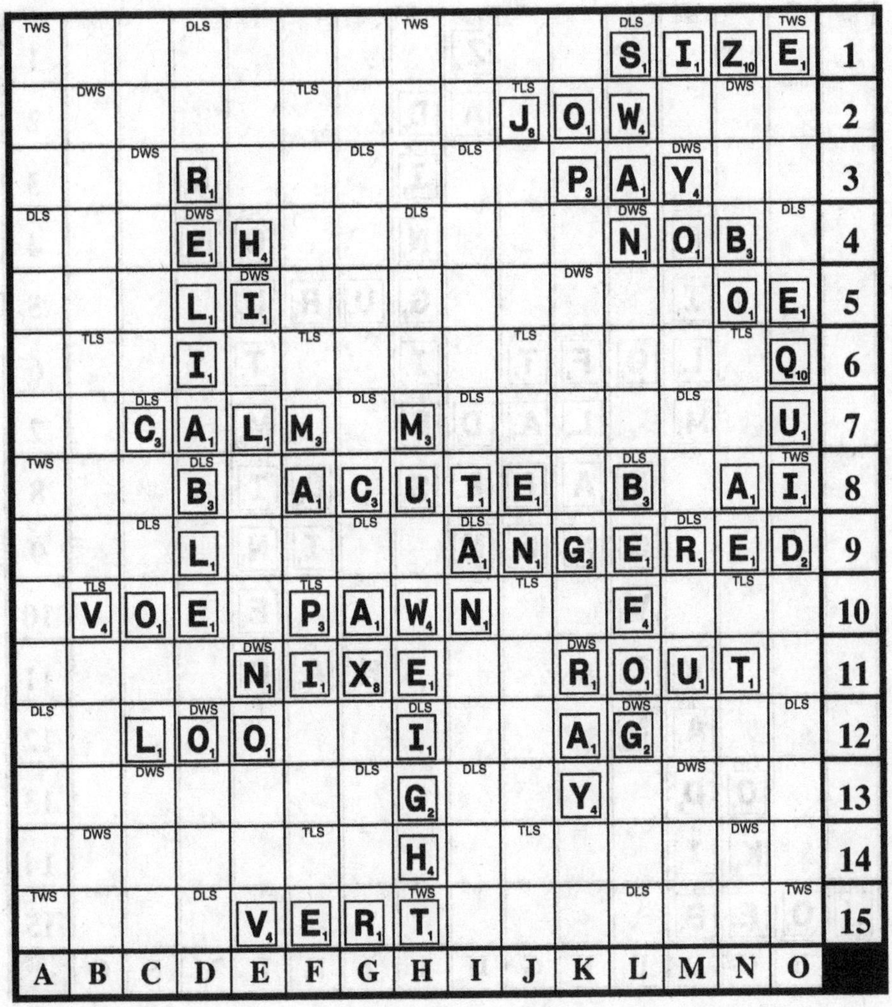

DIAGRAM 22-35

Strieb's rack: **A E I N N T ?**

Some plays just seem to happen. We don't always look for such brilliancies. But if you do, and it's there, is it satisfying! The answer is on page 331.

Bonus Q: If his rack had been AINSTT?, what would his best play have been?

Example 36

March 2007, Calgary, AB, SCRABBLE Club: Esther Matthews

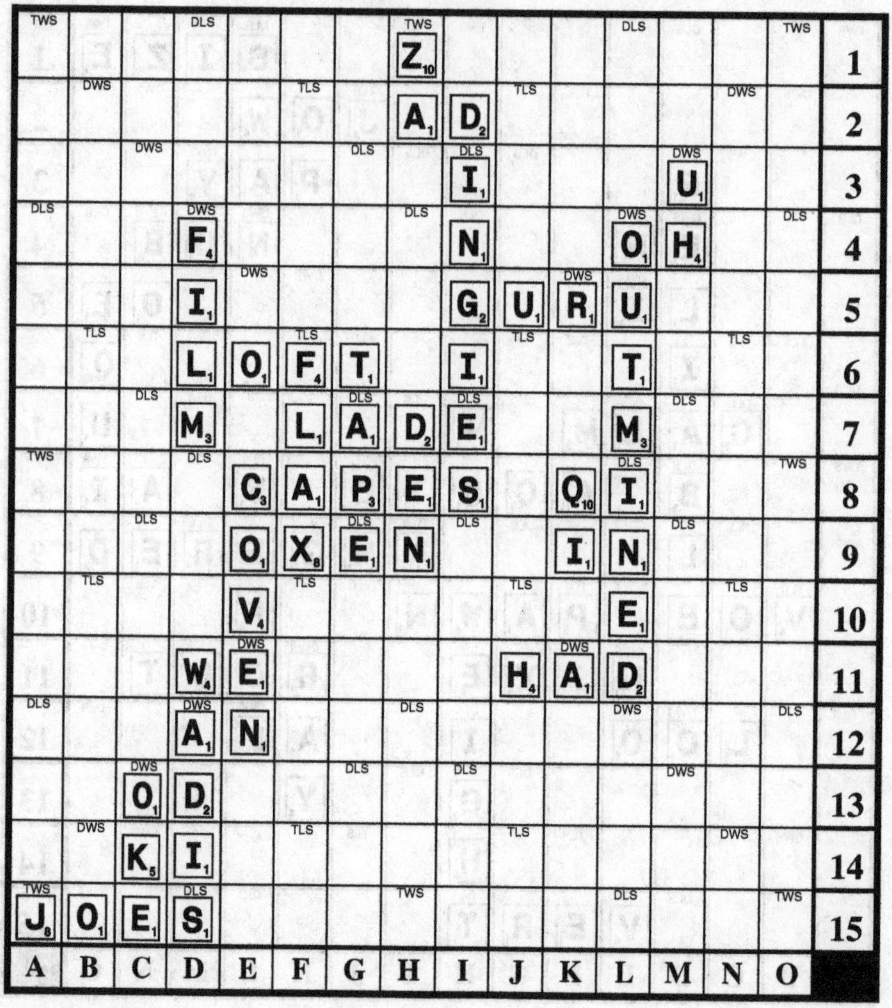

Z
A D
I U
F N O H
I G U R U
L O F T I T
M L A D E M
C A P E S Q I
O X E N I N
V E
W E H A D
A N
O D
K I
J O E S
A B C D E F G H I J K L M N O

DIAGRAM 22-36

Matthews's rack: **A E I S S Y ?**

Usually a bingo is the best play. But here you might want to think twice, particularly if you can save your blank. Can you? The answer is on page 331. (Note that OUTMINED is a phoney.)

Example 37

December 2003, Albany, NY, Championship: John Morse

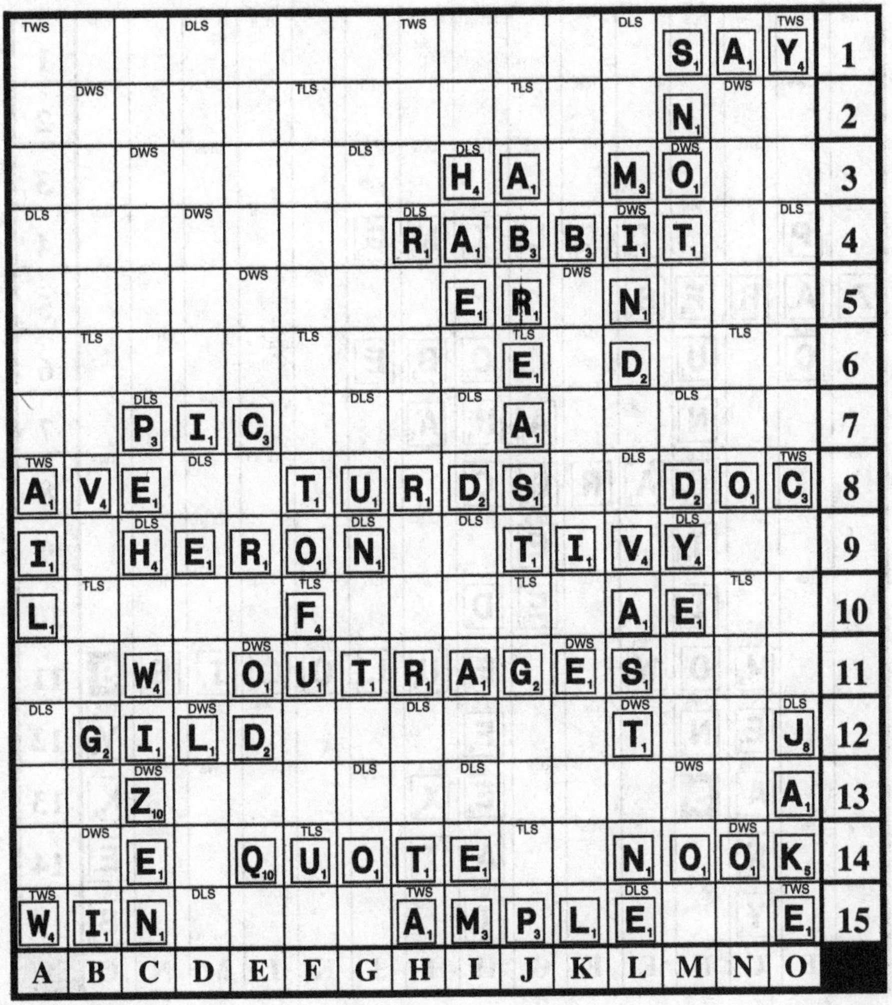

S A Y
N
H A M O
R A B B I T
E R N
E D
P I C A
A V E T U R D S D O C
I H E R O N T I V Y
L F A E
W O U T R A G E S
G I L D T J
Z A
E Q U O T E N O O K
W I N A M P L E E
A B C D E F G H I J K L M N O
1 2 3 4 5 6 7 8 9 10 11 12 13 14 15

DIAGRAM 22-37

Morse's score: 311 *Opponent's score:* 288
Morse's rack: **E F G I N R ?**

Can he bingo and also make an extension play? That's usually tough to do! This is, without a doubt, a cutting-edge play. The answer is on page 331.

Example 38

July 2003, Albany, NY, Championship: Stefan Fatsis

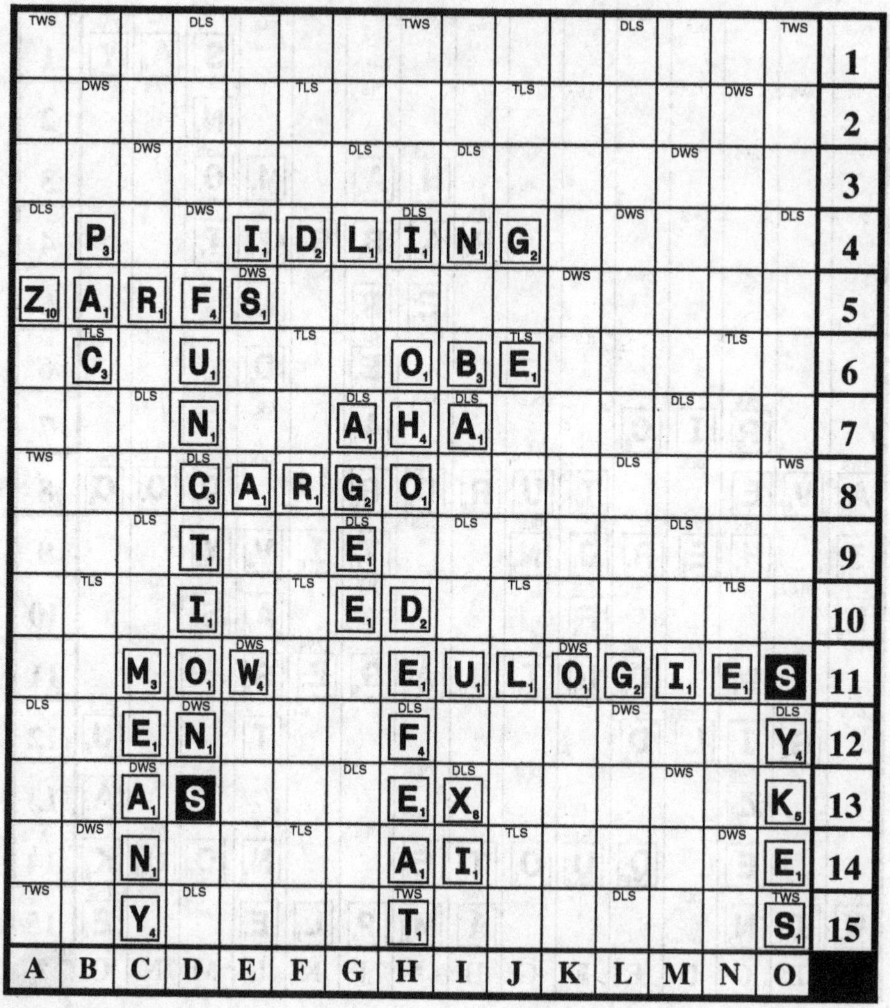

DIAGRAM 22-38

Fatsis's score: 227 *Opponent's score:* 262
Fatsis's rack: **D I I R S T U**

With this play, the author of bestseller *Word Freak*—about the SCRABBLE subculture, his own rise to expert-level player, and some of the colorful tournament "characters" he met—shows his well-earned expertise at the game. The answer is on page 331.

Example 39

December 2003, friendly game: Albert Hahn

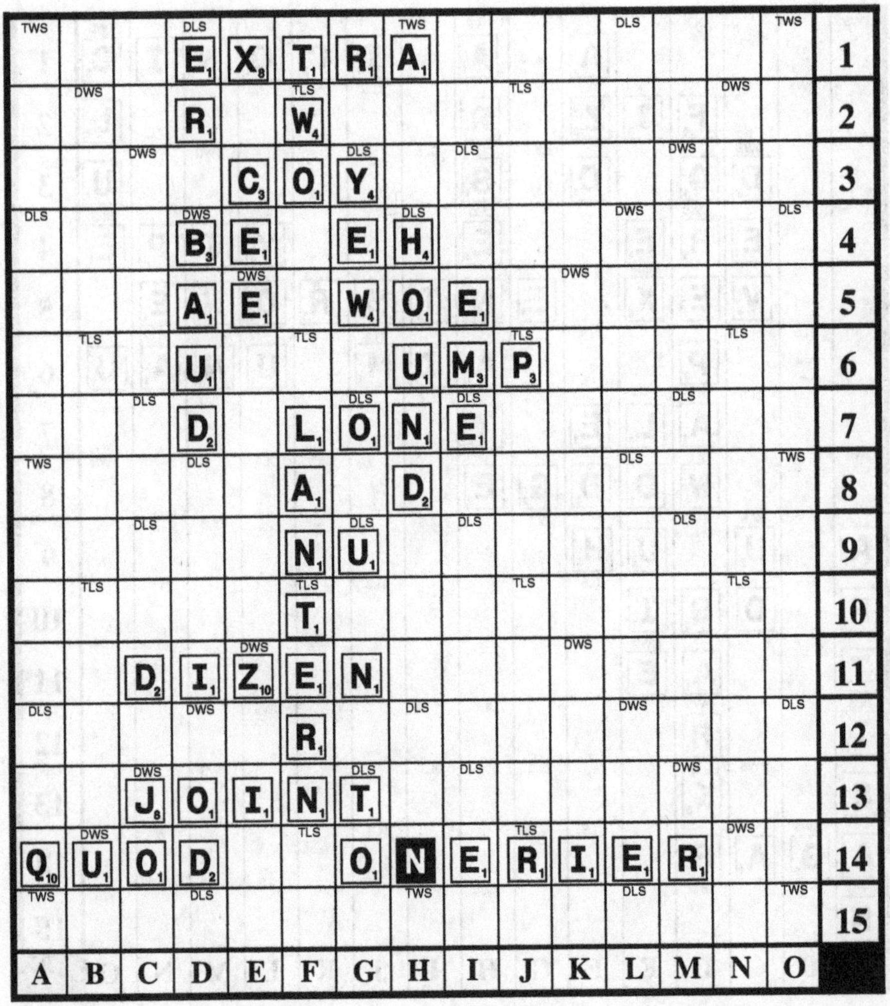

DIAGRAM 22-39

Hahn's score: 150 *Opponent's score:* 263
Hahn's rack: **A A I L M R T**

This onetime runner-up for the Canadian National Championship shows why he deserved to be up there. This is one sparkling play! A word of caution: Don't be satisfied with the first nice play you see! How can he make up his whole point deficit *this turn*? The answer is on page 331.

Example 40

December 2003, Oshawa, ON, Championship: Mark Przybyszewski

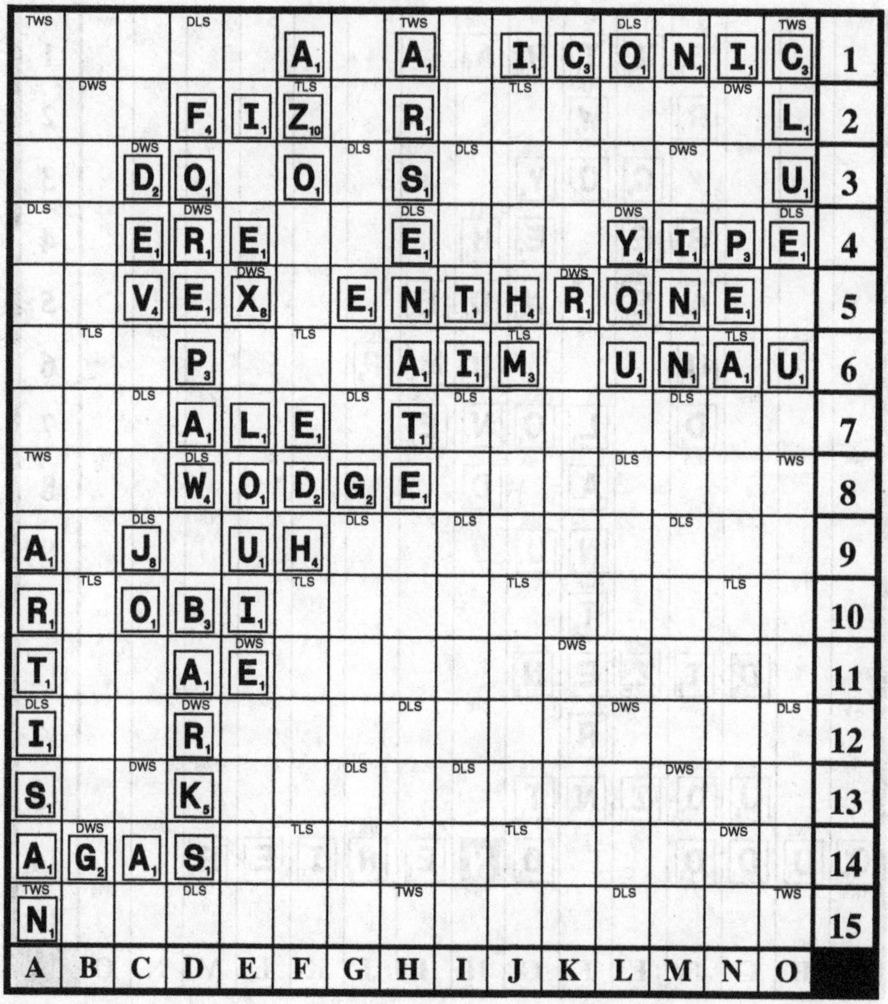

A A I C O N I C 1
F I Z R L 2
D O O S U 3
E R E E Y I P E 4
V E X E N T H R O N E 5
P A I M U N A U 6
A L E T 7
W O D G E 8
A J U H 9
R O B I 10
T A E 11
I R 12
S K 13
A G A S 14
N 15
A B C D E F G H I J K L M N O

DIAGRAM 22-40

Przybyszewski's score: 306 *Opponent's score:* 311
Przybyszewski's rack: **D E E I M R T**

Although he has RETIMED, DIMETER, DEMERIT, and MITERED, none of them play. However, what common word, known to all four-year-olds, can he play? Think "extended bingo"! The answer is on page 331.

Example 41

July 2003, friendly game: Carol Yamashita

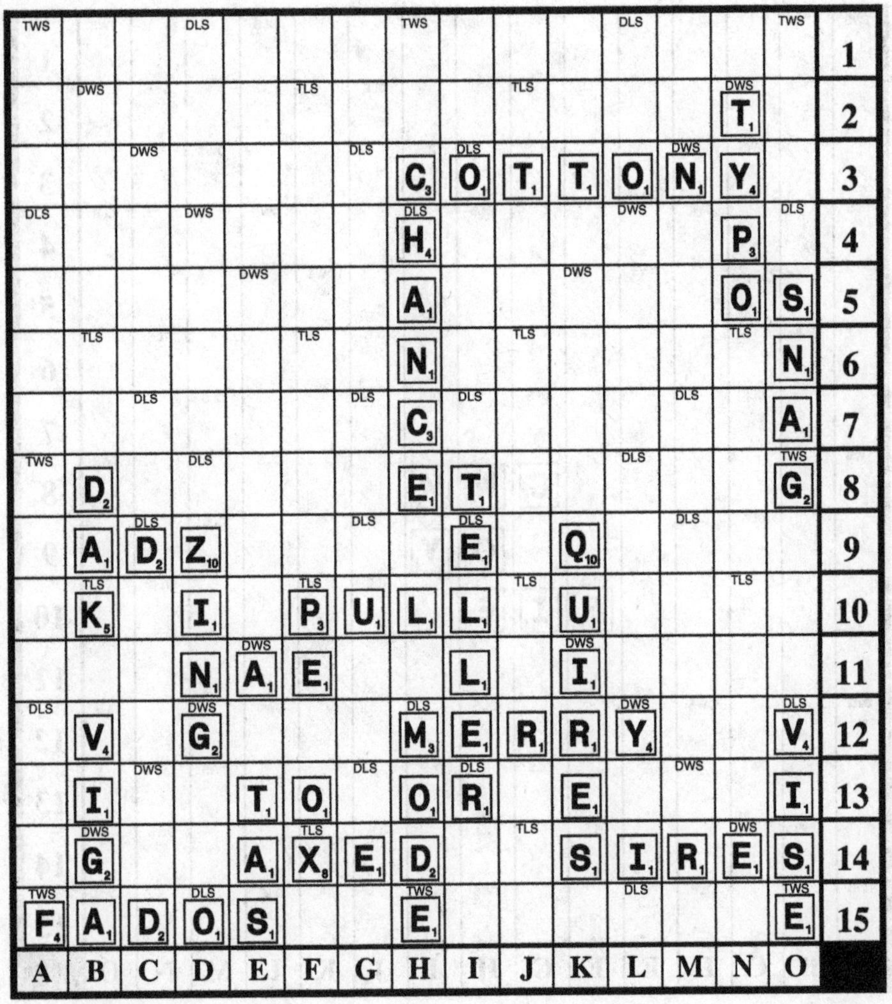

DIAGRAM 22-41

Yamashita's score: 306 *Opponent's score:* 311
Yamashita's rack: **A H I M O R ?**

A bingo? Sure! But can you find one that scores at least 100 points, like Carol did? The answer is on page 331.

Example 42

August 2001, Calgary SCRABBLE Club #374: Randall Thomas

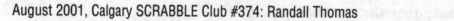

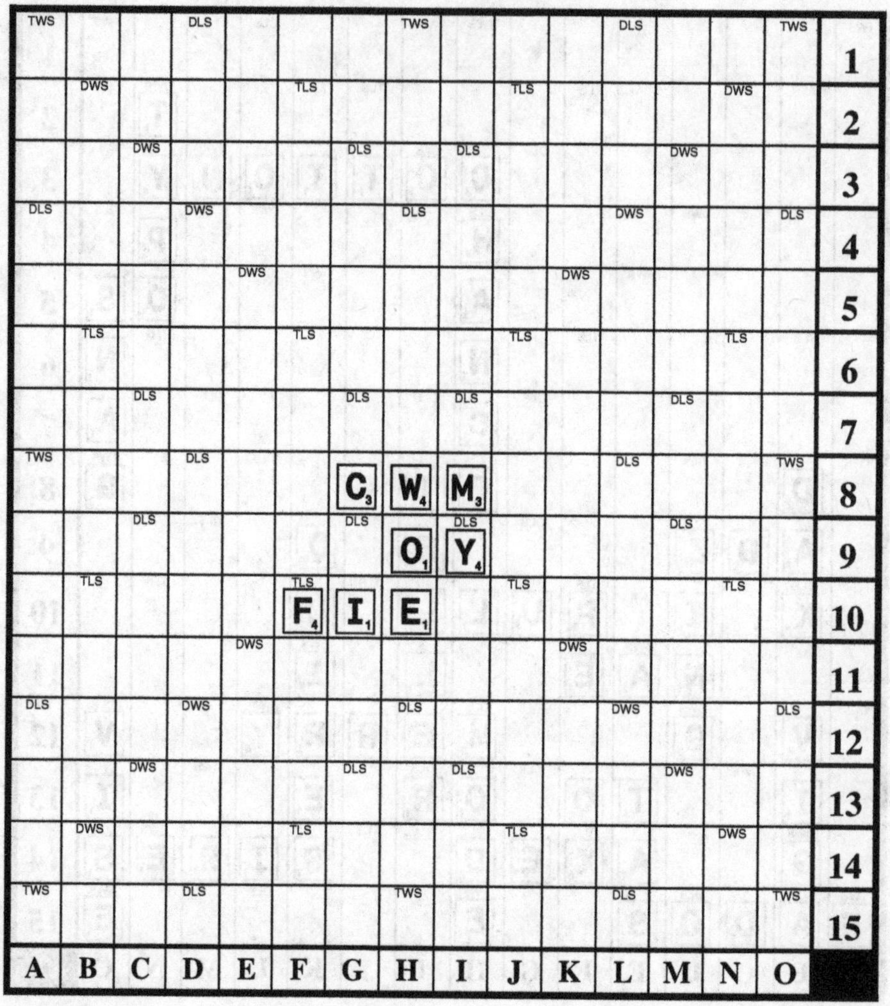
C W M
O Y
F I E
A B C D E F G H I J K L M N O
1 2 3 4 5 6 7 8 9 10 11 12 13 14 15

DIAGRAM 22-42

Thomas's score: 25 *Opponent's score:* 40
Thomas's rack: **E E J N O R T**

There's not much to play with on this board. Does that make it any easier to find a nice play? Not really, because during a game, you never know when to expect the unexpected! And no one would turn down this play if they saw it! The answer is on page 331.

Example 43

March 2003, Rome, GA, tourney: Steve Dennis

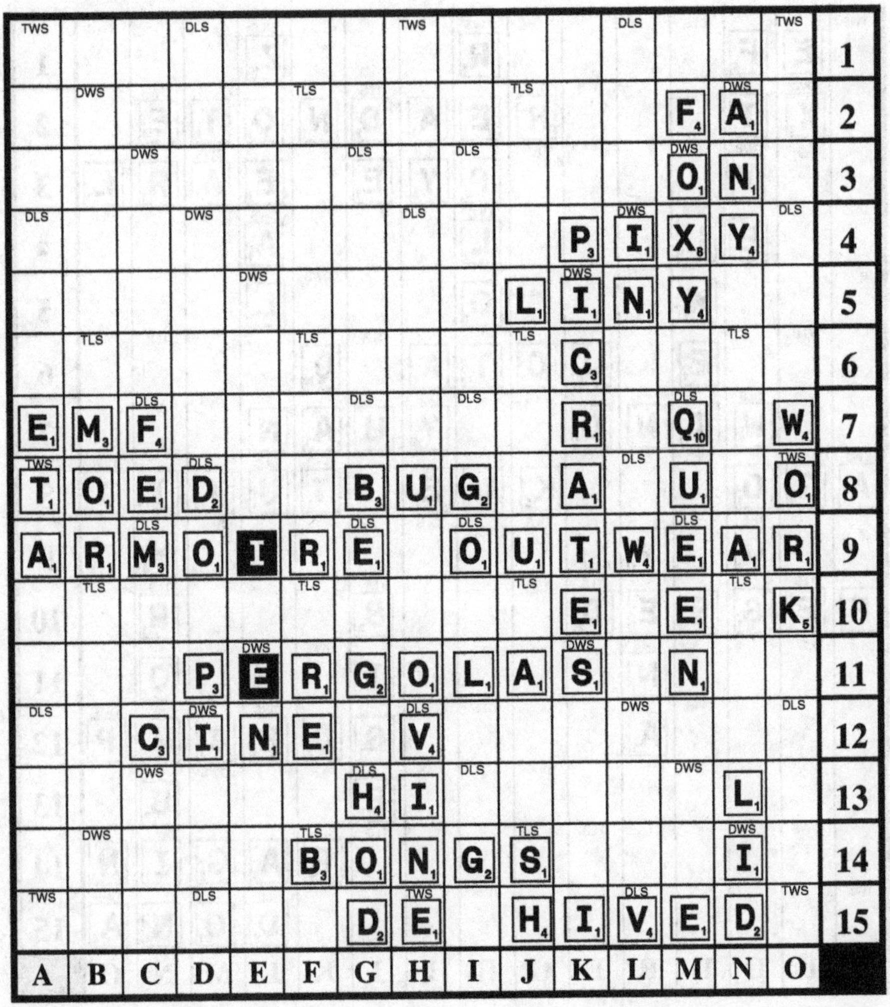

F A
O N
P I X Y
L I N Y
C
E M F R Q W
T O E D B U G A U O
A R M O I R E O U T W E A R
E E K
P E R G O L A S N
C I N E V
H I L
B O N G S I
D E H I V E D
A B C D E F G H I J K L M N O
1 2 3 4 5 6 7 8 9 10 11 12 13 14 15

DIAGRAM 22-43

Dennis's score: 225 *Opponent's score:* 246
Dennis's rack: **A E I L R S T**

He has one of the all-time great racks, but the board is very tight, and none of his several 7-letter bingos will play. Did that stop him? No! Looking further, he finds a longer bingo that works beautifully! The answer is on page 331.

Example 44

October 2003, Philadelphia Championship: Marlon Hill

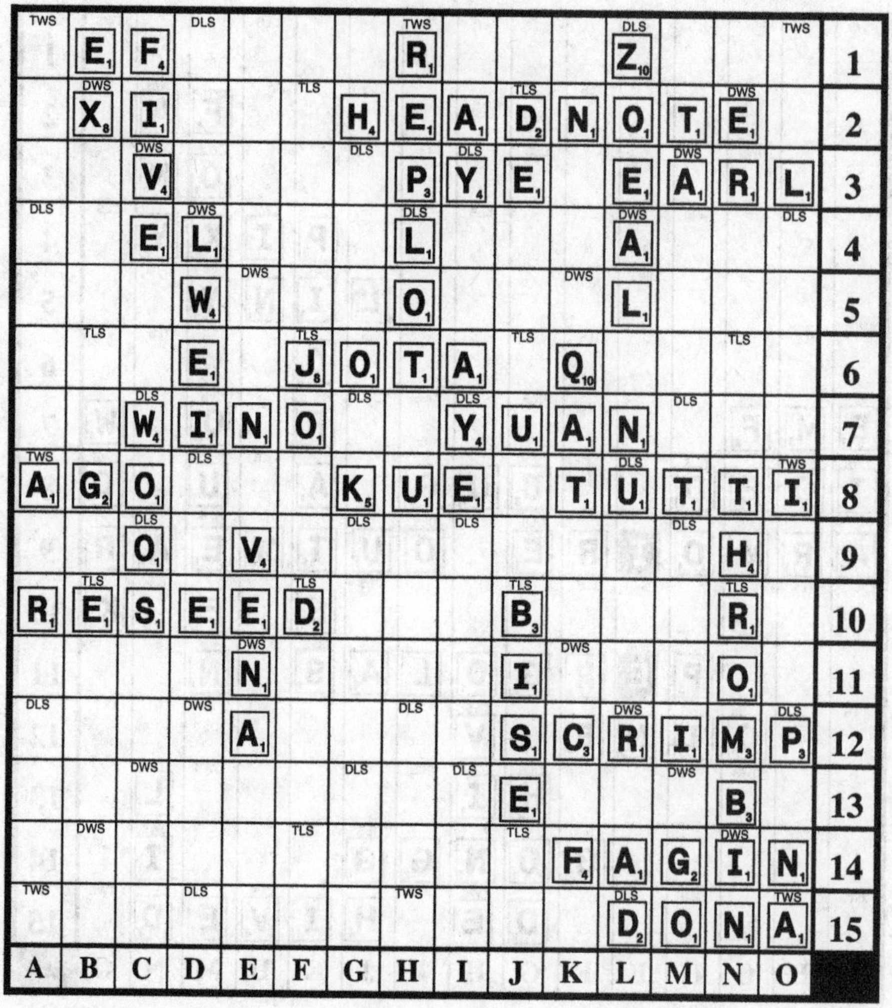
EF R Z 1
XI HEADNOTE 2
V PYE EARL 3
EL L A 4
W O L 5
E JOTA Q 6
WINO YUAN 7
AGO KUE TUTTI 8
O V H 9
RESEED B R 10
N I O 11
A SCRIMP 12
E B 13
FAGIN 14
DONA 15
A B C D E F G H I J K L M N O

DIAGRAM 22-44

Hill's score: 375 *Opponent's score:* 260
Hill's rack: **C D I I M T ?**

Despite his overwhelming lead, he never gives up looking for the best play, nor should he, because the more he wins by, the higher in the standings he'll finish. But here he has to look beyond the obvious. There is a playable bingo here, but it's *not* through the open A on row 12! The answer is on page 332.

Example 45

August 2000, National SCRABBLE Championship: Randy Hersom

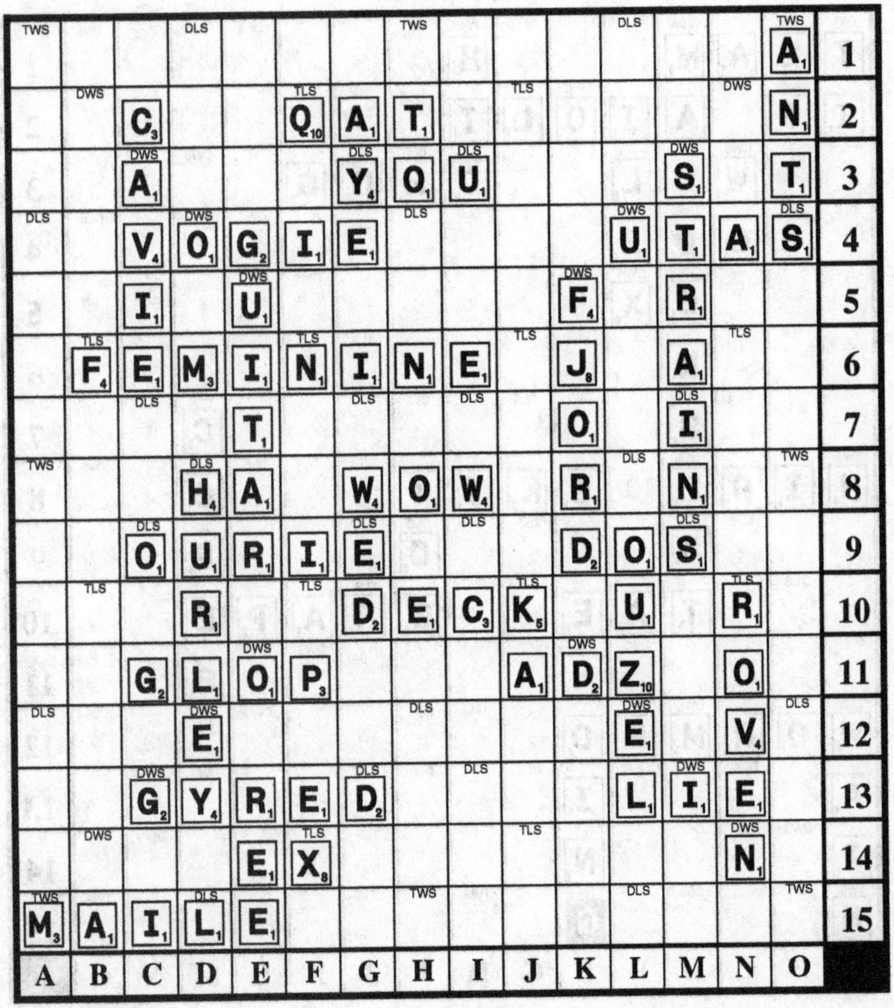

DIAGRAM 22-45

Hersom's score: 342 *Opponent's score:* 390
Hersom's rack: **A E H I L S ?**

With ROVEN taking no back hooks, it looks like it's going to be difficult to find a bingo. But if you look for the UnUsUal, a bingo may be easier to find. Hint, hint! And no, the blank would *not* be a U! While the answer is obscure, we're confident that if you've glanced through this book at the most important topics, you've encountered this word. The answer is on page 332.

Example 46

January 2002, Calgary, AB, SCRABBLE Club #374: Margaret West

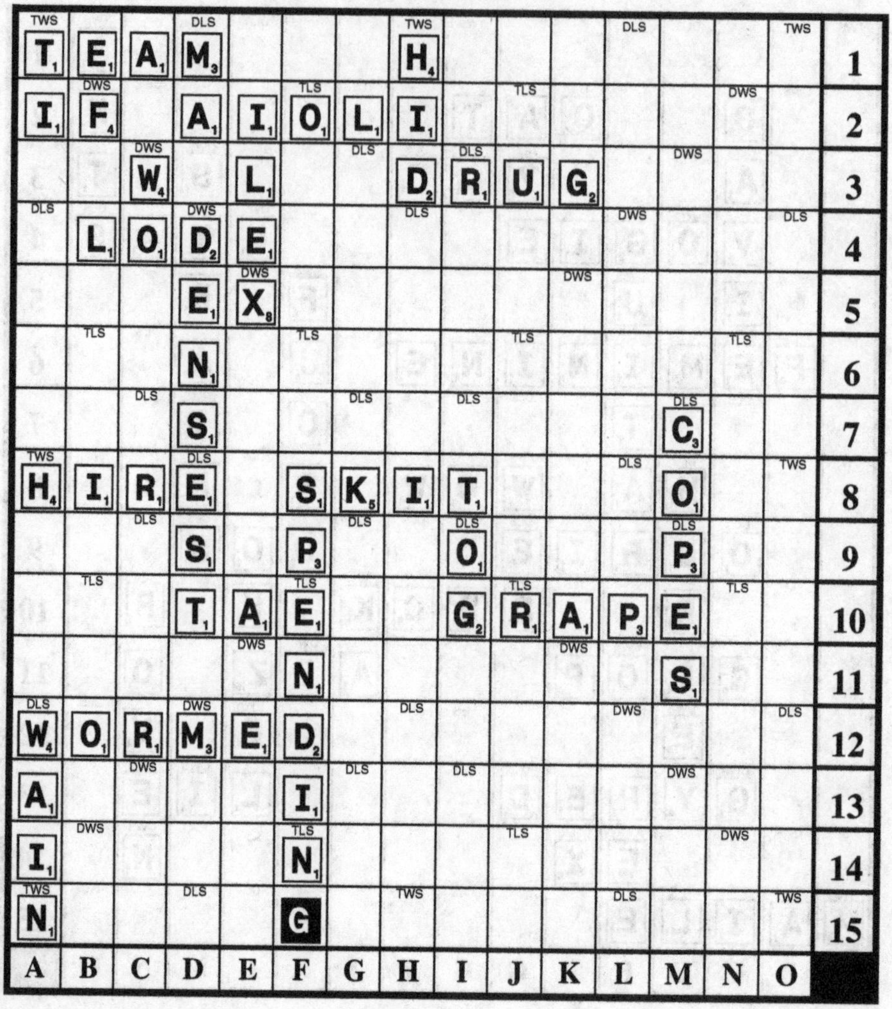

DIAGRAM 22-46

West's score: 126 *Opponent's score:* 184
West's rack: **ADIQRTU**

Good thing she didn't stop after seeing QUOTA 8K 45. There is a better play that is *very* hard to see, unless you're thinking really *big*. This is one of the most dazzling bingos we've ever seen played. Give yourself enormous props if you can find it! Club Director Siri Tillekeratne mentioned to us that Margaret was in her seventies when she made this play! The answer is on page 332.

Example 47

June 2002, friendly game: Mike Turniansky

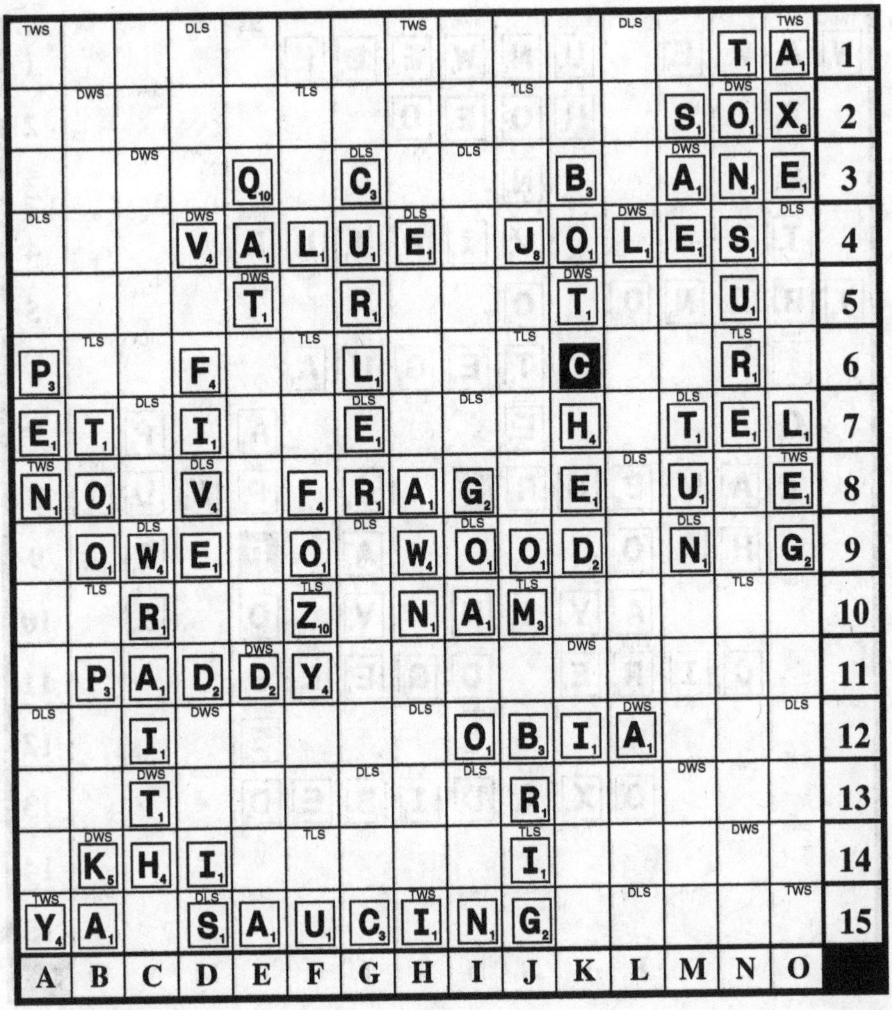

T A 1
S O X 2
Q C B A N E 3
V A L U E J O L E S 4
T R T U 5
P F L C R 6
E T I E H T E L 7
N O V F R A G E U E 8
O W E O W O O D N G 9
R Z N A M 10
P A D D Y 11
I O B I A 12
T R 13
K H I I 14
Y A S A U C I N G 15
A B C D E F G H I J K L M N O

DIAGRAM 22-47

Turniansky's score: 383 *Opponent's score:* 304
Turniansky's rack: **D E I M N R ?**

No, there's no playable bingo, and that wasn't a good sign, but he was able to find a very satisfying 33-point play. In "parallel" we trust. The answer is on page 332. (Note that NEG was not acceptable at that time.)

Example 48

August 2002, National SCRABBLE Championship: Trey Wright

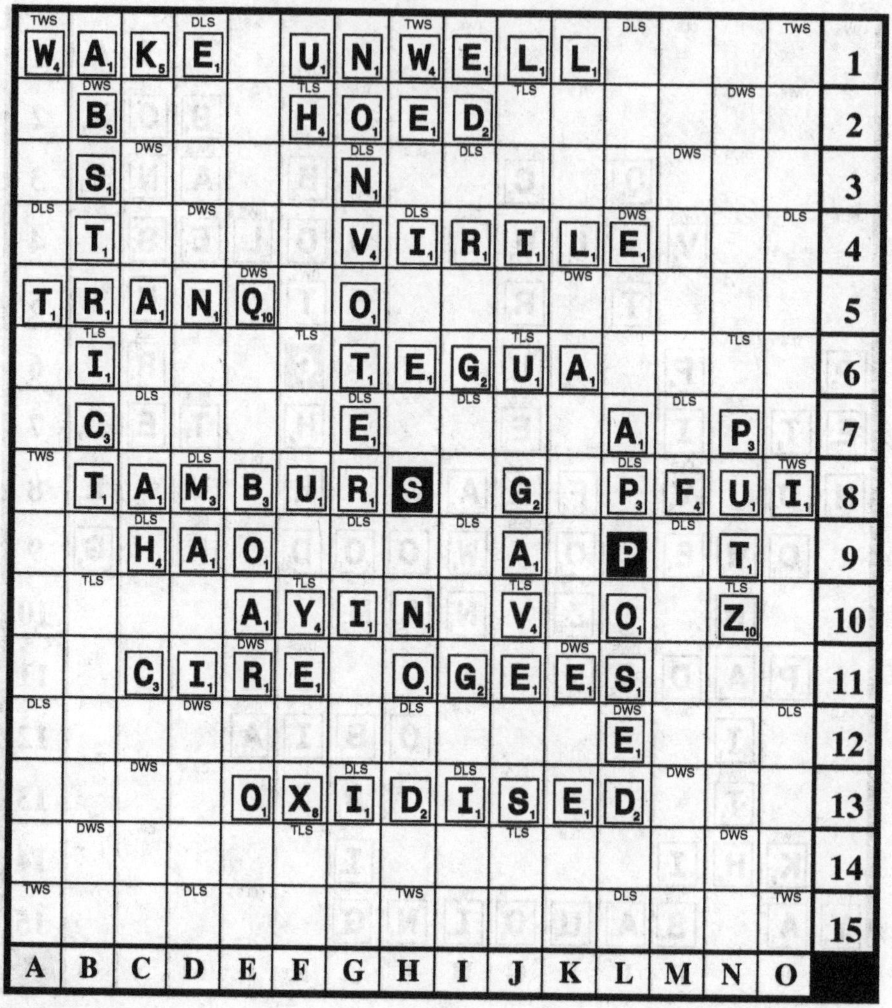

DIAGRAM 22-48

Wright's score: 320 *Opponent's score:* 368
Wright's rack: **D E F N R R T** Unseen tiles: **A I J L M N O O S Y**

With three tiles left to draw, he could have played NODDER H10 30, putting himself only 18 points down, but would that be enough to win? Or does he have another, more strategic resource? To those of us who saw this play, we weren't surprised when Trey went on to win the 2004 National SCRABBLE Championship. The answer is on page 332.

Example 49

December 2003, friendly game: Dennis Stone

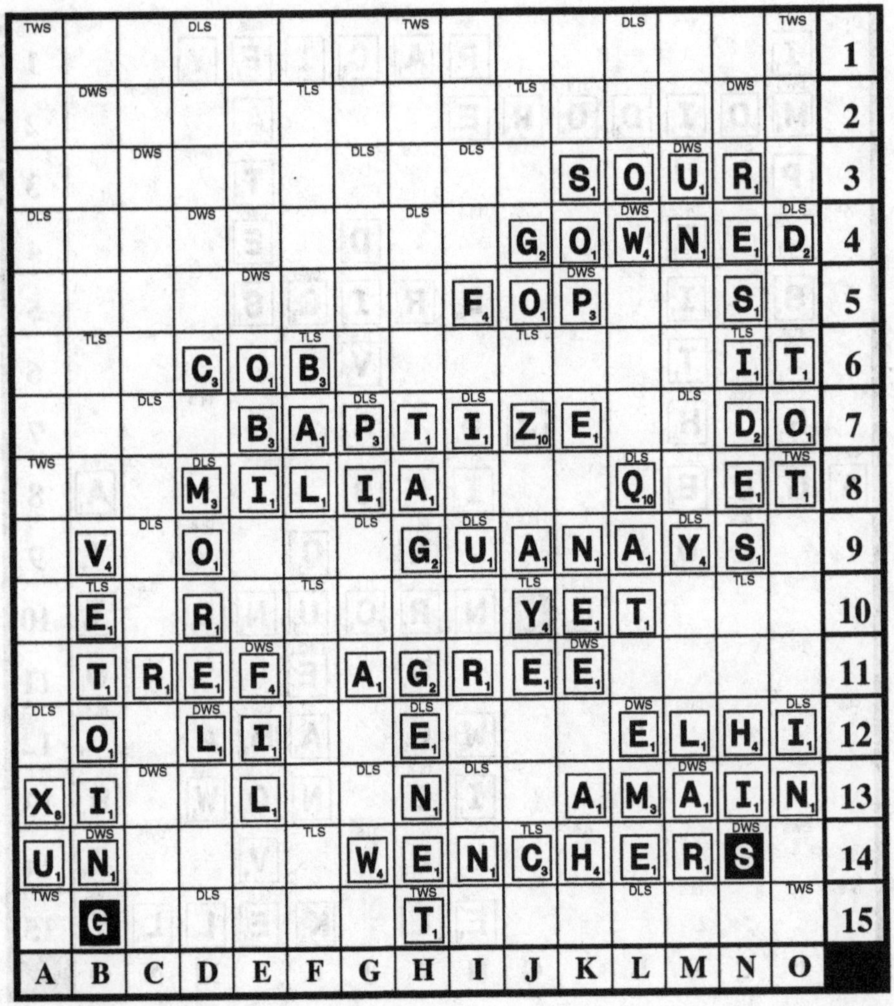

DIAGRAM 22-49

Stone's score: 331 *Opponent's score:* 345
Stone's rack: **A A D J R U V** Opponent's rack: **D I K O S**

With his awkward tiles, it's not easy to find a win here. But since his opponent can't end the game on his next turn, Dennis only needs to find about 55 points (is that all?) in two turns, even if he doesn't go out on his second play. How can he do that? The answer is on page 332.

Example 50

March 2006, Berkeley, CA: Jerry Lerman

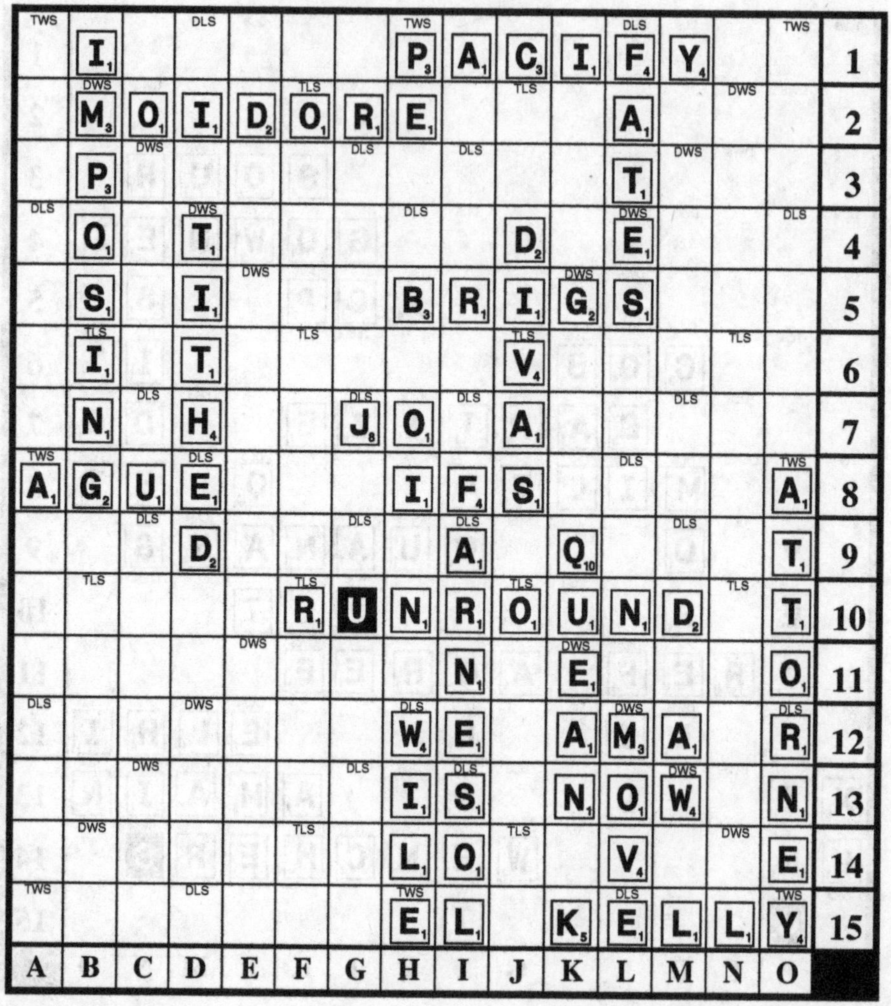

DIAGRAM 22-50

Lerman's score: 317 *Opponent's score:* 394
Lerman's rack: **A C E I R U U** Unseen tiles: **B E E E G H X Z ?**

This looks hopeless, but it is not. If the blank is one of the last two letters in the bag, Lerman has a chance. The answer will explain it in more detail. This position is similar to Example 13, because both require knowing unusual words and being able to set up bingos if the right tile is drawn. The main difference between them is that if the right tile is drawn, Lerman's opponent has no way to block the bingo. We do not expect any but expert players to find the best play, but anyone can appreciate the beauty of the situation, particularly when his current rack is so weak. The answer is on page 332.

Example 51

Mack Meller, NY, vs. Ben Schoenbrun, NY

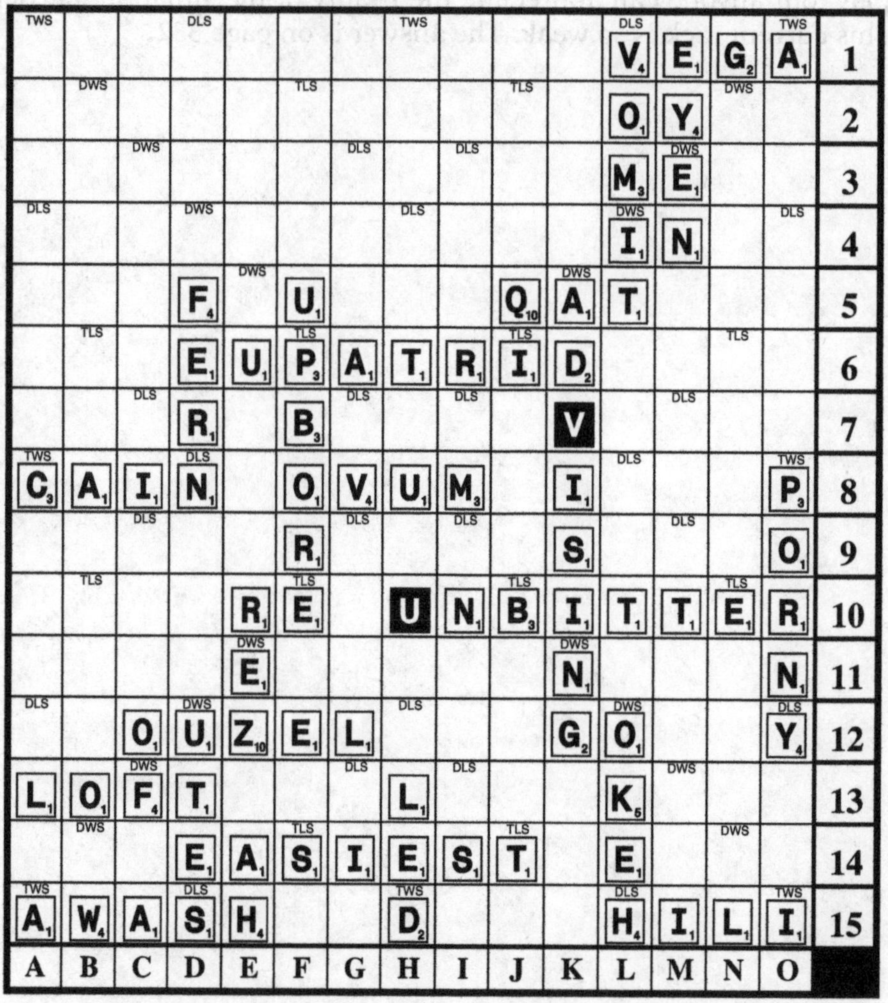

DIAGRAM 22-51

Meller's score: 313 *Schoenbrun's score:* 382

Meller's rack: **A A D N O R X** Unseen tiles: **C D E E G I J O W** (2 in the bag)

Sixteen-year-old Mack Meller is down enough to believe he needs a bingo to win. He might, however, believe that one play, an obscure four-letter word, could give him some hope to outrun his opponent without the bingo—or, at least, save some spread points. This play is worth 45 points. What would you do? The answer is on page 332.

Example 52

Mack Meller, NY, vs. Avery Mojica, KS

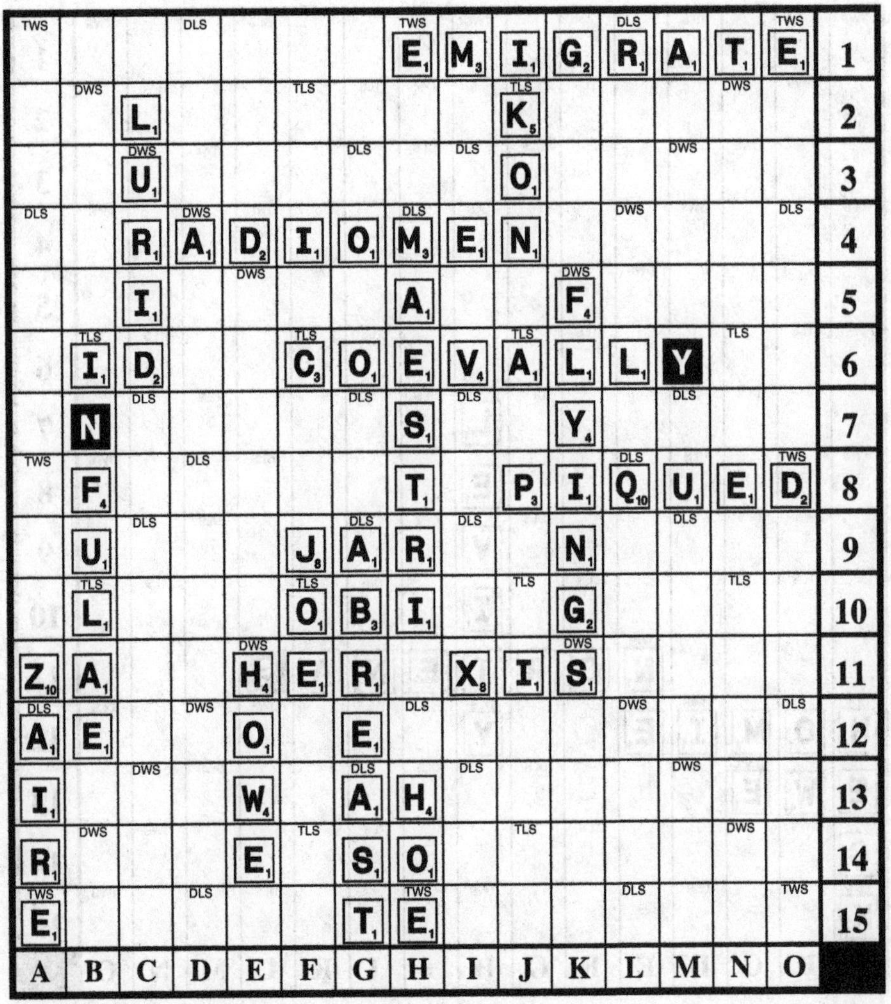

DIAGRAM 22-52

Meller's score: 395 *Mojica's score:* 456
Meller's rack: **C N P R S T Y**

Can Meller find a play with this consonant-heavy rack that makes the game more competitive?

His position looks grim; with no vowels except the sometimes Y, he needs a bingo pronto. Would you get discouraged or optimistic in this position? Meller found a nice resource! The answer is on page 332.

Example 53

Joey Krafchick, GA, vs. Siddharth Murali, TX

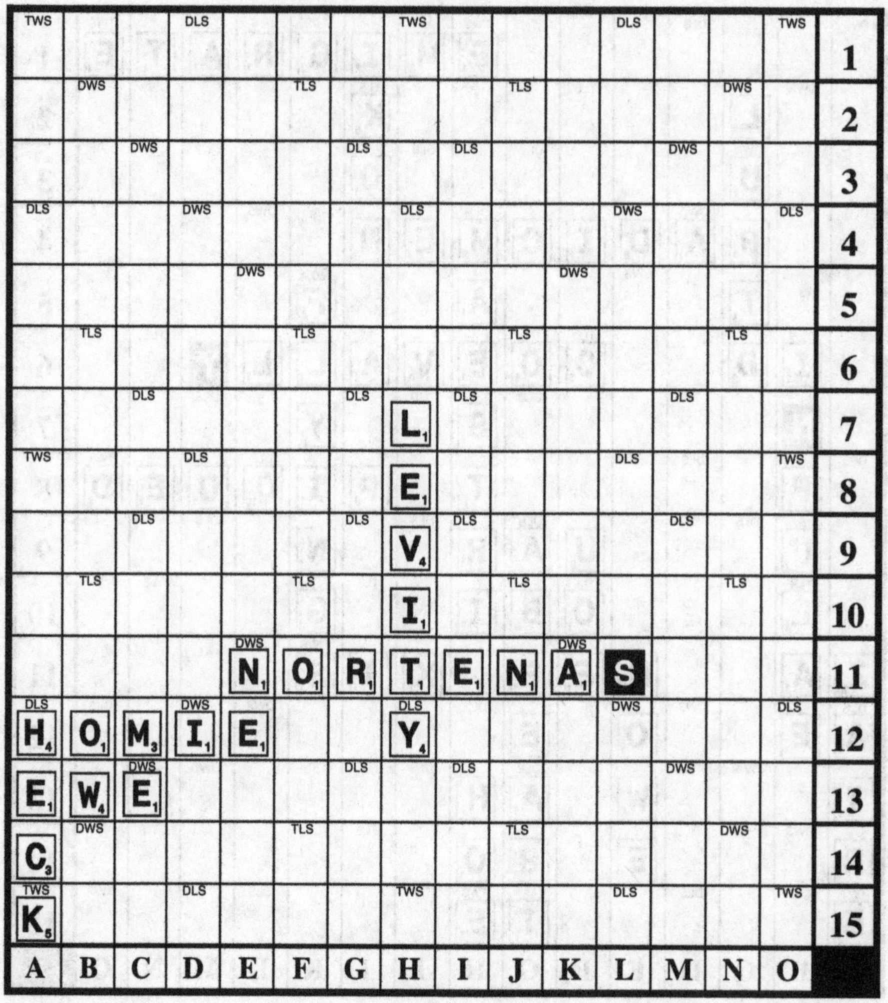

NORTENAS
LEVITY
HOMIE
EWE
HECK
A B C D E F G H I J K L M N O
1 2 3 4 5 6 7 8 9 10 11 12 13 14 15

DIAGRAM 22-53

Krafchick's score: 77 *Murali's score:* 147
Krafchick's rack: **A A C I I O R**

Any way to salvage this rack? Yes!

Down 70 points with a very weak rack. It's time to check all possibilities! The answer is on page 333.

Example 54

Nigel Richards, NZ, vs. Joey Mallick, ME

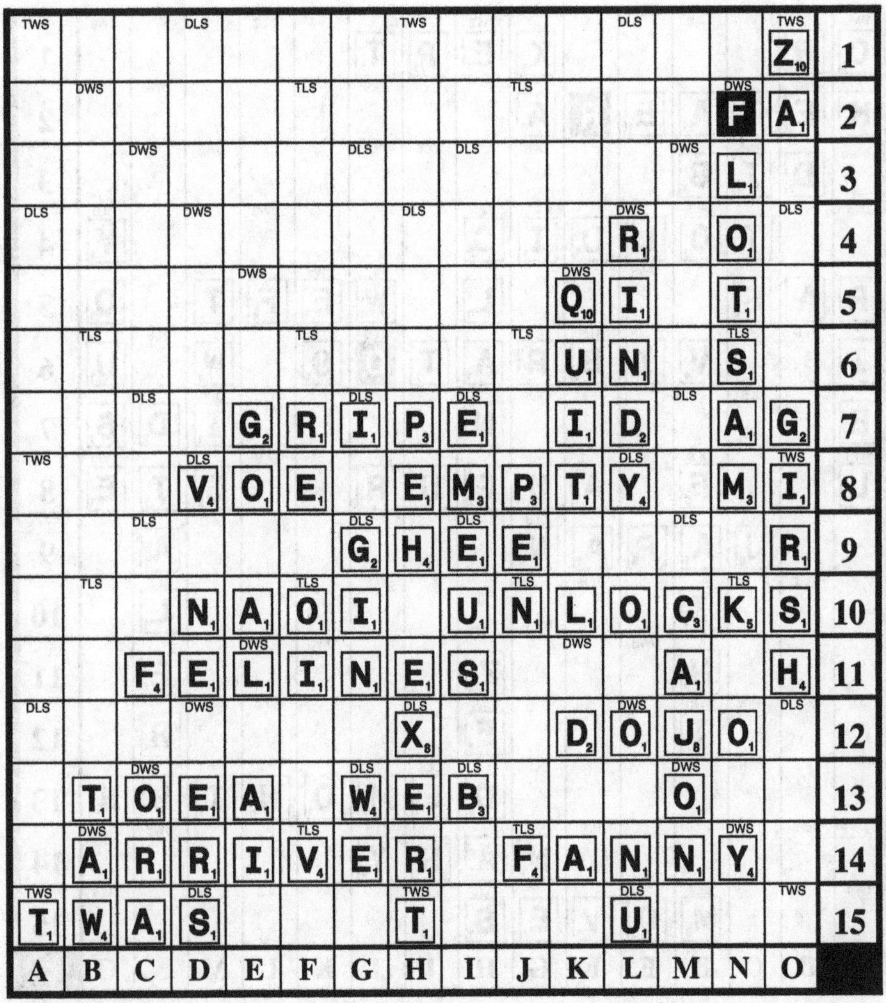

Z
F A
L
R O
Q I T
U N S
G R I P E I D A G
V O E E M P T Y M I
G H E E R
N A O I U N L O C K S
F E L I N E S A H
X D O J O
T O E A W E B O
A R R I V E R F A N N Y
T W A S T U
A B C D E F G H I J K L M N O
1 2 3 4 5 6 7 8 9 10 11 12 13 14 15

DIAGRAM 22-54

Richards's score: 340 *Mallick's score:* 364
Richards's rack: **A B C D E I ?** Mallick's rack: **D E I L T U**

Richards finds a way to win against any defense. Can you?

Down 24 points but with a blank and good tiles, though no easy bingo lines, how does he proceed to win? The answer is on page 333.

Example 55

Joey Krafchick, GA, vs. Paul Holser, TX

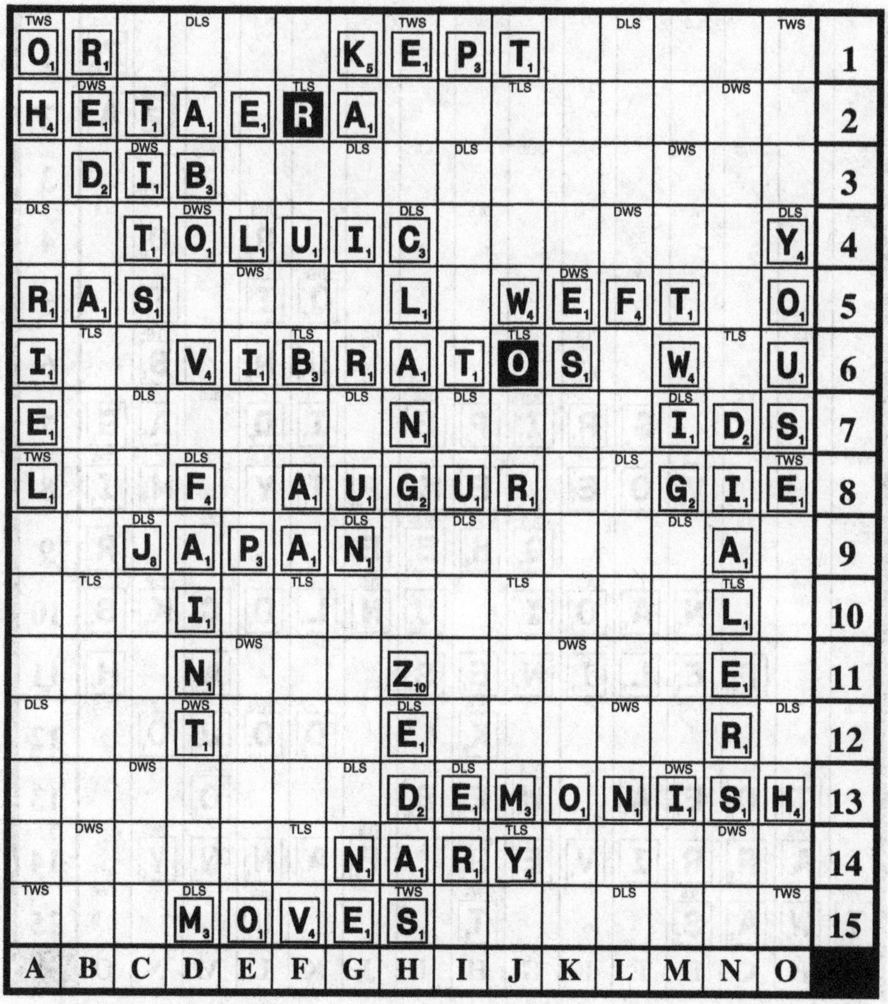

O R K E P T 1
H E T A E R A 2
D I B 3
T O L U I C Y 4
R A S L W E F T O 5
I V I B R A T O S W U 6
E N I D S 7
L F A U G U R G I E 8
J A P A N A 9
I L 10
N Z E 11
T E R 12
D E M O N I S H 13
N A R Y 14
M O V E S 15
A B C D E F G H I J K L M N O

DIAGRAM 22-55

Krafchick's score: 294 *Holser's score:* 383
Krafchick's rack: **C D E G I N X** Holser's rack: **E O O Q**

Can Krafchick find a win in this seemingly hopeless ending? Yes! The answer is on page 333.

Solutions to Excellent Plays

Example 1, Diagram 22-1: Carroll played RETAIL 11A 51 points, simultaneously forming CAJOLER, FAXES, TA, AR, ID, and LI. This was a winning play, though REMAIL in the same position would have been slightly better.

Example 2, Diagram 22-2: Even with the board so devoid of scoring opportunities, Edley found a way to set himself up for a huge score on his next play. In order to solve this, you need to know that DEL and DELE are words. Edley played DEL C5 4 points. It would have been very hard for Norr to have blocked his immediate threat of PREFIXED/DELE 8A 68 points. In fact, even if she could have blocked, it wouldn't have been worth it. That's because from her point of view, Edley might not even have had the play (or SUFFIXED, since DELF is also acceptable), and because blocking (for less than 10 points, by playing either DELI, HILI, PILI, SOLI, or TALI, etc., at 7A) would have left Edley with a huge scoring opportunity along column A. Thus, Edley was able to play PREFIXED.

Example 3, Diagram 22-3: <u>H</u>AM L8 6 points. The only way to win! This brilliant stroke allows Cappelletto to play out with NERTZ K5 28, also forming THERE, and his opponent is powerless to stop him from winning.

Example 4, Diagram 22-4: Glowniak found UNTRUTH A8 39 points. The DEV leave is excellent, considering the collection of awkward tiles on her original rack and the lack of scoring opportunity in the position.

Example 5, Diagram 22-5: Felt challenged LURIDITY off the board and played PUMP G6 14 points, keeping ERST and taking a 50-point lead. If he doesn't challenge and instead plays PURPLEST 1F 89 points, he will then have a 59-point lead, but both he and his opponent will have just drawn seven new tiles. In that situation, there is no way to predict who will draw better tiles. However, by forcing his opponent to keep his poor rack of DIILRTU and keeping the bingo-prone tiles ERST with a 50-point lead, he gives himself a better chance to play a bingo first and take a game-winning lead in the next few turns.

Example 6, Diagram 22-6: Armstrong found METAPHOR B4 69 points.

Example 7, Diagram 22-7: Cohen played COU<u>N</u>TERMEN D1 82 points.

Example 8, Diagram 22-8: Although CILANTRO H1 80 points would have been a very nice play, CONTRALT<u>O</u> H7 83 is worth more, and it is certainly much prettier!

Example 9, Diagram 22-9: Jackson played the wonderful word WOLVERINE 3D 66 points.

Example 10, Diagram 22-10: There are many good possibilities to consider; HEXED O7 48 points and HELPED O6 36 are the first two we saw. However, both of these fall short of a win, since they give the opponent a good place for his P at N10. The only play that wins is UPHELD O6 36, which sets up EX N5 50. The opponent has to block with LIP N3 or PIU 6M, and then Edley plays LEX L11 to win by 3 points or 1, since the opponent gets stuck with the Q and G, and Edley plays out.

Example 11, Diagram 22-11: Norr played OD N12 3 points, because next turn she wanted to play either QUEER or QUEEN O8 48. The truth is that if her opponent ignored the threat and simply played UNDESERVED 13E 14, he would have won by a few points. Not realizing his danger, he blocked with ION 9M 7, thinking that he would now win by a larger margin. That sprung Norr's trap, as she played ER H13 2. Now, with IU left, her opponent can neither end the game nor stop QUEEN 15D 81, which won for Norr. Note that if Norr had played ER H13 first, her opponent would have played ION 15F 15, and would have won.

Example 12, Diagram 22-12: With the possibility of a Q play at either 6K or 7K (QUITE), M6 (QUIZ), or N9 (EQUIP), Edley noticed that DEE N7 9 points would block all of his opponent's Q plays, thereby earning him an extra 20 points and the win. He also saw that if the Q was in the bag, then after DEE his opponent wouldn't be able to stop him from playing the game-winning EQUALS at either 2J or 4H. In the actual game, the Q was the last tile in the bag, and Edley went out and won with EQUALS.

Example 13, Diagram 22-13: Cappelletto knew that the only way he could win was by playing a bingo. That looked hopeless unless the G was the last tile in the bag. With that slim hope, he simply dropped his best tile, the S, on the board to form SQUARERS/ES 8C for 19 points. The G *was* the last tile, which gave him OOGONIA, at either M9 or 13I. However, both places could have been blocked with the play ODIC K9 17.

Instead of blocking, the opponent made her best scoring play and was astonished when Cappelletto emptied his rack with his bingo and won! She told us: "As I was tracking tiles I realized that he had three Os. Even though I knew his whole rack, I simply remember thinking: 'Three Os! There's no way he could have a bingo!' So I didn't bother looking closely at all of his possibilities. I know the word! I was just overconfident. It was a good lesson!"

Example 14, Diagram 22-14: Wapnick played STOLE A6 5 points. This blocks the huge X hot spots at B2–6 and B8–10. The opponent very likely had either VARIX B2 62 or PAX B8 57. The result is that STOLE wins 91 percent of the time. SWEET O11 43 wins only 86 percent of the time. The complete analysis of this position took several pages of text to prove. As it turned out, the two tiles in the bag would have lost the game for Wapnick after SWEET, but kept the win after STOLE.

Briefly, the reason STOLE wins so often is that Wapnick now has a 16-point lead, with only 5 tiles to play. The opponent has no really good X plays. Wapnick will play out first almost all the time, winning by a hair.

Example 15, Diagram 22-15: Baron's thinking was this: 1. Reeves has the blank or he never would have opened up the A column with the word LOCK, allowing BLOCK, CLOCK, or FLOCK and a vertical play to a TWS. 2. He's probably planning the play JAB or JOB A1 for 37 points if he doesn't draw a bingo. 3. The only chance to win is if Reeves plays the J on A1. With that, Baron simply looked up at his opponent and started Reeves's timer! In effect, Baron had passed his turn. Reeves was surprised, but he assumed that Baron was simply frustrated. He shrugged his shoulders as if to say "Sorry, Mike!" and proceeded to play his highest-scoring play, JABOT A1 46 points, emptying the bag and taking a 100-point lead. Whereby Baron plopped down JUNIPERS 1A 104, winning the game by just a few points!

Example 16, Diagram 22-16: The reasonable options are: QUINOA E4 30, JOINT E7 24, JIN 7C 25, and JO E7 9, as well as exchanging just the J. Goldman noticed that there were a number of eight-letter bingos possible with the Q without the J on the rack. He played JO E7 9 and played EQUATING next turn. Computer analysis of this position showed that he made the best play by an overwhelming margin. JO simulated 9 points better than JIN and 10 better than exchanging the J. JOINT was 11 points back, and QUINOA was 15 points behind JO. Here are all the potential bingos with his 6-letter leave: QUANTIC(S), ANTIQUE (D, R, S), QUINATE, QUINTAL(S), QUINNAT(S), QUINTAN(S), PIQUANT, QUINTAR(S), ASQUINT, QUANTIZE, QUANTIFY, QUAINTLY, QUANTITY, ACQUAINT, EQUATING, QUANTING, ALIQUANT, AQUATINT, EQUATION, EQUITANT, QUAINTER, QUANTILE, QUATRAIN, QUINTAIN, and TRANQUIL.

Example 17, Diagram 22-17: POL 2L 20 sets up an unstoppable JEEZ or GEEZ O1 72 to win by 3 after opponent plays XU 1A 29.

Example 18, Diagram 22-18: ENDEAVOR 1H 39. Ironically, the opponent had just played VIRAL instead of RIVAL to make it harder to reach the TWS.

Example 19, Diagram 22-19: SORT A3 5. Any sort of regular-sized bingo would still lose. Pistolese had to hope he could draw one of the four As left along with the S in the next turn or two. He drew ANS, while his opponent, not surprisingly, left the A column alone, playing AA 15E 6. Whereby Pistolese played ASSORTMENT A1 108 and won.

Example 20, Diagram 22-20: RORQUALS A1 243. A "rorqual" is a kind of whale. This play is the highest ever scored for a "non-bingo."

Example 21, Diagram 22-21: EQUESTRIAN 14E 38. Besides being prettier, it's much better than ANSWER 15J 32, because there is only one other S out besides his. Greenspan stands a great chance to play down the O column to the O15 TWS, pluralizing EQUESTRIAN and scoring really well next turn.

Example 22, Diagram 22-22: MALEVOLENT 8A 48. This is one of the finest extension plays we've ever seen.

Example 23, Diagram 22-23: QUINTESSENTIAL L1 96 (the blank is played as a T).

Example 24, Diagram 22-24: VEE 7M 6. With the score so lopsided, Epstein needs to play aggressively. This is the best way to maximize his chances for getting back into the game. He now has two excellent Triple-Triple possibilities. Note that VIE 7M is weaker because the I can be used for an -ING word on row 15. *Note:* His opponent played KEN O6 21, and Epstein responded with DILIGENT 15H 149 to keep the rest of the game exciting and competitive.

Example 25, Diagram 22-25: EVE 2H 17 sets up a huge YEH hook at 1H that will score 50+ points next turn. The opponent can't stop it no matter what tiles he has. This was enough for Alexander to win.

Example 26, Diagram 22-26: HAIRPIECE 5C 98 (the blank is played as an H).

Example 27, Diagram 22-27: ADHESION J7 98 is the first complete eight-tile overlap we've ever seen played in any North American SCRABBLE game tournament or club.

Example 28, Diagram 22-28: SHOWBIZ L7 68. I credit this play, being so psychologically uplifting, for enabling me to maintain the confidence that it was truly possible for me to win the National Championship for a third time, despite the extremely tough competition from players half my age. My opponent was Brian Cappelletto, whom many experts considered the most consistent and best player in North America at that time. Cappelletto and I had identical records of twenty-two wins apiece after the thirty-one-game tournament. I was fortunate to edge him by the slim margin of 100 spread points to take first place. Had I played my first choice, WHIZ, then if my remaining games finished as they did, I would have placed second.

Example 29, Diagram 22-29: ROUNDEST I8 77.

Example 30, Diagram 22-30: MANIA B2 46.

Example 31, Diagram 22-31: ENORMOUS O8 80.

Example 32, Diagram 22-32: MOONSHINE O8 54.

Example 33, Diagram 22-33: COPYING 11E 60.

Example 34, Diagram 22-34: FOSSILIZE 15G 60.

Example 35, Diagram 22-35: INADVERTENT 15A 89. If he had had AINSTT?, he would have played EQUIDISTANT O5 71, saving his blank!

Example 36, Diagram 22-36: SEASCAPES 8A 53.

Example 37, Diagram 22-37: FINGERNAIL A1 95.

Example 38, Diagram 22-38: DISFUNCTIONS D2 52.

Example 39, Diagram 22-39: EXTRAMARITAL 1D 66.

Example 40, Diagram 22-40: DINNERTIME M3 80.

Example 41, Diagram 22-41: HARMONIZING D2 102.

Example 42, Diagram 22-42: REJECTION G4 77.

Example 43, Diagram 22-43: RETALIATES A6 83.

Example 44, Diagram 22-44: MATRICIDE A7 98.

Example 45, Diagram 22-45: SHEQALIM A8 89.

Example 46, Diagram 22-46: LIQUIDATOR B4 94.

Example 47, Diagram 22-47: QMEN L7 33.

Example 48, Diagram 22-48: RIF G12 6. He recognized that no matter what his opponent had, NODDER wasn't going to be enough to win. He also considered that if his opponent didn't have the S or A, he might not have been able to block a bingo. This turned out to be the case. In fact, the A, I, and S were all in the bag, and Wright went out with TINDERS and won. No other play gave him as much hope as RIF.

Example 49, Diagram 22-49: VOW L2 9. This threatens AJAR 1L 47 and wins, since his opponent can't go out in one turn.

Example 50, Diagram 22-50: PE 3B 12. This gives him a chance to play one of two potential bingos if he draws the blank. He *did* draw the blank, and while his opponent blocked PIRARUCU with EX G12 41, Lerman played AURICULA A8 86, catching his opponent with BEEGHZ (42 points for Lerman!) and winning 459–435.

Example 51, Diagram 22-51: The 45-point play is TAXA, but that puts him 24 points down. He expects his opponent to score at least 20, and is likely to go out before he does. It's very unlikely indeed that Meller will outrun him. Thus, he finds a way to fish for a bingo. But where would he play one? The most obvious place is down the A or B columns, and he would expect his opponent to block both lines if Meller drops just one tile on the board. With that in mind, he plays XI/EX 14L 18. If his opponent blocks, as expected, *and* Meller draws the D—a one-in-nine chance (11 percent)—he can play through the ME: ANDROMEDA 3G 67, which will be enough for the win! As it happens, he did *not* draw the D, but that doesn't take away from his conception and resourcefulness. In SCRABBLE, as occasionally in life, your actions won't always bear fruit; it's often the *thought* that counts!

Example 52, Diagram 22-52: With no vowels other than a Y, Meller seems unlikely to do well with this rack. However, he found the terrific ENCRYPTS N8 92.

Example 53, Diagram 22-53: With this poor vowel-laden rack, many players might resign themselves to scoring few points and getting rid of several vowels. However, Joey took a closer look at how the board was changed by his opponent's last play. HECK invited a unique four-tile front extension. He played AIRCHECK A8 57.

Example 54, Diagram 22-54: Richards played the very quiet-looking BI 9C 14. Mallick couldn't go out, nor could he score well, and Richards played DECAGONAL E3 26 to win by just a few. If Mallick had tried to block, he would have only succeeded in giving Richards a different out play.

Example 55, Diagram 22-55: If his opponent had played LEE 14B 10 instead of RIEL, that would have set up QI 15A 35, and the threat would have been enough to win, despite Krafchick's EX 6A 52. Krafchick showed the flaw of RIEL by playing HE O13 5. This set up NIX 15M 69. If his opponent blocked with NOO 13L 4, then Krafchick's HEX O13 39 plus ZING 11H 28, followed by MYC J13 10 and AD B5 14, is enough to win. There followed JO C9 11, NIX 15M 69, OF L4 10, MYC J13 10, JOE C9 12, AD B5 14, PASS, GIDS 7L 6, and 20 points for the unplayed Q left them with a final score of 418–416 in favor of Krafchick.

Where do we go from here? The next generation of SCRABBLE game players is waiting to be taught. If you'd like to join us, chapter 23 will show you how to introduce SCRABBLE games to your children. Let us know how you do! We're always looking for better techniques. Good luck!

23 SCRABBLE® FOR CHILDREN

Most people agree that one of the greatest gifts one can bestow on a child is a lifelong curiosity about words. This curiosity has a way of leading to other things, such as a love of reading, better communication skills, and much more. Playing SCRABBLE games with children has proven to be one of the easiest and most effective ways to ensure this love of words.

This has been shown time and again by parents who encourage their children to play the game, and by teachers who have used the SCRABBLE games extensively in the classroom. Few letters brought more satisfaction to the staff of the National SCRABBLE Association than those that began: "My mother and I have been playing SCRABBLE together for thirty-five years . . ." or "My sixth-grade class improved their vocabulary skills remarkably after we played SCRABBLE this semester."

By the time your children are four or five, you can introduce them to SCRABBLE® for Juniors. At the age of eight, they should be ready to try the regular SCRABBLE game.

Remember, SCRABBLE games will provide your children with a number of educational benefits. And the best part is that they'll be having so much fun, they won't even notice. Among the things youngsters learn from playing SCRABBLE games are:

Vocabulary—This one's pretty obvious.
Spelling—This one's even more obvious!
Math—Remember, SCRABBLE scoring requires ongoing addition, multiplication, counting, recounting, and calculation.
Spatial Relationships—Since words have different values in different places on the board, kids learn to assess and evaluate how many and which tiles to use in their words with the available space on the board.

Critical Thinking—The competition and options provided by the SCRABBLE game make it a necessity for youngsters to plan ahead and to assess and evaluate options.

Social/Personal Skills—As with any good game, it also helps children experience the value of team play, competition, and the need to follow rules. A good score or an unusual word builds self-esteem, and a word challenge teaches positive confrontation.

Despite all the obvious fun and educational benefits, however, playing SCRABBLE with children does require a little thought beforehand. As open as they are to new experiences, many children can still be intimidated by a game that involves spelling or a contest that pits them against an adult. With that in mind, you should always consider measures that will give the child both an advantage and a sense of ease.

The most obvious of these is to allow the child to use a dictionary when making any SCRABBLE game move. It's a terrific safety net and one that the child can be weaned from over time. Early on you may also try playing with two children at once, so the child does not have the threat of a one-on-one confrontation. Play a three-handed SCRABBLE game or let the two kids act as a team against you. Both methods work well.

For the most part, you should approach teaching SCRABBLE games the way you teach a child to ride a bike: Jump right in. There is little to be gained by abstract discussion of the process; both of you are far better off getting out the board and going at it!

If the child has never even observed a game before, a good place to start is to have him or her find the tiles for his or her name—or a favorite word—and place them in the center of the board. Then have him or her calculate the score. Next have the child move the name or word to another place where s/he might encounter a word or letter bonus. A couple of tries should convey the idea of relative scores and the concept of "looking for the hot spots" whenever possible.

Another early exercise might be to place the word ATE on the board. Then have the child find all the letters that can be hooked in front (D, F, R, etc.). Find another word, like BAN, and show what can be placed at the end of a word (D, G, K, etc.). Each time you build a word down with either the front- or end-hook letters illustrates that s/he can make two complete new words! This is especially true with the S. For the most part, children should learn not to use the S unless they are going to make two words.

Take out a rack and have your children draw seven letters from the tile bag. Have them move the tiles around on the rack and wait for words to appear magically. This is a good time to remind them to look for familiar letter combinations: ING, PRE, EST, RE, ATE, ER, etc. Try this several times so that they learn that some letters produce more words than others.

A COUPLE OF TROUBLE SPOTS TO LOOK FOR

There are a couple of areas we've found that tend to confuse youngsters when they first play SCRABBLE. So you'll probably need to reemphasize the following points:

- Plays may be made only in a straight line: horizontally or vertically. Diagonal plays are never acceptable.
- Bonus squares (Double Word Score, etc.) count only the *first time* they are used. Explain to your child that after a bonus square is covered up, it will provide no more bonus points in that game.
- The blank is always scored as zero points, but it can be used to cover a Double or Triple Word bonus square to take advantage of the extra points.
- They are free to exchange all or some of their tiles whenever they wish, as long as there are seven tiles remaining in the pool. But to do so they must skip a turn. Explain why exchanging is sometimes a good strategy.
- A child can challenge your word whenever s/he wishes to, but s/he should be aware that an unsuccessful challenge means that s/he misses his or her turn. However, we recommend a "free challenge" rule when an adult plays with a child—at least early on—as it is less intimidating and helps him or her to learn words.
- Learn to differentiate between proper and common nouns. This can be confusing. After all, Bill, Rose, Mike, and May are all proper names and generic words as well. Explain this to your child.

The overriding goal is to teach your child that words can be fun. Here are a couple of other ways to do this:

- Have your child see how many words s/he can make out of his or her name. For example, the name Thomas has seventy-nine legal words in it. Use your last name if the first isn't workable.
- Teach anagrams. Show how the letters in the word TEA can also spell EAT and ETA, or how CAROB can become COBRA. Find or make up a name and anagram it. For example, Ruth Ardeen can be transformed into: HEAD TURNER, TUNA HERDER, UNDER EARTH, and THUNDER EAR.

Probably the single biggest mistake people make in teaching SCRABBLE games to children is pushing them too fast. In this regard, it is no different from baseball, gymnastics, or any other endeavor that requires one to "crawl before you walk." Remember, it is thrilling for a seven-year-old to find a four-letter word on his or her rack and place it *anywhere* on a SCRABBLE game board.

Only after your child is comfortable and confident should you start to introduce other options s/he might have played. Techniques include asking where else s/he might have played the same word, or what other word(s) might have been made with the same letters. If the game is really tutorial in nature, you can ask to see what his or her original rack was, and then, together with the child, consider plays from that. Try always to "lead" a child, so that s/he discovers the alternate plays rather than your spelling it out.

Remember, when playing SCRABBLE games with children, the operative word is *fun*. The rest will take care of itself.

The NASPA is often asked which SCRABBLE game should be purchased and used in playing with children. Currently, Hasbro offers three options. They are:

SCRABBLE® FOR JUNIORS

Geared to children aged five and up, this game has a two-sided board. One side helps children form words through pictures of familiar objects such as a horse or a barn. The opposite side is more like a traditional SCRABBLE board.

SCRABBLE® BRAND CROSSWORD GAME

This, of course, is the standard SCRABBLE game. It also comes in Deluxe, Deluxe Travel, and Spanish editions. Most children are ready to graduate to this board by eight years of age.

SCHOOL SCRABBLE® KIT

Founded in 1992, the National School SCRABBLE Program is now used in more than 15,000 schools throughout the United States and Canada, with well over half a million children using the game in the classroom or as an after-school activity. The program has been praised by parents and educators alike as an innovative, fresh tool for teaching children numerous skills. Perhaps it's best summed up by one observation heard over and over again by teachers: Students are having so much fun, they don't even realize they're learning!

The National School SCRABBLE Program was conceived by a team from the National SCRABBLE Association and developed along with educational consultants and Hasbro executives. This group spent nearly two years in classrooms, studying a wide group that included elementary schools, middle schools, junior high schools, and high schools. In addition, they visited both public schools and private schools in urban, suburban, and rural areas. While they confirmed that children of all ages can benefit, it was concluded that grades five through eight were the optimal age group.

Regardless of the venue, one constant remained: Although there was almost always skepticism from students on the first visit, by the third visit they couldn't get enough of the game. As a teacher in Massachusetts remarked one afternoon, "If you had told me that I'd one day see a bunch of twelve-year-old boys fighting over a dictionary, I'd have said you were crazy." But that's exactly what happened in school after school, all over the country.

The centerpiece of the National School SCRABBLE Program was the School SCRABBLE Kit, sold to schools by Hasbro at $49.95, which was the manufacturer's cost. In fact, if one were to purchase the items in the kit separately, it would cost well over $150. As of this writing the kit is being reconsidered and may take a different form.

Each kit had everything a classroom needed to get started. It included six modified Deluxe SCRABBLE boards; tiles; racks; an *Official SCRABBLE® Players Dictionary, Fourth Edition*; a curriculum guide; and a video that the students and teacher watched together.

The National School SCRABBLE Kit was designed to encourage creative learning and to act as a catalyst to get children excited about learning. Teachers cite educational benefits such as improved skills in language arts (vocabulary, spelling, and dictionary usage), mathematics (traditional, mental math, and spatial relationships), and social interaction (cooperative learning and conflict resolution).

In 1997 the NSA and Hasbro organized and sponsored the first-ever school SCRABBLE Championship in Springfield, MA. It was a one-day event that featured teams of two from area middle schools. This war of words ended up taking on a definite athletic atmosphere as children arrived in team buses, many wearing team jerseys. Prizes included Hasbro games and toys, books, and more. High-scoring words led to high-fives; victories led to team cheers. The organizers, who'd done this as an experiment, knew they were on to something.

By the year 2001, the school SCRABBLE competitive scene had grown substantially. There were statewide tournaments in Massachusetts, Oregon, and Indiana, as well as large school tournaments in Memphis, Dallas, and San Francisco. In addition, Long Island, New York, held a regional competition with 200 children competing. At all venues, they were serious. It was clear they had been studying word lists, had practiced against one another, and had held marathon sessions against the SCRABBLE® CD-ROM.

The prizes had improved as well. First prize was now an all-expenses-paid trip for two to the Nickelodeon studios in Orlando, FL. Other prizes included gift certificates, toys and games, and more.

The program also saw the first student from the National School SCRABBLE Program competing against adults. Twelve-year-old Leland Fiddler from Massachusetts was the youngest of more than 600 word wizards who competed in the grueling five-day 2001 National SCRABBLE Championship in Providence, Rhode Island. Every one of Leland's opponents was an adult, yet he compiled a respectable 17–14 record and appeared on national television and in dozens of news stories. It was a great day for competitive SCRABBLE, our version of the first time a Little League baseball player made it to the Major Leagues.

In 2003, the first National School SCRABBLE® Championship (NSSC) was held in Boston, which included more than ninety teams of two students each from many different states. In 2018, the sixteenth NSSC was held in Philadelphia, PA, and will continue to be an annual event. Winners earn awards worth up to $2,500 for each student on the team, though every student walks away with prizes of some kind.

24 SHARING THE JOY: Tales from *SCRABBLE® News*

"Around the Board" was a regular feature of *SCRABBLE® News* for many years. We hope you enjoy these news items as much as we did.

BINGO "BEDS"

Sam Kantimathi (CA) wrote to us about two exciting plays he witnessed recently, one of which he found less than thrilling. At an Atlantic City, NJ, tournament he saw Lynn Cushman (NY) play BERATED directly above the opening play of ONETIME, simultaneously forming BO, EN, RE, AT, TI, ME, and DE. Only one month later in San Francisco, Sam's first play against Brian Cappelletto (IL), the 1998 National SCRABBLE Champion, was ENTASIS 8C 66. Brian quickly played REALISE on top of his play, simultaneously forming RE, EN, AT, LA, IS, SI, and ES for 77 points.

PLAYING FAST AND HARD

At the 1988 National SCRABBLE Championship, Vernon Jones (NJ) and Buddy Morton (TN) played their complete game in fourteen minutes. But that's not the story. Vernon's first two plays were EXPAND 8C 48 and UNEXPANDED 8A 63, an excellent acceptable-looking phoney that went unchallenged. He went on to score 471 points—without a bingo. But that's not the story, either. Buddy was drawing so badly that he had to exchange tiles when he was down 130 points late in the game. He then proceeded to draw consecutive bingos, DILLIES and ALIASES, and then he laid down a Triple-Triple BRIDLERS, to win, 504–471.

To Amazing Grace

Amazing aboideau
How sweet the find
That saved a rack
Like mine
I thought I'd pass
But now I've found
A bingo that works
Just fine.

—Steve Oliger (PA)

NEVER TOO TIRED

Joyce Spalding, Director of SCRABBLE® Club #104 in Port Huron, MI, told us about her son's experience in basic training. "He said that at one point his company had to live outdoors for five days. At three in the morning they were awakened and put through various maneuvers all day. By evening he was cold, tired, and hungry. His feet were blistered and his throat was sore. He was exhausted both physically and mentally, and then he saw a sign that read: BIVOUAC, and the first thought to cross his mind was: 'That's a great SCRABBLE game word!'"

PLAYING CATCH-UP

It can often be demoralizing to be behind more than 100 points. We often tell novices to try to find the best play, regardless of the score. Winning will take care of itself. Director Ginger White (NY) remembered this adage at a tournament in New York City a few years ago. She was behind, 70–305, after eight plays. She came back with a flurry of high-scoring plays to win, 387–367!

EXCHANGING THE Q

Years ago, during a crucial game at the San Francisco SCRABBLE® Club Tournament, one of the authors, Joe Edley, had been drawing very poor tiles and was trailing his opponent after five plays. He drew all vowels and exchanged seven tiles, whereby he drew seven consonants, including the Q and an S. After his opponent took an even bigger lead, Edley exchanged again. This time he decided to save one tile, the S. Immediately after drawing tiles, he realized, to his horror, that he had carelessly saved the Q instead! Miraculously, he drew EINRU? and played QUERCINE through an E for 86 points, then went on to win the game and the event.

UNUSUAL HOOK WORD

At a Baltimore, MD, tournament years ago, as the story goes, Gila Lipman's opponent challenged XI. Gila won the challenge, of course. Minutes later, the challenger added I to XI, forming XII. When Gila challenged, her opponent indignantly retorted, "If you can play eleven, I certainly can play twelve."

Racks Man*

Let me tell you how it will be:
Two Vs for you, S blank for me.
'Cause I'm the racks man,
Yeah, I'm the racks man.

Should VV not appeal to you,
Be thankful I don't add a Q.
'Cause I'm the racks man.
Yeah, I'm the racks man.

If you pass the Q, you'll draw four Us.
If you keep "SATIRE," you'll draw the Q.
When you finally bingo, you'll still lose,
'Cause you're trailing by two fifty-two.

—Jim Kramer (MN)

(*sung to "Taxman," with apologies to the Beatles)

PHONEYS

"Quick . . . Is it *harrass* or *harass? Paralell* or *parallel*? Alan S. Brown, associate professor of psychology at Southern Methodist University's Dedman College, argues that all those multiple-choice tests that give several spellings of words . . . simply reinforce incorrect spelling patterns." This was the beginning of an article in the April 1989 issue of *American Teach.* It goes on to say what most SCRABBLE game experts already know, and what newcomers should be aware of: When you see phoneys, or just think about them, as time passes it will become increasingly difficult to remember that they were phoney. The more you see a fake word, the easier it will be to "remember" that it is a word. Our advice is to play a minimum of phoneys and do not study nonwords or such lists.

FIVE BINGOS!

Jerry Lerman (CA), a top West Coast expert, played a tough game against Jeff Widergren (CA), another top player, at a tournament. Jerry lost, 467–469. Less than a month later at another tournament, he and Jeff were paired again. This time Jerry started off the game with LOVESICK, BUCKEENS, GARDENIA, and SUNDERER, all bingos. Later he added AMPERES, for a total of *five* bingos. Unfortunately for him, Widergren played the unusual BARGUEST for a Triple-Triple for 158 points, as well as the bingo LOONIES and other high-scoring plays to win, 502–460.

HOW CLOSE?

How much difference can 100 points make over the course of thirteen games? At the 1993 Waltham, MA, Premier Tournament, which included several past national champions, the difference between first and sixth was only 100 points. The Waltham event was scored using a "credit" system, whereby the winner receives 46 credits for a win and the loser 30 credits. And then, depending on how many points the winner wins by, the winner receives more credits and the loser subtracts some credits. That year the tourney ended with the winners accumulating 565, 564, 562, 559, 557, and 555 credits. When you consider that each of the credits was worth about 10 game points each, that was probably the closest finish ever in any major tournament! Canadian Adam Logan, who at the time was a teenaged Princeton University mathematics student, won top honors.

CURIOUS OVERDRAWS

The rule used to be that when a player overdraws a tile and has eight on his/her rack, the opponent randomly draws two tiles, looks at them both, then returns one to the bag and the other to the player. At the 1991 SCRABBLE® Masters Championship in Cincinnati, Ron Multon (IL) had some unusual coincidences happen to him. The first time an opponent overdrew tiles, Ron randomly drew the E and R off his opponent's rack. Thinking that his opponent was vowel-heavy, he gave him back the E. His opponent promptly played the bingo NEONATES. In another game, after his opponent overdrew tiles, Ron was comfortably ahead. He drew the blank and an I from his opponent's rack, and of course he put the blank back in the bag, thinking that he had really saved himself some plus-points! As it happened, that was a big mistake. His opponent already had one blank and immediately played a bingo. Later, his opponent drew the other blank, used it to bingo again, and won by 10 points.

BINGO OR NOT?

Jim Neuberger (NY), runner-up at the 1980 National SCRABBLE Championship and one of the true gentlemen of the game, was upset at a Niagara Falls tournament a few years ago after a difficult loss in the first round. A few rounds later, when he was watching two players analyze the end of their game, he noticed that GONADES was a better play than the one made, and he said so. When Richie Lund of Brooklyn, another top player, happened to hear Jim's comment, he told him it was not acceptable. Jim was certain it was good and said so. Momentarily the pairings were announced, and Jim and Richie were paired together. After Richie's opening play of WICKER, Jim's rack was GONADE?. There were many sure bingos on the rack (GROANED, TANGOED, CONGAED, BONDAGE . . .), but he was licking his chops for a challenge from Richie as he played GONADES. Without hesitating, Richie challenged and said confidently, "I just looked it up before we started the game." Jim was flabbergasted, but went on to win the game and the tournament with an 8–2 record. Richie finished second.

ADJUDICATIONS

Word judges are correct in their adjudications probably better than 98 percent of the time. However, if you think a mistake has been made, always ask for a second opinion. By doing that, another judge is required to research the challenged play. When a mistake does occur, it's usually because the word judge does not notice that a word is acceptable. What are the consequences of not asking for that second opinion? Just ask Peter Morris (MI). Peter, the 1991 World SCRABBLE Champion and 1989 National Champion, was playing at a club several years ago when he held the following rack: ABELNN?. ADO was on the board and he was pondering his bingo possibilities. Suddenly he found a wonderful ten-letter common-word bingo through the ADO! Needless to say, he was praying his opponent wouldn't take the spot. As luck would have it, his opponent left it for him but played WAPATI on another part of the board. Peter was virtually certain that WAPITI was the correct spelling. So he challenged. The word judge said, "Acceptable!" Peter didn't think he should ask for a second opinion, since someone obviously *saw* the word. What happened next? You guessed it: His opponent blocked ADO and his bingo turned into a "nongo." See the answer for his missed play on page 366.

If I Had a Blank . . .*

If I had a blank
I'd play it in the mornin'
I'd play it in the evenin'
All over this board.
I'd sing out BINGO
I'd sing out BONUS
I'd sing about the gap between
My score and my opponent's
All over this land.

—Steve Oliger (PA)

(*sung to "If I Had a Hammer")

NINE-LETTER PLAY

Finding seven-letter plays is not typically one of the first skills a child learns when starting to play the SCRABBLE game. Nine-letter words are rare even for the best players. That's why we were so excited when we heard this story. At the 1990 National SCRABBLE Championship, Bob Schoenman (OR) was playing in the Expert Division, while his nine-year-old son, Ian, rooted for him on the sidelines. During a break, Ian was playing with another child of a contestant and had the rack DCORTU?, with an AR on the board. He astonished several adults who saw him play a common-word nine-letter bingo. Can you guess his play? The answer is on page 366.

MISSING TILES

SCRABBLE® Club #288 in Huron, SD, met one afternoon at its appointed time only to discover a robbery had occurred and their game cabinet was in much disarray. The thief had used a crowbar and had pulled the hardware off the wall, leaving the lock intact. The deluxe boards were left there, but the culprits had stolen all the little bags of tiles. Club Director Florence Holm was able to identify the bags at police headquarters, but she was unable to convince the police to return them until after the thief had stood trial. It was also discovered that money was taken from the main office of the building, Wilson Center. Imagine the thief's response after opening the little bags and finding not jewels or coins but SCRABBLE game tiles!

AROUND THE GLOBE

Do you know anyone who has played SCRABBLE on all seven continents? National SCRABBLE Association's 1999 Director of the Year, Margaret Bauer, has. She has played in Europe many times, as well as with clubs in Israel and some of the best players down under in Australia. She cruised down the Nile in Egypt and toured Ecuador—always keeping a set nearby. And, on a cruise to Antarctica, she happened to have a roommate who played. We wouldn't have been surprised if she had found her way on to a space shuttle and bingoed where no one had before.

PHONEY ALERT

At the 1988 National SCRABBLE Championship in Reno, NV, Peter Morris (MI) pulled a fast one against dictionary-proof Robert Felt (NY), who has one of the best vocabularies around and actually knows the meanings of many of the obscure words. When Peter tried the bingo FOGHATS, Robert knew he had seen it before, so he did not challenge it. After the game, he found out how right he was. FOGHATS was on Al Weissman's (RI) published list of most outrageous phoneys!

Years later at the same Reno, NV, hotel, Jeff Widergren (CA) used the same phoney, FOGHATS, to steal a game from his opponent, another top player, who also remembered having seen the word before.

SECOND OPINION

Johnny Nevarez (VA), who used to direct one of the largest and longest tournaments each year in Reno, NV, had the opening play against Jerry Lerman (CA) during the 1993 World SCRABBLE Championship. His opening rack was AGORRTT. Johnny realized that GARROTTE was acceptable. Therefore, hoping that Jerry would use an E, Johnny played GARROT, which wasn't an *OSPD* word.

"Acceptable!" came the judge's reply after Jerry's challenge.*

"Wait, that can't be right! I want a second opinion!" declared Johnny.

Turns out it's a British-only word that is acceptable for WSC play. To our knowledge, that's the first time a winner of a challenge ever asked for a second opinion.

QUICK RECOVERY

"At the Michael Wise Memorial Tournament in Toronto last September, Mark Przybyszewski (NY), otherwise known affectionately as EYECHART, had not

*The challenger does not lose a turn at World Championship play, regardless of the play's acceptability.

arrived at the announced start time. And so, at 9:10 A.M. I supervised the start of his game against another expert [Rich Baker]. Mark eventually ran into the room very much out of breath, to find 2:54 left on his clock. Rich agreed to pause the clock for a few minutes to let Mark regain his composure—it hadn't helped that Rich had begun the game with a bingo. I apologized for being out of the room when Mark arrived, and for therefore not reminding him that he might prefer to elect to forfeit the game with a spread of only 50 points. As it turned out, it was a good thing—he won the game, 442–304, using only 6 minutes of his clock, and the win gave him the Last Gasp Prize for the best Sunday record by a non-placer!"

—John Chew, Toronto, Ontario

May I Play?

Upon me has been cast a pall,
I'm suffering from acute withdrawal,
My mind is mired in deep malaise,
I haven't played for 2 whole days!
There IS no cure for my affliction,
I want NO cure for this ADDICTION.
Just lead me to the sacred board!
My passion cannot be ignored.
Sweat is forming on my brow,
I have to play the game right now!!
Breathe in, breathe out—OK, I'm calm,
There is no cause for your alarm.
I don't need any medication
I just need the sublime sensation
Of a bingo on my rack.
So please will you get off my back,
The club will meet tonight at six.
And I really need my fix.
I know it's our anniversary,
But darling, please, please hear my plea!
I'll make it up to you, I swear!
Just let me play 4 games and THEN,
I'll be home real close to ten.
Please understand, I do implore,
See ya, hon, I'm out the door.

—Marty Fialkow (NJ)

EXPLOSIVE FINISH

"In a fun game last year at our Dallas Club #436, Mic Baron (TX), a relative newcomer to organized SCRABBLE game play, and Mike Early, an expert, were nearly through with a game with a score of 280–209 after ten plays each, with Mic winning. After holding a minute and thinking about a potential TWS-TWS through the S on 14O, Mic challenged Early's ORDINES 14I. After it came back acceptable, Early then played ZOEAE 15F to go ahead by 50 points. Mic then found and played PSALMIST O8 176, his first-ever TWS-TWS. Mike then played EGO 6A, opening yet another potential TWS-TWS, and you guessed it: Mic's rack was EEINST? and he found NEEDIEST 1A for 113 points to bingo out. With the 24 points in Mike's rack, the final score was 593–342, Mic's highest game ever!"

—Bryan Pepper, Director, Club #436

TASTY TREAT

Matt Laufer (NY) asked Mark DiBattista (NY) to anagram the following rack of eight letters: AEIIRTY?. Mark wrestled with the rack for a couple of days, not willing to give up on it. A few days later, at the Plainview, NY, tournament, Mark and Matt challenged players at the breakfast table to anagram the rack. This time both Sal Piro (NY) and Chris Economos (NY) came up with the anagram. In his second game that morning, Mark had this rack: AERTY??. On the board, but separated, were an I and a K. Guess what Mark played? The answer is on page 366.

My Favorite Game

There was a time in days of old
When we'd visit friends, some new, some old,
We'd sit and chat and talk of sport
Or sing around the pianoforte,
But now 'tis quiet, no more noise,
For concentration it destroys.
It's a regulated game,
Two minutes, or you're called a name.
Watch the score, don't be unwary,
Be prepared with a dictionary.
Don't waste an X in any old place,
Wait until you have a triple space.
Too late you find you've used your Us,
You've got to watch not Ps but Qs.
So home you go to practice the game,

Vowing next time you'll win the same.
You find yourself thrilled when you read a word
You're sure that the others have never heard.
And next time when you're invited, you say,
"Oh, SCRABBLE, why sure, I'd love to play."

—Florence Weintraub (TX)

NAME EXTENSION

The following anagram has been floating around East Coast anagram circles for a long time. IDA SHAPIRO, a veteran New York player, can add a C to her name and anagram it into a common eleven-letter word. What is it? The answer is on page 366.

FAMILY GAME AND RECORD

The NASPA was tickled when Aileen Osofsky (NY) walked into NASPA headquarters and told us about a great game of SCRABBLE she had recently played. "We were playing four-handed, and my daughter Randy went first. She opened the game with RAPPING, with the first P on the star. My grandson Ryder played next; he's fourteen. He said he could do better. He played DESTINE, front-hooking RAPPING with the T and scoring 90 points. I delighted to one-up them with my own bingo, FELLOWS, pluralizing TRAPPING, for 95 points. Finally, my other grandson, Judd, age seventeen, who didn't like his tiles at all, brightened up considerably when he saw that his EIINOUZ played around the N in TRAPPINGS for the Double-Double UNIONIZE for 118 points! Incredible, was all we could say!"

HAPPY BIRTHDAY, CLUB #248

"On October 2, 1999, the Mid-Cities, Texas SCRABBLE® Club #248 celebrated its fifteenth birthday with a one-day unrated tournament/birthday party, which continued a tradition that started on our first birthday in 1985. I called a local grocery store and ordered a cake with the inscription 'Happy Birthday, SCRABBLE Club #248.' When I picked up the cake, it was beautiful, but complete with a picture of a bedraggled cleaning lady holding pail, mops, and rags. After recovering from the shock and laughter, I asked why the picture? The store employee pulled out the order form and explained that this particular picture was picture #248 from their catalog. I decided to take it instead of an unadorned substitute. The strangely decorated cake garnered many laughs that night! By the way, *no one* could guess why we had the picture."

—Mary Rhoades (TX)

EVAPORATION OF A SURE WIN

Sammy Okosagah (MD) and Steve Polatnick (FL) had a classic game during an early round at the Atlantic City Championship in 1999, Luise Shafritz (PA) reported. "With a comfortable 77-point lead, Steve had AEIOSTZ on his rack when Sammy made a setup of ER at 9L, allowing Steve to play his bingo AZOTISE for 125 points and take a 189-point lead. The E was now in the TWS alley at N15. Steve noticed that he had emptied the bag and his draw included QJ. Sammy's rack was EIMRRST, so down comes the Triple-Triple RIMESTER for 149 points. Steve, thinking his 189-point lead was still enough for the win, said something congratulatory and then was shocked to discover that when they added the 46-plus points from his rack, Sammy had won, 511–505!"

HAIKU

Inward-Bound

Snow sends us inside
Where words drift like flakes across
Terrain of our minds.

—Paul Thompson (WA)

Frustration

Bleak on my last rack
Lurks the kue to filch from me
My scant advantage.

—Vivienne Muhling (CAN)

Life

Letters march in rows,
Scoring points for words you make.
More to life than this?

—Norma Bernhardt (CA)

OTIOSITY

Top experts Charlie Southwell (VA), Steve Polatnick (FL), and Jim Pate (AL) were swapping stories at dinner during the 1994 National SCRABBLE Championship. Jim told the following tale: "I was at a tourney in 1981 where I had the great fortune to play OTIOSITY. In 1983, Chuck Armstrong [one of the top-rated players in the nation at the time] and I were sharing breakfast before a tournament. I told Chuck of my play of OTIOSITY. That day in the first round of the tourney, Chuck played OTIOSITY."

After that conversation, Charlie and Steve were paired together the next morning, and Steve played OTIOSITY against Charlie!

A GAME A DAY

Bill Zoller wrote to us about his parents, Mr. and Mrs. Herbert Zoller, of Farmington Hills, MI. "My parents have been playing the game ever since I can remember. But for the last twenty-four years they have played one game almost every morning after breakfast. They claim it helps them start the day on a positive note and stay mentally alert and active. In addition, they have kept track of who won and their scores. As of August 20, 1994, they had played 7,338 games, with my dad winning 3,670 games and my mom 3,668 games. Very close after twenty-four years of play! The margin of difference has been as high as 400 games in my mom's favor. My dad's highest score was 408 in 1985, and my mom's 421 in 1987. Playing the game every day has helped to keep their minds alert and contributed to their good health. They celebrated their sixty-fifth wedding anniversary on September 14, 2000. Mom is eighty-nine and Dad is ninety-four."

LOOK UP AND SEE YOUR PLAY?

At a recent tournament, Andrea Michaels (CA) had 478 points and her final rack was DEITTU?. "There was an open COBALT, but I spent so much time looking for an N or an I to play INTUITED or an open space to play QUITTED that I ran overtime. Afterward, my opponent pointed out that I could have started with an A and played ATTITUDE, winning the high-scoring prize for my division. The irony? I was sitting across from a player throughout the whole game who wore a T-shirt that said ATTITUDE across it."

TRUSTING FRIENDS

"I futzed with the rack and came up with a word that Alan Stern (CA) told me was good yesterday when he asked me what the anagram of DELEADS is. At the time, I responded that I didn't know one, and he told me that it was DEADLES. I discovered that this 'word' played with six overlaps and played it. My opponent, another expert, held me on it and finally decided that I must know it, because I had so many other options. Ironically, he had a Double-Double bingo himself that I blocked. So I got away with a very unintentional phoney. The moral is: DEADLES is not acceptable and there are *no* anagrams for DELEADS. Alan, are you reading?"

—Jan Dixon (DE)

LONG WORDS

It's not often you hear about an eleven-letter word being played in our game. Even less frequently heard of is two tens played in one game. How about all three of them in the same game? Bernard Gotlieb (Quebec) was playing Ann Sanfedele (NY) in Albany in 1999. First, with the W in the A column, Gotlieb played OUTGROW, 33 points, and later added the ING for 45 points. With IN on the board, he bingoed with OPERATING for 74 points, while Ann added the CO in front of it for 30 points. Finally, Ann added INTER in front of TWINE for 42 points.

Born to Lose

If earthly creatures could but choose,
They'd opt to win and never lose
And even ties would not elate
At crossings with a moving freight.
To lose a fortune would be sad.
To lose a duel would be too bad.
Some politicians lose their clout
And boxing champs get kayoed out.
Luckless gamblers lose their shirt
And Indy losers can get hurt.
Most losing golfers hook and slice
(and mutter words that ain't so nice).
Derby ponies lose by noses
(they don't get to smell the roses).
And poor old Casey couldn't bat,
But swatted flies become a splat.
And Aesop touted the disgrace:
The hare that blew the tortoise race.
(Methinks the loss that caused most dread
was feudal queens who lost a head.)
But SCRABBLE losers are unique.
They take their losses without pique,
They tally scores, emerge all smiles,
They merely shrug and blame the tiles.

—Maxene Johnson (AR)

KENTUCKY MADNESS AND A NOVICE POINT OF VIEW

Each year in late spring the Kentucky marathon tests the abilities and endurance of twenty-some players who get together for twenty-four straight hours of the SCRABBLE game in an unofficial and unrated tournament. In 1999, while several players had to be awakened to make their next play at least once or twice at some time during the night, everyone had a blast. Bob Lipton, frequent World SCRABBLE Championship participant and three-time past winner of this event, won with a 16–6, + 1,498 record. Tobi Wikel (MI), a newcomer to organized play, was thrilled to be able to play with the top experts. "I have been dreaming about this for months. It's every 'baby' player's fantasy. Me, playing face-to-face, eye-to-eye, across the board from those that can really play the game! Drawing EXPERT tiles from EXPERT bags, placing them one by one on EXPERT racks. Surely EXPERT words would magically appear! Yep, no more BABY boards, no more BABY games! Well, folks, it was a dream come true and I did have the time of my life. EXPERT words did appear, but not by magic and not on *my* rack. Words like CRONIES, IGNITOR, SERIOUS, LUSTIER, ERASURE, ASTERIA, and SLIDERS appeared on my rack. Words like NEOTENY, PEPLUM, EUPNOEA, QUAICH, INCASED, UNWALLED, GREENTH, ABOMASA, DOVENING, SEROTINE, and WATTAPES appeared on theirs. I won three and lost nineteen (yeah, last place). After it was over, I returned to my motel room exhausted but with a smile on my face. . . ."

ONE-TILE RECORD SCORE

Late in a recent tournament game against another expert, Tom Kelly (NY) was behind, and so he played the only bingo he found, MOTHERED. Although he was now ahead by 30 points, he wasn't too happy because the M was placed on 15B and just waiting for a front S hook. His opponent, so intent on being able to play the Q, played QUIRK A10. Tom drew the last S and plopped it down on the TWS A15, forming SMOTHERED/QUIRKS for 99 points, winning easily, earning his way into the record books with the highest-scoring one-tile play in NASPA tournament history.

IS IT REAL?

At the January Reno, NV, tournament in 1997, there was a fierce battle for first place between several top players. On the second board during the penultimate round, Lester Schonbrun (CA), perennial top-ten-rated player, played TABOURIN against Jeff Widergren (CA). Both players are quite experienced and generally know virtually all the bingos that have only one high-point tile. Though neither was certain of its acceptability, Widergren decided not to challenge. Ten minutes later, sitting next to them on the top board, Greg Heidler (HI) was playing David Wiegand (OR). When Greg played TABOURIN, all four players chuckled, and the word was accepted, again. Readers, please don't be fooled. Check it for yourself. TABOURIN is a phoney! FYI: David Wiegand won the tourney with a 15–3 record.

Game Plan

There was an old woman
Who lived in a shoe.
She had so many children
That she didn't know what to do.
A good friend advised her,
"What you need to get
Is an *OSPD*
And a nice SCRABBLE set."
Then the woman was astonished,
She had doubted the advice.
For she saw her kids' behavior
Change from naughty into nice.
They studied words and spelling.
They even learned to add
And they found that taking turns
Was really not so bad.
The whining caused by boredom
Was replaced with fun and smiles.
Was elixir in the SCRABBLE bag
Or magic in the tiles?

Now the lady in the brogan
No longer sings the blues
For her brats evolved as cherubs
And they mind their Ps and Qs.
She'll live happy ever after
For her home is filled with cheer
And the governor has proclaimed her
As "The Mother of the Year!"

—Maxene Johnson (AZ)

LOSING IN STYLE

Alan Stern (CA) wrote: "Had lots of fun in Dallas (1996 National SCRABBLE Championship) despite my 13–14 finish, good for fifty-seventh place in Division 1. The carnival-like side room for after-hours was interesting all the time with anagrams, team games, and computer games running simultaneously.

"My high lowlight came on day three, where I stood 7–5. I had the weirdest day of losses ever, probably outscoring most people's winning efforts. I played Joel Sherman (NY) first and lost 466–443. Then came another loss to Ann Ferguson (WA), 443–403, followed by a defeat from Brian Cappelletto (IL) and his four bingos, including THIOTEPA, 573–409! Thank God the lunch break came! After scarfing down bad pizza, I sat down to watch Jan Dixon (DE) hand me a 412–410 setback, making that four consecutive 400-or-better losses for the day. I wasn't finished yet. The tile gods gave me a break and rained all big-ten tiles (4 Ss, JQXZ, + 2?s) on my rack, enabling a 512–289 blistering over Mark Milan (CA).

"The final game of the day saw me get back to my losing ways to Carol Kaplan (CA), 456–437! The damage report: 1–5, – 33, 434 average. Fifteen bingos, five losses of 400+! I did pocket a couple of high-loss prizes to ease some of the pain. Had a great time anyway!"

HALL OF SHAME

David Goodman (NY) writes: "Many players have shared their own personal moments of disgrace, but I think my own experience tops them all and should ensure my automatic entry in the Hall of Shame. I was playing in a one-day seven-game event in Lansing, MI, in February 1991. It was the sixth game, and I had only won one game up to that point.

"Finally, I felt I was playing very well and had built up about a 100-point lead with no tiles left in the bag. Both my opponent and I had seven each on our racks. I was holding the Q and could only find one spot to play it. My opponent played WAS at that spot, scoring 30-plus points. I looked at the word, and in my mind pronounced it WAHS. I then reasoned, rather logically, that WA is not a word, so how could you pluralize it? I decided to challenge it and confidently wrote WAS on the challenge slip.

"As fate would have it, a young boy of perhaps eight or nine was collecting the challenge slips, bringing them up to the director's table, and returning them with their verdicts. When he arrived at my table and saw what I had written on the slip, he shouted out incredulously, 'You're challenging the word WAS?' Probably most of the fifty or so players in the room turned to see who the numbskull was who didn't know the word 'WAS.' I, of course, immediately realized my error and, beet-faced, crumpled up the challenge slip and muttered, 'Never mind.'

"My opponent then added injury to the insult by playing out with another 30-plus points' play, received an extra 34 from my unplayed tiles, and won the game!

"Although I recovered from this mortifying trauma to win the final game big, it remains to this day probably the most memorable of all my tournament experiences. And lest I even try to forget or repress it, I have recounted this tale to enough of my friends who are all quite happy to help me remember it."

A GAME TO REMEMBER

Robert Kahn (FL)

Ian Weinstein, Steve Polatnick, Richard Ross, and I often play on Saturdays at my office in southern Florida. Sometimes only two or three of us will be available, and when we have an odd number we usually play a series of round-robin events, alternating as the singleton. On September 9, 2000, the group consisted of Ian, Steve, and myself. I was the first singleton, and indeed in game one they absolutely clobbered me.

In games two and three I happened to be on the winning side with a number of contributions that made my participation respectable, and game four was now at hand. Once again, I was playing as the singleton.

On the third turn of the game, Steve and Ian played ARSINES for 70, then BAILOUT on the succeeding move. At that point I was down, 156–89.

The T from BAILOUT was on O10, and my rack at the time was EEMNRR?. I could not readily find it, but I decided that my rack had sufficient potential that in order to preserve a shot at the Triple-Triple, my best approach would be to open a second one on the other side. Accordingly, I deployed the letters M, E, and R underneath the O in the word ZONE at B12, forming OMER, thus creating a second Triple-Triple with the R in the second position. With the remaining letters in my rack consisting of ENR?, I drew three tiles and looked at them one by one. First I saw an A . . . then an I . . . and so far I was feeling pretty good. When I looked at the final tile and noted that it was a Q, my initial reaction was one of frustration, but after whining only a few seconds, I discovered the looming possibilities.

As Steve and Ian verbally deliberated about their options, I figuratively crossed my fingers in the hope that the T would remain undisturbed.

The commentary from Steve and Ian was comparable to my own approach. Since they could not substantially benefit from either space, the best plan would be to void their rack of the J, hoping that if I did use a Triple-Triple option, the remaining space would be preserved for their potential comeback.

After JAG was placed on the board for 31 points, putting me at a deficit of

187–111, I felt a rush of excitement, nervously placing the Q on the Double Letter position and announcing my score of 284 points for the play ANTIQUER.

Having played the game since the 1950s, this was by far my highest single turn, and perhaps the best single moment.

Not to be outdone, Steve and Ian, with a new rack of EINOPSU, plopped down PRUINOSE through the R, and within a matter of seconds my play of 284 points had netted me a mere 49-point lead. Nevertheless, I decided to close the board to the maximum extent possible. (In so doing, I had an unplayable ISOBATH.)

With the score 532–451 in my favor, I elected to go for points on the final move, DELF 36, confident that the boost in score would preserve the victory. Steve and Ian then banged down their fourth bingo, ENROOTED, scoring 77 points, and picking up my rack (ADIR) to result in a 568–538 final score.

The game was truly exhilarating for all concerned. In fact, Steve commented that he thought that the score of 538 might be the highest-known losing score in the history of the game. (Wrong! See page 508.)

SCRABBLE SPOTLIGHT (1988)
Millicent King

My students have been labeled "special" because they have various learning problems. They are special to me because they are beautiful young beings with a lot more going for them than people tend to give them credit for. The key to their success is a lot of teacher patience, a boost to their confidence, and plenty of extra love each day. These seventh- and eighth-graders may not be the top academic students at Wiley Middle High in Winston-Salem, but they are definitely the school's SCRABBLE champs.

You may ask: How did all of this happen? Well, things started popping around December 1982, when I excitedly began making preparations for my first authentic SCRABBLE game Christmas party. Students tend to pick up on their teacher's enthusiasm and they wanted to help. My party boasted prizes, refreshments, and great mental fun for all. I designed creative invitations, which my students volunteered to color and decorate for me. It was at that moment the seeds were planted and they wanted to know more about "this game called SCRABBLE."

A couple of days later I took my deluxe game to school and the students all gathered around, their eyes shining with curiosity. Intrigued by the board, they wanted to learn right away. I was amazed! I had taught older students to play but never dreamed that my fidgety junior-high students would be attentive long enough to learn the real mechanics of the game. Was I ever wrong! They were more than eager to learn, and of course, I was a most willing teacher.

Soon, respect and love for the game became highly contagious. They sensed that there was something challenging and mystic about the "SCRABBLE fever" that possessed their teacher.

My floundering students, who were usually hard to motivate academically, were practically begging for instruction of a game that teaches a myriad of excellent academic skills. Naturally, SCRABBLE teaches spelling skills, but that's only the beginning. SCRABBLE also encourages students to have a reason to want to spell correctly. It improves definition skills, hand–eye coordination, strategy, math skills, healthy competitive habits, a sense of positive achievement . . . the list could go on and on.

As a teacher, it was sheer ecstasy for me to watch their daily mental growth as they became skillful players. I watched them become so adept that a transfer of learning took place in all subject areas, each one bringing new words to our master SCRABBLE list for future games. Not only did their reading and spelling skills improve, their self-pride soared. Remarkably, they challenged other seventh- and eighth-grade students who were not in a "special program" and defeated them. For once, these "special kids" were the winners and not the underdogs.

It's interesting to note that my male students were generally more serious than the girls and subsequently became the better players. The skills these young men learned very well were to use the Ss and blanks wisely, play well offensively and defensively, and to make fantastic hook-ons.

Here's something any teacher can appreciate: The main requisite to get SCRABBLE privileges in my classes was to complete one's other work first. Consequently, a higher percentage of assignments began getting completed—another plus for academic improvement!

School is out now and the students are gone. But as I erase the final SCRABBLE scores that are still on the board, I smile triumphantly to myself. I was able to give these "special" students something that no one can ever take away from them. They will continue to improve their games and develop their minds. Who knows, one of them may become a national SCRABBLE champ someday.

Who says "special students" can't become SCRABBLE experts? Nobody at Wiley Middle School, that's for sure. And while Ms. King has passed on, her legacy thrives.

A ZEN MOMENT

I'm down by 105 points (mostly from fooling around, trying to be clever and then challenging MANDARIN—duh . . .) and I have on my rack AEIRST? (nice, eh?) with only two realistic (for me, not for the Table 1 guys) available spots. I see the obvious spot for a word ending in T, but I need the very cramped spot at the bottom of the board, which I would have dismissed as impossible (pre-NSC annotation experience), but I thought about Edley and closed my eyes and breathed deeply and said, "Find me," and opened my eyes and immediately saw ASTRIDE at 15G for 97 points, forming TODS, WEET, LAR, LI, ID, and NE. Probably not an amazing play, but it was just so damn weird how when I closed my eyes and said "Find me" to myself, the play just instantly arrived in my mind. I mean, the entire play from drawing tiles to hitting my clock took about ten seconds. Anyway, back to reality. I lost the game, but not by much. Still, I'm beginning to think there is something to this zen idea. But don't expect to see me with hairy armpits or burning incense at my table anytime soon.

—Eve Wengler, Table 1, Division 1 Game Recorder
for the 2002 National SCRABBLE Championship
(Ed: The game recorder sits next to the players
at Board 1—the top players—throughout the tournament,
recording their racks and plays for posterity so that the
public can analyze the games later.)

EXCESSIVE PLAY

After reading about Wayne Clifford of Calgary, CAN, using five power tiles in one play, I had the good fortune to one-up him in a recent game against fellow St. Louis player Kenton Kloos. In the middle of our friendly game, I found myself with ESSSX?? and was able to play EXCESSES, using six of the ten power tiles in the game in one play!

—Andy Yates (MO) (Ed: The ten power tiles are
the four Ss, two blanks, and J, Q, X, and Z.)

FAMED NAMES

John Morse (NY) wondered how many rated players have first and last names that together anagram into one word. Here are some of our NASPA members' names. Can you find their one-word anagrams? We've only printed the names of those who have common-word anagrams. The answers are on page 366.

1. Ruth Barnes
2. Dan Barry
3. Chet Bartels
4. Fay Bell
5. Ed Davis
6. Al Demers
7. Peter Dicanio
8. Pat Diener
9. Kent Doe
10. Barb Earl
11. Chris Edom
12. Hoyt Ellis
13. R.A. Fontes
14. Amy Fowler
15. Ron Gaines
16. Fran Galt
17. Bert Gittes
18. Pat Gomes

19. Denise Kapp
20. Rose Noel
21. Pearl Rives
22. Paul Root
23. Dawn Russ
24. Ian Sharp
25. Ken Smith
26. Ruth Snead
27. Pat Spaniol
28. Robin Tems
29. Linda Tepper
30. Bo Yu

BINGOS GALORE

At the Western Canadian Championship (WCC), Emil Rem's (AB) first three turns against top expert Ira Cohen (CA) were: exchange 7, exchange 7, and yes, exchange 7. Then he proceeded to draw everything and won by 56 points. At another point in the tourney, Rem found himself with EINRSTU when DEN was about the only hot spot for a bingo. He found a common 10-letter word. Can you? The answers are on page 366.

DELL-ICIOUS

On his way to winning the Wisconsin Dells Tournament, near the end of the game against longtime friend and sparring partner Marty Gabriel (IL), 2001 World SCRABBLE Champion Brian Cappelletto (IL) played a late bingo for a 134-point lead and took the last six tiles. He had seen a couple of unlikely bingo chances for Gabriel, but the makeup of the unseen tiles didn't worry him much. Famous last words! A 269-point turnaround on the final play made Gabriel a 135-point winner. Turns out he had REEQUIPS for a 3 × 3 for 221 points, together with 48 points from the six tiles on Cappelletto's last rack, any one of which on Gabriel's rack would have prevented the win. But, in typical Cappelletto fashion, he shrugged it off and won all the rest of his games.

COMMUNAL DINNER

It's a tradition at the Western Canadian Championship held in Calgary every October that Saturday evenings the local players host the out-of-towners for a nice communal dinner. Among other things, locals are requested to bring a bottle of wine or a six-pack of beer.

On this Saturday afternoon, I was playing Dennis Kaiser (CO) and arrived at a critical position. The score was 247–229 in Dennis's favor. I surveyed the board without much enthusiasm. I was leaning to play CLOD 5J (making OBI and DEN), and I considered also blocking the O column with a play like FOCI. Neither seemed appealing, and as I glanced around, my eyes focused on the six-pack of beer, which I had deposited on the floor in anticipation of the evening's dinner. On the can, in big letters, were the words "cold filtered." Cold? That's an anagram of CLOD! And I noticed a fine play, namely COLD 15A for 48 points!

However, my joy was short-lived, for Dennis, who may or may not have followed my gaze to the beer cans, immediately replied with FILTERED for 86 points!

—Allan Simon, Calgary

STUCK WITH THE BLANK?

At the Masters Championship in 2003, a very interesting position arose between former National SCRABBLE Champion Ron Tiekert and Canadian National Champion Ron Hoekstra. Given the tiles left on each player's rack, what would *you* do?

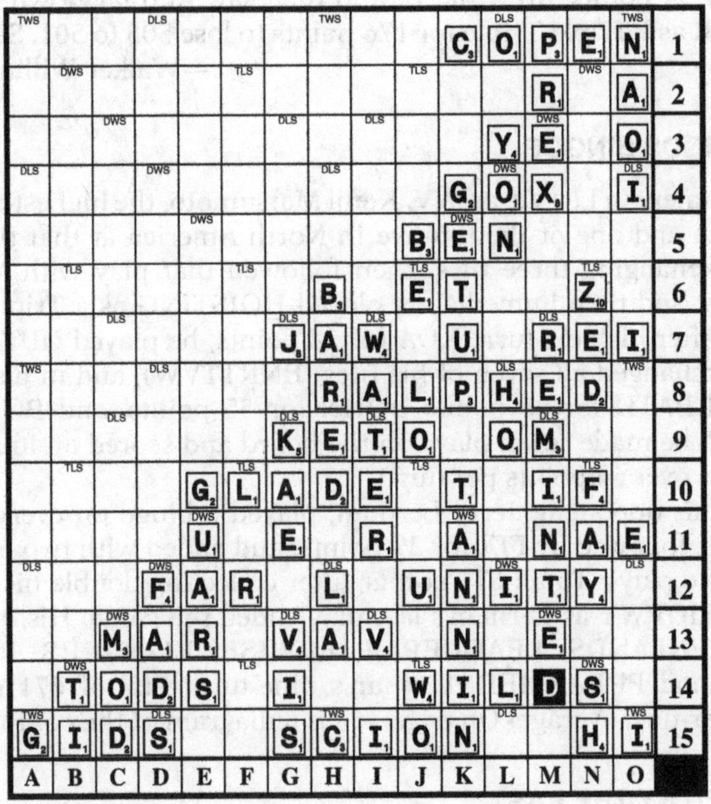
COPEN 1
R A 2
YEO 3
GOXI 4
BEN 5
B ET Z 6
JAW U REI 7
RALPHED 8
KETO OM 9
GLADE TIF 10
U E R A NAE 11
FAR L UNITY 12
MAR VAV N E 13
TODS I WILDS 14
GIDS SCION HI 15
A B C D E F G H I J K L M N O

Your rack: OUT *OPP. rack:* EQ?

Back in 2003 there were no legitimate plays available for either player, and thus it came about that a champion was left stuck with a blank! Of course, this year, one of the players would indeed have been able to play. Can you find the only two plays available? The answer is on page 366.

JUST ASK YOUR OPPONENT

At a recent Philadelphia tournament, Jay Strieb (PA) sat staring at the word HOIDENS on his rack, wondering if it was a legal play. Much to his surprise, his opponent, Jim Kille (PA), played HOIDENS at the spot that Strieb expected to play it. Strieb then played the word, hooking it under the same word!

A MEMORABLE ENDING

There was a remarkable game between two of Seattle's top players, Ann Ferguson and Ken Clark. With his rack EFHIIRS and one tile in the bag, the eight unseen tiles were ADEINSUV. Ken was up 405 to 327. He happily played FISHIER for 94 points, drew the U, and then saw Ann lay down INVADERS through the R as a Triple-Triple for 176 points to lose 505 to 501. See page 366.

—Walker Willingham (WA)

BINGOS BINGOS BINGOS

At a tournament in Las Vegas, NV, Kenji Matsumoto, the highest-rated player in attendance and one of the top five in North America at that time, started one game exchanging three tiles, then followed that play with MAIDENLY for 75 points, and then immediately played HOISTING as a Triple-Triple for 122 points. After his next turn, KOA for 38 points, he played OUTDROVE for 64 points, exchanged all seven of his tiles (BNRTTVW), and in his next three turns played BATH for 48 points, JOHN for 55 points, and BORTZ for 48 points. In all, he made seven plays on the board and scored an incredible 450 points. That's over 64 points per turn!

However, his opponent, Jerry Lerman, played a bingo on every one of his first six turns, followed by FIX for 39 points, and ended with two more bingos on his last two plays. Total: 671 points, after collecting double his opponent's last rack of EIQVWY as Lerman's last play ended the game. His bingos were: FISTULA, FENLANDS, LEAGUER, PALEWISE, ECOCIDES, ROSULATE, TRAINING, and PREARMED. Lerman's nine-turn total of 671 gave him a 74.5-point-per-turn average! On page 363 is a diagram of the completed game.

UN*A*FFECTED BY THE PAST

In a local eight-round tournament in Brooklyn in 2015, Joe Edley was playing expert Jeremy Hall. At one point early in the game, Edley took four minutes to decide on a play, finally laying down two letters and forming three two-letter words in the process, including AF. Hall took one look and immediately—and correctly—challenged the phoney AF. Edley sheepishly removed the play and

Jerry Lerman, CA, vs. Kenji Matsumoto, HI

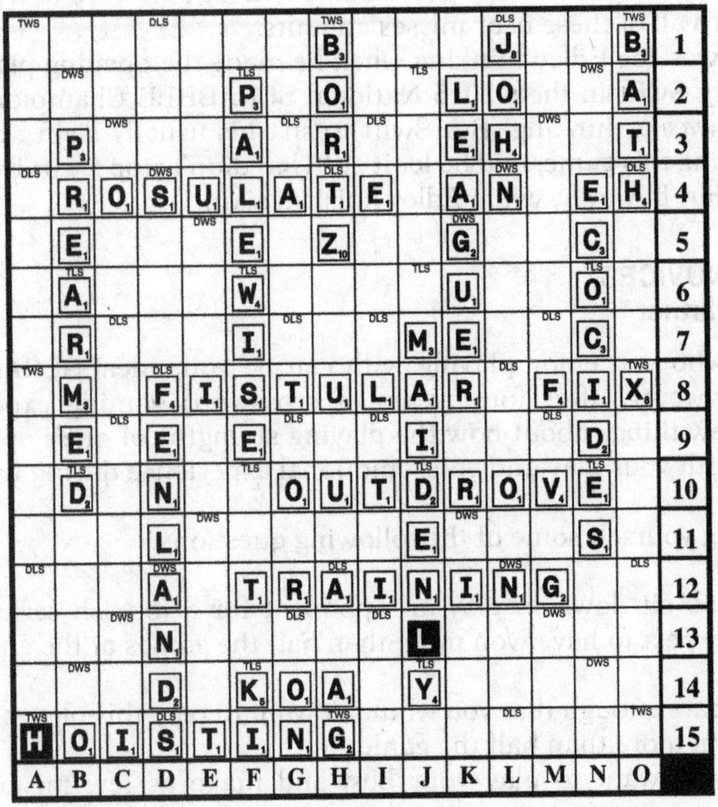

Final score: JL: 671 KM: 450

lamented his accidentally choosing the wrong vowel. Hall then took another three minutes to consider his play and also formed three two-letter words, in the same spot, including—you guessed it—AF. Edley was paying attention and broke into uncontrollable laughter and challenged it off the board. They both agreed that having seen the phoney AF once on the board, it briefly stuck in Hall's subconscious. Lesson: Don't play phoneys if you can avoid it!

WORDS AND NAMES

You don't play MILLCAKE against expert Joey Mallick and expect a challenge (MALLICK +E), nor expect two-time National SCRABBLE Champion

David Wiegand to miss WINDAGE on his rack. And you don't expect former National and World SCRABBLE Champion Joel Sherman to let your play of MARSHEN slide by. When a player's name is close to a word or a phoney, they quickly learn all of these near misses and hits.

So what was Joe Edley thinking when he made the opening play SWIFTED against Orry Swift in their 2015 National SCRABBLE Championship game? He clearly *wasn't* thinking! But Swift wasn't his usually swift self (a top-ten player) during this game, and he let it go! That didn't stop Swift from finishing fifth that year, however, while Edley finished sixth.

TIPS FOR NOVICES

The Ideal Partner

Anyone who you enjoy playing with can be your ideal SCRABBLE game partner. However, after forty years of crossword gaming experience, I've learned a few things about how the playing strengths of one's opponents can influence both your play and your emotional experience during friendly game sessions.

Try asking yourself some of the following questions:

1. When you sit down to play an opponent for a longish series of games, do you expect to have won more than half the games at the end of the session?
2. Do you care enough that you wouldn't want to play this player again if you didn't win more than half the games?
3. Would you want to play your best and make as few mistakes as possible?
4. Do you want your opponent to play as well as they can possibly play?

Depending on your personality and goals, of course, the answers to these questions may vary. However, it's our experience that most players want their opponent's best game, and want themselves to play their best. They don't mind making mistakes, but want both to learn from them and minimize them. And they don't want to *lose* or *win* too many games.

The nuance of this last sentence may surprise you, but it seems clear that there is a dividing line as to how many games a player is comfortable losing to and also winning from his/her regular partner.

Our estimate is that your ideal playing partner is one with whom you will win between 30 and 70 percent of your games. Our reasoning is that if you win too many games, over time you will tend to become more "lazy" regarding how well you look for the best play. You'll realize this as you make mistakes and lose to your partner while recognizing that you were just careless. Why? Because you've won too many games without putting forth your best effort. This is not ideal for either player.

If you lose too many games and aren't improving fast enough to win more over time, then you may develop a "losing" attitude that could work on your subconscious to instill the notion that no matter how you play against this player, you'll mostly just lose unless you get extremely lucky. This attitude can persist when you play others and hinder your progress.

However, if you observe the 70-30 rule when choosing your partner, your opponent will have to pay attention to virtually all of the plays in order to avoid losing. And you will be rewarded just enough so that over time you'll realize you can best your partner as long as you play well and pay attention to making your best play.

By winning or losing to someone within the 70-30 group, you both can enjoy the experience to the fullest by not expecting to win or lose all the time and knowing that if you draw decent tiles and pay attention, you'll win your share of games.

Does this mean you should change your partner if he doesn't fall into the 70-30 category? Absolutely not. Enjoy yourself! Simply be aware that you might benefit from an additional partner who fits this 70-30 theory.

One final note: The law of averages, as well as my own experience, suggests that against someone in your 70-30 group, there will be a time when you win all the games during a session, and then lose all the games at another session. My advice is to enjoy yourself and ride the wave!

ANSWERS: CHAPTER 24

ADJUDICATIONS: BELLADONNA

NINE-LETTER PLAY: COURTYARD

TASTY TREAT: TERIYAKIS

NAME EXTENSION: APHRODISIAC

FAMED NAMES: 1. HEARTBURNS; 2. BARNYARD; 3. STRETCHABLE; 4. FLYABLE; 5. ADVISED; 6. EMERALDS OR DEMERSAL; 7. DEPRECIATION; 8. PERTAINED OR REPAINTED; 9. TOKENED; 10. BARRABLE; 11. CHROMIDES; 12. HOSTILELY; 13. SEAFRONT; 14. MAYFLOWER; 15. REASONING; 16. FLAGRANT; 17. BESETTING; 18. POSTGAME; 19. KIDNAPPEES; 20. LOOSENER; 21. REPRIEVALS; 22. UPROOTAL; 23. SUNWARDS; 24. PIRANHAS; 25. METHINKS; 26. UNTHREADS; 27. PALPATIONS; 28. BRIMSTONE; 29. INTERLAPPED; 30. BUOY

BINGOS GALORE: INDENTURES

STUCK WITH THE BLANK?: ZA 6N 11; IFE 10M 6 OR IFS IOM 6

A MEMORABLE ENDING: CLARK PLAYED FISHIER N9 96, GIVING HIM A TOTAL OF 501 POINTS. THE LAST TILE WAS THE U, AND SO FERGUSON WAS ABLE TO PLAY INVADERS 176, WHICH WITH THE 2 POINTS FROM THE U ON CLARK'S RACK, GAVE HER 505 POINTS!

25 THE DECIDING FACTOR: Finding the Best Play

While we've given you the tools to make better plays, the one thing we've left out is to show you a streamlined process of how it's done for each play of every game. This chapter is devoted to "everyday" SCRABBLE game positions. There are no bingos or superparallel plays among these twenty positions. Instead, we're presenting typical positions where the best play is not always easy to spot. Through a process of asking yourself the right questions and observing the opportunities afforded by score, hot spots, defensive or offensive maneuvers, and rack balancing, you'll learn, over time, how to approach finding the best play. Please note that while the answer words are common, we consider all two-letter words and any three-letter words using the J, Q, X, or Z to also be common. So if you haven't learned those words, you might want to first glance at the lists on pages 19–20 and pages 523–26 to refresh your memory.

The questions beneath the following diagrams are designed to help you find reasonable "choices" for your best play. The answers to the A questions begin on page 397. Once you have these answers, think about which play you'd like to play. Then go to page 399 for the B answers. BP is our abbreviation for Best Play.

Part Two shows you nine positions. You're on your own with these. Three will require knowing an obscure word or two, but that's it. Three are endgame positions. Even if you cannot solve them, they will add to your experience. Endgames are tough, but the principles explained here will serve you well hereafter.

1.

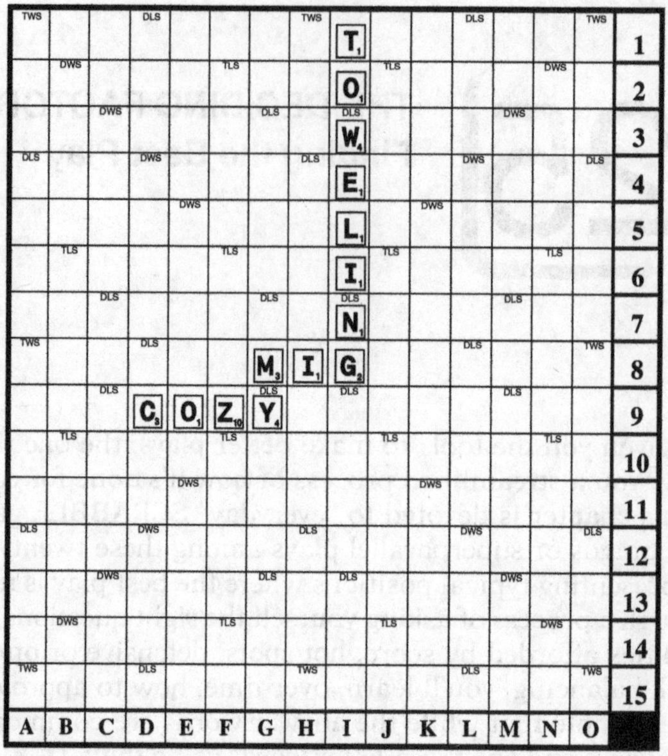

DIAGRAM 25-1

Your score: 33 *Opponent's score:* 79
Opponent's last play: TOWELING I1 67 Rack: **B G N N O S U**

A)

1. Find your BP across Row 1 through the T at 1I.
2. Find your BP down Column E through the O.
3. Find a play on Row 4 that covers both the DLS on 4H and DWS on 4L. Find a word that puts your highest-valued tile on the DLS.
4. Use the I on 6I to form an -ING word. There are no bingos,* but there is a six-letter word.
5. Look at the potential for parallel plays down the H column and find a play that scores well and blocks the TWS on 1H.

B) Which play would you make?

*Since 2014 there actually *is* a bingo available—BONUSING. For the purpose of learning strategic considerations, let's assume you are unaware of its acceptability.

2.

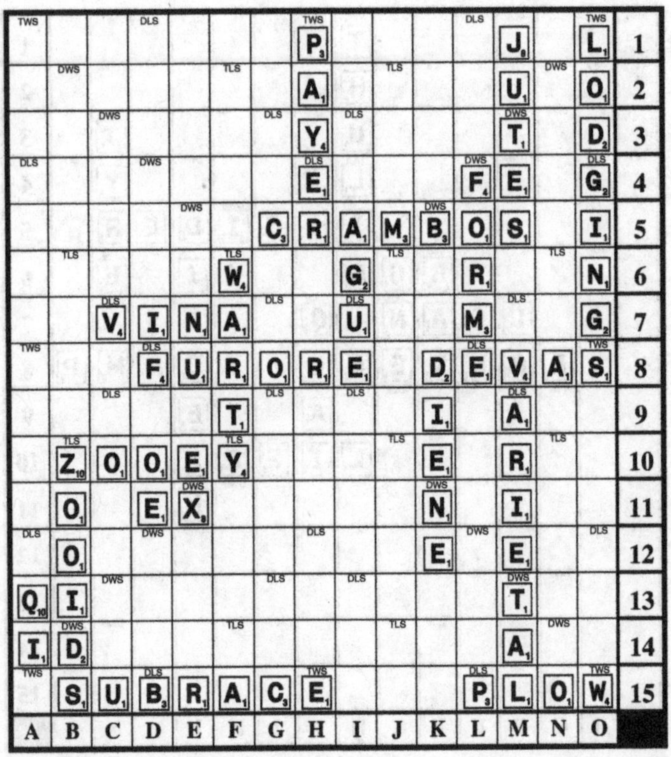

CRAMBOS
VINA
FURORE
DEVAS
ZOOEY
EX
QI
ID
SUBRACE
PLOW
A B C D E F G H I J K L M N O

DIAGRAM 25-2

Your score: 358   *Opponent's score:* 342
Rack: **D H L S T T ?**

A) You want to save your blank for a big play, and possibly your S as well. So look carefully for any plays you can make with your other tiles.

1. Find some good plays across the A on H2.
2. Find the hot spot bonus square that can hold your H, giving you 20 points.
3. If you were to exchange tiles, which should you exchange?
4. Find a certain TLS square to play your H, using another letter as well to score 28 points.
5. Where else can you play three consonants, saving both the S and the blank?

B) Which play would you make?

3.

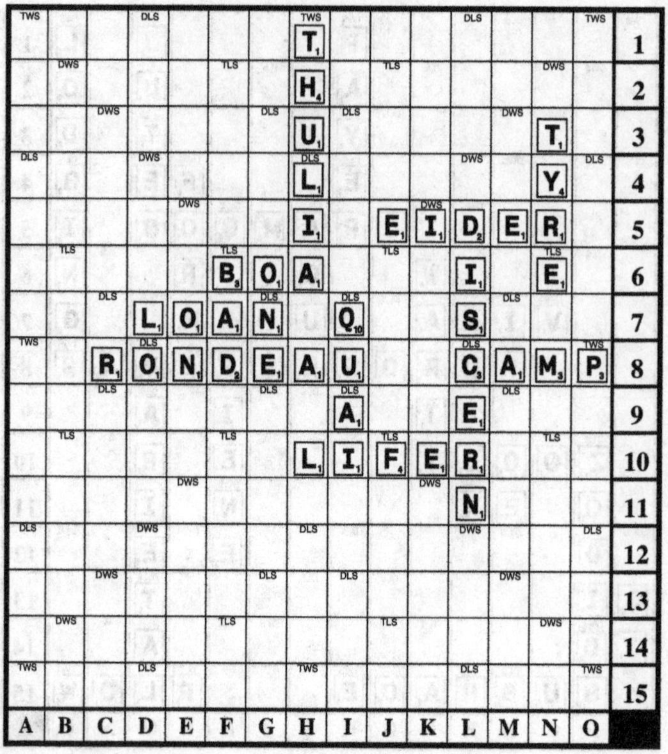
T
H
U T
L Y
I E I D E R
B O A I E
L O A N Q S
R O N D E A U C A M P
A E
L I F E R
N
1 2 3 4 5 6 7 8 9 10 11 12 13 14 15
A B C D E F G H I J K L M N O

DIAGRAM 25-3

Your score: 156 *Opponent's score:* 169
Rack: **E E E I P T V** Opponent's last play: CAMP 8L 30

A)

1. Ideally, you'd like to get rid of both high-point tiles. Can you do that with two different words using the E on J5?
2. Can you use the DWS on M3 to play a word using your V?
3. Can you find two six-letter words playing through the E on J5?
4. Can you find a way to play PEE and score 20 points? Think parallel play.
5. Can you find a six-letter word using the T in TURK?
6. Where's the most dangerous hot spot? Can you take advantage of it? Might your opponent? What can you play near there to block it and score well, using both of your high-point tiles?

B) Which play would you make?

4.

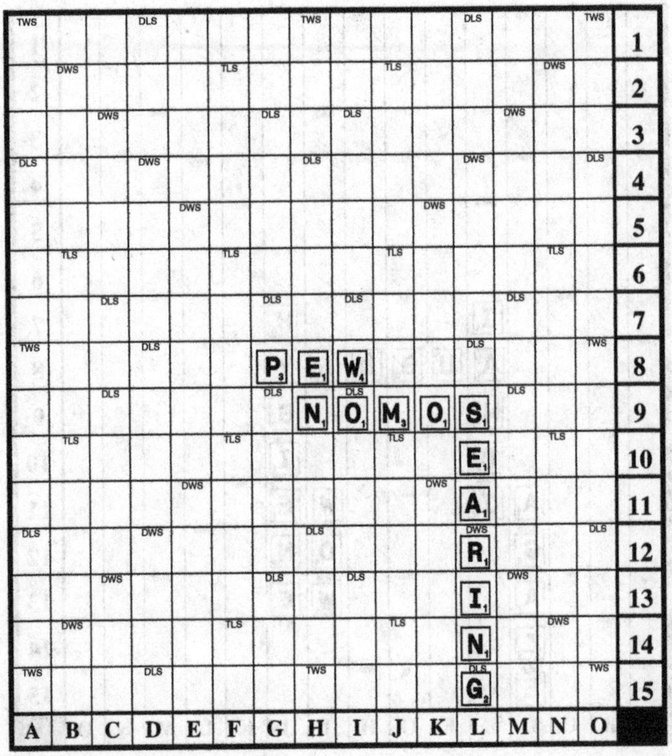

DIAGRAM 25-4

Your score: 24 *Opponent's score:* 100
Rack: **C D E K L U Z**

A)

1. Find a play to one of the TWSs on Row 15.
2. Find a six-letter word that plays across Row 10. On the same row, find a play worth 37, using the Z.
3. Find a word that plays across the A on 11L, covering the DWS on 11K, that uses the Z.
4. Use six tiles and the N on 14L, covering the DWS on 14N, and score 32.
5. Look parallel and find a play that uses the Z and scores more than 46 points. Remember to look for bonus squares next to vowels. How many points does it score?

B) Which play would you make?

5.

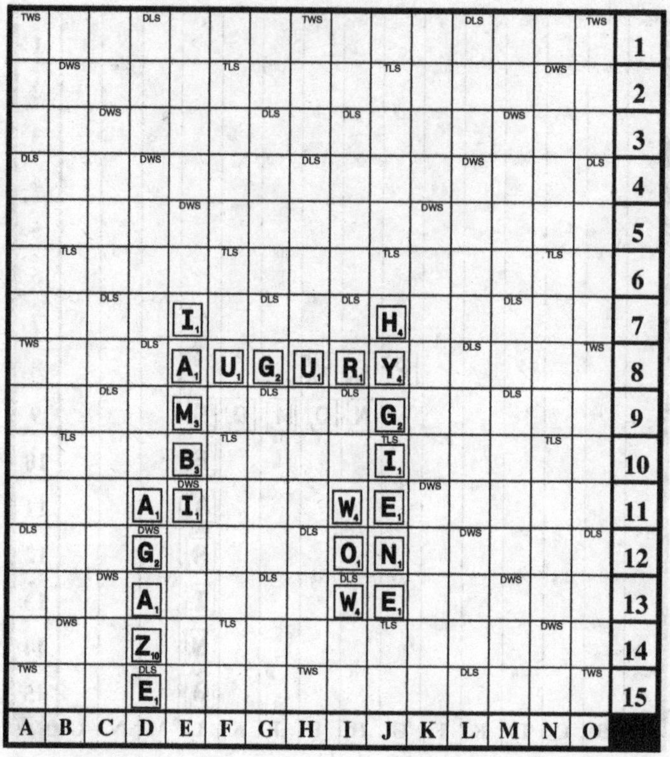

DIAGRAM 25-5

Your score: 93 *Opponent's score:* 24
Rack: **C E I P P V Y**

A)

1. What four-letter plays can be made beginning at 15A that score 27?
2. Find a five-letter word using the Z.
3. Where is the most dangerous hot spot for a four- or five-letter word?
4. Where can you play PEC for 24?
5. How can you block the answer to number 3, covering two bonus squares and scoring 34?

B) Which play would you make?

6.

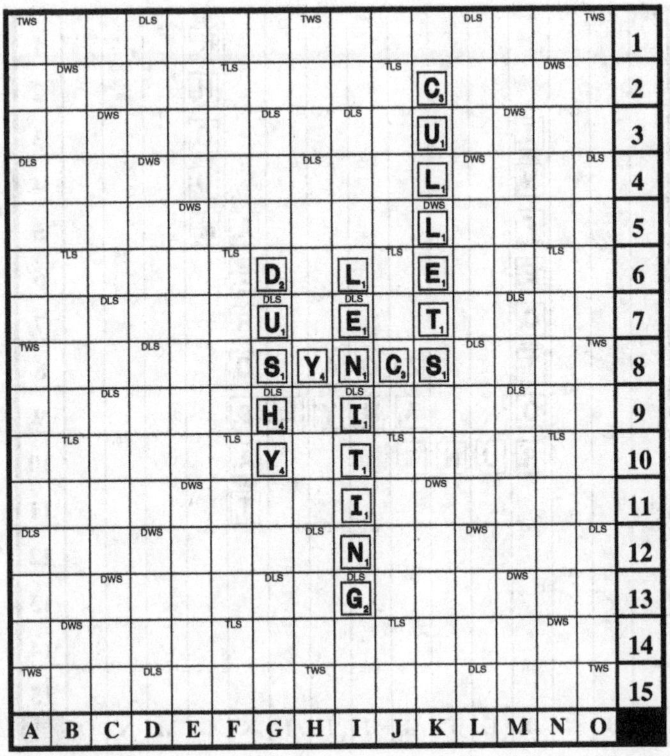

DIAGRAM 25-6

Your score: 94 *Opponent's score:* 84
Rack: **D E E F O O S**

A)

1. Playing parallel to LENITING, find a four-letter play for 22 points that sets up your S to play across a TWS next turn.
2. From the G on 13I, find a play that covers the DWS on 13M.
3. Play FOE such that it sets up a new bingo line.
4. Find a play that covers both a DLS and DWS and uses the F, the D, and three vowels.
5. Notice the possibility of playing the obscure word COOF 2J 18, leaving DEES.

B) Which play would you make?

7.

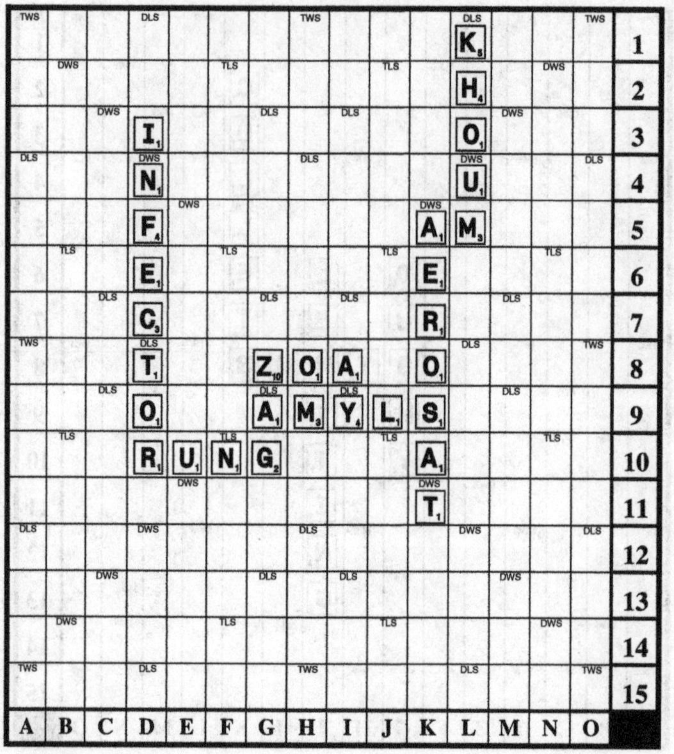

DIAGRAM 25-7

Your score: 132 *Opponent's score:* 159
Rack: **A E E H I I T**

A)

1. Find a word across Row 1, using the K, that covers a TWS square.
2. Find a play across Row 7 that scores at least 24 points.
3. Find at least one four- and five-letter word on Row 8 that covers a TWS square.
4. Look parallel to INFECTOR and find a 29-point play.

B) Which play would you make?

8.

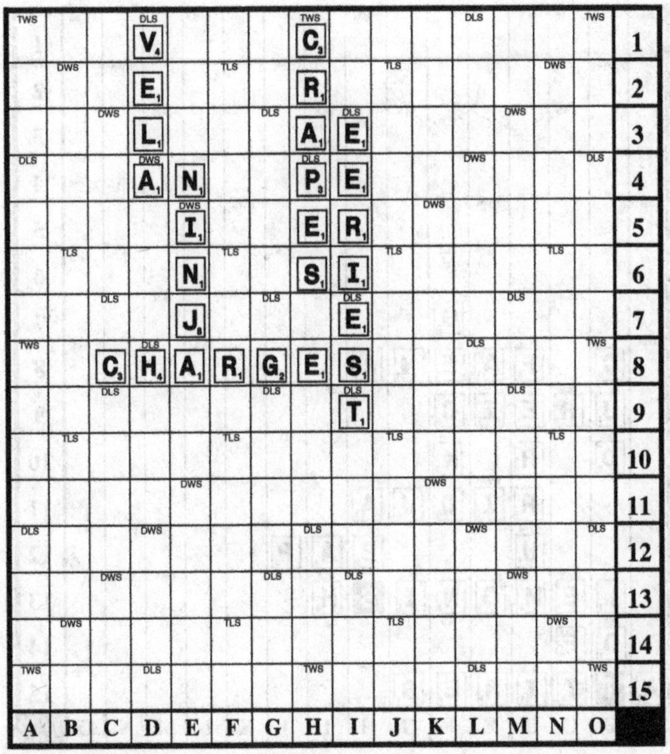

C H A R G E S
V E L A
N I N J
C R A P E S
E E R I E S T

DIAGRAM 25-8

Your score: 105 *Opponent's score:* 133
Rack: **D L O O T U W**

A)

1. Find your best play through the E on 2D.
2. Find a seven-letter word beginning with the H on D8.
3. Play parallel to NINJA to score 23 points.
4. Find a play across Row 2 through the R.

B) Which play would you make?

9.

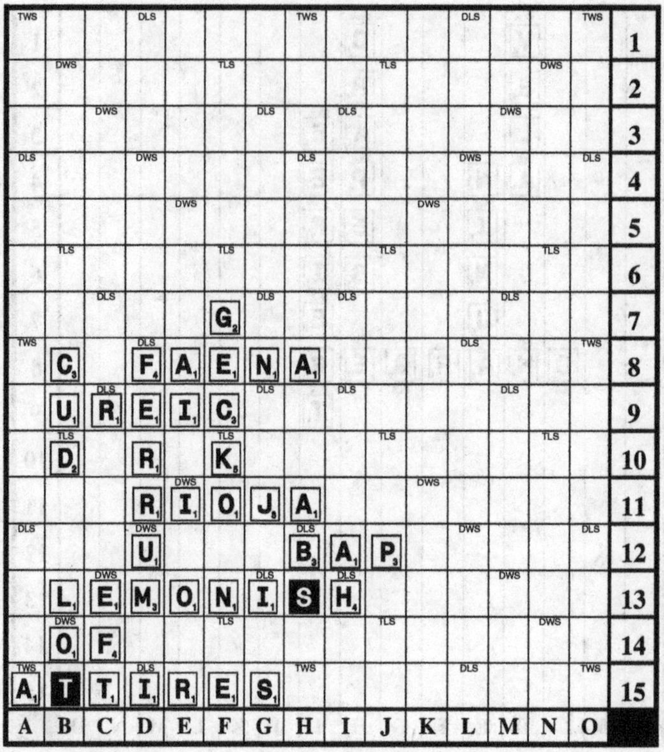

DIAGRAM 25-9

Your score: 155 *Opponent's score:* 177
Rack: **E I L M N S T**

A)

1. Find plays on Row 10 beginning on 10H.
2. What's your best word that pluralizes BAP and plays vertically on Column K?
3. AH takes an S. Find a six-letter word going from 14I to 14N.
4. Which single letter would you play, and where, if you were going to fish off one letter, hoping to draw a bingo? If you then draw a vowel, which vowels give you bingos?

B) Which play would you make?

10.

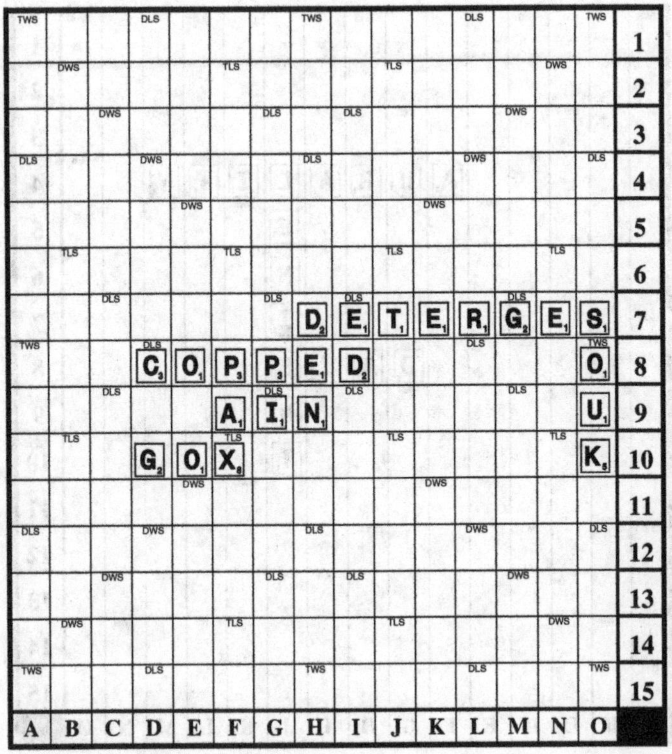

DIAGRAM 25-10

Your score: 123 *Opponent's score:* 82
Rack: **A C G I R T W**

A)

1. Find a two-letter word that scores 28 points. (Hint: TLS)
2. Find a six-letter word ending in the C on 8D.
3. Find a play on Row 10 starting at 10H that uses the W and G.
4. Find a five-letter word through the E on K7 that uses the W and G.
5. Find a seven-letter word that plays through the E on N7 that also covers the N2 DWS.
6. Find a play that uses the W and G and plays to the K on 10O.

B) Which play would you make?

11.

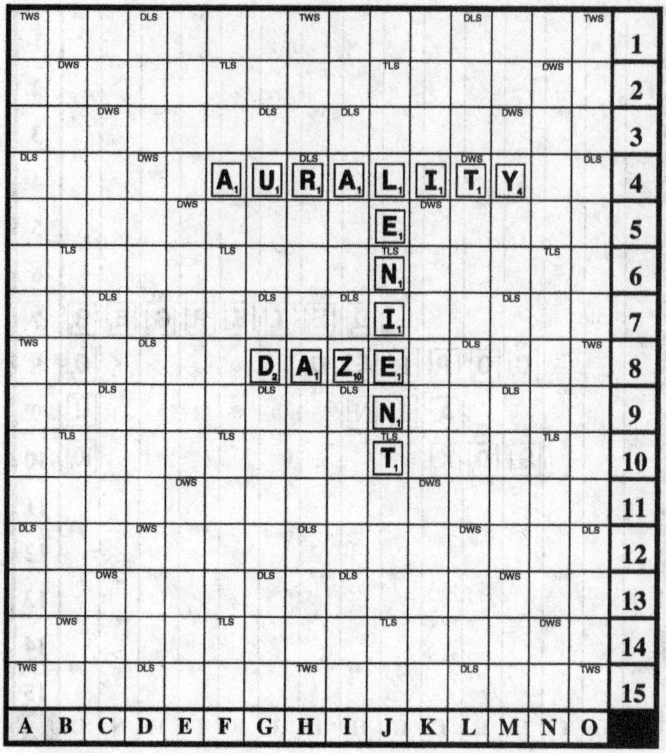

DIAGRAM 25-11

Your score: 76 *Opponent's score:* 102
Rack: **E L O O O U ?**

A)

1. If *not playing* is your preference, which tiles would you choose to exchange?
2. Find places to play just the two Os.
3. You have a four-letter word on your rack, without using the blank. What is it and where would you play it?
4. Play through the Z.

B) Which play would you make?

12.

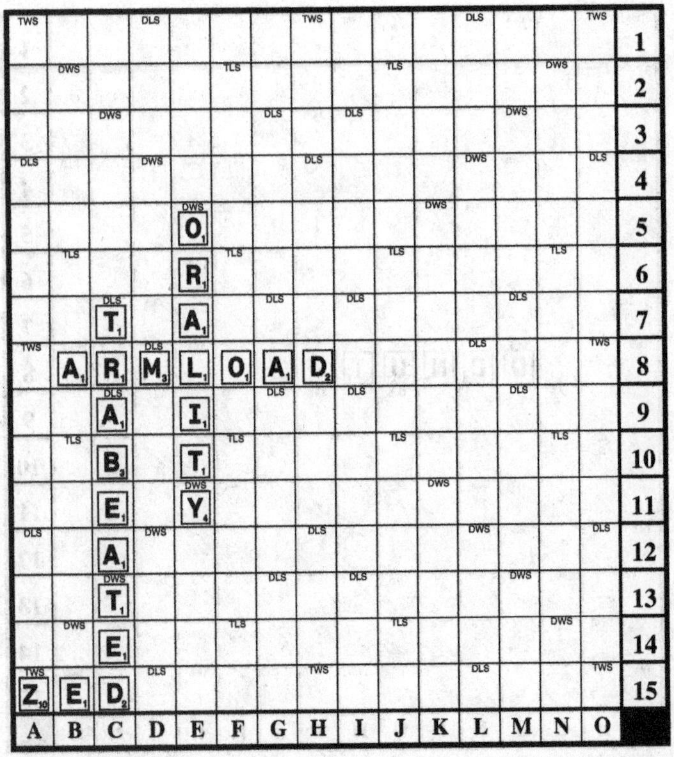

DIAGRAM 25-12

Your score: 127 *Opponent's score:* 114
Rack: **E E N N O R Y**

A)

1. Find a play across Row 14, beginning at 14B.
2. Find plays across Rows 7 and 9, beginning at Column G.
3. Find a play on Column B near the bottom of the board.
4. Find a play on Column F, beginning on the F2 square.
5. Find a play beginning on 12A and ending at the DWS on 12D.
6. Find a play on Column D near the bottom, scoring 26 points.
7. Find a play beginning with the A on 7E, going across.

B) Which play would you make?

13.

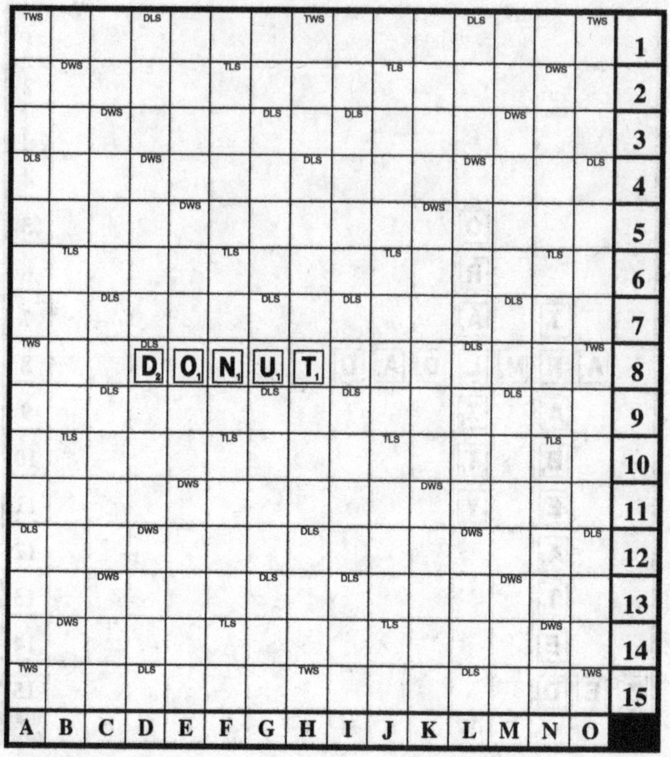

DIAGRAM 25-13

Your score: 0 *Opponent's score:* 24
Rack: **E E G H O R S**

A) You are close, but the bingo is not quite there.

1. Find the best place to play either HOE, HOG, or OH.
2. Find a six-letter word that ends in the D on 8D.
3. Find a play that goes from a DWS to and/or through the O on 8E, without using the S.
4. Find a play that uses the E, G, and H and one letter on the board.
5. Note that the obscure GORHEN plays on F3 for 18.

B) Which play would you make?

14.

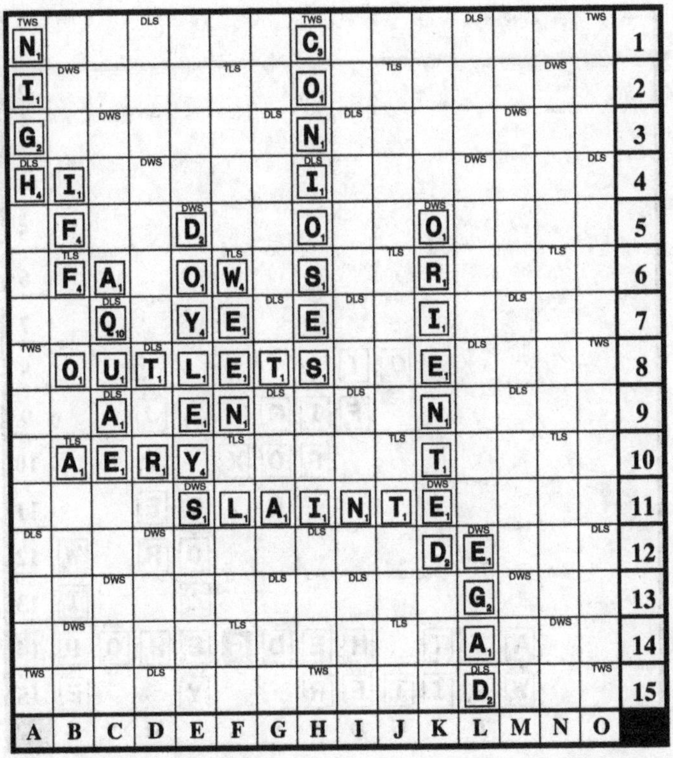

DIAGRAM 25-14

Your score: 269 *Opponent's score:* 244
Rack: **A C I O R T V**

A)

1. Find a play on Column L that covers the DLS on L1 and the DWS on L4.
2. Find a seven-letter word that goes through the A on Row 14. Can you get a high-point tile on the TLS square?
3. Find a six-letter word that plays on Row 8 from 8J to 8O.
4. Find a five-letter word beginning with the E on 8K.
5. Find your best play that goes through the D on 15L and covers a TWS.
6. Find a six-letter word, putting the C on 14J.

B) Which play would you make?

15.

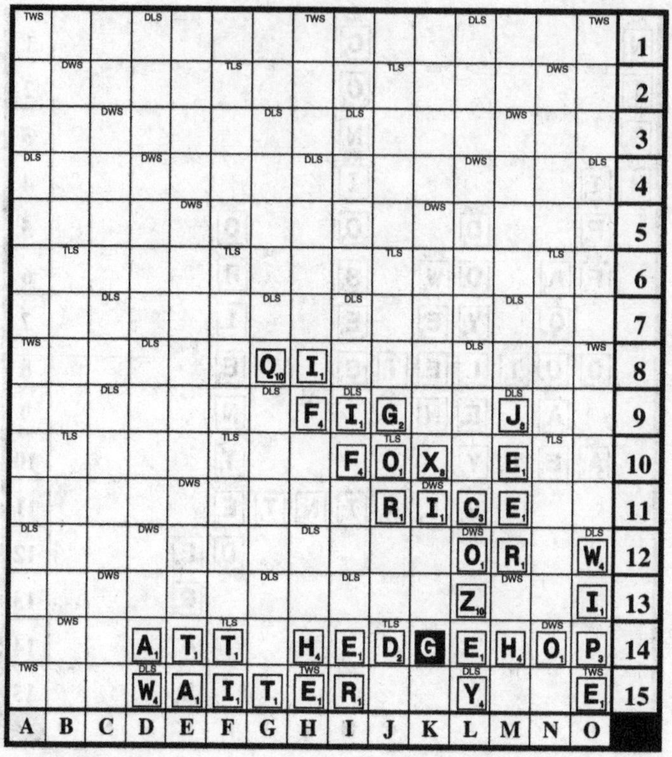

DIAGRAM 25-15

Your score: 186 *Opponent's score:* 180
Rack: **D E E I I R S**

A)

1. Find a choice of plays on Row 7, where either an R or D play on top of IF.
2. Find your best play on Row 12.
3. Would you prefer to exchange? If so, what tile(s)?
4. If you dumped just one tile, which would it be and where?
5. Find a play or two on the left side of Row 13.

B) Which play would you make?

16.

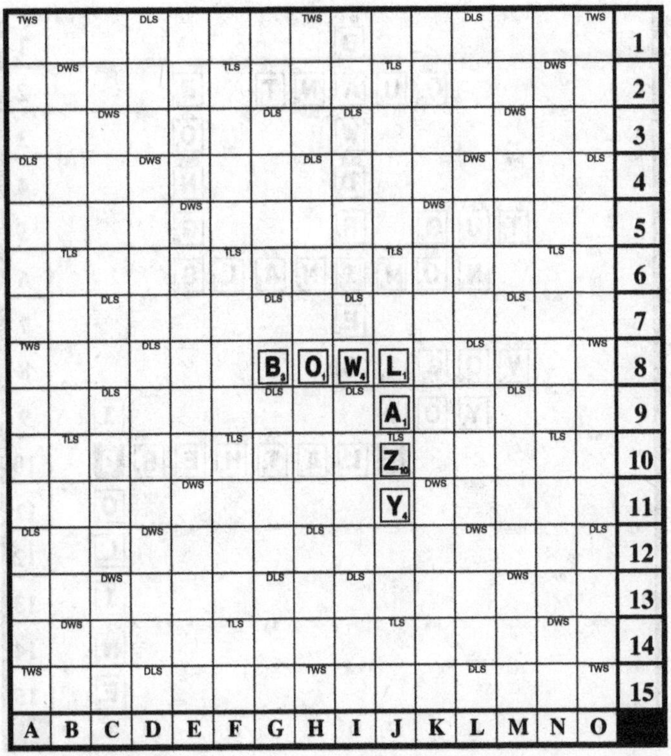

DIAGRAM 25-16

Your score: 16 *Opponent's score:* 45
Rack: **A I I N S T U**

A) You have several RETINAS tiles, and they should be cherished and used for a bingo.

1. Find some good places to play AI.
2. Find some plays using the Z.
3. UNAI is a great vowel dump. Where can you play it?
4. What five-letter word can you play that includes the two Is and an A?
5. If you prefer, which letters would you exchange?

B) Which play would you make?

17.

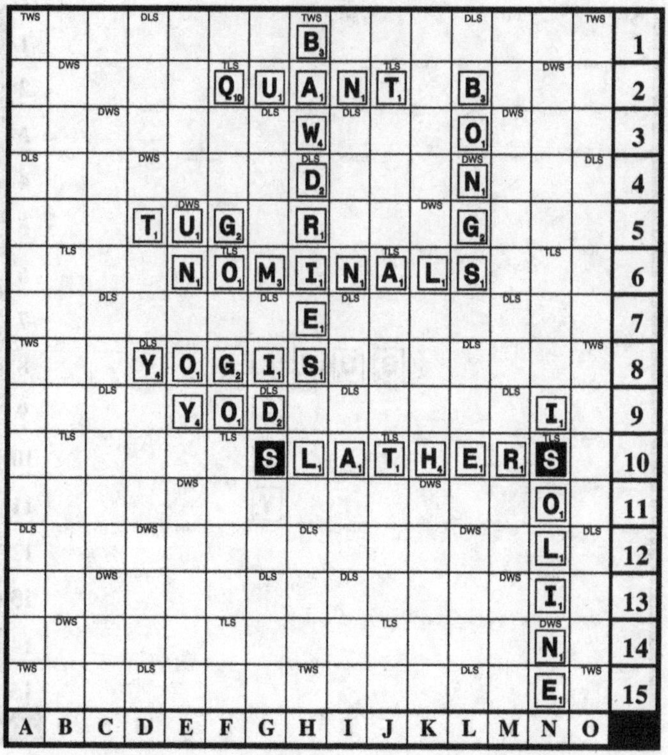

DIAGRAM 25-17

Your score: 205 *Opponent's score:* 156
Rack: **A C E F I I V**

A)

1. Find a +30-point play using only two tiles.
2. Find your highest-scoring play parallel to BONGS.
3. Find your best vertical play using the H on 10K.
4. Find your best play parallel to TUG.
5. Find a play on top of and parallel to <u>S</u>LATHER<u>S</u>.

B) Which play would you make?

18.

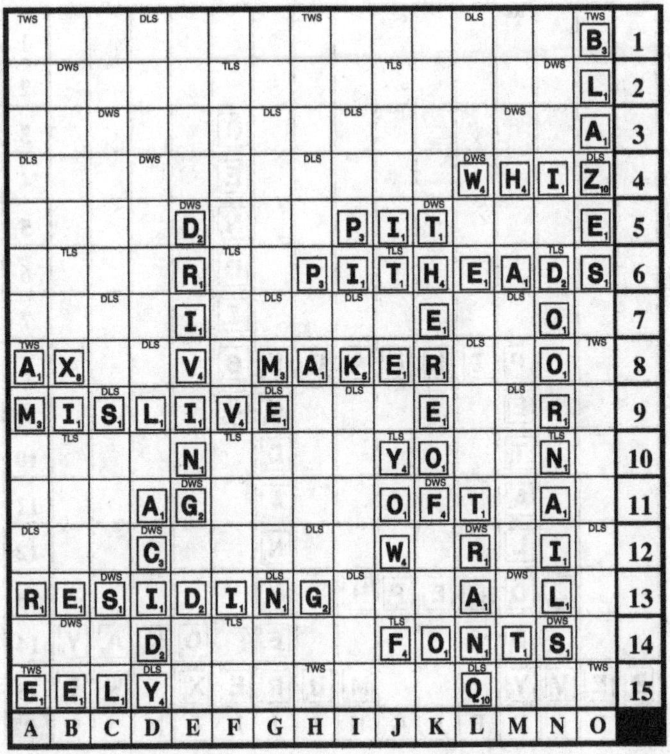

B 1
L 2
A 3
W H I Z 4
D P I T E 5
R P I T H E A D S 6
I E O 7
A X V M A K E R O 8
M I S L I V E E R 9
N Y O N 10
A G O F T A 11
C W R I 12
R E S I D I N G A L 13
D F O N T S 14
E E L Y Q 15
A B C D E F G H I J K L M N O

DIAGRAM 25-18

Your score: 433 *Opponent's score:* 344
Rack: **G J N O O U U**

A)

1. Find your best play parallel to and overlapping WHIZ.
2. Find a 33-point play using your J. "33" is key.
3. Find a play that uses both Us, a four-letter word.
4. Find a way to use both an O and a U with the J. Look for a four-letter word.
5. Note that UNJAM is a good play through the AM, saving GOOU.

B) Which play would you make?

19.

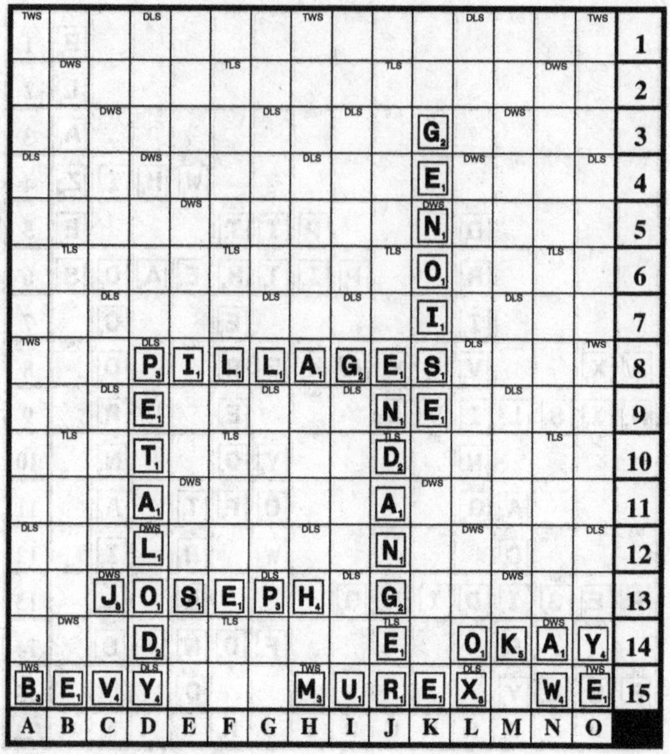

DIAGRAM 25-19

Your score: 258 *Opponent's score:* 255
Rack: **A D E E I O U**

A)

1. Find a play parallel to ENDANGER.
2. Use only three tiles—all vowels—and the G on K3, while covering the DWS. Now use three slightly different vowels with the T on 10D to form a four-letter word.
3. Use the A on 11D (or 11J) to form two different four-voweled five-letter words. Now use the E on 13F to form one of the same words in number 2. That same word plays for more points beginning at 4H.
4. Play parallel to and underneath JOSEPH.
5. Play parallel to PETALODY for 21 points.

B) Which play would you make?

20.

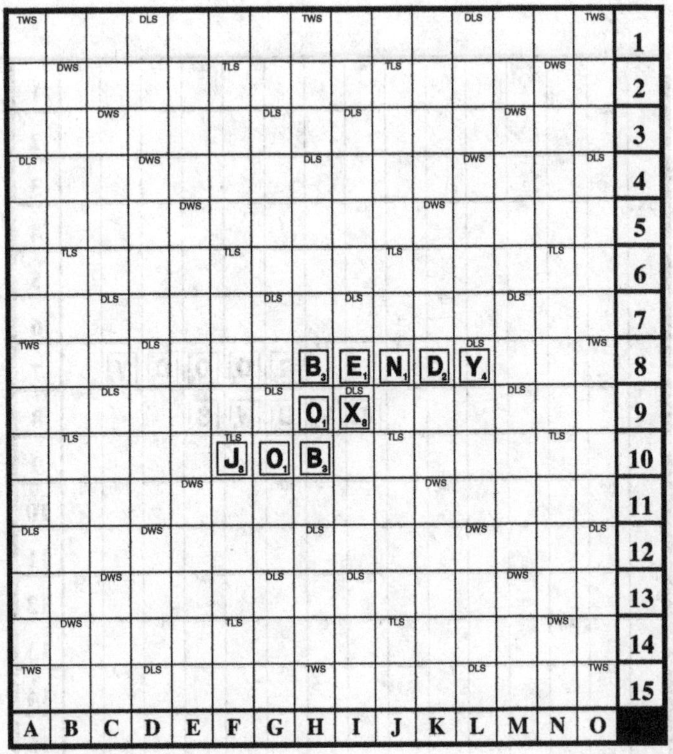

DIAGRAM 25-20

Your score: 38   *Opponent's score:* 61
Rack: **E E T T U V Y**

A)

1. Find a play using the J.
2. Find your best play parallel to BENDY.
3. Find two plays from the D to the DWS square using a Y.
4. Note that OXY is acceptable. Can you use that knowledge to play through the N on 8J?
5. VET is a verb. Can that help you to find a six-letter word?
6. VOX is also acceptable. What's your best play using that knowledge?

B) Which play would you make?

FINDING THE BEST PLAY: PART TWO

21.

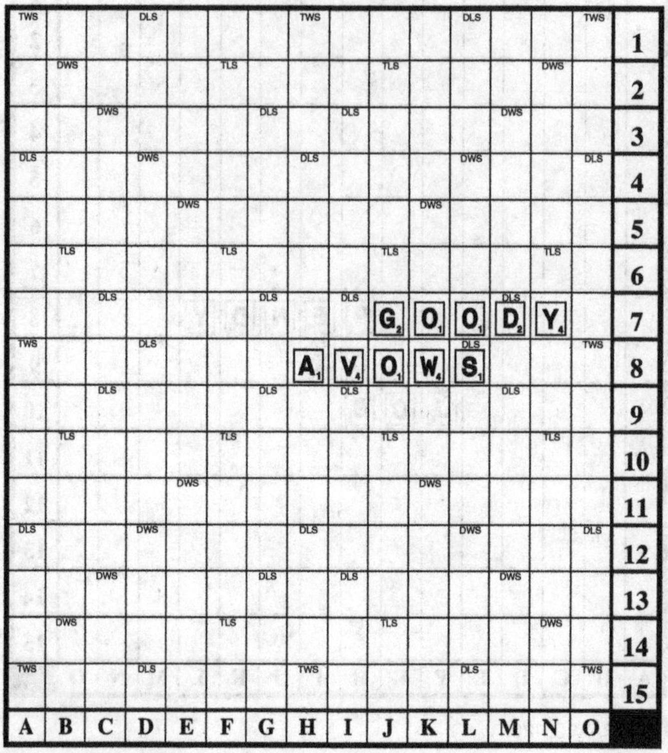
GOODY
AVOWS

DIAGRAM 25-21

Your score: 24 *Opponent's score:* 22
Your rack: **A B E I N R S**

22.

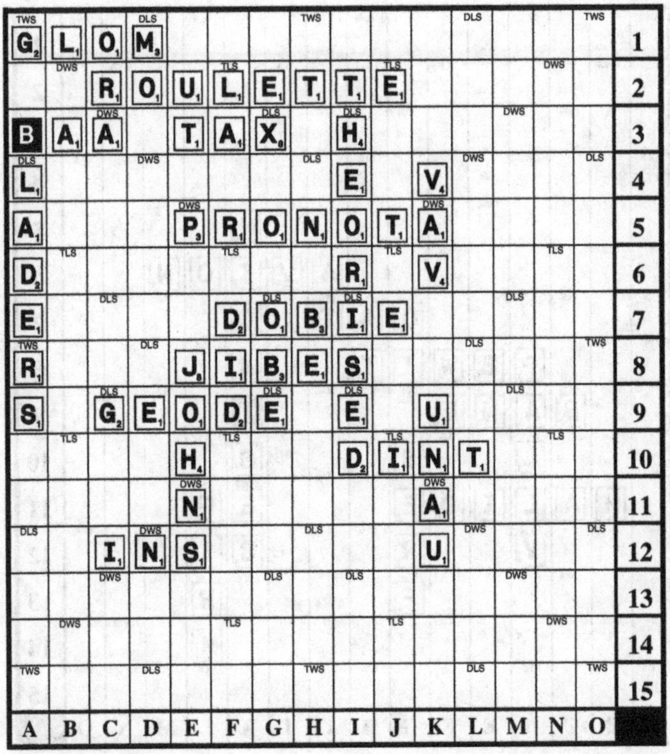

DIAGRAM 25-22

Your score: 228 *Opponent's score:* 276
Your rack: **A M N O R T W**

23.

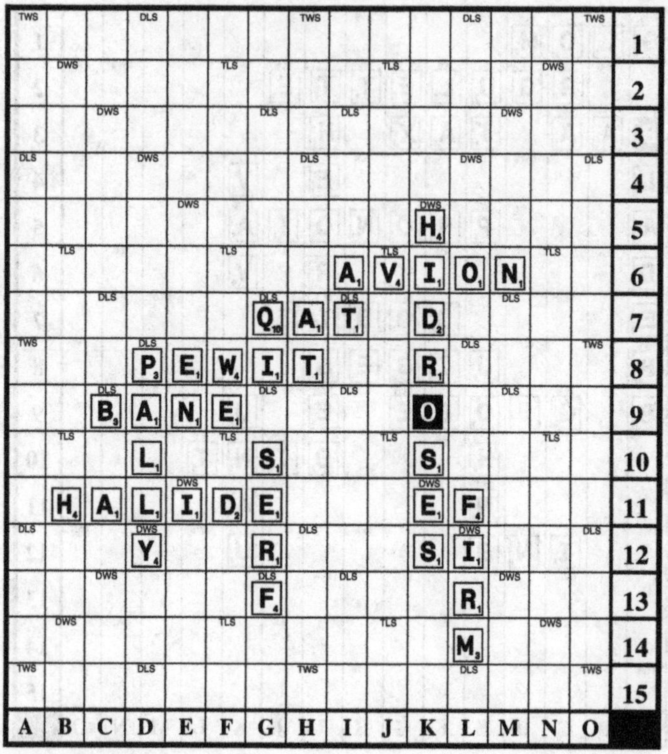

DIAGRAM 25-23

Your score: 151 *Opponent's score:* 131
Rack: **E I O O O U X**

24.

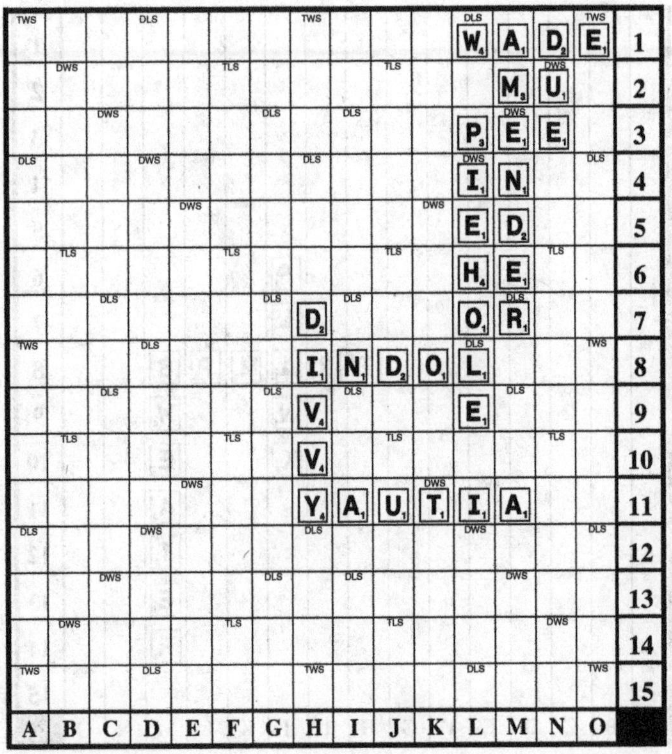

WADE 1
MU 2
PEE 3
IN 4
ED 5
HE 6
D OR 7
INDOL 8
V E 9
V 10
YAUTIA 11
A B C D E F G H I J K L M N O

DIAGRAM 25-24

Your score: 153 *Opponent's score:* 127
Your rack: **A B E E E L R**

25.

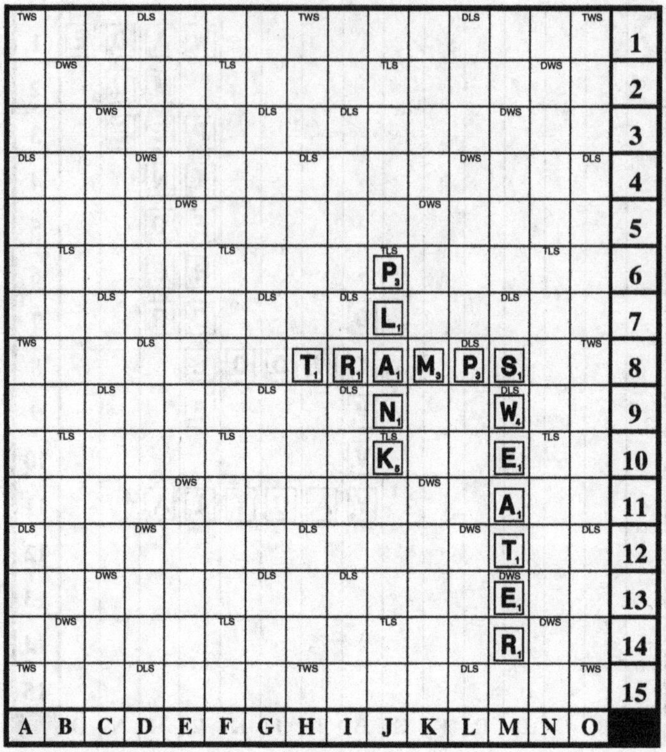

DIAGRAM 25-25

Your score: 27 *Opponent's score:* 112
Rack: **D I I I O Y ?**

26.

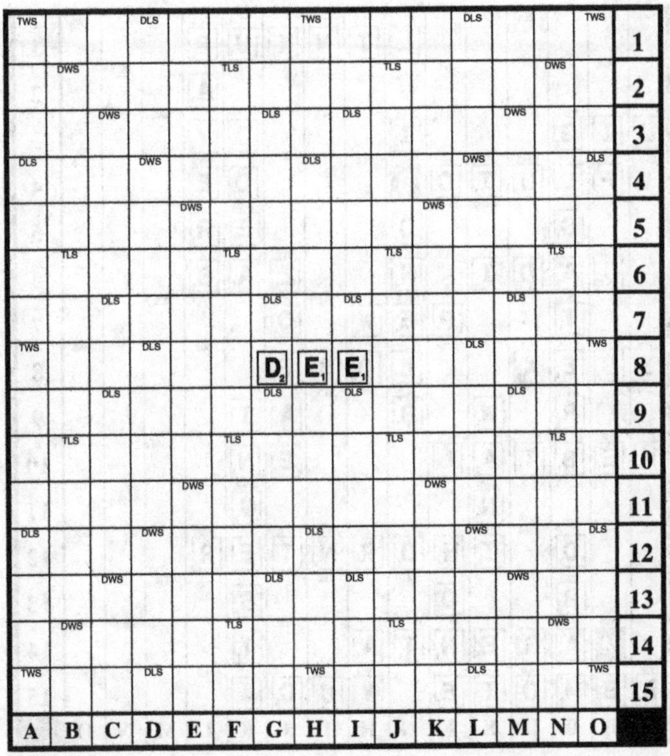

TWS
DLS
DWS
TLS
D
E
E
1
2
3
4
5
6
7
8
9
10
11
12
13
14
15
A B C D E F G H I J K L M N O

DIAGRAM 25-26

Your score: 0 *Opponent's score:* 8
Your rack: **A B I I L M X**

27.

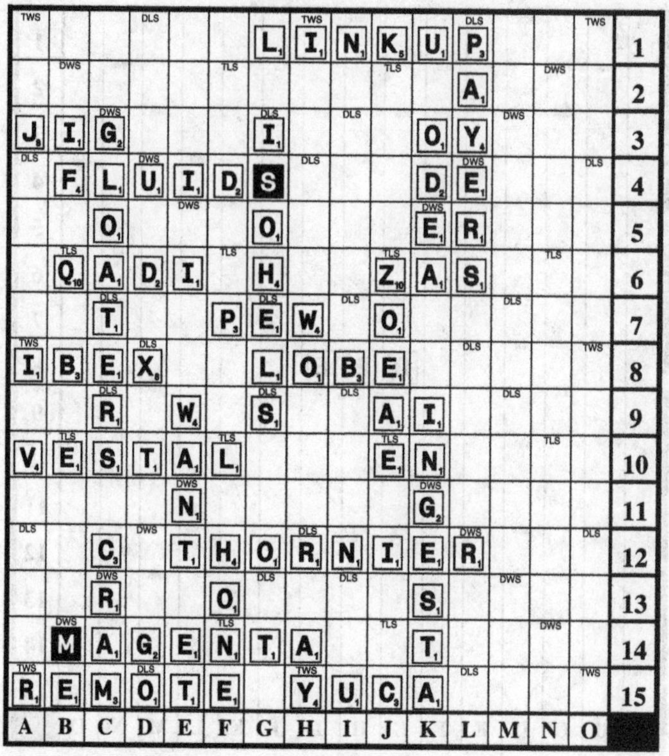

DIAGRAM 25-27

Your score: 373 *Opponent's score:* 379
Your rack: **A E I U V** Opponent's rack: **D M N**

28.

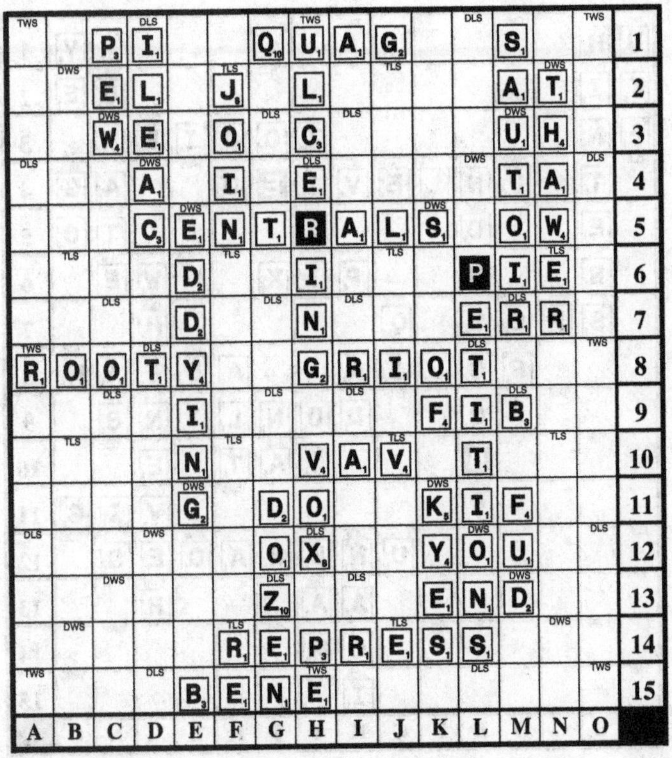

DIAGRAM 25-29

Your score: 394 *Opponent's score:* 415
Your rack: **A A E H I M M** Opponent's rack: **A L N U**

29.

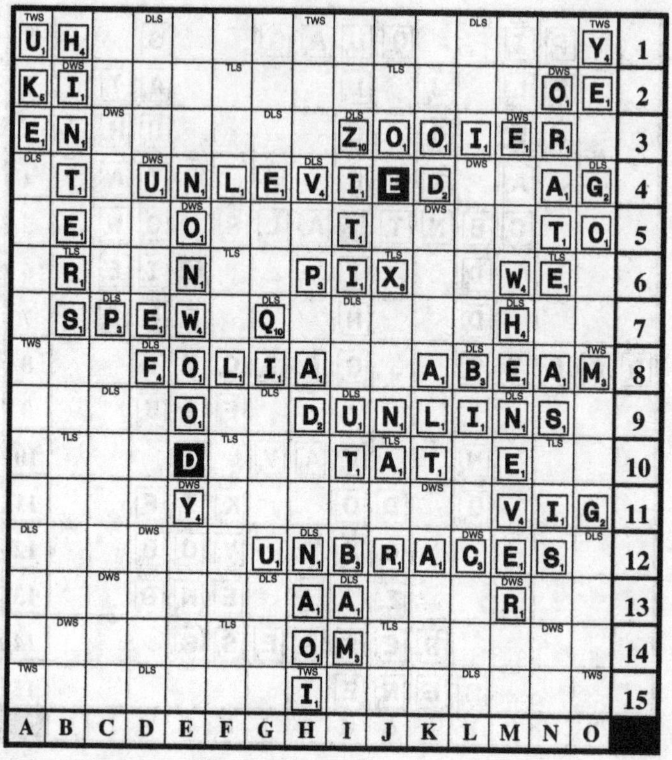

DIAGRAM 25-28

Your score: 379 *Opponent's score:* 398
Your rack: **A C D E L R T** Opponent's rack: **D E F G I R S**

1. 1. BUNT 1F 18; 2. BONGO E5 or E8 16—not BONGOS, because that would waste the S for too few points; 3. BEGUN 4H 22; 4. BONING 6F 17; 5. NOB H1 22

2. 1. LATH 2G 15, SHALT 2F 12, and HALT 2G 9 are three choices; 2. AH 14M 20; 3. Best to keep ST?, exchanging DHLT. The ST go together really well, and you only need one or two vowels to draw a bingo, which you can either play through the P, A, or Y of PAYER or across Row 13, ending in S for DIENES; 4. SH J9 28; 5. TIDAL 9J 20

3. 1. VEEP J3 15 or PEEVE J1 12; 2. VEE or VIE M1 16. These would both be better than EVE because EVE sets up the DLS on 1L, playing to the TWS on 1O, and that could be devastating. For example, if your opponent had the Z or J for, say, ZERO 69 or JEER 57; 3. TEEPEE J1 12 or TEEVEE J1 13; 4. PEE 9D 20; 5. PETITE 3J 16; 6. DISCERN takes an S, but you don't have one, though your opponent might. PEEVE K8 28

4. 1. GLUE 15L 15 and GELD 15L 18. Two others, uncommon, are GUCK 15L 33 and KLUDGE 15H 36; 2. LUCKED 10C 27 and ZED 10F 37; 3. DAZE 11K 28; 4. CLUNKED 14I 32; 5. ZEK K11 62

5. 1. VICE, PIPE; 2. ZIPPY 14D 27; 3. Column H, Rows 12–15; 4. PEC H10 12 24; 5. CONVEY 12H 34

6. 1. FOOD J11 22. This allows you to play FOODS and make another word that can cross either of the TWSs at 15H or 15O. Although, your opponent would have the same opportunity should s/he have an S; 2. GOOFED 13I 22; 3. FOE 4F 13; 4. FOOLED 4H 28; 5. Hmm . . . okay, you've noticed.

7. 1. KITE 1L 24. For experts, note KITH, KHAT, or KHET 1I; 2. HERE 7I 24. *Note also:* HIREE 7I 26 or THERE 7H 30; 3. HEAT, THETA, or TEETH 8A 24; 4. HIE, HAE C3 29 or THEE C2 31

8. 1. LOWED 2A 18 is better than either WOOED or TOWED, because the OUT leave after LOWED is much more synergistic than LTU or LOU. The weakness of LOWED is that the L in the second position between two TWS squares is more vulnerable to higher-scoring plays than the W or the T; 2. HOLDOUT D8 22; 3. DOOR F5 23; 4. WORLD 2F 29

9. 1. There are many such plays. Two are LIMN 10H 17 and LINT 10H 11; 2. MILS K9 20 is good because the ENT leave is the best three-tile leave with your rack that doesn't include the S; 3. SILENT 14I 22; 4. Playing the M at AM H8 4 leaves your best six-tile leave, EILNST. You'll draw playable bingos with vowels A (ENTAILS), E (TENSILE), I (LINIEST), O (ENTOILS), and U (UTENSIL), plus a slew of consonants will also give you many seven- and potentially eight-letter words.

10. 1. AW 6M 28; 2. TRAGIC D3 18 or ARCTIC D3 20; 3. TWIG 10H 15; 4. WAGER K4 18; 5. CIGARET 28; 6. GAWK 10L 20.

11. 1. Exchanging OOOU is the best. By keeping the EL with the blank, you bring a substantial balance to your rack that maximizes your chances for a bingo next turn. The E and the L go very well together; 2. NOO 6J 3, 9J 3, TOO L4 4, ONO 6I 3, or OOT 10H 3 are the only spots to get rid of just the OO; 3. OLEO is playable by hooking either the D beginning at 7E or 9E, or hooking the T beginning at K10; 4. OOZE I6 23.

12. 1. YEN 14B 22 or NEON 14B 12; 2. YEN, YON, or YORE 7G or 9G are all reasonable choices; 3. EYE B13 24; 4. YORE F2 17; 5. YEAN or YEAR 22; 6. YEN D12 26 or YON D12 26; 7. ANYONE 7E 28.

13. 1. HOE and HOG play at 9G for 22 and 24 points, respectively. OH plays best at 9F 20; 2. HORSED D3 20; 3. HERO E5 14 or OGRE E8 10; 4. HUGE G7 14; 5. So noted.

14. 1. VICAR L1 30; 2. AVIATOR 14I 36; 3. VECTOR 8J 42; 4. EVICT 8K 42; 5. AVOID 15H 27 and DIVA 15L 24; 6. CRAVAT 14J 34.

15. 1. RIDE and DIE at 7H are two of the best; 2. DIE 12H saves the bingo-prone EIRS leave; 3. Exchanging EI or even just I are both reasonably good exchanges; 4. Play the I at ID J13 3; 5. IRE 13C 15 or DIRE 13B 19 are two such plays.

16. 1. AI K11 14 and AI 9G 10; 2. NAZI 10H 13, ZIT 10J 12, or ZITI 10J 13; 3. UNAI 9E 13; 4. TIBIA G6 9; 5. Exchange IU. STAIN is a powerful bingo-prone leave.

17. 1. EF O14 32; 2. CAFÉ M1 34; 3. CHIEF K9 26; 4. FIVE 4A 32; 5. FIE 9I 26.

18. 1. GOO 3K 23; 2. JOG 8M. 33 is divisible by 3, potentially indicating a TWS square being covered; 3. GURU 5C 7; 4. JUDO 5C 12; 5. So noted.

19. 1. DUO K11 19; 2. AGUE 3J 10 and IOTA or AUTO 10B 6; 3. AUDIO 11D 12 or ADIEU 11D 12; 4. DIE 14F 27; 5. DOSE E11 21

20. 1. JETTY or JUTTY F10 23; 2. VEE 7I 32; 3. DUTY K8 16 and EYED K5 16; 4. TEENY J5 23; 5. VETTED K3 20; 6. VOTE G9 28

Answers to B Questions

1. Points are important, as is blocking the TWS at 1H and keeping a decent leave. How can you best accomplish these three goals? BUNT blocks the TWS but is not worth as many points as BEGUN or NOB. BONGO gets rid of another tile, but it's worth fewer points and you still leave the TWS open and keep the unwanted U. BEGUN is a great play because it scores very well and keeps a reasonable leave (NOS), but it doesn't block the TWS. NOB scores just as well as BEGUN, and it blocks the TWS. However, if your opponent has an S, he can potentially score a lot of points with SNOB, playing across the top row. What are the odds that your opponent will have an S? Using the simple formula in Appendix 6, the odds are approximately 25 percent (there are three Ss left to draw). We're not worried about him drawing a blank because he likely won't use it unless he can bingo, and that's much less likely. So if your opponent doesn't have the S, *you* can play there and perhaps even score next turn with at least a +40-point play. NOB is likely to benefit you the most. Note that if occasionally your opponent makes a big play there, the best thing to do is shrug it off and chalk it up to bad luck. Even the best players take such gambles sometimes.

2. TIDAL is the ideal play because it does almost exactly what your exchange would do, except it scores 20 points and retains the H, which goes really well with the T.

3. With PEEVE K8 28, you accomplish all of your realistic goals this rack: scoring well, blocking, and retaining a decent leave (EIT).

4. While the leave isn't great, the points are too great to pass up. ZEK is a "killer" play.

5. Because it scores so well and blocks the H12 square from your opponent putting a high-point tile on it and playing to the TWS on 15H, CONVEY 12H 34 is no doubt the best play. Why? The score, the block, the number of tiles played, and the leave all contribute to making this the best play.

6. Setting up your S is unnecessary. There's no need to give your opponent a chance to take extra points with a hot spot you set up for him. Sometimes it's the right play, but not here, because you're not in trouble, scorewise. FOOLED is an excellent way to score points, use five tiles (more chances to draw a blank), save ES (always a plus), and establish a 40-point lead.

7. Of all the plays, HIE gives you a good score and the best leave. If you have to keep three vowels, make it the AEI combo—it's the best of the lot. If you're concerned about the open TWSs on Row 1, note that making a good decision in the game often means compromising one criteria for another. Scoring well and having a reasonable leave often trump any board position considerations. As long as the board is open, both sides have equal chances, so your own leave is often more important than the hot spots you leave for your opponent. One last note: Leaving a letter between two TWSs is *much* less dangerous when that letter covers the DLS. The odds are that your opponent won't get more than 33 points using a TWS square.

8. WORLD saves OUT (which is synergistic even if the O and U are not great tiles individually) and scores much more than any other play. It's ideal for this rack.

9. Given the number of potential bingos after fishing off the M, AM is a good sacrifice this turn for a potentially huge gain next turn. And, by the way, AM is superior to MA because MA will occasionally block more of your bingos next turn than AM will.

10. Your variety of choices this turn may make it a more difficult decision, but there are logical guidelines to help pave your way: Given the leave (CGIRT), AW isn't worth the points because you're likely to have an inflexible, poor next rack. TRAGIC and ARCTIC save either the GW or CW, which are very weak leaves. WAGER is reasonable, and the CIT leave is synergistic. CIGARET is a great point grabber and rack cleaner, but saving the W is very weak, since drawing another high-point tile can severely cripple your next rack. Note that playing with one high-point tile isn't usually all that difficult, but playing with two or more makes it much more difficult to retain a good leave on your following play. GAWK is very interesting in that it scores reasonably well, though not best, but your leave, CIRT, is slightly more synergistic than CIT (CRIT really comes alive with all sorts of possibilities after drawing an A or an E, or even an O—which means twenty out of the unseen seventy tiles will do you a lot of good), plus, you're not improving the board for your opponent as you do after WAGER. WAGER opens the DWS next to the W for very easy parallel plays that allow your opponent good dumps, while GAWK blocks the only -S bingo spot (ending a bingo with the S added to SOUK). All in all, GAWK is slightly superior to WAGER, and much better than all other plays.

11. Scoring 23 points and accomplishing almost everything you would by exchanging, OOZE is a clear favorite.

12. For points and its terrific leave (ER), ANYONE is a clear favorite.

13. Plays like HORSED use the S too cheaply, particularly since you can score more with HOG or HOE and save the S. OH saves three consonants and two vowels, which is probably the best kind of leave, if all the consonants are 1-point tiles. But here the G is clunky since you don't have an I-and-N combo to liven it up. This makes HOG so much more attractive. HUGE leaves a nice EORS, but you're sacrificing too many points for it. Besides, after HOG, the EERS leave is super. Note that while GORHEN leaves the excellent ES, the openness of the board after GORHEN makes it a weak choice. By opening up the G, O, R, and H, you make it easy for your opponent to choose one of those lines to dump just the right tiles to balance his rack perfectly. In general, it's usually better to play parallel and defensive than open and perpendicular, unless you're getting a big bonus in return, like a lot of points or giving yourself the perfect bingo-prone leave, which isn't the case here. All in all, HOG wins the pick easily.

14. It comes down to points and leave. VECTOR and EVICT score so many more than the others that they far outshine them right away. Between these two, the better leave is after EVICT: AOR vs. AI. No contest! EVICT is much superior because the R on your rack with two vowels far outweighs using an extra tile for VECTOR and getting the two-vowel leave.

15. While any and all of the choices are reasonable, the play of ID for just three points shows up as best. Why? Because this board is very "closed," meaning that there are few places for your opponent to score well without opening it up for you. And so your play of ID blocks one of those open spots, along Row 12. Taking that away from your opponent means that he almost certainly won't bingo next turn unless his word begins with an R or a D at 7H. Since you have both an R, a D, and bingo-prone tiles, if your opponent doesn't play on Row 7 and you get your bingo, you'll be sitting pretty. If your opponent takes that spot, many times he'll take it and give you an S-hook to *attach your S to,* so again, you'll do well. ID gives you better odds and more chances to score well next turn, and takes away an important line for your opponent. Even if it doesn't score well for you, you've reached your goal to accomplish something important with your turn, and sometimes that's all you can hope for. By comparison, most of the other plays diminish your chances, because even playing on Row 12 and leaving yourself with good tiles, DEEIRS is an even better one for drawing bingos.

16. Leaves of AINST or INSTU are the best. Exchanging the IU is an excellent play to keep AINST. However, it's not worth sacrificing 14 points. Play AI K11 14, take the points, and leave INSTU. If you're going to keep a U, saving it with a STIN is not a bad way to do it. Lots of synergy there, and plenty of bingo potential.

17. All of the choices require you to compromise something, either points, leave, or board position. In general, in such situations, keep the board open and give yourself the best leave, taking the points if you can. FIVE 4A 32 is your best shot because the ACI leave is quite reasonable given how open the board is. With only a consonant or two, you'll score at least 30 next turn, which is all you can ask for in this position. Other plays don't give you nearly enough, because your leaves are much weaker. You don't want to keep the V or the two Is or five of these tiles, ergo, FIVE is the only choice that doesn't do any of these things.

18. Clearly, nothing you do short of exchanging is going to give you a good leave, so a compromise is required. When you compromise, make sure you get something for it. JOG saving NOOUU is *much* worse than JNUU after GOO. So much so that GOO is a big favorite here. The J in your leave will at least allow you a few points next turn while you try to balance your rack. The other plays simply sacrifice way too many points.

19. Given the points, DIE 14F seems like the best you can do. No matter how you play, your leave won't be good, but you can always exchange next turn. Getting 27 points this turn is worth it.

20. None of the plays will leave anything reasonably good; hence, there's no reason not to take the most points by playing VEE, and next you may still be able to play JUTTY. (Note that VOTE leaves open its own R, D, and S-hook as well as the H12–H15 TWS.)

21. Unfortunately, there are no bingos. He's so close, though! Many players might be tempted to drop the B on N6 for 13 points because many one-tile draws will lead to a bingo next turn. However, instead of getting frustrated after searching and not finding a bingo, look for the next best thing: a Double-Double! BROWNIE K5 48 keeps the AS, and you still have a not-insignificant chance to score a bingo next turn.

22. Where can you score points? A TLS-DWS down the B column might be perfect. However, your best score there is MATRON B10 32, keeping the W. Ugh; not perfect. The other best hotspot is at L12: MOWN L12 28 keeps the perfect leave, ART; however, it opens up the TWS-TWS combo with the N on L15. How to decide? In such cases, your leave is *more* important than the opening. The N will cover the DLS between the two TWSs, and that takes much of the sting out of that opening. Plus, the ART leave gives you a tremendous start for your next bingo. That's a winner!

23. Scoring opportunities are few here, but should be weighed carefully. Here are the two best options: OXIME 14I 30; OXO F13 31. Either of these is better than exchanging. Why? Mostly because of the points! Your bad leaves might turn better after your draw, but even if not, you can exchange next turn. For now, the points will give you a nearly 60-point lead.

But how do you choose between these two plays? Both leaves are very weak. However, if you compare the two resulting board positions, we see that OXIME not only opens the TWS on row 15 but also allows for a huge S double-hook DWS at 14N. In the long run, that's a bigger risk than plopping the O onto 15F with OXO. Plus, the EIOU leave has more potential for better next turns than the OOU leave after OXIME because of the E and I on your rack. So, based on all of the above, OXO is your best chance to win this game.

24. As a general rule, when you have several choices for plays, none of which scores much, and with the board fairly closed (which it is, except for six- or seven-letter words beginning with an S at O3), see if you have a short play that leaves a bingo-ish leave. In this situation, you have a ready-made bingo after getting rid of two Es. ABELR has the dynamic -ABLE and -ER endings. You *will* draw a bingo a reasonable percentage of the time to play beginning at either G1, O3, or A7. There are thirty seven-letter words that include ABELR and end in a vowel that play down to G7, and twelve eight-letter words that include ABELR and end in a D. That's a better chance for a bingo than any other tile dump. And VEE 9H 13 is the highest-scoring EE dump.

25. It's either exchange or use two Is, keeping the blank. The only other choice would be to use IOY (only if you earned a reasonable score, so that saving DII? might be worth it), but that's not possible. So, how can you use two Is? Two choices: IDIOT 12I 12 or IDIOM K4 22. IDIOM is the clear favorite!

26. The most obvious choices are MIX J8 35 or XI 9I 34. However, the less obvious but more productive play is IAMBI 7F 28 (a plural of IAMBUS, a type of metrical foot). Why is IAMBI more productive? Because of the two TLSs that play opens. You're extremely likely to be able to play for 50 points or more next turn at 6F. And if you draw an O, I, or U, you will be able to play the X at 6J (OBE, XU, XI). So, you sacrifice 6 or 7 points now for an excellent chance to score 50 points next turn. IAMBI is best.

27. The first thing to notice in this endgame position is that your opponent cannot go out with their DMN rack. If you can go out in two turns with enough points, you can win. Keep in mind that your opponent has MIDI E3 14, giving them a total of 393 points. So, for you to win, you need 19 points in your two turns (373 + 19 = 392 + 2 (opp. Nx2) = 394). The best way to do that is with VENUE 10I 8, followed by AI 2I 14.

28. You again need to go out in two and score enough to overcome whatever your opponent plays, such as SERFDOM 14C 21 or FRIDGE 10B 21. The only way to do that is with KILT 2A 8. You need to know the word ACRED or ARCED, because after KILT, both of them play at 1D 30, which is enough to win. Or, if your opponent blocks on top, you still have ARCED D11 25, which would also win.

29. You are helped in this position when you realize that your opponent can go out and win with LUNAR or ULNAR A4 6. So, you must block. The key observation is to notice that you have the tropical tree MAMIE in your rack, along with AH. If you know that word, you can set it up by playing RAH A8 6. Next turn you can play either MAMIE B10 43 or the already set up MAMIE B2 38. Your opponent cannot go out, nor block both MAMIEs, and so you win.

26 PLAYER INTERVIEWS: Hear from Four Enthusiastic Players

JOEY KRAFCHICK INTERVIEW
April 16, 2018

When did you start playing SCRABBLE?
I started playing SCRABBLE when I was five, as I learned to read at an early age and the entire family enjoyed playing SCRABBLE. I quickly started getting better at it, which fueled a passion that has escalated to the point that here I am, in my early twenties. I would say that it really hit me that I had SCRABBLE talent when I went 6–0 and made it to the finals of the School SCRABBLE Championship in 2007.

When did you discover the world of competitive SCRABBLE?
I played in my first SCRABBLE club in 2005, and then my first real tournament in 2006 when I was eleven. My local club was very welcoming to me, but like any adults would be they were somewhat alarmed that this whippersnapper

randomly showed up and started beating all of them. I went to that club most weeks for many years, but eventually stopped going. My first tournament was a one-day event in Philadelphia, and that was the day I got hooked on competitive SCRABBLE, without a doubt.

What was it like playing on national television on ESPN?
I really enjoyed playing in front of the cameras at the School SCRABBLE Championships. It motivated me to play well and impress. I generally like spotlight under any circumstance that is positive.

What was the reaction among classmates in regard to your success?
Generally, other students thought it was cool that I played SCRABBLE at the national level. However, being immature and young myself, I felt the need to hide it sometimes because others may have given me a hard time, out of jealousy or whatever. But once high school hit, I had no shame and I just continued to improve, and now I can't believe that I ever had the attitude that someone could frown upon what I do.

Do you have a memory of any particular match, perhaps against a tournament veteran or a SCRABBLE champion?
I don't have a specific memory about beating a former champion, since any single game in a tournament is, well, a single game! It definitely is the marker of significant progress, because as a new tournament player I didn't think I could ever beat someone of that level, let alone get to that level myself. I'm proud to say I can compete with any SCRABBLE player, former champ or not.

Would you tell us about your training and study routine?
I spend a lot of hours each week on SCRABBLE, although it's hard to quantify exactly how many. I used to only study tiny amounts when I was young, and in the summer, I would binge study before the Nationals. However, in 2013, I went 14–17 in Division 1 at the Nationals for the second straight year. This ignited a frustration at my stagnation, so I went into study overdrive. My half-ass study methods had proven ineffective for way too long. Thus, I did a consistent three hours per day, seven days per week, for about two years. Now I do about 60–90 minutes a day studying, and as of the beginning of 2017 I'm attempting to learn the Collins English Dictionary.

You've also become an active tournament director. What's that like?
Tournament organizing is an incredible honor for me. It means the world to me that I can get a hundred or more people to show up to an event of mine. I've learned a lot about dealing with people and business perspectives as a result, but the end goal of my organizing is to get everyone in the same place playing SCRABBLE and to facilitate an incredible weekend. Not many people who play in tournaments want to deal with the aspects of tournament organizing and/or directing. I take that as an opportunity to create an awesome event that will leave nothing but good memories.

A "walk-off bingo"—when one goes out with a play of seven or more tiles—is one of the more exciting plays in the game. Do you have a walk-off bingo memory?
I've played a lot of tournament games at this point, so I have lots of "walk-off" stories, but I'll give you an example. In the last round of a recent Nationals in Indiana, it was a cash game. I was down about 100 points nearing the end of the game, and with the Q unseen, I went for a Hail Mary Q-stick and ended up winning by 2 points. That was a $450 creative sequence that I got lucky to follow through with.

MIKE BARON INTERVIEW
April 16, 2018

Mike Baron is considered one of the godfathers of the SCRABBLE culture worldwide. For nearly four decades he has been a club director, a successful tournament expert and champion, a tournament promoter, a North American SCRABBLE Players Association advisory board member, and a mentor. He is the author of *SCRABBLE® Wordbook* and "The Cheat Sheet."

You've been around the SCRABBLE tournament scene for nearly forty years. What's the chief difference between the early days and now?
My arthritis. :) But seriously, there have been a number of significant differences, and it's hard to know which is greatest. Here are some:

a. **Atmosphere.** There seemed to be "a lightness of being," a lighter atmosphere at clubs and tournaments, a camaraderie and purer love of the game. We played for the joy of word-making and some cheap trophies. With the advent of ratings, which emerged in the late 1980s, and the sorting of players into divisions, the competitive nature of the game certainly rose, but with that, so did an atmosphere that may have compromised the previous camaraderie.

b. **Technology.** Computers allowed the digitization of the dictionary (by 1986) and the spread of online gaming (1990s). Hand-generated word lists, such as the three-to-make-four-letter word list, which took me weeks to generate in the summer of 1983, subsequently could be generated in seconds. It allowed more lengthy lists, such as all the high-probability bingos to even be attempted. While my various shorter word lists were published piecemeal (1981 to 1987), *The Wordbook* (1988), containing all the words and more extensive word lists, would not have been possible without computers. On the gaming front, programming wizards were able to devise "bots," which knew the entire dictionary and, with the algorithms devised, were able to beat the world's best experts. The Internet has now allowed players all over the world to play one another remotely. The upsides include access and the low expense to do so. The downsides include a depersonalization of the gaming experience (the two-dimensionalization of life), smaller club and tourney attendance, and a few cheaters who deny using any assistance while playing. :)

You are legendary for your word knowledge and books. Tell us one word you'd love to play someday and why.
TINTINNABULATION, only because it's a cool word and it can't fit on the board. :) Okay, so TINTINNABULARY would fit. Actually OUGUIYA, as a bingo, because it represents turning absolute drek into gold.

The international tournament scene uses two different SCRABBLE dictionaries depending on the locale—one international and the other North American. Do you think there will ever be just one official word source?
I had advocated for such when I met, as a sort of SCRABBLE emissary from the United States, with the then-head of the British SCRABBLE scene in

1987. I suggested a unified word source and a first World Championship. He pooh-poohed the idea of a combined lexicon, saying the respective publishers would never agree to it. As you know, the first World Championship did occur (1991), where words in either of the two lexica then (call it the North American and British lexica) were considered acceptable. As the years progressed, the lexicon adopted outside North America included ALL the words in the two lexica, now referred to as the International lexicon, while North Americans have held firm to their own lexicon. I believe the majority of North American club and tournament players are so accustomed to their lexicon and the task of learning so many new words seems so onerous, that I would not predict club and tourney aficionados adopting the International lexicon anytime soon. Then there's the disincentive for the North American lexicon publisher—why banish one of its bestsellers?

Is it true you proposed to your wife, Pamina, using a SCRABBLE board?
Yes, on Labor Day 1989, thirteen months and thirteen dates after meeting her at the 1988 National SCRABBLE Championship, I proposed to her on a SCRABBLE board. She did not challenge my play, apparently finding it acceptable. Definitely the best play of my life.

If you could give any advice to anyone contemplating entering a SCRABBLE tournament, what would it be?
Follow your passion, enjoy the game, and enjoy the people you meet through this wonderful, crazy enterprise. On average, you will have thirteen turns per game. Consider each turn a riddle to solve or a question to answer, where the question posed is along the lines of: "Given this rack, this board, my opponent's last play, the present score, and my present word knowledge, what is my best play?" On my thirteen turns, I aspire to go 10–3 or better in terms of best play selections. Realize, too, that there will be better plays possible that are not in your present word arsenal. Find joy in learning (and relearning) such words. When demonstrated, enjoy the beauty of your opponent's playmanship. Congratulate your opponent and yourself when either of you come up with one of those special plays. Take pride in keeping your cool when the Tile Gods frown upon you. Be grateful that you have sufficient health and the opportunity to play this wonderful game and befriend some fairly amazing people who share your passion for the game. The gratitude for connections to such special people may continue, even if or when one's health prohibits or limits one's playing or playmanship.

CORNELIA GUEST INTERVIEW
April 16, 2018

How did you get involved in coaching kids for the National School SCRABBLE® Championship?
I got involved coaching School SCRABBLE in 2004, when my children (triplets) were in fifth grade. I'd been playing tournament SCRABBLE for a few years and thought my children would enjoy it. I started teaching at the Ridgefield Library in Connecticut and at my kids' school in New York State. The first team I brought to the NSSC—my daughter, Aune Mitchell, and her classmate Alex Hodgson—was in 2005.

All kids want to win. How do you manage their expectations in preparing them for competition?
I usually tell the parents, rather than the kids, what their expectations should be. I like to say something nonjudgmental, such as, "Usually the older kids win the championships, but your team should win some games," or, "It's rare for a team to win the first time at Nationals, but your team will have a blast, win or lose." The hardest is when I bring the top-ranked team, as expectations are high. For those teams, I'll say, "They have a great chance, but you never know what tiles they'll pick." I understand they're adding more games this year, which will make luck somewhat less of a factor.

What is your advice on attracting kids to the game and maintaining their enthusiasm?
I try to make SCRABBLE fun. For the last ten years I've had a Halloween-themed tournament the weekend after Halloween. Kids come in costumes, and we have prizes for best costume and best Halloween word. I have several divisions so that the kids who are new to the game aren't over fazed. I have lots of prizes—every kid goes home with something. Other ways to keep it fun include giving bonus points in class for a particular type of word—for example, during the recent election players got a 10-point bonus for an election-related word, such as VOTE.

I also have the kids play a simplified variation of Anagrams if we have enough time. I handicap players, so the newer players can play three-letter words while the more skilled players must play four- or five-letter words. When Mack Meller was playing with us he had to play eight-letter words—and still won many times! I like to encourage kids and keep anagramming fun.

For a while I was running monthly tournaments with youth divisions, and some of the kids who attended those have gone on to be top players, including Matthew O'Connor, Ben Schoenbrun, and Bradley Robbins. I think the more kids get the chance to play with other kids when they start out, the more they'll enjoy the game.

You are an intermediate tournament player. What was it like when some of your middle school players began to occasionally defeat you in a practice game?
I love it when my students start beating me! It means I've done a good job getting them started. With really good students, like Mack Meller (a top-ranked player), I arrange for them to have sessions with better players such as Joe Edley. I refer them to good books and to online study programs such as Quackle, Zyzzyva, and Aerolith. I've also arranged clinics and study sessions for my Nationals-bound teams with other teachers.

Tell us about some of your young players who've gone on to compete against adults in tournament play.
Mack Meller is my most successful student. But I've had many others who have done well in adult competition, including Matthew Silver, Kevin Rosenberg, Noah Kalus, and DeeAnn Guo. I've been fortunate to have some strong players from other states on my Nationals teams, though usually their main coaching is at home (I'll do some online practice). Californians Cooper Komatsu, Zachary Ansell, and Jem Burch are all playing well in open competition.

In addition to being a successful SCRABBLE coach, you are also a tournament organizer for adults. What's the difference between kids and adults in regard to their behavior in competition?
Great question! I generally find the kids behave better at tournaments, especially if something goes wrong. They're used to listening to adults, and they understand good sportsmanship. But I'm also easier on the kids in tournaments. I'm not as concerned about noise and I don't mind explaining a point several times. There tend to be a lot more challenges at a kids' tournament, but the kids usually take a lost challenge in stride. There are also no recounts, which I think is great. On the downside, sometimes you'll have a kid who's very upset and starts crying. But I see very little meanness at kids' tournaments.

Are you a sports fan? Can you tell us of a time you made the equivalent of a "buzzer beater" or "walk-off home run" in a SCRABBLE match?
I'm not really much of a sports fan, though I competed in equestrian events for years and enjoy going to the races at Saratoga. The most exciting SCRABBLE moment for me was when Matthew Silver and my daughter, Aune, found the winning outplay TABLOIDS at the 2007 NSSC to win the championship. They were behind and the clock was ticking down, and I thought they wouldn't find the play in time. It was an unbelievable moment. Kevin McCarthy, who had spent many hours coaching the team, was in tears. That was the first year ESPN filmed the NSSC—and the first year Jimmy Kimmel invited the winners to his show—so the whole experience was amazing.

MACK MELLER
April 23, 2018

You played in your first official SCRABBLE tournament at ten years old. What are your memories from that experience?
I remember I had crammed in, like, eight hours of studying the day before but was still extremely nervous the day of. I lost my first game of the event and was pretty distraught afterwards, but thankfully I had some previous experience with a few chess tournaments and youth SCRABBLE events that I could rely on to calm myself down. I ended up going undefeated for the rest of the day and winning the event.

While still a teenager you've been ranked as high as number 2 among all tournament SCRABBLE players in North America. Does that bring extra pressure for you when you compete?
I generally find that most of the pressure I experience comes from my own internal expectations, but other players having high expectations can certainly increase the stress. I try to just enjoy each game and not get too wrapped up in what others think of my performance. I especially enjoy hanging out with friends between games and at meals since the fun helps me stay calm.

How old were you when you first defeated a world or national SCRABBLE champion in a tournament match, and what was that experience like?
I beat Joel Sherman in a tournament when I was eleven, but I'm sure I got very lucky that game. Obviously, anything can happen in one game, so I don't recall

thinking too much of it. I'd also already played Joel and Joe Edley a bunch of times at a club, and probably won an occasional game there. Both Joel and Joe were always very supportive and happy to give me advice when I was starting out. I've now played over fifty tournament games combined with them, and they're both always gracious, win or lose.

What other activities interest you besides SCRABBLE?

One other activity I enjoy a lot is birdwatching—I regularly go on local birding outings and have attended two teen birder summer camps. I still remember reading about the AEPYORNIS (a huge extinct bird called the "elephant bird") in a bird book and then studying the same word for SCRABBLE later that day. I also enjoy a variety of sports, including frisbee, tennis, golf, and ping-pong. I'm always eager to try new interesting foods; one word I like using to describe myself is a TUROPHILE (someone who loves cheese).

PART • 5

BECOMING A SKILLED ANAGRAMMER

Chapter 27 can take a complete novice anagrammer and turn him/her into an expert. Here you will also learn the tricks to finding seven- and eight-letter words with ease.

27 ANAGRAMMAR

The predominant skill enjoyed by many excellent players of the SCRABBLE® Crossword Game is the ability to find words in a jumbled array of letters. This edition of *Everything SCRABBLE®* provides you the practice necessary to raise your anagramming level to whatever heights you want to attain. Practice with these puzzles and your skills are guaranteed to grow!

There are many online games that help you become adept at finding three- to five-letter words, so we begin with six-letter alphagrams. These alphagrams are organized according to each important letter so that you can become familiar with the way the designated letter shows up in sixes. We've placed them in four-word sets so that you can easily digest and solve them in short spurts, at your convenience. We strongly suggest you use letter tiles and continually rearrange them in a systematic way until you find the common word the letters can spell. We cannot emphasize enough that actually moving the tiles around into different arrangements is so much more effective a method for training your brain than trying to do it all in your head. Enjoy!

Later on we will show you an easy method for finding seven- and eight-letter words with only a very small amount of training, using designated "edge" letters.

A note on the answers throughout Part 5: Our goal is for most twelve- to fourteen-year-old English speakers to know virtually all the puzzle words that follow. We apologize in advance for any words that seem more obscure than you might expect!

Six-Letter Alphagrams B:

SET A

1. AABBNN
2. AABDET
3. AABDLL
4. AABELR

SET B

1. AABGIR
2. ABBCOT
3. ABCDTU
4. ABCEEM

SET C

1. ABCEHL
2. ABCENO
3. ABCFIR
4. ABCLOT

SET D

1. ABDEEH
2. ABDEET
3. ABDEIT
4. ABDINT

SET E

1. ABDNOU
2. ABDRSU
3. ABEEHV
4. ABEENT

SET F

1. ABEFFL
2. ABEFHL
3. ABEGLM
4. ABEHLR

SET G

1. ABEILV
2. ABEKMR
3. ABEKRY
4. ABEKST

SET H

1. ABELRV
2. ABEMNO
3. ABERTT
4. ABERUU

SET I

1. ABGIMT
2. ABHINS
3. ABHIOP
4. ABILNO

SET J

1. ABIMRU
2. ABLLOT
3. ABLRTU
4. ABNRTU

SET K

1. ABNOTY
2. ABNRUU
3. ABPRTU
4. ABSUWY

SET L

1. BBEELP
2. BBRSUU
3. BCEEHR
4. BCEHRU

SET M

1. BCEIST
2. BCEKTU
3. BCENOU
4. BCHLOT

SET N

1. BCILPU
2. BCOOWY
3. BDEEIS
4. BDEEOY

SET O

1. BDEGTU
2. BDEHIN
3. BDELOU
4. BDFIOR

SET P

1. BDHIRY
2. BDIITT
3. BDIOTU
4. BEEELT

SET Q

1. BEEFOR
2. BEELMM
3. BEFFTU
4. BEGILO

SET R

1. BEGLNO
2. BEHLMU
3. BEIRTT
4. BELRTU

SET S

1. BEMNRU
2. BEMORY
3. BENNOT
4. BEOSTW

SET T

1. BGGIIW
2. BGHOTU
3. BGLNOO
4. BHIOPS

SET U

1. BIMSTU
2. BINNOU
3. BLMOSY
4. BMOOTT

SET V

1. BNOTTU
2. BNOTUY
3. BOORRW
4. BNNORU

C:

SET A

1. AACDER
2. AACELP
3. AACFIL
4. AACHTT

SET B

1. AACIRV
2. AACLTU
3. AACNRY
4. AACNTV

SET C

1. ACCELN
2. ACCESU
3. ACCSTU
4. ACDDEE

SET D

1. ACDDIN
2. ACDEHT
3. ACDEIV
4. ACDILP

SET E

1. ACDORW
2. ACEELV
3. ACEEMN
4. ACEERR

SET F

1. ACEGLN
2. ACEGLY
3. ACEGNY
4. ACEHPY

SET G

1. ACEHSW
2. ACEITV
3. ACELOT
4. ACEMNU

SET H

1. ACENNU
2. ACEORS
3. ACFISO
4. ACFORT

SET I

1. ACGILR
2. ACGHTU
3. ACHTTY
4. ACIINN

SET J

1. ACIMOS
2. ACIMOT
3. ACIMPT
4. ACINPT

SET K

1. ACLLOR
2. ACLMOR
3. ACNNOY
4. ACMUUV

SET L

1. ACNORY
2. ACORTV
3. CCIILN
4. CCIRSU

SET M

1. CDDEEO
2. CDEEFT
3. CDEERU
4. CDEINR

SET N

1. CDEMOY
2. CDOORT
3. CEEEFL
4. CEEHMS

SET O

1. CEELRV
2. CEELRY
3. CEEMNT
4. CEENOR

SET P

1. CEFNOR
2. CEGORR
3. CEHMOR
4. CEHNOS

SET Q

1. CEHNRW
2. CEHPSY
3. CEIILT
4. CEIINT

SET R

1. CEIKLP
2. CEIKOO
3. CEILNP
4. CEILOP

SET S

1. CEINOV
2. CEIOPR
3. CEIOPT
4. CEKOPT

SET T

1. CELMSU
2. CELOPU
3. CENOPU
4. CFFINO

SET U

1. CGHIOT
2. CGHORU
3. CHISTT
4. CHMOOS

SET V

1. CHNOOP
2. CIIMTV
3. CIINOR
4. CILNOU

SET W

1. CILOPY
2. CIMOST
3. CINOSU
4. CIMSTY

SET X

1. CIORTV
2. CIPRST
3. CIRSTT
4. CKRSUU

SET Y

1. CLLORS
2. CLMNOU
3. CLNRUU
4. CMOSTU

SET Z

1. CNOOTY
2. CNOTUY
3. CORTUY
4. COOPTU

D:

SET A

1. AADEGN
2. AADEGM
3. AADEPR
4. AADFIR

SET B

1. AADGOP
2. AADILR
3. AADLMY
4. AADMRU

SET C

1. ADDEGO
2. ADDELP
3. ADEEFM
4. ADEFLU

SET D

1. ADEFOR
2. ADEGIN
3. ADEHLR
4. ADEILL

SET E

1. ADEINV
2. ADEMNU
3. ADEMOW
4. ADEOPS

SET F

1. ADEPTU
2. ADFFOR
3. ADFIRT
4. ADGINT

SET G

1. ADFRTY
2. ADHLRY
3. ADGNOR
4. ADHOSW

SET H

1. ADIIMR
2. ADIKNP
3. ADILNS
4. ADIMRY

SET I

1. ADIMSY
2. ADINPU
3. ADIRSU
4. ADLNOU

SET J

1. ADMNOY
2. ADMORR
3. ADNOPR
4. ADNORU

SET K

1. ADNORW
2. ADNRTU
3. ADOPRY
4. BDDEIN

SET L

1. DDIOTU
2. DEEEGR
3. DEEELT
4. DEEGIR

SET M

1. DEEGLN
2. DEEGLP
3. DEEGLU
4. DEEGNR

SET N

1. DEEILY
2. DEEIMP
3. DEELMY
4. DEELST

SET O

1. DEEMRU
2. DEFFNO
3. DEFHIS
4. DEGIMT

SET P

1. DEGIST
2. DEGLSU
3. DEIINO
4. DEIIRT

SET Q

1. DEILMW
2. DEILRV
3. DEIMMU
4. DEIOPS

SET R

1. DEIORW
2. DEIRTV
3. DELMOY
4. DELNOO

SET S

1. DEMOST
2. DENNOT
3. DENORT
4. DEOORV

SET T

1. DENRTY
2. DEOPRW
3. DEOTUV
4. DERSTY

SET U

1. DEGILR
2. DGIINO
3. DFLNOU
4. DGNORU

SET V

1. DGOTUU
2. DHLOSU
3. DHORSU
4. DIIMTW

SET W

1. DIMNOO
2. DIMOPU
3. DINNUW
4. DIOSTU

SET X

1. DIPRTU
2. DLNOTU
3. DNRSUY
4. DRSTUY

F:

SET A

1. AEEFLM
2. AEFFLW
3. AEFGOR
4. AEFILN

SET B

1. AEFIMN
2. AEFIRR
3. AEFIST
4. AAEFLM

SET C

1. AEFLRT
2. AEFLSY
3. AEFNST
4. AEFNSU

SET D

1. AFFIRT
2. AFGLRU
3. AFHIMS
4. AFHMOT

SET E

1. AFILMY
2. AFINRU
3. AFIRTY
4. AFLLOR

SET F

1. AFINNT
2. AFLMOR
3. AFLNTU
4. AFLORV

SET G

1. AFLRTU
2. AFMORT
3. EFGIRU
4. EFGLNU

SET H

1. EFGORT
2. EFIINT
3. EFILLT
4. EFILPR

SET I

1. EFINSU
2. EFIRVY
3. EFLMSY
4. EFLNNU

SET J

1. EFLNOY
2. EFLRUU
3. EFLSUU
4. EFNOST

SET K

1. EFRRSU
2. FGHOTU
3. FGNSUU
4. FHIINS

SET L

1. FHIRTT
2. FHORTU
3. FIIMST
4. FILMSY

SET M

1. FILOSS
2. FILPTU
3. FIMNOR
4. FINOSU

SET N

1. FIOTTU
2. FIPRUY
3. FLRSUU
4. FORRUW

G:

SET A

1. AAEGGR
2. AAEGMN
3. AAGHNR
4. AEEGSW

SET B

1. AEGHRT
2. AEGILO
3. AEGIMP
4. AEGKRW

SET C

1. AEGLPU
2. AEGLRV
3. AEGMNT
4. AEGOTU

SET D

1. AEGRTT
2. AEGOVY
3. AGHNPU
4. AGIMST

SET E

1. AGINSS
2. AGIRTU
3. AGLLNO
4. AGLMOR

SET F

1. AGLNOO
2. AGLRUV
3. EEGINN
4. EEGLMU

SET G

1. EEGLNT
2. EEGRRT
3. EEGRSY
4. EGHILS

SET H

1. EGHIOT
2. EGHITW
3. EGHLNT
4. EGHNOU

SET I

1. EGHSTU
2. EGILMN
3. EGILPT
4. EGINPP

SET J

1. EGINSU
2. EGIOOR
3. EGLLTU
4. EGLNOU

SET K

1. EGLOUY
2. EGMNTU
3. EGMORU
4. EGNORV

SET L

1. EGNOTU
2. EGOORV
3. GHINNO
4. GHLOPU

SET M

1. GHNRUY
2. GHORTW
3. GIIKNS
4. GIINOR

SET N

1. GILRSY
2. GNORST
3. GOORTT
4. GNOPSY

H:

SET A

1. AAHPTY
2. AAHRSS
3. AEEHNV
4. AEHHRT

SET B

1. AEHILN
2. AEHILW
3. AEHINR
4. AEHKNS

SET C

1. AEHLLT
2. AEHLMT
3. AEHLOT
4. AEHLTW

SET D

1. AEHMMY
2. AEHMNU
3. AEHRRT
4. AHILSV

SET E	SET F	SET G	SET H
1. AHIMOR	1. AHMRTW	1. AHORTT	1. EEHLMT
2. AHINSV	2. AHNOPR	2. AHORTU	2. EEHNPW
3. AHISTU	3. AHNOWY	3. AHRTTW	3. EEHRTT
4. AHLPSS	4. AHOORY	4. EEHITV	4. EHHNPY

SET I	SET J	SET K	SET L
1. EHILMU	1. HHMRTY	1. HIINTW	1. HLNOUY
2. EHIRTV	2. HIIMPS	2. HILOPS	2. HMOOST
3. EHLRTU	3. HILLPU	3. HINOPS	3. HNRTUU
4. EHORTY	4. HILLRT	4. HIRTTY	4. HOPRTY

K:

SET A	SET B	SET C	SET D
1. AEIKLT	1. AEKNRT	1. AKMPRU	1. EEKLWY
2. AEIKNT	2. AHKNRS	2. AKNSWY	2. EEKPPU
3. AEKMPU	3. AIKNNP	3. EEEKNR	3. EHIKOR
4. AEKMRT	4. AKMNSU	4. EEKLNR	4. EIKLLR

SET E	SET F	SET G	SET H
1. EIKLNT	1. EIKOOR	1. EKOORT	1. GHIKNT
2. EIKLNU	2. EKNNSU	2. EKRTUY	2. GIKLNY
3. EIKNOV	3. EKNOPS	3. FIKRSY	3. HKNOOU
4. EIKNPR	4. EKNORW	4. FKLOSY	4. IKLNSY

M:

SET A	SET B	SET C	SET D
1. AAEMNS	1. AALMOR	1. AEEKMR	1. AEMNOY
2. AALMNP	2. AAMNRT	2. AEEMSS	2. AEMNRU
3. AALMNW	3. AAMRTU	3. AELMOR	3. AEMNTU
4. AALMNY	4. DEIMTU	4. AELMRV	4. AEMPRT

SET E
1. AEMRTU
2. AEMTTU
3. AIIMPR
4. AILMNY

SET F
1. AILMPR
2. AIMSTU
3. ALMNOR
4. ALLMOS

SET G
1. ALMORT
2. ALMSUY
3. AMNORT
4. AMNTTU

SET H
1. AMOOTT
2. AMORRT
3. AMORRY
4. AMPRUW

SET I
1. AMRRTY
2. BEELMM
3. BEFLMU
4. EEIMNR

SET J
1. EEMNOY
2. EIILMU
3. EILLMT
4. EILMPP

SET K
1. EILMTY
2. EIMMOR
3. EIMNRV
4. EIMOOR

SET L
1. EIMOPS
2. EIMOTV
3. EIMPRT
4. EIMRSY

SET M
1. EIMSSU
2. ELLMOW
3. ELMOPY
4. ELMOTT

SET N
1. ELMOUV
2. EMMNOT
3. EMMRSU
4. EMNORS

SET O
1. FFIMNU
2. FIIMST
3. FIMNOR
4. HIIMPS

SET P
1. HIMSWY
2. IMOPRV
3. IMNOOT
4. LMTTUU

P:

SET A
1. AAELPP
2. AAELPT
3. AELOPR
4. AENOPW

SET B
1. AEOPTT
2. AENPTU
3. AIOPTU
4. AIPRTY

SET C
1. ALLPRU
2. ALOPPT
3. ALOPST
4. ANPRUW

SET D
1. AOOPTT
2. AOPRRU
3. AOPRST
4. APRSTY

SET E
1. EELLPT
2. EELNPS
3. EENPRT
4. EEOPRS

SET F
1. EEOPTU
2. EEPRTY
3. EIIPST
4. EIOPTT

SET G
1. EKNOPS
2. ELLNOP
3. ENOPTT
4. ENNOPU

SET H
1. ENPTUU
2. EOOPPS
3. EOPRTY
4. EPRSUU

SET I

1. FFIOPR
2. IIPRST
3. ILLOPW
4. IOPPTT

SET J

1. IPSTTY
2. IPRTUY
3. PRSUYY
4. OOPRTU

V:

SET A

1. AAARTV
2. AADLNV
3. AAEGRV
4. AAIRVY

SET B

1. AALOVW
2. AALSSV
3. AANSTV
4. ABEERV

SET C

1. ABEEHV
2. ACITVY
3. ADEEVW
4. AENRTV

SET D

1. AIIRTV
2. AILSUV
3. AIORSV
4. BEINOV

SET E

1. CDEEIV
2. CEELRV
3. EILPSV
4. CENOVY

SET F

1. CRSUVY
2. CNOOVY
3. DDEIIV
4. DEIRRV

SET G

1. DELOSV
2. DEORUV
3. EEELNV
4. EEILVW

SET H

1. EELSTV
2. EELTVW
3. EENNUV
4. EERSVW

SET I

1. EIINTV
2. EILOTV
3. EINRTV
4. EIRTUV

SET J

1. ERSSUV
2. ERSUVY
3. IILNOV
4. IINOSV

W:

SET A

1. AAEKNW
2. AAESWY
3. AALSWY
4. AALWYY

SET B

1. ABMOTW
2. ABSUWY
3. ADESWY
4. ADHOSW

SET C

1. ADPRUW
2. AEEGSW
3. AEEKNW
4. AEELSW

SET D

1. AEELWY
2. AEESSW
3. AELRWY
4. AFLLUW

SET E	SET F	SET G	SET H
1. AHNOWY	1. CEFRUW	1. DIMOSW	1. ELLOWY
2. ALLOPW	2. DEGITW	2. DORSWY	2. ENTTWY
3. ALOTUW	3. DEGLOW	3. EEFSTW	3. IINTTW
4. ALRSUW	4. DENOOW	4. EHINTW	4. NOPTUW

Y:

SET A	SET B	SET C	SET D
1. AAHSSY	1. ABBOTY	1. ACLLMY	1. AEERTY
2. AAIRWY	2. ABDNRY	2. ACLNUY	2. AEGRTY
3. AALRSY	3. ABETUY	3. ADEKPY	3. ANRTTY
4. AARSTY	4. ABPSSY	4. ADFGLY	4. AEILSY

SET E	SET F	SET G	SET H
1. AENNOY	1. BDENOY	1. BHIOSY	1. DEPTUY
2. AFFLOY	2. BEFLRY	2. CCOPUY	2. DEPRRY
3. AFLTUY	3. BEILNY	3. CDIIOY	3. DFIMOY
4. AGRSUY	4. IPPTUY	4. DDIOTY	4. EEFLUY

SET I	SET J
1. EHRRSY	1. ELMOTY
2. EINNTY	2. EMSSTY
3. EINTTY	3. GIPSTY
4. ELLOSY	4. GILTUY

JQXZ:

SET A	SET B	SET C	SET D
1. AAAELZ	1. AAGJRU	1. AANSTZ	1. ACIQTU
2. AABELZ	2. AAGLXY	2. AAQRSU	2. ACEJLO
3. AACJKL	3. AAMNOZ	3. ABCEJT	3. ADEIJL
4. AADHRZ	4. AANRTZ	4. ACEJKT	4. ADILRZ

SET E	SET F	SET G	SET H
1. ADENPX	1. AELSUX	1. AEOPQU	1. AEQSUY
2. ADIRWZ	2. AGIJSW	2. AIJLOV	2. AILOTX
3. AEEQTU	3. AGJNOR	3. AHORTX	3. AIMRTX
4. AEILRZ	4. AJLOPY	4. CDEEEX	4. CEEITX

SET I	SET J	SET K	SET L
1. CEIJNT	1. DEELUX	1. DIILQU	1. EEMNYZ
2. CEILQU	2. DEEORZ	2. EEFLRX	2. EERTVX
3. CEJKOY	3. DELPUX	3. EEIPRX	3. EFIPRX
4. CEIOTX	4. DEOTUX	4. EEMPTX	4. EGIJLN

SET M	SET N
1. EGNOXY	1. FFISUX
2. EIINOZ	2. FILNUX
3. EIJNRU	3. IJRSTU
4. EINQUU	4. ILOQRU

LNRST:

SET A	SET B	SET C	SET D
1. AAENSU	1. AEELNR	1. AELSTU	1. AENRTU
2. AAILSS	2. AEENNT	2. AENNTT	2. AEORSU
3. AALNNU	3. AEINNT	3. AENOSS	3. AESTTT
4. AANOST	4. AELNSU	4. AENOTT	4. AIINRS

SET E	SET F	SET G	SET H
1. AILORS	1. ANORTU	1. EELSTT	1. EILOTT
2. AILRTU	2. ANRTTU	2. EENNSU	2. EINNOT
3. ALNSTU	3. EEIRRT	3. EEORST	3. EIORRT
4. ANNSTU	4. EELNST	4. EILOOR	4. ELLNOR

SET I

1. ELNNTU
2. ELOORS
3. ELRTTU
4. ELOTTU

SET J

1. ENRSUU
2. ENRTUU
3. IINSST
4. ILNOOT

SEVEN-LETTER ALPHAGRAMS

The key to learning how to find seven- and eight-letter words is actually fairly simple. Most longer words have a familiar combination of letters either at the beginning or at the end—or, as they will be called here, the "edge" letters. For example: ovaTION, wearIEST, throwING, PROmote, OUTcome. So if you know the "edge," you'll have the edge!

In these first sets, you will be given the edge letters, and your task will be to find the word. In later puzzles, you will be given a variety of edge combos to choose from. As always, the more you practice, the easier this will become.

It is *strongly* suggested that you use letter tiles and put the edge letters in place and then rearrange the non-edge tiles until you've found the word. Why? Because unless you're already very experienced with anagramming, using only your imagination isn't going to be the fastest way to become a highly skilled anagrammer. For example, when I was a child, I took clarinet lessons. My teacher used to say that the most important thing for a student to do is to develop *good habits* when learning the instrument. He would emphasize that some semiskilled musicians hadn't learned good habits and so weren't able to fully develop their skills. These habits included breathing techniques, how one held the instrument, and which skills were vital to continue practicing every day. Of course, my preference was to play games and solve puzzles rather than practice the clarinet. But hey, the principle works here, too!

It's the same thing with anagramming. By using letter tiles and continually rearranging the tiles as you look for the words, you are simultaneously training your brain to mix up the letters in your head! Expert anagrammers don't generally need to use tiles to find the words; they just pop into their minds as they look at the combinations. But that's because they have hundreds of hours of experience using tiles. Either that or they are naturally gifted, or have developed their imaginations from other skills they've learned.

One last piece of advice before you start your journey into sevens and eights: It's a good idea to *pronounce* some of the arrangements you see. You don't need to pronounce them out loud, although that's not a bad idea; just sounding out the arrangements in your head will tend to give your subconscious mind and memory some associations to play with while you move the tiles. And it will give you practice recognizing that some arrangements have more than one pronunciation. For instance, the classic RE-STING can be pronounced two different ways. One way will sound foreign, while the other makes it obvious what the word is. SCRABBLE players often have that auditory blindness. Here are two words that, due to momentary blindness, have been misunderstood and challenged at the expert level in real tournament games: FORTY ("like a fort?") and WAS ("I didn't know WA was a two-letter word, let alone had a plural!"). WA isn't a two-letter word, but WAS has been and likely always will be a good word.

Three- and Four-Letter Edges

Front Edges

COM-

1. ACCMOPT
2. ACMOPSS
3. CEMOOPS
4. CMOOPST

CON-

SET A	SET B
1. ACCELNO	1. CCDEENO
2. CCEINOT	2. CCENNOR
3. CDELNOO	3. CDEFINO
4. CDEMNNO	4. CFIMNOR

DIS-

SET A	SET B	SET C
1. ABDDINS	1. DIPRSTU	1. DGISSTU
2. ACDDIRS	2. ADDIINS	2. DIIMSSS
3. BDIRSTU	3. ADGHIRS	3. ADILPSY
4. DEIPSTU	4. CDDIORS	4. BDEIOSY

FOR-

SET A	SET B
1. ABDEFOR	1. EFGORRY
2. AEFMORR	2. AFLMORU
3. CEFOPRS	3. EFGINOR
4. EEFORRV	4. EFNORTU

MIS-

SET A	SET B
1. ACILLMS	1. ADIMRSW
2. AILMPSY	2. EFIILMS
3. DIMORSW	3. EIMPSST
4. DEIMSSU	4. EIMPSTY

NON-

1. ACFNNOT
2. DFNNOOO
3. ALNNOPY
4. DNNOORW

OUT-

SET A	SET B
1. ABGORTU	1. ACEOPTU
2. ADEOTTU	2. AEORTUW
3. AENORTU	3. ALOPTUY
4. AKLOTTU	4. CEMOOTU

OVER-

1. ACEORTV
2. AELOPRV
3. AENORRV
4. DEEORUV

PRE-

SET A

1. ACEEFPR
2. AEILPRV
3. DEENPRT
4. EENPRTV

SET B

1. CDEIPRT
2. EEIPRVW
3. EEPRTTX
4. AEEHPRT

PRO-

SET A

1. BELMOPR
2. CDOPRTU
3. COOPRRT
4. GLNOOPR

SET B

1. BEOPRRV
2. CEOPRRU
3. DGIOPRY
4. EKOOPRV

SUB-

1. ABENPSU
2. BDEISSU
3. BELRSUU
4. BEPSTUY

Back Edges

-AGE

SET A

1. AABBCEG
2. AAEGMPR
3. AAEGMSS
4. ACEGINO

SET B

1. AEEEGNT
2. AABDEGN
3. AAEGPSS
4. ACEGLLO

SET C

1. AACEEGR
2. AEGILLV
3. AACEGNR
4. AEFGILO

-AND

SET A

1. AABDHNT
2. AADGLNR
3. ABDHNSU
4. ADELNTW

SET B

1. AABDMNR
2. ADFFHNO
3. ADLLNOW
4. ADLNOTU

-ANT

SET A	SET B	SET C	SET D
1. AABLNTT	1. ADINSTT	1. ADHNRTY	1. ABNOTUY
2. AAGLLNT	2. AADINRT	2. AEEGLNT	2. ADINSTT
3. AAINRTV	3. AAGNRTV	3. AAEGNPT	3. AEMNNRT
4. ADEINTV	4. ABINRTV	4. AAILNTV	4. ADMNORT

-ATE

SET A	SET B	SET C	SET D
1. AACEETT	1. ADEEITV	1. ACEEMRT	1. ABEOPRT
2. AADEMNT	2. AACELPT	2. AEEELTV	2. ADEEFLT
3. AEIIMTT	3. AAEGITT	3. AACETTU	3. AEELMTU
4. ACDEITT	4. ABEIRTV	4. AAEISTT	4. AADELTU

SET E	SET F
1. AAENRRT	1. AEIMPRT
2. ACDEETU	2. AEILOST
3. ADEEIMT	3. AEILOTV
4. AEFILNT	4. AEISTTU

-BLE

SET A	SET B	SET C	SET D
1. AABEELT	1. AABEILM	1. ABEIKLL	1. ABEILLV
2. AABELTX	2. ABDELRU	2. AABELPR	2. BEHILMT
3. AABDDEL	3. ABEELNT	3. ABBELMR	3. AABEFFL
4. AABCELP	4. ABELNOT	4. ABELMOV	4. ABDEILU

SET E	SET F
1. ABEILLP	1. BEEGILL
2. BEIILSV	2. BEGLMRU
3. BELORTU	3. BBELSTU
4. ABBELUY	4. ABCELRU

-ENT

SET A

1. ACEINNT
2. AEINPTT
3. CENNOST
4. CENRRTU

SET B

1. AEGNNTT
2. AEMNPTY
3. CENNOTT
4. DEEINTV

SET C

1. EEGMNST
2. EEILNNT
3. EEIMNNT
4. EENPRTV

SET D

1. EILNOTV
2. ELNOPTU
3. CENNOTV
4. ABEIMNT

-ERS

SET A

1. ABDEGRS
2. ABEERSV
3. ADDENRS
4. ADEIRRS

SET B

1. AEGHRST
2. ADENPRS
3. AEFLRST
4. AEKLRSW

SET C

1. AEPPRST
2. AELRSWY
3. BBEORRS
4. BEERRSW

SET D

1. CEEFNRS
2. CEGORRS
3. CEIMNRS
4. CEFNORS

SET E

1. CEILRSS
2. CELRRSU
3. DEHLORS
4. DEIRRSV

-ESS

SET A

1. AEDDRSS
2. BEGINSS
3. EELSSSU
4. EENNSSW

SET B

1. AEEGLSS
2. AELLSSW
3. DDEGOSS
4. EHNOSST

SET C

1. EFOPRSS
2. CDEHSSU
3. DEELNSS
4. DENRSSY

-EST

SET A

1. ABERSTV
2. BEINOST
3. CENOSTT
4. EEENSTV

SET B

1. EIIRSTW
2. ADDESST
3. AEMRSTW
4. CEGNOST

SET C

1. EFOSSTT
2. EINOSST
3. AEEMNST
4. BEGGIST

SET D

1. DEIKNST
2. EGLNOST
3. ELOSSTW
4. AEFIRST

SET E

1. BELNOST
2. EEEIRST
3. EHIMOST
4. ENOOSST

SET F

1. AEGLRST
2. BDELOST
3. EGGSSTU
4. EHOPSST

-FUL

SET A

1. ABFHLSU
2. ACFLTTU
3. AEFFLTU
4. AFHLMRU

SET B

1. AFLLPUY
2. ACEFLRU
3. ADFHLNU
4. AFGILNU

SET C

1. AFILNPU
2. EEFGLLU
3. EFHLOPU
4. EFHLLPU

SET D

1. FIILPTU
2. FLLOSUU
3. FILLLUW
4. FFILSTU

-IAL

1. AACILOS
2. AAILPRT
3. ACDILOR
4. AIILRTV

-IDE

SET A

1. ACDEINY
2. ADEHIRW
3. BDEIMOR
4. CDEFINO

SET B

1. DEIOPRV
2. BDDEEIS
3. BDEISSU
4. DEIORTU

-IER

SET A

1. ABEGGIR
2. AEEIRRT
3. CEEHIRW
4. DEIINRW

SET B

1. EGIMMRU
2. ACEIRRZ
3. AEHIKRS
4. CEIIPRR

SET C

1. EEEINRT
2. EHIPRSU
3. ACEIRSU
4. AEIINRR

SET D

1. CEHIIRT
2. EEIMPRR
3. EHIORSW
4. ADEEIRR

SET E

1. AEIOPRS
2. DDEGIIR
3. EFHIIRS
4. EILLORW

SET F

1. AEEHIRV
2. BEIKLRU
3. DEEEIRS
4. EFINNRU

-IES

SET A

1. ABEEINS
2. AEILPPS
3. CEEIPSS
4. EFIINSU

SET B

1. EIIKNPS
2. ADDEINS
3. AEIMRRS
4. CEIKOOS

SET C

1. EFILLOS
2. EIILMPS
3. ADEIISS
4. BBEHIOS

SET D

1. DDEIMSU
2. EFIOSST
3. EIISSTX
4. AEFIIRS

SET E

1. BDEEIRS
2. EEEIMNS
3. EGIPSSY
4. EIKOORS

SET F

1. AEEIRSW
2. BEEINSW
3. EEINOPS
4. EHINOPS

-IFY

SET A

1. ACFILRY
2. AFGIRTY
3. DFGIINY
4. EFISTTY

SET B

1. AFFILSY
2. AFILMPY
3. EFINRUY
4. FILLMOY

-ILE

1. AEFGILR
2. BEEGILU
3. EEFILRT
4. EFILOPR

-ILY

SET A

1. ACFILNY
2. ACILRSY
3. ADHILNY
4. AGILNRY

SET B

1. CIKLLUY
2. ACILSUY
3. ADEILRY
4. AEHILVY

SET C

1. AHIKLSY
2. FIILNTY
3. FILSSUY
4. GIILMRY

SET D

1. IILTTWY
2. ILLOSUY
3. ABDEILY
4. HILPSUY

SET E

1. IILMSTY
2. IILPSTY
3. ILNTTUY
4. ILORRSY

-INE

SET A

1. ACEHIMN
2. ACCEINV
3. AEGIIMN
4. CEIILNN

SET B

1. EFFILNO
2. AEIILNR
3. AEIINNS
4. BCEIMNO

SET C

1. CEIINSU
2. EIKLNSY
3. BEEEILN
4. BEIMNOR

SET D

1. CDEEILN
2. DEIILMN
3. EINORTU
4. CDEEINO

SET E

1. CEEILNR
2. CEFINNO
3. EEHILMN
4. EEINNTW

-ING

SET A

1. ABBDGIN
2. ABDEGIN
3. ABDGIIN
4. DFGGINU

SET B

1. EGHIMNS
2. GHINOOS
3. ADEGHIN
4. AGGINRU

SET C

1. AGIKNNS
2. DGINSSU
3. EGIKNOV
4. GIIKNNO

SET D

1. ABGINST
2. AGILNUV
3. AGINOPS
4. DGINNOU

SET E

1. EGINNOP
2. GIINNOR
3. AGGINRT
4. ACGILNP

SET F

1. DEFGINU
2. EEGINNV
3. EGINOTV
4. GIINSSU

-ION

SET A

1. ACFINOT
2. AINOORT
3. BIILLNO
4. CFIINOT

SET B

1. CHINOSU
2. AEINOSV
3. AINOSTT
4. CDIINOT

SET C

1. IINOTTU
2. IIMNOSS
3. DEIINOT
4. CINOSTU

SET D

1. EINOORS
2. IINNOOP
3. INOOPRT
4. EIMNNOT

-ISH

SET A

1. ABBHISY
2. AEHIKPS
3. AHIMNNS
4. BEHILMS

SET B

1. ABHILOS
2. AGHINSU
3. AGHIRSY
4. AHINRST

SET C

1. CEHHIRS
2. DHIPRSU
3. FHINRSU
4. HINORSU

SET D

1. CDHILSO
2. FHILOOS
3. GHIILRS
4. HILSSTY

-ISM

1. ACIMNRS
2. AEHIMST
3. EHIMORS
4. IMORSTU

-IST

SET A

1. ACINRST
2. AIINPST
3. CEHIMST
4. EIILSTT

SET B

1. ILOOSST
2. ADDFIST
3. BISSSTU
4. EFILSTT

SET C

1. FILORST
2. ILSSTTY
3. AHIPRST
4. CEILLST

SET D

1. EGIOSTT
2. FILSTTU
3. IORSTTU
4. ADIIRST

-ITE

1. BEEISTW
2. EEIRRTW
3. DEEIPST
4. DEEIRTU

-ITY

SET A	SET B
1. ABIILTY	1. ACILRTY
2. ACDIITY	2. ADILTUY
3. AIRSTVY	3. BEIRTVY
4. IILTTUY	4. AINNTUY

-IUM

1. ACCILMU
2. AIMNRUU
3. HIILMTU
4. ADIMSTU

-IVE

SET A	SET B
1. ABEISUV	1. ACEIPTV
2. BEEEHIV	2. CDEEEIV
3. EEFISTV	3. CEIRSUV
4. EFGIORV	4. EEILSUV

-IZE

SET A	SET B
1. ABEIPTZ	1. EIILNOZ
2. AEGINOZ	2. DEIILOZ
3. DEIIOXZ	3. DEIIMSZ
4. EEIIMTZ	4. EIILTUZ

-LAR

1. AEGLRRU
2. AELLRST
3. AIILMRS
4. ALOPPRU

-LIKE

SET A

1. ACEIKLT
2. AEIKLNU
3. BEEIKLW
4. EIKLNSU

SET B

1. EGIIKLW
2. AEFIKLN
3. AEIKLRW
4. EEIKLOT

SET C

1. EHIIKLP
2. EIKLOTY
3. AEIKLMN
4. DEIIKLS

SET D

1. EGIKLMU
2. EGIKLRU
3. EGIIKLP
4. DEGIKLO

-MAN

1. AABEMNS
2. AAGHMNN
3. AFGMNOR
4. AMNNOSW

-NAL

1. AADELNR
2. AAELNRS
3. ADILNOR
4. AILMNNO

-NCE

SET A

1. ACEFINN
2. CCEEINS
3. CEENOPT
4. ACEMNOR

SET B

1. ABCEENS
2. AACDENV
3. ACEEHNN
4. CEEENSS

-OID

1. ABDILOT
2. ADDEINO
3. DHIORTY
4. ACDFIOT

-OSE

SET A	SET B
1. ABCEOOS	1. EOPPSSU
2. AEMOOSV	2. AEOOPPS
3. CEELNOS	3. DEIOPSS
4. ELNOOSU	4. EOPPRSU

-OUS

SET A	SET B	SET C	SET D
1. ACLLOSU	1. DEIOSUV	1. IMNOOSU	1. CIIOSUV
2. AEGOSSU	2. ACORSUU	2. EIORSSU	2. EHINOSU
3. BDIOSUU	3. AFOSTUU	3. ACOSUUV	3. EIOPSTU
4. DEHIOSU	4. BIOOSUV	4. AINOSUX	4. ADORSUU

SET E

1. BFIORSU
2. CIORSUU
3. ENORSUV
4. FIORSUU

-OWN

1. DELNOTW
2. DNNORUW
3. GINNORW
4. DIMNOTW

-TIC

SET A	SET B
1. AACFINT	1. ACCEIST
2. ACCHIOT	2. ACCISTU
3. ACIPSST	3. ACILPST
4. CEEGINT	4. CIILOPT

-URE

SET A	SET B
1. ACEPRTU	1. EEGRSTU
2. AEEFRTU	2. CEOPRRU
3. AEFILRU	3. EEILRSU
4. CEELRTU	4. EENRTUV

Two-Letter Edges

When given a choice of two edges to search through when looking for seven- and eight-letter words, it's better to focus on the longer edge, because if there's a word that uses that edge, it will take less time to find it—because you'll have fewer letters to rearrange. However, there are many common two-letter edges that supply literally thousands of common words. So, just because you don't see a word having a three- or four-letter edge, that doesn't mean you won't find one with a two-letter edge.

With two-letter edges for seven-letter words, there are 120 permutations available for the remaining five letters, when all five are different. You're not going to want to go through all of them, but with practice you can systematically begin with one choice for the third letter and try to check out most of the possible ways the remaining four letters can be added before moving on to a different third letter. Don't concern yourself if it takes longer; again, you're training your brain to find the common ways that letters go together, and your brain will learn over time so that eventually you'll be able to anagram more easily in your head. And don't forget to pronounce them.

Front Edges

AB-
1. AABDNNO
2. AABINST
3. ABCDNOS
4. ABELOSV

AC-
1. AABCORT
2. AACCILM
3. AACDEMY
4. AACRTUY

AD-

1. AAADMNT
2. ADEEOPT
3. AADILMR
4. AADOPRT

AN-

SET A

1. AACHNRY
2. AAENNNT
3. AAMNOTY
4. AALMNOY

SET B

1. AAGLNRU
2. AAGLNOY
3. AEMNORY
4. AMNNOTY

BE-

SET A

1. ABBELOR
2. BDEEILV
3. BEEEILV
4. BBELLOY

SET B

1. ABDEEHV
2. ABEGINO
3. BCEHITW
4. BDEEIMT

BI-

1. ABCFILO
2. BCCEILY
3. BCIISTU
4. ABEILNP

BL-

1. ABEKLNT
2. BLMOOSS
3. BLOOTUW
4. ABELNRY

BR-

1. AABDORV
2. ABDEHRT
3. ABEKPRU
4. ABCDEOR

CH-

SET A	SET B
1. AACDEHR	1. ACEEHNP
2. ACEEHHT	2. ACEHLNN
3. ACEHNST	3. CEEHIOR
4. CEHIMNY	4. CEHLORT

CL-

1. CCEIKLR
2. CELORSU
3. CELOPSU
4. CELOSST

CR-

1. ACDERSU
2. CCEEIRV
3. CCERTUW
4. ACLRSTY

DE-

SET A	SET B	SET C	SET D
1. AADDENP	1. DEELOSU	1. DEEEFNS	1. CDEFNTU
2. ADEELUV	2. ACDEEES	2. DEEIIST	2. DDEGIMO
3. CDEEILN	3. ADEIILR	3. ACDERTT	3. DEEIPSS
4. DDDEELU	4. CDEFIIT	4. BCDEEIL	4. CDEMORU

EN-

SET A	SET B
1. ACEEHNN	1. AEFGNRT
2. ACEHNNT	2. AENNRTT
3. ACENORT	3. BEELNNO
4. ADEEGMN	4. CDEEIMN

EX-

SET A

1. ACEILMX
2. ACERTTX
3. AEEIMNX
4. AEEIPTX

SET B

1. AEILNPX
2. BEHIITX
3. CDEELUX
4. CEEPRTX

FL-

1. AEFLLNN
2. AEFLPRU
3. AABEFGL
4. AFLMOST

FR-

1. DEEFMOR
2. BEEFIRS
3. EFGLORT
4. AFGHRTU

GL-

1. BEGLLOU
2. EGILMPS
3. EGILRTT
4. AGLMORU

GR-

1. EGILMNR
2. ACEGIMR
3. GNOPRUW
4. EGIOPRU

IN-

SET A

1. ABHIINT
2. AEIINRT
3. BDINNOU
4. CEEINNS

SET B

1. CFIILNT
2. ACEINTX
3. AFINORS
4. BIILNTU

SET C

1. CEFILNT
2. DEIINRS
3. ACFINNY
4. AILLNST

SET D

1. BIKLNOT
2. CEIILNN
3. EEIINTV
4. ADIILNV

SET E

1. AINNSTT
2. BINRSTU
3. CEIINOV
4. EGHIINV

PL-

1. ABCELOP
2. AAELPTU
3. DLOOPWY
4. ACILNPY

RE-

SET A

1. ADEIMRT
2. ACERRTT
3. AEEFMRR
4. AEEGRRU

SET B

1. AEELNRW
2. AEFINRR
3. CCEELRY
4. AELMORV

SET C

1. BEILRTU
2. CEEIPRT
3. CEELRSU
4. CEIRRTU

SET D

1. CEORRTY
2. DDEOORW
3. DERSTUY
4. EEMORRS

SC-

1. AACDLNS
2. AACLPSU
3. ACDENNS
4. ACELLPS

SH-

1. AEHKPSU
2. AHMOOPS
3. BEEHRST
4. GHNOSTU

SP-

1. AANPRST
2. AALPSTU
3. DEIPRSY
4. NOOPRSS

ST-

SET A

1. AAIMNST
2. ABDNSTY
3. ACHMOST
4. AEHLSTT

SET B

1. AERSTTU
2. AILRSTT
3. CEHRSTT
4. EFPSTUY

TH-

1. AEHPRTY
2. AHORTTY
3. BEEHRTY
4. DEHNRTU

TR-

SET A

1. AACEHRT
2. AAILRTV
3. ACFFIRT
4. ACNRTUY

SET B

1. ACORRTT
2. AINRSTT
3. AIORRTT
4. DEINRTT

UN-

SET A

1. AAENRUW
2. ADEKNSU
3. AEHLNSU
4. CNORSSU

SET B

1. DINNSUW
2. ACDEGNU
3. ADENRUY
4. AINRTUY

SET C

1. DEGLNUU
2. EINQRUU
3. ACELNNU
4. AEEGNRU

SET D

1. BDNNOUU
2. ACLNPSU
3. FIMNORU
4. CENORUV

UP-

1. ABDIPRU
2. ACEHPRU
3. ADEGPRU
4. AEEHPUV

Back Edges

-AL

SET A

1. AACDILR
2. AADGLRU
3. AACFLTU
4. AALNRTU

SET B

1. ACILMSU
2. ACELNRT
3. ADEEFLR
4. AEILRSV

-CT

1. AACLPTY
2. AACRTTT
3. CEPSSTU
4. CEOPRTT

-ED

SET A

1. AADDERW
2. ABDEELL
3. ADEGLOT
4. ADELNPT

SET B

1. BDELSTU
2. AADELLY
3. ACCDERU
4. ADEGOVY

SET C

1. ADELRTT
2. CCDEESU
3. AADEMSS
4. ACDEEFT

SET D

1. ADEHMSS
2. ADELOTT
3. CDDEENO
4. ABCDEEH

SET E

1. ACDEEPS
2. ADEILLT
3. ADEMRTU
4. CDEEITV

-EE

1. AADEERW
2. ACEEEPS
3. ACEEEUV
4. ADEEFRT

-ER

SET A

1. ABDELNR
2. ACEHRTW
3. ADENPRR
4. AEERSTW

SET B

1. AEGNRTU
2. CEHRRSU
3. AEORRSU
4. DELORST

SET C

1. EERRSVW
2. BCEKLOR
3. AEGHLRU
4. EFFLMRU

SET D

1. AEILPPR
2. DDEELPR
3. AELLMRS
4. CEEHLRW

-IA

1. AAAHIPS
2. AAEGILR
3. AAIILPT
4. ABEHIMO

-IC

SET A

1. AACCHIR
2. ABCEIOR
3. ACCFIIP
4. ACDIMNY

SET B

1. ACIIRST
2. ACGINOR
3. CCEINRT
4. CCHINOR

-LY

SET A

1. AABILMY
2. AAFLLTY
3. ABDILRY
4. ABDLORY

SET B

1. ABELSTY
2. ACEHLPY
3. ACELLRY
4. ADEILLY

SET C

1. ADILRTY
2. AEHLPSY
3. AEEGLRY
4. AFILLNY

SET D

1. AILLTVY
2. ALMRSTY
3. ALLRRUY
4. BELORSY

SET E

1. BEFILRY
2. CELLRUY
3. BILOSSY
4. CLORTUY

-ND

1. ABDENRT
2. ADNOSTU
3. ADIKMNN
4. DDEGNOS

-ON

1. AAGNOPR
2. ABNOOSS
3. GLNOTTU
4. AHNOOPR

-RD

1. AACDLPR
2. AADERSW
3. AADIRRW
4. ABBDMOR

-RY

SET A	SET B	SET C	SET D
1. ABERRVY	1. ADEPRRY	1. AENNRTY	1. CEENRSY
2. ABERTTY	2. ADLNRUY	2. AILRRVY	2. CEMRRUY
3. ABILRRY	3. AEGIMRY	3. AIMPRRY	3. EFILRRY
4. ACEHRRY	4. AELRSVY	4. AOORRTY	4. ELORTTY

-UM

SET A	SET B
1. ADEMRRU	1. DHLMOOU
2. AMNRTTU	2. IMMOPTU
3. CDIMMOU	3. MOOPPSU
4. CFLMRUU	4. AMRSTTU

Three-Letter Edges: A Potpourri

Find the seven-letter words in each set below. Each word either begins and/or ends with one or more of the following edges:

Front: COM-, CON-, DIS-, FOR-, MIS-, OUT-, OVER-, PRE-, PRO-, SUB-

Back: -AGE, -AND, -ANT, -ATE, -BLE, -ENT, -ERS, -ESS, -FUL, -GUE, -IAL, -IDE, -IER, -IES, -IFY, -ILE, -ILY, -INE, -ING, -ION, -ISH, -ISM, -IST, -ITE, -ITY, -IUM, -IVE, -IZE, -LAR, -LIKE, -MAN, -NAL, -NCE, -OID, -OSE, -OUS, -OWN, -TIC, -URE

If more than one edge might be correct, check out the more likely edge first. For example, in Set A no. 1, you can see -ING and -IUM. There are many more -ING words than -IUM words, so try that edge first.

SET A

1. AGIMNSU
2. EFIIMRS
3. CCENOPT
4. AFGIMNY

SET B

1. EINNORU
2. DEGGHIN
3. CEMMNOU
4. DDEINST

SET C

1. CEMNOSU
2. EMOOPRT
3. EHIKSSU
4. ALOSTTU

SET D

1. BESTTUX
2. ABGLRRU
3. ADGILNO
4. AEFGIRT

SET E

1. ABELLOV
2. EIILMSV
3. AEFILNT
4. BEIIKLR

SET F

1. CCIPRTY
2. BHILPSU
3. AENNRTT
4. AEGSTUV

SET G

1. EFGIOOR
2. AEFGORV
3. ABBELUY
4. EFLOSTU

SET H

1. EFOPRSU
2. AHILLST
3. FGIINSY
4. DEIORSS

SET I

1. ABELLMN
2. DINNOPR
3. AEIPSTT
4. BDEEIKL

SET J

1. EGORTUW
2. BEILMSU
3. CGIINPS
4. EEGIKLL

SET K

1. ABGLOSU
2. CDEOPRU
3. ELOSSTW
4. AEMNRTV

SET L

1. AAEEGRV
2. EMNORTT
3. AEMORRV
4. DOOORTU

SET M

1. AENNNPT
2. BDEFOOR
3. ELNOSTV
4. AEFIMNR

SET N

1. DIORSTT
2. IOORSTU
3. FILLNUY
4. BDEIIRS

SET O

1. ABEILSZ
2. AEGORTU
3. EEILPRU
4. DEEIIST

SET P

1. ACDIMMU
2. ILNNOPS
3. AEGHOST
4. DEEFHLU

SET Q

1. AEEGORV
2. AEEIRRW
3. ACCDEEN
4. BEHIRSU

SET R

1. AEFHLTU
2. AHILSTY
3. AABEGRR
4. CLNOSTU

SET S

1. BEIOOST
2. AELPSTU
3. AGIILTY
4. BEORUVY

SET T

1. EFIRRTY
2. CCEINOS
3. AEGLMPU
4. CIMOPSY

SET U

1. CFMOORT
2. EEHIPSV
3. CDENNOT
4. AHIMNNU

SET V

1. AEIPRTV
2. DFILTUU
3. AINOPSS
4. FHIORRY

SET W

1. AAEGNTV
2. CEMOPTU
3. IILOSTV
4. BCMOSTU

SET X

1. DIILLST
2. FLMOORU
3. ACELLOT
4. BDEIOSY

SET Y

1. DEIOORW
2. AMOORSU
3. AAELNST
4. AAEGTTW

SET Z

1. BHIOORS
2. INNOSTU
3. ALNPSTU
4. CEIIKNT

SET AA

1. EGILORS
2. AANRRTW
3. CIOOPSU
4. AGMOPRR

SET AB

1. ABELOPT
2. KNNNOUW
3. INNOSTU
4. FGILOOY

SET AC

1. ACDMMNO
2. CEFLNOU
3. AGIKNOS
4. ACEORTU

SET AD

1. BLOPSTU
2. EEEORSV
3. AEIKLSW
4. EEMPPRT

SET AE

1. AELOPTU
2. AEEGSTT
3. DEILSTW
4. BDISSUY

SET AF

1. ADEEHIR
2. CEOPRTT
3. AEFGOOT
4. DDEIIOX

SET AG

1. AABELPY
2. ABEGMRU
3. HOOSTTU
4. EGNNPTU

SET AH

1. ACNRRTU
2. EIRSUVV
3. CEGIILN
4. EILMRSU

SET AI

1. AEEISST
2. BDDEISU
3. ACILNTU
4. ADGINOR

SET AJ

1. ACDIRST
2. EIIRTTW
3. EIINSTU
4. AEFOPRW

SET AK

1. AINOOTV
2. AEIKMST
3. ACEMOPR
4. ADILPSY

SET AL

1. EFGNOOR
2. IKMOOST
3. BHINRSU
4. FIMORTY

SET AM

1. LNNOPSU
2. EEIMPRR
3. CDISSSU
4. EELPRTZ

SET AN

1. ADINSTT
2. ACCILRU
3. FFIORTY
4. EFFIORT

SET AO

1. ACEHNNT
2. ADEEFPR
3. AEEGPRS
4. ACEENNP

SET AP

1. CEFIPSY
2. BDEIORV
3. OOPSTTU
4. EMOOPRT

SET AQ

1. AHILSSV
2. FLNOORR
3. FIMSTYY
4. DIKNNOS

SET AR

1. CCILSTY
2. CENORTV
3. AFMNOOT
4. DEGINNY

SET AS

1. AILOSTU
2. EEGRSTY
3. AIIILNT
4. EEEIKLY

SET AT

1. ENNOORZ
2. ACEGOTT
3. AEMNNSW
4. DNOPTUW

SET AU

1. ABEFILX
2. EEFGLOR
3. BHIRSTU
4. AEEOPRT

SET AV

1. DELLSTU
2. ENORRTT
3. DEELPRU
4. EFIPRTY

Two-Letter Edges: A Potpourri

Find the seven-letter words in each set below. Each word either begins and/or ends with one or more of the following two-letter edges:

Front: AB-, AC-, AN-, BE-, BI-, CH-, CR-, DE-, EN-, EX-, IN-, RE-, ST-, SC-, TR-, TH-, UN-, UP-

Back: -AL, -CT, -ED, -EE, -IA, -IC, -LY, -ND, -ON, -RD, -RY

SET A

1. AABELNO
2. DEGLNNO
3. HOOPSTU
4. ACLNPSU

SET B

1. BEEEGIS
2. EIPRRST
3. HPRTTUU
4. GHIPRTU

SET C

1. ENOPSST
2. ACHNOVY
3. DEELOPX
4. EHINNRT

SET D

1. BEFILOU
2. DEMNOST
3. ACEEHIV
4. IILMSTU

SET E

1. EEGGNOR
2. AEENNTU
3. DEERTUX
4. ACEENOT

SET F

1. ACMNORY
2. EEEMRTX
3. EEILNTT
4. CENORUV

SET G

1. AACCLSU
2. AGILNRY
3. ELNRSTY
4. CEIIMPR

SET H

1. EERSTTU
2. EGPRSUU
3. ABGINSU
4. CEEGINR

SET I

1. AAINRTW
2. ABEGHRU
3. EMPRTTU
4. DEFILPU

SET J

1. AABLMSY
2. CDEIMNO
3. ABDIMNR
4. CEENRSY

SET K

1. ABELSTY
2. DEEEOTV
3. EEHNORT
4. CEILNOX

SET L

1. BCEHIOT
2. CEIIMSS
3. CDEEKLR
4. DEELOPR

SET M

1. CEHNTUY
2. EHIINRT
3. ABDEETT
4. BDEILOR

SET N

1. BGILOOY
2. EILOPTX
3. GHHOTTU
4. CFFHINO

SET O

1. ABDEMNO
2. CEILMPR
3. EIINQRU
4. AACDINT

SET P

1. AABGEGN
2. CEHOORT
3. EEENPSX
4. CDEHOPP

SET Q

1. ACELOTY
2. AAAGMNR
3. BIILLNO
4. CEHINOR

SET R

1. BCDEKOR
2. EEHNSTU
3. DEINRSU
4. DFNNOUU

SET S

1. CDEIKRR
2. ADMMNSU
3. EFFINST
4. ACEMNRW

SET T

1. CEFFLSU
2. GILORTY
3. COPRTUU
4. AACDDRW

SET U

1. ADDEEGR
2. EILNOVV
3. CEPRSUW
4. CEIMNRU

SET V

1. CDEOSTU
2. EEHMORT
3. IINRTTY
4. CGIILLO

SET W

1. FGHIINT
2. BCLMRUY
3. AAIMMNO
4. DENORUW

SET X

1. CELPRSU
2. EGGIRRT
3. EEEIRRV
4. CEOQRTU

SET Y

1. DEMNOUV
2. AEINPTU
3. ADEILRV
4. CIILNOS

SET Z

1. EEGMRRS
2. EGHNRSU
3. EEEGNRV
4. DEGNNOU

SET AA

1. AEIOQSU
2. ABDDEES
3. ACDHORR
4. EINNOSV

SET AB

1. EEEILRV
2. EEMPRST
3. DENOPUX
4. BFFNOOU

SET AC

1. EFGLORS
2. AIIILMT
3. ACDEHRT
4. EEGIMNR

SET AD

1. AIIMNTU
2. EELORSV
3. EFRRSSU
4. DDEINPS

SET AE

1. DEELLRY
2. EENRRTY
3. CEEGLNT
4. ACDRSTU

SET AF

1. AILRTUV
2. ADDEHIR
3. AIILMMN
4. ELORTTY

SET AG

1. ADDLLRU
2. EFLORWY
3. AELNRTV
4. ELORSUY

SET AH

1. AELRRSU
2. CDEIRTV
3. ADLORRW
4. CDEISST

SET AI

1. EHIORSY
2. AFLNORT
3. CCELLOT
4. CEEEELT

SET AJ

1. BEEEILL
2. DEELNSY
3. EEEEFRR
4. EILMPTY

EIGHT-LETTER ALPHAGRAMS

Four-Letter Edges

Although eight-letter words can be harder to find, the principle of edge power remains the same. And there are significantly more common eights with four-letter edges than there are sevens with four-letter edges.

Front Edges

ANTI-
1. AAEIKLNT
2. AAIKNNTT
3. ACIKLNOT
4. ADIIKNST

FORE-

SET A	SET B
1. ADEEFHOR	1. DEFLOORT
2. ADEFHNOR	2. DEFOORRW
3. AEFNORRW	3. EFFOOORT
4. BEFILMOR	4. EFMOORST

HAND-
1. AACDHINP
2. AADDEHMN
3. AADHILNR
4. ADEHNNSW

HEAD-
1. AABDDEHN
2. ACDEHKLO
3. ADEEHRST
4. ADEHHNTU

OVER-

SET A
1. ABEEKORV
2. ACEEMORV
3. DEEIORRV
4. EELORRUV

SET B
1. ADEEHORV
2. ADEIOPRV
3. EENOORTV
4. EEIMORTV

SET C
1. AEEFLORV
2. AEEORRTV
3. AELOPRVY
4. BEEIORTV

POST-
1. ACDOPRST
2. ADEOPSTT
3. ADIOPPST
4. ADGOPRST

Back Edges

-ABLE

SET A
1. AABBEELT
2. AABEELRS
3. AABEGLRU
4. ABCDEELU

SET B
1. AABEHKLS
2. AABCEILM
3. AABEILRS
4. ABBDELNO

SET C
1. ABBELOPR
2. AABELLPY
3. ABCELTTU
4. AABBEELR

SET D
1. AABELPSS
2. AABDEELR
3. AABELLPP
4. AABEEHLR

-ALLY

SET A
1. AACLLRSY
2. AALLNNUY
3. AFLLMORY
4. ALLMNORY

SET B
1. ABELLRVY
2. ABLLRTUY
3. ACILLOSY
4. AILLSUVY

-ANCE
1. AABCEIMN
2. AACEINRV
3. ABCEINRV
4. ACEINNSU

-ATOR

SET A	SET B
1. AADIORRT	1. AEOOPRRT
2. AAGIORTT	2. AGIMORRT
3. AAIMNORT	3. AIIMORTT
4. ABIORRTV	4. AILOORTV

-BACK
1. AABBCEKR
2. AABCIKLT
3. ABCCEKMO
4. ABCFKOST

-BALL
1. AABBELLS
2. AABELLMT
3. ABEFILLR
4. ABFLLOOT

-ENCE
1. ACDEEINU
2. CDEENPRU
3. CEEEIMNN
4. CEEILNOV

-ETTE
1. BEENRTTU
2. EEELMOTT
3. EEGINTTV
4. EELORTTU

-FISH
1. ACFHIRSW
2. AFHIRSST
3. DFGHILOS
4. BEFHILSU

-HEAD

1. ABDEEHNO
2. AADDEHHR
3. ADEEHORS
4. AADEHILN

-IBLE

1. BEEILRRT
2. BEEILNSS
3. ABEEFILS
4. BEEGIILL

-ICAL

SET A	SET B
1. AACCILTT	1. ABBCIILL
2. AACILMOT	2. ACEHILOR
3. AACILNTU	3. ACGILRSU
4. ACCEILLR	4. ACHILMTY

-IEST

SET A	SET B	SET C
1. ACEFINST	1. ADEGISTU	1. AEHIIRST
2. ACEIKSTT	2. ADEHIRST	2. AEIKLNST
3. BEHISSTU	3. BEIMPSTU	3. CEIRSTUV
4. DEISSSTU	4. DEIINSTW	4. DEGIPSTU

-IGHT

SET A	SET B
1. ADGHILTY	1. GHIILTTW
2. AGGHILST	2. GHIKLSTY
3. DFGGHIOT	3. AGHIIRTT
4. FGGHINTU	4. GHIORTTU

-INGS

SET A	SET B
1. ACGILLNS	1. AGGINRST
2. ADGILNRS	2. AGHINSSV
3. ABEGINST	3. AGIILNRS
4. AEGIMNNS	4. AGIKMNRS

-LAND

1. AADDEHLN
2. AADFLMNR
3. ADEHLMNO
4. ACDLNOPR

-LATE

SET A	SET B
1. AABELTTU	1. AACEELST
2. ADEELOST	2. ADELNTUU
3. ADELMOTU	3. AEILMSTU
4. AEEGLRTU	4. AELOPPTU

-LESS

SET A	SET B
1. ADEEHLSS	1. ACEEFLSS
2. AEEFLLSS	2. AEEHLSST
3. AEHLMRSS	3. AEILNRSS
4. BEILLMSS	4. CEEKLRSS

-LIER

SET A	SET B
1. AACEILRV	1. CEEILMOR
2. AEEILMRS	2. DEIILMPR
3. AEGILNRR	3. EEEILMRS
4. CDDEILRU	4. EEIILLRV

-LIKE

SET A

1. ABEEIKLN
2. AEEIKLVW
3. AEIKLOPS
4. EEFIIKLL

SET B

1. ACEEIKLL
2. AEHIIKLR
3. ADEIKLLY
4. EEEIKLRT

SET C

1. ADEHIKLN
2. AEIIKLLT
3. DEEIIKLT
4. DEIKLMRU

-LINE

SET A

1. AAEIKLLN
2. ADDEEILN
3. ADEILLNN
4. AEGILNOS

SET B

1. CEEIKLNN
2. BEILNNTU
3. DEEIILNS
4. EEFIILLN

-LIST

1. AAFILSTT
2. ACILOSTV
3. ADEIILST
4. EILNOSTV

-MENT

SET A

1. ABEEMNST
2. AEFGMNRT
3. AEMNNORT
4. EEEMNNTT

SET B

1. EEMMNOTV
2. EIMNNOTT
3. EHIMNPST
4. EMMNNOTU

-NESS

SET A

1. ACEHINSS
2. ADEGLNSS
3. ADEENRSS
4. AEELNSST

SET B

1. ACELMNSS
2. ADEKNRSS
3. AEENNSST
4. CEHINRSS

-OUSE

1. ADEHMOSU
2. AEEHOSTU
3. CEEHIOSU
4. EFHNOSUU

-RATE

1. AACEELRT
2. ABEEILRT
3. ADEEMORT
4. AEELORTT

-ROOM

1. ABHMOORT
2. ACHMOORT
3. AEMNOORT
4. AILMMOOR

-SHIP

1. ADHHIPRS
2. ADHILPSY
3. AFGHILPS
4. HINOPSTW

-SOME

1. ADEHMNOS
2. AEEFMORS
3. EEIMORST
4. EILMOOST

-STER

SET A

1. ADEORRST
2. AEEMRSTT
3. AEGGNRST
4. EEEMRSST

SET B

1. EHOOPRST
2. EINPRSST
3. ELLOPRST
4. EEGIRRST

-TION

SET A	SET B
1. ACFINORT	1. AINOORTT
2. ACIINNOT	2. EINOPRTU
3. ADDIINOT	3. GIMNOPTU
4. AAIINOTV	4. EIINOPTT

-TIVE

SET A	SET B
1. AADEIPTV	1. ADEIOPTV
2. AAEILTVX	2. ACEIRTUV
3. EIIOPSTV	3. ACEIINTV
4. EEIPRTUV	4. EFGIITUV

-TORY

1. ADIORTUY
2. DIMORSTY
3. INOPRTUY
4. AALORTVY

-TURE

1. AAEMRRTU
2. ACEERRTU
3. AEEPRRTU
4. CENPRTUU

-ULAR

1. AACLRSUV
2. ABGLLORU
3. ACCILRRU
4. AGILNRSU

-WORK

1. ADKOORRW
2. BDKOORWY
3. DKOOORWW
4. EHKMOORW

Front Edges

COM-

1. ACILMNOP
2. ACLMMNOU
3. CDMNOOPU
4. CCEEMMOR

CON-

SET A

1. ACCNORTT
2. CEFINOTT
3. ACNORSTT
4. CCDELNOU

SET B

1. CCEENORT
2. CDEINORS
3. CEEGNORV
4. CEINORTV

DIS-

SET A

1. ACDIILMS
2. AADIRRSY
3. ADDEISSU
4. ADEEGIRS

SET B

1. DEEHILSV
2. CDEIILPS
3. DDEIORRS
4. DEILOSSV

FOR-

1. ABDFILOR
2. AEFKNORS
3. EFORRSTY
4. FHOOORST

MIS-

SET A

1. AADIMPST
2. AEGIMSSU
3. AIILMRST
4. BDIILMSU

SET B

1. CIMNOSTU
2. DEGIIMSU
3. EIIMRSTW
4. EIMNPSST

NON-

SET A

1. AAFLNNOT
2. ADINNORY
3. AEGLNNOR
4. CIKNNOST

SET B

1. CINNOOTX
2. EENNNOSS
3. EILNNOTT
4. ENNOORTV

OUT-

SET A

1. ABDOORTU
2. ACHMOTTU
3. AMORSTTU
4. BDNOOTUU

SET B

1. ADELOTUW
2. AFKLNOTU
3. BORSTTUU
4. DEFILOTU

SET C

1. EHINOSTU
2. DIKNORTU
3. EGOSSTUU
4. FGHIOTTU

PRE-

SET A

1. CDEELPRU
2. BEHIPRRT
3. CCEINPRT
4. CEEENPRS

SET B

1. EEGIPRST
2. DEEMPRSU
3. EEEIMPRR
4. DEEOPRRR

PRO-

SET A

1. ACLOPRRU
2. ADGILOPR
3. AEOPRSTT
4. CEHOPPRY

SET B

1. CEINOPRV
2. EEEGOPRT
3. CLOOOPRT
4. DFNOOPRU

SUB-

SET A

1. ABCEPSSU
2. ABCRSTTU
3. ABEELSSU
4. ABELNPSU

SET B

1. ABHMNSUU
2. BEEGMRSU
3. BEILSTTU
4. BGOPRSUU

Back Edges

-AGE

SET A	SET B
1. AACEEGLV	1. AAEGIMRR
2. AABEGOST	2. ABBCEGIR
3. AAEEGMPR	3. ACEEGKRW
4. AAEGGLNU	4. AEGILOPS

-AND

1. AABDEHNR
2. ABDDENST
3. ADGHLNNO
4. ADGMNORU

-ANT

SET A	SET B
1. AABDNNTU	1. ABDENTTU
2. AACENRTT	2. ACEHNNPT
3. AAEHNPST	3. AEEHLNPT
4. AAGNNSTT	4. AELNORTT

-ATE

SET A	SET B	SET C	SET D
1. AABCDEIT	1. AADEEIRT	1. AADEILTV	1. ABEGILOT
2. AABCDETK	2. AADEGRTU	2. ABCEINTU	2. ACDDEEIT
3. AACDEOTV	3. AAEGILTT	3. AAENNOTT	3. AEEEMPRT
4. AACELLOT	4. AAEGNSTT	4. ACEEERRT	4. AEIIRRTT

-BLE

1. BCEFILOR
2. ABEEFILS
3. BEEGIILL
4. BEHILORR

-ENT

SET A

1. AACDEJNT
2. AEFFLNTU
3. CEINNNOT
4. EEENRRTV

SET B

1. EEHINNRT
2. EEINNPTT
3. EEEGMNRT
4. DEGIILNT

-ESS

SET A

1. ABENORSS
2. ACEHINSS
3. ADEEHLSS
4. ADELORSS

SET B

1. AEEMNNSS
2. AEHLMRSS
3. AEIINRSS
4. AELRSSST

SET C

1. CEELLSSU
2. DEEEHLSS
3. DEGNOOSS
4. EEFILLSS

-EST

SET A

1. ABEEKLST
2. ACEELNST
3. DENOSSTU
4. DEIISTVV

SET B

1. ABELSSTT
2. DEIMMOST
3. EGNOSTUY
4. AELLMSST

-FUL

SET A

1. ACEEFLPU
2. ACEFGLRU
3. AEFHLMSU
4. AFHKLNTU

SET B

1. BDFLOTUU
2. BFILLSSU
3. CFLLOORU
4. DEFILPRU

-GUE

1. AAEGHNRU
2. ADEGILOU
3. EEGILOPU
4. EGIINRTU

-IAL

SET A

1. AAEILMRT
2. AAEILRRT
3. ABEIILNN
4. ACFFIILO

SET B

1. ABIILMNO
2. ACILLNOO
3. AEIILMPR
4. AILORTTU

-IDE

1. BCDEIRSU
2. CCDEIINO
3. DEILOOPS
4. DDEILMSU

-IER

SET A

1. ABEEILRR
2. AEFHILRS
3. CEIIKRST
4. EGHIIMRT

SET B

1. ACCEHIRT
2. AEGIINRR
3. DEIRRSTU
4. EFIIPRRU

SET C

1. ADEIINRT
2. CEEIRRSW
3. EEINORRR
4. EIIKNRST

-IES

SET A

1. AAEIIRSV
2. ABEEIKRS
3. AEEFISST
4. AEFIIRST

SET B

1. ACEEGINS
2. ADEEISST
3. AEEIRRST
4. AEIINSTV

SET C

1. ACEFIIPS
2. ACEIISTV
3. AEFIILMS
4. CEEIINST

-IFY

1. ABEFITUY
2. ACFILSSY
3. DEFIINTY
4. FIILMPSY

-ILE

1. AEILLOTV
2. CDEIILMO
3. EEIJLNUV
4. ADEILNPS

-ILY

SET A	SET B
1. ACIKLNRY	1. CEEHILRY
2. ADEILSTY	2. DEILRSSY
3. AEGILRSY	3. DEEGILRY
4. BEEILRYZ	4. EILPRTTY

-INE

SET A	SET B
1. AAEGIMNZ	1. EEFIIMNN
2. ADEIMNOP	2. EIINPRST
3. AEIMNOPT	3. EFGIINRU
4. CEHILNOR	4. EFILNORU

-ING

SET A	SET B	SET C
1. AAGIILNV	1. ABGIINNR	1. ACEGIMNN
2. ADGIINOR	2. ACGIKNOR	2. ACGINNRU
3. AFGGINOR	3. AEGGILLN	3. AEGILNNR
4. EFGINRTU	4. CGHINOOS	4. AGILNNRS

-ION

SET A	SET B
1. AABINORS	1. ACCINOOS
2. ADEHINOS	2. ACHIMNOP
3. AIILNOPV	3. BIILNOOV
4. CDEIINOS	4. CINOOPRS

-ISH

1. EEFHIRSV
2. HIIKMRSS
3. AHILLMSS
4. AHINOSST

-ISM

1. ACIIMSTV
2. ADIMMNSY
3. AILLMOSY
4. CEIMORSX

-IST

SET A	SET B
1. AAILMRST	1. DEHINOST
2. ABINOSTT	2. EFIIMNST
3. AHIOPRST	3. IMOORSTT
4. BBILOSTY	4. FIRSTTUU

-ITE

SET A	SET B
1. ADEIMNTY	1. EEHIMOST
2. AEEIPPTT	2. EFIIINNT
3. AEFIORTV	3. EIILMOPT
4. AEGHIPRT	4. EIOOPPST

-ITY

SET A	SET B
1. AACDITUY	1. ADIIPRTY
2. AAFILTTY	2. AEGILLTY
3. ACEINTTY	3. AILOPRTY
4. ACIITTVY	4. CDIILTUY

-IUM

1. AEGIMNRU
2. AIIMNTTU
3. DEIILMRU
4. EIMMOPRU

-IVE

SET A	SET B
1. ADEEHISV	1. AEIINSVV
2. AABEIRSV	2. DEIORTUV
3. DEEINOSV	3. EEFFISUV
4. CEEEIPRV	4. DEIIISVV

-IZE

SET A	SET B
1. ABEINRUZ	1. AEEGILLZ
2. ACEILLOZ	2. AEFIILNZ
3. ACEINNOZ	3. AEIIRSTZ
4. ADEEIILZ	4. BEIILMOZ

-MAN

SET A	SET B
1. AACHMNNR	1. AEEMNRVY
2. AADIMNRY	2. AEHMNOSU
3. AACHIMNR	3. AFMNNORT
4. ABELMNNO	4. AEMNPRSU

-NAL

SET A	SET B
1. AAELNOSS	1. AAELMNRT
2. AACDILNR	2. AEILNNRT
3. AAILNNOT	3. AGIILNOR
4. ACIILMNR	4. AEELNRTX

-NCE

SET A	SET B
1. ACEEILNS	1. ACEEGNNT
2. CCEENNOS	2. CCEINNOV
3. CEEEILNN	3. CCDEEENR
4. CEEENNST	4. CEELNOPU

-OID

1. AADINOPR
2. ADEIORST
3. CDHIIOSZ
4. ADHIMNOU

-OSE

1. ACEMOOST
2. CEFORSTU
3. EGMNOOOS
4. DEEORSTX

-OUS

SET A	SET B
1. ABFLOSUU	1. CELORSUU
2. AENORSUV	2. DEIORSSU
3. ALOORSUV	3. DNOORSUW
4. BEILLOSU	4. EEGNORSU

-OWN

1. CDKLNOOW
2. CDLNOOOW
3. DELMNOTW
4. DHNOSTUW

-TIC

SET A	SET B
1. ABCDEIIT	1. AACCGILT
2. ACCIOSTU	2. ACDEINPT
3. ACEIOPRT	3. ACIIRSTT
4. ACIMNORT	4. CGIILOST

-URE

1. ACEIMNRU
2. AEELPRSU
3. BCEHORRU
4. CDEEIPRU

Three-Letter Edges: A Potpourri of Eights

Find the eight-letter words in the following sets, each of which includes one or more of the following three-letter edges:

Front: CON-, DIS-, MIS-, OUT-, PRE-, PRO-, SUB-

Back: -AGE, -ANT, -ATE, -ENT, -EST, -FUL, -GUE, -IAL, -IDE, -IER, -IES, -IFY, -ILE, -INE, -ING, -ION, -ISH, -ISM, -IST, -ITE, -ITY, -IUM, -IVE, -IZE, -NAL, -OSE, -OUS, -OWN, -TIC

SET A

1. ACEILOVZ
2. DEEFIINT
3. AAFGLNRT
4. AHIILRTY

SET B

1. BBHINOSS
2. AAELNRTX
3. CCEENRST
4. ACEGINPR

SET C

1. AGIINNTT
2. AEILOPRZ
3. DEEILTUY
4. ACCIRSTY

SET D

1. ADIILTVY
2. DEFIIMOS
3. ACEEHPST
4. AINORSST

SET E

1. AEFIMNST
2. AEEINRSU
3. AADELPTY
4. ACDEFNOW

SET F

1. CEIILLPT
2. ACEHMNRT
3. ALNPPSTU
4. AEEGIRRS

SET G

1. EIINNOSV
2. AEFLLPTU
3. AEIINSTZ
4. DFIILOSY

SET H

1. ACEFIRRT
2. ABGILNOR
3. EEIMQSTU
4. AAEEILNT

SET I

1. ADEEIMRR
2. CEEIKNST
3. GIOORSUV
4. DEILOOPW

SET J

1. EEHINNRS
2. AAEEMMTT
3. AEEGGINR
4. CDEIITWY

SET K

1. AEINOPRT
2. BDEEIMOS
3. ACFINSTY
4. AEILSTWY

SET L

1. BEILMNST
2. ACEFIIPR
3. AGIMNORS
4. ABEEEGRV

SET M

1. AACDIMRT
2. AEIORSTT
3. CDEOORSU
4. AGIINPRT

SET N

1. AEMRSTTU
2. ABEEFILT
3. FHIILLTY
4. CEEINRTT

SET O

1. AILLNOST
2. ABEEGIRV
3. CEFILMRU
4. AEISSSTY

SET P

1. AEGINSTW
2. ENNOOPPT
3. CEIIINSV
4. AFGIMNTU

SET Q

1. EEIINSTT
2. ADKMNORW
3. IIMNOOSS
4. AEGGMORT

SET R

1. CCEIMOST
2. EEIILSTV
3. EFIILSTY
4. AEIMNRSU

SET S

1. ACGIKNRT
2. ADHIMNOS
3. EIILLSUV
4. ACFIILTY

SET T

1. CEILMRSU
2. IIMOPSTT
3. DFHIIMUY
4. AEGOPPST

SET U

1. ADEGNOPU
2. EMNOORSU
3. AEFFGOST
4. AEFLSTUW

SET V

1. GIMNORSW
2. ADEGINRY
3. AEEIKNRS
4. FGLNORUW

SET W

1. FIINNOSU
2. EINNRTTU
3. ACDIIJLU
4. ADDEIORS

SET X

1. EEINSTTW
2. ACILNOSU
3. CDEHIIMO
4. ACILNSTY

SET Y

1. EILOPRSU
2. DGGIRSTU
3. AIINNSTY
4. CFLNORSU

SET Z

1. ACENNOTV
2. AACELLOT
3. EHINNSSU
4. ADFILRTY

SET AA

1. EILNRTUV
2. AEILMMOR
3. GIOORRSU
4. AEGHORST

SET AB

1. CEINORTV
2. AEGGLNPT
3. AACEEIMT
4. AAEMPTTU

Compound Eight-Letter Words

Eight-letter words that are composed of two four-letter words sitting side by side, like BOATYARD, can be some of the toughest words to find. Often they have no common edges, and the letters don't go together in any typical pattern. If you have a rack with fairly common letters but see no edges that work, you might look for four-letter words that might be part of a compound eight-letter word.

Below are sixteen sets of this type of compound eight. As a hint in the first eight sets, the first letter of each four-letter component is underlined. How many can you find?

SET A

1. ABCDILLR
2. ADOPRSSW
3. AEEHRTVW
4. AEEIMMNT

SET B

1. AEELLLTT
2. AEFILNPS
3. AEHMOSTW
4. AEMMOORT

SET C

1. AHHIPLSW
2. AHNOPSST
3. BBNORSTU
4. EHILMOOR

SET D

1. BDKNOOOR
2. CEIKLOSV
3. ABHOOSTW
4. AADDLLNY

SET E

1. AACINORT
2. AACHILNP
3. AACEMRSS
4. AACDELOS

SET F

1. AACCKORT
2. AACCHLOR
3. AABKLLPR
4. AABDLOOT

SET G

1. AABCEKLM
2. AABCCEHK
3. AAACSTWY
4. AAABDEST

SET H

1. AADHLPSS
2. AADKLMNR
3. AAEEKMNS
4. AAEFLMOT

SET I

1. AAEGRSTZ
2. ABBDHIRT
3. ABBEORTW
4. ABCDEFLO

SET J

1. ABDDELOT
2. ABEFHOOT
3. ABEFILOT
4. ABEFOORT

SET K

1. ABEIKNRS
2. ABEILNOT
3. ACCEEKLN
4. ADOOPRRT

SET L

1. ADRSSTTU
2. ADINOPRR
3. ADEIKLSW
4. ADEEHMMO

SET M

1. ACNORTTU
2. ACEPSTTY
3. ACENORRW
4. ACEKOORW

SET N

1. ACEIKMNN
2. ACEFIMPR
3. ACEEKNRW
4. ACEEIRSW

SET O

1. ACEEFPTY
2. ACDFFHNU
3. ACDEHKRU
4. DEFIILRW

SET P

1. DEIINPPW
2. DHILLNOW
3. DIILLMNW
4. DNOOPRUW

More Compound Eights

Each of the following sets includes only common compound words that are composed of a five-letter word and a three-letter word sitting side by side, though not necessarily in that order. How many can you find?

SET A	SET B	SET C	SET D
1. DEELNWWY	1. AHOPSTUW	1. AACHINSW	1. AAEKLMRW
2. DEEHNOWY	2. BCDEEORV	2. AACELNPY	2. ABDHMOTU
3. AEEHNOPR	3. CHORSTTU	3. AABDEKRY	3. ABEEIKRT
4. AEHLNTUZ	4. ACCEHKPY	4. AAEGIMNO	4. ABEOPPRY

SET E	SET F
1. ACCKOPRT	1. ACPSSTUY
2. ACDEOPRS	2. ADEFFORT
3. ACEHIPTW	3. ADGNNORS
4. ACEILLPS	4. BDEEEHST

ANSWERS

Six-Letter Alphagrams

B:

SET A: BANANA, ABATED, BALLAD, ARABLE
SET B: AIRBAG, BOBCAT, ABDUCT, BECAME
SET C: BLEACH, BEACON, FABRIC, COBALT
SET D: BEHEAD, DEBATE, BAITED, BANDIT
SET E: ABOUND, ABSURD, BEHAVE, BEATEN
SET F: BAFFLE, BEHALF, GAMBLE, HERBAL
SET G: VIABLE, EMBARK, BAKERY, BASKET
SET H: VERBAL, BEMOAN, BATTER, BUREAU
SET I: GAMBIT, BANISH, PHOBIA, ALBINO
SET J: BARIUM, BALLOT, BRUTAL, TURBAN
SET K: BOTANY, AUBURN, ABRUPT, SUBWAY
SET L: PEBBLE, SUBURB, BREECH, CHERUB
SET M: BISECT, BUCKET, BOUNCE, BLOTCH
SET N: PUBLIC, COWBOY, BESIDE, OBEYED
SET O: BUDGET, BEHIND, DOUBLE, FORBID
SET P: HYBRID, TIDBIT, OUTBID, BEETLE
SET Q: BEFORE, EMBLEM, BUFFET, OBLIGE
SET R: BELONG, HUMBLE, BITTER, BUTLER
SET S: NUMBER, EMBRYO, BONNET, BESTOW

SET T: BIGWIG, BOUGHT, OBLONG, BISHOP
SET U: SUBMIT, BUNION, SYMBOL, BOTTOM
SET V: BUTTON, BOUNTY, BORROW, UNBORN

C:

SET A: ARCADE, PALACE, FACIAL, ATTACH
SET B: CAVIAR, ACTUAL, CANARY, VACANT
SET C: CANCEL, ACCUSE, CACTUS, DECADE
SET D: CANDID, DETACH, ADVICE, PLACID
SET E: COWARD, CLEAVE, MENACE, CAREER
SET F: GLANCE, LEGACY, AGENCY, PEACHY
SET G: CASHEW, ACTIVE, LOCATE, ACUMEN
SET H: NUANCE, COARSE, FIASCO, FACTOR
SET I: GARLIC, CAUGHT, CHATTY, NIACIN
SET J: MOSAIC, ATOMIC, IMPACT, CATNIP
SET K: COLLAR, CLAMOR, CANYON, VACUUM
SET L: CRAYON, CAVORT, CLINIC, CIRCUS
SET M: DECODE, DEFECT, REDUCE, CINDER
SET N: COMEDY, DOCTOR, FLEECE, SCHEME
SET O: CLEVER, CELERY, CEMENT, ENCORE
SET P: CONFER, GROCER, CHROME, CHOSEN
SET Q: WRENCH, PSYCHE, ELICIT, INCITE
SET R: PICKLE, COOKIE, PENCIL, POLICE
SET S: NOVICE, COPIER, POETIC, POCKET
SET T: MUSCLE, COUPLE, POUNCE, COFFIN
SET U: GOTHIC, GROUCH, STITCH, SMOOCH
SET V: PONCHO, VICTIM, IRONIC, UNCOIL
SET W: POLICY, SITCOM, COUSIN, MYSTIC
SET X: VICTOR, SCRIPT, STRICT, RUCKUS
SET Y: SCROLL, COLUMN, UNCURL, CUSTOM
SET Z: TYCOON, COUNTY, OUTCRY, COPOUT

D:

SET A: AGENDA, DAMAGE, PARADE, AFRAID
SET B: PAGODA, RADIAL, MALADY, MARAUD
SET C: GOADED, PADDLE, DEFAME, FEUDAL
SET D: FEDORA, GAINED, HERALD, ALLIED
SET E: INVADE, UNMADE, MEADOW, SOAPED
SET F: UPDATE, AFFORD, ADRIFT, DATING
SET G: DRAFTY, HARDLY, DRAGON, SHADOW
SET H: MIDAIR, KIDNAP, ISLAND, MYRIAD
SET I: DISMAY, UNPAID, RADIUS, UNLOAD
SET J: DYNAMO, RAMROD, PARDON, AROUND
SET K: ONWARD, TUNDRA, PARODY, BIDDEN
SET L: OUTDID, DEGREE, DELETE, EDGIER
SET M: LEGEND, PLEDGE, DELUGE, GENDER
SET N: EYELID, IMPEDE, MEDLEY, ELDEST
SET O: DEMURE, OFFEND, FISHED, MIDGET
SET P: DIGEST, SLUDGE, IODINE, TIDIER
SET Q: MILDEW, DRIVEL, MEDIUM, POISED

SET R: WEIRDO, DIVERT, MELODY, NOODLE
SET S: MODEST, TENDON, RODENT, OVERDO
SET T: TRENDY, POWDER, DEVOUT, DRYEST
SET U: GIRDLE, INDIGO, UNFOLD, GROUND
SET V: DUGOUT, SHOULD, SHROUD, DIMWIT
SET W: DOMINO, PODIUM, UNWIND, STUDIO
SET X: PUTRID, UNTOLD, SUNDRY, STURDY

F:

SET A: FEMALE, WAFFLE, FORAGE, FINALE
SET B: FAMINE, FAIRER, FIESTA, AFLAME
SET C: FALTER, SAFELY, FASTEN, UNSAFE
SET D: TARIFF, FRUGAL, FAMISH, FATHOM
SET E: FAMILY, UNFAIR, RATIFY, FLORAL
SET F: INFANT, FORMAL, FLAUNT, FLAVOR
SET G: ARTFUL, FORMAT, FIGURE, ENGULF
SET H: FORGET, FINITE, FILLET, PILFER
SET I: INFUSE, VERIFY, MYSELF, FUNNEL
SET J: FELONY, RUEFUL, USEFUL, SOFTEN
SET K: SURFER, FOUGHT, FUNGUS, FINISH
SET L: THRIFT, FOURTH, MISFIT, FLIMSY
SET M: FOSSIL, UPLIFT, INFORM, FUSION
SET N: OUTFIT, PURIFY, SULFUR, FURROW

G:

SET A: GARAGE, MANAGE, HANGAR, SEWAGE
SET B: GATHER, GOALIE, MAGPIE, GAWKER
SET C: PLAGUE, GRAVEL, MAGNET, OUTAGE
SET D: TARGET, VOYAGE, HANGUP, STIGMA
SET E: ASSIGN, GUITAR, GALLON, GLAMOR
SET F: LAGOON, VULGAR, ENGINE, LEGUME
SET G: GENTLE, REGRET, GEYSER, SLEIGH
SET H: HOGTIE, WEIGHT, LENGTH, ENOUGH
SET I: HUGEST, MINGLE, PIGLET, PIGPEN
SET J: GENIUS, GOOIER, GULLET, LOUNGE
SET K: EULOGY, NUTMEG, MORGUE, GOVERN
SET L: TONGUE, GROOVE, HONING, PLOUGH
SET M: HUNGRY, GROWTH, SKIING, ORIGIN
SET N: GRISLY, STRONG, GROTTO, SPONGY

H:

SET A: APATHY, HARASS, HEAVEN, HEARTH
SET B: INHALE, AWHILE, HERNIA, SHAKEN
SET C: LETHAL, HAMLET, LOATHE, WEALTH
SET D: MAYHEM, HUMANE, RATHER, LAVISH
SET E: MOHAIR, VANISH, HIATUS, SPLASH
SET F: WARMTH, ORPHAN, ANYHOW, HOORAY
SET G: THROAT, AUTHOR, THWART, THIEVE

SET H: HELMET, NEPHEW, TETHER, HYPHEN
SET I: HELIUM, THRIVE, HURTLE, THEORY
SET J: RHYTHM, IMPISH, UPHILL, THRILL
SET K: WITHIN, POLISH, SIPHON, THIRTY
SET L: UNHOLY, SMOOTH, UNHURT, TROPHY

K:

SET A: TALKIE, INTAKE, MAKEUP, MARKET
SET B: TANKER, SHRANK, NAPKIN, UNMASK
SET C: MARKUP, SWANKY, KEENER, KERNEL
SET D: WEEKLY, UPKEEP, HOKIER, KILLER
SET E: TINKLE, UNLIKE, INVOKE, PINKER
SET F: ROOKIE, SUNKEN, SPOKEN, KNOWER
SET G: RETOOK, TURKEY, FRISKY, FOLKSY
SET H: KNIGHT, KINGLY, UNHOOK, SLINKY

M:

SET A: SEAMAN, NAPALM, LAWMAN, LAYMAN
SET B: AMORAL, MANTRA, TRAUMA, TEDIUM
SET C: REMAKE, SESAME, MORALE, MARVEL
SET D: YEOMAN, MANURE, UNTAME, TAMPER
SET E: MATURE, MUTATE, IMPAIR, MAINLY
SET F: PRIMAL, AUTISM, NORMAL, SLALOM
SET G: MORTAL, ASYLUM, MATRON, MUTANT
SET H: TOMATO, MORTAR, ARMORY, WARMUP
SET I: MARTYR, EMBLEM, FUMBLE, ERMINE
SET J: YEOMEN, MILIEU, MILLET, PIMPLE
SET K: TIMELY, MEMOIR, VERMIN, ROOMIE
SET L: IMPOSE, MOTIVE, PERMIT, MISERY
SET M: MISUSE, MELLOW, EMPLOY, MOTTLE
SET N: VOLUME, MOMENT, SUMMER, SERMON
SET O: MUFFIN, MISFIT, INFORM, IMPISH
SET P: WHIMSY, IMPROV, MOTION, TUMULT

P:

SET A: APPEAL, PALATE, PAROLE, WEAPON
SET B: TEAPOT, PEANUT, UTOPIA, PARITY
SET C: PLURAL, LAPTOP, POSTAL, UNWRAP
SET D: POTATO, UPROAR, PASTOR, PASTRY
SET E: PELLET, SPLEEN, REPENT, REPOSE
SET F: TOUPEE, RETYPE, PITIES, TIPTOE
SET G: SPOKEN, POLLEN, POTENT, UNOPEN
SET H: TUNEUP, OPPOSE, POETRY, PURSUE
SET I: RIPOFF, SPIRIT, PILLOW, TIPTOP
SET J: TYPIST, PURITY, SYRUPY, UPROOT

V:

SET A: AVATAR, VANDAL, RAVAGE, AVIARY
SET B: AVOWAL, VASSAL, SAVANT, BEAVER
SET C: BEHAVE, CAVITY, WEAVED, TAVERN
SET D: TRIVIA, VISUAL, SAVIOR, BOVINE
SET E: DEVICE, CLEVER, PELVIS, CONVEY
SET F: SCURVY, CONVOY, DIVIDE, DRIVER
SET G: SOLVED, DEVOUR, ELEVEN, WEEVIL
SET H: SVELTE, TWELVE, UNEVEN, SWERVE
SET I: INVITE, VIOLET, INVERT, VIRTUE
SET J: VERSUS, SURVEY, VIOLIN, VISION

W:

SET A: AWAKEN, SEAWAY, ALWAYS, WAYLAY
SET B: WOMBAT, SUBWAY, SWAYED, SHADOW
SET C: UPWARD, SEWAGE, WEAKEN, WEASEL
SET D: LEEWAY, SEESAW, LAWYER, LAWFUL
SET E: ANYHOW, WALLOP, OUTLAW, WALRUS
SET F: CURFEW, WIDGET, GLOWED, WOODEN
SET G: WISDOM, DROWSY, FEWEST, WHITEN
SET H: YELLOW, TWENTY, NITWIT, UPTOWN

Y:

SET A: SASHAY, AIRWAY, SALARY, ASTRAY
SET B: BATBOY, BRANDY, BEAUTY, BYPASS
SET C: CALMLY, LUNACY, KEYPAD, GADFLY
SET D: EATERY, GYRATE, TYRANT, EASILY
SET E: ANYONE, LAYOFF, FAULTY, SUGARY
SET F: BEYOND, BELFRY, BYLINE, UPPITY
SET G: BOYISH, OCCUPY, IDIOCY, ODDITY
SET H: DEPUTY, PREDRY, MODIFY, EYEFUL
SET I: SHERRY, NINETY, ENTITY, SOLELY
SET J: MOTLEY, SYSTEM, PIGSTY, GUILTY

JQXZ:

SET A: AZALEA, ABLAZE, JACKAL, HAZARD
SET B: JAGUAR, GALAXY, AMAZON, TARZAN
SET C: STANZA, QUASAR, ABJECT, JACKET
SET D: ACQUIT, CAJOLE, JAILED, LIZARD
SET E: EXPAND, WIZARD, EQUATE, LAZIER
SET F: SEXUAL, JIGSAW, JARGON, JALOPY
SET G: OPAQUE, JOVIAL, THORAX, EXCEED
SET H: QUEASY, OXTAIL, MATRIX, EXCITE
SET I: INJECT, CLIQUE, JOCKEY, EXOTIC
SET J: DELUXE, ZEROED, DUPLEX, TUXEDO
SET K: LIQUID, REFLEX, EXPIRE, EXEMPT
SET L: ENZYME, VERTEX, PREFIX, JINGLE

SET M: OXYGEN, IONIZE, INJURE, UNIQUE
SET N: SUFFIX, INFLUX, JURIST, LIQUOR

LNRST:

SET A: NAUSEA, ASSAIL, ANNUAL, SONATA
SET B: LEANER, NEATEN, INNATE, UNSEAL
SET C: SALUTE, TENANT, SEASON, NOTATE
SET D: NATURE, AROUSE, ATTEST, RAISIN
SET E: SAILOR, RITUAL, SULTAN, SUNTAN
SET F: OUTRAN, TRUANT, RETIRE, NESTLE
SET G: SETTLE, UNSEEN, STEREO, ORIOLE
SET H: TOILET, INTONE, RIOTER, ENROLL
SET I: TUNNEL, LOOSER, TURTLE, OUTLET
SET J: UNSURE, UNTRUE, INSIST, LOTION

Seven-Letter Alphagrams

Three- and Four-Letter Edges

Front Edges:

COM-
COMPACT, COMPASS, COMPOSE, COMPOST

CON-
SET A: CONCEAL, CONCEIT, CONDOLE, CONDEMN
SET B: CONCEDE, CONCERN, CONFIDE, CONFIRM

DIS-
SET A: DISBAND, DISCARD, DISTURB, DISPUTE
SET B: DISRUPT, DISDAIN, DISHRAG, DISCORD
SET C: DISGUST, DISMISS, DISPLAY, DISOBEY

FOR-
SET A: FORBADE, FOREARM, FORCEPS, FOREVER
SET B: FORGERY, FORMULA, FOREIGN, FORTUNE

MIS-
SET A: MISCALL, MISPLAY, MISWORD, MISUSED
SET B: MISDRAW, MISFILE, MISSTEP, MISTYPE

NON-
NONFACT, NONFOOD, NONPLAY, NONWORD

OUT-
SET A: OUTBRAG, OUTDATE, OUTEARN, OUTTALK
SET B: OUTPACE, OUTWEAR, OUTPLAY, OUTCOME

OVER-
OVERACT, OVERLAP, OVERRAN, OVERDUE

PRE-
SET A: PREFACE, PREVAIL, PRETEND, PREVENT
SET B: PREDICT, PREVIEW, PRETEXT, PREHEAT

PRO-
SET A: PROBLEM, PRODUCT, PROCTOR, PROLONG
SET B: PROVERB, PROCURE, PRODIGY, PROVOKE

SUB-
SUBPENA, SUBSIDE, SUBRULE, SUBTYPE

Back Edges:

-AGE
SET A: CABBAGE, RAMPAGE, MASSAGE, COINAGE
SET B: TEENAGE, BANDAGE, PASSAGE, COLLAGE
SET C: ACREAGE, VILLAGE, CARNAGE, FOLIAGE

-AND
SET A: HATBAND, GARLAND, HUSBAND, WETLAND
SET B: ARMBAND, OFFHAND, LOWLAND, OUTLAND

-ANT
SET A: BLATANT, GALLANT, VARIANT, DEVIANT
SET B: DISTANT, RADIANT, VAGRANT, VIBRANT
SET C: HYDRANT, ELEGANT, PAGEANT, VALIANT
SET D: BUOYANT, DISTANT, REMNANT, DORMANT

-ATE
SET A: ACETATE, MANDATE, IMITATE, DICTATE
SET B: DEVIATE, PLACATE, AGITATE, VIBRATE
SET C: CREMATE, ELEVATE, ACTUATE, SATIATE
SET D: PROBATE, DEFLATE, EMULATE, ADULATE
SET E: NARRATE, EDUCATE, MEDIATE, INFLATE
SET F: PRIMATE, ISOLATE, VIOLATE, SITUATE

-BLE
SET A: EATABLE, TAXABLE, ADDABLE, CAPABLE
SET B: AMIABLE, DURABLE, TENABLE, NOTABLE
SET C: LIKABLE, PARABLE, BRAMBLE, MOVABLE

SET D: LIVABLE, THIMBLE, AFFABLE, AUDIBLE
SET E: PLIABLE, VISIBLE, TROUBLE, BUYABLE
SET F: LEGIBLE, GRUMBLE, STUBBLE, CURABLE

-ENT
SET A: ANCIENT, PATIENT, CONSENT, CURRENT
SET B: TANGENT, PAYMENT, CONTENT, EVIDENT
SET C: SEGMENT, LENIENT, EMINENT, PREVENT
SET D: VIOLENT, OPULENT, CONVENT, AMBIENT

-ERS
SET A: BADGERS, BEAVERS, DANDERS, RAIDERS
SET B: GATHERS, PANDERS, FALTERS, WALKERS
SET C: TAPPERS, LAWYERS, ROBBERS, BREWERS
SET D: FENCERS, GROCERS, MINCERS, CONFERS
SET E: SLICERS, CURLERS, HOLDERS, DRIVERS

-ESS
SET A: ADDRESS, BIGNESS, USELESS, NEWNESS
SET B: AGELESS, LAWLESS, GODDESS, HOTNESS
SET C: PROFESS, DUCHESS, ENDLESS, DRYNESS

-EST
SET A: BRAVEST, BONIEST, CONTEST, EVENEST
SET B: WIRIEST, SADDEST, WARMEST, CONGEST
SET C: SOFTEST, NOSIEST, MEANEST, BIGGEST
SET D: KINDEST, LONGEST, SLOWEST, FAIREST
SET E: NOBLEST, EERIEST, HOMIEST, SOONEST
SET F: LARGEST, BOLDEST, SUGGEST, POSHEST

-FUL
SET A: BASHFUL, TACTFUL, FATEFUL, HARMFUL
SET B: PLAYFUL, CAREFUL, HANDFUL, GAINFUL
SET C: PAINFUL, GLEEFUL, HOPEFUL, HELPFUL
SET D: PITIFUL, SOULFUL, WILLFUL, FISTFUL

-IAL
ASOCIAL, PARTIAL, CORDIAL, TRIVIAL

-IDE
SET A: CYANIDE, RAWHIDE, BROMIDE, CONFIDE
SET B: PROVIDE, BEDSIDE, SUBSIDE, OUTRIDE

-IER
SET A: BAGGIER, TEARIER, CHEWIER, WINDIER
SET B: GUMMIER, CRAZIER, SHAKIER, PRICIER
SET C: TEENIER, PUSHIER, SAUCIER, RAINIER
SET D: ITCHIER, PREMIER, SHOWIER, READIER

SET E: SOAPIER, GIDDIER, FISHIER, LOWLIER
SET F: HEAVIER, BULKIER, SEEDIER, FUNNIER

-IES

SET A: BEANIES, APPLIES, SPECIES, UNIFIES
SET B: PINKIES, DANDIES, MARRIES, COOKIES
SET C: FOLLIES, IMPLIES, DAISIES, HOBBIES
SET D: MUDDIES, SOFTIES, SIXTIES, FAIRIES
SET E: DERBIES, ENEMIES, GYPSIES, ROOKIES
SET F: WEARIES, NEWBIES, PEONIES, PHONIES

-IFY

SET A: CLARIFY, GRATIFY, DIGNIFY, TESTIFY
SET B: FALSIFY, AMPLIFY, REUNIFY, MOLLIFY

-ILE

FRAGILE, BEGUILE, FERTILE, PROFILE

-ILY

SET A: FANCILY, SCARILY, HANDILY, ANGRILY
SET B: LUCKILY, SAUCILY, READILY, HEAVILY
SET C: SHAKILY, NIFTILY, FUSSILY, GRIMILY
SET D: WITTILY, LOUSILY, BEADILY, PUSHILY
SET E: MISTILY, TIPSILY, NUTTILY, SORRILY

-INE

SET A: MACHINE, VACCINE, IMAGINE, INCLINE
SET B: OFFLINE, AIRLINE, ASININE, COMBINE
SET C: CUISINE, SKYLINE, BEELINE, BROMINE
SET D: DECLINE, MIDLINE, ROUTINE, CODEINE
SET E: RECLINE, CONFINE, HEMLINE, ENTWINE

-ING

SET A: DABBING, BEADING, ABIDING, FUDGING
SET B: MESHING, SHOOING, HEADING, ARGUING
SET C: SNAKING, SUDSING, EVOKING, OINKING
SET D: BASTING, VALUING, SOAPING, UNDOING
SET E: OPENING, IRONING, GRATING, PLACING
SET F: FEUDING, EVENING, VETOING, ISSUING

-ION

SET A: FACTION, ORATION, BILLION, FICTION
SET B: CUSHION, EVASION, STATION, DICTION
SET C: TUITION, MISSION, EDITION, SUCTION
SET D: EROSION, OPINION, PORTION, MENTION

-ISH
SET A: BABYISH, PEAKISH, MANNISH, BLEMISH
SET B: ABOLISH, ANGUISH, GRAYISH, TARNISH
SET C: CHERISH, PRUDISH, FURNISH, NOURISH
SET D: COLDISH, FOOLISH, GIRLISH, STYLISH

-ISM
NARCISM, ATHEISM, HEROISM, TOURISM

-IST
SET A: NARCIST, PIANIST, CHEMIST, ELITIST
SET B: SOLOIST, FADDIST, SUBSIST, LEFTIST
SET C: FLORIST, STYLIST, HARPIST, CELLIST
SET D: EGOTIST, FLUTIST, TOURIST, DIARIST

-ITE
WEBSITE, REWRITE, DESPITE, ERUDITE

-ITY
SET A: ABILITY, ACIDITY, VARSITY, UTILITY
SET B: CLARITY, DUALITY, BREVITY, ANNUITY

-IUM
CALCIUM, URANIUM, LITHIUM, STADIUM

-IVE
SET A: ABUSIVE, BEEHIVE, FESTIVE, FORGIVE
SET B: CAPTIVE, DECEIVE, CURSIVE, ELUSIVE

-IZE
SET A: BAPTIZE, AGONIZE, OXIDIZE, ITEMIZE
SET B: LIONIZE, IDOLIZE, MIDSIZE, UTILIZE

-LAR
REGULAR, STELLAR, SIMILAR, POPULAR

-LIKE
SET A: CATLIKE, UNALIKE, WEBLIKE, SUNLIKE
SET B: WIGLIKE, FANLIKE, WARLIKE, TOELIKE
SET C: HIPLIKE, TOYLIKE, MANLIKE, DISLIKE
SET D: GUMLIKE, RUGLIKE, PIGLIKE, GODLIKE

-MAN
BASEMAN, HANGMAN, FROGMAN, SNOWMAN

-NAL

ADRENAL, ARSENAL, ORDINAL, NOMINAL

-NCE

SET A: FINANCE, SCIENCE, POTENCE, ROMANCE
SET B: ABSENCE, ADVANCE, ENHANCE, ESSENCE

-OID

TABLOID, ADENOID, THYROID, FACTOID

-OSE

SET A: CABOOSE, VAMOOSE, ENCLOSE, UNLOOSE
SET B: SUPPOSE, PAPOOSE, DISPOSE, PURPOSE

-OUS

SET A: CALLOUS, GASEOUS, DUBIOUS, HIDEOUS
SET B: DEVIOUS, RAUCOUS, FATUOUS, OBVIOUS
SET C: OMINOUS, SERIOUS, VACUOUS, ANXIOUS
SET D: VICIOUS, HEINOUS, PITEOUS, ARDUOUS
SET E: FIBROUS, CURIOUS, NERVOUS, FURIOUS

-OWN

LETDOWN, RUNDOWN, INGROWN, MIDTOWN

-TIC

SET A: FANATIC, CHAOTIC, SPASTIC, GENETIC
SET B: ASCETIC, CAUSTIC, PLASTIC, POLITIC

-URE

SET A: CAPTURE, FEATURE, FAILURE, LECTURE
SET B: GESTURE, PROCURE, LEISURE, VENTURE

Two-Letter Edges

Front Edges:

AB-

ABANDON, ABSTAIN, ABSCOND, ABSOLVE

AC-

ACROBAT, ACCLAIM, ACADEMY, ACTUARY

AD-

ADAMANT, ADOPTEE, ADMIRAL, ADAPTOR

AN-
SET A: ANARCHY, ANTENNA, ANATOMY, ANOMALY
SET B: ANGULAR, ANALOGY, ANYMORE, ANTONYM

BE-
SET A: BELABOR, BEDEVIL, BELIEVE, BELLBOY
SET B: BEHAVED, BEGONIA, BEWITCH, BEDTIME

BI-
BIFOCAL, BICYCLE, BISCUIT, BIPLANE

BL-
BLANKET, BLOSSOM, BLOWOUT, BLARNEY

BR-
BRAVADO, BREADTH, BREAKUP, BROCADE

CH-
SET A: CHARADE, CHEETAH, CHASTEN, CHIMNEY
SET B: CHEAPEN, CHANNEL, CHEERIO, CHORTLE

CL-
CLICKER, CLOSURE, CLOSEUP, CLOSEST (CLOSETS)

CR-
CRUSADE, CREVICE, CREWCUT, CRYSTAL

DE-
SET A: DEADPAN, DEVALUE, DECLINE, DELUDED
SET B: DELOUSE, DECEASE, DELIRIA, DEFICIT
SET C: DEFENSE, DEITIES, DETRACT, DECIBEL
SET D: DEFUNCT, DEMIGOD, DESPISE, DECORUM

EN-
SET A: ENHANCE, ENCHANT, ENACTOR, ENDGAME
SET B: ENGRAFT, ENTRANT, ENNOBLE, ENDEMIC

EX-
SET A: EXCLAIM, EXTRACT, EXAMINE, EXPIATE
SET B: EXPLAIN, EXHIBIT, EXCLUDE, EXCERPT

FL-
FLANNEL, FLAREUP, FLEABAG, FLOTSAM

FR-
FREEDOM, FRISBEE, FROGLET, FRAUGHT

GL-
GLOBULE, GLIMPSE, GLITTER, GLAMOUR

GR-
GREMLIN, GRIMACE, GROWNUP, GROUPIE

IN-
SET A: INHABIT, INERTIA, INBOUND, INCENSE
SET B: INFLICT, INEXACT, INSOFAR, INBUILT
SET C: INFLECT, INSIDER, INFANCY, INSTALL
SET D: INKBLOT, INCLINE, INVITEE, INVALID
SET E: INSTANT, INBURST, INVOICE, INVEIGH

PL-
PLACEBO, PLATEAU, PLYWOOD, PLIANCY

RE-
SET A: READMIT, RETRACT, REFRAME, REARGUE
SET B: RENEWAL, REFRAIN, RECYCLE, REMOVAL
SET C: REBUILT, RECEIPT, RECLUSE, RECRUIT
SET D: RECTORY, REDWOOD, RESTUDY, REMORSE

SC-
SCANDAL, SCAPULA, SCANNED, SCALPEL

SH-
SHAKEUP, SHAMPOO, SHERBET, SHOTGUN

SP-
SPARTAN, SPATULA, SPIDERY, SPONSOR

ST-
SET A: STAMINA, STANDBY, STOMACH, STEALTH
SET B: STATURE, STARLIT, STRETCH, STUPEFY

TH-
THERAPY, THROATY, THEREBY, THUNDER

TR-
SET A: TRACHEA, TRAVAIL, TRAFFIC, TRUANCY
SET B: TRACTOR, TRANSIT, TRAITOR, TRIDENT

UN-
SET A: UNAWARE, UNASKED, UNLEASH, UNCROSS
SET B: UNWINDS, UNCAGED, UNREADY, UNITARY
SET C: UNGLUED, UNIQUER, UNCLEAN, UNEAGER
SET D: UNBOUND, UNCLASP, UNIFORM, UNCOVER

UP-

UPBRAID, UPREACH, UPGRADE, UPHEAVE

Back Edges:

-AL

SET A: RADICAL, GRADUAL, FACTUAL, NATURAL
SET B: MUSICAL, CENTRAL, FEDERAL, REVISAL

-CT

PLAYACT, ATTRACT, SUSPECT, PROTECT

-ED

SET A: AWARDED, LABELED, GLOATED, PLANTED
SET B: BUSTLED, ALLAYED, ACCRUED, VOYAGED
SET C: RATTLED, SUCCEED, AMASSED, FACETED
SET D: SMASHED, TOTALED, ENCODED, BEACHED
SET E: ESCAPED, TALLIED, MATURED, EVICTED

-EE

AWARDEE, ESCAPEE, EVACUEE, DRAFTEE

-ER

SET A: BLANDER, WATCHER, PARDNER, SWEATER
SET B: GAUNTER, CRUSHER, AROUSER, OLDSTER
SET C: SWERVER, BLOCKER, LAUGHER, MUFFLER
SET D: APPLIER, PEDDLER, SMALLER, WELCHER

-IA

APHASIA, REGALIA, TILAPIA, BOHEMIA

-IC

SET A: ARCHAIC, AEROBIC, PACIFIC, DYNAMIC
SET B: SATIRIC, ORGANIC, CENTRIC, CHRONIC

-LY

SET A: AMIABLY, FATALLY, RABIDLY, BROADLY
SET B: BEASTLY, CHEAPLY, CLEARLY, IDEALLY
SET C: TARDILY, SHAPELY, EAGERLY, FINALLY
SET D: VITALLY, SMARTLY, RURALLY, SOBERLY
SET E: BRIEFLY, CRUELLY, BOSSILY, COURTLY

-ND

BARTEND, ASTOUND, MANKIND, GODSEND

-ON

PARAGON, BASSOON, GLUTTON, HARPOON

-RD

PLACARD, SEAWARD, AIRWARD, BOMBARD

-RY

SET A: BRAVERY, BATTERY, LIBRARY, ARCHERY
SET B: DRAPERY, LAUNDRY, IMAGERY, SLAVERY
SET C: TANNERY, RIVALRY, PRIMARY, ORATORY
SET D: SCENERY, MERCURY, RIFLERY, LOTTERY

-UM

SET A: EARDRUM, TANTRUM, MODICUM, FULCRUM
SET B: HOODLUM, OPTIMUM, OPPOSUM, STRATUM

Three-Letter Edges: A Potpourri

SET A: AMUSING, MISFIRE, CONCEPT, MAGNIFY
SET B: REUNION, HEDGING, COMMUNE, DISTEND
SET C: CONSUME, PROMOTE, HUSKIES, OUTLAST
SET D: SUBTEXT, BURGLAR, LOADING, FRIGATE
SET E: LOVABLE, MISLIVE, INFLATE, RIBLIKE
SET F: CRYPTIC, PUBLISH, ENTRANT, VAGUEST
SET G: GOOFIER, FORGAVE, BUYABLE, FOULEST
SET H: PROFUSE, TALLISH, SIGNIFY, DOSSIER
SET I: BELLMAN, NONDRIP, PATTIES, BEDLIKE
SET J: OUTGREW, SUBLIME, SPICING, LEGLIKE
SET K: SUBGOAL, PRODUCE, SLOWEST, VARMENT
SET L: AVERAGE, TORMENT, OVERARM, OUTDOOR
SET M: PENNANT, FORBODE, SOLVENT, FIREMAN
SET N: DISTORT, RIOTOUS, NULLIFY, BIRDIES
SET O: SIZABLE, OUTRAGE, PUERILE, DEITIES
SET P: CADMIUM, NONSLIP, HOSTAGE, HEEDFUL
SET Q: OVERAGE, WEARIER, CADENCE, BUSHIER
SET R: HATEFUL, HASTILY, BARRAGE, CONSULT
SET S: BOOTIES, PULSATE, AGILITY, OVERBUY
SET T: TERRIFY, CONCISE, PLUMAGE, MISCOPY
SET U: COMFORT, PEEVISH, CONTEND, INHUMAN
SET V: PRIVATE, DUTIFUL, PASSION, HORRIFY
SET W: VANTAGE, COMPUTE, VIOLIST, COMBUST
SET X: DISTILL, ROOMFUL, COLLATE, DISOBEY
SET Y: WOODIER, AMOROUS, SEALANT, WATTAGE
SET Z: BOORISH, NONSUIT, PULSANT, KINETIC
SET AA: GLORIES, WARRANT, COPIOUS, PROGRAM
SET AB: POTABLE, UNKNOWN, NONSUIT, GOOFILY
SET AC: COMMAND, FLOUNCE, SOAKING, OUTRACE
SET AD: SUBPLOT, OVERSEE, SAWLIKE, PREEMPT
SET AE: OUTLEAP, GESTATE, WILDEST, SUBSIDY
SET AF: HEADIER, PROTECT, FOOTAGE, DIOXIDE
SET AG: PAYABLE, UMBRAGE, OUTSHOT, PUNGENT
SET AH: CURRANT, SURVIVE, CEILING, MISRULE
SET AI: EASIEST, BUDDIES, LUNATIC, ADORING
SET AJ: DRASTIC, WITTIER, UNITIES, FOREPAW

SET AK: OVATION, MISTAKE, COMPARE, DISPLAY
SET AL: FORGONE, MISTOOK, BURNISH, MORTIFY
SET AM: NONPLUS, PREMIER, DISCUSS, PRETZEL
SET AN: DISTANT, CRUCIAL, FORTIFY, FORFEIT
SET AO: ENCHANT, PREFADE, PRESAGE, PENANCE
SET AP: SPECIFY, OVERBID, OUTPOST, PROMOTE
SET AQ: SLAVISH, FORLORN, MYSTIFY, NONSKID
SET AR: CYCLIST, CONVERT, FOOTMAN, DENYING
SET AS: OUTSAIL, GREYEST, INITIAL, EYELIKE
SET AT: NONZERO, COTTAGE, NEWSMAN, PUTDOWN
SET AU: FIXABLE, FORELEG, BRUTISH, OPERATE
SET AV: DULLEST, TORRENT, PRELUDE, PETRIFY

Two-Letter Edges: A Potpourri

SET A: ABALONE, ENDLONG, UPSHOOT, UNCLASP
SET B: BESIEGE, STRIPER, THRUPUT, UPRIGHT
SET C: STEPSON, ANCHOVY, EXPLODE, THINNER
SET D: BIOFUEL, ENDMOST, ACHIEVE, STIMULI
SET E: ENGORGE, UNEATEN, EXTRUDE, ACETONE
SET F: ACRONYM, EXTREME, ENTITLE, UNCOVER
SET G: ACCUSAL, ANGRILY, STERNLY, EMPIRIC
SET H: TRUSTEE, UPSURGE, ABUSING, GENERIC
SET I: ANTIWAR, BEARHUG, TRUMPET, UPFIELD
SET J: ABYSMAL, DEMONIC, BIRDMAN, SCENERY
SET K: BEASTLY, DEVOTEE, THEREON, LEXICON
SET L: BIOTECH, SEISMIC, CLERKED, DEPLORE
SET M: CHUTNEY, INHERIT, ABETTED, BROILED
SET N: BIOLOGY, EXPLOIT, THOUGHT, CHIFFON
SET O: ABDOMEN, CRIMPLE, INQUIRE, ANTACID
SET P: BEANBAG, CHEROOT, EXPENSE, CHOPPED
SET Q: ACOLYTE, ANAGRAM, BILLION, CHORINE
SET R: BEDROCK, ENTHUSE, INSURED, UNFOUND
SET S: DERRICK, SUMMAND, STIFFEN, CREWMAN
SET T: SCUFFLE, TRILOGY, UPCOURT, CRAWDAD
SET U: DEGRADE, INVOLVE, SCREWUP, NUMERIC
SET V: SCOUTED, THEOREM, TRINITY, ILLOGIC
SET W: INFIGHT, CRUMBLY, AMMONIA, REWOUND
SET X: SCRUPLE, TRIGGER, REVERIE, CROQUET
SET Y: UNMOVED, PETUNIA, RIVALED, SILICON
SET Z: MERGERS, HUNGERS, REVENGE, DUNGEON
SET AA: SEQUOIA, DEBASED, ORCHARD, VENISON
SET AB: RELIEVE, TEMPERS, EXPOUND, BUFFOON
SET AC: GOLFERS, MILITIA, CHARTED, REGIMEN
SET AD: MINUTIA, RESOLVE, SURFERS, DISPEND
SET AE: ELDERLY, REENTRY, NEGLECT, CUSTARD
SET AF: VIRTUAL, DIEHARD, MINIMAL, LOTTERY
SET AG: DULLARD, FLOWERY, VENTRAL, ELUSORY
SET AH: SURREAL, VERDICT, WARLORD, DISSECT
SET AI: HOSIERY, FRONTAL, COLLECT, ELECTEE
SET AJ: LIBELEE, DENSELY, REFEREE, EMPTILY

Four-Letter Edges

Front Edges:

ANTI-
ANTILEAK, ANTITANK, ANTILOCK, ANTISKID

FORE-
SET A: FOREHEAD, FOREHAND, FOREWARN, FORELIMB
SET B: FORETOLD, FOREWORD, FOREFOOT, FOREMOST

HAND-
HANDICAP, HANDMADE, HANDRAIL, HANDSEWN

HEAD-
HEADBAND, HEADLOCK, HEADREST, HEADHUNT

OVER-
SET A: OVERBAKE, OVERCAME, OVERRIDE, OVERRULE
SET B: OVERHEAD, OVERPAID, OVERTONE, OVERTIME
SET C: OVERLEAF, OVERRATE, OVERPLAY, OVERBITE

POST-
POSTCARD, POSTDATE, POSTPAID, POSTGRAD

Back Edges:

-ABLE
SET A: BEATABLE, ERASABLE, ARGUABLE, EDUCABLE
SET B: SHAKABLE, AMICABLE, RAISABLE, BONDABLE
SET C: PROBABLE, PLAYABLE, CUTTABLE, BEARABLE
SET D: PASSABLE, READABLE, PALPABLE, HEARABLE

-ALLY
SET A: RASCALLY, ANNUALLY, FORMALLY, NORMALLY
SET B: VERBALLY, BRUTALLY, SOCIALLY, VISUALLY

-ANCE
AMBIANCE, VARIANCE, VIBRANCE, NUISANCE

-ATOR
SET A: RADIATOR, AGITATOR, ANIMATOR, VIBRATOR
SET B: OPERATOR, MIGRATOR, IMITATOR, VIOLATOR

-BACK
BAREBACK, TAILBACK, COMEBACK, SOFTBACK

-BALL
BASEBALL, MEATBALL, FIREBALL, FOOTBALL

-ENCE
AUDIENCE, PRUDENCE, EMINENCE, VIOLENCE

-ETTE
BRUNETTE, OMELETTE, VIGNETTE, ROULETTE

-FISH
CRAWFISH, STARFISH, GOLDFISH, BLUEFISH

-HEAD
BONEHEAD, HARDHEAD, SOREHEAD, NAILHEAD

-IBLE
TERRIBLE, SENSIBLE, FEASIBLE, ELIGIBLE

-ICAL
SET A: TACTICAL, ATOMICAL, NAUTICAL, CLERICAL
SET B: BIBLICAL, HEROICAL, SURGICAL, MYTHICAL

-IEST
SET A: FANCIEST, TACKIEST, BUSHIEST, SUDSIEST
SET B: GAUDIEST, HARDIEST, BUMPIEST, WINDIEST
SET C: HAIRIEST, LANKIEST, CURVIEST, PUDGIEST

-IGHT
SET A: DAYLIGHT, GASLIGHT, DOGFIGHT, GUNFIGHT
SET B: TWILIGHT, SKYLIGHT, AIRTIGHT, OUTRIGHT

-INGS
SET A: CALLINGS, DARLINGS, BEATINGS, MEANINGS
SET B: GRATINGS, SHAVINGS, RAILINGS, MARKINGS

-LAND
HEADLAND, FARMLAND, HOMELAND, CROPLAND

-LATE
SET A: TABULATE, DESOLATE, MODULATE, REGULATE
SET B: ESCALATE, UNDULATE, SIMULATE, POPULATE

-LESS
SET A: HEADLESS, LEAFLESS, HARMLESS, LIMBLESS
SET B: FACELESS, HEATLESS, RAINLESS, RECKLESS

-LIER
SET A: CAVALIER, MEASLIER, GNARLIER, CUDDLIER
SET B: COMELIER, DIMPLIER, SEEMLIER, LIVELIER

-LIKE
SET A: BEANLIKE, WAVELIKE, SOAPLIKE, LIFELIKE
SET B: LACELIKE, HAIRLIKE, LADYLIKE, TREELIKE
SET C: HANDLIKE, TAILLIKE, TIDELIKE, DRUMLIKE

-LINE
SET A: ALKALINE, DEADLINE, LANDLINE, GASOLINE
SET B: NECKLINE, BUNTLINE, SIDELINE, LIFELINE

-LIST
FATALIST, VOCALIST, IDEALIST, NOVELIST

-MENT
SET A: BASEMENT, FRAGMENT, ORNAMENT, TENEMENT
SET B: MOVEMENT, OINTMENT, SHIPMENT, MONUMENT

-NESS
SET A: ACHINESS, GLADNESS, DEARNESS, LATENESS
SET B: CALMNESS, DARKNESS, NEATNESS, RICHNESS

-OUSE
MADHOUSE, TEAHOUSE, ICEHOUSE, FUNHOUSE

-RATE
LACERATE, LIBERATE, MODERATE, TOLERATE

-ROOM
BATHROOM, CHATROOM, ANTEROOM, MAILROOM

-SHIP
HARDSHIP, LADYSHIP, FLAGSHIP, TOWNSHIP

-SOME
HANDSOME, FEARSOME, TIRESOME, TOILSOME

-STER
SET A: ROADSTER, TEAMSTER, GANGSTER, SEMESTER
SET B: HOOPSTER, SPINSTER, POLLSTER, REGISTER

-TION
SET A: FRACTION, INACTION, ADDITION, AVIATION
SET B: ROTATION, ERUPTION, GUMPTION, PETITION

-TIVE
SET A: ADAPTIVE, LAXATIVE, POSITIVE, ERUPTIVE
SET B: ADOPTIVE, CURATIVE, INACTIVE, FUGITIVE

-TORY
AUDITORY, MIDSTORY, PUNITORY, LAVATORY

-TURE
ARMATURE, CREATURE, APERTURE, PUNCTURE

-ULAR
VASCULAR, GLOBULAR, CIRCULAR, SINGULAR

-WORK
ROADWORK, BODYWORK, WOODWORK, HOMEWORK

Three-Letter Edges

Front Edges:

COM-
COMPLAIN, COMMUNAL, COMPOUND, COMMERCE

CON-
SET A: CONTRACT, CONFETTI, CONTRAST, CONCLUDE
SET B: CONCRETE, CONSIDER, CONVERGE, CONTRIVE

DIS-
SET A: DISCLAIM, DISARRAY, DISSUADE, DISAGREE
SET B: DISHEVEL, DISCIPLE, DISORDER, DISSOLVE

FOR-
FORBIDAL, FORSAKEN, FORESTRY, FORSOOTH

MIS-
SET A: MISADAPT, MISUSAGE, MISTRIAL, MISBUILD
SET B: MISCOUNT, MISGUIDE, MISWRITE, MISSPENT

NON-
SET A: NONFATAL, NONDAIRY, NONGLARE, NONSTICK
SET B: NONTOXIC, NONSENSE, NONTITLE, NONVOTER

OUT-
SET A: OUTBOARD, OUTMATCH, OUTSMART, OUTBOUND
SET B: OUTLAWED, OUTFLANK, OUTBURST, OUTFIELD
SET C: OUTSHINE, OUTDRINK, OUTGUESS, OUTFIGHT

PRE-
SET A: PRECLUDE, PREBIRTH, PRECINCT, PRESENCE
SET B: PRESTIGE, PRESUMED, PREMIERE, PREORDER

PRO-
SET A: PROCURAL, PRODIGAL, PROSTATE, PROPHECY
SET B: PROVINCE, PROTEGEE, PROTOCOL, PROFOUND

SUB-
SET A: SUBSPACE, SUBTRACT, SUBLEASE, SUBPANEL
SET B: SUBHUMAN, SUBMERGE, SUBTITLE, SUBGROUP

Back Edges:

-AGE
SET A: CLEAVAGE, SABOTAGE, AMPERAGE, LANGUAGE
SET B: MARRIAGE, CRIBBAGE, WRECKAGE, SPOILAGE

-AND
BAREHAND, BEDSTAND, LONGHAND, GOURMAND

-ANT
SET A: ABUNDANT, REACTANT, PHEASANT, STAGNANT
SET B: DEBUTANT, PENCHANT, ELEPHANT, TOLERANT

-ATE
SET A: ABDICATE, BACKDATE, ADVOCATE, ALLOCATE
SET B: ERADIATE, GRADUATE, TAILGATE, STAGNATE
SET C: VALIDATE, INCUBATE, ANNOTATE, RECREATE
SET D: OBLIGATE, DEDICATE, PERMEATE, IRRITATE

-BLE
FORCIBLE, FEASIBLE, ELIGIBLE, HORRIBLE

-ENT
SET A: ADJACENT, AFFLUENT, INNOCENT, REVERENT
SET B: INHERENT, PENITENT, EMERGENT, DILIGENT

-ESS

SET A: BARONESS, ACHINESS, HEADLESS, ROADLESS
SET B: MEANNESS, HARMLESS, AIRINESS, STARLESS
SET C: CLUELESS, HEEDLESS, GOODNESS, LIFELESS

-EST

SET A: BLEAKEST, CLEANEST, SOUNDEST, VIVIDEST
SET B: STABLEST, IMMODEST, YOUNGEST, SMALLEST

-FUL

SET A: PEACEFUL, GRACEFUL, SHAMEFUL, THANKFUL
SET B: DOUBTFUL, BLISSFUL, COLORFUL, PRIDEFUL

-GUE

HARANGUE, DIALOGUE, EPILOGUE, INTRIGUE

-IAL

SET A: MATERIAL, ARTERIAL, BIENNIAL, OFFICIAL
SET B: BINOMIAL, COLONIAL, IMPERIAL, TUTORIAL

-IDE

CURBSIDE, COINCIDE, POOLSIDE, MUDSLIDE

-IER

SET A: BLEARIER, FLASHIER, STICKIER, MIGHTIER
SET B: CATCHIER, GRAINIER, STURDIER, PURIFIER
SET C: DAINTIER, SCREWIER, ORNERIER, STINKIER

-IES

SET A: AVIARIES, BAKERIES, SAFETIES, RATIFIES
SET B: AGENCIES, STEADIES, ARTERIES, VANITIES
SET C: PACIFIES, CAVITIES, FAMILIES, NICETIES

-IFY

BEAUTIFY, CLASSIFY, IDENTIFY, SIMPLIFY

-ILE

VOLATILE, DOMICILE, JUVENILE, SANDPILE

-ILY

SET A: CRANKILY, STEADILY, GREASILY, BREEZILY
SET B: CHEERILY, DRESSILY, GREEDILY, PRETTILY

-INE

SET A: MAGAZINE, DOPAMINE, PTOMAINE, CHLORINE
SET B: FEMININE, PRISTINE, FIGURINE, FLUORINE

-ING

SET A: AVAILING, RADIOING, FORAGING, REFUTING
SET B: BRAINING, CROAKING, ALLEGING, CHOOSING
SET C: MENACING, UNCARING, LEARNING, SNARLING

-ION

SET A: ABRASION, ADHESION, PAVILION, DECISION
SET B: OCCASION, CHAMPION, OBLIVION, SCORPION

-ISH

FEVERISH, SKIRMISH, SMALLISH, ASTONISH

-ISM

ACTIVISM, DYNAMISM, LOYALISM, EXORCISM

-IST

SET A: ALARMIST, BOTANIST, APHORIST, LOBBYIST
SET B: HEDONIST, FEMINIST, MOTORIST, FUTURIST

-ITE

SET A: DYNAMITE, APPETITE, FAVORITE, GRAPHITE
SET B: HOMESITE, INFINITE, IMPOLITE, OPPOSITE

-ITY

SET A: AUDACITY, FATALITY, TENACITY, ACTIVITY
SET B: RAPIDITY, LEGALITY, POLARITY, LUCIDITY

-IUM

GERANIUM, TITANIUM, DELIRIUM, EMPORIUM

-IVE

SET A: ADHESIVE, ABRASIVE, NOSEDIVE, PERCEIVE
SET B: INVASIVE, OUTDRIVE, EFFUSIVE, DIVISIVE

-IZE

SET A: URBANIZE, LOCALIZE, CANONIZE, IDEALIZE
SET B: LEGALIZE, FINALIZE, SATIRIZE, MOBILIZE

-MAN

SET A: RANCHMAN, DAIRYMAN, CHAIRMAN, NOBLEMAN
SET B: EVERYMAN, HOUSEMAN, FRONTMAN, SUPERMAN

-NAL

SET A: SEASONAL, CARDINAL, NATIONAL, CRIMINAL
SET B: MATERNAL, INTERNAL, ORIGINAL, EXTERNAL

-NCE
SET A: SALIENCE, ENSCONCE, LENIENCE, SENTENCE
SET B: TANGENCE, CONVINCE, CREDENCE, OPULENCE

-OID
PARANOID, ASTEROID, SCHIZOID, HUMANOID

-OSE
COMATOSE, FRUCTOSE, MONGOOSE, DEXTROSE

-OUS
SET A: FABULOUS, RAVENOUS, VALOROUS, LIBELOUS
SET B: ULCEROUS, DESIROUS, WONDROUS, GENEROUS

-OWN
LOCKDOWN, COOLDOWN, MELTDOWN, SHUTDOWN

-TIC
SET A: DIABETIC, ACOUSTIC, OPERATIC, ROMANTIC
SET B: GALACTIC, PEDANTIC, ARTISTIC, LOGISTIC

-URE
MANICURE, PLEASURE, BROCHURE, PEDICURE

Three-Letter Edges: A Potpourri of Eights

SET A: VOCALIZE, DEFINITE, FLAGRANT, HILARITY
SET B: SNOBBISH, RELAXANT, CRESCENT, CAPERING
SET C: TAINTING, POLARIZE, YULETIDE, SCARCITY
SET D: VALIDITY, MODIFIES, CHEAPEST, ARSONIST
SET E: MANIFEST, UNEASIER, PLAYDATE, FACEDOWN
SET F: ELLIPTIC, MERCHANT, SUPPLANT, GREASIER
SET G: ENVISION, PLATEFUL, SANITIZE, SOLIDIFY
SET H: CRAFTIER, LABORING, MESQUITE, ALIENATE
SET I: DREAMIER, NECKTIES, VIGOROUS, WOODPILE
SET J: ENSHRINE, TEAMMATE, AGREEING, CITYWIDE
SET K: ATROPINE, EMBODIES, SANCTIFY, SWEATILY
SET L: NIMBLEST, PACIFIER, ORGANISM, BEVERAGE
SET M: DRAMATIC, TOASTIER, DECOROUS, PIRATING
SET N: MATUREST, FLEABITE, FILTHILY, RETICENT
SET O: STALLION, VERBIAGE, MERCIFUL, ESSAYIST
SET P: SWEATING, OPPONENT, INCISIVE, FUMIGANT
SET Q: ENTITIES, MARKDOWN, OMISSION, MORTGAGE
SET R: COSMETIC, LEVITIES, FEISTILY, ANEURISM
SET S: TRACKING, ADMONISH, ILLUSIVE, FACILITY
SET T: CLUMSIER, OPTIMIST, HUMIDIFY, STOPPAGE
SET U: POUNDAGE, ENORMOUS, OFFSTAGE, WASTEFUL
SET V: MISGROWN, READYING, SNEAKIER, WRONGFUL
SET W: INFUSION, NUTRIENT, JUDICIAL, ROADSIDE

SET X: TWENTIES, UNSOCIAL, HOMICIDE, SCANTILY
SET Y: PERILOUS, DRUGGIST, INSANITY, SCORNFUL
SET Z: COVENANT, ALLOCATE, SUNSHINE, DRAFTILY
SET AA: VIRULENT, MEMORIAL, RIGOROUS, SHORTAGE
SET AB: CONTRIVE, EGGPLANT, EMACIATE, AMPUTATE

Compound Eight-Letter Words

SET A: BIRDCALL, PASSWORD, WHATEVER, MEANTIME
SET B: TELLTALE, LIFESPAN, SOMEWHAT, ROOMMATE
SET C: WHIPLASH, SHAPSHOT, STUBBORN, HEIRLOOM
SET D: DOORKNOB, LOVESICK, SHOWBOAT, LANDLADY
SET E: RAINCOAT, CHAPLAIN, MASSACRE, CASELOAD
SET F: COATRACK, CHARCOAL, BALLPARK, BOATLOAD
SET G: CLAMBAKE, BACKACHE, CASTAWAY, DATABASE
SET H: SLAPDASH, LANDMARK, NAMESAKE, MEATLOAF
SET I: STARGAZE, BIRDBATH, BROWBEAT, BOLDFACE
SET J: DEADBOLT, HOOFBEAT, LIFEBOAT, BAREFOOT
SET K: BEARSKIN, TAILBONE, NECKLACE, TRAPDOOR
SET L: STARDUST, RAINDROP, SIDEWALK, HOMEMADE
SET M: TURNCOAT, TYPECAST, CAREWORN, COOKWARE
SET N: NICKNAME, CAMPFIRE, NECKWEAR, WISEACRE
SET O: TYPEFACE, HANDCUFF, ARCHDUKE, WILDFIRE
SET P: WINDPIPE, DOWNHILL, WINDMILL, DOWNPOUR

More Compound Eights

SET A: NEWLYWED, HONEYDEW, EARPHONE, HAZELNUT
SET B: SOUTHPAW, BEDCOVER, SHORTCUT, PAYCHECK
SET C: CHAINSAW, ANYPLACE, DAYBREAK, EGOMANIA
SET D: LAWMAKER, BADMOUTH, TIEBREAK, PAPERBOY
SET E: CRACKPOT, SCOREPAD, WHITECAP, ALLSPICE
SET F: PUSSYCAT, TRADEOFF, GRANDSON, BEDSHEET

PART • 6

APPENDICES: Facts, Trivia, and Word Lists

In Part 6 we've included the following appendices to serve as handy references about the world of SCRABBLE games.

Appendix 1 clarifies some often-misunderstood rules pertaining to the SCRABBLE game.

Appendix 2 lists a variety of facts and trivia that have been accumulated over decades.

Appendix 3 tells you all about the North American SCRABBLE Players Association.

Appendix 4 has some word lists that you may find invaluable.

Appendix 5 shows you how to use flashcards for learning bingos.

Appendix 6 shows a handy way to calculate the odds of your opponent's having any given letter during a game.

APPENDIX 1

Common Questions About Rules and Clarifications

The North American SCRABBLE Players Association receives many letters and calls concerning rules. Because of that, we thought we should devote a chapter to clarifying the rules. As a reminder, we want to assure you that it's perfectly okay to play with any variation of the rules you prefer, as long as all the participants know which rules are in effect at the onset of the game.

OVERDRAWING TILES

Many people want to know what happens if a player discovers eight tiles on his or her rack instead of seven.

There is no discussion in the boxed rules about what to do in this situation. NASPA has devised a rule that seems to work very well for our clubs and tournaments: The opponent randomly draws three tiles from the offending player's rack, looks at the three of them, and then chooses which one to return to the pool of letters. The remaining tiles go back to the player's rack. If a player overdraws two tiles, then the opponent randomly draws four tiles from the player's rack, chooses which two to replace in the pool, and returns the other tiles to the player. And so on. In each case, the offending player may see all the tiles seen by the opponent.

This overdrawing penalty influences most players to draw their tiles more carefully. One further note about overdrawing: If the overdrawing player realizes s/he has overdrawn before mixing any of the new tiles with the old ones, then the opponent should randomly choose tiles *only* from the group of newly drawn tiles, while following the instructions given above.

PLAYING WORDS ON THE BOARD

In chapter 5, we discussed what was acceptable play-making. We'll briefly repeat in a slightly different form what we've previously said:

Given that PART is the only play on the board, the following are acceptable plays:

1. PARTY; DEPART; DEPARTING
   It's acceptable simply to add one or more letters to a word, to either the front or back, or to *both* the front and back.

2. PARTS: If you want, you can add just an S to a word already on the board.

3. You may play at right angles to a word.

```
P A R T Y          G
        O      P A R T
        U          E
                   W
```

4. You may play parallel to a word as long as adjacent letters form words horizontally and vertically. In this case, since FA, OR, and IT are all acceptable, playing FOIL as shown is acceptable.

```
  F O I L
P A R T
```

What is *not* acceptable is playing tiles diagonally across the board.

One further point: **All** the letters played in one turn must be contained in **the same horizontal or vertical word.** *Example:* If PART is on the board and your rack is ADEELMV, it is *not acceptable* to play *in one turn:* the five letters AELMV, forming the words LAME and REV. That's because the five letters are not all contained in one word or played in a straight line.

```
  P A R T
L A M E
      V
```

PLAYING A BLANK

The official rules do not allow a player, later in the game, to change the letter that the blank represents. Likewise, a player may not replace the blank with the letter it represents and use the blank in another word. At the NASPA's clubs and tournaments, this rule is strictly enforced. The NASPA also advises that to avoid later confusion, both players record on his or her score sheet what letter the blank represents at the time it's played.

Those of you who'd like a game with more scoring chances may play the variation that *allows* players to replace a blank on the board with the letter (from your rack) it represents. The drawback (or advantage) to this game is the increased luck factor.

EXCHANGING TILES

A player may exchange tiles (from one to seven) as long as there are at least seven tiles still in the bag. First, decide which tiles you want to exchange. Then remove them from your rack and place them facedown on the table. Only then may you draw your new tiles, place them on your rack, and replace the exchanged tiles back into the pool.

CHOOSING A DICTIONARY

We have discussed *The Official SCRABBLE® Players Dictionary, Sixth Edition*. We recommend it, but whether you use it or not, make sure that all players know exactly which word reference you are using. All words labeled as a part of speech (including those listed of foreign origin, and as archaic, obsolete, colloquial, slang, etc.) are permitted, with the exception of the following: words always capitalized, abbreviations, prefixes and suffixes standing alone, words requiring a hyphen or an apostrophe, and words formed only as part of a two-word phrase. But please remember that some abbreviations and prefixes are acceptable words since they also have separate meanings. For example, RE, which is considered a prefix, is also an acceptable word representing the second tone on the diatonic musical scale (do, re, mi, etc.).

CHALLENGING

When may a player challenge? And how many words may be challenged at one time?

The rules state that a player can challenge until the next turn. The North American SCRABBLE Players Association has developed a more precise definition for when a player may challenge:

A) Using sand timers or no timers: Once a player has announced his or her score, the opponent may "Hold!" or challenge. After the player has drawn at least one tile from the pool, the opponent may *not* challenge or hold anymore. To avoid what we'll call "speedy-draw syndrome," the player must take a few seconds to record the total score before drawing replacement tiles.

B) Using tournament clocks: After the player has started his or her opponent's timer, the opponent may "Hold!" or challenge. As above, once the player has drawn at least one tile from the pool, the opponent may not challenge or hold anymore.

Using clocks: Once an opponent has called "Hold!" at the proper time, s/he has as long as s/he wants to think about challenging, as long as s/he hasn't yet made the next play. The player can insist on drawing tiles after one minute, as long as s/he keeps the replacement tiles separate from the old tiles. This is called the "Courtesy Rule." If there is a successful challenge, the opponent may see the replacement tiles before the player returns them to the pool.

Using sand timers: After calling "Hold!" the opponent has only the length of his or her turn—three minutes—to decide whether to challenge or not. The Courtesy Rule is in effect here as well.

SCORING

In chapter 2, we have already shown how to score the bonus squares. However, there is one scoring question we are asked about so often that we thought it would be helpful to mention it again.

Let's look at two examples:

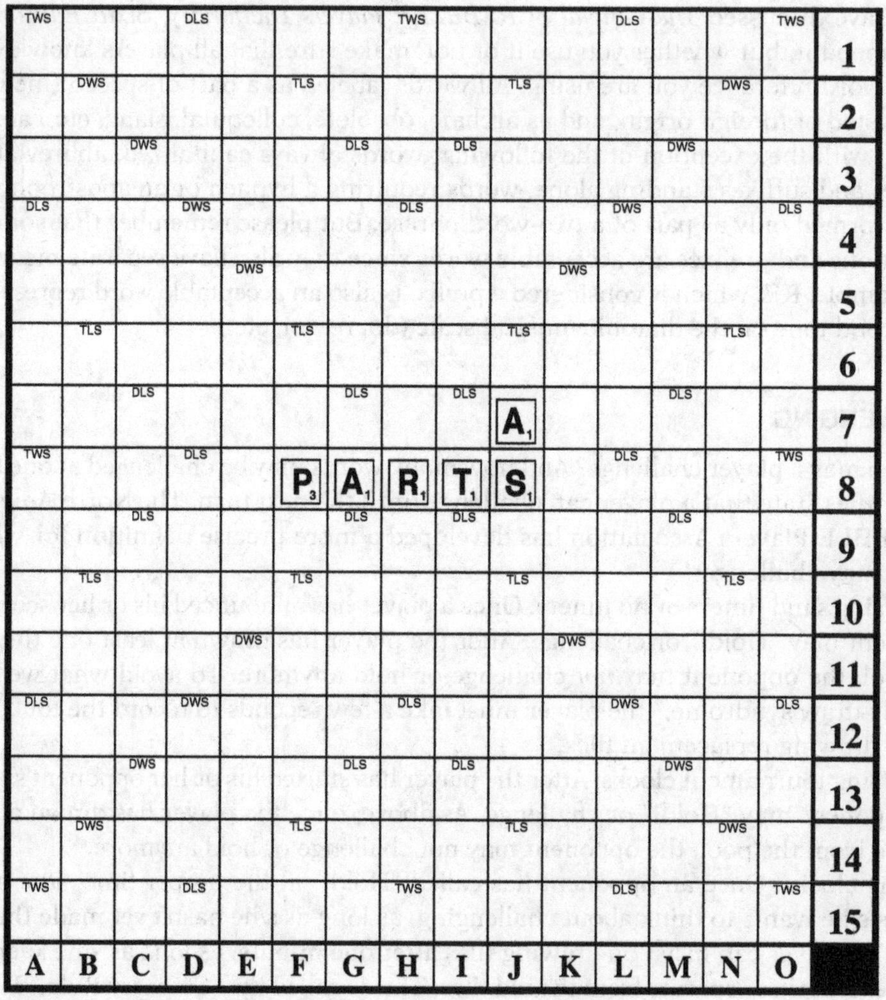
A
P A R T S
1 2 3 4 5 6 7 8 9 10 11 12 13 14 15
A B C D E F G H I J K L M N O

DIAGRAM A-1

You have the above position with the rack: **A C E L R T W**
Play CRAWL 6G.

How much is this play worth?

The play CRAWL 6G forms WAS simultaneously. The W will cover the TLS. Since you form two words at once, and the bonus square is used for both words, and you are *covering* the bonus square *this* turn, the W is scored as a Triple Letter Score square for both CRAWL and WAS. The score for playing CRAWL (spelling both CRAWL and WAS) is: C (3) + R (1) + A (1) + W (12) + L (1) + W (12) + A (1) + S (1) = 32 pts.

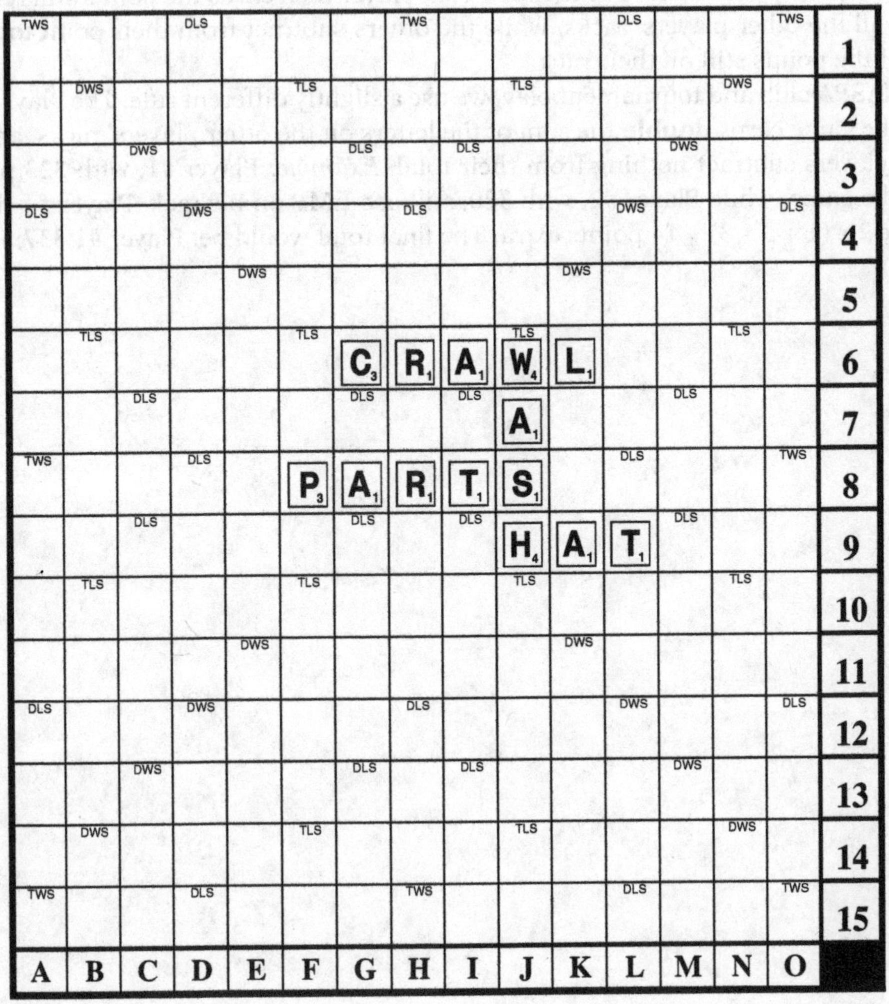

TWS
DLS
DWS
TLS
C R A W L
A
P A R T S
H A T
1 2 3 4 5 6 7 8 9 10 11 12 13 14 15
A B C D E F G H I J K L M N O

DIAGRAM A-2

Next turn your opponent forms the words HAT/WASH. What does this play score? Answer: H (4) + A (1) + T (1) + W (4) + A (1) + S (1) + H (4) = 16 points. Notice that the

W is not counted as a Triple Letter Score because bonus squares can be scored only as such on the turn they are covered.

ENDING THE GAME

The boxed rules mention that the game is over when a player uses all of his or her tiles and there are no more tiles to draw. That player then earns the points still remaining in all the other players' racks, while the others subtract from their point total the sum of the points still on their rack.

In NASPA club and tournament play, we use a slightly different rule. The player who ends the game earns **double** the sum of the letters on the other players' racks, and the other players subtract nothing from their total. *Example:* Player #1, with 323 points, ends the game, while Player #2, with 320, still has EMP on his rack. Player #1 should receive 2 x (1 + 3 + 3) = 14 points extra. The final total would be: Player #1 337; Player #2 320.

APPENDIX 2

Facts and Figures of the World's Favorite Crossword Game

There are an estimated 35 million leisure SCRABBLE game players in the United States and Canada alone. Among those are more than ten thousand enthusiasts who belong to the nearly three hundred sanctioned clubs. Their organization, the North American SCRABBLE Players Association, is headquartered in Dallas, Texas.

Each year, more than 300 sanctioned North American SCRABBLE game tournaments are held. These attract players of all levels, from curious novices to experts, and usually encompass ten to twelve rounds of play over a two-day weekend. At tournaments, players use chess clocks to time their moves, with each player receiving twenty-five minutes to make all his or her plays.

All levels of players are rated by the North American SCRABBLE Players Association in relation to their tournament results. Players rated over 1600 are considered experts. There are more than ten thousand rated players in the United States and Canada, of whom more than five hundred are experts.

The ten best players in the last National SCRABBLE Championship averaged at least 405 points per game.

In tournament play, the following records stand as of November 2007:

The **HIGHEST TOURNAMENT GAME SCORE:** 803 points by Joel Sherman at Stamford, CT, 2011.

The **HIGHEST CLUB GAME SCORE:** 830 points by Mike Cresta vs. Wayne Yorra; Lexington, MA, SCRABBLE Club #108 game on October 12, 2006. Both opponents were rated under 900 at the time. Wayne's losing score was 490 points, and along the way he played four bingos, JOUSTED, LADYLIKE, SCAMSTER, and UNDERDOG. Their combined total of 1,320 points is the **HIGHEST COMBINED SCORE** ever at an NASPA-sanctioned club or tournament. The winner played two 3 × 3s, FLATFISH for 239 points and QUIXOTRY for 365 points, making that bingo the **HIGHEST SINGLE SCORING PLAY** in club or tournament history. Incidentally, after his first *two* plays on the board (not counting several exchanges), he already had over 600 points!

The **HIGHEST LOSING SCORE:** 552 points by Stefan Rau (NY) to Keith Smith (CA) 582 points; Dallas, TX, 2008.

The **HIGHEST TIE GAME:** 502–502 points by John Chew (ONT) and Zev Kaufman (ONT) at a 1997 Toronto Club #3 tournament.

The **HIGHEST-SCORING NON-BINGO:** RORQUALS, 243 points by Karen Merrill (OR), 1997.

The **LARGEST ONE-GAME SPREAD:** 569 points by Ken Lambe (MI) at a New York qualifying tournament in 1981. Final score: 714–147.

The **GREATEST COMEBACK:** 256 points by David Poder (CA); Campbell, CA, 2001. He was behind 6–262 and won 541–539.

The **MOST POINTS SCORED WITH ONE TILE:** 99 by Tom Kelly (NY); Plainview, NY, 1999. He played an S on 15A to form QUIRKS/SMOTHERED.

The **MOST POINTS SCORED ON THE FIRST PLAY:** 128 points MUZJIKS by Jesse Inway (CA).

The **HIGHEST PER TURN AVERAGE** (counting exchanges): 61.2 points by Jim Kramer (MN); Waltham, MA, 2000. In nine plays he scored 551 points. His first four plays were CAROUSED 62, OREGANO 97, DILUTIVE 80, and ASTRINGE 140. His last play was a bingo, RETIRING 72, and his opponent, world champion Joel Wapnick (QUE), went out with a bingo, caught up to Kramer with 22 points, and finished with 453 points. Wapnick averaged 45.13 points per turn in ten plays and their **COMBINED PER TURN AVERAGE** of 52.8 is also a record.

The **HIGHEST AVERAGE SCORE** (two-day or more tourney): 470.11 points by Chris Cree (TX) in Houston on Labor Day Weekend, 2007. He finished with a 16–2, +2117 record. The same record during a one-day tournament was earned by Christopher Sykes (ON), who finished 7–0, +995 and averaged 485.3 points each game at Brantford, ON, in November, 2007.

YOUNGEST EXPERT: Currently, the youngest 2,000-rated expert in North America is Mack Meller (NY), born in 2000. He is rated above 2,100, fourth-highest-rated player in North America.

NATIONAL CHAMPIONSHIP WINNERS (top five in order, beginning with winner):

1978: David Prinz (CA); Dan Pratt (MD); Mike Senkewicz (NY); Linda Gruber (NY); Charles Goldstein (CA)

1980: Joe Edley (CA); Jim Neuberger (NY); Ron Tiekert (NY); Dan Pratt (MD); David Prinz (CA)

1983: Joel Wapnick (QUE); Dan Pratt (MD); Joe Edley (CA); Steven Fisher (QUE); Edward Halper (NY)

1985: Ron Tiekert (NY); Joe Edley (CA); Richie Lund (NY); Chuck Armstrong (MI); Dan Pratt (MD)

1987: Rita Norr (NY); Jere Mead (MA); Chuck Armstrong (MI); Chris Cree (TX); Brian Cappelletto (AZ)

1988: Robert Watson (MN); Peter Morris (ONT); Joel Wapnick (QUE); Chuck Armstrong (MI); Joe Weinike (NY)

1989: Peter Morris (MI); Mark Nyman (ENG); Ron Tiekert (NY); Richie Lund (NY); Darrell Day (TX)

1990: Robert Felt (CA); Lester Schonbrun (CA); Ed Halper (NY); Charlie Southwell (MD); Louis Schecter (NY)

1992: Joe Edley (NY); Joel Wapnick (QUE); Brian Cappelletto (IL); Lester Schonbrun (CA); David Gibson (SC)

1994: David Gibson (SC); David Wiegand (OR); Bob Lipton (FL); Joe Edley (NY); Mark Nyman (ENG)

1996: Adam Logan (NJ); Marlon Hill (MD); Joe Edley (NY); Brian Cappelletto (IL); Paul Epstein (MI)

1998: Brian Cappelletto (IL); Trey Wright (CA); Jere Mead (MA); Jim Kramer (MN); Ron Tiekert (NY)

2000: Joe Edley (NY); Brian Cappelletto (IL); David Wiegand (OR); Adam Logan (CA); Randy Hersom (SC)

2002: Joel Sherman (NY); Nigel Richards (Indonesia); Jakkrit Klaphajone (THAI); Brian Cappelletto (IL); Paul Epstein (MI)

2004: Trey Wright (CA); David Gibson (SC); Nigel Richards (Indonesia); Chris Cree (TX); Brian Cappelletto (IL)

2005: David Wiegand (OR); Panupol Sujjayakorn (THAI); John Luebkemann (DE); Jerry Lerman (CA); Joe Edley (NY)

2006: Jim Kramer (MN); Geoff Thevenot (TX); Pakorn Nemitrmansuk (THAI); Mark Pistolese (HI); Scott Appel (NJ)

2008: Nigel Richards (Malaysia); Brian Cappelletto (IL); David Gibson (SC); Joey Malick (ME); Ian Weinstein (FL)

2009: David Wiegand (OR); Nigel Richards (NZ); Joel Wapnick (OH); Adam Logan (CAN); Chris Cree (TX)

2010: Nigel Richards (NZ); Brian Cappelletto (IL); Laurie Cohen (AZ); Orry Swift (TX); David Wiegand (OR)

2011: Nigel Richards (NZ); Kenji Matsumoto (HI); Brian Bowman (KY); Jim Kramer (WI); Jesse Day (CA)

2012: Nigel Richards (NZ); David Gibson (SC); Jesse Day (CA); Kenji Matsumoto (HI); David Wiegand (OR)

2013: Nigel Richards (NZ); Komol Panyasophonlert (THAI); Will Anderson (PA); Noah Walton (CA); Kenji Matsumoto (HI)

2014: Conrad Bassett-Bouchard (CA); Jim Kramer (WI); Joel Sherman (NY); Jason Li (CAN); Will Anderson (PA)

2015: Matthew Tunnicliffe (CAN); Jesse Day (CA); Will Anderson (PA); Panupol Sujjayakorn (THAI); Orry Swift (TX)

2016: David Gibson (SC); Ian Weinstein (FL); Mack Meller (NY); Matthew Tunnicliffe (CAN); Joel Sherman (NY)

2017: Will Anderson (PA); Mack Meller (NY); Nigel Richards (NZ); Alec Sjoholm (WA); Rafi Stern (MA)

SCRABBLE® SUPERSTARS SHOWDOWN

In 1995 there was a special SCRABBLE® Superstars Tournament held in Las Vegas, NV, that awarded the most money in any SCRABBLE game tournament, and that's still true as of 2001. The winner got $50,000. In all, $100,000 was awarded. The top fifty-four players of North America participated.

SUPERSTARS TOP FIVE WINNERS: David Gibson (SC); Brian Cappelletto (IL); Joe Edley (NY); Jan Dixon (DE); Robin Pollock Daniel (ONT)

In 2003 a second Superstars Tournament was held, this time called the ALL-STARS Championship, and included the top 24 players. David Gibson (SC) once again prevailed, followed by Ron Tiekert (FL), Joel Wapnick (QUE), Brian Cappelletto (IL), and Joey Mallick (ME).

WORLD SCRABBLE® CHAMPIONSHIPS

There have been seventeen English-language World SCRABBLE® Championships (WSC) since 1991. These events are very different from any other sanctioned tournament in North America. Why? One reason is that it's an invitation-only tournament. Each nation or region has a specific allotment of players they may send to the WSC. For instance, the United States now sends fourteen players. Canada sends seven. Another reason is that instead of using our official word list from North America, the British word list is added, which includes approximately twenty-five thousand extra words. That's because most of the other nations in the world use the British word source, and many of these nations now play with both our word source and the British word source.

Once players know they will qualify for the WSC, within a year of the next one, they must review the extra British words in addition to the U.S. words in order to do well. And then forget them for the rest of the next two years in order to do well in North American tourneys. That's not an ideal situation. However, North Americans have done well.

Approximately one hundred players from around the world, many of whom don't even speak English, get together and battle it out in this twenty-four-round tournament. The top two players at that point play a best-of-five finals.

WSC TOP FIVE WINNERS:

1991: Peter Morris (MI); Brian Cappelletto (IL); David Boys (CAN); Joe Edley (NY); Ron Tiekert (NY)

1993: Mark Nyman (ENG); Joel Wapnick (CAN); David Gibson (SC); Gareth Williams (Wales); Allan Saldanha (ENG)

1995: David Boys (CAN); Joel Sherman (NY); Jeff Grant (NZ); Bob Lipton (FL); Joe Edley (NY)

1997: Joel Sherman (NY); Matt Graham (NY); Joe Edley (NY); Robert Felt (CA); Mark Nyman (ENG)

1999: Joel Wapnick (CAN); Mark Nyman (ENG); David Boys (CAN); Adam Logan (CA); Andrew Fisher (ENG)

2001: Brian Cappelletto (IL); Joel Wapnick (CAN); Jim Kramer (MN); Steve Polatnick (FL); Andrew Fisher (ENG)

2003: Panupol Sujjayakorn (THAI); Pakorn Nemitrmansuk (THAI); Andrew Perry (ENG); Mark Nyman (ENG); Jim Kramer (MN)

2005: Adam Logan (CAN); Pakorn Nemitrmansuk (THAI); Fernando Naween (AUS); Ganesh Asirvatham (IND); Gareth Williams (WALES)

2007: Nigel Richards (NZ); Ganesh Asirvatham (MAY); Wellington Jighere (NGR); Joel Wapnick (CAN); Akshay Bhandarkar (UAE)

2009: Pakorn Nemitrmansuk (THAI); Nigel Richards (NZ); David Wiegand (OR); Marut Siriwangso (THAI); Komol Panyasophonlert (THAI)

2010: Nigel Richards (NZ); Pakorn Nemitrmansuk (THAI); Chris May (AUS); Bob Linn (MD); Nathan Bernedict (AZ)

2011: Nigel Richards (NZ); Andrew Fisher (AUS); Pakorn Nemitrmansuk (THAI); David Wiegand (OR); Chris May (AUS)

2013: Nigel Richards (NZ); Komol Panyasophonlert (THAI); David Wiegand (OR); Sammy Okosagah (MD); Craig Beevers (ENG)

2014: Craig Beevers (ENG); Chris Lipe (NY); David Wiegand (OR); Adam Logan (CAN); Brett Smitheram (ENG)

2015: Jighere Wellington (NIG); Lewis Mackay (ENG); Esther Perrins (AUS); Komol Panyasophonlert (THAI); David Wiegand (OR)

2016: Brett Smitheram (ENG); Mark Nyman (ENG); Lewis MacKay (ENG); Adam Logan (CAN); David Webb (ENG)

2017: David Eldar (AUS); Harshan Lamabadusuriya (ENG); Austin Shin (ENG); Goutham Jayaraman (SG); Nigel Richards (NZ)

(Note: For more records and statistics, visit www.cross-tables.com.)

APPENDIX 3

The North American SCRABBLE® Players Association (NASPA)

PO Box 12115
Dallas, TX 75225-0115
www.scrabbleplayers.org

The NASPA website, listed above, is a wealth of information, and is easy to navigate. Headings include: About Us, News, Play SCRABBLE®, Media, Clubs, Tournaments, Members, Directors.

❑ NASPA publishes the following (among other items):

- Lists of upcoming tournaments
- News of tournaments and their results
- News items about what's happening in the world of SCRABBLE games
- Lists of all sanctioned clubs and club changes

❑ NASPA is responsible for:

- Sanctioning official NASPA clubs and directors
- Sanctioning official tournaments and advertising them on its website, as well as allowing cross-tables.com to do the same
- Formulating and regularly updating rules and guidelines for ensuring fair standards and practices at official SCRABBLE game clubs and tournaments
- Maintaining membership records for more than 10,000 SCRABBLE game players
- Making online starter kits available to each new member, including word lists (the twos, the two-to-make-threes, and more), as well as providing all NASPA members access to Zyzzyva, the premier word-list generating program as a study guide and tournament and club word adjudicator
- Organizing and promoting an annual National SCRABBLE Championship tournament open to all rated players who are current members
- Answering all queries about organized SCRABBLE game play and related questions
- Maintaining constant liaison with Hasbro, Inc., the game's manufacturer, to consider mutual promotional ventures

APPENDIX 4

Important Word Lists

The following lists represent some of the most useful SCRABBLE game words to learn. They will appear on your rack repeatedly as you learn to balance your rack. These word lists are adapted from *The Wordbook* by Mike Baron and Jere Guin and *The Wordbook Addendum '91* by Mike Baron and Jim Homan. For information about these books contact Mike Baron at PO Box 2848, Corrales, NM 87048.

THE TOP TEN 6-LETTER STEMS

(in order of usefulness)

SATINE

A: ENTASIA TAENIAS
B: BANTIES BASINET
C: ACETINS CINEAST
D: DESTAIN DETAINS INSTEAD NIDATES SAINTED SATINED STAINED
E: ETESIAN
F: FAINEST
G: EASTING EATINGS GENISTA INGATES INGESTA SEATING TAGINES TEASING
H: SHEITAN STHENIA
I: ISATINE
J: TAJINES
K: INTAKES
L: ELASTIN ENTAILS NAILSET SALIENT SALTINE SLAINTE TENAILS
M: ETAMINS INMATES TAMEINS
N: INANEST STANINE
O: ATONIES
P: PANTIES PATINES SAPIENT SPINATE
R: ANESTRI ANTSIER NASTIER RATINES RETAINS RETINAS RETSINA STAINER STEARIN
S: ENTASIS NASTIES SEITANS SESTINA TANSIES TISANES
T: INSTATE SATINET
U: AUNTIES SINUATE
V: NAIVEST NATIVES VAINEST
W: TAWNIES WANIEST
X: ANTISEX SEXTAIN
Z: ZANIEST ZEATINS

SATIRE

A: ARISTAE ASTERIA ATRESIA
B: BAITERS BARITES REBAITS TERBIAS
C: ATRESIC CRISTAE RACIEST STEARIC
D: ARIDEST ASTRIDE DIASTER DISRATE STAIDER TARDIES TIRADES
E: AERIEST SERIATE
F: FAIREST
G: AIGRETS GAITERS SEAGIRT STAGIER TRIAGES
H: HASTIER
I: AIRIEST
L: REALIST RETAILS SALTIER SALTIRE SLATIER TAILERS
M: IMARETS MAESTRI MISRATE SMARTIE
N: ANESTRI ANTSIER NASTIER RATINES RETAINS RETINAS RETSINA STAINER STEARIN
P: PARTIES PASTIER PIASTER PIASTRE PIRATES PRATIES TRAIPSE
R: ARTSIER TARRIES TARSIER
S: ARTSIES SATIRES
T: ARTIEST ARTISTE ATTIRES IRATEST RATITES STRIATE TASTIER
V: RAVIEST VASTIER VERITAS
W: WAISTER WAITERS WARIEST WASTRIE

THE TOP TEN 6-LETTER STEMS *(cont.)*

RETINA

C: CERATIN
CERTAIN
CREATIN
TACRINE
D: ANTIRED
DETRAIN
TRAINED
E: ARENITE
RETINAE
TRAINEE
F: FAINTER
G: GRANITE
GRATINE
INGRATE
TANGIER
TEARING
H: HAIRNET
INEARTH
THERIAN
I: INERTIA
K: KERATIN
L: LATRINE
RATLINE
RELIANT
RETINAL
TRENAIL
M: MINARET
RAIMENT
N: ENTRAIN
TRANNIE
P: INAPTER
PAINTER
PERTAIN
REPAINT
R: RETRAIN
TERRAIN
TRAINER
S: ANESTRI
ANTSIER
NASTIER
RATINES
RETAINS
RETINAS
RETSINA
STAINER
STEARIN
T: INTREAT
ITERANT
NATTIER
NITRATE
TERTIAN
U: RUINATE
TAURINE
URANITE
URINATE
W: TAWNIER
TINWARE

ARSINE

C: ARCSINE
ARSENIC
CARNIES
D: RANDIES
SANDIER
SARDINE
F: INFARES
G: EARINGS
ERASING
GAINERS
REAGINS
REGAINS
REGINAS
SEARING
SERINGA
H: HERNIAS
NEARISH
I: SENARII
J: INJERAS
K: SNAKIER
L: ALINERS
NAILERS
RENAILS
M: MARINES
REMAINS
SEMINAR
N: INSANER
INSNARE
O: ERASION
P: PANIERS
RAPINES
R: SIERRAN
S: ARSINES
SARNIES
T: *See* SATINE *list*
V: RAVINES

IRONES

A: ERASION
C: COINERS
CRONIES
ORCEINS
RECOINS
D: DINEROS
INDORSE
ORDINES
ROSINED
SORDINE
G: ERINGOS
IGNORES
REGIONS
SIGNORE
H: HEROINS
INSHORE
I: IONISER
IRONIES
IRONISE
NOISIER
J: JOINERS
REJOINS
L: NEROLIS
M: MERINOS
O: EROSION
P: ORPINES
R: IRONERS
S: SENIORS
SONSIER
T: NORITES
OESTRIN
ORIENTS
STONIER
U: URINOSE
V: ENVIROS
RENVOIS
VERSION
W: SNOWIER

TONIES

A: ATONIES
B: BONIEST
C: NOTICES
SECTION
H: ETHIONS
HISTONE
I: INOSITE
L: ENTOILS
ONLIEST
M: MESTINO
MOISTEN
MONTIES
SENTIMO
N: INTONES
TENSION
O: ISOTONE
TOONIES
P: PINTOES
POINTES
R: NORITES
OESTRIN
ORIENTS
STONIER
S: NOSIEST
T: TONIEST
W: TOWNIES
X: TOXINES

THE TOP TEN 6-LETTER STEMS *(cont.)*

SANTER

A: SANTERA
B: BANTERS
C: CANTERS CARNETS NECTARS RECANTS SCANTER TANRECS TRANCES
D: DARNEST STANDER
E: EARNEST EASTERN NEAREST STERANE
G: ARGENTS GARNETS STRANGE
H: ANTHERS THENARS
I: *See* SATINE *list*
K: RANKEST TANKERS
L: ANTLERS RENTALS SALTERN STERNAL
M: MARTENS SARMENT SMARTEN
N: TANNERS
O: ATONERS SANTERO SENATOR TREASON
P: ARPENTS ENTRAPS PARENTS PASTERN TREPANS
R: ERRANTS RANTERS
S: SARSNET
T: NATTERS RATTENS
U: NATURES SAUNTER
V: SERVANT TAVERNS VERSANT
W: WANTERS

SINTER

A: *See* SATINE *list*
C: CISTERN CRETINS
D: TINDERS
E: ENTIRES ENTRIES RETINES TRIENES
F: SNIFTER
G: RESTING STINGER
H: HINTERS
K: REKNITS STINKER TINKERS
L: LINTERS
M: MINSTER MINTERS REMINTS
N: INTERNS TINNERS
O: NORITES OESTRIN ORIENTS STONIER
P: PTERINS
S: ESTRINS INSERTS SINTERS STRINES
T: RETINTS STINTER TINTERS
U: NUTSIER TRIUNES UNITERS
V: INVERTS STRIVEN
W: TWINERS WINTERS

STONER

A: ATONERS SANTERO SENATOR TREASON
B: SORBENT
C: CORNETS CRETONS
D: RODENTS SNORTED
E: ESTRONE
F: FRONTES
G: TONGERS
H: HORNETS SHORTEN THRONES
I: NORITES OESTRIN ORIENTS STONIER
K: STONKER
L: LORNEST
M: MENTORS MONSTER
N: TONNERS
O: ENROOTS
P: POSTERN PRONEST
R: SNORTER
S: NESTORS STONERS TENSORS
T: STENTOR
U: TENOURS TONSURE

EATERS

A: AERATES
B: BEATERS BERATES REBATES
C: CERATES CREATES ECARTES
D: DEAREST DERATES REDATES SEDATER
F: AFREETS FEASTER
G: ERGATES RESTAGE
H: AETHERS HEATERS REHEATS
I: AERIEST SERIATE
K: RETAKES
L: ELATERS REALEST RELATES RESLATE STEALER
M: REMATES RETEAMS STEAMER
N: EARNEST EASTERN NEAREST STERANE
O: ROSEATE
P: EPATERS REPEATS RETAPES
R: RETEARS SERRATE TEARERS
S: EASTERS RESEATS SEAREST SEATERS TEASERS TESSERA
T: ESTREAT RESTATE RETASTE
U: AUSTERE
W: SWEATER
X: RETAXES

THE TOP TEN 7-LETTER STEMS

EASTERN

A: ARSENATE
SERENATA
B: ABSENTER
C: CENTARES
REASCENT
REENACTS
SARCENET
E: SERENATE
F: FASTENER
FENESTRA
REFASTEN
G: ESTRANGE
GRANTEES
GREATENS
NEGATERS
REAGENTS
SERGEANT
H: HASTENER
HEARTENS
I: ARENITES
ARSENITE
ARTESIAN
RESINATE
STEARINE
TRAINEES
J: SERJEANT
L: ETERNALS
TELERANS
O: EARSTONE
RESONATE
R: TERRANES
S: ASSENTER
EARNESTS
SARSENET
STERANES
T: ENTREATS
RATTEENS
U: SAUTERNE
V: RAVENEST
VETERANS

ENTRIES

A: *See* EASTERN +I
C: ENTERICS
ENTICERS
SECRETIN
D: INSERTED
NERDIEST
RESIDENT
SINTERED
TRENDIES
E: ETERNISE
TEENSIER
F: FERNIEST
INFESTER
G: GENTRIES
INTEGERS
REESTING
STEERING
I: NITERIES
K: KERNITES
L: ENLISTER
LISTENER
REENLIST
SILENTER
M: MISENTER
N: INTENSER
INTERNES
O: ONERIEST
SEROTINE
R: INSERTER
REINSERT
REINTERS
RENTIERS
TERRINES
S: SENTRIES
T: INSETTER
INTEREST
STERNITE
TRIENTES
U: ESURIENT
RETINUES
REUNITES
V: NERVIEST
REINVEST
SIRVENTE
X: INTERSEX
Y: SERENITY

NASTIER

A: ANTISERA
RATANIES
SANTERIA
SEATRAIN
B: BANISTER
BARNIEST
C: CANISTER
CERATINS
CISTERNA
CREATINS
SCANTIER
TACRINES
D: DETRAINS
RANDIEST
STRAINED
E: *See* EASTERN + I
F: FAINTERS
G: ANGRIEST
ANGSTIER
ASTRINGE
GANISTER
GANTRIES
GRANITES
INGRATES
RANGIEST
H: HAIRNETS
INEARTHS
THERIANS
I: INERTIAS
RAINIEST
SATINIER
K: KERATINS
NARKIEST
L: ENTRAILS
LATRINES
RATLINES
RETINALS
SLANTIER
TRENAILS
M: MINARETS
RAIMENTS
N: ENTRAINS
TRANNIES
O: NOTARIES
NOTARISE
SENORITA
P: PAINTERS
PANTRIES
PERTAINS
PINASTER
PRISTANE
REPAINTS
R: RESTRAIN
RETRAINS
STRAINER
TERRAINS
TRAINERS
S: ARTINESS
RETSINAS
STAINERS
STEARINS
T: INTREATS
NITRATES
STRAITEN
TERTIANS
U: RUINATES
TAURINES
URANITES
URINATES
W: TINWARES

REALIGN

A: GERANIAL
B: BLEARING
C: CLEARING
RELACING
D: DANGLIER
DRAGLINE
E: ALGERINE
F: FINAGLER
G: GANGLIER
LAGERING
REGALING
H: NARGHILE
NARGILEH
I: GAINLIER
J: JANGLIER
L: ALLERGIN
M: GERMINAL
MALIGNER
MALINGER
N: LEARNING
O: GERANIOL
REGIONAL
P: GRAPLINE
PEARLING
R: GNARLIER
S: ALIGNERS
ENGRAILS
LASERING
NARGILES
REALIGNS
SIGNALER
SLANGIER
T: ALERTING
ALTERING
INTEGRAL
RELATING
SLANTIER
TANGLIER
TRIANGLE
V: RAVELING
X: RELAXING
Y: LAYERING
RELAYING
YEARLING

THE TOP TEN 7-LETTER STEMS *(cont.)*

NAILERS

B: RINSABLE
C: CARLINES LANCIERS
D: ISLANDER
E: ALIENERS
G: *See* REALIGN + S
H: INHALERS
I: AIRLINES
M: MARLINES MINERALS MISLEARN
O: AILERONS ALIENORS
P: PRALINES
R: SNARLIER
S: RAINLESS
T: *See* NASTIER + L
V: RAVELINS
X: RELAXINS
Y: INLAYERS

SAINTED

B: BANDIEST
C: DISTANCE DANCIEST
D: DANDIEST
E: ANDESITE
G: SEDATING STEADING
H: HANDIEST
I: ADENITIS DAINTIES
M: MEDIANTS
O: ASTONIED SEDATION
P: DEPAINTS
R: *See* NASTIER + D
S: DESTAINS SANDIEST
T: INSTATED
U: AUDIENTS SINUATED
V: DEVIANTS

SARDINE

A: ARANEIDS
B: BRANDIES
D: SARDINED
E: ARSENIDE NEARSIDE
G: DERAIGNS GRADINES READINGS
L: ISLANDER
N: INSNARED
O: ANEROIDS ANODISER
P: SPRAINED
R: DRAINERS SERRANID
S: ARIDNESS SARDINES
T: *See* NASTIER + D
U: DENARIUS UNRAISED URANIDES
V: INVADERS

SERIATE

D: READIEST SERIATED STEADIER
E: EATERIES
H: HEARTIES
L: ATELIERS EARLIEST LEARIEST REALTIES
M: EMERITAS EMIRATES STEAMIER
N: *See* EASTERN + I
P: PARIETES
R: ARTERIES
S: SERIATES
T: ARIETTES ITERATES TEARIEST TREATIES TREATISE
W: SWEATIER WASTERIE WEARIEST
Y: YEASTIER

STONIER

A: *See* NASTIER + O
B: BORNITES
C: COINTERS CORNIEST NOTICERS
E: *See* ENTRIES + O
G: GENITORS
H: HORNIEST ORNITHES
I: IRONIEST
J: JOINTERS
K: INSTROKE
L: RETINOLS
N: INTONERS TERNIONS
O: SNOOTIER
P: POINTERS PORNIEST PROTEINS REPOINTS TROPINES
R: INTRORSE
S: OESTRINS
T: SNOTTIER TENORIST TRITONES
U: ROUTINES SNOUTIER
V: INVESTOR
Y: SEROTINY TYROSINE

TRAINEE

C: CENTIARE CREATINE INCREATE ITERANCE
D: DETAINER RETAINED
G: GRATINEE INTERAGE
H: HERNIATE
I: INERTIAE
K: ANKERITE
L: ELATERIN ENTAILER TREENAIL
M: ANTIMERE
P: APERIENT
R: RETAINER
S: *See* NASTIER + E

4- TO 8-LETTER WORDS THAT INCLUDE AT LEAST 62% VOWELS

4

ACAI
AEON
AERO
AGEE
AGIO
AGUE
AIDE
AJEE
AKEE
ALAE
ALEE
ALOE
AMIA
AMIE
ANOA
AQUA
AREA
ARIA
ASEA
AURA
AUTO
AWEE
BEAU
CIAO
EASE
EAUX
EAVE
EEEW
EIDE
EMEU
EPEE
ETUI
EURO
IDEA
ILEA
ILIA
INIA
IOTA
IXIA
JIAO
LIEU
LUAU
MEOU
MOUE
NAOI
OBIA
OBOE
ODEA
OGEE
OHIA
OLEA
OLEO
OLIO
OOZE
OUTA
OUZO
OWIE
PAUA
QUAI
RAIA
ROUE
TOEA
UNAI
UNAU
UREA
UVEA
ZOEA

5

AALII
ADIEU
AECIA
AERIE
AIOLI
AIYEE
AQUAE
AREAE
AUDIO
AURAE
AUREI
COOEE
EERIE
LOOIE
LOUIE
MIAOU
OIDIA
OORIE
OURIE
QUEUE
URAEI
ZOEAE

6

AALIIS
ABASIA
ABELIA
ABULIA
ACACIA
ACAJOU
ACEDIA
ACUATE
ACULEI
ADAGIO
ADIEUS
ADIEUX
AECIAL
AECIUM
AEDILE
AEDINE
AENEUS
AEONIC
AERATE
AERIAL
AERIED
AERIER
AERIES
AEROBE
AERUGO
AGAPAE
AGAPAI
AGORAE
AGOUTI
AIKIDO
AIOLIS
AIRIER
AKEBIA
ALEXIA
ALODIA
ALULAE
AMADOU
AMAUTI
AMEBAE
AMOEBA
AMUSIA
ANEMIA
ANOMIE
ANOPIA
ANOXIA
ANURIA
AORTAE
AOUDAD
APIECE
APNOEA
APOGEE
APORIA
AREOLA
AREOLE
ARIOSE
ARIOSI
ARIOSO
AROUSE
ARUANA
ASIAGO
ATAXIA
ATONIA
AUBADE
AUCUBA
AUDIAL
AUDILE
AUDIOS
AUDISM
AUDIST
AUGITE
AUNTIE
AURATE
AUREUS
AURORA
AUROUS
AUSUBO
AUTEUR
AUTOED
AVENUE
AVIATE
AZALEA
BAILEE
BAILIE
BATEAU
BAUBEE
BEANIE
BEEBEE
BLOOIE
BOOBOO
BOOCOO
BOOGIE
BOOHOO
BOOKIE
BOOKOO
BOOTEE
BOOTIE
BOUBOU
BOUGIE
BUREAU
CAEOMA
CAIQUE
COATEE
CODEIA
COOCOO
COOEED
COOEES
COOKIE
COOLIE
COOTIE
COTEAU
COULEE
CURIAE
DAIMIO
DAUTIE
DEARIE
DOOBIE
DOODOO
DOOLEE
DOOLIE
DOOZIE
EASIER
EASIES
EELIER
EERIER
EIDOLA
EKUELE
ELODEA
ELUATE
ELUVIA
EMEUTE
EOCENE
EOLIAN
EONIAN
EOSINE
EPIZOA
EPOPEE
EQUATE
EQUINE
ETOILE
EUPNEA
EUREKA
EURIPI
EXODOI
EXUVIA
FACIAE
FAERIE
FAUNAE
FEIJOA
FEIRIE
FERIAE
FLOOIE
FOODIE
FOOTIE
FOVEAE
GALEAE
GATEAU
GIAOUR
GOALIE
GOATEE
GOODIE
GOOIER
GOOLIE
GOONIE
GUAIAC
GUINEA
HEAUME
HEINIE
HOAGIE

4- TO 8-LETTER WORDS THAT INCLUDE AT LEAST 62% VOWELS *(cont.)*

6 *(cont.)*

HOODIE
HOODOO
HOOLIE
HOOPOE
HOOPOO
IDEATE
IGUANA
IODATE
IODIDE
IODINE
IODISE
IODIZE
IODOUS
IOLITE
IONISE
IONIUM
IONIZE
IONONE
KOODOO
KOOKIE
KOUROI
LAMIAE
LAOGAI
LAURAE
LEAGUE
LIAISE
LOANEE
LOOGIE
LOOIES
LOOKIE
LOONIE
LOUIES
MEALIE
MEANIE
MEDIAE
MEINIE
MEOUED
MIAOUS
MILIEU
MOIRAI
MUUMUU
NAUSEA
NOOGIE
OAKIER
OATIER
OBELIA
OCREAE
ODIOUS
OEDEMA
OEUVRE
OIDIUM
OILIER
OLEATE
OLEINE
OOLITE
OOMIAC
OOMIAK
OORALI
OOZIER
OPAQUE
OPIATE
OPIOID
OREIDE
ORIOLE
OROIDE
OTIOSE
OUGIYA
OURARI
OUREBI
OUTAGE
OUTATE
OUTEAT
OUTLIE
OUTSEE
OUTVIE
PALEAE
PEERIE
PEEWEE
PEREIA
QUAERE
QUALIA
QUELEA
QUEUED
QUEUER
QUEUES
QUINOA
REALIA
REDIAE
RESEAU
ROADEO
ROADIE
ROOFIE
ROOKIE
ROOMIE
SOIREE
SOUARI
TAENIA
TEEPEE
TEEVEE
TENIAE
TIBIAE
TOONIE
TOUPEE
TOUPIE
UAKARI
UBIQUE
UNCIAE
UNEASE
UNIQUE
URAEUS
URANIA
UREASE
UREDIA
UREIDE
UREMIA
UTOPIA
UVEOUS
UVULAE
VEEPEE
VOODOO
WEENIE
WEEPIE
WEEWEE
WIENIE
WOODIE
WOOLIE
WOOPIE
YAUTIA
ZAIKAI
ZOARIA
ZOECIA
ZOOIER
ZOUAVE

7

ABOULIA
ACEQUIA
AECIDIA
AENEOUS
AEOLIAN
AEONIAN
AERADIO
AEROBIA
ALIENEE
AMOEBAE
ANAEMIA
AQUARIA
AQUEOUS
AREOLAE
AUDITEE
AUREATE
AUREOLA
AUREOLE
AURORAE
AUTOSAVE
COUTEAU
EPINAOI
EUCAINE
EUGENIA
EULOGIA
EUPNOEA
EVACUEE
EXUVIAE
IPOMOEA
MIAOUED
NOUVEAU
OIDIOID
OOGONIA
OUABAIN
OUGUIYA
ROULEAU
SEQUOIA
TAENIAE
URAEMIA
ZOOECIA

8

ABOIDEAU
ABOITEAU
ABOULIAS
ACADEMIA
ACAULINE
ACAULOSE
ACAULOUS
ACEQUIAS
ACICULAE
ACIDEMIA
ACIDURIA
ACIERATE
ACOELOUS
ACQUIREE
ACTINIAE
ACULEATE
ADEQUATE
ADULARIA
AECIDIAL
AECIDIUM
AEQUORIN
AERADIOS
AERATION
AERIFIED
AERIFIES
AEROBIUM
AEROFOIL
AEROLITE
AERONAUT
AGENESIA
AGIOTAGE
AGOUTIES
AGUACATE
AGUELIKE
AGUEWEED
AIGUILLE
AKINESIA
ALEHOUSE
ALEURONE
ALIENAGE
ALIENATE
ALIENEES
ALLELUIA
ALOPECIA
AMEERATE
AMOEBEAN
AMOEBOID
ANABAENA
ANAEMIAS
ANAEROBE
ANALOGUE
ANOOPSIA
ANOREXIA
ANOXEMIA
APIARIAN
APIARIES
APIMANIA
APOLOGIA
APOLOGUE
AQUACADE
AQUAFABA
AQUANAUT
AQUARIAL
AQUARIAN
AQUARIUM
AQUATONE
AQUILINE
ARACEOUS
ARAHUANA
ARAPAIMA
AREOLATE
ATARAXIA
AUBRETIA
AUBRIETA
AUDIENCE
AUDITEES
AUDITION
AUDITIVE
AUGURIES
AUREOLAE
AUREOLAS
AUREOLED
AUREOLES
AURICULA

8 (*cont.*)

AUTACOID
AUTOCADE
AUTOCOID
AUTODIAL
AUTOGIRO
AUTOLOAD
AUTOMATA
AUTOMATE
AUTOSAVE
AUTOSOME
AUTUNITE
AVIANIZE
AVIARIES
AVIATION
AVIFAUNA
AZOTEMIA
AZOTURIA
BAUHINIA
BEAUCOUP
BEAUTIES
BIUNIQUE
BOISERIE
BOOGALOO
BOOHOOED
BOUSOUKI
BOUTIQUE
BOUZOUKI
CAESIOUS
CAESURAE
CAPOEIRA
CAUSERIE
CAUTIOUS
COEQUATE
COOEEING
COUMAROU
COUTEAUX
DAIQUIRI
DEAERATE
DECIDUAL
DEIONISE
DEIONIZE
DETAINEE
DIALOGUE
DIAPAUSE
DIECIOUS
DIOECIES
DIOICOUS
DOUPIONI
DUOLOGUE
EARPIECE
EATERIES
ECAUDATE
ECOTOPIA
EDACIOUS
EGOMANIA
ELUVIATE
EMACIATE
EMEERATE
EMERITAE
ENCAENIA
EOLIPILE
EOLOPILE
EPICEDIA
EPIFAUNA
EPIGEOUS
EPILOGUE
EPIZOITE
EPOPOEIA
EQUALISE
EQUALIZE
EQUATION
EQUATIVE
EQUIPAGE
EQUISETA
EQUITIES
EQUIVOKE
ERADIATE
ETIOLATE
ETOUFFEE
EUCAINES
EUDAEMON
EUDAIMON
EUGENIAS
EULOGIAE
EULOGIAS
EULOGIES
EULOGISE
EULOGIUM
EULOGIZE
EUPEPSIA
EUPHORIA
EUPNOEAS
EUPNOEIC
EUROKIES
EUROKOUS
EUROPIUM
EUROZONE
EUSOCIAL
EUTAXIES
EUXENITE
EVACUATE
EVACUEES
EVALUATE
EXAMINEE
EXEQUIAL
EXEQUIES
EXIGUOUS
EXIMIOUS
EXONEREE
EXONUMIA
EXUVIATE
FACETIAE
FAUTEUIL
FILARIAE
FOVEOLAE
GUAIACOL
GUAIACUM
GUAIOCUM
HEMIOLIA
HETAERAE
HETAIRAI
HONOUREE
HOODOOED
IBOGAINE
ICEHOUSE
IDEALISE
IDEALIZE
IDEATION
IDEATIVE
IDIOCIES
IDONEOUS
IGUANIAN
INERTIAE
INFAUNAE
INITIATE
IODATION
IODINATE
IPOMOEAS
ISOLOGUE
JALOUSIE
KABLOOIE
KAMAAINA
LAUREATE
LEUCEMIA
LEUKEMIA
MAIASAUR
MAIEUTIC
MAIOLICA
MAUSOLEA
MAZAEDIA
METANOIA
MEUNIERE
MIAOUING
MILIARIA
MINUTIAE
MOIETIES
MONILIAE
MOVIEOLA
NAUSEATE
NAUSEOUS
NEURULAE
OCEANAUT
OEDEMATA
OEDIPEAN
OEILLADE
OITICICA
OLIGURIA
OOGAMETE
OOGAMIES
OOGAMOUS
OOGENIES
OOGONIAL
OOGONIUM
OOLOGIES
OOTHECAE
OPTIONEE
ORATORIO
OUABAINS
OUISTITI
OUTARGUE
OUTEATEN
OUTGUIDE
OUTHOUSE
OUTQUOTE
OUTRAISE
OUTVALUE
OUTVOICE
OVARIOLE
PAHOEHOE
PARANOEA
PARANOIA
PATOOTIE
PAURAQUE
PEEKABOO
PEEKAPOO
POACEOUS
PRIEDIEU
QUAALUDE
QUEASIER
QUEAZIER
QUEENIER
QUEUEING
QUIETUDE
QUILLAIA
QUINIELA
RADIALIA
REAROUSE
RELEASEE
RETIARII
ROULEAUS
ROULEAUX
ROUSSEAU
SAUTOIRE
SEAPIECE
SEAQUAKE
SEQUELAE
SEQUOIAS
SILIQUAE
TAENIOID
TAQUERIA
TEAHOUSE
THIOUREA
TOEPIECE
TOXAEMIA
UBIETIES
UINTAITE
UNEASIER
UNIAXIAL
UNIDEAED
UNIONISE
UNIONIZE
URAEMIAS
URAEUSES
UREDINIA
URINEMIA
USQUABAE
USQUEBAE
USURIOUS
UXORIOUS
VIRAEMIA
VOODOOED
WEIGELIA
ZABAIONE
ZOOECIUM
ZOOGLEAE
ZOOGLOEA
ZOOMANIA

THE 2-TO-MAKE-3 WORD LIST

Listed below are all the 107 two-letter words. Before and after each two-letter word are listed each of the letters that can be added to the word to form a three-letter word. *Example:* NU takes a G front hook to form GNU, as well as any of the back hooks—B, G, N, S, and T—to form NUB, NUG, NUN, NUS, and NUT.

b	AA	hls
cdfgjklnstw	AB	asy
bcdfghlmprstw	AD	dosz
ghkmnstw	AE	
bdfghjlmnrstwyz	AG	aeos
abdfhlnpry	AH	ais
r	AI	dlmnrst
abcdgps	AL	abelpst
bcdghjlmnprty	AM	aipu
bcdfgmprstvw	AN	adeity
bcefgjlmoptvwy	AR	bcefkmst
abdfghklmprtvwyz	AS	hkps
bcefghklmopqrstvw	AT	et
cdhjlmnprstvwy	AW	aeln
flmprstwz	AX	e
bcdfghjklmnprswy	AY	es
ao	BA	adghlmnprsty
o	BE	deglnsty
or	BI	bdgnostz
	BO	abdgopstwxy
a	BY	es
o	DA	bdghklmnpswy
o	DE	beflnpvwxy
au	DO	ceghlmnrstw
bfglmprtwx	ED	hs
dkr	EF	fst
fhmpy	EH	
bcdegmst	EL	dfklms
fghmr	EM	eosu
bdfghkmpstwy	EN	dgs
fhpsy	ER	aegnrs
bfhlmoprty	ES	st
bfghjlmnprstvwy	ET	ah
defhmnpsty	EW	e
dhklrsv	EX	
	FA	bdghnrstxy
	FE	dehmnrstuwyz
ae	GO	abdorstx
asw	HA	deghjmopstwy
st	HE	hmnprstwxy
acgkp	HI	cdemnpst
o	HM	m
moprstw	HO	bdegmnoptwy
abdfghklmrv	ID	s
dgkr	IF	fs
abdfghjklprstvwyz	IN	kns
abcdghklmpqstvwx	IS	m
abdfghklnpstwz	IT	s
	JO	begtwy
os	KA	befsty
s	KI	dfnprst
a	LA	bcdghmprstvwxy
	LI	bdenpst

	LO	bgoprtwx
ao	MA	cdegmnprstwxy
e	ME	dghlmnstw
a	MI	bcdglmrsx
hmu	MM	m
e	MO	abcdgilmnoprstw
ae	MU	dgmnstx
	MY	c
a	NA	beghmnpvwy
ao	NE	begtw
o	NO	bdghmorstw
g	NU	bgnst
bcghmnprsty	OD	ades
dfhjrtvw	OE	s
o	OF	ft
dfnops	OH	mos
kmp	OI	kl
wy	OK	ae
dhmnrsty	OM	as
cdefhimstwy	ON	eos
bcfhklmpst	OP	aest
cdfgklmnt	OR	abcegst
bcdgkmnpsw	OS	e
bcdhjlmnprstvwy	OW	elnt
bcfglpsv	OX	oy
bcfhjst	OY	
os	PA	cdhklmnprstwxy
ao	PE	acdeghnprstw
	PI	acegnpstux
a	PO	dhilopstwx
	QI	s
aeio	RE	bcdefgimpstvxz
a	SH	aehoy
p	SI	bcgmnprstx
	SO	bcdhlmnpstuwxy
eu	TA	bdegjmnoprstuvwx
au	TE	acdeglnstw
	TI	celnpstxz
	TO	degmnoprtwy
dh	UH	
bcdghlmrstvy	UM	mps
bdfghjlmnprst	UN	is
cdhpsty	UP	os
bjmnps	US	e
bcghjmnoprt	UT	aes
aeo	WE	bdent
t	WO	eknostw
	XI	s
	XU	
pr	YA	ghkmprswy
abdeklprtw	YE	ahnprstwz
	YO	bdkmnuw
	ZA	gpsx

3-LETTER WORDS

AAH	AMU	BAG	BRR	COW	DIE	EEK	FAN	FOX	GOA	HIC
AAL	ANA	BAH	BUB	COX	DIF	EEL	FAR	FOY	GOB	HID
AAS	AND	BAL	BUD	COY	DIG	EEW	FAS	FRO	GOD	HIE
ABA	ANE	BAM	BUG	COZ	DIM	EFF	FAT	FRY	GOO	HIM
ABS	ANI	BAN	BUM	CRU	DIN	EFS	FAX	FUB	GOR	HIN
ABY	ANT	BAP	BUN	CRY	DIP	EFT	FAY	FUD	GOS	HIP
ACE	ANY	BAR	BUR	CUB	DIS	EGG	FED	FUG	GOT	HIS
ACT	APE	BAS	BUS	CUD	DIT	EGO	FEE	FUN	GOX	HIT
ADD	APO	BAT	BUT	CUE	DOC	EKE	FEH	FUR	GRR	HMM
ADO	APP	BAY	BUY	CUM	DOE	ELD	FEM	GAB	GUL	HOB
ADS	APT	BED	BYE	CUP	DOG	ELF	FEN	GAD	GUM	HOD
ADZ	ARB	BEE	BYS	CUR	DOH	ELK	FER	GAE	GUN	HOE
AFF	ARC	BEG	CAB	CUT	DOL	ELL	FES	GAG	GUT	HOG
AFT	ARE	BEL	CAD	CUZ	DOM	ELM	FET	GAL	GUV	HOM
AGA	ARF	BEN	CAF	CWM	DON	ELS	FEU	GAM	GUY	HON
AGE	ARK	BES	CAL	DAB	DOR	EMO	FEW	GAN	GYM	HOO
AGO	ARM	BET	CAM	DAD	DOS	EMS	FEY	GAP	GYP	HOP
AGS	ARS	BEY	CAN	DAG	DOT	EMU	FEZ	GAR	HAD	HOT
AHA	ART	BIB	CAP	DAH	DOW	END	FIB	GAS	HAE	HOW
AHI	ASH	BID	CAR	DAK	DRY	ENG	FID	GAT	HAG	HOY
AHS	ASK	BIG	CAT	DAL	DUB	ENS	FIE	GAY	HAH	HUB
AID	ASP	BIN	CAW	DAM	DUD	EON	FIG	GED	HAJ	HUE
AIL	ASS	BIO	CAY	DAN	DUE	ERA	FIL	GEE	HAM	HUG
AIM	ATE	BIS	CEE	DAP	DUG	ERE	FIN	GEL	HAO	HUH
AIN	ATT	BIT	CEL	DAS	DUH	ERG	FIR	GEM	HAP	HUM
AIR	AUK	BIZ	CEP	DAW	DUI	ERN	FIT	GEN	HAS	HUN
AIS	AVA	BOA	CHI	DAY	DUM	ERR	FIX	GET	HAT	HUP
AIT	AVE	BOB	CIG	DEB	DUN	ERS	FIZ	GEY	HAW	HUT
AJI	AVO	BOD	CIS	DEE	DUO	ESS	FLU	GHI	HAY	HYP
ALA	AWA	BOG	COB	DEF	DUP	EST	FLY	GIB	HEH	ICE
ALB	AWE	BOO	COD	DEL	DYE	ETA	FOB	GID	HEM	ICH
ALE	AWL	BOP	COG	DEN	EAR	ETH	FOE	GIE	HEN	ICK
ALL	AWN	BOS	COL	DEP	EAT	EVE	FOG	GIF	HEP	ICY
ALP	AXE	BOT	CON	DEV	EAU	EWE	FOH	GIG	HER	IDS
ALS	AYE	BOW	COO	DEW	EBB	EYE	FON	GIN	HES	IFF
ALT	AYS	BOX	COP	DEX	ECO	FAB	FOO	GIP	HET	IFS
AMA	AZO	BOY	COR	DEY	ECU	FAD	FOP	GIS	HEW	IGG
AMI	BAA	BRA	COS	DIB	EDH	FAG	FOR	GIT	HEX	ILK
AMP	BAD	BRO	COT	DID	EDS	FAH	FOU	GNU	HEY	ILL

3-LETTER WORDS *(cont.)*

IMP	KEF	LEG	MAS	MOW	NOW	OOT	PED	PUG
INK	KEG	LEI	MAT	MUD	NTH	OPA	PEE	PUL
INN	KEN	LEK	MAW	MUG	NUB	OPE	PEG	PUN
INS	KEP	LES	MAX	MUM	NUG	OPS	PEH	PUP
ION	KEX	LET	MAY	MUN	NUN	OPT	PEN	PUR
IRE	KEY	LEU	MED	MUS	NUS	ORA	PEP	PUS
IRK	KHI	LEV	MEG	MUT	NUT	ORB	PER	PUT
ISM	KID	LEX	MEH	MUX	OAF	ORC	PES	PYA
ITS	KIF	LEY	MEL	MYC	OAK	ORE	PET	PYE
IVY	KIN	LIB	MEM	NAB	OAR	ORG	PEW	PYX
JAB	KIP	LID	MEN	NAE	OAT	ORS	PHI	QAT
JAG	KIR	LIE	MES	NAG	OBA	ORT	PHO	QIS
JAM	KIS	LIN	MET	NAH	OBE	OSE	PHT	QUA
JAR	KIT	LIP	MEW	NAM	OBI	OUD	PIA	RAD
JAW	KOA	LIS	MHO	NAN	OCA	OUR	PIC	RAG
JAY	KOB	LIT	MIB	NAP	OCH	OUT	PIE	RAH
JEE	KOI	LOB	MIC	NAV	ODA	OVA	PIG	RAI
JET	KOP	LOG	MID	NAW	ODD	OWE	PIN	RAJ
JEU	KOR	LOO	MIG	NAY	ODE	OWL	PIP	RAM
JIB	KOS	LOP	MIL	NEB	ODS	OWN	PIS	RAN
JIG	KUE	LOR	MIM	NEE	OES	OWT	PIT	RAP
JIN	KYE	LOT	MIR	NEG	OFF	OXO	PIU	RAS
JOB	LAB	LOW	MIS	NET	OFT	OXY	PIX	RAT
JOE	LAC	LOX	MIX	NEW	OHM	PAC	PLY	RAW
JOG	LAD	LUD	MMM	NIB	OHO	PAD	POD	RAX
JOT	LAG	LUG	MOA	NIL	OHS	PAH	POH	RAY
JOW	LAH	LUM	MOB	NIM	OIK	PAK	POI	RBI
JOY	LAM	LUN	MOC	NIP	OIL	PAL	POL	REB
JUG	LAP	LUV	MOD	NIT	OKA	PAM	POP	REC
JUN	LAR	LUX	MOG	NIX	OKE	PAN	POS	RED
JUS	LAS	LYE	MOI	NOB	OLD	PAP	POT	REE
JUT	LAT	MAC	MOL	NOD	OLE	PAR	POW	REF
KAB	LAV	MAD	MOM	NOG	OMA	PAS	POX	REG
KAE	LAW	MAE	MON	NOH	OMS	PAT	PRO	REI
KAF	LAX	MAG	MOO	NOM	ONE	PAW	PRY	REM
KAS	LAY	MAM	MOP	NOO	ONO	PAX	PSI	REP
KAT	LEA	MAN	MOR	NOR	ONS	PAY	PST	RES
KAY	LED	MAP	MOS	NOS	OOF	PEA	PUB	RET
KEA	LEE	MAR	MOT	NOT	OOH	PEC	PUD	REV

3-LETTER WORDS *(cont.)*

REX	SAL	SIS	SYN	TIN	ULU	VIN	WOE	YIP
REZ	SAN	SIT	TAB	TIP	UMM	VIS	WOK	YOB
RHO	SAP	SIX	TAD	TIS	UMP	VOE	WON	YOD
RIA	SAT	SKA	TAE	TIT	UMS	VOG	WOO	YOK
RIB	SAU	SKI	TAG	TIX	UNI	VOW	WOS	YOM
RID	SAW	SKY	TAJ	TIZ	UNS	VOX	WOT	YON
RIF	SAX	SLY	TAM	TOD	UPO	VUG	WOW	YOU
RIG	SAY	SOB	TAN	TOE	UPS	VUM	WRY	YOW
RIM	SEA	SOC	TAO	TOG	URB	WAB	WUD	YUK
RIN	SEC	SOD	TAP	TOM	URD	WAD	WUZ	YUM
RIP	SEE	SOH	TAR	TON	URN	WAE	WYE	YUP
ROB	SEG	SOL	TAS	TOO	URP	WAG	WYN	ZAG
ROC	SEI	SOM	TAT	TOP	USE	WAN	XED	ZAP
ROD	SEL	SON	TAU	TOR	UTA	WAP	XIS	ZAS
ROE	SEN	SOP	TAV	TOT	UTE	WAR	YAG	ZAX
ROM	SER	SOS	TAW	TOW	UTS	WAS	YAH	ZED
ROO	SET	SOT	TAX	TOY	VAC	WAT	YAK	ZEE
ROT	SEV	SOU	TEA	TRY	VAN	WAW	YAM	ZEK
ROW	SEW	SOW	TEC	TSK	VAR	WAX	YAP	ZEN
RUB	SEX	SOX	TED	TUB	VAS	WAY	YAR	ZEP
RUE	SEZ	SOY	TEE	TUG	VAT	WEB	YAS	ZIG
RUG	SHA	SPA	TEG	TUI	VAU	WED	YAW	ZIN
RUM	SHE	SPY	TEL	TUM	VAV	WEE	YAY	ZIP
RUN	SHH	SRI	TEN	TUN	VAW	WEN	YEA	ZIT
RUT	SHO	STY	TES	TUP	VEE	WET	YEH	ZOA
RYA	SHY	SUB	TET	TUT	VEG	WHA	YEN	ZOO
RYE	SIB	SUE	TEW	TUX	VET	WHO	YEP	ZUZ
RYU	SIC	SUK	THE	TWA	VEX	WHY	YER	ZZZ
SAB	SIG	SUM	THO	TWO	VIA	WIG	YES	
SAC	SIM	SUN	THY	TYE	VID	WIN	YET	
SAD	SIN	SUP	TIC	UDO	VIE	WIS	YEW	
SAE	SIP	SUQ	TIE	UGH	VIG	WIT	YEZ	
SAG	SIR	SUS	TIL	UKE	VIM	WIZ	YIN	

APPENDIX 5

Flashcards: The Champions' Way

by Joe Edley

This information is in the Appendix for one reason only: It's not for everyone. It's for the player who really wants to excel at the game far beyond the average living room player.

The very best SCRABBLE game players use flashcards of some type to learn and review the thousands of words they need to know. If you're intent on becoming a champion, there is no better time-efficient way to learn the vast SCRABBLE game vocabulary than by using flashcards. Perhaps you know of a software program that can generate specialized word lists. Or, as a NASPA member, you can download Zyzzyva from scrabbleplayers.org, a free program created by Michael Thelen used with computers and mobile devices, that can create many useful word lists and is an excellent study guide that can substitute for the flashcards described below. Or you might want to create your own cards with your own special words.

Each card, about 1 inch × 3 inches, has ten to fifteen seven- and eight-letter words spelled correctly on one side. On the other side each word is printed in alphagram order—that is, the letters of each word are put in alphabetic order. *Example:* On one side is ISOPODAN; on the other side is printed ADINOOPS. After you have fifty to one hundred cards, you can keep them together with a rubber band and put them in your pocket so that no matter where you go, you can always take them out and look at them if you have a few spare moments. Of course, using them effectively is vital to really learn the words and be able to find them quickly on your rack. Let's say you're looking at a deck of flashcards for the first time. Here is the sequence of steps to follow:

1. Look at the side that has the words spelled correctly. Look at the first word and imagine seeing it in your mind's eye. When you can do that successfully, go on to the next word. When you've seen them all in this fashion, reverse the card.

2. Look at the first alphagram. Does the correctly spelled word immediately come to mind? If so, go on to the next word. When you come to an alphagram and do not immediately recognize the word it represents, *do not* try to remember what the word

is. This would be a vital mistake.* Instead, manipulate the letters in your head, putting together likely combinations of two or three letters at a time until some combination of letters looks familiar and you realize you've found the word. If you manipulate the letters in your head and still cannot imagine what the word is, then after thirty seconds or so, look at the other side and see the word spelled correctly. Notice two, three, or four letters of the word and how they go together. Or look for any other distinguishing feature that will help you to visualize the word the next time you look at the alphagram.

Example: The alphagram AAEILNO can be turned into the word AEOLIAN. Notice the second and third letters of the alphagram, AE. By focusing on those two letters when you think AEOLIAN, you may remember that they begin the word when you next see its alphagram. From there it will be a small step to think of the whole word.

Example: If you get stumped on EINNORU, just notice the "INNO" and think "ION," and then the other common beginnings—"RE" and "UN"—and REUNION will likely pop into your awareness quickly. Why would you study REUNION, since it's such a common word? You might want to practice anagramming words you know to increase your speed.

3. Once you see the distinguishing features and can visualize the word, go back to the alphagram, look at the letters you need to put together in order to reach the point when you recognize the word, and then put the remaining letters in place in your mind.

4. When you've completed ten cards in the preceding fashion, start over and review each of those cards again, looking at one alphagram at a time until you figure out what the word is. Review all ten cards two or three times before going on to the next set of ten.

5. Finally, experience the "miracle." Let's say that you've reviewed ten cards twice and you've begun reviewing them a third time. You come across an alphagram that you can't decode. After thirty to forty-five seconds with no success, ask your subconscious for help. Say to yourself, with a good deal of emotion in the request, "Please help me to decode the word!" I've had thousands of individual experiences with this method, and they go something like this: First I'll spend some time trying to determine a word by moving the letters around in my head in all conceivable patterns. At some point I'm frustrated, and so I say, "Please help me find the word!" What happens next

*You want to train your mind to manipulate the letters in your head. You do not want to simply recall the words you saw thirty minutes ago. Recalling the words on a card won't help you when you have an alphagram of a bingo on your rack and you want to find the word quickly. However, if you find yourself using your memory automatically instead of exerting your anagram muscles, that's okay. With enough anagram practice, your skills will grow, regardless.

is usually one of two sequences—either the word will simply pop into my head (this can be almost a "religious" experience, since it happens without apparent cause other than simply desiring it), or, much more often, my mind will be more receptive to trying new letter arrangements. When this "openness" occurs, suddenly I will be aware that I hadn't tried several different possibilities. At that point I will begin to manipulate the letters again, putting them in these new, previously unthought-of orders. Then, bam! Suddenly the word is right there in front of me! The success you'll have with this method will likely be dependent on how determined you are to find the answer without looking at the other side of the card.

If all else fails, don't stay frustrated with not being able to determine the word. This advice is not given lightly, and is *very important.* If you get frustrated and stay there too long, you are likely to get to the point where you find studying flashcards *work.* That's *not* the idea. It can be *play,* and feel like an end in itself. Look at the reverse side of the card and ask yourself, "What could I have thought that would have led me to finding the correct spelling?"

As long as you learn how to visualize a seven- or eight-letter word in your head (remember, start with two- and three-letter words and work your way up), this method is foolproof, and there are a number of reasons why you, as a budding champion, should train in this way:

1. You are training yourself to find words listed in alphagram (alphabetical) order. When you play the SCRABBLE game, if you always start with the tiles on your rack in alphagram order, then it will be easier to find the high-scoring seven- and eight-letter words. That's because you will have trained yourself to see these words with the letters in that specific order.

2. Eventually, no matter how many times it takes you to learn a set of flashcards, this method of study generates mental development, much like lifting weights or jogging will continue to develop your body the more you do it. This means that you'll continue to get faster and better at it. When I first began to use flashcards, it took several hours over the course of several days to get through a deck of 100 cards. Now, after more than three decades, it takes me about forty-five minutes to go through the same number of words. That's one to three seconds per word. That's not bragging. *Most anyone can learn to do it simply by practicing.* With twenty minutes of flashcard practice a day, you'll speed up over time and learn hundreds or thousands of new words each year. After a couple of years you'll be able to learn a new deck in a fraction of the time it originally took.

3. You are training yourself to have fun while learning. How is that possible? First, remember to refrain from staying frustrated—if thirty to fifty seconds pass and you can't determine the answer, look it up. As you start to find the words quicker, you will likely get the thrill of seeing the word. That moment of recognition can be truly joyful. So, take a moment and enjoy it. Multiply that by 1,000,000 and you'll have an inkling

of why I still use this same method. And it's no drudgery. It's fun, and you can do it anywhere for as little or as much time as you prefer.

4. The more you use flashcards, the more you'll see that you're not just memorizing the words—you are actually training your brain how to anagram. You can prove this to yourself when you see an alphagram or anagram of a word you hadn't studied before and suddenly the word pops into your mind. That's not your memory at work! That shows that you've trained your brain to work *without* your conscious mind.

5. With your increased speed at finding more words to choose from for each play, you'll be able to focus more on strategy. That's where you'll start to win even more. Learning the best strategies separates the experts from the true champions. You can read *Everything SCRABBLE®* and the last chapter of *The Official SCRABBLE® Puzzle Book*, as well as former National and World Champion Joel Wapnick's *How to Play SCRABBLE® Like a Champion*. Check Amazon for availability.

6. The more words you find each turn and the more you consider strategy, the more *fun* you'll have. It's that simple!

Following are 100 mostly uncommon but useful seven-letter words to know. None of them has any other anagrams. We've arranged their alphagrams in groups of ten on the left, with the corresponding word spelled correctly on the right. We invite you to try the flashcard method of learning these words so you can have firsthand experience with it. *Note:* Read each of the ten words on the right. Then cover up the words and look only at the left column, following the instructions given earlier. Good luck!

AEROLITH

This edition, we'd like to recommend another study source: www.aerolith.org. Every day you can test yourself and learn up to fifty words of every length from two to fifteen letters long, if you desire.

If you are a newbie, we suggest starting with the Daily Challenges: three- and four-letter words, and then work your way up to fives or longer. Since there are many obscure words shown as alphagrams, if you don't find a word fairly quickly, move on. After you time out, check the answers, then later try the same quiz and see if you have learned those you didn't know before. This site is invaluable both for learning new words and for gaining anagram speed.

Bingo Flashcard Practice

CARD 1

1. ADEIIPR PERIDIA
2. ADEILNP PLAINED
3. ADEIMNU UNAIMED
4. ADENRTV VERDANT
5. ADIINST DISTAIN
6. CEGINOR COREIGN
7. AEGMNOR MARENGO
8. AEGLRTU TEGULAR
9. ADEFIRS FARSIDE
10. ADGILOR GOLIARD

CARD 2

11. ACDINRU IRACUND
12. AAGILRT RAGTAIL
13. ADEFORS FEDORAS
14. CDEIIOR ERICOID
15. EIMOSTU TIMEOUS
16. EHINOSU HEINOUS
17. DEMNORT MORDENT
18. DEHILOT LITHOED
19. AEMNNOR MONERAN
20. BEIORRT ORBITER

CARD 3

21. EFINNOR INFERNO
22. AACINRT ANTICAR
23. EMNOORT MONTERO
24. EIMORTT OMITTER
25. EILNOOV VIOLONE
26. CEILOST CITOLES
27. AAGINRS SANGRIA
28. AEHIMNR HARMINE
29. ACINRST NARCIST
30. AIMNRTU NATRIUM

CARD 4

31. AABDEIS DIABASE
32. ABELNRU NEBULAR
33. AEGLOPR PERGOLA
34. AEGLORV VORLAGE
35. ADENOSY NOYADES
36. AEEGILT EGALITE
37. DEENORT ERODENT
38. ABEEINT BETAINE
39. ADILNOR ORDINAL
40. ACDEEIR DECIARE

CARD 5

41. ACELNOT LACTONE
42. ABENORS BORANES
43. AADELNT LANATED
44. AENOPRS PERSONA
45. AELORTV LEVATOR
46. AEORTUV OUTRAVE
47. AEELOPR PAROLEE
48. AAGINRT GRANITA
49. AAEIPRS SPIRAEA
50. ACEIMOR COREMIA

CARD 6

51. BEEILNR BERLINE
52. AINORSW WARISON
53. AGIORSU GIAOURS
54. AEILNSW LAWINES
55. DDEINOT DENTOID
56. EEILNTV VEINLET
57. DEEHIRT DIETHER
58. ADEEFRT DRAFTEE
59. DEHINOS HOIDENS
60. DEENOPT PENTODE

CARD 7

61.	ACGIORT	ARGOTIC
62.	ADFINRT	INDRAFT
63.	ADGIRSU	GUISARD
64.	AEGILMN	GEMINAL
65.	ABDEISU	SUBIDEA
66.	AEEGMNT	GATEMEN
67.	ADNRSTU	TUNDRAS
68.	BDEIRTU	BRUITED
69.	BEGILNO	IGNOBLE
70.	ADEKORT	TROAKED

CARD 8

71.	ADEINOR	ANEROID
72.	ADELNOR	LADRONE
73.	ABDEOTU	BOUTADE
74.	ADINORT	DIATRON
75.	AEELORS	AREOLES
76.	DEEIORS	OREIDES
77.	ADEGIRT	TRIAGED
78.	ACEIORS	SCORIAE*
79.	ABEIORS	ISOBARE
80.	AADEINS	NAIADES

CARD 9

81.	AEEINPR	PERINEA
82.	AAILNOT	ALATION
83.	ACEILOT	ALOETIC
84.	ADEGNOT	TANGOED
85.	AEGORTU	OUTRAGE
86.	ACEENOT	ACETONE
87.	ADEENST	STANDEE
88.	AAEGILR	REGALIA
89.	ADEIILR	DELIRIA
90.	ADEGILT	LIGATED

CARD 10

91.	ADDEINO	ADENOID
92.	ACEEINU	EUCAINE
93.	AEEGNRU	UNEAGER
94.	AADELNR	ADRENAL
95.	AAELNRS	ARSENAL
96.	ACELNOR	CORNEAL
97.	ACLNRTU	TRUNCAL
98.	ADEIRSU	RESIDUA
99.	ACEEORS	ACEROSE
100.	ADEESTU	SAUTEED

* ORACIES is now acceptable.

APPENDIX 6

Does Your Opponent Have the S?
by Charlie Bond (TX)*

Consider the following scenario. The score is tied. You have a bingo-prone rack, but you would love to be rid of two letters—an O and an M. There's a place on the board to play OM—and it sets up a Triple Word Score. The only way your opponent could use the Triple is by pluralizing OM. Two Ss have been played; so have both blanks. You have one S on your rack, and eighty-three tiles have been played. Does your opponent have the other S?

Often, you wonder whether your opponent has a certain letter. Does your opponent have the Q? Does your opponent have the J? Does he or she have either of the two Ws? Does he or she have any of the five remaining Es?

There are no certain answers to these questions—and not until all the tiles have been drawn. But you can make an educated guess about your opponent's rack. In fact, you can figure out the likelihood that your opponent has a certain letter.

I've computed some probabilities that can help you guess your opponent's rack. More specifically, this is the probability that your opponent is holding a certain letter. The probabilities depend on two things: 1) the number of tiles you are wondering about; and 2) the number of tiles on the board. You can count the number of tiles that are on the board. The number you are wondering about would be 1—if you are wondering about the one Q; 2—if you are wondering about the two Ws; or 5—if you are wondering whether your opponent has even one of the five remaining Es. Here are the probabilities, arranged in a table.

* Mr. Bond taught statistics at Texas Christian University and is an avid SCRABBLE game player.

The Probability That Your Opponent Has a Specific Tile (or Tiles)

# of Tiles on Board	# of Tiles You Are Wondering About 1	2	3	4	5
10	8	16	23	30	36
20	10	18	26	34	40
30	11	21	30	38	46
40	13	25	35	44	52
50	16	30	42	52	61
60	21	38	52	63	72
70	30	52	68	79	87
80	54	81	93	98	99
83	70	93	99	100	100

The numbers in the Table are probabilities. They range from 0 to 100. A probability of 0 means that your opponent cannot possibly have the tile(s) you are wondering about. A probability of 100 means that your opponent is certain to have at least one of the tiles. A probability of 50 means the chances are 50 in 100 (or 1 in 2).

Notice a few things about these probabilities. The more tiles that are on the board, the greater the probability that your opponent is holding a particular tile. So, if it is late in the game, your opponent is more likely to be holding the Q than if it is early in the game. Also, the greater the number of tiles you are wondering about, the greater the probability that your opponent is holding at least one of those tiles. So he or she is less likely to have the Q than one of the four Us.

The probabilities in the Table are based on blind chance. Use them when you are interested in playing the odds. Maybe you can do better. Maybe you have watched your opponent's last few plays and have deduced what his or her tiles are. If so, use your knowledge.

If you would prefer to play the odds, here is how:

Example 1: Does your opponent have the S? If 83 tiles have been played, that means there are only 3 left in the bag. If there is 1 S left to play and you don't have 1, the probability that your opponent has the S is in the lower lefthand corner of the Table. It is 70 in 100. Very likely.

Example 2: Does your opponent have a W? If 40 tiles are on the board, none of them Ws, the probability that your opponent has a W can be read from the Table. It is 25 in 100. Not too likely.

Example 3: Does your opponent have an E? If 25 tiles have been played and 5 Es are unaccounted for, the probability that your opponent has an E is between 40 in 100 and 46 in 100.

A caveat: The numbers in the Table make an assumption—that of all the tiles unaccounted for, each is equally likely to be on your opponent's rack. This assumption may be questionable, particularly if the tiles of interest would tend to be kept on the rack for a long time. In that case, the numbers in the Table will underestimate the true likelihoods. Play accordingly.

A formula for use in games: The Table should be useful for study. But you could not consult it during a game. For games, I have developed a simple mathematical formula for estimating probabilities. With the formula, you can estimate all of the probabilities that are in the Table—and others that are not there, too. Here is the formula:

Let P = the probability you are trying to compute;

Let X = the number of tiles you are wondering about;
and
Let Y = the number of tiles on the board.

The formula is $P = 10X + Y - 30$

So, for Example 1, $P = 10(1) + 83 - 30 = 63$.
For Example 2, $P = 10(2) + 40 - 30 = 30$.
For Example 3, $P = 10(5) + 25 - 30 = 45$.

The formula gives approximate likelihoods. For exact probabilities, use the Table.

GLOSSARY

Abbreviations: DLS: Double Letter Score; **DWS:** Double Word Score; **TLS:** Triple Letter Score; **TWS:** Triple Word Score; **?:** Blank; **PTS.:** Points.

Alphagram: The alphabetic arrangement of a group of letters. *Example:* BEGNU is the alphagram of the word BEGUN.

Anagram: A word that is spelled with the exact same letters as another word. *Example:* KITCHEN is an anagram of THICKEN, and vice versa. GAPE is an anagram of PAGE.

Back Extension: *See* "Extension Play."

Back Hook: *See* "Hook Letter."

Balancing Your Rack: Making a play that leaves the letters on your rack that will most likely help you to score well next turn. This often means leaving a favorable ratio of vowels and consonants. Also known as "Rack Balance."

Bingo: Any word played that uses all seven letters of the rack, earning a bonus of 50 points. British players use the term "bonus" instead of bingo.

Bingo-Prone Tiles: A group of tiles that is likely to produce a bingo; often used to describe a player's set of three to six tiles just before drawing his or her replacement tiles. *Example:* ERS?, AL?, or AERST.

Blank: One of the two tiles that has no letter printed on it. The blank is worth zero points, but it is widely regarded as the most valuable tile due to its chameleonlike ability of being able to represent any letter. Having one increases the odds of playing a bingo.

Blank Bingo: A bingo that includes a blank tile.

Blocking: The act of playing a word on the board that stops the opponent from making a potentially large score.

Braille: To feel the surface of a tile while a player's hand is in the bag in order to draw a blank or other specific letter. This is strictly forbidden.

"Challenge!": An opponent calls "Challenge!" when s/he thinks a word is not acceptable (i.e., not in the *OSPD6*). The opponent records the challenged words on a "challenge slip," and a word judge is called to verify the acceptability of all the words formed on a play. If any of the words challenged are unacceptable, the whole play is unacceptable. The player must then remove his or her play from the board and lose that turn. If all the words are acceptable, then the challenger loses his or her turn. Only one turn is lost on any challenge.

Challenge Slip: The slip of paper upon which the words being challenged are printed by one of the players (and double-checked by the opponent). These slips are generally preferred to a player's simply pointing to the challenged word on the board. That's because mistakes are much more likely to be made unless the words are recorded.

Chess Clock: *See* "Tournament Clock."

Closed Board: The opposite of an open board: when there are few or no places on the board to put down either bingos or other high-scoring plays.

Coffeehousing: To make small talk, crack knuckles, or do any of a number of things meant to distract or mislead your opponent. This is unethical and strictly forbidden in clubs and tournaments. It is generally considered impolite to talk during a tournament game unless it is pertinent to the score or the play.

Contestant Score Card: On this card each player keeps a record of each game's results: opponent's name and signature, who played first, final score, total number of wins, and his or her own total point spread.

Courtesy Rule: If an opponent takes more than a minute to "Hold!" a play, the player may draw new tiles but must keep them separate from the others until the hold is resolved. Often, a third rack is used to hold these new tiles.

Credits: A seldom-used but effective method of deciding tournament results. One "credit" system has each player beginning each game with 30 credits. The winner automatically earns 10 credits, plus 1 credit for each 10 points of point spread (rounded off). The loser subtracts 1 credit from his or her original 30 for each 10 points of spread. Arbitrarily, no more than 60 credits nor fewer than 10 credits can be earned. For example, if Player #1 beats Player #2 400–350, Player #1 earns 30 + 10 (for winning) + 5 (for winning by 5 × 10 points) = 45 credits. Player #2 earns 30 – 5 (for losing by 5 × 10 points) = 25 credits. For ties, both players receive 35 credits.

Double-Double (DWS-DWS): When a player makes a play with letters that cover two Double Word Score squares, it is known as playing a "Double-Double." The bonus for covering two DWSs on one play is four times the sum of the value of the letters of the Double-Double word. The sum should include the extra values earned from any DLS covered that turn.

Dumping: Making a play that scores few points but rids the rack of a poor combination of letters.

Edge Letters (or Edge): Those two, three, or four letters commonly found at the beginning or end of many words. Examples: RE; UN; PRE; ING; TION; IER.

Endgame: That portion of a SCRABBLE game in which there are fewer than eight tiles left to draw from the bag.

Exchanging Tiles (or Trading Tiles): Instead of playing a word on the board, the player may use his or her turn to exchange from one to seven tiles for new tiles drawn from the bag. There must be at least seven tiles in the bag in order to exchange. To exchange, place the unwanted tiles facedown in front of you, announce the number of tiles you are exchanging, draw an equal number of tiles from the bag and place them on your rack. Finally, return the unwanted tiles to the bag.

Extension Play: The extension of one word by adding two or more letters. *Example:* With QUEST on the board, adding CON to the front creates the extension CONQUEST. Also called "Front Extension" or "Back Extension."

Fishing: To play for only a few points or exchange only one or two tiles, keeping five or six really good tiles, with the hope of making a high-scoring play next turn.

Frequency List: *See* "Preprinted Tracking Sheet."

Front Extension: *See* "Extension Play."

Front Hook: *See* "Hook Letter."

"Hold!": An opponent calls "Hold!" when a player plays a word that the opponent considers challenging. Calling "Hold!" signals to the player not to draw new tiles until either the challenge is officially resolved or the hold is canceled. To cancel a "Hold!" the opponent simply tells the player, "I accept the play." Using chess clocks, an opponent may hold as long as s/he desires; with sand timers, a hold may last as long as three minutes. After one minute of holding, the player may draw tiles, but must keep them separate from the others. *See also* "Courtesy Rule."

Hook Letter (or Hook): A letter that will spell a new word when it is played either at the front or end of a word already on the board. *Example:* With HARD on the board, the Y is a hook letter, since HARDY is acceptable. "Hook" is also used as a verb. *Example:* The letter C can "hook" on to HARD, since CHARD is acceptable. Also called "Front Hook" or "Back Hook."

Hot Spots: These are either specific squares or areas on the board that have excellent bonus-scoring opportunities. Players will do well to look for these areas before looking for words on their rack. *Examples:* Triple Letter Score squares or Double Word Score squares adjacent to vowels; a single letter placed between two open Triple Word Score squares; words that take a variety of hook letters (ARE, ON, CARE).

Leave: The group of tiles on a player's rack after s/he makes a play and before s/he draws new tiles.

Natural: A bingo that does not use a blank tile. Also called a "Natural Bingo."

Neutralizing the Timer: Stopping the game clock. Neither player's time continues during challenges, rule disputes, or score verifications.

Nongo: A bingo that won't play on the board.

***Official SCRABBLE® Players Dictionary, Sixth Edition*:** The bible for all North American SCRABBLE Players Association clubs and tournaments. The official source for all of the two- to eight-letter words. For words of more than eight letters, the NASPA uses *Merriam-Webster's Collegiate Dictionary, 11th Edition.*

Open Board: During play, the board is considered "open" when there are many places to play either bingos or other high-scoring words.

Overdrawing Tiles: When one player draws more tiles from the bag than is appropriate.

Parallel Play: A word played parallel to another word. *Example:*

```
  MAR
 LATE
```

With MAR on the board, LATE is a parallel play that simultaneously forms MA, AT, and RE, all of which earn points for the player.

Passing: A player may pass his or her turn by not exchanging tiles and not making a play on the board. The player says "Pass!", scores zero, and starts the opponent's timer. It is now the opponent's turn. In club or tournament play, when there are six consecutive scores of zero in a game, the game is over. A player scores zero when s/he either exchanges, passes, or loses a challenge.

Phoney: Any unacceptable word. An unacceptable word is one that is not found in *The Official SCRABBLE® Players Dictionary*, or, if the root word has more than eight letters, it is not found in the *Merriam-Webster's Collegiate Dictionary, 11th Edition*. However, if a phoney is not challenged, it will stay on the board for the remainder of the game.

Point Spread: The algebraic difference between the winner's and loser's score of a game. *Example:* If Player #1 wins over Player #2 by 400–300, Player #1's point spread is +100; Player #2's is –100. *See* "Total (Cumulative) Spread."

Power Tiles: There are ten power tiles. They are the two blanks, the four Ss, and the J, Q, X, and Z.

Preprinted Tracking Sheet: Also called Frequency List, or, simply, Tracking Sheet. This sheet of paper has printed on it either the alphabet or a partial or complete list of the 100 lettered tiles used in a SCRABBLE game.

Rack Balance: *See* "Balancing Your Rack."

Rack Management: How a player develops his or her series of racks toward the goal of putting down a bingo and other high-scoring plays.

Rating: For each sanctioned North American SCRABBLE Players Association tournament, a new rating is computed for each of the contestants. The rating represents how well a player is doing in relation to other rated players. The higher the rating, the more skillful the player. Ratings currently range from 200 to 2,100.

Rounds: In club or tournament play, one game is one round. Typically, there are five or six rounds (games) per day at most tournaments.

Sand Timer: In some tournaments and clubs where chess clocks are not available, three-minute sand timers are used to time each player's turns.

Second Opinion: If a player believes the word judge has made a mistake, s/he may ask for a second person to research the challenge. That second judgment is known as the "second opinion." If the second opinion contradicts the original one, a third opinion may be called for.

Stems: Certain five- and six-letter combinations of letters are so useful for forming bingos that lists of bingos have been printed that include these stems. Some of the more useful ones are: STARE, STANE, RETINA, SATINE, and SATIRE. By learning these lists and saving these letters, players will learn to play bingos more often.

Team (or Partnership) Game: Two or more players may pool their knowledge and play as one team against another.

Total (Cumulative) Spread: Over the course of many games the + (plus) or – (minus) spread for each game is added together. At the end of a tournament each player has a total spread for the event.

Tournament Clock: Often called a Chess Clock, it is actually two clocks housed in one plastic or wooden case. Sanctioned tournament games are timed using these clocks. Each player has twenty-five minutes to play the entire game. After making a move, the player presses the button on his or her side of the clock, which starts the opponent's time. The clock is used in this fashion until the game is over. Players are penalized 10 points per minute for every minute or fraction thereof used over the allotted twenty-five.

Tracking (or Tile Tracking): The process of keeping track of the letters played on the board. This can give the astute player an advantage as the game progresses. Careful trackers can deduce an opponent's rack after there are no letters left to draw. By knowing the opponent's rack, the player can often make moves to block the opponent's best plays or set up high-scoring plays that the opponent can't block. Players are allowed to play with their own Preprinted Tracking Sheet alongside their score sheet.

Tracking Sheet: *See* "Preprinted Tracking Sheet."

Triple-Triple: When a player makes a play with letters that cover two Triple Word Score squares, it is known as playing a "Triple-Triple." The bonus for covering two TWSs on one play is nine times the sum of the value of the letters of the Triple-Triple word. The sum should include the extra values earned from any DLS covered that turn.

Turnover: Players are playing for "turnover" when they play as many tiles as they can in order to draw as many new tiles as possible. By playing for turnover, a player maximizes his or her chances for drawing the better tiles.

Two-to-Make-Threes: Two-letter words that will take a third letter placed either in front or in back to form a three-letter word. *Example:* AN is a two-to-make-three because BAN, CAN, etc., as well as AND, ANT, and ANY are words. The three-letter words BAN, CAN, ANT, and ANY are also known as three-to-make-fours. This description may seem confusing. When in doubt, consider any word on our 2-to-Make-3 Word List on page 523 to be a two-to-make-three. Also note "three-to-make-fours," etc.

Joe Edley is the only North American to have won the National SCRABBLE Championship three times. He was the director of clubs and tournaments for the National SCRABBLE Association from 1988–2009, and creator of the new nonword puzzle app, NOKORI.

John D. Williams, Jr. was the executive director of the National SCRABBLE Association for twenty-five years and served as the game's national spokesperson. His latest book is *Word Nerd: Dispatches from the Games, Grammar, and Geek Underground* (W. W. Norton).